THE CHILD CLINICIAN'S HANDBOOK

RELATED TITLES

Handbook of Behavior Therapy with Children and Adults:
A Developmental and Longitudinal Perspective
Robert T. Ammerman and Michel Hersen (Editors)
ISBN: 0-205-14583-3

Handbook of Prescriptive Treatments for Children and Adolescents
Robert T. Ammerman, Cynthia G. Last, and Michel Hersen (Editors)
ISBN: 0-205-14825-5

Handbook of Psychotherapy with Children and Adolescents
Thomas R. Kratochwill and Richard J. Morris (Editors)
ISBN: 0-205-14804-2

The Practice of Child Therapy, Second Edition
Thomas R. Kratochwill and Richard J. Morris (Editors)
ISBN: 0-205-14397-0

Child and Adolescent Psychotherapy: Process and Integration
Robert M. Leve
ISBN: 0-205-14907-3

The Clinician's Handbook: Integrated Diagnostics, Assessment, and
Intervention in Adult and Adolescent Psychopathology, Fourth Edition
Robert G. Meyer and Sarah E. Deitsch
ISBN: 0-205-17181-8

Child and Adolescent Therapy
Margaret Semrud-Clikeman
ISBN: 0-205-15026-8

THE CHILD CLINICIAN'S HANDBOOK

WILLIAM G. KRONENBERGER

Indiana University School of Medicine

ROBERT G. MEYER

University of Louisville

ALLYN AND BACON
Boston   London   Toronto   Sydney   Tokyo   Singapore

Library of Congress Cataloging-in-Publication Data

Kronenberger, William G.
    The child clinician's handbook / William G. Kronenberger, Robert
G. Meyer.
        p.   cm.
    Includes bibliographical references and index.
    ISBN 0-205-14752-6
    1. Child Psychiatry—Handbooks, manuals, etc.   I. Meyer, Robert
G.   II. Title.
    [DNLM: 1. Mental Disorders—in infancy & childhood—handbooks.
2. Mental Disorders—diagnosis—handbooks.   3. Mental Disorders—
—therapy—handbooks.   WS 39 K93c 1995]
RJ499.3.K76   1995
618.92´89—dc20
DNLM/DLC
for Library of Congress   95-12659
                                                                      C I P

Printed in the United States of America
10 9 8 7 6 5 4 3 2   99 98 97

DEDICATION

To my parents, Earl and Julie, and to my wife, Dari.
—WGK

To the great new kids on the block, Kenny, Steven,
and of course, Christopher.
—RGM

CONTENTS

PREFACE

One of the common complaints of mental health professionals is the lack of practical clinical references. By "practical" and "clinical," we mean references that show how to assess and treat mental disorders in an office or hospital setting. Graduate students, interns, and residents often lament that they have read extensively about the *theory* behind mental disorders but that they have seen little about the *practice* of assessment and psychotherapy. In other words, they need a reference to connect the theory to clinical work. Likewise, some practitioners and trainees express confidence about their ability to diagnose mental disorders but confusion about how to treat the disorders. Clinicians and researchers know the importance of keeping up with advances in assessment and treatment, but this task becomes increasingly difficult as the knowledge base expands. Literature reviews and theoretical articles are extremely important, but they often seem removed from the daily pragmatics of the clinical mental health practice.

Taken in context, these issues argue for the development of a book that can be used as an up-to-date reference for clinicians and as a practical teaching tool for trainees. In writing this book, we have aimed to keep the practical, clinical issues of assessment and treatment paramount, while integrating major advances in theory and research. This task was made somewhat easier by the adoption of the spirit and organization of Bob Meyer's *Clinician's Handbook*, an adult text that has a similar goal. *The Child Clinician's Handbook* uses a modification of Meyer's organizational scheme to provide a concise, integrated description of the diagnosis, assessment, and treatment of childhood mental disorders.

The Child Clinician's Handbook is intended to facilitate clinical work by anticipating the questions of practitioners and students: What are the characteristics of the disorder? Are there any tests I can use to assess it thoroughly? How do I treat the disorder? For each major childhood mental disorder, these questions are answered in a structured presentation that is uniform throughout the text. Hence, the book is designed for quick and easy use. Extensive references for each disorder direct clinicians to other sources if additional readings are desired. Chapter 1 contains a detailed presentation of the book contents and suggestions for use in daily practice or learning. It is recommended that you begin with a thorough reading of that chapter before proceeding to use the book in your daily work.

We all have "clinical" books on our shelves that look impressive but are gathering dust. Many of these books achieve dust-gathering status because they are simply not applicable to (or are too cumbersome for) our daily clinical work. From start to finish, this book was written to be a frequent reference in everyday clinical work, not a "dust gatherer." We hope that it fills this important niche for you in your work.

The material contained in this book is drawn from several sources, ranging from well-constructed research studies to our own clinical observations. Obviously, child mental health is a constantly evolving field, and we expect the research and clinical database to advance. We welcome comments, feedback, and suggestions about new research and clinical directions in this field. Please send these to William Kronenberger, Ph.D.; Riley Child Psychiatry Clinic; 702 Barnhill Dr.; Indianapolis, IN 46202-5200.

We appreciate the permission of the American Psychiatric Association to use the DSM-IV categories and diagnostic criteria to structure our presentation of child psychopathology. Readers who are interested in an extensive discussion of the formal diagnosis of childhood psychiatric disorders should consult the DSM-IV.

We are grateful to several students and colleagues who provided us with invaluable comments, assistance, and written contributions. We acknowledge David Sabine, Stacy Cambron, and Laura Bolte for their assistance with the writing of the Disruptive Behavior Disorders and Anxiety Disorders chapters. Cathy Morrow and Lori Schober's help with library work was much appreciated. We reserve special thanks for Mylan Jaixen, our editor at Allyn and Bacon, for his guidance and expertise, and to Sue Hutchinson, editorial assistant, for her help. We also acknowledge the professors and colleagues who have been instrumental in our clinical learning experiences: Bob Thompson, Dick Lawlor, George McAdoo, Gina Laite, Suzanne Blix, Madeline Kolar, Matt Galvin, Jim Rizzo, Diane Lanman, Lisa Hill, Rosemary Collins, Bobbi Siccardi, Ted Petti, Bob Ten Eyck, George Karwisch, Ron Stachler, Paul Deardorff, David Hellkamp, Vytautas Bieliauskas, A. I. Rabin, Bertram Karon and many others—their influence is no doubt incorporated in this work as it is in our therapeutic styles. Insightful reviews by Jack W. Finney, Virginia Polytechnic Institute and State University, and Peggy Ollerhead, School Psychologist, Roland Park Country School, Towson, MD, also helped us to improve the quality of the book and were much appreciated. Finally, the support, input, and specialty knowledge of our colleagues Earl Kronenberger, Bryan Carter, and Linn LaClave were essential in our work.

LIST OF TABLES

CHAPTER 1

Diagnosis, Assessment, and Treatment in Clinical Practice

■ ## Introduction

This book is written to be a practical reference and teaching text for child mental health clinicians and trainees. Every day, these clinicians face a common scenario: A child walks in the door, accompanied by (and almost always at the insistence of) a parent. The child and parent are at the clinician's office because the parent or another adult finds the child's behaviors to be problematic. The mental health clinician (*clinician* will be used in this book to refer to a psychologist, psychiatrist, social worker, psychiatric nurse, or advanced student in one of these areas) is expected to perform an evaluation and to provide recommendations in a timely, professional, and informed manner.

The task of the clinician is enormous: They must, in a limited period of time, provide a diagnosis, background information, formulation of the case, and therapeutic recommendations. In many cases clinicians are then called on to do psychotherapy, which requires additional expertise. Added to this increasingly complex picture are the facts that diagnostic systems change every few years, psychotherapy is evolving, and a mountain of assessment and clinical outcome research is published every year. In order to stay current and competent, clinicians must be skilled in therapy, adroit at observation, and knowledgeable about research and clinical literature.

Even if all children presented with similar problems, the clinician's job would be complicated and intellectually demanding. However, diagnostic categories for childhood disorders are growing in number and refinement. The clinician must be prepared to recognize and address problems as varied as Mental Retardation, Separation Anxiety Disorder, and Conduct Disorder. Perhaps the only similarity across children is the clinician's starting point, which usually involves three basic questions:

1. What are the characteristics of the child's problem?
2. How should the child's problem be evaluated in depth?

3. Based on the evaluation results, what can be done to address the child's problem?

Guidelines and suggestions for answering these questions can be found in numerous sources. Question 1 involves establishing a diagnosis and/or description of the child's behaviors, as well as a history of the symptoms and related problems. Traditionally the clinician has referred to the current *Diagnostic and Statistical Manual of Mental Disorders* (since 1980, DSM-III, DSM-III-R, and now DSM-IV; American Psychiatric Association, 1980, 1987, 1994) and to psychopathology books for assistance with this initial question. However, while DSM-IV provides important information about symptoms, features, and epidemiology, it falls short on in-depth evaluation (particularly psychological testing) and therapy recommendations. Hence, the clinician has to look elsewhere to answer Questions 2 and 3.

Question 2 reflects the focus on more in-depth, individual evaluation of the child's problems. For this evaluation, clinicians rely on clinical interviews, psychological assessment, and behavioral assessment. Clinical interviews tap general background information, but they also focus on specific factors common to a diagnostic group. For example, the interview of a child with Attention-Deficit/Hyperactivity Disorder (ADHD) might include observation and questions related to the child's ability to concentrate, sit still, listen, and follow directions. These components would be much less emphasized in the interview of a child with Separation Anxiety Disorder. Clinical interviews with parents would be similarly tailored to the child's problems. Psychological assessment, on the other hand, might focus on test patterns typical of the child's diagnostic group and on the selection of specific test instruments to assess the child's problem in detail. Behavioral assessment investigates the child's behaviors, the events that preceded the behaviors (antecedents), and the events that followed the behaviors (consequences).

In order to address Question 2, then, the clinician needs current knowledge about general interviewing questions, diagnosis-specific features to investigate in the interview, general psychological tests (such as IQ tests and broad personality tests), and diagnosis-specific tests (such as those designed to evaluate a particular cluster of problems, such as ADHD). To use the ADHD example again, the clinician would need background information about the child's development and current circumstances; specific interview information about ADHD features; (ideally) IQ and achievement testing; and tests of attention, concentration, and other ADHD-related behaviors. In addition to the DSM-IV, the clinician draws on knowledge contained in a basic interviewing book, books about the major tests (such as IQ tests and personality tests), and books (or articles) about diagnosis-specific tests to answer Question 2.

Finally, after completing the evaluation process that answers the first two questions, the clinician must provide recommendations for therapy. In many cases, therapy is conducted by the evaluating clinician. Hence, the clinician often must know in detail how to address the problem in therapy. As with the first two questions, many excellent books have been written to address Question 3. Books exist, for example, about cognitive-behavioral, psychodynamic, play, and family therapy to address child behavior problems. Often, however, these books deal with general therapy techniques but lack specific application or modification for different problems.

Looking at the clinician's bookshelf, then, one can see diagnostic books, interviewing books, testing books, and therapy books. Clinicians have probably used these books in the course of their initial learning and continuing education. Unfortunately, however, they rarely take their basic books down to assist with day-to-day clinical issues, except, perhaps, to doublecheck on a diagnostic criterion. Why does this situation exist? Clinicians need the information in their basic books, but they often do not use basic books in their daily practice. Books that have been so important in learning are relegated to the status of decorations in the clinical office.

There appear to be at least three reasons for this state of affairs: First, time is a factor. Busy clinicians do not have time to read a new book (or to review an old one) for each patient; they do not have daily time to do a literature search or to enter a scholarly debate. This is not to belittle the importance of these endeavors. Indeed, it is very important for clinicians to keep up with their field and with scholarly advances. But the everyday office environment is typically not the place for such efforts; continuing education classes, case conferences, seminars, and professional holidays provide opportunities for more basic learning. In the office, interacting with patients, clinicians need access to practical summaries, descriptions, and brief recommendations.

Second, it is rare for a single child mental health book to integrate the topics of diagnosis, interviewing, assessment, and treatment. More commonly, these topics are the subjects of separate, lengthy, detailed books. Although such books provide essential in-depth information, they leave a gap between diagnosis, assessment, and therapy. Assessment-therapy gaps, however, are not present in the clinical setting. Rather, the clinician uses assessment to plan, evaluate, and modify therapy; assessment and therapy are part of the same process. Hence, clinicians need a book that addresses diagnostic, assessment, and therapy issues in a brief, practical, integrated manner.

Third, in day-to-day practice, clinicians need to find information quickly. Often the clinician has 5–10 minutes between appointments in which to review the patient's chart and plan for the session. If questions arise in this brief time, the clinician must find answers immediately or wait until later to search for them. In many cases, current child mental health books require extensive searching to answer simple questions. There are many reasons for this problem, but all of them can be reduced to organization and structure. Some books lack chapter-to-chapter similarity in structure because they are edited volumes, with each chapter author using his or her own style of writing and organizing a chapter. Other books are difficult to follow because they use few or confusing headings within a chapter. The effect of this problem is that clinicians cannot predict from chapter to chapter what will be contained in a book and where it will be in the chapter.

■   Rationale

The problems just outlined are the impetus for the writing of this book. Of course, this is not the first time these problems have been identified. Meyer and Deitsch (1996) have dealt with many similar issues for adult mental health clinicians in their *Clinician's Handbook*. In fact, this work is intended to apply their approach (with some modifications) to the situation of the child mental health clinician.

Addressing these problems and providing a resource that will be useful to busy clinicians has required the definition of a clear set of goals and organizing principles for this book:

1. Integrated consideration of diagnostic, assessment, and therapy issues in each chapter
2. Broad organization of chapters by diagnosis according to DSM-IV
3. Use of consistent structure and headings within each chapter
4. Critique, when possible, of assessment instruments and intervention modalities based on research findings

Adherence to these goals means that this book is intended to be problem-focused, practical, easy to use, concise, and current with the literature. Familiarity with the organizational principles outlined here and with the philosophy of the book will help clinicians use the book as a reference in everyday practice. Because of the organization of the book, clinicians should have a sense of *what* is covered in each chapter and *where* such information can be found. Issues of diagnosis, evaluation/assessment, and therapy are covered in every chapter. Chapters are organized based on the DSM-IV diagnostic system, with which almost every clinician is familiar. All major DSM-IV childhood diagnoses, including some that affect children *and* adults (such as mood disorders) are covered. The age range is approximately birth to 16 years of age; clinicians who are interested in disorders of late adolescence and adulthood are referred to Meyer and Deitsch's (1996) *Clinician's Handbook*.

Although DSM-IV provides extensive and useful diagnostic information, the use of the DSM-IV diagnostic system as one of the organizing components of the *Child Clinician's Handbook* is not intended as a blanket endorsement of all of the contents of the DSM-IV. Certainly, some DSM diagnoses and assumptions have been both criticized and acclaimed. However, an extensive discussion of the advantages and disadvantages of the DSM system is beyond the scope of this book. DSM-IV was chosen to organize the chapters of this book because it is the most widely used and widely accepted system of mental disorders for both clinical and research purposes. Hence, it not only offers a comprehensive diagnostic system, but it also serves as a common language for mental health practitioners and researchers.

■ Some Assumptions

Because this book is intended to be a resource for practicing and training clinicians, it assumes a basic level of clinical knowledge. Essentially, this "basic" level of knowledge means that the user of this book will probably have had (or will be currently taking) introductory courses in counseling or psychotherapy, diagnosis, and assessment. Hence, major interventions and assessment instruments are reviewed in the following section, but comprehensive discussions of specific assessment and intervention techniques are avoided in this introductory chapter. Later chapters discuss assessment instruments and treatment techniques in greater depth, as they pertain to specific clinical problems. Clinicians looking for additional information about specific assessment instruments should refer to the test manuals and to Sattler (1993). Books containing overviews of treatment techniques are referenced in the following Treatment Options section.

■ Basic Organization

☐ INTRODUCTION

All of the chapters in this book follow a similar outline (Table 1.1), which is designed to facilitate the process of rapidly locating and understanding information pertaining to childhood mental health disorders and treatment. The subject of each chapter is a major category of DSM-IV disorders, such as mood disorders or ADHD. Depending on the breadth of the major category, there will be descriptions of one or more disorders contained within the chapter. In the mood disorders chapter, for example, are the diagnoses Bipolar I Disorder, Bipolar II Disorder, Cyclothymic Disorder, Major Depressive Disorder, and Dysthymic Disorder. The ADHD chapter, on the other hand, contains only a single disorder. Characteristics that are shared by all of the disorders within the major category are covered in an introductory section. Then characteristics of the diagnosis, assessment, and treatment of each specific disorder are described.

☐ CLINICAL DESCRIPTION

Coverage of each specific disorder begins with a Clinical Description section. This section gives the clinician an overall picture of the disorder that may be used to guide the clinical interview and initial formulations. Within this section, three major topics are considered, each of which is labeled with a subheading: Diagnostic Considerations, Appearance and Features, and Etiology.

Diagnostic Considerations

The Diagnostic Considerations section begins with a basic description of diagnostic criteria specified in DSM-IV. However, the section does not describe the

TABLE 1.1   Outline of Chapters in *The Child Clinician's Handbook*

I. Clinical Description

    A. Diagnostic Considerations
    B. Appearance and Features
    C. Etiology

II. Assessment Patterns

    A. Broad Assessment Strategies
       1. Cognitive Assessment
       2. Psychological Assessment
       3. Behavioral Assessment
       4. Family Assessment

    B. Syndrome-Specific Tests

III. Treatment Options

    A. Behavioral Interventions
    B. Psychotherapy
    C. Family Interventions
    D. Medication
    E. Inpatient Hospitalization
    F. Special Education
    G. Referral

criteria verbatim (one can use the DSM-IV for that), and it is *not* a substitute for the DSM-IV. Rather, diagnostic criteria are summarized in descriptive form to supplement the formal DSM-IV listings. For example, DSM-IV includes numerous subtypes and specifiers for some disorders. Much of this detail is omitted or only briefly summarized in the Diagnostic Considerations section. In short, the clinician should have and use the DSM-IV.

Instead of simply repeating DSM-IV criteria, the Diagnostic Considerations section addresses issues related to making a diagnosis. These issues include a broad description of the disorder, difficult differential diagnoses, prevalence of the disorder, and subtypes of the diagnosis. In some cases, competing diagnostic systems are so commonly used (as with diagnoses of Autistic Disorder and learning disorders) that the clinician needs to be aware of how these fit with the DSM-IV criteria. Over all, then, the Diagnostic Considerations section provides additional information that the clinician can use in making a diagnosis of the child's problem and in understanding this diagnosis.

Appearance and Features

Following the description of diagnostic issues, the discussion turns to the psychological, behavioral, and social appearance of a child with the disorder. Diagnostic criteria, of course, begin to give a picture of the child's appearance, but they are of necessity restricted to broad and/or key features of the disorder. In addition to key features, the Appearance and Features section describes behaviors, psychosocial characteristics, and risks associated with the child's condition but not necessarily required for diagnosis. For example, children with ADHD are at increased risk for learning disabilities, although this is not a diagnostic criterion for the disorder.

The Appearance and Features section also attempts to bring the diagnosis "to life" by providing a description of a "typical" child with the disorder. This section should be clinically useful in two ways: First, it should familiarize the clinician with what he or she is likely to see from a child with the diagnosis. Second, the section suggests targets for specific questions in the clinical interview. These questions may probe the details and associated features of the disorder, helping the clinician to gain a more comprehensive picture of the child's problems. The Appearance and Features section, then, is intended to assist the clinician with the interview facet of the initial evaluation. In order to improve its usefulness, a table summarizing the primary and associated features of each disorder is included in each Appearance and Features section.

Etiology

The Diagnostic Considerations section concludes with a discussion of the etiology of the disorder. Rather than adopting a set pattern of describing biological, then psychological, then social theories of etiology, the emphasis of the Etiology section differs from chapter to chapter, based on the weight of empirical research and theory. For example, if biological theories of etiology have received more empirical and theoretical attention for a particular disorder, these will be emphasized in the Etiology section of that disorder. Etiological theories that have received little attention or research support are omitted.

Perhaps no section contains more condensed information than the Etiology section of each chapter, because of the volume of writing from different theoretical orientations about the origins of psychopathology. For each disorder in this book an effort was made to cover major etiological theories in sufficient detail to give the clinician a basic knowledge of each. However, this book cannot claim to be comprehensive or extremely detailed in a discussion of etiological theories for all of the childhood disorders. Such a comprehensive, theoretical, and historical view is rarely required in day-to-day clinical work. References are provided in the Etiology sections for clinicians who need additional information about the etiology of a particular disorder.

An overview of disorder etiology can be extremely helpful to clinicians, who are frequently asked by parents "why" their child has a behavior problem. Even if clinicians do not want to answer that question directly (or confidently!) to parents, chances are that they will want to have tentative etiological hypotheses for their own clinical use. In fact, etiological formulations are standard in intake report summary sections. In addition, knowledge about possible etiology can help clinicians select targets for the clinical interview. Awareness about potential causal issues can guide the clinicians' observations and questions. Finally, etiological hypotheses are often important in choosing an intervention. Family etiology, for example, may result in a recommendation for family therapy.

☐   ## ASSESSMENT PATTERNS

Following the basic description of the disorder, an Assessment Patterns section provides recommendations about how the child might be assessed using standardized psychological instruments. The major problem for the clinician at this stage is not finding a test to use, but selecting among the multitude of tests that are available to assess children. Many tests (such as IQ tests, broad personality tests, self-esteem tests, and broad-band behavior problem checklists) are used in the assessment of multiple disorders, while other tests may be designed for a specific disorder or behavior problem. Likewise, tests may assess cognitive, psychological, behavioral, or familial-social characteristics of the child. Finally, tests differ based on who responds to the questions. In the case of a child the parent is often called upon to respond to questions about the child's behaviors. Other respondents are the clinician, the teacher, other adults, or the child.

Clearly, the selection of tests poses a complex situation for the clinician. A similarly complex situation exists for a book (such as this one) that is designed to review major tests and to help the clinician choose a test for use with a particular child. To simplify and organize the presentation of assessment instruments for each disorder, tests are classified based on the breadth of their application (broad application vs. application to a specific disorder), the major type of information that they provide (cognitive, psychological, behavioral, or familial-social), and the major source of information and formulation (clinician, child, parent, or other person) (Table 1.2). To assist the clinician with the selection of tests, a sample assessment battery is included in the Assessment Patterns section for each disorder. This sample battery is illustrative of useful tests for *most* children presenting with the disorder. However, tests may need to be added or deleted based on the particular characteristics of each child.

Broad Assessment Strategies

The Broad Assessment Strategies section reviews tests that are useful in the assessment of more than one disorder. Such tests tap broad psychological, behavioral, and social characteristics of the child, which may pertain to multiple disorders. Specifically, clinicians frequently want information about the child's cognitive functioning, internal psychological functioning, external behavioral functioning, and family environment regardless of the child's specific problems. Information about these areas can be critical in formulation, diagnosis, and intervention.

The selection of which tests to include in the Broad Assessment Strategies section was guided by several criteria: popularity with clinicians, quantity of empirical research, usefulness in the clinical situation, and importance of the

TABLE 1.2   Organization of Psychological Assessment Instruments

TARGET OF ASSESSMENT	PRIMARY INFORMATION SOURCE			
BROAD ASSESSMENT STRATEGIES	**Clinician**	**Child**	**Parent**	**Other**
Cognitive				
Psychological				
Behavioral				
Family				
SYNDROME-SPECIFIC TESTS				

data for diagnosis and therapy. If empirical data exist to support the use of the test or presence of a test pattern in a diagnostic group, it is referenced. In some cases, hypothesized test patterns can be inferred for a diagnostic population, based on clinical experience and observations (but no current empirical support); these hypotheses are stated as being "expected" or "likely," and they are not referenced. Thus, expected assessment patterns that are described without reference to a book, article, chapter, or study are based on clinical experience and expectation as opposed to research data.

Of course, the relevance and importance of each test will vary somewhat based on the features of a specific disorder. Thus, with the exception of cognitive testing, no broad assessment strategy or test cuts across *all* diagnoses. Some chapters, for example, will not consider internal psychological assessment, while others will not cover family assessment. Only relevant assessment strategies are described for each diagnosis.

Although no test is useful for all childhood diagnoses, many broad tests show up repeatedly throughout the book. Summaries and descriptions of these tests are provided later in this chapter. In subsequent chapters, when broad tests are recommended for a specific diagnosis, only a description of their application to the diagnosis will be given. No basic information (e.g., reference, number of items, scoring, etc.) will be provided for broad tests in the later chapters, since the reader may refer to the basic test description in this introductory chapter. (See Table 1.3 for a list of broad assessment instruments and corresponding references.)

In order to simplify the organization of the Broad Assessment Strategies section, broad tests are divided into four groups based on the type of informa-

TABLE 1.3   Broad Assessment Instruments

NAME (ABBREVIATION)	REFERENCE	INFORMATION SOURCE
Cognitive Assessment		
Bayley Scales of Infant Development: Second Edition (Bayley-II)	Bayley, 1993	Clinician
Wechsler Preschool and Primary Scale of Intelligence—Revised (WPPSI-R)	Wechsler, 1989	Clinician
Wechsler Intelligence Scale for Children—Revised (WISC-R)	Wechsler, 1974	Clinician
Wechsler Intelligence Scale for Children—Third Edition (WISC-III)	Wechsler, 1991	Clinician
Wechsler Adult Intelligence Scale—Revised (WAIS-R)	Wechsler, 1981	Clinician
Woodcock-Johnson Tests of Educational Achievement— Revised (WJ-R)	Woodcock and Johnson, 1989a	Clinician
Wechsler Individual Achievement Test (WIAT)	The Psychological Corporation, 1992	Clinician
Vineland Adaptive Behavior Scales (VABS)	Sparrow et al., 1984	Clinician
Psychological Assessment		
Minnesota Multiphasic Personality Inventory (MMPI)	Hathaway and McKinley, 1967	Clinician
Minnesota Multiphasic Personality Inventory—Adolescent Form (MMPI-A)	Butcher et al., 1992	Clinician
Rorschach Inkblot Test (Rorschach)	Exner, 1986	Clinician
Thematic Apperception Test (TAT)	Murray, 1943	Clinician

Diagnostic Interview for Children and Adolescents— Revised (DICA-R)	Herjanic and Campbell, 1977	Clinician
Diagnostic Interview Schedule for Children—Revised (DISC-R)	Costello et al., 1984	Clinician
Child Assessment Schedule (CAS)	Hodges, 1985	Clinician
Schedule for Affective Disorders and Schizophrenia for School-Age Children (K-SADS)	Puig-Antich et al., 1983	Clinician
Piers-Harris Self Concept Scale (PHSCS or Piers-Harris)	Piers, 1984	Child
Symptom Checklist-90— Revised (SCL-90-R)	Derogatis, 1983	Child

Behavioral Assessment

Child Behavior Checklist (CBCL)	Achenbach, 1991a	Parent
Teacher's Report Form (TRF)	Achenbach, 1991b	Teacher
Youth Self-Report (YSR)	Achenbach, 1991c	Child
Conners Parent Rating Scale (CPRS)	Conners, 1990	Parent
Conners Teacher Rating Scale (CTRS)	Conners, 1990	Teacher
Missouri Child Behavior Checklist (MCBC)	Sines et al., 1969	Parent

Family Assessment

Family Environment Scale (FES)	Moos and Moos, 1981	Parent Child
Family Adaptability and Cohesion Evaluation Scales—III (FACES-III)	Olson et al., 1985	Parent Child

tion that they give: cognitive assessment, psychological assessment, behavioral assessment, and family assessment. These four test groups have specific definitions in this book, which are described later in this chapter. Within each group, attention is given to the primary respondent and/or administrator of the test. Tests that require administration or extensive formulation by the clinician are considered to be *clinician-administered*. Examples of such tests are IQ tests, achievement tests, neuropsychological tests, projective tests, and interviews. The Minnesota Multiphasic Personality Inventory (MMPI) is also considered to be clinician-administered because it requires extensive formulation by the clinician and is not completely face-valid. Although all clinician administered tests use data provided by the child and/or parent, considerable effort, expertise, and/or observation are required by the clinician. Hence, these are grouped under the "clinician-administered" rubric to alert clinicians that these tests require additional time and expertise.

Tests that are essentially face-valid and self-administered are grouped into three additional categories: *Child-report tests* involve the self-report of the child; essentially the child reads (or is read) questions and provides answers. Answers are face-valid and require little inference on the part of the clinician. These tests are susceptible to bias, social desirability, lack of insight, and other factors that may distort the meaning of the data obtained. The clinician must consider these factors in evaluating the meaning of child report tests. *Parent-report tests* involve the parent's response to questions involving the child, parent, or family. Again, answers are face-valid, and the clinician must consider effects of social desirability, bias, lack of insight, lack of observational skill, and other personality factors in interpreting the data obtained. *Other-report tests* are face-valid tests completed by other persons familiar with the child. Inpatient unit staff, teachers, and siblings are examples of such persons. These tests carry the same caveats as child and parent-report tests.

The organization of tests into clinician-administered, child-report, parent-report, and other-report categories has several advantages. First, interpretation of the tests should involve a consideration of who is the respondent to the test. Correlations between clinician administered tests, child-report tests, and parent-report tests are typically quite low (Kaslow & Racusin, 1990), indicating that a comprehensive assessment must integrate information from multiple sources. Second, interpretation should involve a consideration of the degree to which the items are face-valid, projective, and/or interpreted by the clinician. Projective tests and tests requiring additional inferences take clinical formulation into account, while face-valid instruments are more "pure" measures of what the child or parent wants to say to the clinician. Third, tests involve varying degrees of preparation, time, and effort. Clinician-administered tests almost always require the use of the clinician's (or a technician's) time in order to gather data. Hence, these tests must be worked around clinical interviews and the rest of the clinician's schedule. Child-, parent-, and other-report tests may be completed without requiring significant additional clinical time. Fourth, the tests give different types of information, all of which can be valuable. Children and parents, for example, can have different viewpoints on the same behavior, and nothing is a substitute for the clinician's observation and probing of specific issues. Hence, it is usually important to give a variety of tests based on the respondent and the type of information obtained. Such a variety can give a more complete clinical picture.

Cognitive Assessment

The broad assessment strategies for each disorder can be divided into four major categories (cognitive, psychological, behavioral, and family) based on the type of information obtained. Cognitive assessment is defined in this book as tests that provide information about the child's intellectual abilities, specific cognitive capacities, understanding of the environment, ability to engage in adaptive behavior, and level of basic knowledge. With few exceptions, cognitive assessment tests are clinician-administered and require considerable expertise to administer and interpret.

Intelligence Tests.   Perhaps the most widely used cognitive assessment tests in the clinical setting are intelligence tests. Intelligence tests are used to gain an overall impression of the child's cognitive ability as well as to measure specific intellectual abilities, such as verbal comprehension and nonverbal reasoning. While numerous intelligence tests exist, the most extensively used are the *Bayley Scales of Infant Development: Second Edition* (Bayley-II; Bayley, 1993) for children age 0–42 months, the *Wechsler Preschool and Primary Scale of Intelligence—Revised* (WPPSI-R; Wechsler, 1989) for children age 3–7 years, the *Wechsler Intelligence Scale for Children—Third Edition* (WISC-III; Wechsler, 1991; however, much of the research that applies to the WISC-III is based on the older Wechsler Intelligence Scale for Children—Revised (WISC-R; Wechsler, 1974) for children age 6–17 years) the *Wechsler Adult Intelligence Scale—Revised* (WAIS-R; Wechsler, 1981) for adolescents and adults over age 16, and the *Stanford-Binet Intelligence Scale: Fourth Edition* for age 2–adult (SB:FE; Thorndike, Hagen, and Sattler, 1986).

The Bayley-II is a measure of mental-behavioral development in infants age 1 month to 42 months. Its items require the presentation of a stimulus or request to the child, followed by observation and scoring of the response. Items test age-appropriate mental and motor development. The Bayley-II yields a Mental Developmental Index (MDI), a Psychomotor Developmental Index (PDI), and Behavior Rating Index (BRI). The MDI may be used as an approximation of IQ, although IQ at very young ages is only moderately predictive of IQ at later ages. Based on a large normative sample, Bayley-II MDI, PDI, and BRI raw scores can be converted to standard scores with a mean of 100 and standard deviation of 15 (Bayley, 1993).

At older ages (roughly 3 or 4 years and up), the Wechsler scales (WPPSI-R, WISC-III, and WAIS-R) become the measures of choice for child intelligence and cognitive status. Each Wechsler scale consists of a variety of subscales; most subscales appear on all three age-based versions of the Wechsler IQ tests (Tables 1.4 and 1.5). As measures of specific cognitive abilities the Wechsler

TABLE 1.4   Wechsler Intelligence Scale Verbal Subtests

SUBTEST	CONTENT	WPPSI-R	WISC-III	WAIS-R
Sentences	Short-term auditory memory for sentences	O	N	N
Digit Span	Short-term auditory memory for numbers	N	O	S
Information	Fund of basic information	S	S	S
Comprehension	Practical knowledge and judgment	S	S	S
Arithmetic	Mental computation	S	S	S
Vocabulary	Word knowledge	S	S	S
Similarities	Relationships between concepts	S	S	S

S = Standard subtest
O = Optional subtest
N = Not on test

subscales may be helpful in the diagnosis and understanding of certain disorders. More importantly, however, subscales can be combined into higher-order ability composites.

The most well-known and widely used composites are based on Wechsler's *a priori* conceptualization of intelligence as having Verbal and Performance components. Hence, in addition to an overall measure of intelligence (Full Scale IQ or FIQ), the WPPSI-R, WISC-III, and WAIS-R yield measures of Verbal IQ (VIQ—comprehension and knowledge of verbal concepts) and Performance IQ (PIQ—visual-spatial, visual-motor, and visual sequencing ability). However, the Verbal–Performance differentiation of subtests appears to hold empirically only for the WPPSI-R (Sattler, 1990).

Factor analyses of the WISC-III and WAIS-R support the existence of Verbal (usually called Verbal Comprehension or VC) and Performance (usually called Perceptual Organization or PO) clusters of subtests, but additional clusters have also been identified (Sattler, 1993; Wechsler, 1991). The most widely accepted "other" factor-analytically derived clusters of subtests are Freedom from Distractibility (FFD, a measure of attention, concentration, and short-term memory; Arithmetic and Digit Span subtests) and Processing Speed (PS, a measure of rapid response to simple visual-motor tasks; Coding and Symbol Search subtests)(Sattler, 1993; Wechsler, 1991).

Hence, in addition to subtest scores, the Wechsler scales give FIQ, VIQ, PIQ, VC, PO, FFD, and PS (WISC-III only) scores. Subtest raw scores are con-

TABLE 1.5   Wechsler Intelligence Scale Performance Subtests

SUBTEST	CONTENT	WPPSI-R	WISC-III	WAIS-R
Geometric Design	Visual-motor organization	S	N	N
Animal Pegs	Concentration, finger dexterity, and persistence	O	N	N
Mazes	Planning and perceptual organization	S	O	N
Object Assembly	Synthesis of parts into meaningful wholes	S	S	S
Block Design	Analysis and synthesis of abstract part–whole relationships	S	S	S
Picture Completion	Identification of essential detail	S	S	S
Picture Arrangement	Social-temporal sequencing	N	S	S
Coding/Digit-Symbol	Psychomotor speed of association and reproduction	N	S	S
Symbol Search	Psychomotor speed of matching of details	N	O	N

S = Standard subtest
O = Optional subtest
N = Not on test

verted to scaled scores (mean [m] = 10; standard deviation [s.d.] = 3) based on excellent normative samples. FIQ, VIQ, and PIQ scores are reported as standard scores (m = 100; s.d. = 15). The WISC-III manual provides norms for VC, PO, FFD, and PS scores that allow conversion to "Index" scores with a mean of 100 and standard deviation of 15. WAIS-R scores for VC, PO, and FFD (a PS factor has not been identified on the WAIS-R) can be derived using conversion tables in Sattler (1993). Over all, the WPPSI-R, WISC-III, and WAIS-R provide excellent data concerning the cognitive-intelligence status of children age 3 and older. Additional interpretive strategies and tables for these tests can be found in Wechsler (1981, 1989, 1991) and Sattler (1993).

After the Wechsler scales, the SB:FE is probably the next most used intelligence test in the clinical setting. The SB:FE consists of fifteen subtests that cluster into four broad intelligence areas: Verbal Reasoning (VR), Abstract/ Visual Reasoning (AVR), Quantitative Reasoning (QR), and Short-Term Memory (STM). Depending on age, children are administered from eight to fifteen of the subtests. Based on a large normative sample, subtest scores are converted to Standard Age Scores (SASs), which are standard scores with a mean of 50 and a standard deviation of 8. Area (VR, AVR, QR, and STM) standard scores and an overall IQ score are reported based on a population mean of 100 and standard deviation of 16.

The SB:FE has received criticism for its normative sample, factor structure, difficulty of administration, and length of administration (which can easily exceed 2 hours). Sattler (1993) found no evidence to support the existence of the four area composites. He proposed an alternate grouping of subtests into Verbal Comprehension, Nonverbal Reasoning/Visualization, and Memory areas. Despite these problems, the SB:FE is still widely used. Its widespread use is probably a result of its historical significance, broad age range, extensive sampling of abilities, and utility with older mentally retarded individuals. However, psychometrically and practically, the SB:FE is a less desirable test than the Wechsler scales, except in special cases (which are noted in later chapters).

In addition to the intelligence tests already described, several less widely used measures of intelligence have good psychometric properties and provide clinically relevant data. These scales will not be covered extensively in later chapters, but they deserve mention because they may provide valuable information in specific cases. The *McCarthy Scales of Children's Abilities* (McCarthy, 1972; ages 2½ to 8½), the *Kaufman Assessment Battery for Children* (K-ABC; Kaufman and Kaufman, 1983; ages 2½ to 12½), and the *Woodcock-Johnson Tests of Cognitive Abilities—Revised* (Woodcock and Johnson, 1989b; McGrew, 1994) are excellent measures of global and specific cognitive abilities. Selected subtests from the SB:FE and the *Woodcock-Johnson Tests of Cognitive Abilities—Revised* can be used by clinicians to assess specific areas of cognitive functioning as well as global intelligence.

Achievement Tests.   While intelligence tests seek to evaluate intellectual ability (reflected in basic knowledge and skills obtained in the everyday environment), achievement tests focus more on knowledge gained in the school and home settings. These tests measure the extent to which children have learned what they have been formally taught. At later ages, achievement tests reflect the effects of formal schooling. As with intelligence tests, there are many achievement tests, several of which are psychometrically quite good. Two such tests are the *Woodcock-Johnson Tests of Educational Achievement—Revised* (WJ-R; Woodcock and Johnson, 1989a) and the *Wechsler Individual Achievement Test* (WIAT; The Psychological Corporation, 1992). Several other excellent tests exist, such as the *Kaufman Test of Educational Achievement* (K-TEA; Kaufman and Kaufman, 1985) and the *Peabody Individual Achievement Test—Revised* (PIAT-R; Markwardt, 1989). The WJ-R and WIAT will be considered in more detail here because they have newer norms, more subtests, and excellent psychometric properties.

The WJ-R is an individually administered achievement test with nine standard subtests that fall into four achievement clusters: Reading (pronunciation and comprehension), Mathematics (basic arithmetic and applied problems), Written Language (spelling and writing skills), and Knowledge (science, social studies, and humanities). Subtest and cluster scores are converted to standard scores (m = 100; s.d. = 15) based on a large, representative normative sample. In addition to the nine standard subtests, the WJ-R includes a variety of "supplementary" subtests that are not required in order to obtain cluster scores. However, they can be useful in detailed analysis of a specific achievement problem. Like standard subtests, supplementary subtests yield standard scores relative to a normative sample.

The WJ-R covers an extremely wide age range, from age 2½ to adulthood, and it yields an extensive body of scores. In addition to standard scores, the WJ-R gives age-equivalent, grade equivalent, percentile, confidence interval, and Relative Mastery Index (RMI) scores. The RMI is a measure of the percent of mastery of a topic obtained by the tested child when the average child would score a 90%. For example, an RMI of 95 on Calculation indicates that, when the average child has achieved a 90% mastery level of Calculation, the tested child is likely to show 95% mastery of Calculation.

Like the WJ-R, the WIAT has excellent psychometric properties, although its age range is substantially smaller than that of the WJ-R (age 5 to 19-11). The WIAT consists of eight subtests and four composite areas: Reading, Mathematics, Language, and Writing. The Reading, Mathematics, and Writing areas are similar to those on the WJ-R. However, the Language area includes tests of listening comprehension and oral expression that are unlike any test in the WJ-R achievement battery (although there are tests of Oral Vocabulary and Listening Comprehension in the *Woodcock-Johnson Tests of Cognitive Abilities*). In addition, the WIAT does not include Knowledge tests like those on the WJ-R.

WIAT subtest and composite raw scores yield age- or grade-based standard scores (m = 100; s.d. = 15) based on a representative normative sample. Unlike the WJ-R, the WIAT includes no supplementary subtests, but the WIAT can be used as a brief screening test by eliminating some of the more lengthy and complex subtests. Because the WIAT was co-normed with the WISC-III (i.e., some of the children in the WIAT and WISC-III standardization samples took both the WIAT and WISC-III), WIAT scores can be directly linked to WISC-III scores. In other words, a "predicted" score for each WIAT area can be calculated from the WISC-III IQ score, and the statistical significance of the IQ-achievement difference can be calculated.

Adaptive Functioning Tests. It is sometimes important to consider the results of an adaptive functioning test in addition to the results of intellectual testing, particularly for children with low IQ. Adaptive functioning reflects the extent to which the child functions effectively within his or her environment. Specifically, adaptive functioning tests investigate the child's performance of daily living skills, communication with others, functioning in social situations, and use of motor skills to interact with the environment. Hence, tests of adaptive functioning can give the clinician an idea of the child's ability to engage in self-care and interaction with the environment. Children with adequate adaptive functioning skills can interact appropriately with their environment and can care adequately for themselves. A child with low IQ but high adaptive functioning would be treated quite differently than a child with low IQ and low adaptive functioning.

Most adaptive functioning tests have significant psychometric or practical drawbacks. In the clinical setting the most widely used and psychometrically sound adaptive functioning test is the *Vineland Adaptive Behavior Scales* (VABS; Sparrow, Balla, and Cicchetti, 1984). The VABS assesses social competence and adaptive behavior in children from birth to 19 years old. It is administered in interview format to a respondent who is familiar with the child's behavior. Adaptive behavior is tapped by four VABS subscales: Communication (receptive and expressive language, written language), Daily Living Skills (hygiene, personal care, independence in personal living), Socialization (social behavior), and Motor Skills (gross and fine motor coordination). Subscales can be combined to give an Adaptive Behavior Composite. In addition to adaptive behavior scores, the VABS also gives a score for Maladaptive Behavior (behavior problems).

All VABS scales can be converted to standard scores (m = 100; s.d. = 15) based on a normative sample. In addition to the Expanded Form, there is a briefer Survey Form of the VABS and a Classroom Edition for teachers. The Expanded or Survey forms are typically given to the primary caretaker (usually a parent) and take from 30 to 90 minutes to administer. The VABS has good psychometric properties and is the most widely used adaptive behavior scale. Overall, it is the scale of choice for assessing adaptive behavior. However, its norms have been criticized (Sattler, 1990).

Psychological Assessment

Psychological assessment instruments are defined in this book as tests that measure the internal psychological thoughts, affects, beliefs, issues, or states of the child. They differ from behavioral assessment instruments in that they are internally focused on the child's thoughts and feelings. Psychological assessment instruments are valuable in the clinical setting because they provide a window on the internal states that are presumed to underlie the child's behavior. Thoughts, feelings, and beliefs are important in clinical formulations and in many treatment modalities, particularly psychodynamic and cognitive. Included in the category of psychological assessment are clinician administered tests of personality and structured interviews, as well as child-report tests of self-esteem, stress appraisal, and coping.

Clinician-Administered Tests of Personality.   Clinician-administered tests of personality are often divided into "objective" and "projective" tests. Objective tests present the child with a structured set of questions and a finite set of answers. The child chooses a preworded answer for each question. Projective tests present an ambiguous or incomplete stimulus and ask the child to make something (e.g., a percept, story, or drawing) out of the stimulus.

An extremely useful objective personality test for adolescents is the *Minnesota Multiphasic Personality Inventory* (MMPI; Hathaway and McKinley, 1951, 1967). Recently the MMPI has been revised, and a version was created specifically for use with adolescents, the *Minnesota Multiphasic Personality Inventory—Adolescent* (MMPI-A; Butcher et al., 1992). The MMPI is the most widely used and researched personality test, although most of its use has been with adults. The MMPI consists of 566 true-false items that cluster into three validity and ten clinical scales (Table 1.6). A fourth validity scale, the "Cannot Say" scale

TABLE 1.6   MMPI/MMPI-A Validity and Clinical Scales

SCALE	ABBREVIATION (NUMBER)	DESCRIPTION
VALIDITY SCALES		
Lie	L	Presenting overly favorable picture of self, denial of faults
Infrequency	F	Unusual, atypical responding
Defensiveness	K	Minimizing problems, denial of distress
CLINICAL SCALES		
Hypochondriasis	Hs (1)	Somatic complaints
Depression	D (2)	Dysphoria, tired, inhibited, low self-esteem, attention/concentration problems
Hysteria	Hy (3)	Self-centered, superficial, demands attention
Psychopathic Deviate	Pd (4)	Nonconforming, resists rules, authority conflict, social maladjustment, impulsive
Masculinity-Femininity*	Mf (5)	Dependent, passive, sensitive, traditional female interests, nurturant
Paranoia	Pa (6)	Suspicious, self-righteous, guarded
Psychasthenia	Pt (8)	Anxiety, self-critical, ruminates
Schizophrenia	Sc (9)	Thought problems, alienation
Hypomania	Ma (9)	Impulsive, energetic, egocentric
Social Introversion	Si (0)	Social discomfort, inhibition

* Scale is scored in the opposite direction for females. Note: This table is for review purposes and is not intended to serve as the basic resource for interpretation of the MMPI.

(abbreviated as "?"), is a count of the number of items left unanswered by the respondent. In addition to the basic validity and clinical scales, hundreds of other MMPI validity, clinical, and content scales have been developed, as well as subscales to enhance the interpretation of the basic clinical scales (see Greene [1991] and Graham [1990] for a description of additional MMPI scales). With the exception of the Lie (L) scale, the other basic validity and clinical scales were developed using an empirical approach for item selection. This approach selects items based on the extent to which they differentiate between a normal group and a target clinical group. For example, items for the Hypochondriasis (Hs) scale were selected because they differentiated between normals and psychiatric patients with functional somatic problems (the empirical item selection process was, in fact, not quite this simple or clean; see Dahlstrom, Welsh, and Dahlstrom (1972) for a detailed analysis of item selection).

MMPI scale scores can be converted to T-scores based on a nonrepresentative Minnesota sample tested in the 1930s and 1940s. However, T-scores obtained using these norms are remarkably similar to those using more representative samples (Greene, 1991). Interpretation of the MMPI is complex because of the number of potential MMPI scales to interpret, the meaning of profile patterns, the variety of items contained in each scale, and the volume of MMPI research. At the very least, knowledge of psychometrics, a graduate-level course, and clinical supervision are required to use the MMPI competently. Readers interested in additional information concerning the MMPI are encouraged to consult Graham (1990), Greene (1991), and Dahlstrom et al. (1972).

The lower age range of the MMPI has been a subject of disagreement between clinicians. Relative to adult norms, adolescents tend to elevate most MMPI scales. Marks, Seeman, and Haller (1974) addressed the problem of elevated adolescent scores by providing actuarial data and norms for children as young as 14. Using age 14 as the cutoff is probably wise, considering that the reading ability required for most MMPI items is approximately sixth to eighth grade. Marks et al.'s (1974) adolescent norms are probably the most widely used for the MMPI. However, because those norms use non–K-corrected scores (adult MMPI norms use K-corrected scores), they should be interpreted with caution for adolescents with high K-scales.

Interpretation of the MMPI for adolescents has also been the subject of some disagreement. Perhaps the best interpretation strategy is to look at the adolescent's profile compared to both adult and adolescent norms. Interpretation of the meaning of the profile may begin with the usual descriptors for scales and code types, with the understanding that a developmental view must be taken. For example, alienation in the adolescent years may reflect more of an identity-growth process than would alienation for a 45-year-old person. The tendency to "overpathologize" the MMPI profiles of adolescents, particularly relative to adult norms, must be resisted by the clinician. Nevertheless, elevated profiles can indicate personality traits and even psychopathology in the adolescent. Profiles can also be compared to "typical" presentations of two-point code types described in Marks et al. (1974).

The venerable original MMPI was revised in 1989 to form a new (but very similar) instrument, the MMPI-2 (Butcher et al., 1989). The MMPI-2 retained most of the original items from the basic clinical and validity scales (although some of these were slightly reworded to reflect more modern views). However, many of the other items were changed, deleted, or added, requiring most other MMPI subscales to be changed as well. A new, modern, more representative normative sample was used, and the calculation of T-scores was changed for most scales (not scales 5 and 0) to achieve a somewhat more "normal" distribution of scores. These T-scores are called "uniform T-scores" and are not normalized T-scores per se (see Butcher et al. [1989] for a discussion of T-score derivation). T-scores of 65 (not 70 as on the original MMPI) and higher were considered clinically significant. The issue most relevant to child/adolescent assessment, however, was the authors' recommendation that the MMPI-2 *not* be used with adolescents under the age of 18 (Butcher et al., 1989). Hence, the MMPI remained the authors' test of choice for use with adolescents age 14 to 17/18 (until the development of the MMPI-A a few years later).

The MMPI-A (Butcher et al., 1992) was developed as the adolescent companion to the MMPI-2. An effort was made to retain (with occasional wording changes) most MMPI items in order to maintain congruence between the MMPI-A and MMPI/MMPI-2, although some items were deleted because of offensive or inappropriate content for adolescents. Validity and clinical scales that are most changed on the MMPI-A are F (27 items deleted from the original MMPI), 5 (16 items deleted), and 0 (8 items deleted); other validity and clinical scales have only minor changes. Norms for the MMPI-A were derived from a national sample of 1620 adolescents between the ages of 14 and 18. Efforts were made to make the normative sample representative of geographic region and ethnicity; however, the sample may be of somewhat higher socio-economic status (SES) than the national population of adolescents. Like the MMPI-2, the MMPI-A uses uniform T-scores for most validity and clinical scales (not scales 5 and 0).

The MMPI-A is a 478-item true-false instrument that can be administered to adolescents age 14 to 18. It includes the same basic validity and clinical scales as the MMPI and MMPI-2, and most scales retain their original interpretive meaning. Numerous new validity and clinical scales were also developed for the MMPI-A (Butcher et al., 1992). Unlike the MMPI-2 (but similar to earlier MMPI adolescent norms), scales 1, 4, 7, 8, and 9 do not have K-corrections on the MMPI-A; in other words, non–K-corrected norms are used for all scales. T-scores of 65 and higher are considered clinically significant.

The decision of which form of the MMPI to use for adolescents is a complex one. Perhaps the easiest decision is that the MMPI-2 should *never* be used with an adolescent under age 18. For children 14–18 the original MMPI has the advantage of decades of research and clinical use, but some items are inappropriate for adolescents, and norms are less than ideal. The MMPI-A, on the other hand, is briefer, has more appropriate items for adolescents, has better norms, and is a generally more "modern" test. However, it does not have the volume of research and clinical support of the MMPI. Over all, interpretation of MMPI scales L, K, 1, 2, 3, 4, 6, 7, 8, 9, and 0 should be similar for the MMPI and MMPI-A, because only very minor changes were made in these scales. Scales F and 5, however, have undergone major changes on the MMPI-A, and they should be interpreted cautiously until further research is done. As research accumulates on the MMPI-A, this test will clearly become the test of choice over the MMPI for adolescents. Until this body of research exists, however, both instruments will probably continue to be used.

Of the projective personality tests, the most well-known are the *Rorschach Inkblot Test* (Exner, 1986) and the *Thematic Apperception Test* (TAT; Murray, 1943). The Rorschach consists of ten cards, each of which is a picture of a symmetric inkblot. Numerous systems exist for administering and scoring the Rorschach, but all ask children to say what they see on the blot (the "percept"). Later the children are asked to show in detail the characteristics that led them to see the percept in the way they did. Scoring is done on the basis of response characteristics ("determinants") such as color, form, achromatic color, shading, dimensionality, and texture. The content and form quality of the children's responses are also used in scoring. The widely accepted Exner (1986) Rorschach scoring and interpretation system is used in this book.

The TAT (Murray, 1943) is one of a multitude of storytelling tests. Numerous other such tests exist, several of which were designed specifically for children. However, the TAT is the oldest, best known, and most widely used of these tests. Hence, it serves as the prototypical storytelling test in later chapters. Many hypotheses about TAT patterns may be readily applied to other storytelling tests.

The TAT presents the child with a picture of a person or people in a certain setting or activity. The child is asked to tell a story about the characters in the picture, what they are doing, what they are thinking, and what they are feeling. No widely accepted scoring system exists for the TAT. Stories are typically analyzed for repetitive, unique, intense, or problematic themes, beliefs, or affects. The TAT can provide a picture of how the child expects sequences of events to occur, as well as predominant affects and thoughts of the child related to these stories.

Clinician-Administered Structured and Semistructured Interviews. Structured and semistructured diagnostic interviews use an organized set of questions and probes to evaluate a child's behaviors and feelings. They are typically based on a diagnostic system (e.g., DSM-III-R or DSM-IV) and have as their major goal the delineation of a specific diagnosis. Diagnostic interviews are considered here as clinician-administered psychological assessment measures because they require the clinician's time and judgment and they ask about the child's internal thoughts/feelings as well as about behaviors.

Examples of structured or semistructured interviews are the *Diagnostic Interview for Children and Adolescents—Revised* (DICA-R; Herjanic and Campbell, 1977; Mokros and Poznanski, 1992), the *Diagnostic Interview Schedule for Children—Revised* (DISC-R; Costello et al., 1984; Hodges and Zeman, 1993), the *Child Assessment Schedule* (CAS; Hodges, 1985, 1987; Hodges and Zeman, 1993), and the *Schedule for Affective Disorders and Schizophrenia for School Age Children* (Kiddie-SADS or K-SADS; Puig-Antich, Chambers, and Tabrizi, 1983; Puig-Antich and Ryan, 1986; Orvaschel and Puig-Antich, 1987). These interviews all consist of a set of diagnostic questions that are asked directly to the child and/ or parent and are used to arrive at a diagnosis for the child; they have both parent and child forms, although the integration of these forms varies between interviews. The interviews differ somewhat on the skill required of the interviewer, the diagnostic criteria covered, and psychometric properties. All of these interviews have been updated with changes in the DSM diagnostic systems, from DSM-III to DSM-III-R, and eventually (although not yet for some of the interviews) for DSM-IV.

The DICA-R and DISC-R are very structured and assess a wide range of diagnoses of childhood and adolescence. The DICA-R may be administered to children age 6–17. Despite having adequate test-retest reliability, the DICA-R has questionable or unknown interrater reliability and needs more psychometric study (Finch, Casat, and Carey, 1990; Hodges and Zeman, 1993). Like the DICA-R, the highly structured DISC-R requires little clinical experience to administer and yields a DSM diagnosis. In addition to the diagnosis, the DISC-R can yield "scores" (actually counts of number of symptoms) for each diagnosis category; these scores can be used as subscales. The DISC-R may be administered to children age 6–18, although it should probably not be used with children younger than 11 (Hodges and Zeman, 1993). The psychometric properties of the DISC and DISC-R have been severely criticized (Finch et al., 1990). At this time, both the DICA-R and the DISC-R are in need of further development before they should see extensive clinical use.

The K-SADS and the CAS, on the other hand, are less structured and therefore require a skilled interviewer and more clinical judgment than the DICA-R and the DISC-R (Mokros & Poznanski, 1992). The CAS contains open-ended as well as yes-no questions, and the K-SADS uses severity ratings as well as symptom presence questions. In addition, both the CAS and the K-SADS call on the interviewer to make a judgment as to the presence or absence of symptoms as opposed to simply recording the child's yes-no answers.

Two forms of the K-SADS exist, one to assess the child's present symptoms (K-SADS-P), and one to assess past and current psychopathology (K-SADS-E). Both forms are intended to be administered to the parent and the child, with a diagnosis evolving from the interview results. The K-SADS appears to have adequate reliability (Mokros and Poznanski, 1992) and has been used with children age 6–17 (Hodges and Zeman, 1993). It is perhaps the most widely used clinical interview and is strongly endorsed by some authors (Mokros and Poznanski, 1992).

The CAS has been used primarily with children age 7–12, although it appears to apply to children as young as 5 and as old as 17 (Hodges and Zeman, 1993). It tends to be less symptom oriented in its organization and does not assess less common diagnoses of childhood and adolescence. However, the CAS appears to have the best psychometrics of the clinical interviews considered here, with extensive validity studies and good reliability (Finch et al., 1990). CAS diagnoses have been found to relate correctly to child self-report of depression and anxiety (Hodges, 1990). Like the DISC-R, the CAS can yield scores for different content areas, and these scores can be used as subscales.

Despite their potential utility as diagnostic tools, the DICA, DISC, CAS, and K-SADS are rarely used in actual clinical practice. A major problem is their length, which ranges in time from 1 to 4 hours, depending on whether both parent and child are interviewed. This significantly limits their clinical utility and makes them unpleasant for clinicians and families. On the other hand, the interviews are vitally important for research, which demands standardization and replication. Hence, they have seen most widespread use in research. Because of their limited clinical applicability, these interviews are considered only in the context of diagnoses for which they have seen extensive clinical or research use. However, because of their breadth, they could be used diagnostically for almost any diagnosis covered in this book.

Child-Report Psychological Assessment Instruments. Child self-report instruments are sometimes used to gather information about internal psychological thoughts and feelings, but these instruments are used sparingly before early adolescence. Before age 10 to 12, children lack the insight, reading ability, and word knowledge to respond to most broad-band psychological questionnaires. Some diagnosis-specific tests, on the other hand, appear to give valid results with children as young as 6. These latter tests are considered in the context of specific diagnoses.

For older children and adolescents, two useful self-report psychological tests are the *Piers-Harris Self Concept Scale* (PHSCS; Piers, 1984) and the *Symptom Checklist-90—Revised* (SCL-90-R; Derogatis, 1983). The PHSCS is an eighty-item self-report scale of self-concept/self-esteem in children (Piers, 1984). In addition to a Total Self-Concept Score, it yields subscale scores of self-concept in six areas: Behavior, Intellectual and School Status, Physical Appearance and Attributes, Anxiety, Popularity, and Happiness and Satisfaction.

PHSCS subscale and Total Self-Concept raw scores convert to T-scores (m = 50, s.d. = 10) based on a large normative sample. For all scales, higher T-scores indicate better self-concept. The Piers-Harris can be a valuable tool for assessing different types of self-esteem in children. For example, a child who feels good about himself or herself over all, may have very low self-esteem related to intellectual status. The Piers-Harris can help to isolate these self-esteem "problem areas." The psychometric properties of the Piers-Harris are good, with adequate test-retest reliability, internal consistency, and validity. However, its norms may overestimate self-esteem; clinical experience suggests that T-scores of 55–60 are average, as opposed to T-scores of 50.

The SCL-90-R is a ninety-item self-report scale that asks the respondent to rate the subjective severity of psychological symptoms in nine areas: Somatization, Obsessive-Compulsive, Interpersonal Sensitivity, Depression, Anxiety, Hostility, Phobic Anxiety, Paranoid Ideation, and Psychoticism. It also yields a Global Severity Index of overall symptom severity. Items are face-valid and are rated on a 0–4 scale of severity. Item scores are added to give subscale raw scores, which may then be converted to T-scores (m = 50, s.d. = 10) based on a normative sample of adolescents. The SCL-90-R can be administered to adolescents as young as 13 and has been shown to be reliable and valid (Derogatis, 1983). It can be a useful instrument for quantifying the severity of an adolescent's symptoms along several symptom parameters. Although it is more face-valid (and thus more subject to manipulation) than the MMPI, the SCL-90-R is briefer and more symptom-focused. Clinical experience with this scale suggests that the norms for adolescents may provide T-scores that are too low, minimizing the actual severity of symptoms.

Behavioral Assessment

Unlike psychological assessment instruments, behavioral assessment instruments focus on the external behaviors of the child. Behavioral assessment scales provide a structured, systematic way for the clinician to gather information about the child's behavior as it is perceived by an observer in a certain setting. Because they are usually administered in checklist form, behavior assessment scales are also called behavior checklists.

Achenbach Child Behavior Checklists. Perhaps the most widely used behavior checklists are those developed by Achenbach: the *Child Behavior Checklist* for parents (CBCL; Achenbach, 1991a, 1992), the *Teacher's Report Form* for children age 5–18 years (TRF; Achenbach, 1991b), and the *Youth Self Report* for children age 11–18 years (YSR; Achenbach, 1991c). Recent efforts have standardized the format and meaning of the Achenbach scales across ages and respondents. Hence, the CBCL, TRF, and YSR share many similar items and yield essentially the same subscales. This congruence is extremely valuable when comparing data obtained from different respondents.

The CBCL has separate forms for children age 2–3 years (CBCL/2–3; Achenbach, 1992) and children age 4–18 years (CBCL; Achenbach, 1991a). Because the CBCL for 4–18-year-olds is much more widely used than the 2–3-year-old version, it will be emphasized here. CBCL items fall into two categories: competence items and problem items. The seven competence items (each item has several subparts) ask for information about the child's participation in sports, activities, groups, chores, peer relationships, and academics. Three competence scales are obtained based on sums of item scores: Activities, Social, and School competence. Higher scores on the competence scales indicate better adjustment in these areas.

In addition to the competence items, the CBCL contains 113 behavior problem items, one of which has eight subparts and one of which asks the parent to list up to three problems that are not covered on other checklist items. Each CBCL item describes a specific behavior or belief of the child. For the behavior problem items, the parent rates on a 0 (not true) to 2 (very or often true) scale the extent to which the item is true of the child's behavior during the past 6 months. Behavior problem items cluster into eight factor-analytically derived subscales (with certain modifications to create congruence between the CBCL, TRF, and YSR), although items may appear on none, one, or more than one subscale. The CBCL subscales are Withdrawn, Somatic Complaints, Anxious/Depressed, Social Problems, Thought Problems, Attention Problems, Delinquent Behavior, and Aggressive Behavior. Certain subscale scores (adjusted so that items are not counted twice in a single scale or for both scales; see Achenbach, 1991a) are combined to yield two "higher-order" subscales: Internalizing (Withdrawn, Somatic Complaints, and Anxious/Depressed) and Externalizing (Delinquent Behavior and Aggressive Behavior). An overall Total Problem score is obtained by summing all CBCL items except items 2 (allergy item) and 4 (asthma item).

CBCL Competence and Problem Subscale raw scores are converted to T-scores based on a large national sample of children age 4–18. T-scores are normalized such that a large proportion of normal children receive high competence and low problem scores. Problem subscale T-scores of 67–70 and higher may be considered clinically elevated, while Total Problem T-scores of 60–63 and higher may be considered clinically elevated. In interpreting CBCL subscale scores, the clinician must look at what items are driving the subscale score. A high Anxious/Depressed score, for example, could reflect perfectionistic worry or feelings of isolation and worthlessness depending on item endorsement patterns.

The CBCL/2–3 resembles the CBCL, but it has no Competence items and fewer (100) problem items. Like the CBCL, it gives Anxious/Depressed, Withdrawn, Somatic Problems, Aggressive Behavior, and Destructive Behavior subscales, but it lacks the Social Problems, Thought Problems, and Attention Problems subscales. The CBCL/2–3 also has a Sleep Problems subscale. Internalizing (Anxious/Depressed and Withdrawn subscales), Externalizing (Aggressive and Destructive Behavior subscales), and Total Problem scores are obtained, and conversion to T-scores occurs as on the CBCL. Interpretation is also similar to the CBCL.

The TRF is the teacher-completed analogue to the CBCL. Although it lacks the Competence section of the CBCL, it includes an Academic/Adaptive Functioning section (Academic Performance, Working Hard, Behaving Appropriately, Learning, and Happy subscales, and a Total Adaptive score) and a Problem Items section (same subscales as CBCL, with very minor item differences on subscales). The TRF and CBCL have the same number of items, most of which are virtually identical. Scoring and interpretation are essentially the same as for the CBCL.

The YSR has the same number and type of Competence and Problem items as the CBCL, with few exceptions. In fact, almost all YSR items are CBCL items worded in the first person. YSR subscales are virtually identical to CBCL subscales, with the exception of the School Competence subscale (missing on the YSR). Total scores, T-scores, and scale interpretation are similar to the CBCL.

Clinicians can use the different Achenbach scales to obtain a picture of the child's behavior from the viewpoint of multiple respondents in multiple situations. For example, a problem-ridden TRF profile coupled with a relatively normal CBCL profile suggests that the child may behave adequately in the less structured, more individualized home environment while becoming disorganized and misbehaving at school. Alternatively, the child may behave poorly only around a particular teacher, or the parent may be minimizing the child's behavior problems. In cases where the YSR, TRF, and/or CBCL show markedly different profiles, the clinician should expect the child, teachers, and parents to disagree about the child's behavior problems.

Conners Rating Scales.   Like the Achenbach scales, the Conners scales include forms for parents (*Conners' Parent Rating Scales;* CPRS) and teachers (*Conners' Teacher Rating Scales;* CTRS)(Conners, 1990). Several forms of the CPRS exist, differing primarily in breadth and in number of items. The CPRS has a 93 item form (CPRS-93) and a forty-eight–item form (CPRS-48), a revised version. A shorter form of the Conners scales that is sometimes used is the ten-item "Hyperactivity Index" (HI; also called the Conners Abbreviated Symptom Questionnaire or ASQ), which is embedded in the longer CPRS forms (Conners, 1990). The ten HI items are the items that are most responsive to ADHD drug treatment effects, but they are not sufficient for the diagnosis of ADHD; hence, although they are widely used, they should *not* be separated from the scale for independent use in ADHD assessment (Atkins and Pelham, 1991; Barkley, 1987; Conners, 1990).

Each Conners form consists of behavioral items to be rated by the parent, with items clustering into factor-analytically derived subscales. Parents rate each item on a 0–3 (CPRS-48) or 1–4 (CPRS-93) scale of "how much you think your child has been bothered by this problem during the past month" (Conners, 1990, p. 22). Norms (for conversion to T-scores) are available based on age-sex groups for all Conners scales except the CPRS-93 (Conners, 1990), and norms are not available for the HI on the CPRS-93.

The CPRS-48 checklist can be administered to parents of children age 3–17. It yields five subscales (Conduct Problem, Learning Problem, Psychosomatic, Impulsive-Hyperactive, and Anxiety) and the Hyperactivity Index. No age range is specified for the CPRS-93, although norms are based on children between the ages of 6 and 14. CPRS subscales are Conduct Disorder, Anxious-Shy, Restless-Disorganized, Learning Problem, Psychosomatic, Obsessive-Compulsive, Antisocial, and Hyperactive-Immature. A major disadvantage of the CPRS-93 is its use of a single set of norms (based on children age 6–14) for all age-sex groups. Unlike the Achenbach scales, which were not designed to focus on any particular disorder, the Conners scales tend to include items that are more focused on externalizing symptomatology (such as conduct problems, attention-deficit, and hyperactivity), giving a more in-depth assessment of these behaviors at the expense of breadth of assessment (although the Conners scales do have some internalizing items).

As with the CPRS, two major forms of the CTRS exist, the CTRS-39 and a revised twenty-eight–item form (CTRS-28). The CTRS is intended to be administered to a teacher who is familiar with the child's classroom behavior. Both forms of the CTRS use a 0–3 rating scale and 1 month time frame for items, similar to the CPRS-48. The CTRS-39 has six factor subscales (Hyperactivity, Conduct Problem, Emotional-Overindulgent, Anxious-Passive, Asocial, and Daydream-Attention Problem), while the shorter CTRS-28 has only three scales (Conduct Problem, Hyperactivity, and Inattentive-Passive). Both teacher forms also include the Hyperactivity Index. The derivation of raw and T-scores for the CTRS scales are similar to the CPRS.

A short form of the CTRS-39, the IOWA-Conners Rating Scale, was developed to delineate problems of inattention/overactivity from problems of aggression/defiance. The IOWA-Conners consists of ten items, five of which measure inattention/overactivity and five of which measure aggression. It appears to have promise as a brief screen for inattention, oppositionality, and aggressiveness, although use of the full CTRS-39 or CTRS-28 is recommended because of their comprehensiveness and superior psychometrics.

Conners (1990) suggests that, in general, the revised versions of his scales (CPRS-48 and CTRS-28) should be used. However, the older CPRS-93 and CTRS-39 have larger norm samples and broader symptom coverage. On the other hand, the CPRS-48 and CTRS-28 were co-normed (same normative samples), providing better comparisons between parent and teacher data. Furthermore, they are briefer than the older versions. For example, Barkley (1987) recommends use of the CPRS-48 because of its brevity and better psychometric properties.

Many of the interpretive comments for the Achenbach scales apply to the Conners scales. Specifically, comparison of parent- and teacher-completed checklists is recommended, and individual items should be examined to guide the interpretation of elevated scale scores. Conners (1990) does not suggest a specific cutoff T-score to identify problems of clinical significance, but he calls scores above 60 "above average," scores above 65 "much above average," and scores above 70 "very much above average" (Conners, 1990, p. 27).

Missouri Children's Behavior Checklist.   Another behavior checklist that can be valuable in clinical practice is the *Missouri Children's Behavior Checklist* (MCBC; Sines et al., 1969). The MCBC is a seventy-seven–item parent-completed checklist of child behaviors. Parents answer (yes-no) whether their child has shown each behavior in the previous 6 months. The items yield seven subscales: Aggression, Inhibition, Activity Level, Sleep Disturbance, Somatization, Sociability, and Depression; raw scores are simply the number of items answered "yes" for each subscale. MCBC subscale raw scores can be converted to T-scores based on a large sample of 9–14-year-old children (separate norms exist for sex but not age).

Thompson, Kronenberger, and Curry (1989) factor-analyzed MCBC subscale scores to give three higher-order factor subscales: Internalizing (Inhibition and Somatization), Externalizing (Aggression, Activity Level, and Sleep Disturbance), and Sociability (Sociability subscale). The Depression subscale was not included in the derivation of factors, although later research suggests that it loads on the Internalizing factor (Thompson, Kronenberger, and Johndrow, 1992). Factor scores are the sum of the T-scores of their constituent subscales. Over all, then, the MCBC gives scores for Aggression, Inhibition, Activity Level, Sleep Disturbance, Somatization, Sociability, and Depression behavior subscales as well as for Internalizing, Externalizing, and Sociability behavior factors. Subscale T-scores greater than 62 may be considered to be in the clinical range, along with Internalizing scores greater than 110 and Externalizing scores greater than 180 (Thompson et al., 1989).

The MCBC has been extensively used and validated in research, and it appears to have clinical utility as well (Thompson, 1986). Unlike the Achenbach and Conners scales, the MCBC subscales were not factor-analytically derived. Hence, while they may have weaker internal consistency, they have greater rational/intuitive appeal. In addition, the MCBC has fewer items than the CBCL and wider symptom coverage than the Conners scales. The yes-no answer format of the MCBC also allows faster completion time than the CBCL. However, the yes-no answer format of the MCBC does not allow parents a midpoint "sometimes" choice for behaviors that occur at moderate frequencies. In addition, the CBCL and CPRS may have stronger psychometric properties and are more widely used than the MCBC. Furthermore, the CBCL has better norms and wider symptom coverage than the MCBC. Nevertheless, the MCBC is extremely useful because of its brevity, ease for parents to understand, and clinical relevance. Clinical experience suggests that the MCBC may identify milder problems better than the CBCL.

Ultimately the clinician's choice of what behavior problem checklist to use depends on the needs and characteristics of a particular clinical case. In general, it is wise to gain input from parents, teachers, and, when possible, the child. The Achenbach scales (CBCL, TRF, YSR) provide broad symptom coverage, good norms, good psychometric properties, and congruence across respondents. The Conners scales (CPRS and CTRS) give more detailed and circumscribed (but briefer) information about externalizing problems (particularly attention, hyperactivity, and conduct problems). The MCBC is briefer than the CBCL, broader in symptom coverage than the CPRS, and possibly more sensitive to mild behavior problems.

Family Assessment

A final set of broad-band instruments that are commonly used in clinical practice with children are family assessment scales. Family assessment scales quantify family characteristics that are believed to be important in the adjustment of the child. They augment the clinician's observations of in-session family interactions and allow the clinician to assess different points of view of family members. Parents, for example, might see the family level of control much differently than children do. Because the respondent to a family assessment instrument must have an intimate knowledge of the family situation, parents and children are the primary information sources.

Two tests that yield clinically useful information about the family are the *Family Environment Scale* (FES; Moos and Moos, 1981) and the *Family Adaptability and Cohesion Evaluation Scales—III* (FACES-III; Olson et al., 1985). The FES is a ninety-item true-false scale designed to assess basic characteristics of the family environment. It is composed of ten subscales: Cohesion (commitment and support in the family), Expressiveness (open expression of feelings and behaviors), Conflict (open expression of hostility, conflict, and aggression),

Independence (self-reliance, assertiveness, and acceptance of intrafamily differences), Achievement Orientation (values of competition and drive to succeed), Intellectual-Cultural Orientation (interest in intellectual and cultural activities), Active-Recreational Orientation (participation in recreational-social activities), Moral-Religious Emphasis (religiosity and use of religious rules to guide the behavior of family members), Organization (structure and planning in the family), and Control (firm rules and hierarchy in the family).

Kronenberger and Thompson (1990) factor analyzed FES subscales and found three higher-order factors: Supportive (Cohesion, Expressiveness, Independence, Active-Recreational Orientation, and Intellectual-Cultural Orientation scales), Conflicted (Conflict, Cohesion [reverse scored], and Organization [reverse scored]), and Controlling (Control, Moral-Religious Emphasis, Achievement Orientation, and Independence [reverse scored]). The Supportive factor measures a sense of openness, team spirit, and shared interests and activities. The Conflicted factor assesses family conflict and a lack of the support and organization that could control conflict when it arises. The Controlling factor measures the use of overt rules and implicit religious and achievement expectations to maintain family stability.

The FES can be completed by parents and adolescents. Raw scores are converted to T-scores based on a large normative sample of families. The sample is not nationally representative, however. Factor scores are sums of subscale T-scores (T-scores of scales with negative factor loadings are subtracted; Kronenberger and Thompson, 1990). It is often instructive to compare the results of parent- and child-reporting to see discrepancies in how the family is viewed. These discrepancies can be helpful in formulations and interventions.

The FACES-III is a twenty-item scale that yields two subscales: Cohesion (the extent to which family members are connected and feel a sense of unity) and Adaptability (the extent to which the family is open to change in its structure). Each item is a family description that is rated on a 1–5 scale of similarity to the family. Items are summed to yield subscale scores. Based on their circumplex theory, Olson et al. (1985) expect that very high and very low Cohesion (enmeshed and disengaged, respectively) and Adaptability (chaotic and rigid) scores denote family problems. Mid-range scores reflect positive family attributes. However, clinical experience indicates that there is a positive linear relationship between Cohesion and the psychological adjustment of family members. Adaptability does not appear to relate to adjustment. Despite these problems, the FACES-III can be used to signal family problems and to assess basic characteristics of family closeness and change. Like the FES, it can be administered to adolescents and adults.

Also included in the Family Assessment section of each chapter are any assessment patterns pertaining to parents. For example, if the mother's MMPI may be particularly useful for a diagnosis, maternal MMPI patterns are described in the Family Assessment section. Parent assessment can be helpful in planning family interventions and in formulations of a case. However, it is infrequently used because some parents object to being the target of assessment.

Syndrome-Specific Tests

Syndrome-specific tests are instruments designed to assess features character-istic of a single diagnosis or a very closely related group of diagnoses. In each chapter, following a discussion of broad assessment test patterns, syndrome-specific tests are described for each disorder. Like the broad assessment in-struments, syndrome specific tests differ based on respondent; some tests are intended to be administered and interpreted by the clinician, and a few are designed to be completed by other adults, usually teachers or inpatient unit staff. However, most syndrome-specific instruments are completed by parents and by the child. Hence, the division of clinician-administered, child-report, parent-report, and other-report is retained under each chapter heading of Syn-drome-Specific Tests, with most attention given to child- and parent-report. Syndrome-specific tests are presented and critiqued under their respective diagnoses.

Syndrome-specific tests can be invaluable in the detailed evaluation of a particular problem or diagnosis. Because most are child- or parent-report, they are easy to obtain and interpret. It is notable that the quantity and quality of syndrome-specific tests vary greatly from one diagnosis to another. Depres-sion and ADHD, for example, have a number of extremely good syndrome-specific tests, while there are almost no such tests for enuresis, encopresis, and tic disorders.

TREATMENT OPTIONS

Coverage of each diagnosis concludes with a consideration of treatment op-tions. Only treatment options that have been the topic of theoretical and re-search work pertaining specifically to a disorder are considered. Furthermore, discussion of treatment options is problem-focused; that is, the treatment is discussed as it pertains to the disorder. Thus, basic descriptions of such tech-niques as family therapy and behavioral interventions will not be found in later chapters; however, applications of different interventions to the specific diagnosis will be considered in detail.

Essentially, such a problem-focused approach is what is needed in the clini-cal situation. Background books on different therapy orientations are abun-dant. These books are important for training, but they are often too general for application to specific, day-to-day clinical issues. In other words, what is fre-quently lacking on the clinician's bookshelf is a book that describes the appli-cation of therapy interventions to specific clinical problems. Across the vari-ous diagnoses in this book, seven types of interventions are applied to the specific problems of the child, as described next.

Behavioral Interventions

These interventions have the common theme of a focus on the child's problem behaviors, their antecedents and their consequences. Internal psychological processes, developmental history, and past stressors are irrelevant. External behaviors and environmental characteristics, manifest in the A-B-C approach (Antecedents-Behaviors-Consequences), are all that matters.

Behavioral interventions are often used with children because adults have a great deal of control over the child's environment. Furthermore, behavioral interventions require little understanding or thought on the part of the child. Hence, even very young or intellectually impaired children can benefit from them. Although the exact content and form of behavioral interventions vary widely depending on the specific target behaviors, at a basic level, they take a similar approach.

Behavioral modification, for example, follows a fairly consistent pattern: First, the problem behavior is operationalized. It is analyzed in detail, with specific descriptors. Vague, overly inclusive language is discouraged. "Disobedience," for example, may be reconceptualized as "sticks out tongue following a request to perform a behavior". Second, the behavior is monitored, with attention also given to the situation that leads up to the behavior (antecedents) and to the situation that follows the behavior (consequences). Third, reinforcing and punishing consequences are identified. Fourth, antecedents and consequences are modified. This may involve removing some antecedents that encourage the behavior and some consequences that reinforce it. In addition, negative consequences may be added. Alternatively, the child may be encouraged to perform different behaviors that are incompatible with the problem behavior. Reinforcing consequences could then be attached to these incompatible behaviors.

Admittedly, this is an oversimplification of one type of behavioral intervention. Other behavioral interventions, such as desensitization and positive practice exist (see Redd, Porterfield, and Andersen, 1979, for additional comments about behavioral interventions). These are described in greater detail as they are applied to specific disorders.

Psychotherapy

"Psychotherapy" means different things to different professionals. Some professionals use the word *psychotherapy* to refer to any intervention performed by a psychologist or psychiatrist that does not use medication. According to this definition, behavioral interventions are psychotherapy. Other professionals reserve the use of *psychotherapy* only for therapy that deals with thought processes. Still others take an even more restrictive view, equating psychotherapy with psychodynamic psychotherapy.

In this book the term *psychotherapy* will be used to group techniques that directly or theoretically address the thought processes, affects, or beliefs of the child. One could argue that behavioral interventions fit into this definition. However, there are two reasons for separating behavioral interventions from psychotherapy. The first is pragmatic. Behavioral interventions for childhood disorders are so important and prevalent that they merit their own heading. Furthermore, the volume of writing and research on behavioral interventions would overwhelm other "psychological" interventions. The second reason is the behavioral approach's repudiation (or at least avoidance) of a focus on internal psychological processes. If behavioral interventions affect thought, it is not because they directly intended to.

Five types of psychotherapy are mentioned with some regularity throughout the following chapters. *Psychodynamic psychotherapy* involves a focus on internal, sometimes unconscious, conflicts that are driving the child's behaviors. Their goal is to process the child's memories such that the child can gain insight, experience the memories, and integrate them into the self. In some cases, psychodynamic psychotherapy also involves having a corrective experience with the therapist, in which the therapist acts in such a way as to allow the child to re-experience a stage of development in a positive way. For example, the therapist could give the child the experience of an accepting parental figure.

Play therapy involves the use of play to allow the child to demonstrate and experience conflicts, affects, fears, hopes, and other thought/affect processes. The experience occurs in the context of an accepting therapist who validates the child and, ideally, teaches the child to accept himself in the process. Some therapists interpret the child's play behavior in the hopes of facilitating insight, while others are staunchly nondirective and accept any nondangerous, nonaggressive, nondestructive behaviors from the child. The child presumably benefits from increased self-acceptance and insight, which is learned from and encouraged by the play therapist (see Axline, 1969)

Cognitive-behavioral interventions encompass a variety of techniques that seek to increase the child's awareness of how thought processes drive behavior and affect. The child is taught to monitor, challenge, and alter thought processes (see Kendall, 1991). Unlike psychodynamic interventions, cognitive-behavioral interventions do not relate to the past history of the development of behavior. Rather, they focus on how present thought drives present feelings and behaviors.

There is some inevitable overlap between behavioral and cognitive-behavioral interventions, since both focus on the behaviors of the child. Self-monitoring, for example, may serve the behavioral purpose of evaluating performance and dispensing reinforcement, or it may serve the cognitive purpose of enhancing insight into one's behavior and the situations in which it occurs. Such "overlapping" interventions may be described in either of the categories for which they are relevant.

Hypnotic techniques involve the use of the altered state of hypnosis to allow the child to gain greater control over physiological or thought states. Following induction of hypnosis, suggestions are made to experience physiological change, to view a situation differently, or to have a hypnotic experience that will assist with memory and/or insight into problems (see Olness and Gardner, 1988).

Group therapy is a generic term used to refer to delivery of a psychotherapeutic intervention in a group format. In many cases the presence of the group is used to facilitate the intervention. For example, group members may model disclosure, affect, and change for other group members. On the other hand, interaction between group members may facilitate insight into a personal or social problem. Group members can also act as motivators for other group members. In some cases the group is used to deliver another type of intervention; cognitive-behavioral techniques, for example, are often taught in a group format. Hence, group therapy and the other psychotherapy techniques are not mutually exclusive (see Yalom, 1985).

Family Interventions

Family interventions refer to the group of psychological techniques that focus on the family as the unit of change for the child. This focus may result in the entire family being present for therapy, or it may result in one other family member (usually a parent) entering therapy in order to benefit the child by changing his or her own behavior.

Family therapy follows the theory that the child's problems emerge in and are shaped by a family system. Eventually, the problem comes to serve a role in the family system, and the family system is reluctant to give up the symptom and the child's role as a "sick" child. The family may be especially reluctant to give up the child's problem if it is deflecting the family's energy and attention from an even greater family problem, such as conflict between the parents. To address the child's problems, then, the therapist must address the problems inherent in the family system. It is these problems and the family's reluctance to change that are maintaining the child's problem.

Family therapists seek to change the family system by pointing out the role of the child's symptom, by restructuring the family, and by demonstrating more positive styles of family interaction. Structural family therapists seek to create appropriate boundaries between family subsystems (such as the parental and child subsystems) and to weaken boundaries that isolate certain family members. Family therapists with a more interactional focus show how the communication in the family creates problems for members. Strategic family therapists emphasize the importance of the child's symptom in maintaining the family system's integrity. Regardless of specific orientation, however, the family therapist's focus is on the family as the source of the problem and not on the child. Change in the child's symptoms can and will occur only when the family changes (see Haley, 1976; Minuchin, 1974).

Parent intervention and training encompasses a number of techniques ranging from individual psychotherapy for the parent to psychoeducational classes directed at parenting skills. These techniques share in common a focus on the parent as the unit of intervention and change. Parent interventions are indicated in cases when the parent's psychological problems are interfering with the child's treatment or are responsible for maintaining the child's problem. *Parent psychotherapy,* for example, involves a referral for the parent to work on individual issues that may or may not directly relate to the child. This therapy may be focused on a diagnosis carried by the parent or on parent behaviors that are provoked by interactions in the parent-child relationship (see Meyer and Deitsch, 1996, for a summary of adult assessment and intervention)

Parent psychoeducation, on the other hand, is directed at educating parents about the details of their child's problem and how to deal with it. Often, behavioral therapy incorporates psychoeducational components; thus, behavioral interventions and psychoeducation often overlap. Forehand (1993), for example, describes a parent behavioral training program in which parents are taught skills for managing child misbehavior. First, parents are taught to attend and interact with the child without attempting to alter the child's behavior. Second, parents learn to reinforce the child's positive behaviors (primarily using praise) and to ignore the child's misbehavior. Third, parents are encouraged to make requests one at a time and in simple terms. Fourth, parents are taught the principle of time-out, which involves removal of the child from the current situation and placement of the child in a nonstimulating environment for a *brief* (3–5 minutes) period of time. Forehand (1993) uses didactics, modeling, role playing, in-session practice with the child, and discussion of home application to teach parents these skills.

Like parent intervention, *marital therapy* centers on the parents as opposed to the child. Marital therapy is warranted for families in which parental conflict contributes to the child's problems or to the parents' inability to manage the child's problems. Open parental conflict, for example, is stressful to children and provides models of hostile interaction. In addition, conflict between parents is often played out in the family in the form of inconsistent discipline and lax rules (see Weeks and Treat, 1992).

Medication

Medication is a common intervention for a number of childhood disorders and a preferred intervention for several (such as ADHD). Medications that are commonly used to treat childhood disorders are briefly summarized in the Treatment Options section for each disorder. The rationale, effectiveness, and pros/cons of medication are considered along with the types of medication used for particular disorders. However, dosages and detailed administration instructions are not described in this book. Furthermore, only medications that have received significant research or clinical attention in published sources are considered. Hence, the medication section is intended only as a brief overview of the major documented medications for a disorder; it is strictly for illustrative purposes and not for clinical use.

Inpatient Hospitalization

Inpatient hospitalization is sometimes used as a "last resort" for children with severe behavioral and psychological problems. Children are typically hospitalized only when they are unmanageable in the home environment, dangerous to themselves or others, severely incapacitated by their disorder, and/or unresponsive to outpatient management. Over all, it is generally wise to use inpatient hospitalization sparingly because it labels the child as "very sick," it places the child in an environment with negative behavioral models, it separates the child from potential social support in the family, it creates a discontinuity of care (e.g., treatment in the hospital abruptly ends or converts to outpatient when the child is returned to the family), and it is costly. Nevertheless, inpatient treatment is warranted for some children, and many children benefit from it.

Of course, inpatient hospitalization is not actually a treatment modality but rather an environment in which various treatments can be administered. Medication is a nearly universal treatment on inpatient units, as is group psychotherapy. Also common (but not universal) are individual psychotherapy, behavior modification plans, and milieu therapy. Less common are family therapy and marital therapy.

Special Education

For some childhood disorders (such as Mental Retardation and Learning Disorders), special provisions must be made in the content and process of the child's schooling. When these provisions concern the child's behavior, they are covered under the Behavioral Interventions section. However, sometimes special provisions are made to help the child's *learning* at school. These educational interventions are considered in the Special Education section. Because this book is written for mental health clinicians as opposed to educators, educational recommendations are limited to referrals and broad interventions.

Referral to Other Professionals or to Authorities

Certain disorders are associated with medical, legal, or other risks that require close work with other disciplines. When these risks exist, they are noted in the introductory paragraphs of the Assessment Patterns or Treatment Options sections. More detailed information about referral needs may also be covered in a special Referral to Other Professionals or to Authorities subsection in the Treatment Options section. Examples of medical and legal risks are mental health conditions that are associated with neurological complications and conditions that are associated with abuse/neglect.

Medical and legal issues, however, may arise in any child therapy case, and the clinician must be observant for warning signs. A few of the warning signs for organic impairment include recent severe injury/illness, sudden behavioral change, lack of psychosocial explanations for behavior, very severe symptoms, loss of consciousness, and significant change in mental status. Warning signs of abuse include fearfulness toward adults, physical signs (bruises, etc.), use of clothing or absence from school to hide injury, social withdrawal, avoidance of certain people or situations, extreme parental defensiveness over discipline, family stress, aggression, fixation on sexual themes and behaviors, and repeated complaints of injury or illness. The clinician must be cautious, however, about jumping to conclusions based on the presence of only a few warning signs. The warning signs noted here could indicate other problems as well.

In general, children being seen for mental health assessment and interventions should—like all children—at the very least be regularly seen by a pediatrician. Any psychological-behavioral complaint that may have a physical basis (such as an eating problem) should be referred to a pediatrician for specific medical evaluation concurrent with psychological evaluation.

Conclusion

The aim of this book is to provide clinicians with an up-to-date handbook for daily use in the diagnosis, assessment, and treatment of children's mental health problems. To this end, the remaining chapters of this book are focused on the assessment and treatment of specific DSM-IV diagnoses. The organizational scheme outlined here indicates what type of material is included for each diagnosis and where it can be found.

Of course, no book can anticipate the variety of individuals presenting with a specific diagnosis. Furthermore, some individuals will respond to certain treatments, while others will not. Ultimately the clinician must marshal all available resources for the assessment and treatment of the child, using a mix of clinical skill and knowledge. This book is intended to be on the front line of those resources.

References

American Psychiatric Association. (1980). *Diagnostic and statistical manual of mental disorders* (3rd ed.). Washington, DC: Author.

_____ . (1987). *Diagnostic and statistical manual of mental disorders* (3rd ed., rev.). Washington, DC: Author.

_____ . (1994). *Diagnostic and statistical manual of mental disorders* (4th ed.). Washington, DC: Author.

Achenbach, T. M. (1991a). *Manual for the Child Behavior Checklist/4-18 and 1991 Profile.* Burlington: University of Vermont Department of Psychiatry.

_____ . (1991b). *Manual for the Teacher's Report Form and 1991 Profile.* Burlington: University of Vermont Department of Psychiatry.

_____ . (1991c). *Manual for the Youth Self-Report and 1991 Profile.* Burlington: University of Vermont Department of Psychiatry.

_____ . (1992). *Manual for the Child Behavior Checklist/2-3 and 1992 Profile.* Burlington: University of Vermont Department of Psychiatry.

Atkins, M. S., and Pelham, W. E. (1991). School-based assessment of attention-deficit hyperactivity disorder. *Journal of Learning Disabilities, 24,* 197–203.

Axline, V. M. (1969). *Play therapy.* New York: Ballantine.

Barkley, R. A. (1987). The assessment of attention-deficit hyperactivity disorder. *Behavioral Assessment, 9,* 207–233.

Bayley, N. (1993). *Bayley scales of infant development: Second edition.* San Antonio, TX: Psychological Corporation.

Butcher, J. N., Dahlstrom, W. G., Graham, J. R., Tellegen, A. M., and Kaemmer, B. (1989). *MMPI-2: Manual for administration and scoring.* Minneapolis: University of Minnesota.

Butcher, J. N., Williams, C. L., Graham, J. R., Archer, R. P., Tellegen, A., Ben-Porath, J. S., and Kaemmer, B. (1992). *MMPI-A: Manual for administration, scoring, and interpretation.* Minneapolis: University of Minnesota.

Conners, C. K. (1990). *Conners' Rating Scales manual.* North Tonawanda, NY: MHS.

Costello, A .J., Edelbrock, C. S., Dulcan, M. S., Kales, R., and Klavic, S. H. (1984). *Report on the NIMH Diagnostic Interview Schedule for Children (DISC).* Bethesda, MD: National Institute of Mental Health.

Dahlstrom, W. G., Welsh, G. S., & Dahlstrom, L. E. (1972). *An MMPI handbook: I. Clinical interpretation.* Minneapolis: University of Minnesota Press.

Derogatis, L. R. (1983). *SCL-90-R administration, scoring, and procedures manual—II.* Towson, MD: Clinical Psychometric Research.

Exner, J. E., Jr. (1986). *The Rorschach: A comprehensive system. I. Basic foundations* (2nd ed.). New York: Wiley.

Finch, A .J., Jr., Casat, C. D., & Carey, M. P. (1990). Depression in children and adolescents. In S. B. Morgan and T. M. Okwumabua (Eds.), *Child and adolescent disorders: Developmental and health psychology perspectives* (pp. 135–173). Hillsdale, NJ: Erlbaum.

Forehand, R. (1993). Twenty years of research on parenting: Does it have practical implications for clinicians working with parents and children? *The Clinical Psychologist, 46,* 169–176.

Graham, J. R. (1990). *MMPI-2: Assessing personality and psychopathology.* New York: Oxford University Press.

Greene, R. L. (1991). *MMPI-2/MMPI: An interpretive manual.* Boston: Allyn & Bacon.

Haley, J. (1976). *Problem-solving therapy.* San Francisco: Jossey-Bass.

Hathaway, S. R., and McKinley, J. C. (1951). *The Minnesota Multiphasic Personality Inventory manual.* New York: Psychological Corporation.

———— . (1967). *The Minnesota Multiphasic Personality Inventory manual.* New York: Psychological Corporation.

Herjanic, B., and Campbell, W. (1977). Differentiating psychiatrically disturbed children on the basis of a structured interview. *Journal of Abnormal Child Psychology, 5,* 127–134.

Hodges, K. K. (1985). *Manual for the Child Assessment Schedule.* Unpublished manuscript, University of Missouri-Columbia.

———— . (1987). Assessing children with a clinical interview: The Child Assessment Schedule. In R.J. Prinz (Ed.). *Advances in behavioral assessment of children and families* (pp. 133–166). Greenwich, CT: JAI Press.

———— . (1990). Depression and anxiety in children: A comparison of self-report questionnaires to clinical interview. *Psychological Assessment, 2,* 376–381.

Hodges, K., and Zeman, J. (1993). Interviewing. In T. H. Ollendick & M. Hersen (Eds.), *Handbook of child and adolescent assessment.* Boston: Allyn & Bacon.

Kaslow, N. J., & Racusin, G. R. (1990). Childhood depression: Current status and future directions. In A. S. Bellack, M. Hersen, and A. E. Kazdin (Eds.), *International handbook of behavior modification and therapy* (2d ed., pp. 223–243). New York: Plenum.

Kaufman, A. S., & Kaufman, N. L. (1985). Manual for the Kaufman Test of Educational Achievement (K-TEA) Comprehensive Form. Circle Pines, MN: American Guidance Service.

Kendall, P. C. (1991). *Child and adolescent therapy: Cognitive-behavioral procedures.* New York: Guilford.

Kronenberger, W. G., and Thompson, R. J., Jr. (1990). Dimensions of family functioning in families with chronically ill children: A higher order factor analysis of the Family Environment Scale. *Journal of Clinical Child Psychology, 19,* 380–388.

Marks, P. A., Seeman, W., and Haller, D. L. (1974). *The actuarial use of the MMPI with adolescents and adults.* Baltimore, MD: Williams & Wilkins.

Markwardt, F. C. (1989). *Manual for the Peabody Individual Achievement Test - Revised (PIAT-R).* Circle Pines, MN: American Guidance Service.

McCarthy, D. A. (1972). *Manual for the McCarthy Scales of Children's Abilities.* San Antonio, TX: Psychological Corporation.

McGrew, K. S. (1994). *Clinical interpretation of the Woodcock-Johnson Tests of Cognitive Ability—Revised.* Boston: Allyn & Bacon.

Meyer, R. G., and Deitsch, S. (1996). *The clinician's handbook* (4th ed.). Boston: Allyn & Bacon.

Minuchin, S. (1974). *Families and family therapy.* Cambridge, MA: Harvard University Press.

Mokros, H. B., and Poznanski, E. O. (1992). Standardized approaches to clinical assessment of depression. In M. Shafii and S. L. Shafii (Eds.), *Clinical guide to depression in children and adolescents* (pp. 129–155). Washington, DC: American Psychiatric Press.

Moos, R. H., & Moos, B. S. (1981). *Family Environment Scale manual.* Palo Alto, CA: Consulting Psychologists Press.

Murray, H. A. (1943). *Thematic Apperception Test manual.* Cambridge, MA: Harvard University Press.

Olness, K., and Gardner, G. G. (1988). *Hypnosis and hypnotherapy with children* (2nd ed.). Philadelphia: Grune & Stratton.

Olson, D. H., McCubbin, H. I., Barnes, H., Larsen, A., Muxen, M., and Wilson, M. (1985). *Family Inventories.* St. Paul, MN: Family Social Science.

Orvaschel, H., and Puig-Antich, J. (1987). *Schedule for affective disorders and schizophrenia for school-age children—epidemiologic version (Kiddie-SADS-E [K-SADS-E]).* Unpublished manuscript, University of Pittsburgh.

Piers, E. V. (1984). *Piers-Harris Children's Self-Concept Scale Revised manual 1984.* Los Angeles: Western Psychological Services.

The Psychological Corporation. (1992). *Wechsler Individual Achievement Test manual.* San Antonio, TX: Author.

Puig-Antich, J., Chambers, W., and Tabrizi, M. A. (1983). The clinical assessment of current depressive episodes in children and adolescents: Interviews with parents and children. In D. Cantwell and G. Carlson (Eds.). *Childhood depression* (pp. 157–179). New York: Spectrum.

Puig-Antich, J., and Ryan, N. (1986). *Schedule for affective disorders and schizophrenia for school-age children (6–18 years) - Kiddie-SADS-Present Episode (K-SADS-P).* Unpublished manuscript, University of Pittsburgh.

Redd, W. H., Porterfield, A. L., and Andersen, B. L. (1979). *Behavior modification: Behavioral approaches to human problems.* New York: Random House.

Sattler, J. M. (1990). *Assessment of children* (3d ed.). San Diego, CA: Author.

———. (1993). *Assessment of children* (3d ed., rev.). San Diego, CA: Author.

Sines, J. O., Pauker, J. D., Sines, L. K., and Owen, D. R. (1969). Identification of clinically relevant dimensions of children's behavior. *Journal of Consulting and Clinical Psychology, 33,* 728–734.

Sparrow, S. S., Balla, D. A., and Cicchetti, D. V. (1984). *Vineland adaptive behavior scales*. Circle Pines, MN: American Guidance Service.

Thompson, R. J., Jr. (1986). Behavior problems in children with developmental and learning disabilities. *International Academy for Research and Learning Disabilities Monograph Series, 3*, 1–125.

Thompson, R. J., Jr., Kronenberger, W. G., and Curry, J. F. (1989). Behavioral classification system for children with developmental, psychiatric, and chronic medical problems. *Journal of Pediatric Psychology, 14*, 559–575.

Thompson, R. J., Jr., Kronenberger, W. G., & Johndrow, D. (1992). Behavior patterns in nonreferred children: Replication of the factor structure of the Missouri Children's Behavior Checklist. *Journal of Clinical Psychology, 48*, 292–298.

Thorndike, R. L., Hagen, E. P., and Sattler, J. M. (1986). *Guide for administering and scoring the Stanford-Binet Intelligence Scale: Fourth Edition*. Chicago: Riverside.

Wechsler, D. (1974). *Manual for the Wechsler Intelligence Scale for Children—Revised*. San Antonio, TX: Psychological Corporation.

_____ . (1981). *Manual for the Wechsler Adult Intelligence Scale—Revised*. San Antonio, TX: Psychological Corporation.

_____ . (1989). *Manual for the Wechsler Preschool and Primary Scale of Intelligence—Revised*. San Antonio, TX: Psychological Corporation.

_____ . (1991). *Manual for the Wechsler Intelligence Scale for Children—Third Edition*. San Antonio, TX: Psychological Corporation.

Weeks, G. R., and Treat, S. (1992). *Couples in treatment: Techniques and approaches for effective practice*. New York: Brunner/Mazel.

Woodcock, R. W., and Johnson, M. B. (1989a). *Woodcock-Johnson psycho-educational battery—revised, tests of achievement*. Allen, TX: DLM Teaching Resources.

_____ . (1989b). *Woodcock-Johnson psycho-educational battery—revised, tests of cognitive abilities*. Allen, TX: DLM Teaching Resources.

Yalom, I. D. (1985). *The theory and practice of group psychotherapy* (3d ed.). New York: Basic Books.

CHAPTER 2

Attention-Deficit Hyperactivity Disorder

■ **Attention-Deficit Hyperactivity Disorder**

☐ CLINICAL DESCRIPTION

Diagnostic Considerations

Attention-Deficit/Hyperactivity Disorder (ADHD) is one of the most common Axis I childhood disorders, occurring in as many as 3–5% of children (Anderson et al., 1987; American Psychiatric Association, 1994; Biederman, 1991). It is characterized by inattention, restlessness, impulsivity, and hyperactivity. These symptoms are disruptive or create social-environmental problems for the child (American Psychiatric Association, 1994; Barkley, 1990; Munoz-Millan and Casteel, 1989). The disorder is much more common in boys than girls, with ratios of 2:1 to 10:1 reported in the literature (American Psychiatric Association, 1994; Barkley, 1991b).

DSM-IV divides ADHD criteria into two groups. The *Inattention* group consists of symptoms reflecting lack of attention to details, difficulty sustaining attention, failure to listen, organizational problems, distractibility, failure to complete activities, and forgetfulness. The *Hyperactivity-Impulsivity* group consists of excessive behavior, squirming, difficulty remaining seated, inappropriate noise/vocalization, and difficulty waiting. Children must meet *either* six of the Inattention symptoms *or* six of the Hyperactivity-Impulsivity symptoms to qualify for ADHD diagnosis. Furthermore, the symptoms must be present in two or more situations. Children who meet only Inattention criteria in a 6-month period are coded as being Predominantly Inattentive Type, while those who meet only Hyperactivity-Impulsivity criteria in a 6-month period are coded as being Predominantly Hyperactive-Impulsive Type. Children who meet both the Inattention and the Hyperactivity-Impulsivity criteria are coded as being Combined Type. Hence, ADHD is coded in DSM-IV as having three subtypes, depending on whether the predominant features are Inattention, Hyperactivity-Impulsivity, or both. An additional ADHD Not Otherwise Specified (ADD NOS) category can be used for children who have problems with attention, hyperactivity, or impulsivity but who do not meet ADHD criteria.

The DSM-IV criteria represent a departure from DSM-III-R, which listed a single group of fourteen criteria for ADHD and required the presence of eight for a diagnosis (American Psychiatric Association, 1987). Children with only inattention symptoms had been classified as Undifferentiated Attention-Deficit Disorder in DSM-III-R (American Psychiatric Association, 1987). The use of a single list of ADHD symptoms in DSM-III-R had been criticized based on factor-analytic studies that suggested that ADHD symptoms fall into two categories: inattention-restless and impulsive-hyperactive (Barkley, 1990). DSM-IV more closely approximates factor-analytic findings by splitting ADHD symptoms into two groups and allowing for an Inattentive subtype. Most children who would have qualified for the Undifferentiated ADD diagnosis in DSM-III-R will qualify for ADHD, Predominantly Inattentive Type, or for ADHD NOS in DSM-IV.

The age of the child is critical in making the ADHD diagnosis. Moderate levels of diffuse activity and a short attention span are not uncommon in very young children. Attention, concentration, and purposeful, controlled activity increase with age. Nevertheless, half of ADHD cases have onset before age 4, and onset of some symptoms must occur prior to age 7 for a diagnosis to be made (American Psychiatric Association, 1994). For some children the disorder is not apparent until the child begins school. The school environment can magnify or illuminate ADHD-type problems, because school activity is more structured and a large amount of comparison children are present. ADHD usually is diagnosed before the age of 7 (Biederman, 1991). When the diagnosis is made after age 7, retrospective accounts show the onset of the behaviors to be prior to age 7.

ADHD is associated with a plethora of medical, behavioral, cognitive, and academic disorders. Children with ADHD frequently do poorly in school; they are more likely to have physical problems than are other children; they have increased difficulties with peer acceptance; and they are more likely to be anxious and depressed (Barkley, 1991b; Biederman, 1991). ADHD sometimes co-occurs with low IQ, in which case ADHD criteria should be applied based on the child's mental age. Perhaps the most common features associated with ADHD, however, are those of Oppositional-Defiant or Conduct Disorder. Stated simply, many children with ADHD have difficulties with compliance and antisocial behavior. In fact, the overlap of ADHD and Conduct Disorder (CD) is so great that some authors have questioned whether they are different disorders (Munoz-Millan and Casteel, 1989). However, empirical evidence and factor analytic studies indicate that, while there is substantial overlap between ADHD and CD, they are distinct syndromes (Carlson and Rapport, 1989; Munoz-Millan and Casteel, 1989).

The large but incomplete overlap between ADHD and CD suggests that subtypes of ADHD may exist in addition to those recognized by DSM-IV. Several authors have noted the heterogeneity of the ADHD population (Whalen and Henker, 1991), which argues for the importance of delineating ADHD subtypes. A first division of subtypes is based on the degree to which the ADHD child shows conduct problems. As many as 50% of children with ADHD have an associated CD or Oppositional Defiant Disorder (ODD; Barkley, 1991a; Biederman and Steingard, 1989). These children (hereafter referred to as ADHD-CD) channel their overactivity into oppositional, aggressive, antisocial, or dangerous behavior; children with ADHD alone present with more attention/impulsivity problems (Carlson and Rapport, 1989). Furthermore, children with ADHD-CD are at risk for later antisocial-aggression problems, while those with simple ADHD are not (Biederman, 1991).

Biederman (1991) suggests two other subtypes of ADHD based on co-occurring diagnoses: ADHD with major depression symptoms (as many as 30% of ADHD cases; Barkley, 1991a) and ADHD with anxiety disorder (as many as 30% of ADHD cases; Barkley, 1991a). These subtypes represent children who have emotional difficulties superimposed on their inattention-hyperactivity problem. The delineation of ADHD subtypes suggests that children with ADHD should routinely be evaluated for related conduct, mood, or anxiety problems. The presence of an associated problem may require more intensive intervention and may signal increased risk for negative long-term outcome.

Children with ADHD can also be grouped into subtypes based on whether their symptoms are primarily cognitive or behavioral (August and Garfinkel, 1989). Children with behavioral ADHD show features of inattention, impulsivity, and hyperactivity, with no associated learning or other disability. Over half of these children may have associated CD. Children with cognitive ADHD, on the other hand, have significant learning and/or other cognitive disabilities in addition to problems with inattention, impulsivity, and hyperactivity. However, they typically have fewer problems with CD than do children in the behavioral group (August and Garfinkel, 1989).

Halperin et al. (1990) suggest yet another parameter along which ADHD children can be divided into subgroups: attentive (Halperin uses the designation "noninattentive," which is shortened here) versus inattentive. Attentive ADHD children show more conduct problems and (by definition) fewer inattention problems than do inattentive ADHD children. Halperin's attentive ADHD group resembles the DSM-IV ADHD, Predominantly Hyperactive-Impulsive (or a behavioral-CD) subtype, while the inattentive ADHD group resembles the DSM-IV ADHD, Predominantly Inattentive (or a cognitive, non-CD) subtype. Educational programming and psychological interventions would be expected to differ between the groups.

Appearance and Features

Despite the apparent existence of ADHD subtypes, certain features are common across many ADHD children (see Table 2.1). Perhaps the most salient feature is difficulty sustaining attention during relatively long, monotonous, group-oriented, or repetitive tasks (Barkley, 1991b; Frick and Lahey, 1991). In some cases the child is distracted by extraneous stimuli, but in other cases the child simply loses interest and fails to persist with the task (Barkley, 1991b).

TABLE 2.1   Appearance and Features of ADHD

COMMON FEATURES

Attention problems

Overactivity: restlessness, inability to sit still, fidgeting, constant movement

Impulsivity, adoption of an acting as opposed to reflective style: interrupting others, difficulty waiting for turn, blurting out answers, making simple mistakes because of impulsive answers, acting without considering consequences

Onset prior to age 7

Poor school performance, learning disability

Peer relationship problems

Oppositionality/defiance or conduct problems

Able to attend to interesting, changing, reinforcing activities that are chosen by the child

Responsive to immediate, salient reinforcement

Negative interactions/relationships with authorities

Negative reputation among authorities

Sleep disturbance

Risk of negative adolescent/adult outcome

OCCASIONAL FEATURES

More common in boys

Onset prior to age 4, although diagnosis may not be made until child enters school

Physical problems, including higher injury risk and motor coordination problems

Aggressive and/or antisocial behavior

Note: The features listed above are often seen but are not universal. Some features may be diagnostically relevant or required, while others may not be required for diagnosis. "Common" features are typical of the disorder; "occasional" features appear frequently but are not necessarily seen in a majority of cases.

On tasks that are interesting; unstructured; and involve shifts of focus, freedom to choose activity, or immediate reinforcement, behavioral differences between ADHD children and normal children may be unnoticeable (Frick and Lahey, 1991). Thus, an ADHD child may appear focused at home or in front of a video game but is quite inattentive and disruptive at school. These situational differences suggest that behavioral data must be gathered from multiple observers in multiple settings in order to diagnose ADHD. Diagnostically, the ADHD behavior need occur in only two settings, although ADHD children often manifest the behavior in more than two situations (American Psychiatric Association, 1994).

In addition to showing poor sustained attention, ADHD children frequently manifest difficulty with impulse control (Barkley, 1991b; Carlson and Rapport, 1989). This leads to behaviors such as interrupting others, difficulty waiting for turn, and poor performance on tasks requiring waiting or thoughtful decisions (Brown and Quay, 1977; Carlson and Rapport, 1989). Impulsivity also affects the ADHD child's compliance with rules or requests, especially when the child acts before considering consequences. Such impulsive behaviors can be dangerous to the child or others, possibly explaining the higher frequency of injury in children with ADHD (American Psychiatric Association, 1994). Impulsivity may decrease in situations involving immediate and valued consequences (Barkley, 1990).

A third common feature of ADHD is overactivity, which may be more prevalent in younger children with ADHD (Barkley, 1990). Overactivity is particularly noticeable in situations requiring the child to sit or to remain in the same place for an extended period of time. At these times, ADHD children tend to squirm, stretch, change position, make noises, play with anything within reach, and stand. The extent of this hyperactivity, however, varies considerably with time, stress, and situation (Barkley, 1991b).

Although not inherent in the ADHD diagnosis, noncompliance, aggression, and other antisocial behaviors are also common features of children with ADHD (Battle and Lacey, 1972; Frick and Lahey, 1991). These behaviors may result from difficulties with sustained attention, impulsivity, or an associated CD. In other cases the child with ADHD is seeking attention by being noncompliant and aversive to the other person. Noncompliance may result from a variety of other ADHD-related deficits, including difficulty sustaining attention to instructions, difficulty sitting still, and difficulty delaying gratification (Barkley, 1991b).

Not surprisingly, the disruptions, interruptions, noncompliance, and antisocial behaviors of ADHD children create social problems for them. Interactions with adults are frequently aversive and involve cycles of commands, noncompliance, and punishment. Empirical study indicates that hyperactive children often receive harsh, controlling, conflict-laden responses from parents and teachers, who may ignore periods of good behavior (Frick and Lahey, 1991; Danforth, Barkley, and Stokes, 1991). ADHD children who exhibit antisocial behaviors such as aggression and interruption also have problems with peer relationships (Carlson and Rapport, 1989). Excessive talking, interruption of ongoing activity, failure to wait for turn, and provocative behavior are all annoying to peers, leading to social problems for over 50% of children with ADHD (Barkley, 1991a). Despite talking more, ADHD children listen and respond less to peers, robbing their social interactions of a sense of balance (Barkley, 1991a). In some cases, peer rejection leads to anger, alienation, and further antisocial behavior from the ADHD child, causing a vicious circle of rejection (Frick and Lahey, 1991).

In the academic realm the effects of ADHD are significant and pervasive. In fact, many children with ADHD present initially because of academic difficulties. Academic difficulty among ADHD children is common, with 20–30% of children with ADHD having a learning disability (Barkley, 1991a; Barkley,

DuPaul, and McMurray, 1990; Lambert and Sandoval, 1980). Over all, ADHD children have achievement testing scores 10–15 points below scale norms, and 35% of ADHD children will be retained a grade at least once before high school (Barkley, 1991a). Expressive language and organization of ideas may be particular problems (Barkley, 1990a), although studies show deficits across virtually all academic areas (e.g., Barkley et al., 1991). The academic difficulties of ADHD children have been attributed to motivational problems, attention problems, lower IQ, and poor test taking skills (Barkley, 1990a).

In addition to academic problems, ADHD is associated with a host of other risks. Children with ADHD show a higher rate of motor coordination problems (as high as 52% have coordination difficulty) and sleep difficulties such as trouble falling asleep, frequent waking, and tiredness after waking (Barkley, 1991a). Health problems and injuries are also common; between 10% and 25% of ADHD children experience multiple serious accidents or poisonings (Barkley, 1991a).

Recently more attention has been given to the persistence of ADHD throughout adolescence and adulthood. As many as 30–50% of children with ADHD show symptoms persisting through adolescence and into adulthood (Biederman, 1991; Weiss et al., 1985); 50–80% of ADHD children continue to meet ADHD criteria in adolescence (Barkley et al., 1991; Barkley, Fischer et al., 1990). Behavioral symptoms such as impulsivity, inattention, immaturity, oppositionality/defiance, social-skills deficits, and distractibility often endure into adolescence. However, symptoms of hyperactivity decline (Barkley et al., 1991; Hechtman, 1991). Elevated rates of academic failure, antisocial personality, substance abuse, criminal behavior, and depression have been reported in adolescents and adults who were diagnosed with ADHD as children, although the risk of these negative long-term outcomes is probably limited to the ADHD-CD subtype (Barkley et al., 1991; Biederman, 1991; Hechtman, 1991; Klein and Mannuzza, 1991). These negative outcomes are less prevalent in adults than in adolescents (Klein and Manuzza, 1991).

Hechtman (1991) reviews literature supporting three types of ADHD adult outcome: normal functioning (probably fewer than half of children; Weiss et al., 1985), moderate disability (serious concentration, social, and emotional problems, low self-esteem; anxiety, and irritability; perhaps as high as 66% [Weiss et al., 1985]), and significant disability (major depression, substance abuse, antisocial behavior). Those with co-occurring CD or Mood Disorder diagnoses are particularly at long-term risk. Factors related to more positive adult outcome are higher IQ, internal locus of control, better social skills, higher family SES, supportive family, and good health (Hechtman, 1991).

Etiology

Biological Theories

Biological factors hypothesized to account for ADHD have received ample attention. Nutrition and toxins have created occasional excitement in the mass media, but little evidence exists to support their causal role. Lead poisoning can create overactivity, but very few cases of ADHD have been attributed to lead. Other ingested substances, such as food additives and sugar, have been suggested as reasons for the development of ADHD. Although it is conceivable that food allergies or sugar cause overactivity in an occasional child, empirical research has not supported the role of food as a factor causing ADHD in most children (Barkley, 1991a; Hynd et al., 1991).

Genetic factors have also been implicated in the development of ADHD, primarily based on two lines of research. First, many genetic disorders (Fragile X, XYY, neurofibromatosis, and certain types of mental retardation) are associated with increased activity and attention deficits in the child (Hynd et al., 1991). Although these observations indicate that some cases of ADHD can result from a genetic disorder, they do not confirm that *all* cases of ADHD result from such disorders. The vast majority of children with ADHD have no known genetic disorder.

A second line of genetic research shows increased incidence of ADHD in biological relatives of children with ADHD. First-degree relatives of children with ADHD show an increased incidence of ADHD, depression, alcoholism, conduct problems, and antisocial disorders (Barkley, 1991a, 1991b; Biederman, 1991; Biederman et al., 1990). Furthermore, 20–32% of immediate family members of ADHD children show symptoms of ADHD (Barkley, 1991a, 1991b; Zametkin, 1989). Hyperactivity in particular appears to have a significant genetic basis, with heritability studies showing greater concordance for hyperactivity among monozygotic (genetically identical) than among dizygotic (not genetically identical) twin pairs (Goodman and Stevenson, 1989). These results suggest a genetic link, but the increased family incidence of ADHD could also be a result of environmental factors that remain stable from generation to generation (e.g., poor parenting, low SES). Hence, the genetic hypothesis shows promise but remains to be confirmed in future research.

A third biological explanation for ADHD suggests that ADHD children have a neuroanatomical abnormality in the brain regions that regulate attention and motor behavior. For example, brain damaging conditions such as closed head injury, perinatal oxygen deprivation, poor prenatal care, and hydrocephalus often result in overactivity and attention deficits (Barkley, 1991a; Hynd et al., 1991). These observations led to the hypothesis that ADHD is caused by damage affecting brain regions responsible for attention and behavioral control.

However, fewer than 5% of ADHD children have a history of documented brain injury. To accommodate this finding, researchers hypothesized that deficits in brain structure, regardless of injury history, account for ADHD (Barkley, 1991b). The dysfunctional brain areas implicated most consistently are the frontal lobes and the reticular activating system (Barkley, 1991a; Hynd et al., 1991). Research has shown smaller frontal lobe areas in ADHD children, decreased frontal lobe blood flow and metabolism, functional abnormalities suggesting frontal lobe dysfunction, and possible EEG abnormalities in certain frontal lobe areas (Barkley, 1991a; Hynd et al., 1991). Although the results of ADHD-neuroanatomy studies are not always consistent (Hynd et al., 1991), the bulk of the research supports the hypothesis that some neuroanatomical mechanism contributes to the development of some ADHD cases (Barkley, 1991a).

A fourth biological explanation for ADHD focuses on the neurophysiology of ADHD children. Because the neurotransmitters most responsible for attention and motor behavior are the catecholamines (dopamine, norepinephrine, epinephrine), they have received the most attention. Most of the evidence supporting the catecholamine hypothesis of ADHD comes from studies showing that medications that reduce the symptoms of ADHD (dextroamphetamine [Dexedrine], methylphenidate [Ritalin], and pemoline [Cylert)] increase the amount of catecholamines in the brain (Barkley, 1991b; Hynd et al., 1991). However, there is no direct evidence that ADHD children suffer from a catecholamine deficit. Numerous investigations of neurotransmitter function, metabolite excretion, and biochemical markers yield largely inconclusive and contradictory results (Barkley, 1991b; Zametkin, 1989; Zametkin and Rapoport, 1987).

Behavioral Theories

Although biological factors are thought to have a significant role in the development of most cases of ADHD, psychological and environmental factors are likely to contribute to the severity and specific characteristics of the disorder. Parents may inadvertently reinforce hyperactive behaviors by giving children added attention when they exhibit ADHD behaviors. In addition, the positive behavior of ADHD children may be ignored by parents who are exhausted from scolding for undesirable behavior. Children with ADHD may not respond as well to typical contingencies; they may need more immediate and obvious rewards (Munoz-Millan and Casteel, 1989). Negative behavioral contingencies combined with a deficit in responding to positive reinforcement may exacerbate ADHD behaviors.

Behavioral theories may also explain the development of oppositionality and noncompliance in the ADHD child. Danforth et al. (1991) note that Patterson's (1982) theory on the development of coercive interactions between parent and child applies to the ADHD child. These interactions occur when a parent makes a command to the child. The child resists the command, for example, by yelling. The parent escalates the command with a threat, pleading, or physical guidance. In return, the child escalates resistance. If the parent gives in to the child's resistance before the child complies, the child is reinforced for the resistant behavior. The frequency and intensity of this resistant behavior then increase, creating future coercive interactions and future reinforcement for defiant behavior. This behavior pattern is likely to emerge in ADHD families, in which immediate compliance by the child is unusual. Parents who fall into the pattern of coercive interaction are at risk for having ADHD-CD children (Danforth et al., 1991; Patterson, 1982).

Psychological Theories

Hyperactive or inattentive behavior may also result from environmental stress, such as family dysfunction or traumatic stress. It is unlikely, however, that the full ADHD syndrome would result from such problems, in the absence of a biological predisposition to ADHD. Instead, these factors are likely to exacerbate existing ADHD symptoms or to create transient overactivity in an otherwise normal child (Frick and Lahey, 1991).

☐ ASSESSMENT PATTERNS

Thorough assessment of a child referred for ADHD is extremely important, since the diagnosis has become a catch-all for describing children who have behavior problems. Ideally an ADHD assessment battery will gather information from multiple informants who have observed the child in diverse situations. This multidimensional approach to behavioral assessment is crucial because ADHD children often behave differently in different environments. In addition, both cognitive and behavioral components of ADHD must be assessed in order to understand the pattern of symptoms for the individual child. As previously noted, some ADHD children show primarily hyperactive symptoms, while others have attention and concentration deficits. Hence, a comprehensive ADHD assessment leads to conclusions about the presence, severity, type, and characteristics of the disorder in each individual child. (A sample assessment battery is shown in Table 2.2.)

TABLE 2.2   Sample Assessment Battery for ADHD

COGNITIVE

Wechsler IQ test (WPPSI-R, WISC-III, WAIS-R)
WJ-R or WIAT
California Verbal Learning Test for Children

BEHAVIORAL

CBCL
CPRS-48
Teacher Report Form
CTRS-28

SYNDROME-SPECIFIC

Continuous performance test
ADHD Rating Scale (Parent and Teacher)
Home Situations Questionnaire
School Situations Questionnaire

Note: Assessment instruments are intended to supplement (not substitute for) a good clinical interview and, when possible, a structured diagnostic interview.

Broad Assessment Strategies

Cognitive Assessment

Clinician-Administered—IQ Testing. ADHD is a cognitive, as well as a behavioral, disorder. Hence, children with ADHD should be assessed for cognitive problems. Cognitive measures used with ADHD children seek to identify deficits of attention, cognitive control, memory, and global intelligence that may be associated with the disorder. Clinicians must remember that, while ADHD children as a group score lower on a variety of cognitive tests, they are a heterogeneous group with regard to test score performance. Some ADHD children ("behavioral" subtype) show remarkably few cognitive deficits, while other children ("cognitive" subtype) show marked deficiencies.

As a group, ADHD children score lower than matched controls on measures of intelligence (Loge, Staton, and Beatty, 1990; Lufi, Cohen, and Parish-Plass, 1990), although most ADHD children score in the broad normal range (Forness et al., 1992). Loge et al. (1990) found ADHD children to score lower than normal controls on Full Scale IQ, Information, Arithmetic, Digit Span, Block Design, and Coding of the WISC-R. However, virtually all IQ scores and subtest scores from the ADHD sample were in the normal range (the matched controls scored above the normal range). This result reflects the so-called "ACID" (*A*rithmetic, *C*oding, *I*nformation, *D*igit Span) profile frequently seen in children and adults with learning disabilities and ADHD (Kaufman, 1990; Sattler, 1990). Lufi et al. (1990) found ADHD children to score lower than controls on virtually all WISC-R subtests, with the largest differences occurring on the Arithmetic, Block Design, Digit Span, and Coding subtests. On the Arithmetic and Coding scales, ADHD children also scored lower than a mental health clinic sample.

The Arithmetic, Digit Span, and (sometimes) Coding subscales have been found in factor analytic studies to constitute a "Freedom from Distractibility" (FFD) factor that measures attention and concentration skills (Sattler, 1990). More recently the FFD factor has been defined as consisting of only the Arithmetic and Digit Span scales on the WISC-III. Children with ADHD often score lower on the scales composing the FFD factor (Forness et al., 1992; Loge et al., 1990; Lufi et al., 1990). Furthermore, evidence exists that ADHD children score below average on the Symbol-Digit Modalities Test (Smith, 1973), which is virtually identical to the WISC-R/WISC-III Coding subtest (Loge et al., 1990). However, one study (Cohen, Becker, and Campbell, 1990) found that WISC-R FFD scores did not correlate with parent and teacher ratings of hyperactivity.

Clinician-Administered—Achievement Testing. Achievement tests are also routinely administered to children with suspected ADHD because of the risk of learning difficulty associated with the disorder. In addition to the WJ-R and WIAT, the Wide Range Achievement Test-Revised (WRAT-R; Jastak and Wilkinson, 1984) and the Kaufman Test of Educational Achievement (K-TEA;

Kaufman and Kaufman, 1985) are commonly used broad achievement tests for assessing learning problems in ADHD children (Sattler, 1990). More specific tests capture areas such as reading and mathematics in a briefer format or in greater detail (Sattler, 1990). Of the achievement tests, the WIAT, K-TEA, and WJ-R appear to have the best psychometric properties and the greatest utility with the ADHD population. The WRAT-R remains widely used, despite having significant problems (Sattler, 1990).

As a group, ADHD children tend to score lower on achievement tests than do control groups. Barkley et al. (1991), for example, found a sample of ADHD adolescents to show WRAT scores in the 88–99 standard score range (m = 100; s.d. = 15), with the lowest scores in mathematics; these scores were lower than those of a control group. Likewise, Forness et al. (1992) suggest that ADHD children may have deficits in reading comprehension. However, August and Garfinkel (1989) note that there are subgroups of ADHD children who score in normal ranges on achievement tests. Using the WRAT-R, they found that behavioral ADHD subtypes scored in the 96–104 standard score range in reading, spelling, and arithmetic. The cognitive subtype, by contrast, scored in the 80–91 range.

Clinician-Administered—Other Cognitive Testing. In addition to intelligence and achievement tests, virtually any test of attention or concentration may be helpful in the understanding of the ADHD child. However, such tests are used less frequently because of lack of knowledge about the test or because an alternative test is more widely used.

Garfinkel and Klee's (1983) Progressive Maze Test, for example, is a computer administered measure of visual-spatial planning ability and goal direction that is also sensitive to impulsive responses. The child moves a square through a maze-like screen to hit a target. Errors occur when the child hits a side or obstacle of the maze; errors reflect impulsivity, erroneous planning, or lack of attention. Other maze tests can also be used to test impulsivity and planning ability in ADHD children. Maze tests discriminate ADHD children from controls and are responsive to medication effects (Barkley, 1991b).

Intelligence tests other than the Wechsler instruments are sometimes used in assessing the child with ADHD (e.g., August and Garfinkel, 1989). However, the proven psychometrics of the WISC-III argue strongly for its use. Reasons for administering an alternative test include recent administration of a Wechsler instrument, need for brevity, and problems with floor or ceiling effects. In these cases a test such as the SB:FE or the Kaufman Brief Intelligence Test (K-BIT; Kaufman and Kaufman, 1990) may be substituted.

Memory tests, such as the Selective Reminding Test (Hannay and Levin, 1985), indicate that ADHD children have poorer short-term recall, long-term storage, and long-term retrieval than do controls. Similarly, ADHD children score more poorly on California Verbal Learning Test (Delis et al., 1994) measures of short- and long-term memory (Loge et al., 1990).

Children with ADHD may have greater problems with tasks that are sensitive to frontal lobe functioning, although some disagreement exists on this point. "Frontal lobe" tasks include verbal fluency, nonverbal fluency, and ability to shift problem-solving set. Loge et al. (1990) found no difference between their ADHD sample and matched controls on the Controlled Oral Word Association Test (Borkowski, Benton, and Spreen, 1967) or on the Wisconsin Card Sorting Test (Heaton, 1981). Chelune et al., (1986) and Felton et al., (1987), on the other hand, did find differences in fluency and problem-solving set. In general, however, these fluency/response set problems do not appear to be the focal issues for ADHD children.

Over all, the most parsimonious strategy for the cognitive assessment of a child with ADHD is to begin with a broad Wechsler intelligence test. Scores on subscales and factors may provide insight into the child's deficits and suggest areas for further probing. These additional areas can be evaluated with more syndrome-specific tests. ADHD children with school problems should also be administered an achievement test to rule out the possibility of a learning disability.

Behavioral Assessment

Parent-Report.   Child behavior checklists are vital in the assessment of a child with ADHD. Such checklists quantify the adult's view of the child's behavior and compare this view to age-based normative samples. In addition, behavior checklists allow the probing of specific behaviors from multiple informants without using valuable interview time. Despite these advantages, the scales must be used with several caveats. Most importantly, the clinician must remember that checklists are affected by the motives and personality of the adult completing them. Factors such as social desirability, exasperation with the child, parental psychopathology, and halo effects can affect scores. This may be particularly true in the case of the ADHD child who places stress on the parent. Hence, behavior checklists should be interpreted with caution in cases where an adult may be motivated to distort scores or may be incapable of giving accurate ratings.

A related problem is the lack of agreement between respondents about the child's behavior. While agreement between adults in the same environment is relatively good (parent and parent), agreement between adults in different environments (parent and teacher) is poor (Whalen and Henker, 1991). This disagreement is due in part to rater bias and in part to the fact that children behave differently with different caretakers and in different environments. At the very least, it argues for the importance of assessing the child's behavior from the viewpoint of several adults.

The *Child Behavior Checklist* (CBCL) can be a valuable tool in identifying the specific behavior pattern shown by a child. The CBCL includes some items that are essential features of ADHD (Attention Problems subscale), some items that are likely associated features of ADHD (Aggressive Behavior and Social Problems subscales), and some items that are not typically related to ADHD (Anxious/Depressed subscale). Hence, the child's CBCL scores indicate the level of attention-related problems, the level of associated problems, and other behavioral problems that may be co-occurring with the ADHD (Achenbach, 1991). CBCL subscale items do not, however, correspond to DSM-IV criteria.

The CBCL discriminates ADHD children from normal and other clinically referred children (Barkley, 1987). A typical child with ADHD would be expected to elevate the Attention Problems scale of the CBCL, with other elevations likely on the Aggressive Behavior scale and the Social Problems scale. Social competence scores are often low relative to norms. Problematic CBCL profiles are also typical of adolescents with ADHD. Adolescents show lower social competence scores and higher Anxiety-Depression, Somatic Complaints, Withdrawal, and Aggressive Behavior scores (Barkley et al., 1991).

Like the CBCL, the *Conners Parent Rating Scales* (CPRS) include items that resemble both essential and associated features of ADHD. A shorter form of the Conners scales that is sometimes used is the ten-item "Hyperactivity Index" (HI), which is embedded in the forty-eight–item parent scale (Conners, 1990). The ten HI items are the items that are most responsive to treatment effects, but they are not sufficient for the diagnosis of ADHD. Hence, although they are widely used, they should not be separated from the scale for independent use in ADHD assessment (Atkins and Pelham, 1991; Barkley, 1987; Conners, 1990).

Barkley (1987) recommends use of the forty-eight–item parent form of the CPRS (CPRS-48) because of its brevity and better psychometric properties. Children with ADHD will most likely show significant elevations on the Impulsive-Hyperactive, Learning Problems, and Conduct Problems scales, and the pattern of elevation of these scales may provide insight into the exact manifestation of the disorder. With the exception of Anxious-Shy, Psychosomatic, and Obsessive-Compulsive, all CPRS-93 scales reflect dimensions of ADHD (particularly Restless-Disorganized and Hyperactive-Immature) and related disorders. A major disadvantage of the CPRS-93 is its use of a single set of norms (based on children age 6–14) for all age-sex groups. ADHD children and adolescents tend to elevate most CPRS scales, with peaks on the Impulsive-Hyperactive (CPRS-48) and Hyperactive-Immature (CPRS-93) scales (i.e., Barkley et al., 1991).

The Conners scales have received considerable research and clinical use in the assessment and treatment of ADHD, and they may be the most widely used scales in ADHD assessment (Barkley, 1987; Conners, 1990). Unlike the Achenbach scales, the items on the Conners scales are largely focused on ADHD and related symptomatology. This gives a more in-depth assessment of ADHD at the expense of breadth of assessment across disorders. The Conners scales discriminate ADHD children from normals in the classroom and at home, and they are sensitive to treatment effects (Barkley, 1987; Conners, 1990; Fischer and Newby, 1991; Newcorn et al., 1989). Conners scale scores also relate significantly to impulsivity on cognitive tests (Newcorn et al., 1989).

In addition to the Conners and Achenbach scales, numerous other broad behavior checklists exist, although none are as well researched in the ADHD area. Virtually all broad behavior checklists include a hyperactivity or inattention scale. The Activity Level subscale of the MCBC, for example, is elevated by ADHD children. If a different checklist is used, scales measuring inattention, hyperactivity, aggression, and social problems should be examined for elevations.

Other-Report.   In addition to the parent-completed CBCL, teachers may complete the *Teacher Report Form* of the CBCL (TRF), which is similar (although not identical) in form, content, scoring, norms, and interpretation to the CBCL. As with parent-reports, teacher-reports of ADHD children's behavior show elevations on the Attention Problems, Aggressive Behavior, and Social Problems scales; similar results are found for ADHD adolescents (Barkley et al., 1991). Comparison of results from the CBCL and TRF can provide insights into the child's relative behavior at school and at home. A problem-ridden TRF profile coupled with a relatively normal CBCL profile suggests that the child may behave adequately in the less structured, more individualized home environment while becoming disorganized and hyperactive at school. When the TRF and CBCL show markedly different profiles, the clinician should expect parents and teachers to disagree about the accuracy of the ADHD diagnosis.

Like the CPRS, the *Conners Teacher's Rating Scales* (CTRS) have two forms, a thirty-nine–item form and a twenty-eight–item form. Barkley (1987) suggests that the shorter form is generally sufficient for ADHD cases, although the longer form has been more widely used in research and provides more comprehensive data. Norms for the thirty-nine–item form apply to ages 3–14, while those for the 28 item form apply to ages 3-17. Hence, if the child is over 14, the twenty-eight–item form is most appropriate. Both forms include the HI, which specifically targets items that are most sensitive to the effects of medication on ADHD. ADHD children are expected to elevate Hyperactivity, Conduct Problem, and Inattention subscales on both CTRS forms, as well as the Asocial scale of the CTRS-39. The Hyperactivity and Inattention scales, however, are most central to the ADHD diagnosis. The teacher HI is often used as a brief ADHD screen in schools, with children scoring 15 (2 standard deviations above the mean) or above considered to be hyperactive (Atkins and Pelham, 1991).

A short form of the CTRS-39, the IOWA-Conners Rating Scale, was developed to delineate problems of inattention/overactivity from problems of aggression/defiance. The IOWA-Conners consists of ten items, five of which measure inattention/overactivity and five of which measure aggression. It appears to have promise as a brief screen for ADHD, Conduct Disorder, and Oppositional-Deviant Disorder (Atkins and Pelham, 1991). However, use of the full CTRS-39 is recommended because of its comprehensiveness and superior psychometrics.

The CTRS has received empirical support similar to that given to the CPRS. Like the CPRS, the CTRS focuses on behaviors typical of ADHD or related disorders, giving a more detailed view then the TRF of ADHD behaviors. However, the TRF taps a wider range of behavior than does the CTRS. Correlations between parent- and teacher-ratings of behavior on the Conners scales are modest (Conners, 1990). In ADHD samples the highest correlations are found between parent- and teacher-ratings of conduct disorder and hyperactivity/

attention (r's in the .40–.42 range; Cohen, Becker, and Campbell, 1990). Extremely high correlations between parent and teacher ratings should not be expected, since the environments, rules, and discipline differ. This fact argues for the use of *both* parent- and teacher-report behavioral checklists in evaluating the ADHD child.

Child-Report. Child self-report behavior checklists are also used as a standardized, rapid means of assessing the child's view of his or her condition. *The Youth Self-Report* (YSR) form of the CBCL, for example, allows older children and adolescents to report on symptoms they experience. On the YSR, ADHD adolescents have been found to elevate scales measuring social problems and delinquent conduct, although depression, somatization, thought disorder, and aggression were not elevated (Barkley et al., 1991).

Syndrome-Specific Tests

Clinician-Administered

Continuous Performance Tests. A continuous performance test (CPT) is a test that assesses attention, impulsivity, and distractibility using letters or numbers projected on a screen (usually a computer screen; Barkley, 1987; Gordon, 1983; Guevremont, DuPaul, and Barkley, 1990; Klee and Garfinkel, 1983). The child watches the screen while stimuli (letters or numbers) flash quickly and in succession on the screen. The object of the task is for the child to execute a response (push a button) when a certain sequence of stimuli is presented. For example, the object may be to push the spacebar on the computer every time the numbers 6 and 4 appear in immediate succession. Thus, if a 6 appears, followed by a 5, the child should NOT push the space bar. Likewise, if a 5 appears, followed by a 4, the child should also *not* push the bar. However, if a 6 appears, followed by a 4, the child *should* push the bar.

From this task, measures of hits (correct responses to the stimulus sequence), misses (presentations of the stimulus sequence that are not responded to, also called omissions), and errors of commission (responses by the child that do not follow the correct stimulus sequence, also called commissions) are derived. Hits measure accurate, sustained attention; misses measure distractibility or wavering attention; commissions measure impulsivity or poor attention to the stimuli. Hence, a child with many hits, few misses, but many commissions is reflecting good sustained attention but significant impulsivity. On the other hand, a child with few hits, many misses, and few commissions is showing distractibility and poor sustained attention but less impulsivity. Some CPTs speed up the presentation of the stimuli when the child is doing well or slow down the presentation of stimuli if the child is doing poorly. These CPTs yield a fourth score, the interstimulus interval, which is a measure of the average speed at which numbers were presented to the child. Shorter interstimulus intervals indicate that the child was able to attend to briefer, more rapid stimuli.

Commonly used CPTs are the Vigilance Task of the *Gordon Diagnostic System* (GDS; Gordon, 1983; Gordon and Mettelman, 1987) and Klee and Garfinkel's (1983) computerized CPT. Barkley (1987) also reviews several other CPTs. The GDS is a small, computerized device that assesses sustained attention and impulsivity in ADHD children, using several tests. The 9-minute CPT measure in the GDS (the Vigilance Task) requires the child to press a button when the sequence 1 then 9 appears on the screen. Scores are obtained for hits, misses, and commissions, as well as for variability of performance across three 3-minute time intervals. Klee and Garfinkel's CPT runs on a personal computer and uses letters.

The CPT is a good measure of inattention and distractibility. CPT scores correlate with observer measures of ADHD symptoms as well as with other cognitive measures of attention, distractibility, and impulsivity (Barkley, 1987; Guevremont et al., 1990; Klee and Garfinkel, 1983; Newcorn et al., 1989). Grant et al., (1990), for example, found scores from the GDS Vigilance Task to correlate with Verbal IQ, Performance IQ, FFD, finger oscillation, auditory perception, visual-motor integration, and nonverbal reasoning scores in a sample of ADHD children. Furthermore, ADHD children and adolescents do more poorly on the CPT than do normal children (Loge et al., 1990), and CPT scores improve with stimulant medication (Barkley, 1987; Barkley et al., 1991; Fischer and Newby, 1991). Commissions may be particularly sensitive to ADHD (Loge et al., 1990).

A variant of the CPT, the Distractibility Task of the GDS (Gordon and Mettelman, 1987), also discriminates ADHD from normal children (Loge et al., 1990). This task is identical to the Vigilance Task of the GDS except that number stimuli flash in three separate columns at the same time (giving the appearance of a three-digit number). The child is to respond when a 1 appears followed by a 9, but only when *both* numbers are in the center column. Numbers in the other columns are intended as distractions. Number correct and errors of commission are scored.

Matching Familiar Figures Test. The Matching Familiar Figures Test (MFFT; Kanan, 1966) is a twelve-item measure of impulse control, visual discrimination ability, and attention to detail. There is also a twenty-item version of the MFFT (Cairns and Cammock, 1978). The child is shown a picture of an object and must choose from a group of six nearly identical pictures the one that exactly matches the target picture. The child is scored for latency time (mean time taken to respond to each picture) and number of errors. Raw scores can be compared to norms (Salkind and Nelson, 1980). The MFFT discriminates ADHD from normal children, and it relates to behavioral measures of activity (Barkley, 1987). However, at least one study questions the MFFT-20's ability to discriminate between ADHD and control adolescents (Barkley et al., 1991). The MFFT has been criticized because of its high correlations with intelligence and achievement as well as for reliability problems (Barkley, 1987; DuPaul et al., 1991; Milich and Kramer, 1984). Nevertheless, it remains one of the most widely used measures of impulsivity in ADHD children.

Waiting Tasks. Waiting tasks require the child to wait a specified amount of time before executing a simple response. For example, in the Delay Task from the GDS (Gordon, 1983) the child must wait, then press a button after a certain amount of time. The child is not told that the amount of waiting time is 6 seconds. When the child presses the button after the requisite amount of time, he or she receives a point, the time is reset, and the child must wait again. If the child presses the button before 6 seconds have elapsed, a point is not awarded, and the timer returns to a 6 second delay. Scores are given for the number of correct responses, the number of times that the button was pressed, and a ratio of correct responses to button presses. Waiting tasks such as the Delay Task measure impulsivity, although their ability to discriminate ADHD children from normals is uncertain (Barkley, 1987; Loge et al., 1990).

Parent-Report/Other-Report

ADHD Rating Scales. ADHD rating scales consist of a list of the DSM ADHD symptoms, which are rated by an observer as to the frequency of their occurrence. ADHD rating scales based on DSM-III-R criteria have been widely used, relevant, and convenient for clinicians. Rating scales based on DSM-IV criteria are emerging but are less researched than the DSM-III-R scales. ADHD rating scales are convenient and valuable because they standardize the assessment of diagnostic symptoms and require little clinician administration time.

Newcorn et al. (1989), for example, developed a scale consisting of all DSM-III ADDH symptoms and all DSM-III-R ADHD symptoms (except for the sleep symptom on the DSM-III, because teachers were the raters for the study). Teachers rated children on a 4-point scale ranging from "not at all" to "very much" for each item. Symptoms rated as "not at all" or "just a little" present (the two low-end points) were considered to be not present for diagnostic purposes. Symptoms rated as "pretty much" or "very much" present (the two high-end points) were present for diagnostic purposes. Symptom presence/absence was then compared to DSM criteria to arrive at a diagnosis. ADHD rating scale scores correlated extremely strongly with the CTRS-28 Hyperactivity Index ($r = 0.92$), Conduct Problems ($r = 0.79$), Inattention-Passivity ($r = 0.79$), and Hyperactivity ($r = 0.89$) subscales (Newcorn et al., 1989). ADHD scores also related to parental ratings of Impulsivity-Hyperactivity and Conduct Problems on the CPRS-48, as well as to errors of commission on a test of impulsivity (Newcorn et al., 1989).

A similar scale was developed by DuPaul (1991) to measure the presence of DSM-III-R symptoms of ADHD. DuPaul's ADHD Rating Scale consists of fourteen items, each of which is a DSM-III-R criterion of ADHD. Parents rate on a 4-point scale the extent to which their child shows each symptom. The scale yields a total score and two subscale scores (Inattention-hyperactivity and Impulsivity-Hyperactivity). Other similar ADHD rating scales exist (Atkins and Pelham, 1991).

Home Situations Questionnaire/School Situations Questionnaire.   The Home Situations Questionnaire (HSQ; Barkley, 1981) consists of sixteen items that describe situations around the home in which ADHD children may have behavioral difficulties. A revised version of the HSQ has fourteen items (DuPaul, 1990). Parents state whether their child has a problem in that setting and the severity of the problem. Scores are obtained for the number of problem situations and the mean severity of these problems when they occur. Scores may be compared to norms derived by Barkley and Edelbrock (1987) or DuPaul (1990). The HSQ provides information about the pervasiveness, severity, and location of the ADHD symptoms at home. Such situation-specific information can be helpful in behavioral interventions. ADHD children score higher than normal children on the scale, which is sensitive to treatment effects (Barkley, 1987; Fischer and Newby, 1991).

The School Situations Questionnaire (SSQ; Barkley, 1981) is a twelve-item scale consisting of school situations that could be problematic for the ADHD child. A revised version of the SSQ has eight-items (DuPaul, 1990). As with the HSQ, teachers state whether the child has a problem in each situation and rate the severity of the problem. Number of problem situations and mean severity are scored and compared to norms (Barkley and Edelbrock, 1987; DuPaul, 1990). ADHD children score higher than normal children on number of situations and situation severity (Barkley, 1987), and the SSQ is sensitive to treatment effects (Fischer and Newby, 1991).

Unlike other rating scales, the HSQ and SSQ provide information about the situations in which inattention, impulsivity, or hyperactivity are likely to occur. This delineation of situational differences tends to fit the observations of most parents or teachers, who have difficulty completing global items about behavior. Frequently, for example, observers state that a child is "sometimes" impulsive, meaning that the child *does* show impulsivity, but not in all situations. The HSQ and SSQ allow the clinician to investigate whether "sometimes" means that the child is somewhat impulsive (or inattentive, or hyperactive) in *all* situations, or whether "sometimes" means that the child is very impulsive in some situations but not in others.

Attention Deficit Disorders Evaluation Scale (ADDES).   The ADDES (McCarney, 1989a; 1989b) is a forty-six–(parent version) or sixty-(teacher version) item questionnaire of typical ADHD behaviors. Raters use a 0–4 scale to rate the frequency with which a child age 4–20 years shows various behaviors. Item scores are summed to yield three subscales (Inattentive, Impulsive, Hyperactive) and a Total Score, which can be compared to scores from large normative samples to give standard scores and percentiles. Children with subscale scores more than 2 standard deviations below the mean are considered to have a problem in that subscale area. The reliability of the ADDES is very good, although more validity studies are needed. In addition, there appears to be some conceptual and statistical overlap between the subscales, suggesting that they may not be pure measures of their stated construct. The ability of the ADDES to discriminate ADHD and other children is not well established, although it appears to correlate moderately with other specific behavioral measures of ADHD (Adesman, 1991). Adesman (1991) cautions against widespread clinical use of the ADDES until further studies are completed.

ADD-H Comprehensive Teacher Rating Scale (ACTeRS). The ACTeRS (Ullmann, Sleator, and Sprague, 1984) is a twenty-four–item teacher-completed measure of four major symptom groups typically shown by ADHD children: Attention, Hyperactivity, Social Skills, and Oppositional Behavior. Items are rated on a 5-point scale, and the scale may be given to the teacher several times per day. Repeated administration allows the clinician to monitor changes in the child's behavior throughout the day. Subscale scores can be compared to those of a normative group (Ullmann et al., 1984). In addition, relative elevations of the subscales may suggest which symptom groups are the most significant problem for the child at school throughout the day. The ACTeRS differentiates ADHD from normal children and is sensitive to treatment effects (Ullmann et al., 1984).

Like the HSQ and SSQ, the ACTeRS allows a finer delineation of ADHD behaviors. While the HSQ and SSQ differentiate behaviors across situations, the ACTeRS can be used to differentiate behaviors across time. This information can be particularly helpful for children whose ADHD worsens with fatigue or for children whose medication appears to "wear off" at some point during the school day.

Self-Control Rating Scale (SCRS). The SCRS (Kendall and Wilcox, 1979) is a thirty-three–item, teacher-completed scale measuring the extent to which the child can control impulsive behavior and conform to rules. Items are added to give a total score that reflects self-control, which is typically a problem in ADHD children. Scale scores can be used to evaluate the child's degree of self-control or to evaluate change in self-control as a result of cognitive-behavioral intervention (Kendall and Wilcox, 1980).

TREATMENT OPTIONS

Treatment options for ADHD are outlined in Table 2.3.

Medication

Medication is perhaps the most well-known, most widely used, and one of the most effective interventions for ADHD (Greenhill, 1992). Specifically, psychostimulant medications are frequently prescribed to assist in the management of ADHD, with improvement rates of as high as 70–80% (Anastopoulos, DuPaul, and Barkley, 1991; Barkley, 1977; Greenhill, 1989, 1992; Munoz-Millan, 1989), compared to placebo response rates of 10–18% (Greenhill, 1989, 1992). The stimulant medications most prescribed for children with ADHD are methylphenidate (Ritalin), dextroamphetamine (Dexedrine), and pemoline (Cylert)(Greenhill, 1992). Ritalin is the most widely prescribed, with one study

TABLE 2.3   Treatment Options for ADHD

MEDICATION

Psychostimulants
Tricyclic antidepressants
Other medications (clonidine, thioridazine)

BEHAVIORAL INTERVENTIONS

Home-based/Office-based
  Psychoeducation
  Attention training/special time
  Reinforcement techniques
  Relaxation techniques

School-based
  Stimulus reduction
  Seating modification
  Increasing task structure and stimulation
  Contingency management

PSYCHOTHERAPY

Cognitive-behavioral interventions
  Self-talk
  Self-monitoring
  Sequenced problem solving

Play therapy
Psychodynamic psychotherapy

Note: This outline of options summarizes major treatments covered in the text. Specific treatments are often combined into an intervention package. Refer to the text for additional descriptions of each treatment. This table is not necessarily an exhaustive list of all treatments available.

showing 88% of a sample of ADHD children to be medicated with Ritalin (Wolraich et al., 1990). Cylert is a longer-lasting, less addicting stimulant, but it may have more significant side effects and less effectiveness than Ritalin (Greenhill, 1989).

Stimulant medications often improve the performance of ADHD children across a variety of tasks. Stimulants have been shown to result in increased attention, reduced impulsivity, decreased overactivity, decreased restlessness, increased compliance, reduced aggressiveness, improved memory, improved social interaction, and improved classroom behavior (Anastopoulos et al., 1991; Barkley et al., 1988; Danforth et al., 1991; Greenhill, 1992; Rapport et al., 1988). Teachers report that 75% of ADHD children improve in global behavior following medication with stimulants (Greenhill, 1992). Evidence also exists that positive effects of Ritalin occur for adolescents and adults as well (Biederman, 1991; Greenhill, 1992; Klorman, Coons, and Borgstedt, 1987). Although the stimulants may have some cognitive effects on as many as 60% of children

(Swanson et al., 1991), they are less effective in improving ADHD children's grades (Whalen and Henker, 1991). CPT scores generally improve following medication (Fischer and Newby, 1991; Greenhill, 1992), but the evidence for improved grades is weak at best (Whalen and Henker, 1991).

The most common complaints about stimulant medication (aside from the fact that they fail to work for some children) are side effects. Stimulants are associated with decreased appetite, weight loss, headache, increased crying, heart rate elevation, slowing of growth, increased tension, and difficulty sleeping in some children (Anastopoulos et al., 1991; Greenhill, 1992). Furthermore, a "behavioral rebound" (Greenhill, 1992) may occur when children experience stimulant withdrawal, usually at the end of the school day. This behavioral rebound consists of irritability, hyperactivity, and excitability. It is usually managed by administering the child an additional dose of the stimulant or by using a longer-lasting stimulant (Greenhill, 1992). More severe but less common side effects are an increase in hyperactive behavior and the development of tics (Greenhill, 1989). The latter effect is rare but argues against the use of stimulants with children who have a positive family history for tic disorder (Biederman, 1991; Greenhill, 1989). The severity of stimulant side effects can be managed by altering the doses or providing "drug holidays," during which stimulant use is discontinued (Anastopoulos et al., 1991). Parents should be informed about possible side effects and should be instructed to monitor them, with severe effects brought immediately to the attention of the prescribing physician.

Despite their effectiveness with many ADHD children, psychostimulants may not be the drug of choice for certain children with ADHD. Some children, for example, fail to respond to stimulant medication (20–30% of cases), while other children, as just discussed, are at risk for tics. Sometimes children or family members may abuse the stimulant medication. Finally, some children need longer-acting medications or have co-occurring depression (Biederman, 1991; Greenhill, 1989, 1992). In these cases the tricyclic antidepressants (TCAs) may be tried as an alternative treatment. TCAs are longer lasting, may have an effect on depression, generally do not affect tics, and do not result in addiction. One common TCA for ADHD is desipramine (Norpramin), which has been found to have a 68% improvement rate for ADHD children (Greenhill, 1992). Imipramine (Tofranil) has also shown response rates greater than those of placebo (Pliszka, 1991).

As with stimulants, however, problems exist with TCA treatment. Side effects of TCA treatment are cardiotoxicity, dry mouth, decreased appetite, headaches, tiredness, dizziness, insomnia, and abdominal discomfort (Biederman, 1991). Furthermore, almost one-third of children will show no response to TCAs (Greenhill, 1992; Pliszka, 1991). Because of side effects and lack of placebo-controlled studies, Greenhill (1992) recommends that TCAs be used with caution for preadolescent children, and parents should closely monitor the child for physical reactions.

Numerous other medications, including clonidine (Catapres), monoamine oxidase inhibitors (MAOIs), thioridazine (Mellaril), lithium, and bupropion

(Wellbutrin), have been suggested as potential treatments for ADHD, although little data exist on the use of these medications (Greenhill, 1992). Clonidine may be promising for ADHD children with high levels of motor activity and aggression, as well as for children with co-occurring ADHD and Tourette's syndrome (Biederman, 1991; Greenhill, 1989). MAOIs are effective but rarely used, since they require strict dietary adherence that children are likely to violate (Biederman, 1991; Greenhill, 1989). Studies of lithium for ADHD treatment have produced disappointing results (Greenhill, 1989).

As a general rule, medication alone is often helpful but rarely sufficient for the treatment of ADHD. Additional treatment components, such as parent psychoeducation, behavioral modification, and interventions to address co-occurring learning problems, are often essential in the management of ADHD.

Behavioral Interventions

Special Considerations for ADHD Children

Medication is frequently combined with behavioral treatments in a package to reduce the child's negative behavior while enhancing attention and concentration. In other cases, medication fails or parents are opposed to medication in principle, leading to the use of behavioral interventions alone. Next to medication, behavior treatments are the most used ADHD treatments (Whalen and Henker, 1991).

Behavioral influences on ADHD symptoms are always present. The behavior of hyperactive children can be annoying and disruptive, leading to negative attention from adults. This attention reinforces hyperactive behavior or angers the child (Newby, Fischer, and Roman, 1991). Ultimately a negative cycle occurs, in which the child is reinforced with (or angered by) attention for hyperactive behavior. The child then engages in further hyperactive behavior, which brings additional parental attention and a continuation of the cycle. Alternatively, the behavior of the child may lead to power struggles between the child and parent. These struggles consist of a cycle in which the parent, frustrated by the child's aversive behavior, makes an unpleasant command to the child. The child, responding to the challenging tone of the parent, refuses to comply, provoking an escalation of parental commands and threats. The child escalates resistance similarly, until the parent gives in, negatively reinforcing the child for oppositional-hyperactive behavior ("giving in" may also consist of engaging the child in a continuing interaction; Newby et al., 1991). Hence, regardless of the etiology of ADHD, behavioral contingencies almost always play a role in its manifestation and perpetuation. Behavioral interventions aim to reinforce task-focused behavior while ignoring or punishing hyperactive, inappropriate behaviors. Most such interventions involve teaching parents or teachers strategies to reduce the child's ADHD behaviors (Abramowitz and O'Leary, 1991; Barkley, 1981).

Virtually all behavioral interventions for ADHD have several basic principles in common:

1. Thorough pre-treatment assessment, using cognitive tests and behavior checklists in addition to interview data
2. Evaluation of the child's environment, as well as the child
3. Involvement of the parents and/or teachers in the treatment of the child.
4. Education of the parents or family about ADHD
5. Screening and treatment for problems that may hamper the implementation of a behavioral plan, such as marital dysfunction or lack of motivation
6. Homework assignments to be performed between sessions
7. Understanding of the stress of parenting and/or teaching a child with ADHD, with appropriate attention to parent and teacher difficulties in implementing a behavioral plan
8. Flexibility in how the plan is implemented, according to the needs and wants of each family or classroom
9. Frequent monitoring of the child's behavior
10. Immediate feedback and reinforcement
11. Ongoing assessment of plan effectiveness
12. Modification of the plan based on feedback about its effectiveness

Home-Based Behavioral Interventions

Five-Step Behavioral Plan. A variety of home-based behavior management plans have been proposed for children with ADHD. Anastopoulos et al. (1991), for example, describe a systematic plan based on one of the most popular behavioral treatments for ADHD (Barkley, 1981). The plan can be implemented in an individual or group format and does not specify a necessary number of sessions. Using plans described by Anastopoulos et al. (1991), Barkley (1981), and Newby et al. (1991), a recommended behavioral plan for ADHD is as follows.

Phase 1—Assessment and Psychoeducation: In this phase, parents are taught the basics of behavior management in general and of the ADHD treatment plan in particular. First, the family is thoroughly assessed for problems and symptoms, particularly as they pertain to the child with ADHD. Second, ADHD is explained in detail, with attention to specific symptoms, etiology, appearance, features, prevalence, course, and treatment. Handouts and books can be used to facilitate understanding and retention of information. Third, behavior management is explained as a general technique. Principles of reinforcement, reinforcement schedules, attention as reinforcement, punishment, and operant conditioning are then explained. Fourth, these principles are then specifically applied to ADHD, with particular attention to the effects of ADHD on the parent–child relationship. During this discussion the automatic nature of parent-child interaction and conflict is explored. Examples of sequences in which children and parents act (usually in a mutually hostile or aggravating way) are given. Parents are taught that the goal is for them to reduce automatic, negative behavior and to increase purposeful, positive contingencies in the environment. Fifth, three special issues about the use of behavior techniques with ADHD children are covered: need for immediate reinforcers, need for consistency, and need for the identification of specific behaviors (Newby et al., 1991). Contingencies must also be able to change to fit changes in the child's behavior.

Phase 2—Attention Training: In this phase, parents are taught the power of parental attention and techniques for harnessing this power. First, attention is necessary to monitor the behavior of the child. Parents must attend to know when to reinforce, and attention is necessary for the assessment of the child's behavior throughout the week. Second, parents are encouraged to spend a certain amount of positive time (typically 15–20 minutes per day) with their child, in which they interact with him or her in a nondirective, nonjudgmental way. Ideally, this "special time" allows parents to make attention salient to the child, to improve the quality of the attention, to make the child's range of behavior salient to the parent, and to improve the parent–child relationship. Parents are eventually encouraged to provide attention when their child is behaving appropriately or is on task and to ignore inappropriate, off-task behavior. Punishment is not used at this time. Third, parents are encouraged to use attention as a reinforcer in other situations, providing attention when the child is engaged in positive behavior and withdrawing attention during hyperactive, off-task behavior. Finally, parents are taught to increase the child's frequency of independent behavior by giving occasional attention-reinforcement when the child is not depending on the parent for entertainment. The largest obstacle to this task is the parental inclination to let the child alone when he or she is behaving well. These times typically allow the parent to take a break, and parents sometimes fear provoking their child with parental attention. Parents are taught that providing attention during times of positive behavior increases the probability of future positive behavior, bringing additional benefits.

Phase 3—Reinforcement Techniques: Initially in this phase, parents select a single behavior to be controlled, and this behavior is tied to a clear reinforcement system. A system of token reinforcement may be used, or primary reinforcers may be provided at the time of the behavior. The behavior selected should be easily observable, clearly defined, and relatively frequent. Anastopoulos et al. (1991), for example, select "compliance with initial parental requests" (p. 216) as the target behavior, using a token system for reinforcement. In addition to having a specific, observable target behavior, a reinforcer must be selected and administered. Reinforcers that have shown the greatest effect on ADHD children's behavior are delivered immediately following the behavior (Hersher, 1985). The plan is fully explained to the child before its implementation. Behaviors are charted by the parent and discussed each week, with appropriate modification of the plan. One or 2 weeks after the instigation of the token system, negative reinforcement and punishment techniques are phased into the plan (following explanation to the child). Specifically, time-out and response cost (in which a reinforcer, such as a token, is removed) are used to reduce the frequency of negative behaviors. As with reinforcement, punishment must be immediate and tied to specific behavior. Time-out, for example, typically involves sitting on a chair in a relatively unstimulating part of the room immediately following the target negative behavior. The time-out period should be relatively brief (1 minute for each year of the child's age is a rough guideline, although this often must be modified for individual children), with extensions of the period for noncompliance with the time-out directive. Continued careful charting and flexibility in the implementation of the plan are essential. Finally, parents are encouraged to extend the principles of the plan to other child behaviors.

Phase 4—Maintenance: The final phase deals with the future implementation of the behavior plan to new situations, without the therapist as a guide. Parents review and plan with the therapist the future of behavioral management in the home, anticipating problems and events. Follow-up sessions are scheduled, and the parents are encouraged to continue monitoring behaviors for discussion at follow-up.

Phase 5—Follow-Up: Finally, several weeks after termination of weekly therapy, the parents meet with the therapist to discuss their progress. Follow-up observational data are collected and problems are discussed. If the system has completely broken down, several weeks of additional therapy may be required.

Other Behavioral Interventions. Other home-based behavioral techniques resemble the program just outlined, with minor modifications. Forehand and McMahon (1981), for example, rely heavily on observations of the parent–child interaction in the clinic and extensive in-clinic training of parenting skills to produce behavior change in the parent as well as in the child. Patterson's (1976, 1982) Social Learning Program for defiant, oppositional children, on the other hand, focuses on power struggles in parent–child interactions, a common problem in families with ADHD children. Although it shares many similarities with the plan previously described, Patterson's program includes several additional components that may be helpful additions to an ADHD behavior plan. For example, parents are taught how they may be subtly reinforcing defiant behavior by engaging their child in a power struggle or by giving in after a battle with the child. Immediacy of feedback, consistency of implementation, and clarity of feedback are emphasized. Time-out is used as in other behavior modification plans, with the exception that the child is placed in a separate room with the door closed, and a timer is used to monitor the duration of the punishment. The closed door presumably reduces escalation that might be provoked if the child could interact with the parent. Patterson's use of the closed door and the timer may be useful components for families who have difficulties with escalating parent–child power struggles.

School-Based Behavioral Interventions

Antecedent Management Techniques. Behavioral techniques applied at school are often used for children with ADHD (DuPaul, Guevremont, and

Barkley, 1992), and communication between parents and teacher is essential for managing the child's behavior across environments (and for evaluating the generalization of treatment effects). One group of school-based techniques targets stimuli which may elicit inattention, impulsivity, or hyperactivity (antecedents to ADHD behavior). "Stimulus reduction," for example, involves buffering the child from extraneous stimuli, presumably reducing distractibility and impulsivity. In stimulus reduction the child is put in a quiet room or quiet place. Stimulus reduction techniques have received little empirical support, and they are rarely used to treat ADHD (Abramowitz and O'Leary, 1991). A second school-based technique is "seating modification", in which the child's seat is moved to a place that will provide more task-appropriate stimulation and less extraneous stimulation. Typically, seating modification involves moving the child to the front of the room or away from other overly active groups of children. In other cases the seating arrangement of the entire classroom may be changed, to reduce distractions from other children (Abramowitz and O'Leary, 1991). Seating modification apparently does produce less off-task behavior. Other specific techniques suggested by Abramowitz and O'Leary (1991) include reducing background classroom noise, reducing difficulty of tasks, allowing the child to pace himself or herself on tasks, increasing task structure, and increasing the stimulation of tasks by using audio or visual components.

Contingency Management. In addition to techniques directed at stimuli, school-based behavioral techniques also emphasize modification of contingencies to change ADHD behavior (DuPaul et al., 1992). Teacher attention is a commonly used reinforcer or punisher to shape the child's behavior. Teachers are encouraged to praise appropriate behavior and to ignore or punish inappropriate behavior. Praise may be verbal-direct (a statement that the child is engaging in good behavior), verbal-indirect (a pleasant verbal interaction with the child that does not specifically refer to good behavior but is contingent upon it), nonverbal-direct (a smile or friendly nod), or nonverbal-indirect (standing near the child or otherwise engaging in pleasant nonverbal interaction). Ideally praise follows good behavior as soon as possible and never follows inappropriate behavior.

Behaviors that are inappropriate but not dangerous, destructive, or disruptive may be ignored by the teacher, although research indicates that some punishment adds to the effectiveness of a praise-ignore plan (Abramowitz and O'Leary, 1991; DuPaul et al., 1992). It is essential that the teacher's method of ignoring be carefully studied for subtle reinforcing components. In some cases, teachers will "ignore" by saying repeatedly to the child, "I am ignoring you." Such a statement communicates that the child is in fact *not* being ignored. Similar patterns of verbal and nonverbal interaction can create a very reinforcing situation out of supposed ignoring.

Certain behaviors exhibited by the ADHD child cannot be ignored. Generally these behaviors are disruptive, dangerous, destructive, or impinge on the freedom of other children. In these cases, punishment techniques can be effective, if properly administered. Reprimands, for example, are particularly effective if they are administered in a brief, matter-of-fact, consistent, firm, direct (standing close to the child and requiring eye contact), and immediate manner (Abramowitz and O'Leary, 1991). Because teachers must deal with large classes, anger, delay, and inconsistency are common problems for them in administering social punishment to children with ADHD. Furthermore, overly long explanations are aversive and irritating to the child, reducing the likelihood that they will be heard and understood.

In addition to reprimands, time-out techniques can be used to punish negative behavior. Because time-out involves restricting the child from access to reinforcement, time-out is perceived by the child as negative, and it produces the same effects as other punishment techniques. School-based time-out may take the form of ineligibility for reinforcers that are being distributed to the class, for a specified period of time (Abramowitz and O'Leary, 1991). For example, if each child is given a piece of candy for solving a math problem correctly, the punished child would not be eligible for the candy. Social time-out involves removing the child from the class, by moving the chair to a remote area of the room or out into the hall. Time-out is most effective when it is announced in a firm, brief, clear, matter-of-fact way, when the child does not desire isolation, when the amount of time for the punishment is clear, when the duration is reasonable for age, and when the child receives additional punishment (an extension of the time-out period) for anything short of immediate compliance with the time-out order (Abramowitz and O'Leary, 1991). Because of its severity and duration, time-out should be used sparingly and only for severe negative behavior. If implemented properly, time-out can have a significant effect on the target child's behavior.

Token Economies. In some cases of ADHD a token economy may be established in the classroom. This technique awards the child points for desirable behaviors (usually on-task behavior) and sometimes removes points for undesirable behaviors (response cost). (Although response cost is not included in all token interventions, it appears to be a critical component of token interventions for ADHD children [DuPaul et al., 1992].) Points may then be exchanged for rewards.

Token economies are powerful shapers of behavior, particularly when the response-cost component is included. However, they are not without risk: First, other children in the classroom may be jealous of the ADHD child and misbehave in the hopes of getting their own token economy. Second, if the parameters of good and bad behavior are too stringent, the ADHD child may be unable to earn any tokens. Such failure may lead to frustration and an increase in negative behavior. This scenario can be avoided by making the target behaviors initially very simple and increasing their difficulty with time. Third, the token economy motivates the child with external rewards, which will not always be present throughout the child's life. Ultimately the child must acquire an intrinsic motivation for good behavior. Fourth, the token economy must be simple enough for the child to understand. Fifth, the token economy may not generalize to the home or to other classrooms. Sixth, token economies require attention and consistency from the teacher, which may be difficult in large classes. Despite these risks, a well-designed token economy can be a potent modifier of children's behavior, justifying its use with ADHD children who do not respond to less intense interventions (DuPaul et al., 1992).

One well-designed token-type intervention is the Attention Training System (ATS; Gordon et al., 1991; Rapport and Gordon, 1987). The ATS uses an apparatus to deliver and deduct the reinforcement points in a token-type behavioral modification plan. The apparatus displays on a screen (placed on the child's desk) points earned by the child for on-task behavior. Each minute, a point is automatically added to the total on the screen. If the teacher observes the child in off-task behavior, he or she pushes a button on a remote-control device, triggering a red light on the child's screen. The red light remains lit for 15 seconds, and a point is subtracted from the child's point total. Thus, as long as the teacher observes on-task behavior, points accumulate automatically at a rate of one per minute. A response-cost procedure deducts one point when the teacher observes off-task behavior. At the end of the class (or day), the child can trade points for rewards.

The ATS has several advantages over traditional token systems (Gordon et al., 1991). First, rewards are frequent and require no modification of the teacher's behavior. Second, rewards are prominent and immediate. Third, the target behavior is not difficult for most ADHD children. Fourth, response cost is built into the program and requires little teacher effort. However, the ATS suffers from many of the same problems of other token interventions, and the apparatus costs several hundred dollars (DuPaul et al., 1992). Nevertheless, the ATS has been found to result in large improvements in on-task behavior for children with ADHD (DuPaul et al., 1992; Gordon et al., 1991). Several authors (DuPaul et al., 1992; Gordon et al., 1991) note the importance of response cost in the ATS and in other token-type procedures. Response cost, as used in the ATS, is an essential component for significant change and has no demonstrable negative long-term effects.

Multi-Site Behavioral Packages

In some cases, collaboration between parents and school is used to increase the effectiveness of a behavioral plan. For example, the teacher may write a note each day describing the child's behavior in class. Based on the note, the parents award reinforcement or punishment at home (Abramowitz and O'Leary, 1991). Such a plan is particularly effective if the child does not respond to a school-based reinforcement plan. In other cases the teacher may rate the child's on-task behavior, which is plotted on a conspicuous chart at home. The child receives verbal and social praise for the chart.

Over all, behavior modification plans are quite effective in managing the behavior of many ADHD children (Anastopoulos et al., 1991; Barkley, 1991b; Newby et al., 1991; Whalen and Henker, 1991). Combined with medication, behavior modification plans create a potent treatment package for ADHD (Greenhill, 1989). Newby et al. (1991) review studies attesting to the short- and long-term effectiveness of several behavior-modification programs in reducing ADHD and defiant behavior. Abramowitz et al., (1992), for example, used a simple method of social punishment (immediate reprimand) and achieved effects comparable to those of medication in one child. They conclude that individual differences in children determine the relative effectiveness of behavior modification versus medication and that a multimodal (e.g., behavior modification *and* medication) approach may be wisest. Greenhill (1989) also suggests that a combination of medication and behavior management may have the greatest effect on ADHD.

The additive effects of medication and behavior management may occur because both interventions reduce the frequency of aversive interactions between the child and parent. This reduction breaks the cycle of misbehavior, power struggles, and negative attention. Medication reduces the frequency of aversive behavior on the part of the child, which is complemented by the behavior plan's effects on the behavior of the parent. Each member of the parent–child system sees the other as improved, leading to positive interaction (Danforth et al., 1991). Thus, behavioral techniques may be particularly important in cases of ADHD that are seen as annoying or aversive by the parents (such as cases with oppositional-defiant features (Biederman, 1991). In addition to beneficial effects on the child, parents may feel more efficacy and parenting self-esteem as they see the beneficial effects of the behavior plan they implement.

Ultimately, the success of a behavior plan depends on how well it is carried out in the environment. Factors such as parental psychopathology, family dynamics, sibling rivalry, and peer relationships can affect a behavioral plan. Furthermore, behavioral plans are demanding on parents and teachers, particularly because ADHD children require frequent monitoring and immediate response (Munoz-Millan and Casteel, 1989). Hence, the clinician should conduct a careful environmental evaluation prior to implementing a behavior plan for ADHD.

Psychotherapy

Cognitive-Behavioral Interventions

Cognitive-behavioral interventions for ADHD directly address attention and concentration deficits with cognitive self-control strategies (Whalen and Henker, 1991). These interventions teach children to use a combination of self-talk, self-monitoring, and cognitive problem-solving strategies that enhance attention, motivation, and behavioral self-control. *Self-talk* generally takes the form of reminding oneself of the cognitions and behaviors to be executed in order to achieve a goal. Additional self-talk uses are for self-reinforcement and for encouraging planful, systematic problem solving over reflexive, maladaptive behavior. *Self-monitoring*, on the other hand, involves increasing the child's awareness of situations, behaviors, and cognitions that precede or accompany

ADHD symptoms. This increased awareness is used to anticipate problems and circumvent them. Finally, *problem solving* consists of systematic efforts to generate and select behaviors that will result in positive consequences for the child and a reduction of ADHD symptomatology (Hinshaw and Melnick, 1992).

Self-talk is present in most cognitive-behavioral treatments. It is used to enhance self-monitoring and problem solving as well as to assist children in controlling their thoughts. Self-talk is typically used to teach children to remind themselves about cognitive control strategies (Baer and Nietzel, 1991). For example, children may mentally go through a list of problem solving steps. Another use of self-talk is for positive self-statements (e.g., I *can* control my behavior) and self-reinforcement (e.g., I did really well in class paying attention to the teacher).

An example of self-monitoring is provided by Hinshaw and Melnick's (1992) description of the "match game." In this game a target behavior (sitting still, for example) is chosen, and positive and negative examples of the behavior are demonstrated by the therapist, along with ratings for each behavior on a 1 (bad) to 5 (good) scale. The child is then engaged in an activity with other children. Following the activity, the therapist and the child independently rate the child's performance on the target behavior. The ratings are then compared, along with the rationale for each. Discussion promotes the child's self-awareness and self-monitoring of the target behavior. Reinforcement for correct matches can be used to increase the child's motivation.

Problem-solving strategies are exemplified by a group intervention developed by Fehlings et al. (1991). They taught ADHD children to use a five-step process for problem solving: (1) Define the problem, (2) set a goal, (3) generate solutions, (4) choose a solution, and (5) evaluate the outcome. Various techniques, including modeling, role playing, homework, and reinforcement, were used to teach the problem-solving process. This process was applied to specific problems, which were eventually generalized to include several areas of particular difficulty for ADHD children. Parents were also taught the problem-solving process and encouraged their children to use it at home. Bloomquist, August, and Ostrander (1991) also used a five-step problem-solving process, although their steps were: (1) Recognize the problem, (2) generate solutions, (3) think of consequences for the solutions, (4) anticipate obstacles to the solutions, and (5) implement the solution. Teachers and parents encouraged children to use the strategies. Horn et al. (1990) added relaxation training and self-monitoring to their problem-solving intervention to increase the ability of the children to recognize and manage threats to adaptive problem solving.

The excitement generated by the theoretical underpinnings of cognitive treatments for ADHD has not been matched by outcome studies. Most studies of the efficacy of cognitive-behavioral treatment for ADHD have shown it to be minimally effective. Cognitive-behavioral interventions are often found to be less effective than medication or behavioral treatment (Abikoff, 1987, 1991; Hinshaw and Melnick, 1992). On the other hand, some studies (Fehlings et al., 1991) have shown cognitive-behavioral treatments to result in some improvement for ADHD children (Baer and Nietzel, 1991). However, improvements are typically small, and studies with positive findings are in the minority (Abikoff, 1991; Baer and Nietzel, 1991; Bloomquist et al., 1991). Cognitive-behavioral treatments generally have not resulted in improvements in the cognitive functioning, academic performance, or behavior of children with ADHD (Abikoff, 1991). Furthermore, cognitive-behavioral treatments require a minimum level of cognitive development in the child, which excludes most preschool- and early–school-age children (Whalen and Henker, 1991).

It is important to note that cognitive-behavioral interventions have been shown to be effective for anger management and oppositional behavior (Hinshaw & Melnick, 1992). Hence, they may have some usefulness in managing associated features of ADHD. Furthermore, the combination of cognitive-behavioral techniques with more traditional behavioral techniques may result in an additive therapeutic effect, although preliminary findings suggest that these effects are likely to be small (Horn et al., 1990). Finally, the existence of some studies demonstrating positive effects of cognitive behavioral therapy for ADHD suggests that these treatments deserve further study (Abikoff, 1991; Baer and Nietzel, 1991; Barkley, 1991b).

Play Therapy/Psychodynamic Psychotherapy

Little has been written on the use of play therapy with ADHD children, with most experts dismissing it as an ineffective treatment for ADHD symptoms (Barkley, 1991b). Nevertheless, play therapy for younger children or supportive/psychodynamic psychotherapy for older children may be important in managing the low self-esteem, anger at authority, and frustration/aggression that can accompany ADHD (Biederman, 1991). The current literature suggests that the use of play or psychodynamic therapy alone for ADHD is usually not appropriate, unless the hyperactivity is resulting from some traumatic event that needs to be processed by the child. However, play therapy may be warranted to address anxious, depressed, or angry symptomatology resulting from the experiences of a child with ADHD.

Other Treatments

In addition to the major treatments covered here, numerous other treatments have been suggested for ADHD. Many of these amount to fads that generate considerable pop-psychology interest but little scientific support. Others have shown promise and need further investigation.

In the fad category are most dietary interventions. While it is true that certain toxins (e.g., lead, mercury) can lead to disorganized or overactive behavior, toxins are very rarely responsible for the development of ADHD behavior. Nevertheless, families in particularly hazardous or toxic living situations should be screened for the possibility of toxic effects. Food additives, vitamins, and sugar have also received attention, but the scientific data in these areas generally do not support their role in ADHD (Barkley, 1991a; Conners, 1980).

More promising are relaxation and biofeedback techniques that encourage ADHD children to gain some measure of control over their impulsivity and overactivity. The development and evaluation of treatment packages using these techniques are in their infancy, so the efficacy of relaxation and biofeedback techniques is largely unknown. Nevertheless, case studies and clinical experience have been encouraging (Barkley, 1991a; Lubar, 1991).

■ References

Abikoff, H. (1987). An evaluation of cognitive-behavior therapy for hyperactive children. In B. B. Lahey and A. E. Kazdin (Eds.), *Advances in clinical child psychology* (vol. 10, pp. 171–216). New York: Plenum.

_____ . (1991). Cognitive training in ADHD children: Less to it than meets the eye. *Journal of Learning Disabilities, 24,* 205–209.

Abramowitz, A. J., Eckstrand, D., O'Leary, S. G., and Dulcan, M. K. (1992). ADHD children's responses to stimulant medication and two intensities of a behavioral intervention. *Behavior Modification, 16,* 193–203.

Abramowitz, A. J., and O'Leary, S. G. (1991). Behavioral interventions for the classroom: Implications for students with ADHD. *School Psychology Review, 20,* 220–234.

Achenbach, T. M. (1991). *Manual for the Child Behavior Checklist/4–18 and 1991 profile.* Burlington: University of Vermont Department of Psychiatry.

Adesman, A. R. (1991). The Attention Deficit Disorders Evaluation Scale. *Journal of Developmental and Behavioral Pediatrics, 12,* 65–66.

American Psychiatric Association. (1987). *Diagnostic and statistical manual of mental disorders* (3rd ed., rev.). Washington, DC: Author.

_____ . (1994). *Diagnostic and statistical manual of mental disorders* (4th ed.). Washington, DC: Author.

Anastopoulos, A. D., DuPaul, G. J., and Barkley, R. A. (1991). Stimulant medication and parent training therapies for Attention Deficit-Hyperactivity Disorder. *Journal of Learning Disabilities, 24,* 210–217.

Anderson, J. C., Williams, S., McGee, R., and Silva, P. A. (1987). DSM-III disorders in preadolescent children: Prevalence in a large sample from the general population. *Archives of General Psychiatry, 44,* 69–76.

Atkins, M. S., and Pelham, W. E. (1991). School-based assessment of Attention Deficit-Hyperactivity Disorder. *Journal of Learning Disabilities, 24,* 197–203.

August, G. J., and Garfinkel, B. D. (1989). Behavioral and cognitive subtypes of ADHD. *Journal of the American Academy of Child and Adolescent Psychiatry, 28,* 739–748.

Baer, R., and Nietzel, M. T. (1991). Cognitive and behavioral treatment of impulsivity in children: A meta-analytic review of the outcome literature. *Journal of Clinical Child Psychology, 20,* 400–412.

Barkley, R. A. (1977). A review of stimulant drug research with hyperactive children. *Journal of Child Psychology and Psychiatry, 18,* 137–165.

_____ . (1981). *Hyperactive children: A handbook for diagnosis and treatment.* New York: Guilford Press.

_____ . (1987). The assessment of Attention Deficit-Hyperactivity Disorder. *Behavioral Assessment, 9,* 207–233.

_____ . (1990). A critique of current diagnostic criteria for Attention Deficit-Hyperactivity Disorder: Clinical and research implications. *Journal of Developmental and Behavioral Pediatrics, 11,* 343–352.

_____ . (1991a). Attention-deficit hyperactivity disorder. *Psychiatric Annals, 21,* 725–733.

_____ . (1991b). Diagnosis and assessment of attention-deficit hyperactivity disorder. *Comprehensive Mental Health Care, 1,* 27–43.

Barkley, R. A., Anastopoulos, A. D., Guevremont, D. C., and Fletcher, K. E. (1991). Adolescents with ADHD: Patterns of behavioral adjustment, academic functioning, and treatment utilization. *Journal of the American Academy of Child and Adolescent Psychiatry, 30,* 752–761.

Barkley, R. A., Du Paul, G., & McMurray, M. B. (1990). A comprehensive evaluation of attention deficit disorder with and without hyperactivity as defined by research criteria. *Journal of Consulting and Clinical Psychology, 58,* 775–789.

Barkley, R. A., and Edelbrock, C. S. (1987). Assessing situational variation in children's behavior problems: The Home and School Situations Questionnaires. In R. Prinz (Ed.), *Advances in behavioral assessment of children and families* (vol. 3, pp. 157–176). Greenwich, CT: JAI Press.

Barkley, R. A., Fischer, M., Edelbrock, C. S., and Smallish, L. (1990). The adolescent outcome of hyperactive children diagnosed by research criteria, I: An 8-year prospective follow-up study. *Journal of the American Academy of Child and Adolescent Psychiatry, 29,* 546–557.

Barkley, R. A., Fischer, M., Newby, R., and Breen, M. (1988). Development of multi-method clinical protocol for assessing stimulant drug responses in ADHD children. *Journal of Clinical Child Psychology, 17,* 14–24.

Battle, E. S., and Lacey, B. (1972). A context for hyperactivity in children, over time. *Child Development, 43,* 757–773.

Biederman, J. (1991). Attention Deficit Hyperactivity Disorder (ADHD). *Annals of Clinical Psychiatry, 3,* 9–22.

Biederman, J., Faraone, S. V., Keenan, K., Knee, D., and Tsuang, M. T. (1990). Family-genetic and psychosocial risk factors in DSM-III Attention Deficit Disorder. *Journal of the American Academy of Child and Adolescent Psychiatry, 29,* 526–533.

Biederman, J., and Steingard, R. (1989). Attention-Deficit Hyperactivity Disorder in adolescents. *Psychiatric Annals, 19,* 587–596.

Bloomquist, M. L., August, G. J., and Ostrander, R. (1991). Effects of a school-based cognitive-behavioral intervention for ADHD children. *Journal of Abnormal Child Psychology, 19,* 591–605.

Borkowski, J. G., Benton, A. L., and Spreen, O. (1967). Word fluency and brain damage. *Neuropsychologia, 5,* 135–140.

Brown, R. T., and Quay, L. C. (1977). Reflection-impulsivity of normal and behavior-disordered children. *Journal of Abnormal Child Psychology, 5,* 457–462.

Cairns, E., and Cammock, T. (1978). Development of a more reliable version of the Matching Familiar Figures Test. *Developmental Psychology, 11,* 244–248.

Carlson, G. A., and Rapport, M. D. (1989). Diagnostic classification issues in Attention-Deficit Hyperactivity Disorder. *Psychiatric Annals, 19,* 576–583.

Chelune, G. J., Ferguson, W., Koon, R., and Dickey, T. O. (1986). Frontal lobe disinhibition in attention deficit disorder. *Child Psychiatry and Human Development, 16,* 221–234.

Cohen, M., Becker, M. G., and Campbell, R. (1990). Relationships among four methods of assessment of children with Attention Deficit-Hyperactivity Disorder. *Journal of School Psychology, 28,* 189–202.

Conners, C. K. (1980). *Food additives and hyperactive children.* New York: Plenum.

_____ . (1990). *Conners' Rating Scales manual.* North Tonawanda, NY: MHS.

Danforth, J. S., Barkley, R. A., and Stokes, T. F. (1991). Observations of parent-child interactions with hyperactive children: Research and clinical implications. *Clinical Psychology Review, 11,* 703–727.

Delis, D. C., Kramer, J. H., Kaplan, E., and Ober, B. A. (1994). *California Verbal Learning Test—Children's Version manual.* San Antonio, TX: Psychological Corporation.

DuPaul, G. J. (1990). *The Home and School Situations Questionnaire—Revised.* Unpublished manuscript. University of Massachusetts Medical Center, Worcester, MA.

_____ . (1991). Parent and teacher ratings of ADHD symptoms: Psychometric properties in a community based sample. *Journal of Clinical Child Psychology, 20,* 245–253.

DuPaul, G. J., Guevremont, D. C., and Barkley, R. A. (1991). Attention Deficit-Hyperactivity Disorder in adolescence: Critical assessment parameters. *Clinical Psychology Review, 11,* 231–245.

_____ . (1992). Behavioral treatment of Attention-Deficit Hyperactivity Disorder in the classroom. *Behavior Modification, 16,* 204–225.

Fehlings, D. L., Roberts, W., Humphries, T., and Dawe, G. (1991). Attention Deficit Hyperactivity Disorder: Does cognitive behavioral therapy improve home behavior? *Journal of Developmental and Behavioral Pediatrics, 12,* 223–228.

Felton, R. H., Wood, F. B., Brown, I. S., Campbell, S. K., and Harter, M. R. (1987). Separate verbal memory and naming deficits in attention deficit disorder and reading disability. *Brain and Language, 31,* 171–184.

Fischer, M., and Newby, R. F. (1991). Assessment of stimulant response in ADHD children using a refined multimethod clinical protocol. *Journal of Clinical Child Psychology, 20,* 232–244.

Forehand, R. L., and McMahon, R. J. (1981). *Helping the noncompliant child: A clinician's guide to parent training.* New York: Guilford Press.

Forness, S. R., Youpa, D., Hanna, G. L., Cantwell, D. P., and Swanson, J. M. (1992). Classroom instructional characteristics in Attention Deficit Hyperactivity Disorder: Comparison of pure and mixed subgroups. *Behavioral Disorders, 17,* 115–125.

Frick, P. J., and Lahey, B. B. (1991). The nature and characteristics of Attention-Deficit Hyperactivity Disorder. *School Psychology Review, 20,* 163-173.

Garfinkel, B. G., and Klee, S. H. (1983). A computerized assessment battery for attention deficits. *Psychiatry Hospitals, 14,* 163–166.

Golden, C. J. (1978). *The Stroop Color and Word Test.* Chicago: Stoelting.

Goodman, R., and Stevenson, J. (1989). A twin study of hyperactivity, II: The aetiological role of genes, family relationships, and perinatal adversity. *Journal of Child Psychology and Psychiatry, 30,* 691–709.

Gordon, M. (1983). *The Gordon diagnostic system.* Boulder, CO: Gordon Systems.

Gordon, M., and Mettelman, B. B. (1987). *Technical guide to the Gordon Diagnostic System.* New York: Gordon Systems.

Gordon, M., Thomason, D., Cooper, S., and Ivers, C. (1991). Nonmedical treatment of ADHD/Hyperactivity: The attention training system. *Journal of School Psychology, 29,* 151–159.

Grant, M. L., Ilai, D., Nussbaum, N. L., and Bigler, E. D. (1990). The relationship between Continuous Performance Tasks and neuropsychological tests in children with Attention-Deficit Hyperactivity Disorder. *Perceptual and Motor Skills, 70,* 435–445.

Greenhill, L. L. (1989). Pharmacologic treatment of Attention Deficit Hyperactivity Disorder. *Pediatric Psychopharmacology, 15,* 1–27.

_____ . (1992). Treatment issues in children with Attention-Deficit Hyperactivity Disorder. *Psychiatric Annals, 19,* 604–613.

Guevremont, D. C., DuPaul, G. J., and Barkley, R. A. (1990). Diagnosis and assessment of Attention Deficit-Hyperactivity Disorder in children. *Journal of School Psychology, 28,* 51–78.

Halperin, J. M., Newcorn, J. H., Sharma, V., Healey, J. M., Wolf, L. E., Pascualvaca, D. M., and Schwartz, S. (1990). Inattentive and noninattentive ADHD children: Do they constitute a unitary group? *Journal of Abnormal Child Psychology, 18,* 437–449.

Hannay, H. J., and Levin, H. S. (1985). Selective Reminding Test: An examination of the equivalence of four forms. *Journal of Clinical and Experimental Neuropsychology, 7,* 251–263.

Heaton, R. K. (1981). *Wisconsin Card Sorting Test manual.* Odessa, FL: Psychological Assessment Resources.

Hechtman, L. (1991). Resilience and vulnerability in long term outcome of Attention Deficit Hyperactive Disorder. *Canadian Journal of Psychiatry, 36,* 415–421.

Hersher, L. (1985). The effectiveness of behavior modification on hyperkinesis. *Child Psychiatry and Human Development, 16,* 87–97.

Hinshaw, S. P., and Melnick, S. (1992). Self-management therapies and Attention-Deficit Hyperactivity Disorder. *Behavior Modification, 16,* 253–273.

Horn, W. F., Ialongo, N., Greenberg, G., Packard, T., and Smith-Winberry, C. (1990). Additive effects of behavioral parent training and self-control therapy with Attention Deficit Hyperactivity Disordered Children. *Journal of Clinical Child Psychology, 19,* 98–110.

Hynd, G. W., Hern, K. L., Voeller, K. K., and Marshall, R. M. (1991). Neurobiological basis of Attention-Deficit Hyperactivity Disorder (ADHD). *School Psychology Review, 20,* 174–186.

Jastak, S., and Wilkinson, G. S. (1984). *Wide-range achievement test—revised.* Wilmington, DE: Jastak Associates.

Kagan, J. (1966). Reflection-impulsivity: The generality and dynamics of conceptual tempo. *Journal of Abnormal Psychology, 71,* 17–24.

Kaufman, A. S. (1990). *Assessing adolescent and adult intelligence.* Boston: Allyn & Bacon.

Kaufman, A. S., and Kaufman, N. L. (1985). *Kaufman test of educational achievement.* Circle Pines, MN: American Guidance Service.

_____ . (1990). *Kaufmann Brief Intelligence Test manual.* Circle Pines, MN: American Guidance Service.

Kendall, P. C., and Wilcox, L. E. (1979). Self-control in children: Development of a rating scale. *Journal of Consulting and Clinical Psychology, 47,* 1020–1029.

_____ . (1980). A cognitive-behavioral treatment for impulsivity: Concrete versus conceptual training in non–self-controlled children. *Journal of Consulting and Clinical Psychology, 48,* 80–91.

Klee, S. H., and Garfinkel, B. D. (1983). The computerized continuous performance task: A new measure of inattention. *Journal of Abnormal Child Psychology, 11,* 487–496.

Klein, R. G., and Mannuzza, S. (1991). Long-term outcome of hyperactive children: A review. *Journal of the American Academy of Child and Adolescent Psychiatry, 30,* 383–387.

Klorman, R., Coons, H. W., and Borgstedt, A. D. (1987). Effects of methylphenidate on adolescents with a childhood history of attention deficit disorder: I. Clinical findings. *Journal of the American Academy of Child and Adolescent Psychiatry, 26,* 363–367.

Lambert, N. M., and Sandoval, J. (1980). The prevalence of learning disabilities in a sample of children considered hyperactive. *Journal of Abnormal Child Psychology, 8,* 33–50.

Loge, D. V., Staton, D., and Beatty, W. W. (1990). Performance of children with ADHD on tests sensitive to frontal lobe dysfunction. *Journal of the American Academy of Child and Adolescent Psychiatry, 29,* 540–545.

Lubar, J. F. (1991). Discourse on the development of EEG diagnostics and biofeedback for Attention-Deficit/Hyperactivity Disorders. *Biofeedback and Self-Regulation, 16,* 201–225.

Lufi, D., Cohen, A., and Parish-Plass, J. (1990). Identifying Attention Deficit Hyperactive Disorder with the WISC-R and the Stroop Color and Word Test. *Psychology in the Schools, 27,* 28–34.

McCarney, S. B. (1989a). *The Attention Deficit Disorders Evaluation Scale, Home Version, technical manual.* Columbia, MO: Hawthorne Educational Services.

_____ . (1989b). *The Attention Deficit Disorders Evaluation Scale, School Version, technical manual.* Columbia, MO: Hawthorne Educational Services.

Milich, R., and & Kramer, J. (1984). Reflections on impulsivity: An empirical investigation of impulsivity as a construct. In K. Gadow and I. Bialer (Eds.), *Advances in learning and behavioral disabilities* (vol. 3, pp. 117–150). Greenwich, CT: JAI Press.

Munoz-Millan, R. J., and Casteel, C. R. (1989). Attention-Deficit Hyperactivity Disorder: Recent literature. *Hospital and Community Psychiatry, 40,* 699–707.

Newby, R. F., Fischer, M., and Roman, M. A. (1991). Parent training for families of children with ADHD. *School Psychology Review, 20,* 252–265.

Newcorn, J. H., Halperin, J. M., Healey, J. M., O'Brien, J. D., Pascualvaca, D. M., Wolf, L. E., Morganstein, A., Sharma, V., and Young, J. G. (1989). Are ADDH and ADHD the same or different? *Journal of the American Academy of Child and Adolescent Psychiatry, 28,* 734–738.

Patterson, G.R. (1976). *Living with children: New methods for parents and teachers.* Champaign, IL: Research Press.

_____ . (1982). *Coercive family process.* Eugene, OR: Castalia.

Pliszka, S. R. (1991). Antidepressants in the treatment of child and adolescent psychopathology. *Journal of Clinical Child Psychology, 20,* 313–320.

Rapport, M., and Gordon, M. (1987). *The attention training system (ATS).* DeWitt, NY: Gordon Systems.

Rapport, M. D., Stoner, G., DuPaul, G. J., Kelly, K. L., Tucker, S. B., and Schoeler, T. (1988). Attention deficit disorder and methylphenidate: A multi-level analysis of dose-response effects on children's impulsivity across settings. *Journal of the American Academy of Child and Adolescent Psychiatry, 27,* 60–69.

Robin, A. L., and Foster, S. (1988). *Negotiating adolescence: A behavioral-family systems approach to parent–teen conflict.* New York: Guilford Press.

Salkind, N. J., and Nelson, C. F. (1980). A note on the developmental nature of reflection-impulsivity. *Developmental Psychology, 16,* 237–238.

Sattler, J. M. (1990). *Assessment of children* (3d ed.). San Diego, CA: Author.

Smith, A. A. (1973). *Symbol Digit Modalities Test manual.* Los Angeles: Western Psychological Services.

Swanson, J. M., Cantwell, D., Lerner, M., McBurnett, K., and Hanna, G. (1991). Effects of stimulant medication on learning in children with ADHD. *Journal of Learning Disabilities, 24,* 219–231.

Ullmann, R. K., Sleator, E. K., and Sprague, R. L. (1984). A new rating scale for diagnosis and monitoring of ADD children. *Psychopharmacology Bulletin, 20,* 160–164.

Weiss, G., Hechtman, L., Milroy, T., and Perlman, T. (1985). Psychiatric status of hyperactives as adults: A controlled prospective 15-year follow-up of 63 hyperactive children. *Journal of the American Academy of Child Psychiatry, 24,* 211–220.

Whalen, C. K., and Henker, B. (1991). Therapies for hyperactive children: Comparisons, combinations, and compromises. *Journal of Consulting and Clinical Psychology, 59,* 126–137.

Wolraich, M. L., Lindgren, S., Stromquist, A., Milich, R., Davis, C., and Watson, D. (1990). Stimulant medication use by primary care physicians in the treatment of Attention-Deficit Hyperactivity Disorder. *Pediatrics, 86,* 95–101.

Zametkin, A. J. (1989). The neurobiology of Attention-Deficit Hyperactivity Disorder: A synopsis. *Psychiatric Annals, 19,* 584–586.

Zametkin, A.J., and Rapoport, J. L. (1987). Neurobiology of ADDH: Where have we come in 50 years? *Journal of the American Academy of Child and Adolescent Psychiatry, 26,* 676–686.

CHAPTER 3

Disruptive
Behavior Disorders

Conduct Disorder (CD) and Oppositional Defiant Disorder (ODD), referred to as "disruptive behavior disorders," are among the most common psychiatric disorders seen in children and adolescents (Shamsie and Hluchy, 1991). The CD and ODD diagnoses share the characteristics of disruptive, disobedient behavior and the breaking of societal norms. Because the community is often victimized by children with CD and ODD, there is strong consensus that these disorders deserve special attention. School- and court-referred children, for example, often exhibit some CD/ODD components.

Because CD and ODD fall into the broader category of disruptive behavior disorders, they are often combined for research, theory, and teaching purposes. In fact, initial research challenged the distinction between CD and ODD (Anderson et al., 1987; Reeves et al., 1987; Rey et al., 1988). More recent work, however, supports the CD–ODD distinction. Achenbach (1978, 1991), for example, has consistently found two "disruptive behavior" factors in his studies with the CBCL. One factor ("Aggressive Behavior" in the 1991 CBCL version) captures components of aggression, anger, and disobedience, while the other factor ("Delinquent Behavior" in the 1991 CBCL version) includes components of lawbreaking and violation of norms. Achenbach's Aggressive Behavior and Delinquent Behavior factors roughly correspond to ODD and CD, respectively. This finding has been replicated in other factor-analytic studies and literature reviews (Achenbach et al., 1989; Loeber and Schmaling, 1985; Quay, 1986; Quay and Peterson, 1982).

Over all, then, empirical research suggests that CD and ODD represent different but related constructs. Reviews by Lahey et al. (1992) and Loeber, Lahey, & Thomas (1991) summarize the relationship of ODD and CD:

1. ODD and CD demonstrate distinct patterns of co-variation. Children who exhibit one of the symptoms of either of these disorders are more likely to have another of the symptoms of the same diagnosis than a symptom of the other diagnosis.

2. The mean age of onset for ODD symptoms is earlier than for CD symptoms.

3. ODD and CD are developmentally related. Many children with ODD do not ever develop CD, but almost all children with CD have had an earlier ODD diagnosis. CD, in turn, predicts Antisocial Personality Disorder in adulthood.

4. Familial correlates of ODD and CD are similar, but children with CD have a greater number or intensity of the correlates.

5. Treatments for ODD are more likely to be effective than treatments for CD, probably because of lower symptom severity and younger age of children with ODD.

Oppositional Defiant Disorder

CLINICAL DESCRIPTION

Diagnostic Considerations

DSM-IV defines ODD as "a recurrent pattern of negativistic, defiant, disobedient, and hostile behavior toward authority figures" (American Psychiatric Association, 1994, p. 91). Diagnostically, ODD is characterized by symptoms such as arguing with authorities, refusal to comply with requests, losing temper, irritability, externalizing blame for misbehavior, vengeful behavior, annoying and provocative behavior, and appearing angry or resentful. Because the disturbance must cause "significant" impairment, typical child oppositionality generally does not qualify for ODD. ODD is not diagnosed if the child qualifies for the CD diagnosis; without this exclusionary criterion, virtually all children with CD would also receive the ODD diagnosis.

Many ODD symptoms are more intense or more frequent versions of typical child behaviors. Hence, the child's disruptive behaviors must exceed the duration, intensity, and frequency of behaviors typical for the child's age. ODD is usually diagnosed in children before 8 years of age and almost always prior to adolescence. ODD is a common disorder, with prevalence rates of 2–16% in the child population (American Psychiatric Association, 1994). Males are diagnosed with ODD approximately three times as often as females (Anderson et al., 1987).

Appearance and Features

Although noncompliant behavior is a frequent target of research study, DSM-defined ODD has been the subject of relatively little research. Unlike CD, which is more severe in its manifestation and consequences, ODD is more likely to be "tolerated" by some parents. Furthermore, because many ODD symptoms resemble typical childhood behavior, parents may be unaware that their child's "misbehavior" warrants a psychiatric diagnosis.

As previously noted, ODD behaviors differ from typical childhood disobedience in severity and frequency. (Appearance and features of ODD are listed in Table 3.1.) At preschool ages this is manifest in frequent, severe temper tantrums and intolerance of frustration. The preschooler with ODD has difficulty delaying gratification; typically, he or she responds to frustration with an extremely hostile and vocal display. Kicking, thrashing, power struggles, and destruction of property are common. If the parent gives in to the child's demands, the child learns that escalation of the power struggle results in gratification.

At older ages, tantrum behavior may persist, but oppositionality and defiance usually become more sophisticated. "Talking back" and passive-aggressive refusal to comply are typical at latency and adolescent ages. Destructive and aggressive behavior persist and are often incorporated into power struggles. Parents may feel held hostage by their child's threats to destroy property or to become physically aggressive. At times the child may appear to be provoking or testing adults for the limits of acceptable behavior. The child may be described by parents as touchy, stubborn, argumentative, and provocative.

Oppositional behavior may be affected by environmental or social factors.

TABLE 3.1   Appearance and Features of Oppositional Defiant Disorder

COMMON FEATURES

Short temper; easily angered
Argues frequently
Provokes peers or authorities
Seeks revenge; vindictive
Externalizes blame
Defiant; noncompliant
Poor frustration tolerance
Stubborn
Unwilling to compromise
Angry/hostile
Irritable

OCCASIONAL FEATURES

Inconsistent caretakers
Harsh or neglectful caretakers
Hyperactivity

Note: the features listed above are often seen but are not universal. Some features may be diagnostically relevant or required, while others may not be required for diagnosis. "Common" features are typical of the disorder; "occasional" features appear frequently but are not necessarily seen in a majority of cases.

ODD children tend to be most oppositional toward certain adults or in certain situations. Many parents, for example, can identify one parent who receives most of the oppositional and defiant behavior. Alternatively, the child may be oppositional at home but not at school. Many ODD children are adversely affected by hyperactive or disobedient peers who put them in situations of conflict with authority. If such conflicts occur repeatedly, the child may get a "reputation" for oppositional behavior. This reputation may lead to increased intolerance of oppositional behavior by authorities, worsening the child's relationship with adults in the environment.

The ODD child almost always comes to clinical attention at the request of a parent or teacher who is frustrated with the child's behavior. Parents usually describe a plethora of oppositional and defiant symptoms. They often report trying various interventions, although more extensive investigation usually reveals that the interventions were half-hearted, inconsistent, or doomed to fail for some reason. The ODD child frequently presents without symptoms in the clinical interview. Many ODD children refuse to recognize that they have a problem, externalizing blame for their behaviors. For example, hitting a parent may be warranted, in the child's view, because the parent put an unreasonable constraint on the child. Despite a denial of problems, children with ODD may be at risk for depression or a developmental disorder. Hence, co-occurring or underlying problems should be carefully examined.

Etiology

There is mounting evidence that parental psychopathology, family problems, and behavioral factors are responsible for the oppositional, noncompliant, negative, and defiant behaviors typical of ODD (Frick et al., 1992). Families of children with ODD show a higher rate of parental depression, substance abuse, and Antisocial Personality Disorder than do families of other clinic-referred children (Billings and Moos, 1983; Griest, Wells, and McMahon, 1980). Behavioral factors, such as parental discipline and parental involvement, are also associated with the development of ODD symptoms (Frick et al., 1992; Griest et al., 1980). Harsh physical punishment of children, for example, can create anger, reduce attachment, and provide a model of aggression. Inconsistent discipline can reward children for escalating until the parents give them what they want; the children then learn to escalate the pattern of defiant, aggressive, and destructive behavior in order to be rewarded by getting their way (Patterson, 1982). Oppositional behavior is reinforced when the child gains attention and control as a result of it. To the extent that attention, control, and gratification result from oppositional behavior, the child will be prone to show ODD symptoms.

Despite the popularity of familial-behavioral explanations of ODD, some data suggest that genetic factors may also play a role. Epidemiologic studies indicate that adopted children of antisocial biological fathers are more likely to exhibit antisocial behavior than are adopted children of normal fathers

(Mednick and Hutchings, 1978). Twin studies also support a genetic component to ODD (American Psychiatric Association, 1994). Nevertheless, biological factors appear to explain only a portion of the variance in emergence of ODD symptoms.

ASSESSMENT PATTERNS AND TREATMENT OPTIONS

Although research supports the existence of ODD and CD as separate syndromes, they share the major characteristics of oppositionality, defiance, authority problems, and rule breaking. Hence, ODD and CD are assessed and treated similarly. Furthermore, because ODD may develop into CD, any ODD assessment must take into account the possible presence of CD symptomatology. CD often warrants closer monitoring, involvement of authorities, and more intensive treatment than does ODD, but the basics of the interventions for the disorders are quite similar. Hence, assessment and treatment of ODD and CD will be considered jointly, following a discussion of CD.

Conduct Disorder

CLINICAL DESCRIPTION

Diagnostic Considerations

DSM-IV defines CD as "a repetitive and persistent pattern of behavior in which the basic rights of others or age-appropriate societal norms or rules are violated" (American Psychiatric Association, 1994, p. 85). This behavior occurs across multiple social arenas, including home, school, and community. Symptoms of CD include bullying, intimidating others, fighting, use of weapons, stealing (with and without confrontation of a victim), cruel behavior toward people or animals, sexual coercion, lying, fire setting, running away, breaking into a house or car, and truancy. CD occurs in 6–16% of boys and 2–9% of girls (American Psychiatric Association, 1994).

DSM-IV notes two CD subtypes: Childhood-Onset type requires at least one conduct problem prior to age 10. Adolescent-Onset type requires no conduct problem prior to age 10. Childhood-onset type is typically more persistent and severe as the individual develops; it is more likely to evolve into Antisocial Personality Disorder.

Numerous other CD subtypings have been identified, but four have received the most attention (Loeber, 1982; Lahey et al., 1992; Loeber and Schmaling, 1985):

1. *Overt versus Covert Behaviors:* Overt CD behaviors include confrontational behavior such as fighting, stealing with confrontation of the victim, and being physically cruel. Covert behaviors include manipulating others, stealing without confrontation, destroying property, and running away.

2. *Group (Socialized) versus Solitary (Undersocialized) CD:* This division distinguishes between those who are likely to act out in the context of peer relationships (Socialized) and those who commit their antisocial acts in a solitary manner (Undersocialized). Undersocialized boys with CD tend to be more aggressive and to have a poorer prognosis (Jenkins and Hewitt, 1944; Jenkins & Glickman, 1947). There may also be physiological differences between the subgroups (Rogeness et al., 1983; Bowden, Deutsch, and Swanson, 1988), including lower resting heart rate for Undersocialized CD. The Socialized—Undersocialized distinction was made in DSM-III-R and has been subsequently dropped in DSM-IV.

3. *Aggressive versus Nonaggressive CD:* Aggressive CD children tend to engage in more fighting, confrontation, and harmful behaviors directed at people. Nonaggressive CD children, on the other hand, are less confrontive and engage in more property-related misbehavior. Hence, this distinction mirrors the overt/covert subtyping.

4. *Early versus Late Onset CD:* This subtyping is recognized in DSM-IV, and, as previously noted, may predict the severity and stability of CD, with Early-Onset CD being more severe and stable. Late-Onset CD children are more likely to be female, are less likely to be aggressive, have less family adversity, are of higher SES, and exhibit higher verbal and reading ability (Moffitt, 1990; McGee et al., 1992). Late-Onset CD is also less likely to be developmentally related to ODD (Lahey et al., 1992).

CD is associated with a number of other Axis I and II disorders. Myers, Burket, and Otto (1993) reported that a majority of their sample of hospitalized CD adolescents also met criteria for substance abuse, ADHD, Major Depressive Disorder, and/or a personality disorder. In another clinical sample, one in three children with an Affective Disorder also qualified for a Conduct Disorder (Kovacs et al., 1988; Puig-Antich, 1982). Substance abuse (Myers et al., 1993), Bipolar Disorder (Kutcher, Marton, and Korenblum, 1989), and Eating Disorders (Myers et al., 1993) have been found to co-occur with CD.

ADHD may be the most frequent co-occurring diagnosis with CD; CD or ODD is found in 20–60% of ADHD cases (Barkley, 1981; Biederman, Munir, and Knee, 1987). When ADHD and CD co-occur, the onset of ADHD generally precedes the onset of CD. Furthermore, a co-occurring ADHD and CD condition is worse than either condition alone, with greater symptom severity, increased risk for later Antisocial Personality Disorder, more environmental problems, more social problems, and deficient processing of social information (Barkley, 1981; Milich and Dodge, 1984).

Appearance and Features

(Appearances and features of CD are listed in Table 3.2.) Children with CD show a consistent pattern of rebellion and violation of societal norms. These norms may be formal (legal), informal (social mores), or specific to the household (parental rules). In most cases, CD develops as a gradual process of

TABLE 3.2   Appearance and Features of Conduct Disorder

COMMON FEATURES

Physical aggression; fighting; intimidation
Cruelty to people or animals
Theft
Destruction of property; fire setting
Use of weapons or other means to cause serious injury
Lawbreaking
Truancy
Running away
Substance abuse
Friends with conduct problems
Manipulative; deceitful; lying
Hostile attribution bias

OCCASIONAL FEATURES

Harsh, neglectful, or inconsistent discipline
Criminal record
Thrill seeking, dangerous behavior
Academic problems

Note: The features listed above are often seen but are not universal. Some features may be diagnostically relevant or required, while others may not be required for diagnosis. "Common" features are typical of the disorder; "occasional" features appear frequently but are not necessarily seen in a majority of cases.

oppositionality that expands from oppositionality toward parents to oppositionality toward adults, all authorities, and eventually to society as a whole (Dishion et al., 1991).

In the typical scenario of CD development the young child displays ODD-type symptoms in the context of maladaptive parent–child interactions. These patterns worsen as the child escalates defiance, disobedience, and aggression to "win" power struggles with the parent. As these interaction patterns become ingrained and severe, the child generalizes them to situations outside the home. The child expects that oppositional-defiant behavior outside the home will bring reinforcement as it has in the home environment. This expectation can take on an air of entitlement, in which the child focuses on gratifying his or her own needs and ignores the presence of rules or the feelings of others.

Often the school and/or peer group are the first non-home settings in which the child exhibits oppositional and rule-breaking behaviors. Most CD-type school/social problems emerge in middle or junior high school. These antisocial behavior problems are annoying to teachers and most peers, leading to failures in the school and social situation. Such failures further alienate the child from peers, rules, and norms.

Separated from mainstream peers and norms, the child may then identify with a deviant peer group. The deviant peer group provides negative social modeling and social reinforcement for antisocial behavior. Eventually the child internalizes a self-concept of "troublemaker," seeks reinforcement in rule violation (e.g., lying, stealing, manipulation), and associates with other CD children. Activities that lead to immediate or effortless gratification are chosen (e.g., drug use, stealing) as alternatives to "unattainable," socially acceptable means of gratification. Angry feelings resulting from alienation and isolation may also contribute to the emergence of CD in late childhood and adolescence.

Achenbrock and Edelbrock (1981) provide a description of CD behaviors at various ages, based on parent-report. In young children, parents tend to report arguments, poor cooperation, disruptiveness, restlessness, boisterousness, attention seeking, domination of others, stubbornness, and tantrums. In middle childhood, oppositional behaviors, negativity, identification with the "bad crowd," poor academic performance, poor peer relations, disrespectfulness, and aggressiveness emerge. In addition to these behaviors, truancy, fire setting, vandalism, and substance abuse occur in late childhood and adolescence. Hence, CD appears to emerge out of early power struggles and academic and social failures that develop into oppositional, defiant, and, eventually, lawbreaking behaviors.

In addition to behavioral problems with oppositionality and rule breaking, there is ample evidence that CD children score lower on intelligence tests, and they often perform poorly in school. In one study, low academic achievement and failing a grade occurred three times more frequently in conduct-disordered junior high school students than in a matched control group (Safer, 1984). Deficits in various academic skills, especially reading, have also been correlated with adolescent delinquency (Dishion et al., 1984; Sturge, 1982). CD children are often perceived by their teachers as uninterested in school, unenthusiastic, and careless. However, it is unclear whether CD arises as a reaction to educational failure or whether CD causes failure (Rutter, Tizard, and Whitmore, 1970; Sturge, 1982).

A number of studies indicate that the intellectual deficiencies of aggressive children extend to social problem-solving and processing skills (Dodge, 1985; Lochman, White, and Wayland, 1991). Compared to peers, aggressive children more often perceive neutral social cues as having aggressive meaning (Dodge, 1985; Milich and Dodge, 1984). CD children are less able to generate relevant means to a social end, to anticipate obstacles blocking a social goal, and to generate directly assertive social responses to a difficult social situation (Joffe et al., 1990). Furthermore, aggressive boys are more likely to act aggressively when they respond impulsively, and they do not perceive obstacles to their problem solutions (Dodge and Newman, 1981). In short, CD children tend to interpret neutral situations as hostile, to fail to generate appropriate solutions to problem situations, and to act inappropriately in problem situations.

Because they interpret neutral situations as hostile, aggressive children feel threatened by peers and adults. Their aggressive behavior, which they see as justified given their interpretation of the situation, may appear misplaced and excessive to others. These attributional distortions, coupled with an impulsive response style, contribute to a greater likelihood of antisocial and aggressive behaviors.

CD is often a precursor of Antisocial Personality Disorder (APD) in adulthood; almost half of children with CD develop significant APD symptomatology (Myers et al., 1993; Robins, 1966). One variable that predicts the development of APD is the number of CD symptoms the child exhibits; early age of onset of CD (especially before age 12) also predicts APD. CD may also predict later chronic substance abuse and overall poor quality of life in adulthood (American Psychiatric Association, 1994). For example, CD is associated with early death, unemployment, marital conflict, financial instability, and poor interpersonal relationships (Robins, 1966).

Etiology

Biological Theories

Several biological theories have been proposed for CD, with mixed empirical results. Most children with CD are boys, although whether this is a biological (e.g., hormonal) or cultural factor is not yet known. Children with conduct problems show less reactivity to and faster recovery from laboratory stimuli (Mednick and Christiansen, 1977). Slow heart rate has also been linked to conduct problems (Wadsworth, 1976). Taken together, these findings suggest that CD children may be less responsive to external stimuli and may need a higher level of external stimulation.

Additional support for a neurological explanation is found in neuroanatomical and neuropsychological studies. Researchers have found correlations between frontal lobe functioning and delinquency (Moffitt and Henry, 1989). A well-known function of the frontal lobes is the inhibition and planning of behavior. Presumably, then, these findings suggest that CD children have less frontal lobe–mediated inhibition of behavior, increasing the probability that they will behave impulsively.

Family and genetic studies also support a biological component to CD. Parental APD, for example, has been found to be associated with CD independent of maternal parenting behavior (Frick et al., 1992). Adoption and twin studies also show a concordance of CD in biologically related children (Cadoret, 1978; Cadoret and Cain, 1980; Jarey and Stewart, 1985; Mednick and Hutchings, 1978).

Over all, results of biological studies are suggestive but preliminary in explaining the emergence of CD. It appears that CD runs in families and is associated with cognitive deficits. However, the effects of environmental factors, as well as the magnitude of the effect of biological factors, remain to be determined.

Family-Behavioral Theories

Virtually all major psychological theories of the etiology of CD cite a role for parent and family functioning in the emergence of symptoms. In fact, issues as fundamental as attachment problems have been suggested as predictive of later CD (Holland et al., 1993). Because attachments formed during infancy and toddlerhood are the basis for later social behavior, disruption in the attachment process may produce later problems with social interaction and adherence to social norms. Examples of attachment disruptions and social deprivation, such as extended separation from the parent, multiple caretakers, marital conflicts, and poor child care, predict later antisocial behavior (Loeber and Dishion, 1983). The child develops little loyalty to rules and social relationships because attachment figures have done little to earn such loyalty.

Later parenting behaviors may also predispose a child to the development of attachment problems, and, later, CD. Insecure-ambivalent attachment patterns, for example, are related to harsh, punitive, and abusive parenting (Holland et al., 1993; Crittenden and Ainsworth, 1989). Many insecurely attached CD children also have histories of negative parent–child interactions characterized by lack of warmth and negotiation, high defensiveness, harsh discipline, and inconsistent discipline (Henggeler et al., 1986; Kazdin, 1987). Out of these negative interactions, a feeling of distrust and suspicion of authority may develop. Instead of nurturance, the child expects rejection and punishment from authorities and society. Thus, the child attempts to meet his or her own needs, with little regard for the advice or rules of society.

In addition to the dyadic parent-child interaction, broader family factors may predispose the child to CD. Children of criminal or alcoholic parents are more likely to have CD (Robins, 1966; Robins, West, and Herjanic, 1975; Quinton, Rutter, and Gulliver, 1990; Rutter, 1985). Family factors such as large size, parental discord, substance abusing parents, parental psychopathology, and parental depression predict CD in the child (Frick et al., 1992; West and Farrington, 1977). These factors may contribute to CD by disrupting attachment, by reducing parental attention to the child, by delaying gratification of the child's needs, by encouraging inconsistent parenting, and/or by providing a negative model for the child.

The association between parental depression and CD could be due to problems with the observational report of a depressed parent: First, depressed parents tend to overestimate externalizing problems in their children (Griest, Wells, and Forehand, 1979; Fergusson, Lynskey, and Horwood, 1993); hence, some "CD" children may come to the attention of clinicians because of catastrophizing on the part of a depressed parent. Second, parent-reports of behavior problems in children of depressed women are frequently discrepant with teacher-reports or child self-reports (Fergusson et al., 1993). Finally, maternal depression and maternal report of child behaviors may be influenced by spurious external factors such as SES, education, and attributional style (Baden and Howe, 1992; Fergusson et al., 1993; Wahler and Dumas, 1989).

Despite the intriguing associations of CD with attachment, parent, and family variables, poor parental disciplinary practices remain the single most emphasized factor in the development of CD. Patterson's (1982) coercion theory is one of the best-known and well-researched explanations of how poor discipline may lead to ODD and CD. Coercion theory suggests that oppositional, aggressive, and antisocial behaviors emerge through a process of reciprocal, negative, coercive interchanges between the child and parent. The scenario begins with a child who exhibits distress behavior as a result of temperament, stress, or other factors. Such behaviors may be developmentally normal (such as crying in an infant) or responses to a negative environment. In healthy parent-child relationships, child distress behavior quickly shapes the behavior of caretakers, who respond to the needs of the child. As the child matures, more appropriate social and verbal skills replace the rudimentary negative distress behaviors, and the child learns to respond appropriately and positively to caretakers.

For some children, however, this rudimentary negative distress behavior is irritating to caretakers, who avoid and/or harshly discipline the child. The child responds to the avoidance or harsh discipline with increasingly hostile and unrewarding behavior, leading to further avoidance and mistreatment from parents. As the parents' avoidance and mistreatment increase, the child must increasingly escalate his or her behavior to gain their attention and force them to attend to the child's needs. Eventually the parent unintentionally reinforces the child's coercive behavior by giving in or modifying demands placed on the child whenever the child displays escalating, oppositional behavior.

This pattern of interaction evolves into a simple power struggle: The child makes a request, refuses to behave, or performs an undesirable behavior. In response the parent imposes a consequence (punishment) or refuses a privilege. The child reacts by escalating forbidden, antisocial, or upset behavior, and the child persists at this behavior until the parent removes the consequence or restores the privilege. The escalation of conflict between child and parent may involve screaming, threats, and even physical fighting, but the child persists in the conflict until the parent gives in.

An example of coercion theory begins with a mother instructing her child to pick up his toys. The child whines and refuses. The mother yells and threatens to spank the child. The child throws a tantrum with loud screaming and thrashing. Finally the mother withdraws and cleans up the toys herself. In this process the child learns that if he tantrums enough, he can get his way with his mother. The mother learns not to upset the child, lest he throw a tantrum.

Such coercive interchanges are not always "won" by the child, but the intermittent reinforcement of periodic "wins" is sufficient to cause the negative behaviors to persist. Because intermittently reinforced behavior is difficult to extinguish, CD children give up their symptoms slowly and reluctantly. Parental inconsistency and harshness can contribute to a relapse of such behaviors.

Psychodynamic Theories

Psychodynamic theories continue to receive considerable attention in the etiology of CD, despite little empirical evidence of their validity. Nevertheless, their intuitive appeal keeps them in the forefront of theorizing on the development of antisocial and CD behaviors. All psychodynamic theories of CD are based on the assumption that children adopt rule-following behaviors as a result of "internalizing" and "identifying" with the beliefs and behaviors of significant others. Normally children form a strong attachment to their caretakers, who gratify their needs adequately, if not completely and immediately. The experience of need gratification and caretaking creates a bond between the child and caretaker, which results in the child identifying with the identity and behaviors of the caretaker. This caretaking bond also encourages the child to please the parent and to retain the parent as a loving, protective, gratifying caretaker. The child thus learns to relinquish the desire for immediate and/or complete gratification in favor of more cooperative, trusting behavior and a strong bond with the caretaker. Over time, and after many instances of steady, nonpunitive caretaking, the child forms an internalized representation of a benevolent, available parent. This internal representation sustains the child's behaviors during separations from the parent and during times of frustrated needs (Matthys et al., 1989).

In some cases the development of the internalized caretaker is disrupted, and the child is left without the representation of the benevolent authority. Traumatic events, inconsistent or harsh parenting, separation from parents, emotionally distant parenting, and family conflict, for example, may disrupt the internalization process, leaving the child with little regulation of his or her needs and impulses. Hence, the child is unable to tolerate limits, frustration, delayed gratification, and other rules. The child lacks respect for others because the child did not have the respect and understanding of caretakers to internalize. In the end the child acts impulsively and immediately to gratify his or her needs, constrained only by the limits of reality but not by the limits of internalized standards of behavior.

ASSESSMENT PATTERNS

Assessment issues for CD and ODD are presented together because of similarities in development and symptoms of the two disorders. CD/ODD assessment must proceed with the understanding that oppositional, antisocial behavior varies by context and social relationships. Hence, informants tend to differ on ratings of the child's behavior, and the symptom picture may vary somewhat based on the source and context of information. Discrepancies in observer reports may reflect influences as diverse as rater bias, secondary gain, social desirability, differing behavior in different contexts, differing behavior in the presence of different raters, and rater psychopathology. Regardless of the hypothesized influences, a proper assessment of a CD/ODD child must make use of multiple methods completed by multiple informants in reference to multiple settings. This multirater-multimethod approach provides a good starting point in capturing the complexity of behavior of the typical CD/ODD child. (A sample assessment battery for ODD and CD is shown in Table 3.3.)

TABLE 3.3   Sample Assessment Battery for Oppositional Defiant Disorder and Conduct Disorder

PSYCHOLOGICAL

Thematic Apperception Test

BEHAVIORAL

Child Behavior Checklist
Teacher Report Form

FAMILY

Family Environment Scale

SYNDROME-SPECIFIC

Means-End Problem-Solving Procedure

Note: Assessment instruments are intended to supplement (not substitute for) a good clinical interview and, when possible, a structured diagnostic interview.

Broad Assessment Strategies

Cognitive Assessment

Clinician-Administered.   As a group, CD/ODD children are more likely to suffer from academic deficiencies than are their normal peers. Because poor school performance is characteristic of CD/ODD children, it is important to assess intellectual deficits or learning disabilities that may be masked by oppositional behavior. Socialized CD/ODD children tend to provide less variability between subtests of the WISC-III. On the other hand, less socialized, more aggressive CD/ODD children may have higher Performance than Verbal IQ, reflecting their weaker knowledge of learned facts and social convention (Meyer, 1993). Truancy or school misbehavior may also result in lower WISC-III Verbal subtest scores (especially Information, Vocabulary, or Arithmetic) as well as in lower achievement test scores.

Meyer (1993) reports that the ability to abstract is important in curbing aggression, possibly because abstraction is important for social problem solving. Problems with abstract verbal thinking may be apparent on the Similarities and Comprehension subtests of the WISC-III. Undersocialized children may score lower on Picture Arrangement and Comprehension than those who are aware of social norms and expectations. On the other hand, children with CD/ODD who are more involved with passive or status offenses are likely to have higher intellectual abilities over all than those who commit more aggressive acts.

Psychological Assessment

Clinician-Administered. Psychological test responses in children with CD/ODD often are characterized by aggressiveness, alienation, anger, and/or socialization problems. Such test patterns may alert the clinician to potential problems, situational interpretations, or personality predispositions that may put the child at risk to misbehave or to behave impulsively.

Resistance, negativism, and rejection of cards characterize CD/ODD children's general approach to the Rorschach. Undersocialized CD children give more personalized (PER) responses and show more violent and bizarre content than do more socialized individuals. More undersocialized children also tend to give fewer overall responses, lower W percentage, lower M percentage, more C and CF responses, more animal responses, higher white-space responses, and more popular responses (Meyer, 1993). This response pattern often reflects a fixation of such individuals on egocentric and violent issues, as well as a mix of defensiveness and emotional undercontrol. CD/ODD children who give Rorschach response patterns with few responses, many form responses, high lambda, low color and shading responses, and many animal responses are probably responding to the test with an extremely defensive and resistant style. Such children may be extremely reluctant to change their behavior or to admit problems.

On the TAT, CD/ODD children have a higher involvement of authorities in their stories, give more aggressive stories, and give responses related to material gain. Often the hero is aggressive or antisocial, and stories involving murder, burglaries, and other crimes are common. Story endings are frequently characterized by unreasonable punishment, escape from punishment, or the demise of authorities. Empathy and relationship themes are absent (Meyer, 1993). Repetitive or unique TAT themes can provide an indication of the beliefs underlying the child's antisocial behaviors. Some CD/ODD children, for example, tell stories involving unreasonable behavior by authorities and hopeless situations for story heroes. The oppositional or antisocial behaviors of these children may be driven by a distrust of authorities and some unhappiness with their situation.

MMPI/MMPI-A profiles of CD/ODD adolescents usually show lack of identification with societal rules, family problems, problems with authorities, rebellion against expectations, anger, and distrust. Hence, the typical MMPI profile for a CD/ODD adolescent includes an elevation on scale 4. The "Persecutory Ideas" subscale of MMPI scale 6 is also generally elevated, although the overall scale 6 score may be within normal ranges (because of the presence of many naively optimistic items on this scale—the "Naiveté" subscale). An elevated scale 8 may indicate social alienation and unusual beliefs, which may drive some of the antisocial behavior. Elevated scale 2, combined with depressed scale 9, typically reflects some unhappiness with the current situation, perhaps as a result of having needs repeatedly unmet or as a result of being punished (e.g., by the legal system). Elevation on scale 9, on the other hand, often suggests that the child acts on antisocial impulses and is extremely resistant to internal and external efforts to control his or her behavior.

The Adolescent Conduct Problems Scale (A-con) of the MMPI-A taps specific conduct behaviors. A-con items include impulsivity, risk-taking behaviors, and antisocial behaviors. Elevated A-con scores may predict school suspension, legal difficulty, and conflict with societal norms (Butcher et al., 1992). Because A-con is a relatively face-valid scale, a CD adolescent may deliberately answer questions to receive a low score. When this is the case, L and K scale scores should be inspected for a defensive response set.

Behavioral Assessment

Parent-Report. Almost all child behavior checklists include items assessing aggressive, oppositional, rule-breaking, and antisocial behaviors. Factor analyses and internal consistency studies indicate that these items cluster into one or two groups. The first group characterizes aggressive, disobedient, and mildly oppositional behaviors (ODD-type behaviors); subscales tapping this dimension generally carry labels such as "Aggression," "Aggressive Behavior," and "Oppositional Behavior." The second group of behaviors represents more serious antisocial behaviors such as truancy, firesetting, destruction of property, and drug use; subscales tapping this dimension are labeled "Delinquent Behavior" and "Conduct Problems" (Achenbach, 1991).

On the CBCL, CD/ODD children tend to elevate the Delinquent Behavior and Aggressive Behavior subscales and the broad-band Externalizing score. Delinquent Behavior elevations are more typical of CD children, while Aggressive Behavior elevations suggest ODD behaviors. On average, CD/ODD children do not differ from other clinically referred children on other CBCL subscales (McMahon and Forehand, 1988). For any individual child, however, other CBCL subscale scores may suggest contributing or co-occurring behavior problems. It is important to note that many children who elevate the Delinquent Behavior and Aggressive Behavior scales do *not* qualify for a CD diagnosis. Hence, the CBCL should not be used exclusively to make a CD or ODD diagnosis (McMahon and Forehand, 1988).

On the CPRS-48, CD/ODD children elevate the Conduct Problem subscale. The Learning Problem subscale is also frequently elevated, indicating that the child's problem behaviors may interfere with school learning. Elevations of the Impulsive-Hyperactive Scale and/or Hyperactivity Index may suggest that the child's disobedient behavior is related to behavioral undercontrol and hyperactivity. In this case a diagnosis of ADHD should be considered. Similar considerations apply for the MCBC Aggressive (corresponding to CPRS Conduct Problem) and Activity Level (corresponding to CPRS Impulsive-Hyperactive) subscales.

Teacher-Report. In addition to parent-completed checklists, a teacher-report measure is essential to understanding the cross-situation behavior of the CD/ODD child. Discrepancies between parent- and teacher-report may suggest that one source is minimizing or exaggerating problems, or that the child's behavior differs in different contexts. When the latter is true, the child is likely to respond to changes in the behavioral contingencies in the "problem" environment. Interpretation of teacher-completed Achenbach (TRF) and Conners (CTRS) scales is essentially the same as for the parent-completed versions of these scales.

Family Assessment

Parent-Report. The family is almost always important in the etiology or treatment of CD/ODD. Hence, a family assessment component is indicated in the evaluation of the CD/ODD child. Based on research indicating that inconsistent supervision and lack of household rules may contribute to CD/ODD (Wilson, 1980), the FES Organization subscale is likely to show deficits in CD/ODD families. The Controlling factor and Control subscale, however, may be elevated, especially in families with a strong hierarchy and harsh discipline. If this is the case, the child may be rebelling against the weight of expectations and lack of independence. Harsh discipline and family conflict also cause elevations of the Conflicted factor and Conflict subscale in some CD/ODD families. The Supportive factor and its components, on the other hand, may show deficits in the CD/ODD family, reflecting a dearth of mutual interest, expression of beliefs, and shared activities. The configuration of FES subscale and factor scores may suggest intervention targets and potential problems that may arise during the course of therapy.

In some cases (especially when the legal system is involved) the family may be motivated to present an overly positive picture of the family environment. Because the FES is largely face valid, deliberate attempts to present a positive characterization of the family will result in an inaccurate profile. A quick screen for defensive or socially desirable responding in these cases is to add the raw scores for the Cohesion and Expressiveness subscales to the reverse raw score of the Conflict subscale (e.g., reverse score every Conflict subscale item, or subtract the Conflict raw score from 9, since 9 is the maximum raw score on the Conflict subscale). The Cohesion and Expressiveness subscales are considered socially desirable by almost all families, and the Conflict subscale is considered undesirable. Hence, this sum is the number of "family relationship" items that the respondent answered in a socially desirable way, with the maximum score being 27. Scores of 25 or higher are extremely rare, even in model families, and they probably indicate some defensiveness or positive bias.

Syndrome-Specific Tests

Clinician Administered

Semistructured Interviews. Semistructured interview formats for CD/ODD children have been suggested by Hanf (1970), Forehand and McMahon (1981), and others. These interviews may use parents, teachers, and/or the child as informants. Hanf's (1970) and Forehand and McMahon's (1981) interviews use a problem guidesheet that allows the clinician to inquire about potential problem areas such as peers, school, or discipline. If the parent reports a particular situation as problematic, the clinician explores the antecedent stimulus (before the behavior), the child's behavior (specific, observable behavior), the environmental response (consequences of the behavior), and the child's reaction (response to consequences). This line of questioning is continued until the clinician has an understanding of the sequence of events in the parent–child interaction (Forehand and McMahon, 1981; McMahon and Forehand, 1988).

Behavioral Coding Systems in a Clinic Setting. Direct behavioral observation is a valuable but expensive procedure for obtaining a reliable and valid description of parent–child interactions. Two widely used structured observation systems for assessing parent-child interaction in the clinic setting are the Dyadic Parent–Child Interaction Coding System (DPICS; Eyberg and Robinson, 1983) and the Forehand Observation System (FOS; Forehand and McMahon, 1981). These systems code parent–child interaction in 5–10-minute intervals based on predefined parent–child tasks.

The DPICS also uses "cleanup time," in which the parent attempts to direct the child to pick up toys in the playroom. The observer records the frequency of behaviors using twenty-three coding categories. Parent behaviors include direct and indirect commands, descriptive/reflective questions, acknowledgment, irrelevant verbalization, unlabeled and labeled praise, physical positive and negative, and critical statement. Child behaviors include cry, yell, whine, smart talk, destructive, physical negative, and change activity. Two behavioral sequences are scored: parental response to deviant child behavior (respond/ignore) and child response to commands (compliance/noncompliance/no opportunity). The DPICS successfully discriminates families of CD children and those of normal children. It also differentiates between CD children and their siblings (Robinson and Eyberg, 1981) and is sensitive to treatment changes (Eyberg and Robinson, 1982; Webster-Stratton, 1984).

In the FOS, scored parent behaviors include rewards (praise or positive attention), attends, questions, commands, warnings, and time-out. The child behaviors are compliance, noncompliance, and inappropriate behavior. The Forehand system is sensitive to treatment effects (McMahon and Forehand, 1984).

Behavioral Coding Systems in a Home Setting. Several behavioral coding systems have been developed to measure the behavior of CD/ODD children and their families in the home setting. Two of the systems that have been most frequently used are the Family Interaction Coding System (FICS; Patterson et al., 1969) and the Standardized Observation Codes system (SOC; Wahler, House, and Stambaugh, 1976). These coding systems are similar in that certain rules are imposed on the family during the observation period (e.g., all members present; no TV, radio, or telephone). During the observation period the child's behavior and the responses by family members are coded in order to provide a sequential account of the child's interactions with family members.

The FICS yields a summary of the child's behavior by computing the frequency of each type of aversive behavior and the frequency of total aversive behaviors. A total of twenty-nine behavioral categories are used to describe the subject–family interaction. Examples include approval, humiliate, command negative, no response, and play. The FICS is effective in discriminating between clinic-referred and nonreferred children and among various subtypes of CD children (Patterson et al., 1969).

The SOC contains twenty-five behavioral response categories, such as sustained work, social approach—child, aversive opposition, self-talk, and social attention adult—nonaversive. A percentage-of-occurrence score is given for each category. The SOC includes a greater focus on positive behaviors than do most other observation systems (Wahler et al., 1976).

Parent Report

Eyberg Child Behavior Inventory (ECBI). The ECBI (Eyberg and Ross, 1978) is one of the most widely used parent rating scales of CD/ODD behaviors in children age 2–17. It contains descriptions of thirty-six behaviors commonly reported by parents of oppositional, defiant, conduct-disordered children. Parents rate each behavior on a 7-point scale indicating frequency of occurrence (Intensity score) and on a yes-no problem identification scale (Problem score). Based on factor analyses, the ECBI appears to be a unidimensional scale measuring conduct problems in children and adolescents. A cutoff criterion of eleven or more behaviors has been suggested for the identification of clinically significant conduct problems (Eyberg and Ross, 1978; McMahon and Forehand, 1988).

Parent Daily Report (PDR). The PDR (Chamberlain and Reid, 1987; Patterson et al., 1975) is a parent observation measure that is completed during a 10-minute telephone interview. It consists of thirty-three child behaviors and one item asking if the child has been spanked in the last day. The PDR yields two scores: Targeted Behaviors (the sum of occurrences of behaviors identified as problematic by parents at the initial interview) and Total Behaviors (the sum of all occurrences on the total list of behaviors).

A revised version of the PDR has been developed for the longitudinal investigation of CD children and their families (Patterson and Bank, 1986). This version asks parents whether they have disciplined their child in the past 24 hours for twenty-three behaviors characteristic of CD. If parents answer an item affirmatively, they are asked to describe the discipline procedure. The Revised PDR also includes sections on parental monitoring of the child, positive reinforcement directed to the child, and the occurrence of crises and social support. A parallel, child-report version of this form asks the child about occurrence of the CD behaviors, the state of his or her mood, and whether the parents have engaged in any of several monitoring behaviors (Patterson and Bank, 1986).

Original Ontario Health Study (OCHS). The OCHS (Boyle et al., 1993) was developed to provide a simple, rapid means of identifying childhood psychopathology in the general population. The OCHS consists of thirty-four behavior problems that cluster into three subscales: CD (physical violence, severe violation of social norms), Hyperactivity (inattention, impulsiveness, and hyperactivity), and Emotional Disorder (tension, obsessions, compulsive behavior). Each item is scored on a 0–2 scale from "never or not true" to "often or very true," and sums of items give subscale raw scores. Separate versions of the OCHS exist for parents, teachers, and adolescents age 12–16. The OCHS can be useful as a quick screen for conduct problems.

Overt Aggression Scale (OAS). The OAS (Yudofsky et al., 1986) was developed for observer rating of child physical or verbal aggression. Aggressive behavior on the OAS is rated in four categories: Verbal Aggression, Physical Aggression against Objects, Physical Aggression against Self, and Physical Aggression against Others. For each category the OAS rater indicates the severity of the behavior on a four-level scale. For example, on the Verbal Aggression scale, "makes loud noises" is a first-level behavior, while "makes clear threats of violence" is a fourth-level behavior. The OAS can be used as a brief measure of the severity and frequency of aggressive behavior.

Generalized Parental Expectancies Questionnaire (GPEQ). The GPEQ (Howe et al., 1989). measures parents' beliefs concerning the general effectiveness of four parenting actions (verbal or physical punishment, withdrawal of positive reinforcement, contingent reinforcement of alternative behavior, and ignoring child misbehavior) with their CD/ODD children. For each of nine hypothetical misbehaviors, the parent rates the effectiveness of the four parenting responses on a 7-point scale. The GPEQ yields four expectancy scores, one for each of the four types of parental actions. It can be used to gauge parental beliefs and preferences for responses to child misbehaviors. These beliefs and preferences may need to be addressed if a change in parenting behavior is required as a part of therapy.

Child Report

Means-End Problem-Solving Procedure (MEPS). The MEPS (Platt and Spivak, 1975) is a commonly used measure of social problem-solving ability. Measurement of social problem solving ability may be particularly important for CD children, since social problem-solving deficits have been implicated in CD/ODD behavior (Dodge, 1985; Lochman et al., 1991). In the MEPS, children are presented with stories that have a beginning and end, but no middle. Children must provide a middle portion for the story by suggesting a behavioral means by which subjects can achieve the ending goals of the story. The means are then scored for relevance to achieving the goal. The MEPS also examines the children's awareness of obstacles to the goals and their awareness of sequencing and the passage of time. CD/ODD children give a lower overall number of relevant means to the story ends and perceive fewer obstacles to the attainment of social goals.

Social Situations Analysis (SSA).   The SSA (Conolly et al., 1987) presents five series of photos that portray problematic social situations. For each situation the child must define the problem and generate possible social responses. Responses are coded as directly assertive, indirectly assertive, passive, aggressive, or vague. The child then indicates the positive and negative outcomes that might ensue from the response. The outcomes are further classified into short- and long-term categories. The SSA has good interrater reliability and differentiates clinic-referred from normal adolescents (Conolly et al., 1987). CD adolescents are expected to perform worse on the SSA because of social problem solving deficits.

Buss-Durkee Hostility Inventory (BDHI).   Aggression inventories typically consist of a list of statements related to hostile attitudes and aggressive behavior. The seventy-five–item, true-false BDHI (Buss and Durkee, 1957) is one of the best known and most used of these inventories. It measures eight dimensions of anger: Assault, Indirect Aggression, Irritability, Negativism, Resentment, Suspicion, Verbal Hostility, and Guilt. Factor analysis of the BDHI has produced two factors: Attitudinal Hostility/Suspicion (e.g., "I know that people tend to talk behind my back") and Motoric Hostility/Assault (e.g., "If somebody hits me first, I let him have it"). Although the BDHI has been employed by numerous researchers, the reliability of the subscales and the predictive validity of the scale have been challenged (Biaggio, 1980). Research indicates that the BDHI provides a global impression of hostile feelings (Biaggio, Supplee, and Curtis, 1981) and discriminates between violent and nonviolent offenders (Biaggio et al., 1981; Selby, 1984). The BDHI is not appropriate for preadolescent children.

Novaco Anger Inventory (NAI).   The NAI (Novaco, 1975) consists of eighty items designed to assess the antecedents of anger. Each item describes a potentially anger arousing situation. The respondent rates the degree to which each situation would arouse anger on a 5-point scale. The NAI has been shown to measure the potential for becoming angry when provoked (Biaggio, 1980). Like the BDHI, the NAI should be used with children of adolescent age.

Adolescent Antisocial Behavior Checklist (AABCL).   The AABCL (Ostrov et al., 1980) is a 350-item scale of antisocial behaviors typically displayed by adolescents in an institutional setting. Staff rate the occurrence and severity of behaviors on a 0–6-point scale. AABCL scores cluster into four subscales: (Activities Directed) Against Staff, Against Property, Against Rules, and Against

Visitors. AABCL scores appear to be internally reliable and to predict differences in antisocial behavior in the institutional setting (Ostrov et al., 1980).

TREATMENT OPTIONS

Many approaches to the treatment of CD/ODD have been tried, with varying success (Shamsie and Hluchy, 1991). In fact, the broad range of therapies attempted testifies to how difficult these disorders are to treat effectively. Effectiveness in the long term is particularly difficult to achieve, especially when the child is returned to the environment that produced or maintained the disorder in the first place.

Another major difficulty in treating children with CD/ODD is co-morbidity with other disorders (Holland et al., 1993). Research on the relationship between CD/ODD and other disorders indicates that co-morbidity is the rule rather than the exception (Myers et al., 1993; Biederman, Newcorn, and Sprich, 1991). Clinicians should be particularly alert for signs of ADHD and Depressive Disorders in the CD/ODD child, since these disorders are often masked by the more dramatic CD/ODD symptoms. When a co-morbid condition is suspected, treatment should include components for both disorders.

Often children with CD/ODD symptoms are already extensively involved with the school, legal, or mental health system by the time that they present for psychological intervention. Because of this involvement with "the system," a rich database of the child's history often exists in the form of school, legal, and past mental health records. Review of these records may assist with preliminary formulations and selection of intervention techniques. Prior treatment failures should be examined closely so that earlier mistakes are not repeated in treatment. Consultation with school and legal agencies may be warranted in some cases as well, and appropriate permission to release information should be obtained from the parent or guardian.

Behavioral Interventions

Social Learning Family Interventions

Because many CD/ODD behaviors violate rules set by authorities, behavioral interventions involving authorities are among the most common and most effective for CD/ODD. Although teachers are sometimes folded into the behavioral plan, most behavioral interventions rely primarily on parents. Such parent management interventions, collectively referred to as "social learning family interventions" (SLFI; Miller and Prinz, 1990), have produced some of the most impressive research results on treatment efficacy (McMahon and Forehand, 1984; Patterson, Chamberlain, and Reid, 1982; Webster-Stratton, 1984). The rationale for SLFI is founded in the theory that coercive parent–child interchanges and environmental contingencies are instrumental in the development and maintenance of oppositional, defiant, and antisocial behaviors. Improvements in parent ratings of child behaviors and in parent attitudes toward the child have consistently been obtained with SLFI-type interventions. In some cases these gains have been maintained for clinically meaningful periods (Webster-Stratton, 1984).

One of the most influential parent training programs was developed by Patterson and colleagues at the Oregon Social Learning Center (Patterson, 1982). Patterson's therapy approach is based on research indicating that oppositional and defiant behaviors are learned and maintained primarily in family interactions. Through the process of social learning within the family, the child is reinforced for escalating defiant, aggressive, and antisocial behaviors, which coerce parents into yielding to the child's demands. Behavioral change occurs when the coercive interchange is broken and the focus of family interaction changes from coercive, antisocial behavior to prosocial behavior, family communication, and mutual social problem solving (Miller and Prinz, 1990).

Patterson's group originally developed their parent training program for preadolescent children who were engaged in overt conduct disorders. In the basic training model, parents first read a programmed teaching text and complete a test on the reading material. Following the satisfactory completion of this psychoeducational intervention, parents learn a step-by-step approach for managing the child's CD/ODD behavior. This step-by-step approach has undergone some modification, and variants of it have been adopted by others (e.g., Clark, 1985). Essentially, behavioral programs based on Patterson's (1982) and similar approaches (Clark, 1985) include some combination of the following six steps:

1. *Psychoeducation.* SLFI programs often begin with teaching of basic behavioral and CD/ODD concepts, such as coercion, reinforcement, punishment, rule violation, and operationally defined behaviors. Parents may also receive some background information about the disorder, such as symptoms, etiology, prevalence, and common treatments. Finally, an overview of the treatment plan is given, with clear expectations of the parents and child.

2. *Observation and monitoring.* Target problem behaviors are identified, and parents are asked to monitor the occurrence of these behaviors at home. This process clarifies the parents' views of the child's behaviors and establishes a baseline by which to measure the effectiveness of future intervention. Ideally, target behaviors are easily identifiable, discrete, and clearly operationally defined.

3. *Reinforcement of prosocial behavior.* In this third step, parents learn reinforcement techniques to focus the child's (and parents') attention away from antisocial behavior and onto prosocial goals. The provision of reinforcement for prosocial behaviors also encourages such behaviors. Examples of reinforcers include social, material, and activity rewards (Clark, 1985).

Social rewards consist of components of parent–child interaction, such as smiles, hugs, and praise. These rewards are implemented as specific parental behaviors that maximize their social impact on the child. For example, praise is more effective if specific feedback is given regarding the behavior rather than more general praise (e.g., "I'm so proud of you for picking up your room" as opposed to "What a good boy you are"). Material rewards include points, tokens, and other reinforcers that may be used by the child to "purchase" tangible objects. Alternatively, the child may be given such objects directly. Activity rewards include access to favored games, areas, or other things to do (e.g., staying up late). Social, material, and activity rewards are combined in this step to encourage specific prosocial behaviors identified by the parent and therapist. The connections of rewards and specific behaviors is planned and purposeful.

4. *Discipline of unacceptable behavior.* At this stage of parent training, parents are taught the correct use of time-out. Time-out consists of removal of the child from a reinforcing or stimulating situation and placement in a situation that is free of reinforcement or stimulation. Time-out should occur for a discrete period of time, and attempts on the part of the child to escalate behavior and escape time-out should be met with further punishment or ignoring. For example, if the child is screaming and taunting from his room, the door may be shut and an extra 2 minutes added to time-out time. Physical punishment is strongly discouraged, and alternatives to physical punishment (especially time-out, withdrawal of privileges, and ignoring) are taught. Parents also learn to "actively ignore" mild attention-getting behaviors to avoid reinforcing the child's negative behaviors with attention.

5. *Supervision-monitoring.* Parents are encouraged to provide close supervision for their child, even when the child is away from home. This involves such behaviors as knowing where the child is at all times, what the child is doing, and when he or she will be home. Supervision by other adults should occur only if the parent knows, trusts, and is comfortable with the adult.

6. *Communication strategies.* Finally, parents learn problem solving, negotiation strategies, and effective communication. Children often respond favorably to being made a part of the problem-solving process, and joint solutions are more likely to be adhered to than decisions imposed by parents without discussion. However, the parents must be careful not to allow the child to start a power struggle. Ultimately, parents must retain responsibility and control for the decision, but the child should feel that his or her input is valued and important. In order to accomplish these goals, parents practice basic skills of reflective listening, negotiation, and avoidance of power struggles (Clark, 1985).

Parents are taught these six steps with a combination of techniques. Initially, a didactic role is adopted by the therapist, who teaches the parent a principle and answers questions about it. The therapist may then model the parenting behavior, anticipating problem situations and solutions. The parent may then practice and role play the new parenting behavior in therapy. When the parent and therapist are comfortable with the technique, the parent then uses it at home and reports on its effectiveness. The therapist then gives feedback, and, if necessary, parent and therapist may modify the technique.

For older children and adolescents the parent-training program described here must undergo some modification. Targeted behaviors, for example, should include those that put the adolescent at immediate risk for delinquency or legal trouble. Parental monitoring and supervision may be more difficult, since the adolescent expects greater freedom than the child. Chores and restriction of free time may be added to punishment procedures, and the adolescent may have a greater involvement in the therapy sessions. For example, the adolescent may be present as contingencies and reinforcers are developed, and the adolescent may be involved in the development of a behavioral contract with target behaviors and reinforcers (Clark, 1985). In addition to providing a therapeutic experience for the adolescent, involvement of the adolescent in decision making allows the therapist to model communication strategies.

Patterson's and related programs are typically used for children in middle grade school (grades 3–4) through junior high or high school (grades 7–10). A second parent training program targets noncompliant behavior in younger children, age 3–8 years (Hanf and Kling, 1973; Forehand and McMahon, 1981). Like the Patterson-type program, it includes a series of steps to train parents in a behavioral intervention:

1. *Nondirective play.* Parents are taught to play with their children in a nondirective way. This is accomplished by teaching the parent to watch the child play as opposed to encouraging a certain type of play by the child. When the parent is engaged by the child, the parent behaves (within reason) in the manner suggested by the child. Parents are coached to reduce the frequency of competing verbal behavior (e.g., commands, questions, and criticisms) and to allow the child to lead the interaction. Parents are also encouraged to ignore minor inappropriate behaviors.

2. *Reinforcement of prosocial behaviors.* As in the Patterson model, parents learn to identify and reward the child's prosocial behavior. The preferred reinforcers are praise and attention.

3. *Simple, effective commands.* Parents are taught to state commands simply, and one at a time. This is accomplished by the parent being in proximity to the child and having a stern facial expression (e.g., laughing or shouting from another room are discouraged). The parent then says the child's name and maintains eye contact to ensure that the child's attention is focused on the parent. Finally, the parent gives the command in simple, clear language. Angry, demanding, or irritated tone of voice is discouraged. Based on the child's compliance or noncompliance with the command, the child receives attention or time-out.

4. *Use of time-out for noncompliance.* Parents are taught the basic principles and use of time-out, which immediately follows a period of noncompliance.

In addition to teaching techniques noted earlier, Forehand and McMahon (1981) use a "bug in the ear" device to teach their behavioral intervention to parents. This device consists of a small speaker in or near the parent's ear.

During playtime with the child the therapist, who observes the parent-child interaction from another room, can provide instructions to the parent through this speaker.

A third example of a comprehensive parent-training program for CD children was developed by Webster-Stratton (1981a, 1981b, 1982a, 1982b). In addition to components of the other programs, this program uses videotape modeling methods. The videotapes show models of differing sexes, ages, cultures, socioeconomic backgrounds, and temperaments in an effort to promote positive modeling effects. Parent models in the tapes provide examples of effective and ineffective parenting behaviors. Webster-Stratton's basic program includes a series of ten videotape programs of modeled parenting skills (250 vignettes of 1–2 minutes each), which are shown by the clinician to groups of parents. Based on the vignettes, the clinician leads a discussion of the interactions and encourages parents' ideas and problem solving, as well as role playing and rehearsal. The effectiveness of the clinician-led group discussion of the modeling videotape has been demonstrated in a series of studies (Webster-Stratton, 1984, 1991).

Alternatives to SLFI

Despite the impressive results of SLFI outcome studies, a substantial proportion of families experience less favorable outcomes following SLFI (Griest and Wells, 1983; Sanders and James, 1983). Limited initial and long-term improvement in families with severe CD children is not uncommon, especially in severely disadvantaged or stressed families (Dumas & Wahler, 1983; Ferber, Keeley, and Shemberg, 1974; McMahon and Forehand, 1984). If the family is marked by socioeconomic disadvantage, if the mother is depressed, if the parents are socially isolated, or if there is marital conflict, SLFI may have diminished effectiveness (Dumas and Wahler, 1983; Wahler, 1980; Webster-Stratton, 1985). The therapeutic success of parent training depends on the parents' ability and willingness to learn and implement the behavioral plan at home. Homes with stress, poverty, chaos, conflict, unmotivated parents, and social isolation are often poor sites for these plans. In these situations, additional intervention and/or a modification of SLFI is warranted. Two such modifications are "synthesis teaching" (ST) and "self-sufficiency training" (SS).

In ST (Wahler et al., 1993), parents learn to discriminate between stressful stimuli emanating from the child care arena and other arenas. The procedure uses a conversational format in which clinician and parent discuss the parent's child care experiences and other experiences that affect child care. The purpose of this discussion is to accentuate the differences between child care and external (usually stressful) experiences, which influence the parent's emotional state. This discussion of differences in experiences enables the parent to approach the task of child care with greater objectivity. The separation of child care stresses from other stresses in the home environment is an extremely difficult task, since the emotional upset resulting from general stress renders the parent vulnerable to the child's negative (e.g., stressful) behaviors. If this separation is accomplished, however, the parent can implement behavioral interventions without the sabotaging effects of extraneous stress and chaos.

SS (Blechman, 1981, 1984) teaches parents to analyze their reactions to stressful events and to find practical solutions. A patterned problem-solving sequence is used to accomplish this goal. First, a particular life problem is targeted. Next, antecedents to the problem and consequences of the problem are identified through intensive discussion in therapy. As parents gain greater insight into the effects of stress on their behavior toward the child, they position themselves to anticipate and control their behavior in stressful situations. This enhanced control prevents the emergence of negative parent–child interaction patterns.

Both ST and SS emphasize a broad range of environmental events that may contribute to poor parenting. Thus, they differ from strict SLFI approaches because they do not concentrate exclusively on child management. Furthermore, both ST and SS focus initial efforts on improving parental awareness and communication of the impact of extraneous factors on child management. Although ST and SS appear promising, few studies have been conducted to specifically assess the relative contribution of these expansion approaches to basic SLFI. Less structured parent psychotherapy may accomplish goals similar to those of ST and SS.

Psychotherapy

Psychotherapeutic approaches to CD/ODD treatment have been dominated by the cognitive-behavioral model. This model targets the child's thoughts and behaviors relative to three primary, overlapping deficits found in CD/ODD children: social relationships, problem solving, and anger management.

Social Relationships/Social Skills

The rationale for a social-skills training approach with CD/ODD children is suggested by research findings that these children demonstrate social behavior deficits (Webster-Stratton, 1991). CD/ODD children are not only aggressive within the family, but they are also less competent socially and more likely to be rejected by peers than are nonaggressive children (Coie, 1990; Loeber and Dishion, 1983). There is some evidence of positive results from social-skills training programs, but contradictory results exist and more efficacy research is needed (Kolko, Loar, and Sturnick, 1990).

Most socially oriented cognitive-behavioral approaches attempt to teach the child social behaviors based on a hypothesized social-skills deficit. These programs coach children in play skills, friendship and conversational skills, academic skills, and behavior control strategies. For example, children are taught to question others for information, clarification, and invitation; they learn to help by giving support and suggestions; they are encouraged to cooperate; and they are reinforced for sharing. Therapeutic activities include cooperative projects, games, constructive activities with blocks and clay, and playing with toys. As the children play, the coach praises successful skill performance and rewards each positive behavior by labeling the behavior and delivering a reinforcement (e.g., placing a token in a cup with the child's name on it). In some cases, such interventions include a response-cost component, in which a child loses a previously gained reinforcer following performance of an undesired behavior. The addition of a response cost component improves the effectiveness of a reinforcement program, but response cost alone is ineffective (Bierman, Miller, and Staub, 1987).

In some cases, more specific, simple social skills are targeted for improvement. This approach may be necessary with children who have fundamental skills deficits or who are having difficulty learning more complicated social interaction skills. Specific social skills include eye contact, smiling, physical space, voice volume and inflection, content of conversation, compliments, acknowledgments, conversational openers, assertive requests, and ignoring. These simple skills are taught using an introductory explanation followed by videotaped modeling, role playing, repeated rehearsal of the skill, feedback, modification based on feedback, and anticipation of "real-life" situations in which the skill can be used. It is usually wise to include a reinforcement component in the skill-learning process, in order to increase the child's motivation.

In addition to the more behaviorally oriented interventions just described, some social-skills interventions emphasize cognitive components. These interventions train children in the cognitive processes of problem solving, self-control, self-statements, empathy training, and perspective taking. Psychoeducational and group discussion methods are commonly used to initially teach these techniques. Children then practice the skills with the therapist and other group members; games and stories can also be used to teach the cognitive skills. Finally, the children are then given homework assignments to try the cognitive techniques in their everyday peer interactions. They report on their homework the next session, with feedback and reinforcement from the therapist and group (Webster-Stratton, 1991).

Problem Solving

Problem-solving interventions combine cognitive and behavioral techniques to teach problem-solving skills, such as generating alternative solutions, means-ends and consequential thinking, and taking the perspective of others (Kazdin et al., 1987a, 1987b). Typically such interventions teach children to approach a problem using some variant of a five-step process (Kazdin et al., 1987a, 1987b):

1. Define the problem.
2. Identify the goal.
3. Generate options.
4. Choose the best option.
5. Evaluate the outcome.

This process is applied primarily to social problems and is taught using a variety of techniques: didactic teaching, practice, modeling, role playing, feedback, social reinforcement, and therapeutic games. Response cost and token reinforcement are also frequent components of problem-solving interventions. Following successful learning of the problem-solving skill, children are given homework assignments to apply the skill in their daily lives. Reinforcement and response cost may again be used to encourage compliance with homework (Kazdin et al., 1987a, 1987b).

Kazdin et al. (1987a, 1987b) report that a combination of problem solving training and parent management training resulted in improvement at study completion and at 1 year follow-up. Behavioral improvement and reduced aggression following problem-solving training were obtained in hospitalized aggressive antisocial children, the majority of whom had a CD diagnosis. Improvements persisted at 1 month and 1 year follow-up (Kazdin et al., 1987a, 1987b).

Anger Management

Several anger-management programs have shown promise in the treatment of CD/ODD children. Goldstein et al. (1987), for example, developed a 10-week anger-control program emphasizing ten techniques that are designed to increase insight, skill, and motivation in managing anger:

1. *Increasing personal power by self-control.* This anger-management technique introduces children to the concept that anger can create problems in the child's life. Admired people who have achieved success with self-control are introduced as role models. Children are taught that they are more powerful when they do not react angrily or respond to provocation.

2. The A-B-C model: This technique and the next technique teach children to identify situations and cues that lead to anger behavior. Identification and insight precede the learning of control techniques, which can be implemented only when the child can identify targets for self-control. This second technique teaches children that each conflict situation has three steps:

   a. Trigger (*Antecedent*): What led up to it? What caused the problem?
   b. Response (*Behavior*): How did the child react to the problem?
   c. Consequence: What were the results of the conflict situation and the child's behavior?

Children give examples of A-B-C in various problem situations. By learning the A-B-C's of their own anger behavior, children may begin to understand, anticipate, and control it.

3. *Cues of being angry* (muscle tension, clenched fists). Children identify the physical signs that indicate anger in themselves and others. Again, this identification can increase the anticipation and control of anger outbursts.

4. *Anger reducers 1, 2, and 3.* Once children learn the warning signs of anger (Steps 2 and 3), they are taught to use an anger reducer to increase self-control and personal power. Five anger reducers are introduced during the program, with the first three in this intervention step:

   a. Reducer 1: Deep breathing can increase concentration and relieve physical symptoms of anger.
   b. Reducer 2: Backward counting is used to distract the child from a provoking situation and gain time to consider choices.
   c. Reducer 3: Pleasant imagery is a relaxation technique used to reduce tension.

5. *Internal and external triggers.* Children are reminded that each conflict situation begins with a trigger. Internal triggers are typically self-statements that consist of cognitive distortions (e.g., "He thinks that I'm a wimp"). External triggers are verbal or nonverbal communications by another person (e.g., pushing or taunting). Children are taught to identify and monitor these triggers, eventually pairing then with an anger reducer.

6. *Using reminders* (Reducer 4). Children are taught positive self-statements to increase control in pressure situations (e.g., "Slow down," "Chill out"). Reminders are introduced to replace internal triggers.

7. *Self-evaluation.* These self-statements are used after a conflict situation to assess response and prepare for next time.

   a. Self-reward (e.g., "I really kept my cool"; for successful or desired behavior)
   b. Self-coaching (e.g., "I need to tune in to my cues"; for failure or undesired behavior)

8. *Thinking ahead* (Reducer 5). Children are encouraged to think of the "C" (consequences) component of the anger situation. Identification of short- and long-term consequences is taught, with children focusing on external (loss of privileges), internal (loss of self-respect, disappointment), and social (alienation, rejection) consequences of aggression. This reducer increases both motivation and insight.

9. *Angry behavior cycle.* Children are instructed to identify behaviors that are likely to anger others. Using the thinking-ahead procedure, children agree to try to change their provoking behavior in order to avoid creating conflict situations.

10. *Using structured learning skills to replace aggression.* Structured learning skills address the psychological and social deficits common to aggressive children. Hence, in this final skill, children review the implementation of the skills they have been taught. Additional deficits, if identified, are remediated. The child commits to continued implementation of the anger-management plan.

Four broad techniques are used to accomplish the learning goals of Goldstein et al.'s (1987) program:

1. *Modeling.* The presentation of each particular skill is carefully demonstrated by the therapist or on videotape, with verbal explanation of the skill performance. In order to avoid confusion and improve retention, only one skill is presented at a time, and at least two modeling examples of each skill are presented.

2. *Role playing.* A second skill teaching technique includes the child as a participant in the learning. Comments are solicited from the children regarding how the presented skill might be useful in everyday situations. Examples of past or future events may be given. One child then becomes the actor, and information concerning the problem situation is identified by group discussion. The actor then chooses a co-actor, and the behavior steps of the skill are reviewed prior to the role play. Finally, the scenario is role played and observed by the therapist and other children. Role reversal may be helpful in understanding another's perspective following the initial role play.

3. *Performance feedback.* A brief feedback period follows each role play. This period helps the main actor discover how well he or she followed the behavioral steps of the specific skill. Reinforcement is provided, consistent with the quality of the performance and improvement over previous performances: Initial role plays are reinforced for "trying", while later role plays must be successful to be reinforced.

4. *Transfer training.* Learning in the training session must be transferred to everyday situations in order for the intervention to be effective. This goal can be facilitated in several ways. Overlearning, for example, is a transfer technique that involves being exposed to the skill repeatedly in multiple settings and in multiple forms (e.g., verbal, written, modeled, acted). Role plays that closely resemble actual problem situations also facilitate transfer; use of props, for example, can add to the reality of the role play. Assigning homework to practice skills provides opportunities to evaluate and enhance performance, as well as to receive reinforcement outside of the therapy session. A "Hassle Log" is also used for the child to record daily events in which skills can be implemented (Goldstein et al., 1987).

In addition to Goldstein et al.'s (1987) program, numerous other anger management programs exist. An anger-coping program developed by Lochman et al., 1991), for example, targeted teacher-referred elementary school boys with highly disruptive, violent, antisocial behavior. The boys initially set goals and received behavioral contracts that were monitored daily by classroom teachers, with reinforcement for goal behaviors. Anger-coping interventions included self-statements about angry feelings, videotapes of adult men modeling anger control and self-management, role plays of difficult situations, and problem-solving skills. The addition of goal setting to the cognitive intervention resulted in greater reduction in aggressive behavior than the cognitive intervention alone (Lochman et al., 1991).

Medication

Abikoff and Klein (1992) conclude that there is uncertain benefit associated with stimulant treatment of CD/ODD. Some studies show significant improvement following stimulant treatment in institutionalized and outpatient antisocial adolescents (Eisenberg et al., 1963; Maletsky, 1974), while other research indicates no improvement (Conners et al., 1971). Stimulants may have the greatest effect on CD/ODD children with co-occurring attention problems or hyperactivity, especially if these co-occurring symptoms are contributing to the oppositional, antisocial behavior. Over all, the benefit of stimulant medication for CD/ODD seems to be on an individual, as opposed to group, basis.

Neuroleptics are sometimes used when agitation or excessively violent behavior is a primary feature of CD/ODD, but they also vary in effectiveness from individual to individual (Klein, Gittelman, Quitkin, and Rifkin, 1980). Furthermore, the side effects of neuroleptics, especially with long-term use, limit their utility with children. Lithium has been used with some effectiveness in explosively aggressive CD/ODD children, but group research support for lithium treatment is equivocal (Klein, Abikoff, Klass, and Shah, 1989). Antidepressants are occasionally used for CD/ODD with a strong affective component.

Over all, there is no single, widely accepted pharmacological treatment for CD/ODD. Instead, multiple medications are used to treat severe or dangerous symptoms, based on the individual presentation of the child. Medication is rarely the sole treatment modality for the CD/ODD child, unless the CD/ODD symptoms are felt to be exclusively the result of another disorder (e.g., Dysthymia or ADHD). In general, medication is used in conjunction with psychotherapy and behavior modification to treat the CD/ODD behaviors.

Inpatient Hospitalization

In some cases the child's oppositional or antisocial behaviors are of sufficient severity or threat to warrant more intensive interventions. The most common of these interventions are hospitalization, partial hospitalization (day treatment), or residential placement. In the case of severe CD/ODD the first decision for the clinician concerns the level of dangerousness presented by the child and/or situation. Children with co-occurring CD/ODD and depression, for example, should be closely evaluated for self-injurious or suicidal inclinations. Alternatively, CD/ODD children are may be placing themselves in dangerous situations or engaging in dangerous pursuits. In other cases CD/ODD children are a danger to others. Threats, revenge themes, or predatory behaviors may suggest behavior that will be dangerous to others. Finally, many CD/ODD children are at risk because of their environment. Signs of physical, verbal, or sexual abuse in the home environment should receive immediate attention. The home environment may have a less overt but still negative effect by encouraging CD/ODD behavior because of poor discipline. If children's behavior, safety, and psychological status are substantially deteriorating in the home environment, short-term inpatient or longer-term residential treatments should be considered. Three placements are commonly used for CD/ODD children: inpatient hospitalization, day treatment, and residential placement.

Inpatient hospital settings provide an opportunity to remove children from the stresses and contingencies of their environment. Free of these factors, a new behavioral plan can be implemented in the relatively safe milieu of the hospital. Such a plan generally targets compliance, following rules, and prosocial behaviors. Rewards in the form of privileges, praise, and access to favored activity are used to reinforce positive change. Ideally, cognitive-behavioral techniques are taught in group or individual therapy, and family issues are addressed in family therapy. The inpatient hospital milieu tends to be a short-term placement intended to break the negative cycle of behaviors at home, to protect the child from stress or danger, to allow the child to learn cognitive-behavioral strategies in intensive therapy, and to stabilize the child's behavior. Followup outpatient therapy is generally necessary for continued improvement and maintenance of gains.

Day treatment programs provide an intensive (usually 5–8 hours per day, 5 days a week) outpatient experience and allow the child to spend nights and weekends at home. Like inpatient units, day treatment programs have special education, activities, individual therapy, group therapy, family therapy, and behavioral programs to encourage behavioral and psychological change. However, they cost far less than an inpatient stay and allow the child to maintain a daily connection with the family. Day treatment programs are effective in reducing CD behavior and improving social skills, self-perceptions, and family functioning (Grizenko, Papineau, and Sayegh, 1993).

Residential placements are sometimes necessary for the most severe CD cases or for CD children who are removed from abusive family environments. The Response Program (RP; Holland et al., 1993), for example, is a time-limited residential program based on the belief that a bonding injury or attachment failure of some sort has occurred in CD children. RP focuses on three goals: understanding the role of attachment and bonding insults in the development and maintenance of behavior problems, working to develop conditions within the child's environment that will lead to the development of attachment, and working to ensure the continuation of care for children regardless of the nature or persistence of their behavior problems. Two processes are central to the development of attachment based on the RP model: affiliation, the feeling of belonging and being connected with others; and mutuality, the understanding that the actions and feelings of one person affect others. Children are in residence at RP for 4 weeks at a time (a short residential or a long hospital stay, depending on perspective). Staff formulate a care plan in which the RP staff, parents, alternative caregivers, the child, social service representatives, and school representatives outline personal and family dynamics and management strategies for helping the child to cope with attachment/interpersonal problems. Living arrangements, therapeutic experiences, and group activities are structured to achieve affiliation and mutuality in residents. Preliminary findings from a 12-month followup indicate that parents report fewer symptoms of CD than at intake (Holland et al., 1993).

A second residential program is based on Aggressive Replacement Training (ART; Goldstein et al., 1987), described earlier as Goldstein et al.'s (1987) ten-step anger-management technique. The ART program is based on the assumption that anger and aggression are last-resort methods of coping. ART groups consist of six to twelve CD/ODD boys ranging from 13–21 years in age. ART includes anger-control training, "structured learning" (social-skills intervention), and "moral education" (moral reasoning skills). Participants complete the program during an approximately 10-week residential stay. Outcome studies of ART suggest that it improves social skills and prosocial behavior while decreasing impulsivity and acting out behaviors (Goldstein et al., 1987).

In addition to the two prototypical residential programs just described, there are myriad residential programs and settings for delinquent children. These vary in quality from residential "warehouses," which do little more than house the children, to residential therapeutic settings, which include components of cognitive-behavioral interventions and behavior-management programs. Although there is evidence that residential therapeutic programs such as ART and RP result in improvement in CD/ODD symptoms, residential settings without a clear intervention sequence may not have the same success. Ultimately, the clinician must screen each program individually for its therapeutic value.

There has been considerable debate regarding the removal of CD/ODD children from the home environment and treatment in inpatient or residential settings. Removal of children from their home environment may harm already fragile affiliations with others, including caregivers (Holland et al., 1993). In some cases (e.g., prison or some inpatient units), removal from the community is followed by placement in an environment where the only attachments to be made are predominantly with an antisocial subculture. These attachments provide negative models and an "education" in antisocial behavior. An additional argument against intensive placements is based on economics: The cost of residential care and the large number of children with severe conduct problems make it impossible to provide residential treatment to all children in need. On the other hand, day treatment programs may be an alternative to higher-cost residential care. Grizenko et al. (1993) report that day treatment and residential treatment have similar outcomes, although day treatment accomplishes its goals in a shorter time and with far less cost (approximately $9200 versus $61,000 for residential).

Over all, then, inpatient/residential settings should be considered for CD/ODD children in situations of danger or extreme deterioration in functioning. Because CD/ODD children often are in situations of risk, the clinician should be aware of the potential need for an inpatient placement. However, such referrals should be made with prudence. Less-restrictive day treatment programs may accomplish the same goals with less personal and financial cost. Such day treatment programs, of course, assume that the home environment is sufficiently safe for the child to return there for the evening and night.

Summary/Integration of Treatments

Behavioral and cognitive-behavioral treatments for CD/ODD have met with the greatest successes, with medication as a useful adjunct. Common factors across treatment modalities include modifying coercive family interactions, implementation of a family behavioral plan, changing the child's cognition system, teaching the child social problem-solving skills, providing positive models and removing negative peer models, reinforcement for attainment of therapy goals, and strengthening social relationships in general (Awad, 1985). The common problems in treatment appear to be resistance of the child to change and difficulty of the family in following through on the therapy plan. Early intervention appears to produce greater results and prevents a downward spiral of deteriorating behavior; at older ages, CD/ODD is extremely difficult to change and requires extensive, persistent intervention. Selection of a treatment plan should be guided by the individual assessment, but it will probably include cognitive, behavioral, and, in the case of severe behavioral problems or co-occurring disorders, medication components. (Treatment options for ODD and CD are listed in Table 3.4.)

TABLE 3.4   Treatment Options for Oppositional Defiant Disorder and Conduct Disorder

BEHAVIORAL INTERVENTIONS

Psychoeducation
Observation and monitoring by adults
Reinforcement of prosocial behavior
Time-out for unacceptable behavior
Involvement of child in problem-solving communication
Nondirective play
Use of simple commands
Videotape modeling
Synthesis teaching—separation of child care stresses from other demands
Self-sufficiency training—patterned problem solving applied to stressful situations

PSYCHOTHERAPY

Cognitive-behavioral interventions

    1. Social-skills training
    2. Problem solving
    3. Anger management
    4. Modeling
    5. Role play

MEDICATION

Neuroleptics
Antidepressants

INPATIENT HOSPITALIZATION

Traditional inpatient settings
Day treatment
Residential settings

Note: This outline of options summarizes major treatments covered in the text. Specific treatments are often combined into an intervention package. Refer to the text for additional descriptions of each treatment. This table is not necessarily an exhaustive list of all treatments available.

■ References

Abikoff, H., and Klein, R. G. (1992). Attention-Deficit Hyperactivity and Conduct Disorder: Comorbidity and implications for treatment. *Journal of Consulting and Clinical Psychology, 60,* 881–892.

Achenbach, T. M. (1978). The Child Behavior Profile: I. Boys aged 6–11. *Journal of Consulting and Clinical Psychology, 46,* 478–488.

———. (1991). *Manual for the Child Behavior Checklist/4–18 and 1991 Profile.* Burlington: University of Vermont Department of Psychiatry.

Achenbach, T. M., Conners, C. K., Quay, H. C., Verhulst, F. C., and Howell, C. T. (1989). Replication of empirically derived syndromes as a basis for taxonomy of child/adolescent psychopathology. *Journal of Abnormal Child Psychology, 17,* 223–233.

Achenbach, T. M., and Edelbrock, C. S. (1981). Behavioral problems and competencies reported by parents of normal and disturbed children aged 4 through 16. *Monographs of the Society for Research in Child Development, 46,* No. 188.

American Psychiatric Association. (1994). *Diagnostic and statistical manual of mental disorders* (4th ed.). Washington, DC: Author.

Anderson, J. C., Williams, S., McGee, R., and Silva, P. A. (1987). DSM-III disorders in preadolescent children: Prevalence in a large sample from the general population. *Archives of General Psychiatry, 44,* 69–76.

Awad, G. (1985). Responsiveness in psychotherapy with antisocial adolescents. *American Journal of Psychotherapy, 39,* 490–497.

Baden, A. D., and Howe, G. W. (1992). Mothers' attributions and expectancies regarding their conduct-disordered children. *Journal of Abnormal Psychology, 88,* 467–485.

Barkley, R. A. (1981). Hyperactive children: A handbook for diagnosis and treatment. New York: Guilford Press.

Biaggio, M. K. (1980). Assessment of anger arousal. *Journal of Personality Assessment, 44,* 289–298.

Biaggio, M. K., Supplee, K., and Curtis, N. (1981). Reliability and validity of four anger scales. *Journal of Personality Assessment, 45,* 639–648.

Biederman, J., Munir, K., and Knee, D. (1987). Conduct and oppositional disorder in clinically referred children with attention deficit disorder: A controlled family study. *Journal of the American Academy of Child and Adolescent Psychiatry, 26,* 724–727.

Biederman, J., Newcorn, J., and Sprich, S. (1991). Comorbidity of attention deficit hyperactivity disorder with conduct, depressive, anxiety, and other disorders. *American Journal of Psychiatry, 148,* 564–577.

Bierman, K. L., Miller, C. L., and Staub, S. D. (1987). Improving the social behavior and peer acceptance of rejected boys: Effects of social skill training with instructions and prohibitions. *Journal of Consulting and Clinical Psychology, 55,* 194–200.

Billings, A. G., and Moos, R. H. (1983). Comparisons of children of depressed and nondepressed parents: A social-environment perspective. *Journal of Abnormal Child Psychology, 11,* 463–486.

Blechman, E. A. (1981). Toward comprehensive behavioral family interventions: An algorithm for matching families and interventions. *Behavior Modification, 5,* 221–235.

———. (1984). Competent parents, competent children: Behavioral objectives of parent training. In R.F. Bangel and R. A. Polster (Eds.), *Parent training* (pp. 34–66). New York: Guilford Press.

Bowden, C. L., Deutsch, C. K., and Swanson, J. M. (1988). Plasma dopamine-beta-hydroxylase and platelet monoamine oxidase in attention deficit disorder and conduct disorder. *Journal of the American Academy of Child and Adolescent Psychiatry, 27,* 171–174.

Boyle, M. H., Offord, D. R., Racine, Y., Sanfors, M., Szatmari, P., and Fleming, J. E. (1993). Evaluation of the Original Ontario Child Health Study Scales. *Canadian Journal of Psychiatry, 38,* 397–405.

Buss, A. H., and Durkee, A. (1957). An inventory for assessing different kinds of hostility. *Journal of Consulting Psychology, 21,* 343–348.

Butcher, J. N., Williams, C. L., Graham, J. R., Archer, R. P., Tellegen, A., Ben-Porath, J. S., and Kaemmer, B. (1992). *MMPI-A: Manual for administration, scoring, and interpretation.* Minneapolis: University of Minnesota.

Cadoret, R. J. (1978). Psychopathology in adopted-away offspring of biological parents with antisocial behavior. *Archives of General Psychiatry, 35,* 176–184.

Cadoret, R. J., and Cain, C. (1980). Sex differences in predictors of antisocial behavior in adoptees. *Archives of General Psychiatry, 37,* 1171–1175.

Chamberlain, P., and Reid, J. B. (1987). Parent observation and report of child symptoms. *Behavioral Assessment, 9,* 97–109.

Clark, L. (1985). *SOS: Help for parents.* Bowling Green, KY: Parents Press.

Coie, J. D. (1990). Adapting intervention to the problems of aggressive and disruptive rejected children. In S. R. Asher and J. D. Coie (Eds.), *Peer rejection in childhood* (pp. 309–337). Cambridge, MA: Cambridge University Press.

Conners, C. K., Kramer, R., Rothschild, G. H., Schwartz, L., and Stone, A. (1971). Treatment of young delinquent boys with diphenylhydantoin sodium and methylphenidate. *Archives of General Psychiatry, 24,* 156–160.

Conolly, J., Burstein, S., Stevens, R., and White, D. (1987). *Interpersonal skill deficits of emotionally disturbed adolescents: Social problem solving, self-reports of social behavior, and self-esteem.* Unpublished manuscript.

Crittenden, P. M., and Ainsworth, M. D. S. (1989). Child maltreatment and attachment theory. In D. Cichetti and V. Carlson (Eds.), *Child maltreatment: Theory and research on the causes and consequences of child abuse and neglect* (pp. 494–528). Cambridge, MA: Cambridge University Press.

Dishion, T. J., Loeber, R., Stouthamer-Loeber, M., and Patterson, G. R. (1984). Skill deficits and male adolescent delinquency. *Journal of Abnormal Child Psychology, 12,* 37–54.

Dishion, T. J., Patterson, G. R., Stoolmiller, M., and Skinner, M. L. (1991). Family, school, and behavioral antecedents to early adolescent involvement with antisocial peers. *Developmental Psychology, 27,* 172–180.

Dodge, K. A. (1985). Attributional bias in aggressive children. In P. C. Kendall (Ed.), *Advances in cognitive-behavioral research and therapy* (vol. 4, pp. 73-110). Orlando, FL: Academic Press.

Dodge, K. A., and Newman, J. P. (1981). Biased decision making processes in aggressive boys. *Journal of Abnormal Psychology, 90,* 375–379.

Dumas, J. E., and Wahler, R. G. (1983). Predictors of treatment outcome in parent training: Mother insularity and socioeconomic disadvantage. *Behavioral Assessment, 5,* 301–313.

Eisenberg, L., Lachman, R., Molling, P. A., Lockner, A., Mizelle, J. D., and Conners, C.

K. (1963). A psychopharmacological experiment in a training school for delinquent boys. *American Journal of Orthopsychiatry, 33,* 431–447.

Eyberg, S. M., and Robinson, E. A. (1982). Parent–child interaction training: Effects on family functioning. *Journal of Clinical Child Psychology, 11,* 130–137.

Eyberg, S. M., and Robinson, E. A. (1983). Dyadic Parent–Child Interaction Coding System: A manual. *Journal of Clinical Child Psychology, 12,* 347–357.

Eyberg, S. M., and Ross, A. W. (1978). Assessment of child behavior problems: The validation of a new inventory. *Journal of Clinical Child Psychology, 7,* 113–116.

Ferber, H., Keeley, S. M., and Shemberg, K. M. (1974). Training parents in behavior modification: Outcome and problems encountered in a program after Patterson's work. *Behavior Therapy, 5,* 415–419.

Fergusson, D. M., Lynskey, M. T., and Horwood, L. J. (1993). The effect of maternal depression on maternal ratings of child behavior. *Journal of Abnormal Child Psychology, 21,* 245–269.

Forehand, R., and McMahon, R. J. (1981). *Helping the noncompliant child: A clinician's guide to parent training.* New York: Spectrum.

Frick, P. J., Lahey, B. B., Loeber, R., Stouthamer, M., Christ, M. A. G., and Hanson, K. (1992). Familial risk factors to oppositional defiant disorder and conduct disorder: Parental psychopathology and maternal parenting. *Journal of Consulting and Clinical Psychology, 60,* 49–55.

Goldstein, A. P., Glick, B., Reiner, S., Zimmerman, D., and Coultry, T. M. (1987). *Aggression Replacement Training: A comprehensive intervention for aggressive youth.* Champaign, IL: Research Press.

Griest, D., Wells, K. C., and Forehand, R. (1979). An examination of predictors of maternal perceptions of maladjustment in clinic-referred children. *Journal of Abnormal Psychology, 88,* 277–281.

Griest, D., Wells, K. C., and McMahon, R. J. (1980). An examination of differences between nonclinic and behavior problem clinic referred children and their mothers. *Journal of Abnormal Psychology, 89,* 497–500.

Griest, D., and Wells, K. C. (1983). Behavioral family therapy and conduct disorders in children. *Behavior Therapy, 14,* 37–53.

Grizenko, N., Papineau, D., and Sayegh, L. (1993). A comparison of day treatment and outpatient treatment for children with disruptive behavior problems. *Canadian Journal of Psychiatry, 38,* 432–435.

Hanf, C. (1970). *Shaping mothers to shape their children's behavior.* Unpublished manuscript.

Hanf, C., and Kling, J. (1973). *Facilitating parent–child interactions: A two stage training model.* Unpublished manuscript.

Henggeler, S. W., Rodick, J. D., Bordin, C. M., Hanson, C. L., Watson, S. M., and Urey, J. R. (1986). Multisystemic treatment of juvenile offenders: Effects on adolescent behavior and family interaction. *Developmental Psychology, 22,* 132–141.

Holland, R., Moretti, M. M., Verlaan, V., and Peterson, S. (1993). Attachment and conduct disorder: The response program. *Canadian Journal of Psychiatry, 38,* 420–431.

Howe, G. W., Baden, A. D., Lewis, W. W., Ostroff, J., and Levine, B. (1989). *Parents' expectations of the efficacy of behavioral parenting techniques.* Unpublished manuscript available from George Howe, Center for Family Research, 613 Ross Hall, 2300 Eye St. N.W., Washington, DC 20037.

Jarey, M. L., and Stewart, M. A. (1985). Psychiatric disorder in the parents of adopted children with aggressive conduct disorder. *Neuropsychobiology, 13,* 7–11.

Jenkins, R. L., and Hewitt, L. E. (1944). Types of personality structure encountered in child guidance clinics. *American Journal of Orthopsychiatry, 14,* 84–89.

Jenkins, R. L., and Glickman, S. (1947). Patterns of personality organization among delinquents. *Nervous Children, 6,* 329–339.

Joffe, R. D., Dobson, K. S., Fine, S., Marriage, K., and Haley, G. (1990). Social problem-solving in depressed, conduct-disordered, and normal adolescents. *Journal of Abnormal Child Psychology, 18,* 565–575.

Kazdin, A. E. (1987). *Conduct disorders in childhood and adolescence.* Newbury Park, CA: Sage.

Kazdin, A. E., Esveldt-Dawson, K., French, N. H., and Unis, A. S. (1987a). Effects of parent management training and problem-solving skills training combined in the treatment of antisocial child behavior. *Journal of the American Academy of Child and Adolescent Psychiatry, 26,* 416–424.

_____. (1987b). Problem-solving skills training and relationship therapy in the treatment of antisocial child behavior. *Journal of Consulting and Clinical Psychology, 55,* 76–85.

Klein, D. F., Gittelman, R., Quitkin, F., and Rifkin, A. (1980). *Diagnosis and drug treatment of psychiatric disorders: Adults and children.* Baltimore, MD: Williams & Wilkins.

Klein, R. G., Abikoff, H., Klass, E., and Shah, M. (1989). Preliminary findings from a controlled trial of lithium, placebo, and methylphenidate in children and adolescents with conduct disorders. Paper presented at the annual meeting of the New Clinical Drug Evaluation Unit, Key Biscayne, FL.

Kolko, D. J., Loar, L. L., and Sturnick, D. (1990). Inpatient social-cognitive skills training groups with conduct disordered and attention deficit disordered children. *Journal of Child Psychology and Psychiatry, 31,* 737–748.

Kovacs, M., Paulaskas, S., Gatsonis, C., and Richards, C. (1988). A longitudinal study of comorbidity with and risk for conduct disorders. *Journal of Affective Disorders, 15,* 205–217.

Kutcher, S. P., Marton, P., and Korenblum, M. (1989). Relationship between psychiatric illness and conduct disorder in adolescents. *Canadian Journal of Psychiatry, 34,* 526–529.

Lahey, B. B., Loeber, R., Quay, H. C., Frick, P. J., and Grimm, J. (1992). Oppositional-defiant and conduct disorders: Issues to be resolved for DSM-IV. *Journal of the American Academy of Child and Adolescent Psychiatry, 31,* 539–545.

Lochman, J. E., White, K. J., and Wayland, K. W. (1991). Cognitive-behavioral assessment and treatment with aggressive children. In P. C. Kendall (Ed.), *Child and adolescent therapy: Cognitive-behavioral procedures* (pp. 25–65). New York: Guilford Press.

Loeber, R. (1982). The stability of antisocial and delinquent child behavior: A review. *Child Behavior, 53,* 1431–1446.

Loeber, R., and Dishion, T. J. (1983). Early predictors of male adolescent delinquency: A review. *Psychological Bulletin, 94,* 68–99.

Loeber, R., Lahey, B. B., and Thomas, C. (1991). Diagnostic conundrum of oppositional-defiant disorder and conduct disorder. *Journal of Abnormal Psychology, 100,* 379–390.

Loeber, R., and Schmaling, K. B. (1985). Empirical evidence for overt and covert patterns of antisocial conduct problems: A meta-analysis. *Journal of Abnormal Child Psychology, 13,* 337–352.

Maletsky, B. M. (1974). D-amphetamine and delinquency: Hyperkinesis persisting? *Diseases of the Nervous System, 35,* 543–547.

Matthys, W., Walterbos, W., Nijo, L., and van Engeland, H. (1989). Person perception in children with conduct disorders. *Journal of Child Psychology and Psychiatry, 30,* 439–448.

McGee, R., Feehan, M., Williams, S., and Anderson, J. (1992). DSM-III disorders from age 11 to age 15 years. *Journal of the American Academy of Child and Adolescent Psychiatry, 31,* 50–59.

McMahon, R. J., and Forehand, R. (1984). Parent training for the noncompliant child: Treatment outcome, generalization, and adjunctive therapy procedures. In R. F. Dangel and R. A. Polster (Eds.), *Parent training: Foundations of research and practice* (pp. 298–328). New York: Guilford Press.

_____ . (1988). Conduct disorders. In E. J. Mash and L. G. Terdal (Eds.), *Behavioral assessment of childhood disorders: Selected core problems* (2d ed., pp. 105–153). New York: Guilford Press.

Mednick, S. A., and Christiansen, K. O. (1977). *Biosocial bases of criminal behavior.* New York: Gardner.

Mednick, S. A., and Hutchings, B. (1978). Genetic and psychophysiological factors in asocial behavior. In R. D. Hare and D. Schalling (Eds.), *Psychopathic behavior: Approaches to research.* Chichester, UK: Wiley.

Meyer, R. G. (1993). *The Clinician's Handbook* (3rd ed.). Boston: Allyn & Bacon.

Milich, R., and Dodge, K. A. (1984). Social information processing in child psychiatric populations. *Journal of Abnormal Child Psychology, 12,* 471–490.

Miller, G. E., and Prinz, R. J. (1990). Enhancement of social learning family interventions for childhood conduct disorder. *Psychological Bulletin, 108,* 291–307.

Moffitt, T. E. (1990). Juvenile delinquency and attention deficit disorder: Boys' developmental trajectories from age 3 to age 15. *Child Development, 61,* 893–910.

Moffitt, T. E., and Henry, B. (1989). Neurological assessment of executive functions in self-reported delinquents. *Development and Psychopathology, 1,* 105–118.

Myers, W. C., Burket, R. C., and Otto, T. A. (1993). Conduct disorder and personality disorders in hospitalized adolescents. *Journal of Clinical Psychiatry, 54,* 21–26.

Novaco, R. (1975). *Anger control: The development and evaluation of an experimental treatment.* Lexington, MA: Lexington Books.

Ostrov, E., Marohn, R. C., Offer, D., Curtiss, G., and Feczko, M. (1980). The adolescent antisocial behavior checklist. *Journal of Clinical Psychology, 36,* 594–601.

Patterson, G. R. (1982). *Coercive family process.* Eugene, OR: Castalia.

Patterson, G. R., and Bank, L. (1986). Bootstrapping your way in the nomological thicket. *Behavioral Assessment, 8,* 49–73.

Patterson, G. R., Chamberlain, P., and Reid, J. B. (1982). A comparative evaluation of a parent-training program. *Behavior Therapy, 13,* 638–650.

Patterson, G. R., Ray, R. S., Shaw, D. A., and Cobb, J. A. (1969). *Manual for coding of family interactions.* New York: Microfiche Publications.

Patterson, G., Reid, J., Jones, R., and Conger, R. (1975). *A social learning approach to family intervention. 1: Families with aggressive children.* Eugene, OR: Castalia.

Platt, N. J., and Spivak, G. (1975). *Manual for the Means End Problem Solving Procedure (MEPS): A measure of interpersonal cognitive problem solving skill.* Unpublished manuscript.

Puig-Antich, J. (1982). Major depression and conduct disorder in prepuberty. *Journal of the American Academy of Child Psychiatry, 21,* 118–128.

Quay, H. C. (1986). Classification. In H.C. Quay (Ed.), *Handbook of juvenile delinquency* (pp. 188–238). New York: Wiley.

Quay, H. C., and Peterson, D. R. (1982). *Interim manual for the Revised Behavior Problem Checklist.* Coral Gables, FL: University of Miami.

Quinton, D., Rutter, M., and Gulliver, L. (1990). Continuities in psychiatric disorders from childhood to adulthood in the children of psychiatric patients. In L. N. Robins and M. Rutter (Eds.), *Straight and devious pathways from childhood to adulthood.* Cambridge, MA: Cambridge University Press.

Reeves, J. C., Werry, J. S., Elkind, G. S., and Zametkin, A. (1987). Attention deficit, conduct, oppositional, and anxiety disorders in children: II. Clinical characteristics. *Journal of the American Academy of Child and Adolescent Psychiatry, 26,* 144–155.

Rey, J. M., Bashir, M. R., Schwartz, M., Richards, I. N., Plapp, J. M., and Stewart, G. W. (1988). Oppositional disorder: Fact or fiction? *Journal of the American Academy of Child and Adolescent Psychiatry, 27,* 157–162.

Robins, L. N. (1966). *Deviant children grow up: A sociological and psychiatric study of sociopathic personality.* Baltimore, MD: Williams & Wilkins.

Robins, L. N., West, P. A., and Herjanic, B. (1975). Arrests and delinquency in two generations: A study of two black urban families and their children. *Journal of Child Psychology and Psychiatry, 16,* 125–140.

Robinson, E. A., and Eyberg, S. M. (1981). The Dyadic Parent-Child Interaction Coding System: Standardization and validation. *Journal of Consulting and Clinical Psychology, 49,* 245–250.

Rogeness, G. A., Hernandez, J. M., Macedo, C. A., and Mitchell, E. L. (1983). Biochemical differences in children with conduct disorder socialized and undersocialized. *American Journal of Psychiatry, 139,* 307–311.

Rutter, M. (1985). Family and school influence on behavioral development. *Journal of Child Psychiatry, 26,* 349–368.

Rutter, M., Tizard, J., and Whitmore, K. (1970). *Education, health, and behavior.* London: Longman.

Safer, D. J. (1984). Subgrouping conduct disordered adolescents by early risk factors. *American Journal of Orthopsychiatry, 54,* 603–612.

Sanders, M. R., and James, J. E. (1983). The modification of parent behavior: A review of generalization and maintenance. *Journal of Applied Behavior Analysis, 14,* 223–237.

Selby, M. J. (1984). Assessment of violence potential using measures of anger, hostility, and social desirability. *Journal of Personality Assessment, 48,* 531–544.

Shamsie, J., and Hluchy, C. (1991). Youth with conduct disorder: A challenge to be met. *Canadian Journal of Psychiatry, 36,* 405–414.

Sturge, C. (1982). Reading retardation and antisocial behavior. *Journal of Child Psychology and Psychiatry, 23,* 21–31.

Wadsworth, M. E. J. (1976). Delinquency, pulse rates, and early emotional deprivation. *British Journal of Criminology, 16,* 245–256.

Wahler, R. G. (1980). The insular mother: Her problems in parent-child treatment. *Journal of Applied Behavioral Analysis, 13,* 207–219.

Wahler, R. G., Cartor, P. G., Fleischman, J., and Lambert, W. (1993). The impact of synthesis teaching and parent training with mothers of conduct-disordered children. *Journal of Abnormal Child Psychology, 21,* 425–440.

Wahler, R. G., and Dumas, J. E. (1989). Attentional problems in dysfunctional mother-child interactions: An interbehavioral model. *Psychological Bulletin, 105,* 116–130.

Wahler, R. G., House, A. E., and Stambaugh, E. E. (1976). *Ecological assessment of child problem behavior: A clinical package for home, school, and institutional settings.* New York: Pergamon Press.

Webster-Stratton, C. (1981a). Modification of mothers' behaviors and attitudes through videotape modeling group discussion. *Behavior Therapy, 12,* 634–642.

_____ . (1981b). Videotape modeling: A method of parent education. *Journal of Clinical Child Psychology, 10,* 93–98.

_____ . (1982a). The long-term effect of a videotape modeling parent education program: Comparison of immediate and one year follow-up results. *Behavior Therapy, 13,* 702–714.

_____ . (1982b). Teaching mothers through videotape modeling to change their children's behavior. *Journal of Pediatric Psychology, 7,* 279–294.

_____ (1984). Randomized trial of two parent-training programs for families with conduct-disordered children. *Journal of Consulting and Clinical Psychology, 52,* 666–678.

_____ . (1985). Predictors of treatment outcome in parent training for conduct disordered children. *Behavior Therapy, 16,* 223–243.

_____ . (1991). Strategies for helping families with conduct disordered children. *Journal of Child Psychology and Psychiatry, 31,* 737–748.

West, O. J., and Farrington, D. P. (1977). *The delinquent way of life.* London: Heinemann.

Wilson, H. (1980). Parental supervision: A neglected aspect of delinquency. *British Journal of Criminology, 20,* 203–235.

Yudofsky, S. C., Silver, J. M., Jackson, W., Endicott, J., and Williams, D. (1986). The Overt Aggression Scale for the objective rating of verbal and physical aggression. *American Journal of Psychiatry, 143,* 35–39.

CHAPTER 4

Elimination Disorders

Two elimination disorders are identified in DSM-IV: *Enuresis* is the inappropriate and often involuntary discharge of urine after an age at which bladder control is expected. *Encopresis* is the discharge of feces into inappropriate places. Although these two disorders occasionally co-occur, they are different in presentation, etiology, and treatment, sharing few underlying characteristics. They do, however, share the common feature of being behavior patterns that are appropriate and expected at one age (infancy) and unusual, shameful, and deviant at another age. Hence, much of the informal, "parental" definition of these disorders hinges on the age at which a particular family believes that their child should be toilet trained. Parents who hold the unspoken opinion that toilet training must be achieved at a very young age may believe that their child has an elimination disorder when this is not the case; parents who err in the other direction may ignore or even foster an elimination disorder in their child.

Although DSM-IV attempts to account for normative development as well as developmental differences in toilet-training age by setting minimum age criteria for the elimination disorders, parents rarely make referrals based on DSM-IV criteria. Furthermore, the parental response to elimination problems in the child is dictated not by scientific knowledge of normative development but by the parent's *belief system* regarding normative development. Therefore, despite the effort to include normative criteria in the diagnostic nomenclature, the role of parental opinion in at least the initial referral cannot be ignored.

■ Enuresis

☐ CLINICAL DESCRIPTION

Diagnostic Considerations

Functional enuresis (hereafter simply referred to as "enuresis") is defined in DSM-IV as the inappropriate and often involuntary discharge of urine after an age at which bladder control is expected. In order to meet diagnostic criteria, a child must have at least two enuretic events a week for 3 consecutive months, or the enuresis must have a significant effect on the child's functioning. Enuresis cannot be diagnosed in children below the age of 5. If a child is significantly developmentally delayed, the clinician should use the child's mental or developmental age instead of chronological age. Because physical disorders must be ruled out before a diagnosis of enuresis is made, examination by a physician is advised for any child presenting for enuresis.

Two overlapping groupings for enuresis exist: Primary-Secondary and Nocturnal-Diurnal. The term *primary enuresis* is used to denote an enuretic child who has never had bladder control. "Having bladder control" is defined in various time frames ranging from 2 weeks to 6 months (Scharf et al., 1987; Fritz and Armbrust, 1982). *Secondary enuresis,* on the other hand, describes a child who had bladder control at one time before regressing to enuretic behavior. It is extremely rare for a child to have no accidents immediately following (or during) successful toilet training; secondary enuresis is diagnosed only when these accidents reach sufficient frequency to be diagnosed as enuresis.

As many as 90% of enuretics are of the primary type (Scharf et al., 1987). Although this percentage seems extremely high based on clinical experience, it does indicate at the very least that the bulk of enuretics are primary. A significant risk exists that primary enuresis may be the result of genetic, physiological, or developmental factors (Scharf et al., 1987). Hence, consultation with a pediatrician is extremely important in the case of a child with primary enuresis. Because the child with secondary enuresis had bladder control at one time, genetic-maturational causes are less likely. For these children, acute illness (or similar change in physiological status) and psychological-behavioral factors are considered as the strongest potential causes (Scharf & Jennings, 1988).

The nocturnal-diurnal distinction is based on whether wetting occurs during the day (diurnal enuresis) or at night (nocturnal enuresis); this distinction is coded in the DSM-IV diagnosis as Nocturnal Only, Diurnal Only, or Nocturnal *and* Diurnal. Nocturnal enuresis is much more common than diurnal enuresis (hence the colloquial description of enuresis as "bedwetting"), and most enuresis treatment and research is directed at nocturnal enuresis. Diurnal enuresis is often regarded by parents as more "intentional" than nocturnal enuresis, and it is true that many cases of diurnal enuresis involve power struggles between the parents and child. However, diurnal enuresis can also be caused by factors such as failure of the child to recognize the need to urinate or weak urinary sphincter (or poor sphincter control).

Studies of the prevalence of enuresis (reviewed by Fritz and Armbrust, 1982) indicate that 12–25% of 4-year-olds, 10–13% of 6-year-olds, 7–10% of 8-year-olds, 3–5% of 10-year-olds, and 1–3% of 12-year-olds and older are enuretic. Comparable but slightly lower prevalence rates are reported in other sources, with estimates of 7% for 5-year-old males and 3% for 5-year-old females; prevalence decreases to 2–3% at age 10 (American Psychiatric Association, 1994). The disorder is more common in boys, with estimates of the sex ratio ranging from 1.5:1 to 3:1 (Fritz and Armbrust, 1982; Scharf et al., 1987). Particularly for young boys, then, enuresis is a common disorder.

Appearance and Features

The appearance and features of an enuretic child depend (see Table 4.1) on whether the enuresis is primary or secondary and whether it is diurnal or nocturnal. The most common presentation in the office of the mental health professional appears to be a primary nocturnal enuretic (although secondary nocturnal enuretics are also common). Ideally, the child will have had a full medical workup and physiological causes will be ruled out. The typical enuretic child is a boy between the ages of 4 and 8 who has significant problems with bedwetting. In many cases this problem has created exasperation in the parents who have tried interventions ranging from reward to punishment. The child usually sleeps through the bedwetting incident, only to find himself in a wet bed in the morning (occasionally the child will wake earlier because of the wet feeling, but rarely in response to the enuretic incident as it is occurring). Because the wet bed must be changed, bedwetting is often an unpleasant occurrence in family life. The child's room (and the child) may smell, constantly reminding the parent and child of the problem. Parental upset and resentment of the child may be noticed by the child, and siblings may tease the child. In other cases the parents give the child attention and nurturance after a bedwetting incident because they feel sorry for him and do not want to shame him.

Diurnal enuresis typically has a different presentation. The child may urinate only at certain times (e.g., at home), while behaving appropriately at other times (e.g., at school). The reasons for the urination may be multiple. Common reasons are anger at parent, secondary gain for enuresis, and/or refusal to leave a fun activity to go to the bathroom until it is too late. Parents are often less forgiving about diurnal enuretic events than they are about nocturnal events, since they tend to perceive diurnal events as intentional. If the enuretic events occur in the presence of peers (or if the child does not change clothes before seeing peers), the child's odor may be a source of ridicule and isolation. Hence, the enuresis has significant social implications.

TABLE 4.1   Appearance and Features of Enuresis

COMMON FEATURES

Urinating into bed or clothes
Age 5 to 8 years
Child sleeps through bedwetting incident

OCCASIONAL FEATURES

Parental upset and/or resentment
Peer or sibling rejection

Note: The features listed above are often seen but are not universal. Some features may be diagnostically relevant or required, while others may not be required for diagnosis. "Common" features are typical of the disorder; "occasional" features appear frequently but are not necessarily seen in a majority of cases.

Etiology

Several potential etiological factors have been suggested for enuresis: medical problems, sleep disorder, bladder capacity, genetics, and psychological factors (Fritz and Armbrust, 1982; Scharf et al., 1987). Although enuresis caused by a physiological problem is not psychogenic enuresis in the technical sense, medical problems are mentioned as an etiological factor here to underscore the importance of considering the possibility that the enuresis is the result of a medical problem. Fritz and Armbrust (1982), for example, cite research indicating that 2–4% of enuresis cases result from urologic problems; urinary tract infections frequently account for secondary enuresis in girls. Other potential organic contributors to enuresis are diabetes, sickle cell disease, and spina bifida (Fritz and Armbrust, 1982).

Nocturnal enuresis has traditionally been thought to be the result of sleep disorders such as deep sleep, narcolepsy, and sleep apnea, but little evidence exists to support this view. In fact, enuresis occurs during any sleep stage and is unrelated to factors such as depth of sleep and dreams (Fritz and Armbrust, 1982; Scharf et al., 1987). Another etiological hypothesis for enuresis is that children with enuresis have a smaller bladder capacity than normal children. This hypothesis suggests that enuretic children can hold less urine volume in the bladder before feeling the need to urinate (Scharf et al., 1987). Evidence for this etiological hypothesis is indirect and sketchy, although treatment programs have been designed to help enuretic children by increasing functional bladder capacity (Geffken, Johnson, and Walker, 1986).

Genetic causes for enuresis are zealously advocated by some authors (Fritz and Armbrust, 1982) and downplayed by others (Kanner, 1972). Enuresis does show a significant tendency to run in families. Studies reviewed by Fritz & Armbrust (1982), Scharf et al. (1987), and Scharf and Jennings (1988) indicate that as many as 70–85% of children who are enuretic have a family member who is enuretic (Shaffer, Gardner, and Hedge, 1984). The risk appears to increase with increasing genetic similarity. However, the extent to which this familial concordance is due to genetic factors or environmental factors is unclear. Enuretic families sometimes appear to regard the enuresis as normal, a type of "family tradition," which may encourage enuretic behavior in children (Kanner, 1972). The most reasonable conclusion at this point appears to be that genetic factors may contribute to some cases of enuresis, but they are neither necessary nor sufficient and must be activated by other etiological factors such as psychosocial factors. Unfortunately, the communication to parents that their child's enuresis may have a genetic component sometimes results in the mistaken belief that nothing can be done to treat the enuresis or that the only effective treatments will be medical. Absolutely no evidence exists to support this belief.

Psychological factors are frequently cited as etiologically responsible for enuresis. Hypothesized factors range from permissive or restrictive toilet-training experience to emotional problems to faulty learning. Some cases of secondary enuresis may develop as a regressive response to stress; as many as four in five cases of secondary enuresis have encountered a significant stressor in the month prior to the development of the problem (Fritz and Anders, 1979). Evidence also exists supporting the notion that enuresis may arise because of faulty learning, particularly as a result of the failure to associate a full bladder with waking up at night. Many treatment modalities are based on this assumption (Mowrer & Mowrer, 1938). Psychodynamic factors such as toilet training history and emotional disturbance may be important in individual cases, but no research exists supporting these hypothesized factors. Finally, family factors such as enmeshment between the child and parent(s) or adoption of an infantile role by the child may account for the development of enuresis in some cases.

ASSESSMENT PATTERNS

A sample assessment battery for enuresis is shown in Table 4.2.

Broad Assessment Strategies

Cognitive Assessment

Clinician-Administered.   Little has been written on the assessment of enuretic children using traditional standardized psychological tests. WISC-R and WISC-III IQ scores of enuretic children appear to be in normal ranges, with one study finding a mean Full Scale IQ score for a sample of enuretic children to be 96 (Shaffer et al., 1984). Another study (Steinhausen and Gobel, 1989) found 77% of enuretic children to have IQ scores between 86 and 115. No differences have been found between verbal and performance skills (Shaffer et al., 1984), and there is no reason to expect any particular constellation of subtest scores. The finding of normal intelligence levels in enuretic children is at odds with the view that enuretic children may be developmentally delayed across a range of abilities. Rather, empirical research suggests that their intellectual ability varies

TABLE 4.2   Sample Assessment Battery for Enuresis

BEHAVIORAL

Child Behavior Checklist or Missouri Child Behavior Checklist

SYNDROME-SPECIFIC

Child Attitude Scale for Nocturnal Enuresis
Tolerance Scale

Note: Assessment instruments are intended to supplement (not substitute for) a good clinical interview and, when possible, a structured diagnostic interview.

much like that of normal children. It is important to note, however, that most of these findings are based on groups that included both primary and secondary enuretics; some evidence exists that primary enuretics may have lower IQ scores and more developmental delays than do secondary enuretics (Shaffer et al., 1984).

Achievement test scores of enuretic children appear to be average to slightly below average (Shaffer et al., 1984), although not enough research exists to come to a definitive conclusion. Children with enuresis appear to qualify for learning disability–type diagnoses at a lower rate than do children with other psychiatric problems (Steinhausen and Gobel, 1989). Again, however, it is important to note that primary enuretics may be more at risk than secondary enuretics for a developmental disability diagnosis. Over all, current research suggests that children with enuresis show much the same performance and variability on intelligence and achievement tests as do normal children.

Psychological Assessment

Child-Report.   Because of the young age of many enuretic children, few self-report psychological tests apply to this group. Results of two studies using the Piers-Harris Children's Self Concept Scale (PHSCS) suggest that the broad self-reported self-concept of enuretic children is in the normal range (total raw score 59–60; Wagner and Geffken, 1986; Wagner and Johnson, 1988). However, this result may reflect social desirability and denial as much as positive self-concept.

Behavioral Assessment

Parent-Report.   Parent-report behavioral checklists are important components of the assessment of children with enuresis, in order to rule out co-occurring or contributing psychobehavioral problems. Studies report that as few as 15% or as many as 50% of children with enuresis may have accompanying emotional or behavior problems (Shaffer et al., 1984; Steinhausen and Gobel, 1989). Two studies using the Behavior Problem Checklist (BPC; Quay, 1977) do not report substantially higher scores on the BPC for enuretics as compared to normal children (Wagner and Geffken, 1986; Wagner and Johnson, 1988). Hence, an enuretic child should not necessarily be expected to obtain clinically elevated scores on broad-based behavior problem checklists such as the BPC, although some enuretics certainly will show associated behavior problems. In addition to the BPC, the Child Behavior Checklist (CBCL) and Missouri Children's Behavior Checklist (MCBC) can be used to investigate the presence of other or associated behavior problems. The BPC, CBCL, or MCBC should be routinely used to determine the extent to which enuresis is a focal problem or part of a behavior problem constellation.

Syndrome-Specific Tests

Child-Report

The Child Attitude Scale for Nocturnal Enuresis (Wagner and Geffken, 1986), consists of twenty-five yes-no items tapping four areas: knowledge of enuresis, feelings regarding enuresis, current child behaviors, and reactions of significant others. On the Child Attitude Scale, most children with enuresis (65%) report unhappiness about their wetting behavior. In one study, all children reported the desire to overcome enuresis (Wagner and Geffken, 1986). Hence, while general self-concept (assessed by the PHSCS) appears to be positive, children with enuresis express some focal distress about their problem. The Child Attitude Scale for Nocturnal Enuresis is also a useful measure of the child's perceptions of the environmental-parental response to their problem.

Parent-Report

A specific parent-report scale that can be useful in the assessment of enuresis is the Tolerance Scale (Morgan and Young, 1975; Butler, Brewin, and Forsythe, 1990), which measures parental attitudes toward and tolerance of enuresis. The Tolerance Scale consists of twenty yes-no items that yield a score reflecting tolerance of enuretic behavior in the child. More intolerance has been found to be related to premature withdrawal from enuresis treatment, although no evidence exists that Tolerance Scale scores are correlated with effectiveness of treatment for those families that remain in treatment (Morgan and Young, 1975). Unfortunately, the Tolerance Scale is poorly developed and described in its scale development article, which limits its usefulness (Morgan and Young, 1975). In fact, even the scoring of the Tolerance Scale is not clearly explained in Morgan and Young's (1975) article; those interested in using this scale should also consult the Method section of an article by Butler et al. (1990) to understand how the scale is scored.

Clinician-Administered

In addition to standardized psychological tests, several authors have stressed the importance of clinician-gathered interview data in diagnosing and treating the enuretic child (Copeland, Baucom-Copeland, and Perry, 1982; Scharf and Jennings, 1988). Copeland et al. (1982) suggest that the following questions are critical to an interview assessment of enuresis: family history of enuresis, child's sleeping patterns, soundness of sleeping, difficulty in awakening, dreams in conjunction with enuresis, indications of CNS problems (i.e., seizures), diabetes, urinary tract problems or infections, and indications of regressive or anxious behavior. They base their selection of these data points on the need to determine the extent to which the enuresis is the result of physiological (CNS problems, diabetes, urinary tract problems), genetic (family history), behavioral (sleeping pattern, soundness of sleep), or emotional problems (regressive/anxious behavior). Scharf and Jennings (1988) also suggest that interview questions should determine the following: primary or secondary enuresis; age at which enuresis reappeared, if it is secondary; developmental history; number of wet nights per week; timing of wetting; total sleep time; frequency and urgency of daytime urination; history of toilet training; presence of sleep disorders; attitude of child and family toward bedwetting; consequences of bed wetting; and "aggravating conditions" (Scharf and Jennings, 1988) such as major stressors.

TREATMENT OPTIONS

Behavioral Interventions

Unidimensional Behavioral Interventions

Although numerous treatments for enuresis have been suggested, the treatment programs of choice for nocturnal enuresis rely on behavioral principles. Nine unidimensional behavioral treatments have been consistently used with enuretic children and have been systematically investigated in research: urine alarm, positive practice, reinforcement for dryness, retention control training, avoidance contingency, overlearning, cleanliness training, waking schedule, and stop/start training. These techniques share several characteristics in common. First, all involve standardized responses to observable child behavior. Second, all are based on the assumption that enuresis occurs as a result of faulty learning; that is, the child either never learned to voluntarily retain urine, or the child learned a response that is incompatible with the retention of urine. Finally, they can be combined as components of multidimensional treatment programs. (These and other treatment options for enuresis are outlined in Table 4.3.)

Urine Alarm (UA) and Cleanliness Training (CT). The oldest and most widely used treatment for enuresis is the UA or "bell and pad" intervention (Mowrer and Mowrer, 1938). The bell and pad, sold commercially under such names as the "Sears Wee Alert" (see Mountjoy, Ruben, and Bradford, 1984, for a list of such devices and manufacturers), consists of two metal sheets separated by a cloth. The child sleeps on top of this device, which, when the cloth is wet, triggers an auditory alarm. In most cases the alarm wakes the child before the child has fully urinated; in other cases, the parents must wake the child. UA intervention is almost always accompanied by CT intervention (in fact, UA generally implies a combination of UA and CT), which requires the child to go to the toilet, clean himself or herself, change clothing, strip and clean the bed, remake the bed, and reset the UA apparatus (e.g., Kaplan et al., 1988). It is extremely important that the child carry out the CT on his or her own in order to assume some responsibility for the bedwetting behavior. In some cases, children's bedwetting behavior is subtly reinforced when the parent strips, cleans, and remakes the child's bed, while having a pleasant interaction with the child. Parents should be neutral rather than punitive or pleasant during

TABLE 4.3	Treatment Options for Nocturnal Enuresis

BEHAVIORAL INTERVENTIONS

Unidimensional Behavioral Interventions

> Urine alarm (UA)
> Cleanliness training (CT)
> Positive practice (PP)
> Reinforcement for dryness (RD)
> Retention control training (RCT)
> Avoidance contingency (AC)
> Overlearning (OL)
> Waking schedule (WS)
> Stop/start training (SST)

Multidimensional Behavioral Interventions

> Dry-Bed Training—UA, PP, WS, CT, RD, OL
> Full-Spectrum Home Training—UA, CT, RCT, OL

FAMILY INTERVENTIONS

Family therapy (systemic, dealing with enmeshment-disengagement issues)

MEDICATION

Imipramine

PSYCHOTHERAPY

Hypnotic techniques
Play therapy

Note: This outline of options summarizes major treatments covered in the text. Specific treatments are often combined into an intervention package. Refer to the text for additional descriptions of each treatment. This table is not necessarily an exhaustive list of all treatments available.

CT. Although numerous UA devices are commercially available, there is no evidence that one device is more effective than any other (Doleys, 1977).

Reviewing literature concerning the effectiveness of the UA, Doleys (1977) reports that it is effective in arresting enuresis in 75% of cases but that the relapse rate is 41%. Hence, the UA is an effective tool in initial arrest of enuresis, with significant risk of relapse. The risk of relapse may be decreased if the alarm is programmed to sound on a variable ratio schedule of 50-70% (70% is probably a more effective figure); that is, the alarm sounds after 70% of wetting episodes and fails to sound after 30% of episodes. Use of a variable ratio schedule may reduce the percentage of relapse by 10–20% (Doleys, 1977). Supervision of the parents during treatment and follow-up also increases the effectiveness of the UA, possibly because it encourages the parents to follow the behavior plan closely (Doleys, 1977). The UA is less effective with children who have multiple wetting episodes at night, diurnal as well as nocturnal enuresis, unsatisfactory sleeping arrangements, family problems, fear of the UA apparatus, or parents with emotional problems (Butler, Brewin, and Forsythe, 1988; Fritz and Armbrust, 1982; Dische et al., 1983).

Two major theories exist concerning the mechanism by which the UA alleviates enuretic symptoms. Classical conditioning theory suggests that repeated presentation of the bell (unconditioned stimulus) in temporal contiguity with a full bladder (conditioned stimulus) leads to association of a full bladder (conditioned stimulus) with waking up (conditioned response). Initially a full bladder while asleep is a neutral stimulus for the child and is not associated with any behavior. On the other hand, the bell or tone sounded by the enuresis alarm, if sufficiently loud, is a stimulus that interrupts sleep in the absence of any prior learning. When the child wets the bed, the bell sounds immediately, waking the child while the bladder is still full. After numerous events such as this, the child begins to associate the full bladder with the sounding of the bell and waking up.

Classical conditioning theory suggests that the bell must sound immediately in order for the child to have a full bladder which is associated with waking; delayed sounding of the bell would allow the child to empty the bladder before waking. Evidence exists that immediate sounding of the bell is associated with faster and more complete training, supporting classical conditioning theory (Doleys, 1977). Classical conditioning theory also predicts that when the unconditioned stimulus (bell) is removed, extinction of the learned response (waking up) will occur. Extinction is less likely to occur when a criterion behavior has been learned under a variable schedule. This phenomenon may account for the increased effectiveness of variable schedules in preventing relapse in enuretic children.

Operant conditioning theory posits that the UA causes behavior change by acting as an aversive event that follows a behavior. Hence, the child learns not to wet the bed in order to escape the aversive event of being awakened by a loud noise (Azrin, Sneed, and Foxx, 1974). In addition, many children regard components of cleanliness training, which follows the bell-waking sequence, as aversive. Evidence supporting this point of view is largely anecdotal and based on observations that children seem to dislike being awakened by the bell. In addition, some children express dislike and fear of the UA apparatus. In some cases the child fears being shocked or harmed by the apparatus. Practice and desensitization should reduce these concerns.

Positive Practice (PP).   PP is a technique that involves the child repeatedly acting out the process of waking up, walking to the bathroom, and going to the toilet. One specific PP technique involves having the child lie in the bed for 3 minutes, then get up and go to the bathroom; this process is repeated nine times following each bedwetting incident (Azrin et al., 1973). Modifications on this scheme are common. For example, another PP routine involves the child counting to 50, then getting out of bed, going to the bathroom, and trying to urinate; this sequence is repeated twenty times (Scharf et al., 1987). PP is rarely, if ever, used alone to treat enuresis, and its effectiveness when used alone has not been investigated. It is common as a part of multidimensional treatment packages for enuresis.

Reinforcement for Dryness (RD).   RD involves the use of praise or other rewards for dry nights. In its simplest form, RD involves having the child feel the dry sheets and then being praised for having a dry night (Azrin et al., 1973). If the child needs more frequent reinforcement, RD may be combined with a waking schedule in which the child is awakened every hour or two and asked to check the sheets; dry sheets are rewarded with praise. More extensive RD interventions involve the parents, child, and therapist agreeing on some reward that the child will receive for each dry night. These rewards may reflect primary (i.e., going out for an ice cream cone) or secondary (i.e., star chart) reinforcers (Kaplan et al., 1988). Like PP, RD is rarely used alone to treat enuresis.

Retention Control Training (RCT).   RCT (Paschalis, Kimmel, and Kimmel, 1972) is based on the theory that children with enuresis have a smaller functional bladder capacity than do normal children. This small functional bladder capacity may make it difficult for enuretic children to sleep through the night without having the need to urinate. The goal of RCT is to eliminate enuresis by increasing the functional bladder capacity (Geffken et al., 1986). Functional bladder capacity is increased by having the child drink fluids and delay urination for increasing time periods. In one specific example (Houts, Peterson, and Whelan, 1986), children drank 8 ounces of water and practiced postponing urination for a 45-minute period. For each 3-minute period that they were able to postpone urination, the children received 5 cents. The criterion of adequate functional bladder capacity was considered to have been reached when the child could postpone urination for the entire 45 minute period.

Studies of the effectiveness of RCT have yielded mixed results, leading Doleys (1977) to conclude that "(the) data do not provide strong support for retention control training as a treatment procedure for enuresis. . . . Nevertheless, there appears to be enough evidence to warrant further investigation" (pp. 46–47). RCT has been more effectively used as one component of a treatment package (Houts et al., 1986). Some evidence exists that, as part of a treatment package, RCT can be an effective contributor to outcome, at least for children with small functional bladder capacity (Houts et al., 1986; Geffken et al., 1986). Hence, it does not appear to be advisable to use RCT as the exclusive treatment for childhood nocturnal enuresis.

Avoidance Contingency (AC).   AC treatments for enuresis involve the administration of a noxious stimulus or removal of a pleasant stimulus following a wetting episode. Although punishment-based treatments were common early treatments for enuresis (Glicklich, 1951), they are relatively unusual today, primarily because of the effectiveness of less aversive methods. Some clinicians conceptualize UA treatments as AC-type treatments, since (according to operant conditioning theory) the child stops wetting to avoid being awakened by the bell. Time-out contingencies, which involve the removal of access to reinforcing places or activities following a wetting episode, are sometimes used to treat diurnal enuresis (Foxx, 1985). Although time-out does not involve the presentation of a noxious stimulus, it is a condition that the child avoids (hence an AC treatment) because pleasant activities are removed. Some evidence exists that time-out treatment may be an effective component in eliminating diurnal enuresis (Foxx, 1985). AC methods appear to have insufficient effectiveness to warrant their use in cases of nocturnal enuresis. As with all punishment techniques, AC interventions should be administered cautiously and with assurance that no harm is being done to the child.

Overlearning (OL).   OL techniques are implemented after an enuretic child has attained some criterion of dryness. They aim to reduce the relapse rate of enuretic children by giving them large amounts of liquid prior to bedtime so that they learn to retain the liquid until waking. In a typical OL regimen the child is trained (usually using a UA) until he or she achieves 14 consecutive nights of dryness. The child is then asked to drink up to 2 pints of liquid in the hour prior to bedtime and is monitored for enuretic accidents as before. Again, the child is trained to a criterion of 14 consecutive nights without bedwetting. Some evidence exists that this additional component reduces the relapse rate in enuretic children (Young and Morgan, 1972a, 1972b; Taylor and Turner, 1975). OL can be modified in terms of the dryness criterion required before OL is implemented (7–14 days is typical) and in the amount of water the child drinks prior to bedtime (1–2 pints is typical)(Taylor and Turner, 1975). Given the relatively high relapse rate found in UA treatments, OL should be considered as an adjunct to UA treatment of any child at risk of having a relapse. By definition, OL is never used alone to treat enuresis.

Waking Schedule (WS).   Waking schedules are common components of multifaceted approaches to the treatment of enuresis (Azrin et al., 1973; Whelan and Houts, 1990; Fournier et al., 1987), although their design and implementation tend to vary widely from one research study and clinical case to another. WS interventions share in common the characteristic of waking the child one or more times during the night and having the child attempt to urinate in the bathroom. In some cases the WS involves waking the child every hour throughout the night, although this rigorous schedule is usually implemented for only the first night or two of treatment (Azrin et al., 1974; Whelan and Houts, 1990). Less rigorous, ongoing WS interventions require the parents to awaken the child one to three times at prescribed intervals throughout the night. Whelan and Houts (1990), for example, used an intensive, every-hour waking schedule for the first night of their intervention, but then had parents awaken the child once, approximately 3 hours after falling asleep. Following each dry night, the waking time was moved 30 minutes earlier to the child's time of falling asleep until the WS was not required. Controversy exists as to the value of including a WS in a treatment package (Whelan and Houts, 1990), but there is agreement that a WS alone is not an effective intervention and certainly not as effective as a UA (Fournier et al., 1987). The WS schedule should not be removed from effective treatment packages until more research data are available.

Stop-Start Training (SST). SST is a less common, minimally effective treatment for enuresis that is based on the belief that bedwetting results from a weakness of the bladder sphincter muscle (Bennett et al., 1985). In SST, children are told to stop and start the flow of urine at regular intervals during daytime urination. During urination the child should pass a small amount of urine, then stop and count to 3 before continuing urination. Again, after the passing of a small amount of urine, the child should stop and count to 3. The start-stop-count sequence should be repeated six times during each urination event. This exercise is assumed to strengthen the sphincter muscle, allowing the child to retain urine more easily while asleep. The child's compliance with this regimen is expected to be monitored and reinforced by parents (Bennett et al., 1985). SST is, at best, minimally effective, with a 17% effectiveness rate (14 consecutive dry nights) reported in one study (Bennett et al., 1985). Based on this effectiveness rate, SST is clearly inferior to UA and multidimensional treatments.

Multidimensional Behavioral Interventions

In actual clinical practice it is rare to see one of the unidimensional behavioral treatments for enuresis applied alone. Even the venerable UA treatment is virtually always combined with CT, and RD is a common component of most clinical plans for enuresis. Other methods, such as OL, are *always* used in conjunction with other methods. Most clinicians combine the unidimensional behavioral treatments based on considerations for the individual case or past experiences with the behavioral treatments. UA and CT are most likely to show up in these idiosyncratic treatment plans, largely because of their demonstrated effectiveness.

Dry Bed Training. Several clinician-researchers have attempted to standardize multidimensional behavioral treatments so that they can be evaluated in outcome research. Probably the most extensively researched and well known of these is the Dry-Bed Training Procedure (DBT) developed by Azrin and colleagues (Azrin et al., 1973, 1974). DBT is a combination of UA, PP, WS, CT, RD, and OL techniques. It is implemented as follows:

The first night of training consists of intensive interventions in a variety of areas. One hour before bedtime the child is given an explanation of the DBT procedure. Then the child is given a glass of liquid to drink and the UA is placed on the child's bed. Next, the child engages in PP, which consists of laying in bed and counting to 50, then rising and walking to the bathroom, followed by an attempt to urinate. PP is repeated twenty times. When PP is over, the child is asked to drink as much as possible and is sent to bed. At hourly intervals throughout the night the child is awakened by parents and required to walk to the bathroom and attempt to urinate (Azrin et al., 1974, suggest that, for children over the age of 6, parents request that the child wait until the next hour before urinating, but this does not appear to be a consistent component of DBT [see Azrin et al., 1973]). Also at these hourly intervals the parent feels the child's sheets and praises the child for dry sheets. The child is then given something to drink and sent back to bed (Azrin et al., 1973, 1974).

On subsequent nights the UA is placed on the bed and PP is given if an accident occurred on the previous night. Then the child is reminded of the goal of remaining dry and of the procedures that will occur if he or she wets the bed. The child is then sent to bed. The child is awakened at the parents' bedtime and sent to the bathroom to attempt to urinate; the awakening time is reduced by 30 minutes following each dry night. If the child sleeps through the night without a bedwetting incident, he or she is praised at least five times during the day for not wetting the bed. Praise is withheld if the child wets the bed (Azrin et al., 1973, 1974).

When a bedwetting incident occurs, the parent disconnects the alarm, awakens the child (if the child is not already awake), gives a brief verbal reprimand, and sends the child to the bathroom to finish urinating. The child then engages in CT, and the parent resets the UA. Finally, the child engages in twenty PP trials before going to sleep. The child must also engage in twenty PP trials the next evening before bedtime when an accident has occurred the previous night (Azrin et al., 1973, 1974).

After 7 consecutive dry nights, the UA is no longer placed on the bed, and the parents inspect the child's bed each morning. If the bed is wet, CT occurs immediately and PP is implemented the following evening. If the bed is dry, the child is praised. If two accidents occur within a week, the child returns to the previous phase of treatment (Azrin et al., 1973, 1974).

Initial studies with normal (Azrin et al., 1974) and developmentally delayed (Azrin et al., 1973) children showed DBT to be extremely successful in eliminating enuresis. In normal children, enuresis was eliminated in all twenty-four subjects within 1 month; there were no major relapses during a 6-month followup. In developmentally delayed children, enuresis was eliminated in twelve subjects within 1 month; no major relapses were reported in a 3-month followup. DBT has been shown to reduce enuretic accidents by as much as 85% within a week and 95% within a month (Azrin et al., 1973).

Following the initial DBT studies, numerous researchers have attempted to replicate the original findings, to identify the most important components of DBT, and to compare DBT to other techniques. No researchers have duplicated Azrin et al.'s (1973, 1974) finding of 100% success rate and low (30%) relapse rate. Most replications find success rates of DBT of between 40% (Fincham and Spettell, 1984; Bennett et al., 1985) and 80% (Kaplan et al, 1988; Butler et al., 1988; Breit et al., 1984). Relapse rates for DBT appear to be in the 40-50% range (Breit et al., 1984). Over all, it appears to be safest to assume effectiveness rates for DBT to be in the 70–80% range and relapse rates for DBT to be in the 30–50% range.

Studies investigating important components of DBT have shown that the mode of delivery (meeting with parents in therapist's office, therapist going to the child's home, meeting with parents and child in therapist's office) is unrelated to DBT effectiveness (Keating et al., 1983). It appears that the UA is an important component of DBT (Azrin and Thienes, 1978; Besalel et al., 1980; Bollard, Nettelbeck, and Roxbee, 1982), although some variations of DBT call for omitting the UA (Azrin and Thienes, 1978). RCT does not appear to add to the effectiveness of DBT (Bollard and Nettelbeck, 1982), while a WS does appear to enhance DBT outcome (Kolko, 1987). Insufficient evidence exists to evaluate the other DBT components. Over all, the evidence appears to indicate that the UA should be included in DBT, while the other components should probably not be eliminated because of lack of knowledge in the literature to date.

Studies comparing DBT to other techniques have generally not shown DBT to be superior to UA-CT alone (Butler et al., 1988; Fincham and Spettell, 1984; Kaplan et al., 1988; Bennett et al., 1985). Relapse rates also apparently do not differ between DBT and UA-CT (Butler et al., 1990). The major disadvantage with DBT relative to UA is the commitment that DBT requires on the part of parents. The first night of intensive training, for example, allows virtually no sleep for parent or child. In addition, children sometimes rebel against the PP component of DBT, and parents sometimes find this component overly tedious. UA, on the other hand, requires minimal pre-bedtime preparation, and nighttime wakings occur only following bedwetting. Parents tend to rate UA more favorably than DBT, although there is no evidence that the effectiveness of UA or DBT is related to ratings of favorability (Fincham and Spettell, 1984). Regarding other treatments, DBT has been shown to be superior to SST and no treatment (Bennett et al., 1985). The relative effectiveness of DBT and other unidimensional behavioral treatments has not been extensively researched, but it is likely that DBT and UA-CT are the most effective treatments for enuresis. Unfortunately, it is not possible to predict for any single child whether DBT or UA-CT will be more effective, although across groups of children they seem to have similar effectiveness. UA is clearly the treatment of choice if parents seem less motivated or are willing to devote less time to treatment.

Full Spectrum Home Training. A second standardized multidimensional behavioral treatment package is Full Spectrum Home Training (FSHT; Houts, Peterson, and Whelan, 1986; Whelan and Houts, 1990). FSHT consists of UA, CT, RCT, and OL components. Parents are given a treatment manual that explains each component of FSHT and are required to record bedwetting incidents throughout the training period. The UA-CT components of FSHT are identical to the unidimensional UA-CT treatments previously described. The RCT component involves the child drinking 8 ounces of water during a "RCT Training Period" during the day. Then the child practices postponing urination for 3-minute increments of time, eventually building to a 45-minute period without urination (money at the end of each 3-minute period is used as a reward to encourage learning). The OL component is implemented following 14 consecutive dry nights. At this point the child drinks 16 ounces of water in the hour before bedtime. FSHT is considered successful when the child has achieved 14 consecutive dry nights in the OL phase.

FSHT has initial success rates of 60–75% (Houts et al., 1986; Whelan and Houts, 1990), with very low relapse rates (Houts et al., 1986). In a study comparing FSHT to UA-CT and UA-CT-RCT, Houts et al. (1986) found similar initial success rates for all three treatments. However, FSHT resulted in significantly lower relapse rates than the other two treatments; relapse rate for FSHT was only 11% at 3- and 6-month followup, compared to 44% (3-month) and 33% (6-month) for UA-CT. The lower relapse rate for FSHT has been attributed to the OL component, although replication of this result is needed. Addition of a WS component to FSHT has not been shown to increase its efficacy (Whelan and Houts, 1990). Overall, FSHT should be considered as a relatively simple multidimensional treatment for enuresis that is initially as effective as UA and may result in lower relapse rates.

Family Interventions

The need for family therapy as a component of enuresis treatment is demonstrated by studies indicating that family difficulties are significantly related to the effectiveness of UA treatment for enuresis (Dische et al., 1983). Hence, it is advisable to assess the family prior to treatment for enuresis in order to identify families who may be in need of additional intervention. Self-report scales such as the FES and the FACES-III may be particularly helpful in this regard. High scores on the FES Conflicted or Controlling factors and low scores on the FES Supportive factor may indicate the need for additional family intervention. In addition, the clinician's observations of a family structure that is covertly maintaining the enuretic behavior (Haley, 1976) would suggest the need for family intervention.

Protinsky and Dillard (1983), for example, suggest that in many cases enuresis is maintained by a coalition between one parent and the enuretic child, with the other parent disengaged from the system. Although this coalition is not acknowledged overtly by the family, it results in characteristic repetitive sequences of behavior that bring the enmeshed parent and child together. Enuresis is one such behavior sequence. In many cases this family structure serves the purpose of deflecting attention away from the marital dyad, so marital issues must be carefully observed in therapy. In order to address this problem, Protinsky and Dillard (1983) suggest a multi-part family intervention based on strategic family therapy (Haley, 1976). First, the therapist accepts the family's interpretation that the child is the presenting problem. In doing this, the therapist is able to join with and influence the family system. Second, the therapist assigns the family direct tasks that require the disengaged parent to join with the enuretic child and that create some distance between the enmeshed parent and the enuretic child. For example, the disengaged parent may be put in charge of handling the child's enuresis. Third, the therapist may use paradox in order to prevent a relapse to enuretic behavior or to maladaptive family interaction. Protinsky and Dillard (1983) suggest telling the child to deliberately engage in the enuretic behavior again. The use of paradox, however, requires considerable caution and a skillful therapist. In many cases, paradox is neither appropriate nor advised. Fourth, marital issues must be addressed, either through marital therapy or homework assignments that require more pleasant interactions between the couple. Protinsky and Dillard (1983) report some success using this technique with a sample of eight families with enuretic children.

Medication

The medication of choice for enuresis is imipramine, which is approved for use with children as young as 6 years of age (Wagner, 1987). Imipramine has been repeatedly shown to be more effective than placebo (Wiener, 1984), and it sometimes produces a therapeutic response faster than a UA (Fournier et al., 1987). The mechanism by which imipramine prevents enuresis is unclear, although it has been suggested that its antidepressant effects, effect on sleep patterns, and/or peripheral anticholinergic effects may be factors in its effectiveness (Fritz and Armbrust, 1982).

Imipramine appears to be not as effective as UA, with significant improvement shown in 20–40% of children (see Fritz and Armbrust, 1982, and Wagner, 1987, for reviews), compared with 75% rates for UA (Doleys, 1977). In fact, Wagner (1987) suggests that the effects seen in imipramine may reflect a temporary suppression of enuretic behavior, followed by spontaneous remission. Relapse rates following imipramine treatment are extremely high (40–60%; Fritz and Armbrust, 1987), probably reflecting the fact that no new behavior has been learned by the child. Some authors report relatively high rates of effectiveness for imipramine (Wiener, 1984), but these studies appear to be the exception rather than the rule. For example, at least one study (Fournier et al., 1987) reports equivalent effectiveness of imipramine and UA. Combining imipramine and UA treatments appears to result in faster improvement but does not improve the overall success rate of UA.

Wiener (1984) suggests that treatment with imipramine is appropriate for cases in which behavioral treatments are unsuccessful and for cases in which the child is extremely distressed or depressed. Other indications for imipramine use include cases in which rapid response is necessary and cases in which the parents are unable to effectively carry out a behavioral intervention. Because of the side effects and potential toxicity of imipramine, it should be used with caution. Given the efficacy of behavioral approaches, initial use of imipramine for simple cases of enuresis is generally not warranted.

Other medications such as desipramine, methedrine, amitriptyline, and nortriptyline, are sometimes prescribed for enuresis. Much less is known about the effectiveness of these medications, although none appears to be more effective than imipramine (Wagner, 1987; Fritz and Armbrust, 1982).

Psychotherapy

Hypnotic Techniques

Hypnosis is infrequently used for enuresis. However, it is occasionally cited as a treatment option for cases who have failed with standard behavioral treatment or who seem to have a strong psychodynamic component. The relatively few studies that address the use of hypnosis with enuretic children report good success rates (as high as 70%; Olness, 1975; Edwards and Van Der Spuy, 1985). However, these studies are generally not as methodologically sound as studies focusing on behavioral treatments for enuresis.

Edwards and Van Der Spuy (1985) designed a treatment plan for enuresis that involved hypnosis as its major feature. First, they seated the child in a comfortable chair and places headphones on his ears. They then played a tape that induced hypnosis with suggestions of relaxation, eye heaviness, eye closure, and drowsiness. Following induction, hypnosis was deepened by a counting-deepening technique. Once the child was in trance, suggestions were made for general relaxation, confidence, and waking up at night when experiencing a full bladder.

Edwards and Van Der Spuy (1985) report that their hypnotic technique resulted in significant increases in number of dry nights per week. Hypnotherapy was more effective than no treatment, trance alone, and brief psychotherapy. Interestingly, hypnotherapy and behavioral treatment (UA) did not differ in effectiveness. Because of the limited research on hypnotherapeutic treatment of enuresis, hypnotherapy should be considered either as an adjunct to behavioral therapy or as an option for treatment-resistant enuretics.

Other Psychotherapy Techniques

In addition to hypnotherapy, psychotherapeutic modalities such as play therapy (e.g., Axline, 1969), psychodynamically oriented therapy, or supportive psychotherapy are occasionally used for enuresis. Little has been written about any of these techniques, but what little evidence exists indicates that they have minimal effects on enuretic symptoms (Werry and Cohrssen, 1965; Fritz and Armbrust, 1982). Play and psychodynamic psychotherapy focus on themes of bladder control, toileting, and parental response to enuresis. Particularly in play therapy, it is important to have a play house with bathroom and bedroom to allow the child to express themes relevant to enuresis.

Psychotherapy is indicated in cases involving other psychopathology in addition to enuresis. In these cases, psychotherapy should be used in conjunction with one of the behavioral interventions for enuresis. When enuresis is combined with other forms of psychopathology, the enuresis sometimes results from the psychopathology; as the psychopathology abates, the enuresis wanes as well. In addition, enuresis can create its own stresses, which can then be managed in play therapy.

TREATMENT OF DIURNAL ENURESIS

In contrast to the explosion of research and clinical techniques to address nocturnal enuresis, little has been written on treatment of diurnal enuresis. Parents tend to regard diurnal enuresis as more "deliberate," perhaps because sleep does not serve as an excuse for the enuretic episodes. The causes of diurnal enuresis, however, are multiple, ranging from poor monitoring of need to urinate to power struggles between the child and parents. In most cases a reinforcement schedule for appropriate urination in the toilet and dryness during the day (RD), combined with cleanliness training (CT) and conspicuous monitoring of enuretic behavior, results in a remission of the diurnal enuretic behavior (Foxx, 1985). Regular bathroom trips during the day also assist in the elimination of this behavior. The effectiveness of RCT for diurnal enuresis has not been extensively studied, although it seems as though this may be a potential intervention as well. For cases in which the enuresis seems to be a result of other child or family psychopathology, psychotherapy or family therapy may be warranted. (Treatment options for diurnal enuresis are outlined in Table 4.4.)

A common problem in the case of diurnal enuresis is the hiding of wet underwear by the child. This can undermine CT and RD interventions by giving the appearance of dryness when the child is actually continuing to wet his or her pants during the day. Hiding underwear can be discouraged by the use of two methods: First, each pair of the child's underwear can be labeled with a day of the week, with the child given access to seven labeled pairs of underwear for each week. Each morning when waking up and evening before sleeping, the child must show that he or she is still wearing the proper underwear. Alternatively, each pair of underwear can be numbered, and the number of the underwear for the day is then recorded and checked by the parent. When underwear is wet or soiled, the child is given a different pair of underwear, and the new number is recorded (if days of the week are used, the parent must have an additional supply of day-labeled underwear for use if the primary underwear is soiled). A second method of discouraging underwear hiding (often combined with the first method) involves punishing the child (usually with time-out or restriction of privileges) if hidden underwear is found.

TABLE 4.4   Treatment Options for Diurnal Enuresis

BEHAVIORAL INTERVENTIONS

Cleanliness training (CT)
Reinforcement for dryness (RD)
Toileting schedule
Retention control training (RCT)
Underwear marking

FAMILY INTERVENTIONS

Family therapy (systemic, dealing with enmeshment-disengagement issues)

PSYCHOTHERAPY

Play therapy

Note: This outline of options summarizes major treatments covered in the text. Specific treatments are often combined into an intervention package. Refer to the text for additional descriptions of each treatment. This table is not necessarily an exhaustive list of all treatments available.

■ Encopresis

☐ CLINICAL DESCRIPTION

Diagnostic Considerations

Functional encopresis is defined by DSM-IV as the discharge of feces into inappropriate places; the encopretic behavior may or may not be voluntary. As with enuresis, encopresis involves the diagnosis of a behavior that is normal at one stage of life (e.g., infancy) and abnormal at a later time in life. The stage at which such behavior becomes worthy of psychiatric diagnosis is arbitrarily set at age 4. In order to be diagnosed with encopresis, children must have one or more encopretic events per month for at least 3 months. Because encopresis cannot be the result of a physical disorder (unless constipation is involved), a medical examination is recommended before encopresis is diagnosed.

Encopresis can be subdivided based on several parameters: involuntary vs. intentional; retentive versus not retentive; primary versus secondary; and diurnal versus nocturnal. Involuntary encopresis is often the result of the retention of feces, which results in constipation and fecal impaction. When feces overflows the impaction (usually in liquid form), encopresis occurs. The retention of feces in the first place may be caused by a multiplicity of factors, including fear of defecating, oppositional tendencies, unwillingness to defecate, or a previous physical illness; functional retention of feces need not be intentional. Intentional encopresis usually occurs as the result of anger, oppositional behavior, or a power struggle between parent and child; it is rarely associated with constipation or impaction. Involuntary/retentive encopresis appears to be more common than intentional/nonretentive encopresis (Wald and Handen, 1987). Involuntary/retentive encopresis is subtyped and coded in DSM-IV as Encopresis "With Constipation and Overflow Incontinence"; intentional/ nonretentive encopresis is diagnosed as being "Without Constipation or Overflow Incontinence."

As with enuresis, the primary-secondary distinction in encopresis is based on the prior acquisition of toileting skills. For primary encopresis a child may not have achieved total fecal continence for 1 year. Secondary encopresis follows a year of total fecal continence (Doleys, 1989). Also mirroring the enuresis classifications, diurnal encopresis occurs during the day, while nocturnal encopresis occurs at night.

Estimates of the incidence of functional encopresis vary widely, from 1% to nearly 8% of children, becoming more rare at older ages (Doleys, 1989; Fritz and Armbrust, 1982; American Psychiatric Association, 1994). The 1% prevalence estimate for children age 5 and older is most widely accepted (American Psychiatric Association, 1994). Some authors (i.e., Protinsky and Kersey, 1983; Fritz and Armbrust, 1982) report that most encopresis is of the diurnal type, although these conclusions appear to be based on clinical observation rather than epidemiological study. The incidence of encopresis appears to decrease sharply at about age 7, to less than 1% (Knopf, 1979). Males outnumber females by as much as 6 to 1 (Doleys, 1989; Protinsky and Kersey, 1983).

Appearance and Features

(Appearance and features of encopresis are listed in Table 4.5.) Encopretic children rarely give advance notice that an encopretic event is about to occur, aside from adopting characteristic postures or facial expressions. Following occurrence of the event, they may resume their activity until it is convenient to change pants, or, more rarely, they may seek to change their clothing immediately. Typically, children with encopresis attempt to hide their problem, often by hiding the soiled clothing. Upon confrontation by the parent, they may continue to deny the problem, even in the face of physical evidence. The degree of discomfort that the child has about the encopresis varies from child to child. Some children (probably more involuntary encopretics) are upset and ashamed about the episodes, but the majority (probably more intentional encopretics) act unconcerned about the symptom (Fritz and Armbrust, 1982). Deliberate smearing of feces is unusual (Fritz and Armbrust, 1982), although encopretic children sometimes accidentally spread the feces in their attempt to clean it up or to hide it.

Upon interview, it is sometimes found that the encopretic child has unusual beliefs about toileting. Some children have a fear of the toilet, while others simply do not see the importance of using the toilet. In some cases of encopresis the children indicate that they do not want to leave a favored activity to go to the bathroom. They then wait until it is too late to make it to the toilet in time. Family patterns of response to encopresis also may reveal insufficient motivation for the child to become toilet-trained. For example, children

---

TABLE 4.5   Appearance and Features of Encopresis

COMMON FEATURES

Defecating into inappropriate place
Retention of feces with overflow of impaction (retentive type)
Use of defecation to manipulate environment (intentional type)
Age 4–7 years
Primarily males
Adoption of characteristic location, posture, or expression prior to encopretic event
Hiding soiled clothing

OCCASIONAL FEATURES

Unusual beliefs about toileting
Not wanting to interrupt activity to defecate
Family response patterns rewarding encopresis (e.g., attention)
Peer rejection/isolation

Note: The features listed above are often seen but are not universal. Some features may be diagnostically relevant or required, while others may not be required for diagnosis. "Common" features are typical of the disorder; "occasional" features appear frequently but are not necessarily seen in a majority of cases.

who are allowed to continue with a favored activity even after an encopretic even are being rewarded for being encopretic.

As the child becomes older, encopresis can have familial and social effects. Similar to enuresis, encopresis can become a significant family stressor, although many families with an encopretic child simply incorporate the encopresis into usual family life. For example, the child may be sent to school with an extra pair of pants and underpants; in more extreme cases the child may be forced by parents to wear a diaper or training pants. On family outings a "clean-up kit" may be brought along, acting as a silent recognition that the encopresis will occur and nothing can be done about it. Parents may adopt an attitude of sympathy and indulgence toward the encopretic child, particularly if one of the parents was encopretic. This adoption of encopresis as a family trait often indicates that the child and family will not give up the encopretic symptoms easily.

The social effects of encopresis depend on where the child has an encopretic event. Many encopretic children have problems only in one place or situation. As long as they are cleaned up before leaving the situation, their problem does not affect their relationships in other situations. Other encopretic children have unpredictable encopretic events that occur in many situations. When an event or its aftermath is noticed by peers, ridicule and isolation may result. The encopretic child may be seen as "dirty" or as a "baby." This teasing and isolation can occur even after the encopresis is cured.

Etiology

Multiple etiological factors are likely to be responsible for encopresis, and the factors are likely to vary from one case to another (Fritz and Armbrust, 1982; Wald and Handen, 1987; Protinsky and Kersey, 1983). The tendency for encopresis to run in families has been noted by several authors (Bellman, 1966; Wald and Handen, 1987), suggesting a possible genetic component. However, the family incidence of encopresis, while higher than chance levels, is relatively low (1% of mothers, 15% of fathers, and 9% of siblings of encopretic children were found to be encopretic by Bellman [1966]). In addition, methods of and attitudes toward toilet training tend to run in families and could be as responsible as genetics for any family history of encopresis. Over all, the genetic etiology of encopresis has not been thoroughly studied, and existing evidence suggests that any genetic influence is likely to be weak (Doleys, 1989).

Toilet-training behavior has also been suggested as a possible etiological factor (Bemporad et al., 1978). Wald and Handen (1987), for example, review studies suggesting that inconsistent toilet training approaches, such as alternating between rigidity and permissiveness, cause encopresis in children. Harsh or premature toilet training may also be responsible for some cases of encopresis (Fritz and Armbrust, 1982; Levine, 1975). Fritz and Armbrust (1982) suggest that the toddler may use encopretic behavior as one of the few outlets for demonstrating independence and retaliating against parents during toilet training. The potential etiological role of toilet training suggests that toilet-training history should be carefully evaluated prior to treatment.

Other potentially significant etiological factors in the development of encopresis are family pathology (Protinsky and Kersey, 1983), co-occurring psychopathology in the child (Fritz and Armbrust, 1982), secondary gain for encopretic behavior (Wald and Handen, 1987), fear of being flushed down the toilet (Fritz and Armbrust, 1982), desire to remain in a dependent role, and stress. Some children are encopretic simply because their parents have not sufficiently emphasized the importance of going to the toilet. Although these factors may explain individual cases of encopresis, insufficient evidence exists to establish any of them as significant for a large percentage of encopretic children. Stress has been the most consistently cited contributing factor in clinical and research work (Fritz and Armbrust, 1982; Bellman, 1966; Wald and Handen, 1987). Stressful events such as starting school, parental separation, birth of a sibling, and family conflict have been found to be present in a large percentage of encopretic children (70% in Bellman's [1966] study). Stressful events may be more important in cases of secondary encopresis.

ASSESSMENT PATTERNS

A sample assessment battery for encopresis is shown in Table 4.6.

Broad Assessment Strategies

Cognitive Assessment

Clinician-Administered.   A first consideration in the assessment of the child with encopresis is developmental maturity. Encopresis cannot be diagnosed in a child with a mental age of less than 4 years. Informally, developmental maturity can be observed and discussed with the parent. More formal assessment would involve giving an intelligence test such as the WISC-III (WPPSI-R if the child is under age 6) or SB:FE, in addition to gathering information about social-developmental maturity and level of independent functioning. A subgroup of encopretics are mentally retarded or have neurological problems that will emerge in lower performance on intelligence tests. However, the vast majority of encopretics are intellectually and neurologically normal and score in the average ranges (IQ of 90–110) on intelligence tests (Doleys, 1989; Fritz and Armbrust, 1982; Kolko, 1989). The risk that the encopresis is due to a medical

TABLE 4.6   Sample Assessment Battery for Encopresis

BEHAVIORAL

Child Behavior Checklist or Missouri Child Behavior Checklist

Note: Assessment instruments are intended to supplement (not substitute for) a good clinical interview and, when possible, a structured diagnostic interview.

or developmental problem is greater in the mentally disabled/neurologically impaired subgroup of encopretics.

Psychological Assessment

Child-Report. A major concern in the assessment and treatment of the child with encopresis is the effect of the disorder on the self-esteem of the child. Such children routinely receive messages from peers, siblings, and parents that their behavior is undesirable, dirty, and embarrassing. Because these messages occur at a time of formation of self-esteem, justifiable concern exists about the way in which these children integrate their encopretic behaviors and the responses of others into their self-concept. Using the PHSCS, Owens-Stively (1987) found that encopretics had lower total, behavior, happiness, and popularity self-esteem than did normal children. These results indicate that encopretic children are at risk to feel that they are a problem, that they are disliked by other children, that they are unhappy, and that they are dissatisfied with themselves. On the other hand, Stark et al. (1990) found that encopretics' self-esteem is higher than that of psychiatric outpatient children. Hence, the self-esteem of encopretics appears to fall between that of normals and psychiatric outpatients. Self-esteem does not appear to predict treatment outcome, although children who are successfully treated report significant increases in self-esteem (Stark et al., 1990).

Behavioral Assessment

Parent-Report. Several authors suggest that children with encopresis will show higher levels of overall behavior problems, particularly those characteristic of an attention deficit (Fritz and Armbrust, 1982; Gabel et al., 1986). These behavior problems are thought to be a result of the social consequences and embarrassment that result from encopresis (Gabel et al., 1986), although behavior problems may be the cause of encopresis in some cases.

On the CBCL, children age 6–11 with encopresis scored, on average, 10 T-score points above the normative sample on the schizoid, uncommunicative, depressed, obsessive-compulsive, somatic, social withdrawal, hyperactive, aggressive, sex problems, delinquent, and cruel scales (Gabel et al., 1986). Nearly 50% of these encopretic children had total behavior problem scores at or above the 90th percentile. The most frequently endorsed CBCL items involved disobedience at home, being constipated, arguing a lot, and being self-conscious. Interestingly, only 10% of the sample reported smearing feces (Gabel et al., 1986). The CBCL scores of the encopretics were lower than those of other children brought for outpatient mental health services (Gabel et al., 1986). Over all, then, encopretic children appear to have a higher-than-average level of behavior problems, as rated by parents. This elevation, however, appears to occur across most or all behavior problem categories. No evidence exists that encopretic children show a particular pattern of behavior problems such as stubbornness or social withdrawal (Gabel et al., 1986).

Although studies have found that encopresis treatment outcome is related to the child's initial level of behavior problems, some disagreement exists as to the exact nature of this relationship. Using the CBCL, Gabel, Chandra, and Shindledecker (1988) found that very high and very low CBCL Internalizing (withdrawal, depression, internal emotional problems) and Externalizing (acting-out, aggressive, overactive problems) behavior problem scores were associated with poor treatment outcome. Average CBCL scores were associated with positive treatment outcome. Stark et al. (1990), on the other hand, found only high levels of behavior problems to be associated with poor treatment outcome. In their study, 25% of treatment successes had other behavioral problems, while 80% of treatment failures experienced other behavioral problems. Both studies support the conclusion that significant levels of behavior problems, as measured on parent-report checklists, are associated with poorer treatment outcome. The relationship between low reported behavior problems and poor treatment outcome found by Gabel et al. (1988) may reflect parental beliefs that their child's behaviors (including encopresis) did not present a significant problem. This may have been subtly communicated to the child in the form of reduced parental pressure to change.

Family Assessment

Parent-Report. Despite the potential importance of the family for the etiology and treatment of encopresis (Protinsky and Kersey, 1983), little research has been done on the standardized assessment of the encopretic family. Administration of the FES may provide some insight into the family dynamics of the encopretic family. Encopretic families who are overly permissive may be expected to show low scores on the Control and Organization subscales, coupled with high scores on the Independence subscale. An overly restrictive/punitive family would be expected to show high Conflict, Control, Moral-Religious Emphasis, and Achievement Orientation scale scores, and low Independence scores. Particularly important to note are discrepancies between father- and mother-report of the family environment (the same goes for behavior problems) because these may indicate inconsistent parenting or subtle family conflict.

Syndrome-Specific Tests

Clinician-Administered

No widely recognized scale of encopretic behaviors and related issues exists. Therefore, the clinician must rely on interview to assess encopretic-specific issues. Important issues to assess on interview are frequency of encopretic episodes, time of occurrence, toilet training history, parental beliefs/attitudes about toilet training, family history of encopresis, whether the child had ever been toilet trained, current stresses, and antecedents and consequences of encopresis. Although no evidence exists that these variables are related to treatment outcome when a standard treatment regimen is used (Stark et al., 1990), knowledge of these variables may assist in the selection of a treatment modality for encopresis.

☐   TREATMENT OPTIONS

Four major types of treatments (see Table 4.7) are routinely used for encopresis, with substantial overlap between all types. In fact, with the exception of medical treatments, it is rare to see only one type of treatment used for encopresis. Treatment for encopresis should always be accompanied by careful recording of encopretic and related behavior. A typical simple behavior-recording plan asks parents to record the time of encopretic event, type of stool, what the child was doing, antecedents of the behavior, and consequences of the behavior. Records can be compiled into weekly charts of encopretic behavior to track trends in the child's progress. In addition to recording encopretic events, events of independent toileting may also be recorded. For example, number of times the child enters the bathroom independently may be a goal of therapy that is tracked carefully.

TABLE 4.7   Treatment Options for Encopresis

MEDICAL MANAGEMENT

Cathartic medications (enemas and suppositories)—for cases involving constipation
Dietary changes

BEHAVIORAL INTERVENTIONS

Self-monitoring
Toileting schedule
Reinforcement for clean underwear
Reinforcement for use of toilet
Time-out for soiling
The "bathroom game" (see Bornstein et al., 1983)
Biofeedback
Underwear marking

FAMILY INTERVENTIONS

Family therapy (systemic, dealing with enmeshment-disengagement issues)

PSYCHOTHERAPY

Play therapy
Cognitive-behavioral challenges of irrational toileting beliefs

Note: This outline of options summarizes major treatments covered in the text. Specific treatments are often combined into an intervention package. Refer to the text for additional descriptions of each treatment. This table is not necessarily an exhaustive list of all treatments available.

Medication and Related Medical Interventions

Because the majority of secondary encopretic cases involve or result from constipation, medical management of the encopretic behavior is routine. Often this is combined with a behavioral intervention, but medical treatment sometimes occurs alone as well. Medical treatment begins with the use of cathartic medications (enemas and suppositories) to eliminate constipation (Kolko, 1989; Waksman, 1983; Stark et al., 1990). This initial phase may last from several days (Stark et al., 1990) to 2 weeks (Kolko, 1989; Waksman, 1983), depending on treatment protocol and response of the child to the medications. During (or sometimes following) the cathartic medication period the child is administered mineral oil two or three times per day in order to maintain adequate bowel functioning (Kolko, 1989; Stark et al., 1990). Finally, diet is changed to include more high-fiber foods that promote regular bowel functioning (Houts, Mellon, and Whelan, 1988; Wald and Handen, 1987). Behavioral components such as sitting on the toilet for 10 minutes following each meal (Stark et al., 1990) and regular toileting trips (Kolko, 1989) are common additional components to these medical regimes.

Medical management of encopresis appears to be frequently effective, although a lack of adequately controlled studies prevents a firm estimate of its success rate. Stark et al. (1990) report a success rate of 33% for medical treatment alone. Success rates for combined medical and behavioral treatment packages appear to be higher, in the 60-70% range (Wald & Handen, 1987). However, numerous case-study reports document the effectiveness of medical treatments in individual cases (Waksman, 1983; Houts et al., 1988). Because of the relative ease with which behavioral components can be added to medical treatments, a combined medical-behavioral approach appears to be the most prudent.

Behavioral Interventions

Behavioral treatments for encopresis generally focus on the use of reinforcement to shape or encourage appropriate toileting behavior. As just noted, they are generally combined with medical treatments because of the high proportion of encopretic children with retentive encopresis. Retentive encopresis generally necessitates the use of some type of enema and dietary plan, but the actual use of the toilet often needs to be shaped using behavioral principles.

The magnitude of the behavioral intervention is largely dependent on the attitude and motivation of the child. Some children are highly motivated to overcome the encopretic symptomatology. For these children, some simple self-monitoring, dietary change, and a toileting schedule are sufficient. Other children merely need encouragement from parents in the form of talking about the encopresis, explaining the need for the child to change behavior, and praising appropriate behavior. In reality, however, these types of children rarely come to the clinician's notice because they are "cured" by their parents. More extensive behavioral plans are designed for resistant and/or unmotivated encopretic children.

Knell and Moore (1990), for example, describe a behavioral plan for use with children who appear to have little motivation to be toilet trained. Their plan reinforces the encopretic child for clean underwear and appropriate use of the toilet. Parents check the child for soiled underwear four times a day: 12:30 p.m., 3:30 p.m., 6:30 p.m., and bedtime. If the child's underwear is not soiled, the parents give a sticker that can be displayed on a prominent, colorful chart. If the child's underwear is soiled, the child must clean his or her pants, change underwear, and place the soiled clothing in an appropriate place. The child is also placed on the toilet for 10 minutes approximately one-half hour after each meal. Although not described by Knell and Moore, a valuable addition to this scheme would be the awarding of a star for each (half-hour) post-meal bathroom trip that the child performs completely on his or her own. This component, which resembles the behavioral intervention suggested by Kolko (1989), would further encourage independent toileting skills. Knell and Moore also suggest telling the child that the daily enema will not have to be administered on days when the child has a bowel movement; this negative reinforcement component is intended as a further motivation for the child to engage in positive toileting skills.

O'Brien, Ross, and Christophersen (1986) describe a medical-behavioral intervention designed for treatment-resistant children. Their plan consists of initial evaluation for medical causes, followed by administration of two enemas to eliminate constipation. Each morning the child is required to sit on the toilet for 5 minutes; if the child fails to defecate, a suppository is administered. Each afternoon, the child's pants are monitored for soiling at 90-minute intervals, and the child is required to sit on the toilet for 5 minutes once. After soiling occurs, the child is required to clean himself or herself, clean the underwear, and change clothes. After appropriate toilet use the child is reinforced by engaging with the parent in a preferred activity for 15 minutes. Finally, diet is modified to include more bulk and fiber foods. O'Brien et al. (1986) found their intervention to be highly effective with two of the four children in their study and mildly effective with the other two children. To address intermittent accidents in the other two children, they added a punishment component in which soiling incidents were followed by correction, ten positive practice (PP) trials, a 5-minute time-out, and six hourly 5-minute toilet sits. This mild punishment procedure further reduced soiling incidents.

Bornstein et al. (1983) suggest a unique behavioral plan that they call the "bathroom game." This game makes use of the belief that variable reinforcement of appropriate toileting behavior will produce more rapid and longer-lasting changes in behavior. In the bathroom game the child is given a blank card with seven rows (one for each day of the week) and two columns (labeled "Soiling" and "Bowel Movement"), for a total of fourteen day-behavior cells. If the child soils on a particular day, a "Y" is marked in the "Soiling" column for that day; if the child has an appropriate bowel movement, a "Y" is marked in the "Bowel Movement" column for that day. At the end of the week the child's card is compared to a card held by the therapist. The therapist's card is identical to the child's, except that half (i.e., seven) of the therapist's day-behavior cells have stars in them. For each Bowel Movement cell in which the child has a "Y" and the corresponding cell on the therapist's card has a star, the child is awarded 50 cents; for each starred Soiling cell in which the child has a "Y", 25 cents are taken away (other reinforcers could be used as well). The proportion of stars on the therapist's card can gradually be reduced to allow fading of the treatment. Bornstein et al. (1983) report positive results of their technique in a case study, but common sense suggests that their complex technique could be used only with older or fairly intelligent children.

In general, behavioral techniques for encopresis rely primarily on positive reinforcement and practice to achieve a decrease in encopretic behavior. However, punishment, if properly used in certain cases, may also assist in decreasing the behavior. Punishment is most likely to be appropriate in cases of voluntary encopresis when the child does not have sufficient negative contingencies to engage in normal toileting behavior. Such children are typically encopretic only at home and do not regard the smell or sensation of feces as aversive (hence reducing the effectiveness of CT). Furthermore, they are not motivated by their parents' admonitions or by the responses of their siblings.

When punishment is incorporated into a behavioral plan for encopresis, several points must be covered. First, the parents should speak with the child before the implementation of the plan. The child should be told that the encopretic behavior is no longer acceptable, and a description of the punishment contingency should be given. If an encopretic event occurs, the punishment should be administered matter of factly, and every effort should be made *not* to shame or scold the child. Examples of punishments that are typically used are time-out (which technically is time out from reinforcement, but is regarded by most children as a punishment), withholding TV time, or removal of a favored toy for a specified period of time. PP and a toileting schedule are also seen by encopretic children as a form of punishment. Punishment should be used extensively only if more basic medical-behavioral interventions (including the mild punishment of CT) have failed.

Numerous variations of these behavioral schemes exist, but all have in common the collection of behavioral data, the utilization of underwear checks and toileting trips, control of access to underwear, CT, reinforcement for appropriate toileting behavior, and eventual fading of the intervention (Doleys, 1989). Most include a simultaneous medical regimen of enemas, suppositories, and dietary change, while some have punishment as a component. Biofeedback is becoming integrated into some behavioral packages, particularly for use with children who appear to have difficulty monitoring rectal sensations or who have poor sphincter control (Kaplan, 1985).

Wald and Handen (1987) review studies suggesting success rates of 61–78% for behavioral-medical treatments, although many of these studies rely on small samples. Some authors suggest that behavioral treatments are effective for nocturnal as well as diurnal encopresis (O'Brien et al., 1986), although the rarity of nocturnal encopresis makes systematic study of this point difficult. Perhaps because of these high success rates, behavioral treatments are commonly used for encopresis.

As with diurnal enuresis, hiding soiled underwear is a common problem in encopresis. Solutions for preventing hidden underwear are also similar to those for diurnal enuresis: First, each pair of the child's underwear can be labeled with a day of the week, with the child given access to seven labeled pairs of underwear for each week. Each morning when waking up and each evening before sleeping, the child must show that he or she is still wearing the proper underwear. Alternatively, each pair of underwear can be numbered, and the number of the underwear for the day is then recorded and checked by the parent. When underwear is soiled, the child is given a different pair of underwear, and the new number is recorded (if days of the week are used, the parent must have an additional supply of day-labeled underwear for use if the primary underwear is soiled). Underwear marking is generally combined with punishment (usually with time-out or restriction of privileges) if hidden underwear is found.

Family Interventions

Family therapy is occasionally used to treat encopresis, sometimes as an adjunct to behavioral therapy (e.g., Berrigan and Stedman, 1989). The value of a family approach to the treatment of encopresis can be inferred from three points of view: First, encopresis often has a significant *effect* on family life, provoking negative responses from parents and siblings and sometimes serving as a source of excitement. Second, parents occasionally have difficulty implementing a behavior plan because of family pathology such as differing discipline styles. In such cases the behavioral treatment of the encopresis activates a maladaptive family interaction pattern. Third, encopresis could be maintained by family pathology, as when a child and mother enmesh over the encopretic symptom.

Protinsky and Kersey (1983) propose a family theory and family therapy for encopresis that closely resembles the intervention proposed by Protinsky and Dillard (1983) for enuresis (see first section of this chapter). Similar to the family treatment for enuresis, Protinsky and Kersey's (1983) family therapy for encopresis borrows heavily from the strategic principles of Haley (1976) and follows a sequence of steps. First, the therapist joins with the family and accepts the child as the presenting problem. Second, the therapist identifies maladaptive coalitions in the family (usually enmeshment between one parent and the child, accompanied by disengagement of the other parent) and uses direct tasks to restructure the family organization. For example, the disengaged parent may be required to implement the behavioral plan. Third, paradoxical interventions may be used to counter any actual or anticipated resistance from the family (these interventions can be risky and require a trained therapist). Finally, the parents are encouraged to engage in marital counseling if this is needed. Protinsky and Kersey (1983) report success (86% success rate) in the implementation of this method in the clinical setting; however, no controlled research is available.

Other types of family therapy use a general systems approach that combines principles of structural (Minuchin, 1974) and strategic (Haley, 1976) family therapy to restructure a maladaptive family organization. The systems approach conceptualizes the family as an interactional system within which the encopretic symptom serves a function. Because the symptom has a function within the system, it cannot be changed without a corresponding change in the system. Structural techniques (Minuchin, 1974) emphasize direct manipulation of boundaries and coalitions in the therapy situation, while strategic techniques (Haley, 1976) require the use of homework assignments and paradox to alter family interaction patterns. Systems family therapy for encopresis begins with an "assessment" of the family structure (McColgan, Pugh, and Pruitt, 1985). In this assessment the role of the child in the structure of the family is determined. Certain maladaptive interaction patterns are common and thus are routinely sought in such families. These include coalitions between one parent and the encopretic child, disengagement of one parent, difficulty expressing conflict in the family, marital conflict, weak boundaries, and enmeshment throughout the entire family system.

Following the assessment phase the disengaged parent is brought into the family system (by use of therapist attention, homework, and/or paradox), and the enmeshed relationship between the other parent and child is weakened. Traditional behavioral interventions for encopresis are implemented, and failures of these interventions are used to show problems in the family system. If marital conflict exists, marital therapy sessions are encouraged. Sibling boundaries are strengthened in the case of disengaged siblings and are weakened in the case of enmeshed siblings. Over all, the encopresis is treated as a symptom of family pathology, which is the focus of therapy (McColgan et al., 1985; Wells and Hinkle, 1990).

Psychotherapy

Play Therapy

Play therapy is a commonly used component of therapy for encopresis, although virtually no studies exist documenting its effectiveness for this particular disorder. Nondirective play therapy such as that described by Axline (1969) can be helpful in assisting young children with expression of feelings. This goal may be particularly important in the case of the child who has endured overly restrictive toilet training and is rebelling against the structure imposed by parents. In Axlinian Play Therapy for encopretic children, the therapist is warm, accepting, patient, permissive, nondirective, respectful of the child, and reflects the child's feelings. Only a few restrictions and expectations exist: The child may not inflict self-damage or hurt the therapist, and the child may not damage the playroom or any materials in it (Axline, 1969). Within these parameters the child chooses the topic, range, speed, and emotional tone of the play. Axline (1969) believed that the child would develop a sense of self and would grow to his or her self-potential within such an open, permissive atmosphere. While this admittedly may not be beneficial for all encopretic children, it may be helpful for those who have experienced conditional acceptance, shame, and loss of self-esteem during toilet training.

Knell and Moore (1990) suggest a more directive form of play therapy that incorporates cognitive-behavioral principles to combat encopresis. Their technique begins with nondirective play. When specific encopresis-related themes emerge, the therapist addresses these with cognitive-behavioral techniques. For example, Knell and Moore (1990) describe a shaping technique in which the child is playing with a toy bear near the toilet. The child, however, avoids any toileting play with the bear. In response to this avoidance, the therapist has the bear gradually approach the toilet and use the toilet appropriately. If phobic or anxious behavior is played out (e.g., child flushes a doll down the toilet), the therapist can allow the child to experience the anxious situation by sitting the doll on the toilet (the cognitive-behavioral technique of exposure) but without the negative consequence of being flushed. Irrational beliefs are addressed by having the dolls express them and then having other dolls comment on their irrationality or model positive beliefs. Over all, the technique involves encouraging the child to express and address toileting problems through play. Although the initial free expression of feelings and concern is Axlinian, the directive play response of the therapist is designed to deliberately move the child to more adaptive toileting attitudes and behavior.

Evaluation of Encopresis Treatments

Unlike enuresis, comparative studies of treatment outcome have not been performed for the various encopresis treatments. Clinically the most widely used (and probably most effective) treatment is a combination of the medical and behavioral approaches, implemented by a mental health clinician-physician team. If the child appears to have associated behavioral problems or significant psychodynamic issues related to toilet training, play therapy should be added to this medical-behavioral therapy. Likewise, if family pathology is apparent or the family is having obvious trouble implementing the behavioral-medical plan, a family therapy component will likely be valuable. Flexible choice in the modality of treatment combined with consistent application of treatment principles appears to be the key in addressing encopresis.

■ References

American Psychiatric Association. (1994). *Diagnostic and statistical manual of mental disorders* (4th ed.). Washington, DC: Author.

Axline, V. M. (1969). *Play therapy*. New York: Ballantine.

Azrin, N. H., Sneed, T. J., and Foxx, R. M. (1973). Dry Bed: A rapid method of eliminating bedwetting (enuresis) of the retarded. *Behavior Research and Therapy, 11,* 427–434.

_____ . (1974). Dry-Bed Training: Rapid elimination of childhood enuresis. *Behavior Research and Therapy, 12,* 147–156.

Azrin, N. H., and Thienes, P. M. (1978). Rapid elimination of enuresis by intensive learning without a conditioning apparatus. *Behavior Therapy, 9,* 342–354.

Bellman, M. M. (1966). Studies on encopresis. *Acta Paediatrica Scandinavia, 56* (Suppl. 170), 1–151.

Bemporad, J. R., Kresch, R. A., Asnes, R., and Wilson, A. (1978). Chronic neurotic encopresis as a paradigm of a multifactorial psychiatric disorder. *Journal of Nervous and Mental Disease, 166,* 472–479.

Bennett, G. A., Walkden, V. J., Curtis, R. H., Burns, L. E., Rees, J., Gosling, J. A., and McQuire, N. L. (1985). Pad-and-Buzzer Training, Dry-Bed Training, and Stop-Start Training in the treatment of primary nocturnal enuresis. *Behavioral Psychotherapy, 13,* 309–319.

Berrigan, L. P., and Stedman, J. M. (1989). Combined application of behavioral techniques and family therapy for the treatment of childhood encopresis: A strategic approach. *Family therapy, 16,* 51–57.

Besalel, V. A., Azrin, N. H., Thienes-Hontos, P., and McMorrow, M. (1980). Evaluation of a parent's manual for training enuretic children. *Behavior Research and Therapy, 18,* 358–360.

Bollard, J., and Nettelbeck, T. (1982). A component analysis of dry bed training for treatment of bedwetting. *Behavior Research and Therapy, 20,* 383–390.

Bollard, J., Nettelbeck, T., and Roxbee, L. (1982). Dry bed training for childhood bedwetting: A comparison of group with individually administered parent instruction. *Behavior Research and Therapy, 20,* 209–217.

Bornstein, P. H., Balleweg, B. J., McLellarn, R. W., Wilson, G. L., Sturm, C. A., Andre, J. C., and Van Den Pol, R. A. (1983). The "Bathroom Game": A systematic program for the elimination of encopretic behavior. *Journal of Behavior Therapy and Experimental Psychiatry, 14,* 67–71.

Breit, M., Kaplan, S. L., Gauthier, B., and Weinhold, C. (1984). The Dry-Bed Method for the treatment of enuresis: A failure to duplicate previous reports. *Child and Family Behavior Therapy, 6,* 17–23.

Butler, R. J., Brewin, C. R., and Forsythe, W. I. (1988). A comparison of two approaches to the treatment of nocturnal enuresis and the prediction of effectiveness using pretreatment variables. *Journal of Child Psychology and Psychiatry, 29,* 501–509.

_____ . (1990). Relapse in children treated for nocturnal enuresis: Prediction of response using pre-treatment variables. *Behavioral Psychotherapy, 18,* 65–72.

Copeland, E. T., Baucom-Copeland, S., and Perry, L. L. (1982). A behavioral approach to enuresis for the family physician. *Journal of the National Medical Association, 74,* 1035–1040.

Dische, S., Yule, W., Corbett, J., and Hand, D. (1983). Childhood nocturnal enuresis: Factors associated with outcome of treatment with an enuresis alarm. *Developmental Medicine and Child Neurology, 25,* 67–80.

Doleys, D. M. (1977). Behavioral treatments for nocturnal enuresis in children: A review of the recent literature. *Psychological Bulletin, 84,* 30–54.

_____ . (1989). Functional enuresis and encopresis. In C. G. Last and M. Hersen (Eds.), *Handbook of child psychiatry diagnosis* (pp. 427–442). New York: Wiley.

Edwards, S. D., and Van Der Spuy, H. I. J. (1985). Hypnotherapy as a treatment for enuresis. *Journal of Child Psychology and Psychiatry, 26,* 161–170.

Fincham, F. D., and Spettell, C. (1984). The acceptability of Dry Bed Training and Urine Alarm Training as treatments of nocturnal enuresis. *Behavior Therapy, 15,* 388–394.

Fournier, J. P., Garfinkel, B. D., Bond, A., Beauchesne, H., and Shapiro, S. K. (1987). Pharmacological and behavioral management of enuresis. *Journal of the American Academy of Child and Adolescent Psychiatry, 26,* 849–853.

Foxx, R. M. (1985). The successful treatment of diurnal and nocturnal enuresis and encopresis. *Child and Family Behavior Therapy, 7,* 39–47.

Fritz, G. K., and Anders, T. F. (1979). Enuresis: the clinical application of an etiologically based classification system. *Child Psychiatry and Human Development, 10,* 103–113.

Fritz, G. K., and Armbrust, J. (1982). Enuresis and encopresis. *Psychiatric Clinics of North America, 5,* 283–296.

Gabel, S., Chandra, R., and Shindledecker, R. (1988). Behavioral ratings and outcome of medical treatment for encopresis. *Journal of Developmental and Behavioral Pediatrics, 9,* 129–133.

Gabel, S., Hegedus, A. M., Wald, A., Chandra, R., and Chiponis, D. (1986). Prevalence of behavioral problems and mental health utilization among encopretic children: Implications for behavioral pediatrics. *Journal of Developmental and Behavioral Pediatrics, 7,* 293–297.

Geffken, G., Johnson, S. B., and Walker, D. (1986). Behavioral interventions for childhood nocturnal enuresis: The differential effect of bladder capacity on treatment progress and outcome. *Health Psychology, 5,* 261–272.

Glicklich, L. B. (1951). An historical account of enuresis. *Pediatrics, 8,* 859–876.

Haley, J. (1976). *Problem-solving therapy.* San Francisco: Jossey-Bass.

Houts, A. C., Mellon, M. W., and Whelan, J. P. (1988). Use of dietary fiber and stimulus control to treat retentive encopresis: A multiple baseline investigation. *Journal of Pediatric Psychology, 13,* 435–445.

Houts, A. C., Peterson, J. K., and Whelan, J. P. (1986). Prevention of relapse in Full-Spectrum Home Training for primary enuresis: A components analysis. *Behavior Therapy, 17,* 462–469.

Kanner, L. (1972). *Child psychiatry.* Springfield, IL: Thomas.

Kaplan, B. J. (1985). A clinical demonstration program of a psychobiological approach to childhood encopresis. *Journal of Child Care, 2,* 47–54.

Kaplan, S. L., Breit, M., Gauthier, B., and Busner, J. (1988). A comparison of three nocturnal enuresis treatment methods. *Journal of the American Academy of Child and Adolescent Psychiatry, 28,* 282–286.

Keating, J. C., Butz, R. A., Burke, E., and Heimburg, R. G. (1983). Dry Bed Training without a urine alarm: Lack of effect of setting and therapist contact with child. *Journal of Behavior Therapy and Experimental Psychiatry, 14,* 109–115.

Knell, S. M., and Moore, D. J. (1990). Cognitive-behavioral play therapy in the treatment of encopresis. *Journal of Clinical Child Psychology, 19,* 55–60.

Knopf, I. J. (1979). *Childhood psychopathology: A developmental approach.* Englewood Cliffs, NJ: Prentice-Hall.

Kolko, D. J. (1987). Simplified inpatient treatment of nocturnal enuresis in psychiatrically disturbed children. *Behavior Therapy, 2,* 99–112.

———— . (1989). Inpatient intervention for chronic functional encopresis in psychiatrically disturbed children. *Behavioral Residential Treatment, 4,* 231–252.

Levine, M. D. (1975). Children with encopresis: A descriptive analysis. *Pediatrics, 56,* 412–416.

McColgan, E. B., Pugh, R. L., and Pruitt, D. B. (1985). Encopresis: A structural/strategic approach to family treatment. *American Journal of Family Therapy, 13,* 46–54.

Minuchin, S. (1974). *Families and family therapy.* Cambridge, MA: Harvard University Press.

Morgan, R. T. T and Young, G. C. (1975). Parental attitudes and the conditioning treatment of childhood enuresis. *Behavior Research and Therapy, 13,* 197–199.

Mountjoy, P. T., Ruben, D. H., and Bradford, T. S. (1984). Recent technological advancements in the treatment of enuresis. *Behavior Modification, 8,* 291–315.

Mowrer, O. H., and Mowrer, W. M. (1938). Enuresis: A method for its study and treatment. *American Journal of Orthopsychiatry, 8,* 436–459.

O'Brien, S., Ross, L. V., and Christophersen, E. R. (1986). Primary encopresis: Evaluation and treatment. *Journal of Applied Behavioral Analysis, 19,* 137–145.

Olness, K. (1975). The use of self-hypnosis in the treatment of childhood nocturnal enuresis: A report on 40 patients. *Clinical Pediatrics, 14,* 273–279.

Owens-Stively, J. A. (1987). Self-esteem and compliance in encopretic children. *Child Psychiatry and Human Development, 18,* 13–21.

Paschalis, A. P., Kimmel, H. D., and Kimmel, E. (1972). Further study of diurnal instrumental conditioning in the treatment of enuresis nocturna. *Journal of Abnormal Child Psychology, 5,* 277–287.

Protinsky, H., and Dillard, C. (1983). Enuresis: A family therapy model. *Psychotherapy: Theory, Research, & Practice, 20,* 81–89.

Protinsky, H., and Kersey, B. (1983). Psychogenic encopresis: A family therapy approach. *Journal of Clinical Child Psychology, 12,* 192–197.

Quay, H. (1977). Measuring dimensions of deviant behavior: The Behavior Problem Checklist. *Journal of Abnormal Child Psychology, 5,* 277–287.

Scharf, M. B., and Jennings, S. W. (1988). Childhood enuresis: Relationship to sleep, etiology, evaluation, and treatment. *Annals of Behavioral Medicine, 10,* 113–120.

Scharf, M. B., Pravada, M. F., Jennings, S. W., Kauffman, R., and Ringel, J. (1987). Childhood enuresis: A comprehensive treatment program. *Psychiatric Clinics of North America, 10,* 655–667.

Shaffer, D., Gardner, A., and Hedge, B. (1984). Behavior and bladder disturbance of enuretic children: A rational classification of a common disorder. *Developmental Medicine and Child Neurology, 26,* 781–792.

Stark, L. J., Spirito, A., Lewis, A. V., and Hart, K. J. (1990). Encopresis: Behavioral parameters associated with children who fail medical management. *Child Psychiatry and Human Development, 20,* 169–179.

Steinhausen, H. C., and Gobel, D. (1989). Enuresis in child psychiatric clinic patients. *Journal of the American Academy of Child and Adolescent Psychiatry, 28,* 279–281.

Taylor, P. D., and Turner, R. K. (1975). A clinical trial of continuous, intermittent, and overlearning 'bell and pad' treatments for nocturnal enuresis. *Behavior Research and Therapy, 13,* 281–293.

Wagner, W. G. (1987). The behavioral treatment of nocturnal enuresis. *Journal of Counseling and Development, 65,* 262–265.

Wagner, W. G., and Geffken, G. (1986). Enuretic children: How they view their wetting behavior. *Child Study Journal, 16,* 13–18.

Wagner, W. G., and Johnson, J. T. (1988). Childhood nocturnal enuresis: The prediction of premature withdrawal from behavioral conditioning. *Journal of Abnormal Child Psychology, 16,* 687–692.

Waksman, S. A. (1983). A multimodal treatment for secondary psychogenic encopresis: A case study. *Psychological Reports, 53,* 271–273.

Wald, A., and Handen, B. L. (1987). Behavioral aspects of disorders of defecation and fecal continence. *Annals of Behavioral Medicine, 9,* 19–23.

Wells, M. E., and Hinkle, J. S. (1990). Elimination of childhood encopresis: A family systems approach. *Journal of Mental Health Counseling, 12,* 520–526.

Werry, J. S., and Cohrssen, J. (1965). Enuresis: An etiologic and therapeutic study. *Journal of Pediatrics, 67,* 423–431.

Whelan, J. P., and Houts, A. C. (1990). Effects of a waking schedule on primary enuretic children treated with Full-Spectrum Home Training. *Health Psychology, 9,* 164–176.

Wiener, J. M. (1984). Psychopharmacology in childhood disorders. *Psychiatric Clinics of North America, 7,* 831–843.

Young, G. C., and Morgan, R. T. T. (1972a). Overlearning in the conditioning treatment of enuresis: A long-term follow-up study. *Behavior Research and Therapy, 10,* 419–420.

_____ . (1972b). Overlearning in the conditioning treatment of enuresis. *Behavior Research and Therapy, 10,* 147–151.

CHAPTER 5

Mood Disorders

DSM-IV does not include separate diagnostic criteria for childhood mood disorders. Instead, DSM-IV incorporates a few developmental considerations into the adult mood disorder diagnoses. This characterization of childhood mood disorders reflects two developing trends in the mental health field: the recognition that children can be depressed and the recognition that depression in childhood has some components that are different from depression in adulthood.

Change in the assessment, diagnosis, and treatment of childhood mood disorders has been rampant in the past century. At one time the predominant psychoanalytic view of depression held that depression could not occur in childhood because children do not have a fully formed superego (Kazdin, 1989a; Mahler, 1961). Later theorists maintained that depression does occur in childhood, but that its symptoms are different than depression in adulthood. DSM-IV takes the position that depression does occur in children and that depression is basically the same syndrome in children as in adults. Hence, diagnostic criteria for the mood disorders vary little by age.

■ Bipolar Disorder and Cyclothymic Disorder

☐ CLINICAL DESCRIPTION

Diagnostic Considerations

Essentially, two groups of mood disorders can be diagnosed in DSM-IV: Bipolar Disorders and Depressive Disorders. Of these two groups the Bipolar Disorders are more unusual in preadolescent children (Keller and Wunder, 1990; Pataki and Carlson, 1992). The Bipolar Disorders have as their defining characteristic the presence of Manic, Mixed, or Hypomanic Episodes of behavior. Manic and Hypomanic Episodes involve such symptoms as elevated or irritable mood, grandiose self-image, little need for sleep, being overly talkative, flight of ideas, distractibility, overactivity, and dangerous behavior. Manic and

Hypomanic Episodes differ based on duration and severity. A Manic Episode must involve symptom presence for at least 1 week and marked impairment in daily functioning. A Hypomanic Episode, on the other hand, may last only 4 or more days, and it involves less severe symptoms that are noticeable but do not cause marked problems. Mixed Episodes occur when a child meets the criteria for a Manic Episode AND a Major Depressive Episode "nearly every day" for 1 week or more, with marked impairment in functioning (for a more extensive discussion of diagnostic criteria, refer to DSM-IV; American Psychiatric Association, 1994).

In addition to manic symptoms, Bipolar Disorders are classified based on the presence of depressive symptoms, in the form of a Major Depressive Episode. A Major Depressive Episode involves the presence of numerous (five or more) depressive symptoms during a 2-week period. At least one of the symptoms must be depressed mood or anhedonia. Other symptoms characteristic of a Major Depressive Episode are weight (or appetite) change, insomnia or hypersomnia, psychomotor agitation or retardation, fatigue, sense of worthlessness or guilt, concentration problems, and preoccupation with death or suicide. In children, irritable mood may be substituted for depressed mood. A Major Depressive Episode may only be diagnosed if the person has significant distress or problems in daily functioning, without sufficient manic symptoms for a Mixed Episode to be diagnosed.

Based on the number of Major Depressive, Manic, Mixed, and Hypomanic Episodes, a number of variants of Bipolar Disorder can be diagnosed. Bipolar I Disorders are diagnosed when the person has had or is having a Manic or Mixed Episode. Diagnostic qualifiers are added depending on the presence of past or current Manic or Mixed Episodes, current Hypomanic Episodes, past Major Depressive Episodes, and current Major Depressive Episodes (American Psychiatric Association, 1994). Bipolar II Disorder is diagnosed when the person has *never* had a Manic Episode but has had Hypomanic and Major Depressive Episodes. Cyclothymic Disorder is diagnosed when the child has multiple occurrences of hypomanic symptoms and multiple occurrences of depressed mood/anhedonia during a 1-year period (2 years for adults), without the presence of a Major Depressive Episode or a Manic Episode. Hence, Cyclothymic Disorder has a more chronic but less severe symptom picture.

The Bipolar Disorders are rarely seen in children, although their incidence jumps in adolescence (Keller and Wunder, 1990; Pataki and Carlson, 1992). In fact, no large studies report on the incidence of Bipolar Disorder in children under the age of 13. Nevertheless, Bipolar Disorder probably does occur extremely rarely in children under age 13 (Keller and Wunder, 1990; Weinberg and Brumback, 1976). Controversy exists as to whether Bipolar Disorder in adolescents (age 13–19) has a different manifestation than Bipolar Disorder in adults. Some authors (Anthony and Scott, 1960; Weinberg and Brumback, 1976) have suggested special criteria for childhood mania, but their criteria do not differ substantially from those used by DSM-IV for a manic episode in children or adults. The predominant view at this point is the use of a single set of symptoms for mania and hypomania in adolescents and adults. Furthermore, treatment for Bipolar Disorder is very similar in adolescents and adults (Pataki and Carlson, 1992; Strober, 1992).

The Bipolar Disorders should be diagnosed cautiously in children and adolescents for several reasons: First, the base rate of Bipolar Disorder in children is very low. Hence, the probability of Bipolar Disorder occurring in any one child, even a clinical case, is small. Second, many diagnostic features of other childhood disorders overlap with manic features or could be interpreted as manic features. Hyperactivity, distractibility, and lack of goal direction, for example, could be symptoms of Attention-Deficit Hyperactivity Disorder (ADHD) as opposed to a Bipolar Disorder; dangerous behavior could be symptomatic of Conduct Disorder (CD). Both ADHD and CD occur much more commonly in children than do the Bipolar Disorders, making either of these diagnoses more likely in any given child. Third, children and particularly adolescents are often prone to greater, more frequent mood swings than are adults. These mood swings can be triggered by apparently minor events (e.g., getting a good grade; having a bad hair day for the prom). Hence, euphoria over minor events may be developmentally normal (or at least not bizarre) for adolescents. To diagnose such mood swings as Cyclothymic Disorder or Bipolar II would result in astronomically high rates of these disorders in adolescents.

Appearance and Features

In order to avoid the pitfalls of misdiagnosing Bipolar Disorders in children and adolescents, the clinician is advised to bear the following features of the disorder in mind:

1. Familial incidence of Bipolar Disorder is considered a risk factor in the disease, even for children and adolescents (Keller and Wunder, 1990; Strober, 1992).

2. A significant change from previous functioning, involving manic symptoms, may be more symptomatic of a Bipolar Disorder than of ADHD or CD in children (Pataki and Carlson, 1992). However, the presence of an organic factor or a traumatic stressor would be a more likely explanation than Bipolar Disorder in the case of a significant change in functioning.

3. Consistently bizarre, pressured behavior, regardless of stressors or environmental factors, may suggest Bipolar Disorder, particularly if flight of ideas and pressured speech are consistently seen in an adolescent. Psychotic behaviors are more characteristic of mania than of other childhood disorders, with the exception of schizophrenia (Pataki and Carlson, 1992).

4. Psychotic behaviors seen during Bipolar Disorder are manic mood–congruent (usually related to grandiosity or overactivity), while those of other disorders may not be as influenced by mood (Keller and Wunder, 1990).

5. The risk of overdiagnosing Bipolar Disorder in adolescents is high if developmentally appropriate norms for "euphoria," "elevated mood," and "overactivity" are not used. Some mood swings and overactivity are typical of the adolescent phase of life.

6. Although Bipolar Disorder is rare and difficult to diagnose in children, clinicians should not overlook it as a diagnosis. In other words, clinicians should be careful not to attribute real bipolar symptoms to adolescent behavior.

7. Grossly inflated self-esteem is more typical of a Bipolar Disorder in a child or adolescent, while most other disorders involve low self-esteem (Keller and Wunder, 1990).

8. Bipolar Disorder in children and adolescents is cyclic, while other disorders such as ADHD, CD, and ODD more consistently affect the behavior of the child or are affected strongly by environment.

(Appearances and features of the Bipolar Disorders are listed in Table 5.1.)

☐   ASSESSMENT PATTERNS AND TREATMENT OPTIONS

Because of the rarity of Bipolar Disorder in children, little is known about its assessment in childhood. Furthermore, the efficacy of lithium as a treatment for children is not known and may differ from its efficacy for adults (Rancurello, 1985). Bipolar Disorders in adolescents, although they may differ somewhat from those of adults, bear sufficient resemblance to adult-presentation Bipolar Disorder that adult assessment techniques and treatments are typically applied to these cases. Additional information about the assessment and treatment of adolescent-onset Bipolar Disorder can be found in adult texts (Meyer and Deitsch, 1996).

■   Major Depressive Disorder and Dysthymic Disorder

☐   CLINICAL DESCRIPTION

Diagnostic Considerations

Depressive disorders in children can be classified in one of two categories: Major Depressive Disorder is typically more severe, often recurrent, and of

TABLE 5.1   Appearance and Features of the Bipolar Disorders

COMMON FEATURES

Manic/Hypomanic behavior: elevated mood, grandiosity, decreased sleep, talkativeness, flight of ideas, distractibility, overactivity
Major depressive episodes or depressive symptoms (not required, but frequently present)
Rare before age 13
Cycling presentation of symptoms

Note: The features listed above are often seen but are not universal. Some features may be diagnostically relevant or required, while others may not be required for diagnosis.

shorter duration; it involves the presence of one or more Major Depressive Episodes with no Manic, Mixed, or Hypomanic Episodes. Dysthymic Disorder, on the other hand, is typically less severe and lasts longer than 1 year in children and adolescents. Depressive disorders that do not fit one of these two categories must be classified as Depressive Disorder, NOS, or as Adjustment Disorder with Depressed Mood (which is technically an Adjustment Disorder and not a Mood Disorder). Adjustment Disorder with Depressed Mood is qualitatively different from the depressive disorders; onset and recovery are relatively rapid, unless it develops into a depressive disorder (Burgin, 1986).

There are few age-based diagnostic differences in the DSM-IV Depressive Disorders. For Dysthymic Disorder the duration of depressed mood is reduced from 2 years for adults to 1 year for children and adolescents. For both Major Depressive Disorder and Dysthymic Disorder, depression in children may be shown by irritable (as opposed to depressed) mood. Essentially, then, children and adults are diagnosed using the same criteria, with minor developmental considerations. This use of similar criteria for children and adults fits the prevailing view that, with some developmental differences, depression is manifest in similar ways for children and adults (Stark, Rouse, and Livingston, 1991).

Much of the research and clinical literature on childhood depression, however, does not mirror the diagnostic nosology of DSM-IV. Instead, most literature refers to "Childhood Depression" or a "depressed group," which may consist of Major Depressive Disorder only, Major Depressive Disorder *and* Dysthymic Disorder, or some other set of criteria for determining depression. Childhood Dysthymic Disorder is rarely mentioned or studied alone in the literature. Other authors develop their own categories and criteria for depression (Shafii and Shafii, 1992). A further complication is the fact that some literature is based on DSM-III or DSM-III-R definitions of depression, while other literature uses DSM-IV. Unfortunately, this plethora of definitions for "depression" complicates the review of childhood depression literature. To simplify this process, *depression* will be used in this section to describe a syndrome that resembles closely the definitions of Major Depressive Disorder *and* Dysthymic Disorder. However, the use of *depression* in this section implies only the approximate and not the exact application of DSM-IV criteria, because DSM-IV criteria are not always used in research. Furthermore, some older studies use earlier DSM criteria, which resemble but are not identical to DSM-IV criteria. Differing definitions of depression will be noted when they stray significantly from the Major Depressive Disorder/Dysthymic Disorder presentation.

The hallmark of depression is depressed mood, although irritable mood has been added for child diagnoses. DSM-IV adds loss of interest or pleasure (anhedonia) as a key symptom for a Major Depressive Episode and then provides a smorgasbord of somatic (weight loss or gain, sleep disturbance, fatigue), cognitive (sense of worthlessness or guilt, difficulty concentrating, suicidal ideation), and behavioral (psychomotor agitation, psychomotor retardation) symptoms. Importantly, depression should not be diagnosed within 2 months of the death of a loved one, unless impairment is marked. This latter criterion reflects the belief that depression should not be diagnosed if the symptoms are part of a normal grief reaction.

Differentiating depression from a "normal" grief reaction can be a difficult task. Weller et al. (1991) compared recently bereaved children with inpatient depressed children and found some differences that may be of diagnostic assistance. In general, bereaved children commonly (more than 20% of sample) reported depressive symptoms, such as dysphoria, loss of interest, appetite disturbance, sleep disturbance, psychomotor retardation/agitation, guilt, and suicidal ideation. However, bereaved children reported fewer symptoms over all than did depressed children. Large differences were found between the groups on sleep disturbance (74% of depressed vs. 29% of bereaved), psychomotor retardation (66% of depressed vs. 32% of bereaved), fatigue (47% of depressed vs. 8% of bereaved), guilt/worthlessness (76% of depressed vs. 21% of bereaved), and trouble thinking (47% of depressed vs. 5% of bereaved). Importantly, 26% of the bereaved sample had symptoms of sufficient severity to be diagnosed as having a Major Depressive Episode. Thus, some overlap between depression and bereavement is seen.

The varying definitions of childhood depression make incidence and prevalence difficult to determine. The incidence of Major Depressive Disorder in school-age children is generally found to be around 1.5–2%, while that of Dysthymic Disorder is slightly higher (2–2.5%) (Anderson et al., 1987; Kashani and Schmid, 1992; Kashani et al., 1983). Depression appears to become more common with age, increasing to 4.7% and 3.3% for adolescents with Major Depressive Disorder or Dysthymic Disorder, respectively (Kashani et al., 1987). In preschoolers, on the other hand, Major Depressive Disorder appears to be uncommon (perhaps less than 1%; Kashani, Holcomb, and Orvaschel, 1986; Kashani and Ray, 1983; Kashani and Schmid, 1992), although large epidemiological studies have not been conducted. The distribution of school-age depression by sex is unclear, with some studies claiming more prevalence among males, while others find equal rates by sex. In adolescence, depressed females outnumber males by as many as 5 to 1 (Kashani and Schmid, 1992; Kashani et al., 1987; Kazdin, 1989a).

In contrast to rates for depressive syndromes, the prevalence of single depressive symptoms is quite high in children. Rates of 7% for preschoolers with one or more depressive symptoms and 40% for adolescents with one or more depressive symptoms have been reported (Kashani et al., 1986; Kashani et al., 1987; Pataki and Carlson, 1990). Hence, it is not surprising to find one or two symptoms of depression in a child. Furthermore, the presence of a depressive symptom does not necessarily indicate that the child has a diagnosable depressive syndrome. Symptoms may be isolated or transient, while the syndrome will be more pervasive and long-lasting.

In DSM-IV, Bipolar I and II Disorders and Major Depressive Disorder can also be specified as having a seasonal pattern if the onset and remission of the Major Depressive Episodes occur at the same time of the year for the last 2 years. During the last 2 years there cannot have been any affective disorders out of this seasonal pattern, and over the individual's lifetime, seasonal episodes must outnumber nonseasonal episodes. The most typical presentation of this subtype in children (referred to as Seasonal Affective Disorder or SAD) is for depression to occur throughout the winter and to remit in spring (Rosenthal et al., 1989; Sonis, 1992). SAD is more common in adolescents than in children, with mean ages in various studies of SAD children of between 12 and 16 years (Sonis, 1989; 1992).

Because SAD is hypothesized to be caused by seasonal patterns of light that disrupt biological rhythms (particularly the decreased light of winter), the common treatments for SAD attempt to reorient the person's biological rhythms (Sonis, 1992). Most common is phototherapy, which involves exposure to bright light at a certain time each day (Sonis, 1989). Hypothetically, this mimics summer light and resets biological rhythms. The ideal intensity, wavelength, site, timing, and duration of the light are under investigation, with indications that ultraviolet light is not necessary and that the eyes should be used as the focus site (Rosenthal et al., 1989; Sonis, 1992). Some success has been reported following the use of phototherapy with small samples of SAD children (Sonis, 1992). Other treatments sometimes used to treat SAD are sleep deprivation and pharmacotherapy (lithium for SAD—Bipolar), although these have been used almost exclusively with adults.

Appearance and Features

Appearance and features of depression in early and middle childhood are listed in Table 5.2.

Developmental Appearance

Numerous authors have suggested that the appearance and features of depression differ somewhat by age. Shafii and Shafii (1992), for example, provide an integrated synopsis of age-based types of depression categorizing by ages: birth–2, 3–5, 6–12, and 12–18.

1. Depression from ages birth–2: In this category are the syndromes of anaclitic depression (Spitz, 1946), hospitalism (Spitz, 1945, 1965), sensory-motor depression, and toddler depression. Compared to depression in school-age children, these syndromes have a weaker cognitive component. Hence, the extent to which infant and toddler syndromes actually represent depression is a source of controversy (Burgin, 1986). Those who oppose depression diagnoses in infancy note that depression requires a substantial and relatively sophisticated cognitive component, of which infants are largely incapable. Nevertheless, deprivation syndromes do occur in infants and their manifestation at times resembles depression.

Anaclitic depression is characterized by whining, withdrawal, weight loss, slowed or stunted growth, susceptibility to infection, dazed and immobile facial expression, intellectual decline, impaired social interaction, and withdrawal (Shafii and Shafii, 1992; Spitz, 1965). It occurs in infants who are emotionally

TABLE 5.2   Appearance and Features of Depression in Early and Middle Childhood

COMMON FEATURES

Affective features: sad or irritable affect
Cognitive features: negative attribution bias, low self-esteem, guilt, worthlessness, helplessness, difficulty concentrating
Somatic features: sleep and appetite disturbance, fatigue
Anhedonia, apathy, repeated claims of being "bored"
Anxiety, fears
Social withdrawal
Decline in academic or social functioning
Suicidal ideation
Decline in self-care behaviors
Physical complaints

OCCASIONAL FEATURES

Suicide attempt
Oppositionality
Poor peer relationships
Psychomotor agitation or retardation

Note: The features listed above are often seen but are not universal. Some features may be diagnostically relevant or required, while others may not be required for diagnosis. "Common" features are typical of the disorder; "occasional" features appear frequently but are not necessarily seen in a majority of cases.

deprived, usually because of separation or infrequent contact with a major attachment figure within the first year of life (Burgin, 1986). Separation is usually physical, although extreme emotional unavailability may also lead to an anaclitic depression. Depressed mothers, for example, are at risk for having depressed infants and children (Burgin, 1986). If the separation lasts several weeks or months, whining gives way to withdrawal, expressionless looks, and resisting interaction with adults. Spitz (1965) suggests that separations of greater than 4 months that occur when the infant is approximately 6–8 months of age greatly increase the risk and longevity of the anaclitic depression.

Hospitalism (so named because it was initially seen in hospitalized or institutionalized infants) is a more severe form of anaclitic depression typically caused by long periods of separation from a consistent, nurturant attachment figure within the first year of life (Shafii and Shafii, 1992; Spitz, 1965). Superimposed on the anaclitic depression are more severe symptoms of slowed motor responsiveness, expressionless face, bizarre/self-stimulating behaviors (hand waving, rocking), extreme intellectual decline (to the point of mental retardation), unresponsiveness to social interaction, and high mortality rate (Shafii and Shafii, 1992; Spitz, 1965).

Sensory-motor depression is a term coined by Shafii and Shafii (1992) to describe a type of infant depression that is not consistent with an anaclitic depression but nevertheless involves the appearance of sadness/irritability that suggests a depressive disorder. The hallmarks of sensory-motor depression are sad facial expression, irritable crying, whining, prolonged and wistful eye contact or no eye contact at all, retardation of language development, disappearance of the smile, motor retardation, sleep disturbance, lack of curiosity, poor feeding, attachment disturbance, delayed cognitive development, and poor health. These symptoms last only hours to days, but duration may increase if the child's problem does not receive attention from caretakers. Shafii and Shafii (1992) do not state the exact differences between sensory-motor and anaclitic depression, but sensory-motor depression appears to be characterized by less emotional deprivation, less withdrawal by the child, and shorter duration than anaclitic depression.

Toddler depression affects children in the 1–2 age range. Some age-specific symptoms of toddler depression are irritable mood, delay in developmental challenges of toddlerhood (walking, standing, language, toilet training, cognitive development), nightmares and night terrors, self-stimulating behaviors (rocking, head banging, masturbation), clinginess, oppositional behavior, excessive fears, and decrease in play. At younger toddler ages, many of the symptoms of anaclitic depression may emerge or persist.

2. Depression at ages 3–5: In preschoolers, common symptoms of depression are sadness, weight loss, motor retardation, tiredness, suicidal ideation, anger, apathy, illness, irritability, and social withdrawal (Kashani et al., 1986). As a result of these symptoms, depressed preschoolers typically play less with other children and verbally express feelings of sadness, worthlessness, and fearfulness (Shafii and Shafii, 1992).

3. Depression at ages 6–12: At school ages, depression in children comes to resemble more closely that of adults. Depressed mood is more clear, and the child more often attempts to verbalize depressive cognitions and affects (Shafii and Shafii, 1992). Anhedonia, apathy, and low self-esteem are also more apparent. Other symptoms commonly seen at these ages are eating disturbances (over- or under-eating), fatigue, suicidal ideation, social withdrawal, moodiness, irritability, lack of motivation, and motor retardation. Although children at these ages will sometimes try to communicate their distress, they often do not have the vocabulary to express their internal experience. Hence, the child may complain of boredom or feeling stupid as a way of communicating anhedonia or low self-esteem, respectively (Shafii and Shafii, 1992). At times the clinician is forced to act as a translator of latency-age vocabulary into psychologically meaningful jargon in order to make sense of the child's symptoms.

Often the presence of depression in a school-age child is first manifest by declining performance, which is more clearly evaluated at school ages than before. Thus, declines in grades, failure to complete chores, or declining performance in sports makes the reality of depression more apparent to caretakers. In addition, peer relationships take on greater importance at these ages, and the status of a child as popular, average, rejected, or neglected may have an impact on the development of depressive symptoms. Reciprocally, depression may have a major impact on the child's social standing.

In addition to the more typical depressive symptomatology, school-age children may show depression through a variety of other symptoms. So-called "masked" depression infers the presence of depression from symptoms such as oppositionality, anger, delinquency, overactivity, fears, somatization, social problems, and poor school performance (Cytryn and McKnew, 1972; Glaser, 1968). Unfortunately, any symptom can be assigned to masked depression without any verification of the validity of the assignment. Because masked depression is, by definition, hidden, it can *only* be inferred and thus yields little clinically useful information. It has been proposed that masked depression should be diagnosed when some depressive symptoms are observed in addition to the masked symptoms. Of course, in this case the depression is no longer masked (Angold, 1988).

4. Depression from ages 12–18: Some characteristics of adolescent depression are seen more frequently in this age group than at other ages. Volatile mood, rage, intense self-consciousness, low self-esteem, poor school performance, delinquent behaviors, substance abuse, sexual acting-out, and social withdrawal are common symptoms of adolescent depression (Shafii and Shafii, 1992). In addition, adolescents may have oversleeping and overeating problems at higher rates than do adults (Simeon, 1989). A significant risk of suicidal behavior also exists in the adolescent group, and any suicidal ideation or threat should be taken extremely seriously.

Normal, nondepressed adolescents go through periods of unhappiness, loneliness, dissatisfaction with themselves, and emotional turmoil. Adolescents face significant developmental tasks that expose them to failure, social stresses, and loss of social support. Establishing romantic relationships, orienting in a career direction, establishing an identity, maintaining standing in the peer group, separating from parents, and becoming independent are all examples of these major developmental tasks of adolescence. Confronting, dealing with, and, occasionally, failing at these tasks can create considerable unhappiness and turmoil for the average adolescent. Symptoms of depression in adolescence are distinguished from developmentally normal problems largely by severity and uniqueness. For example, low self-esteem following rejection by a girlfriend may be a typical response for an adolescent boy. However, when the low self-esteem becomes pervasive, long-lasting, and extremely maladaptive, a diagnosis of depression should be considered.

General Appearance

It should be clear from the preceding discussion that the appearance and features of childhood depression vary somewhat by age and subtype. However, certain features of depression are relatively common in children between the ages of approximately 4 and 12 years old. At ages younger than 4, a restricted cognitive capacity limits the presentation of depression to infant/toddler features. After age 12 or 13, depression tends to resemble adult depression, within the parameters of adolescence previously described (Burgin, 1986). Hence, the remainder of the chapter will focus on depression in the preschool/school-age group of children. Readers interested in adolescent and adult depression should consult Meyer and Deitsch (1996).

Many of the depressive features observed in adults can be downwardly extended to children. Depressed mood and irritable mood are some of the most common symptoms in children, occurring in approximately 80% and 40% of depressed children, respectively (Stark et al., 1991). This mood disturbance is frequently manifest by flat, sad, angry, or tearful facial expression, although the child may deny a mood problem when directly questioned. Because children tend to act out their mood states, oppositional and hostile behavior may follow from depressed or irritable mood (Burgin, 1986). For example, depression may manifest itself in the previously well-behaved child who suddenly resists all requests and throws temper tantrums for small reasons. Power struggles brought on by parental hostility and poor response patterns, on the other hand, are less likely to be primarily driven by mood.

Diminished interest or pleasure, another DSM-IV criterion, occurs in as many as half of depressed children (Stark et al., 1991). Such anhedonia is manifest as complaints of boredom, resistance to take part in any activity, reluctance to leave the room or house, and lack of motivation (Dennison, 1989). This may be particularly noticeable when one attempts to engage the child in play. However, anhedonia in children is rarely total, and the ability of the child to enjoy some activities should not be used to exclude a diagnosis of depression (Pataki and Carlson, 1990). Instead, anhedonia in children is often shown in a diminished pleasure with respect to everyday activity.

Anhedonia frequently combines with fatigue, which affects as many as 50–70% of depressed children (Stark et al. 1991). Children with anhedonic fatigue complain that any adult suggestion requires too much effort. These protests may balloon into temper tantrums or ignoring of the social environment. Psychomotor agitation is seen in depressed children who engage in extensive, often purposeless activity. This activity serves the apparent goal of providing distraction from painful cognitions and affects. Agitation occurs in about 35% of depressed children (Stark et al., 1991).

Cognitive symptoms of depression, such as feelings of worthlessness, guilt, and difficulty concentrating, may be difficult for a child to articulate (Burgin, 1986). Behaviorally, feelings of worthlessness may be seen when a child expects to be criticized, ignored, or rejected by other children. Likewise, the way in which the child interprets neutral situations may show underlying thoughts and schemas. Depressed children with feelings of worthlessness or hopelessness will often enter situations expecting to fail or with a sense of futility; these feelings may be expressed by anxiety, reluctance, or defensive hostility. Ambiguous behaviors of other children are interpreted as reinforcing the child's belief that he or she is worthless, and failure experiences are likely to be catastrophized and overgeneralized. Worthlessness and hopelessness may also be seen in a lack of interest in self-care and appearance behaviors (Dennison,

1989). The depressed child may not show interest in wearing appealing clothing, grooming, or keeping clean. Feelings of guilt may emerge in defensive or anxious behaviors surrounding a negative situation. Often this situation involves a major stressor and is not the fault of the child.

The depressed child's inability to concentrate may be misinterpreted as an attention deficit. However, when it is combined with a sad appearance, anxiety, low self-esteem, fatigue, and a negative outlook, it is likely to be a depressive symptom. "Pure" ADHD children typically do not have the anxiety, low self esteem, and fatigue shown by depressed children unless depression and ADHD are co-occurring.

Depression is also manifest in the social environments of children, which often provide the first noticed symptoms (Simeon, 1989; Pataki and Carlson, 1990). In school, performance typically declines with the onset of depression, and this symptom is often what brings depression to the attention of adults (Pataki and Carlson, 1990). Depressed children score lower on reading and mathematics achievement than do nondepressed peers (Edelsohn et al., 1992). The decline in school performance is both a result of depressive symptoms (difficulty concentrating, lack of motivation, sense of hopelessness, anhedonia) and a confirmation to the child of worthlessness.

School problems can grow and have a "domino effect" on other areas of the child's life (Simeon, 1989). For example, school failure is sometimes viewed by parents and teachers as a sign that the child is being lazy or oppositional, leading to conflict between the child and authorities (Simeon, 1989). Peer relationships may be extremely disrupted, especially since children are typically less willing than adults to accept and sympathize with a peer who is depressed and withdrawn. This may result in the loss of friends, loss of popularity within the classroom, and increased isolation; almost three-fourths of depressed children may be socially withdrawn (Stark et al., 1991). At the extremes, irritability and fighting with peers may lead to complete isolation and rejection by the group (18% of depressed children; Stark et al., 1991). Depressed children are rated as less likable by peers (Edelsohn et al., 1992). At home the child's irritable, moody, and oppositional behavior is alternately distressing and frustrating to the parents. Discipline attempts may be perceived by the child as yet another confirmation of his or her negative world-view.

Somatic symptoms of depression are typically less prevalent in children than in adults (Pataki and Carlson, 1990). Trouble going to sleep is relatively common, but early awakening is often less of a problem for children than for adults. Physical complaints are very common in young children who are depressed, since these are often used as a way of obtaining help and comfort from parents. Furthermore, young children have less insight and, therefore, less understanding of the nature of depression. Their experiences and vocabulary thus lead them to physical complaints as a way of experiencing and expressing their distress. Somatic complaints are also common in adolescents, with 70% of depressed adolescents reporting significant somatic symptomatology (McCauley, Carlson, and Calderon, 1991). Change in appetite is occasionally seen in children and adolescents (one-third to one-half of children;

Pataki and Carlson, 1990), although this rarely results in actual weight loss (less than one-third of the time; Pataki and Carlson, 1990; Stark et al., 1991). Psychomotor retardation is also less common in children than in adults, occurring in only about 20% of depressed children (Stark et al., 1991).

Another common feature of childhood depression is anxiety, which co-occurs so often with depression that it is often difficult to tease the two apart. Depressed children worry about a multitude of things, from their own self-esteem and performance to disasters that may befall themselves or their family. Hence, separation anxiety is a common associated problem for young children (Simeon, 1989).

The long-term course of depression indicates general stability of depressive symptoms over a short-term (e.g., 1–3-month) period (Kaslow and Racusin, 1990). The vast majority (about 90%) of cases of Major Depressive Disorder go into remission within 1.5 years, while Dysthymic Disorder takes longer to remit (6 years to reach 89% remission rate). For children the median duration of an episode of Major Depressive Disorder is 32 weeks, while that for Dysthymic Disorder is over 3 years. Furthermore, Dysthymic Disorder typically has an earlier onset (7–7.5 years of age) than Major Depressive Disorder (10–11 years of age) (Kovacs et al., 1984a; Shafii and Shafii, 1992). By comparison, Adjustment Disorder with Depressed Mood typically lasts only 9 months (Kovacs et al., 1984a). Children who have Dysthymic Disorder or Major Depressive Disorder are also at considerable risk for a future Major Depressive Episode. Approximately 70% of children with Dysthymic Disorder develop a Major Depressive Episode within 5 years of diagnosis of their disorder (Kovacs et al., 1984b). Only a fraction of depressed children later develop Bipolar Disorder (Pataki and Carlson, 1990).

Suicide

Perhaps one of the most troublesome and dangerous features of depression is an increased risk of suicidal ideation, suicidal intent, and suicide attempts (Kotsopoulos, 1989). Significant suicidal ideation may be present in as many as 27% of depressed children (Stark et al., 1991). Suicidal ideation and attempts follow from the feelings of hopelessness and low self-esteem that are characteristic of depression (Pataki and Carlson, 1990), although some authors emphasize that unbearable psychological pain is the key stimulus in suicide (Leenaars and Wenckstern, 1991). As the pain becomes unbearable, the child increasingly views suicide as a reasonable or exclusive option for dealing with his or her feelings.

Fortunately, completed suicide rarely occurs before the age of 10, although suicide risk increases dramatically in adolescence (Pataki and Carlson, 1990). Suicide attempts in adolescents may be as high as 8% (Smith and Crawford, 1986). Completed suicides in adolescents have increased by 300% over the past 30 years, with prevalence rates of nearly 0.01% (quite high considering the seriousness of suicide). Adolescent girls make more suicide attempts, but adolescent boys complete suicide four to five times as often as girls (Simeon, 1989).

This is not the case for children under age 12; preadolescent boys and girls tend to make suicide attempts of equivalent severity, and the rate of completed suicide is roughly equal between the sexes (Leenaars and Wenckstern, 1991). Although many child and adolescent suicides are associated with depressive symptomatology, not all children and adolescents who commit suicide are depressed (Leenaars and Wenckstern, 1991; Simeon, 1989). Two other problems accounting for many suicides are conduct disorders (usually accompanied by drug abuse) and a withdrawn/depressed/anxious syndrome characterized by fear of failure in the social or academic realm.

Identification of individuals at risk for suicide is obviously of paramount importance, and this identification is particularly relevant in the case of depressed children, who already carry an increased risk for suicidal ideation and behavior; 60–80% of suicide victims have a depressive disorder (Pfeffer, 1992; Myers et al., 1991a). In addition to depression, several authors have suggested the following issues to be considered in assessing suicide risk in children (Leenaars and Wenckstern, 1991; Myers et al., 1991a; Myers et al., 1991b; Pfeffer, 1992):

1. Precipitating events: Precipitating events often are a factor in adolescent suicide, but they are less frequently a factor for children. Rather, cumulative stressful events coupled with vulnerability (unsupportive environment, poor coping skills) are often responsible for a child suicide attempt; life stress scores are predictive of suicide attempts by children (Harris and Ammerman, 1986; Myers et al., 1991a). In addition, the fit between the person and the stress must be taken into account. Leenaars and Wenckstern (1991) suggest that certain huge stresses, such as death of a parent by suicide, significantly increase the risk of child suicide. Pfeffer (1992) cites disciplinary crises as another risk event for suicide. Anticipated painful events may also increase risk, if suicide is seen as a way to avoid them.

2. Poor coping skills: Some children rapidly exhaust their coping options or do not know how to cope with stressful experiences. For example, if a boy feels that he cannot talk to his parents, cannot change or avoid his stressful situation, and is facing a catastrophic stress, he will become desperate and resort to maladaptive behavior. To the extent that he considers suicide an option in removing his problems, he will have suicidal ideation and, possibly, attempt suicide. On the other hand, a child who is willing to use any adaptive coping behaviors might reduce his stress appraisal sufficiently to avoid the desperation and psychological pain that could lead to suicidal behavior.

3. Maladaptive family environment: Among the family risk factors for suicide are (a) lack of boundaries, (b) inflexibility, (c) severe stress, (d) parental psychopsychology, and (e) a suicide attempt in the family.

One risk factor is lack of boundaries, with family members overly attached to each other, to the point of a lack of individual independence. This is often manifest in an enmeshed parent–child relationship. In these cases, death of the parent, a disappointing performance by the child, or the drive of the child to be independent are extremely threatening to the child and strip the child of coping behaviors and resources.

Inflexibility in the family system, in which any change is perceived as a mortal threat to the family as a unit, can be a risk factor. In these families, children may resort to suicidal behavior to get the family's attention and force change. On the other hand, the child may commit suicide out of fear over an upcoming change in the system, such as a divorced mother remarrying.

When severe stress, such as neglect or abuse, occurs within the family, the child may feel particularly desperate, since the family is often seen as the only safe haven from stress. Hence, neglect or abuse not only stresses the child, but it also leaves the child with fewer coping resources and less security.

Parental psychopathology (Harris and Ammerman, 1986; Myers et al., 1991a) can contribute to feelings of chaos, unpredictability, and lack of support in the family. Bizarre or depressed parental behavior can distort the child's world view, making suicide seem a viable option.

Suicide attempts in the family increase family stress and provide a dangerous model of maladaptive behavior (Harris and Ammerman, 1986; Pfeffer, 1992).

4. Previous attempts. The best predictor of future behavior is past behavior, particularly when the environmental and precipitating circumstances are similar. Hence, a child who has attempted suicide once is more likely to do so again than is a child who has never attempted suicide. The ratio of attempts to completed suicides is somewhere between 8:1 and 100:1 (Leenaars and Wenckstern, 1991), indicating that most attempts are not successful. However, the fact that previous suicide attempts have failed is *not* a good reason to take future attempts lightly. The child might be more serious the next time around, or might kill himself or herself by accident. The rate of attempted *and* completed suicide is much higher for those who have attempted before than for the general population (Myers et al., 1991b; Pfeffer, 1992).

5. Threats. As with attempts, many more threats occur than do actual suicides. Because of this, threats are often downplayed or even replied to with taunts by angry family members (e.g., "If you want to kill yourself, go ahead!"). The risk involved in missing even one serious threat, however, is so great that any threat should be taken seriously. Most threats occur in verbal or written form, although a child will occasionally communicate with nonverbal behavior (e.g., looking for a gun) that he or she is suicidal. The fact that the child is communicating the threat suggests belief that something can be done to redress the situation. Although the parent or clinician does not want to reward suicidal threats, provision of support, understanding, or restraint can buy valuable time to enhance the child's coping skills and reduce future threats. Communication of suicidal ideation or oblique references to suicide should be managed in the same way as direct threats.

6. Cognitive constriction. Children who are seriously considering suicide often acquire a focused view of their problems and of suicide as a solution.

This desperation and distortion of one's world view can make suicide seem not only reasonable, but necessary. Hence, this and other cognitive distortions put children at risk for seriously considering suicide.

7. Emotional turmoil: Suicide is rarely considered by a calm, rational child or adolescent. Rather, suicidal children are typically in great emotional distress. They are extremely anxious, distraught, agitated, and desperate. Anger and hostility are often present, particularly in "angry" suicides in which the child attempts to kill himself or herself in order to punish a parent or other person.

8. Cognitive desperation: Cognitive desperation is usually manifest as thoughts of hopelessness and helplessness toward the environment and the future. Things will not change or improve; often the expectation is that they will get worse. Cognitive constriction contributes to the feeling of desperation, the elimination of other coping behaviors, and the interpretation of incoming information as universally terrible. Hopelessness and low self-esteem have been shown to be empirically related to suicidality (Myers et al., 1991a).

9. Sudden behavioral changes: A dramatic increase in risky or life-threatening behavior may indicate self-hate and may portend a suicide attempt. Likewise, sudden "completion" behaviors that involve finishing things and getting one's affairs in order suggest some motive such as suicide. For example, children will sometimes give things away or make arrangements for pets before a suicide attempt.

10. Preoccupation with death: This may take the form of simple curiosity, desire to join a loved one, or bizarre delusion. Children are inherently curious about a number of things, including death, but repeated focus on death in the absence of other interests suggests a problem (Harris and Ammerman, 1986).

11. Suicide notes: Most children and adolescents who commit suicide do not leave a note, but some do. In some cases this note is written well before the attempt and is found before the attempt. As with suicide threats, suicide notes should be taken seriously.

12. Lack of perceived support: In many cases, children and adolescents who attempt suicide feel lonely and unsupported by family and friends. This lack of perceived support robs them of one of the most effective coping behaviors: seeking social support. Social support provides a sense of security, belonging, options, and meaning, all of which argue against suicide. Furthermore, social supports can provide different points of view and can temporarily restrain a desperate child from a desperate act.

13. Conduct problems/antisocial behavior. The combination of antisocial behavior, anger, impulsivity, and disrespect for rules seen in children with conduct problems is a risky combination that sometimes leads to suicide attempts or ideation (Myers et al., 1991; Pfeffer, 1992). Conduct problems combined with depression are particularly risky features.

14. Use of drugs and/or alcohol: Substance abuse both dulls inhibition and impairs judgment, increasing the risk of suicide (Pfeffer, 1992).

15. Psychomotor agitation/poor impulse control: Psychomotor agitation increases the risk for suicide by creating impulsivity and a press for action within the person (Pfeffer, 1992). Children who are hyperactive and feel that they must act immediately are at greater risk for suicide because of their inclination to act without thinking. Poor impulse control is often considered as a related risk factor for suicide, because children who lack impulse control are more likely to engage in drastic or irresponsible behavior. However, studies are mixed as to the relationship between poor impulse control and suicide (Harris and Ammerman, 1986).

16. Borderline Personality Disorder: The hallmarks of this disorder (instability, lability, unhappiness, desire for attention) often draw the borderline adolescent into suicidal behavior or self-injury. Borderline Personality Disorder is most dangerous when the adolescent has a co-occurring diagnosis of depression (Pfeffer, 1992).

Etiology

Biological Theories

Numerous explanations exist for the development of depressive disorders, but the two theories that have received the most attention are cognitive-behavioral and genetic-biological. Other authors have used psychoanalytic theory, family systems theory, and stress-and-coping theory to explain the development of depression in children.

Genetic-biological theories of depression note that depression tends to run in families. Proponents of these theories look for biological markers to explain the presence and development of depression in individuals. The risk of depression in children increases markedly if a parent or other close relative has depression, and children who have two depressed parents are at even higher risk (Beardslee et al., 1983; Kashani and Sherman, 1988; Weissman et al., 1987). Furthermore, the concordance rates for depression in monozygotic twins exceed 50% (even when the twins are reared apart), while those for dizygotic twins are under 20% (Gershon et al., 1977; Kashani and Sherman, 1988; Tsuang, 1978). Some preliminary evidence suggests that children who develop depression before puberty may have a greater genetic loading for the disorder, although this evidence generally does not control for environmental influences (Finch, Casat, and Carey, 1990; Kashani and Sherman, 1988). Over all, considerable evidence exists supporting a genetic role in depression, although the magnitude of this role remains to be discovered. It appears based on present data that genetics may create a mild predisposition for depression but that other environmental and biological factors are necessary for its full development.

The possibility of genetic transmission of depression suggests some mechanism of biological development of the disorder. Research in this area has focused on the neurochemical effects of antidepressant medications and the identification of biological markers for depression. Several neurotransmitters have been associated with the regulation of mood by the hypothalamus and limbic system: acetylcholine (ACH), norepinephrine (NE), and serotonin (5-HT). Because of the importance of these neurotransmitters for mood, imbalances in their production, secretion, or reuptake have been suggested as potential causes for depression. The catecholamine hypothesis, for example, focuses on disturbances of the catecholamine neurotransmitters, particularly NE. An initial test of this hypothesis found increased production of MHPG, a metabolite of NE, in depressed adults. However, these results have not been consistently replicated (Finch et al., 1990; Schildkraut, 1965). Similar theories have been posited for 5-HT, ACH, and a combination of neurotransmitters, although no single theory has yet been affirmed (Kashani and Schmid, 1992). Additional support for the importance of NE and 5-HT in the development of depression comes from evidence that their levels are affected by medications that have antidepressant effects. Amitriptyline (Elavil) and imipramine (Tofranil), for example, block reuptake of NE and 5 HT, while nortriptyline (Pamelor) and desipramine (Norpramin) affect NE (Finch et al., 1990; Kashani and Schmid, 1992).

A second direction of biological research on depression is the identification of biochemical markers for depression. Most of these biochemical markers are the result of presumed neuroendocrine abnormalities that may cause or result from depression. Perhaps the most well known marker of depression in adults is the dexamethasone suppression test (DST). The DST consists of oral administration of dexamethasone followed by repeated blood sampling over the next day. The DST is based on the principle that, in normal people, the production of cortisol is suppressed following administration of a dose of dexamethasone. However, a significant minority (40–50%) of depressed adults fail to suppress cortisol following administration of dexamethasone, compared to about 13% of the normal population (Arana, Baldessarini, and Ornsteen, 1985; Yaylayan, Weller, and Weller, 1992). Hence, the nonsuppression of cortisol following a dose of dexamethasone has been hypothesized to be a biological marker for depression. This effect may be a result of disregulation of NE and 5-HT, which control the inhibition and release of cortisol, respectively. Related tests of cortisol secretion involve monitoring the rhythm of secretion of cortisol and the baseline level of plasma cortisol (Finch et al., 1990; Kashani and Schmid, 1992; Weller and Weller, 1988).

The results of child DST studies have yielded minimally adequate sensitivity (50–80% probability of labeling a child as depressed when depression is actually present; 20–50% miss rate) and specificity (60–90% probability of labeling a child as *not* depressed when she is actually *not* depressed; 10–40% false positive diagnoses), and adolescent studies have shown similar or worse figures (30–70% sensitivity but 80–90% specificity; Casat, Arana, and Powell, 1989; Finch et al., 1990; Kashani and Schmid, 1992; Yaylayan et al., 1992). Other studies have found poorer DST sensitivity/specificity in child populations

(Kashani and Schmid, 1992; Yaylayan et al., 1992). Furthermore, the utility of the DST in predicting treatment response/relapse is unknown (Yaylayan et al., 1992), calling into question its use in clinical situations (Finch et al., 1990).

Other tests of biological markers measure the levels of growth hormone (GH) and melatonin, production of thyroid-stimulating hormone (TSH), and sleep abnormalities (Kashani and Schmid, 1992). Levels of GH are reported to be elevated in adult and adolescent depressives, who show blunted GH increases in response to doses of imipramine, desipramine, clonidine, and insulin (Finch et al., 1988; Yaylayan et al., 1992). Depressed children show hypersecretion of GH during sleep (Yaylayan et al., 1992). Melatonin levels show less of a nighttime rise in children and adults with Major Depressive Disorder, compared to controls (Brown et al., 1985; Cavallo et al., 1987). While hypothyroidism and hyporesponse of TSH in response to thyroid releasing hormone have been found in a small minority of depressed adults, no studies have found similar effects in children to date (Khan, 1987; Yaylayan et al., 1992). Sleep abnormalities, sometimes found in depressed adults (e.g., shortened REM latency, increased first REM period, decreased delta-wave sleep time, frequent awakenings, early morning awakening), are not typically found in depressed children, with the possible exception of shortened REM latency for adolescents (Kashani and Schmid, 1992; Yaylayan et al., 1992). In general, then, these other biological tests should be considered experimental and as providing only preliminary evidence for a biological theory of depression.

Psychological Theories

Cognitive-Behavioral Theories.   Perhaps the most widely accepted psychological theories of the etiology of depression use a cognitive-behavioral approach. Cognitive-behavioral theory emphasizes the role of the child's beliefs and behavioral contingencies in causing depression (Stark et al., 1991). A Beck (1976)-type cognitive-behavioral model, for example, holds that depressed children hold maladaptive thoughts and beliefs that distort the way they process information. These maladaptive beliefs consist of negative views of themselves, their world, and their future. Incoming information is interpreted based on their beliefs that they are incompetent, that their world is threatening, and that their future is hopeless. Hence, they see everyday events as hopeless, sad, and aversive, leading predictably to unhappiness. Cognitive errors such as overgeneralization (applying a specific event to all events) and minimization (trivializing the meaning of a positive event) result from this cognitive style. Evidence exists, for example, that depressed children evaluate their performance on a task more negatively than do controls, even when the groups show no difference on performance (Kendall, Stark, and Adam, 1990). Furthermore, studies indicate that depressed children have poorer self-concepts than do controls and that changes in cognitions cause changes in mood (Kashani and Sherman, 1988).

A second cognitive-behavioral model is the Seligman (1975) learned helplessness model. This model posits that depression results when children, through repeated experience with uncontrollable events, come to believe that they have no control over events in their lives. This leads to apathy and lack of motivation to modify aversive events, since the children can do nothing to change them (Kashani and Sherman, 1988). Because of some empirical inadequacies of the model, Seligman and colleagues (Abramson, Seligman, and Teasdale, 1978) have extended it to include the faulty attributions typically made by depressed people. These maladaptive attributions focus on internal, stable, and global attributions for negative life events. Hence, the individuals see themselves as responsible (internal); little can be done to change the situation (stable); and the situation is pervasive (global). Changes in any one of these three attributional dimensions could potentially protect the individuals from depressive symptomatology because they would not blame themselves for the situation, or the stability/pervasiveness of the situation would be seen as minimal and therefore not catastrophic. Depressive attributional styles have been found to be related to depressive symptoms in children over a relatively long (6 months) period of time (Seligman et al., 1984).

Other cognitive-behavioral models resemble the Beck and Seligman models, with slight differences in the emphasized maladaptive thoughts and beliefs. Rehm's (1977) self-control model, for example, centers on self-regulatory processes used by people to cope with stress. Depressive symptoms occur when self-monitoring, self-evaluation, and self-reinforcement are deficient or distorted. When these distortions occur, individuals overemphasize negative events, set unreachable self-standards, and fail to reward themselves for good performance. This interpretation of stressful events leads ultimately to unhappiness, desperation, hopelessness, and feelings of being helpless.

Lewinsohn (1974), on the other hand, proposes a more behaviorally based model that attributes depression to a reduction in reinforcement from the environment, with particular emphasis given to social reinforcement. People at risk for depression have social-skills deficits that cause them to elicit negative responses from others. A lack of positive responses from others (and other reinforcements), in turn, causes them to view the world negatively and withdraw, leading to depressive cognitions and maladaptive social behaviors. This cycle creates a continuing lack of environmental reinforcement and additional feelings of unhappiness. Social skills deficits are of central etiological importance in this and related cognitive theories (Kashani and Sherman, 1988; Kazdin, 1989a), which may apply particularly well to children, given the importance of the peer group and socialization to their psychological well-being.

Stress and Coping Theories. In addition to cognitive-behavioral theories, a second group of etiological theories of depression emphasizes stress, coping, and social support. These theories hold that stress renders individuals vulnerable to negative interpretations and emotions regarding themselves and their environment. If individuals feel overwhelmed by stress, they may become unhappy, hopeless, and desperate, resulting in the development of depressive symptoms. Factors that buffer individuals from stress, such as adaptive coping and social support, attenuate the effects of the stress and reduce risk of depression. Evidence exists, for example, that depressed people have experienced more stressful life events than have controls and that stressful events often immediately precede the development of depression (Kazdin, 1989a). Furthermore, depressed people tend to appraise stresses more negatively than do nondepressed people, creating additional feelings of being overwhelmed or stressed.

Stress, coping, and social support within the family may be especially important in the etiology of depression. Family stresses can contribute to the development of depressive symptoms, and the family can be a source of support to buffer its members from the negative effects of stress (Kaslow et al., 1990; Kronenberger, 1990). These effects may be particularly pronounced for children, who are emotionally and physically dependent on the family. Furthermore, modeling of affective responses to situations and of coping behaviors can have a profound effect on child behavior. Thus, the presence of a depressed parent in the household provides both a family stress and a maladaptive model for the children. Depressed children perceive their family more negatively than do nondepressed children, and depressed children are likely to have families with more psychopathology (Kaslow et al., 1990). In addition, depressed clinic children are more likely to have a depressed mother than are nondepressed clinic children (Kaslow et al., 1990), and the timing of child depression is closely related to the manifestation of maternal depression (Hammen, Burge, and Adrian, 1991). This latter finding argues against the mother–child concordance rate for depression being merely a result of genetic influence. It appears that high stress and the presence of a maternal model of depression put children at substantially greater risk than stress alone. Such depression evolves from the interpersonal relationship with a currently depressed parent as opposed to a purely genetic influence (Hammen et al., 1991). Once the depression emerges in the family system, it may be perpetuated by the system as a way of deflecting future stresses on the family (Teichman, 1989).

Psychoanalytic Theories. Psychoanalytic theories of adult depression attribute the low self-esteem, hopelessness, unhappiness, and other symptoms of the disorder to situations involving loss. A person who experiences the loss of a loved object, may feel anger at being abandoned or at having some issues unresolved. This anger, however, is threatening, since it is directed at the one who is loved and lost. To repress the feelings of anxiety and shame related to having this anger, the person represses the anger or unconsciously turns it on the self. This "anger turned inward" is then manifest on the surface in the form of negative cognitions, low self-esteem, hopelessness, guilt, and unhappiness. Other analytic theorists have taken somewhat different points of view from the starting point of loss. For example, the loss may be seen as creating feelings of anxiety about one's ability to continue effectively in the world, or the loss may remove an object/person who was the target of strong identification (Kashani and Schmid, 1992).

Applying these concepts to children is somewhat difficult, leading some psychoanalytic theorists to believe that children could not be depressed because they lacked the critical superego development to cause self-anger or self-punishment (Kazdin, 1989a). On the other hand, depression in very young children may be seen as the loss of the attachment object, creating a void in the development of the self through object relations and identification (Petti, 1989; Shafii and Shafii, 1992). Other analytic concepts such as repressed desires, unsatisfied need to be the center of the mother's attention, and frustrated desire for narcissistic gratification have also been invoked to explain the development of depression in children (Kazdin, 1989a).

ASSESSMENT PATTERNS

Perhaps no childhood psychological disorder has spawned a plethora of psychological and biological tests as large as the body of tests assessing childhood depression. Biological tests of depression (described earlier in the chapter) include the DST as well as growth hormone, melatonin, thyroid, and sleep EEG tests. None of these tests has proven wholly satisfactory in the assessment of childhood depression, although they are all widely used (especially sleep EEG and the DST). Psychological tests for childhood depression ask the child and/or parent specifically about depressive symptoms, either in interview or questionnaire form. In addition, most broad-band tests of childhood disorders, such as structured diagnostic interviews and behavior checklists, include a section on depression. Over all, the clinician's task is not to find an instrument assessing depression, but to select from the large body of instruments the ones that are reliable, valid, and clinically useful. (A sample assessment battery for depression in early and middle childhood is shown in Table 5.3.)

TABLE 5.3   Sample Assessment Battery for Depression in Early and Middle Childhood

PERSONALITY

Rorschach
Thematic Apperception Test
Sentence Completion Test

BEHAVIORAL

Child Behavior Checklist
Missouri Children's Behavior Checklist
Teacher's Report Form
Youth Self Report

SYNDROME-SPECIFIC

Children's Depression Inventory
Hopelessness Scale

Note: Assessment instruments are intended to supplement (not substitute for) a good clinical interview and, when possible, a structured diagnostic interview.

Broad Assessment Strategies

Cognitive Assessment

Clinician-Administered. At least one study (Kendall et al., 1990) suggests that depressed children do not have a cognitive processing deficit (not to be confused with the cognitive distortions seen in these children). Severe depression may affect a child's performance on cognitive testing if it results in deficits in concentration or in psychomotor retardation. Either of these deficits would result in substantially lower WISC-III Freedom from Distractibility and Processing Speed scores, and, to a lesser extent, lower Perceptual Organization scores (since these subtests are timed). Verbal Comprehension scores are unlikely to be affected by depression, since the tests are not timed, do not require extensive concentration, and involve material that is typically overlearned.

Achievement testing scores may be low relative to those of peers, particularly if the depression has affected the child's ability to learn at school. An equally plausible explanation, however, is that the child's poor performance at school has led to feelings of inadequacy and hopelessness that have developed into depression.

Psychological Assessment

Clinician-Administered. Perhaps the most common clinician-interpreted test for depressed adults is the MMPI. While the MMPI and MMPI-A can be administered to adolescents, their lower age range of 14 years severely limits their utility in the diagnosis of child depression (see Meyer, 1993, for MMPI patterns of depressed older adolescents and adults). Hence, clinician-based psychological assessment of depressed children relies primarily on interviews and projective testing. Depression is assessed by all of the major structured and semistructured diagnostic interviews, such as the Diagnostic Interview for Children and Adolescents (DICA-R), the Diagnostic Interview Schedule for Children (DISC-R), the Child Assessment Schedule (CAS), and the Schedule for Affective Disorders and Schizophrenia for School Age Children (K-SADS).

Projective testing can also be useful in the assessment of the depressed child, particularly if the child lacks insight or is denying symptoms. A variety of techniques can be used in this endeavor, ranging from sentence completion tests to storytelling tests to the Rorschach. All of these assessment instruments are based on the assumptions that the depressed child sees the world differently than a normal child and that the child will project this distorted perception onto an ambiguous stimulus. Ultimately this projected perception should provide the clinician with some insight into the child's unconscious conflicts or cognitive processing.

On the TAT and other storytelling tests, many depressed children tell one of two types of stories. The first type is the brief, unelaborated story, with little plot, excitement, or emotion. This story type often reflects the child's cognitive fatigue, hopelessness, lack of motivation, negative outlook, and/or passive resistance to change. Such children often feel so helpless, hopeless, and, sometimes, angry that they do not want to try anything, including a projective test. Hence, they provide the minimum amount of effort needed to overtly comply with the task, and, hope they bring it to an end.

The second type of TAT story often told by depressed children reflects their cognitive errors and negative affective state. These stories are dominated by negative themes and affects of sadness, anger, anxiety, and hopelessness. Main characters are often very unhappy, malicious, or victims of negative circumstances. Plots are dominated by death, separation, conflicts, or unhappiness, and story endings are either negative or miraculously, stereotypically positive. Careful analysis of the stories can provide the clinician with insight into the child's cognitive errors, fears, and current stresses. Particular attention should be paid to themes that are repeated across stories, strong affects within stories, unique story lines, and omissions of major card features.

The Rorschach also has several indicators of depression, most of which involve responses to achromatic or shading features of the card. Achromatic color responses presumably reflect depressive affects, while the shading responses may reflect psychic pain, stress, or negative self-views. Ultimately Rorschach responses should not be analyzed individually, but need to be viewed in the context of the content and other determinants of the response. Exner (1986) provides an excellent step-by-step approach to scoring and interpreting the Rorschach protocols of children and adults (see also Meyer, 1993). In addition to the determinants of the response, the content can be helpful in understanding the depressed child. Malicious or morbid contents, such as bugs, dead or injured animals or people, and blood, can be indicators of depression. As with the TAT, repeated content and unique answers may reflect salient features of the depression.

Numerous other projective techniques exist for the evaluation of depressed children, including countless variations of sentence completion and drawing tests. Interpretation of these tests varies by clinician, but the targeted responses are those that presumably reflect low self-esteem (such as small pictures, distorted pictures, or pictures missing important parts; or completed sentences that reflect negative comparisons of the child with other children), cognitive distortion (such as sentence endings that indicate catastrophizing, minimization, or other cognitive errors), or negative affect (such as frowns on pictures, cloudy days on pictures; or completed sentences that use words like "sad," "mad," or "worried"). Virtually any ambiguous stimulus can be used, but more established tests such as the Rorschach and TAT have the advantages of a greater data base and more research.

Several authors have expressed significant reservations about the use of projective tests in the assessment of depressed children. Kazdin (1987, 1990) notes that differences between depressed and nondepressed children are often not found in research using projective tests. Likewise, Finch et al. (1990) note problems with the validity of Exner's (1986) Depression Index and suggest that this measure be used only for experimental purposes, if at all. Ball et al.

(1991) found similar problems with Exner's Depression Index, with no relationships between it and other depression scores or depression diagnosis. Overall, little good research has been done to verify the utility of projective instruments in the diagnosis of depression, which is surprising given their widespread use.

Given these caveats, it appears that the wisest use of projective tests with depressed children is to generate hypotheses, which may then be followed up with interviews, other testing, or interventions. Projective tests should never be used alone in arriving at a depression diagnosis, and any conclusions drawn from projectives should be regarded as potentially important, but tentative. However, because of the numerous problems with child self-report and parental report of depressive symptoms, projectives are likely to remain an integral, if tentative, component of the assessment of childhood depression.

Behavioral Assessment

Parent-Report. Most broad-band measures of child behavior problems and psychopathology include a measure of depression. The Achenbach scales (CBCL, TRF, and YSR), for example, have several items measuring depressive symptoms. The most recent revisions of these scales include three subscales that contain depressive symptoms: Anxiety-Depression, Withdrawal, and Social Problems. Depressed children would likely elevate these three subscales into the 70–90 T-score range (Achenbach, 1991a, 1991b, 1991c).

The Achenbach scales have numerous advantages including meticulous scale development, good psychometric properties, and content congruence between respondents. Their principal disadvantages are that they are lengthy, do not include a "pure" depression subscale (because depression items clustered with anxiety items in the factor analyses), and do not mirror DSM-IV criteria. Hence, the Achenbach subscales should not be used for diagnostic purposes, although they may provide considerable insight into broad-band problems and respondent disagreement over symptoms.

Another broad band parent-response scale that can be used in the assessment of depressed children is the Personality Inventory for Children—Revised (PIC-R; Lachar, 1982). The PIC-R is a lengthy (420 true-false items) scale for parents of children between the ages of 3 and 16, which provides data about a range of behavior problems in addition to depression. The PIC-R Depression scale includes questions about depressed mood, social withdrawal, pessimism, anhedonia, and lethargy. It has good reliability and validity, although the length of the entire PIC is a drawback.

Child-Report. In addition to the Youth Self-Report (YSR), the Symptom Checklist-90—Revised (SCL-90-R) includes a depression scale. Unfortunately, however, both the YSR (which can be administered to children 11 years of age and older) and SCL-90-R (which can be administered to children 13 years of age and older; Derogatis, 1983) can be completed only by adolescents and thus are not appropriate for younger children.

Syndrome-Specific Tests

A growing body of research indicates that different informants differ considerably on ratings of behavior problems for the same child. Correlations between almost any combination of parent, child, teacher, and mental health worker ratings of the same behavior tend to be quite low (usually in the 0.20s; Achenbach, McConaughy, and Howell, 1987), although mother–father correlations may be somewhat higher (Kaslow and Racusin, 1990). In other words, child self-ratings of depression often do not correspond with parent-ratings of the child's depression, and neither set of ratings may correlate extremely highly with the clinician's DSM-IV diagnosis (Kaslow and Racusin, 1990; Kazdin, 1989b). Most research indicates that parents underestimate the child's self-reported depression, although this is not always the case, particularly for clinically referred samples (Kaslow and Racusin, 1990). In addition, reports of depressive symptoms and associated features tend to be consistent within respondents but not between respondents. Thus, child-ratings of depression correlate well with child-ratings of self-esteem, hopelessness, loneliness, and so on, but correlate poorly with parent ratings of self-esteem, hopelessness, etcetera. Parent-ratings of child depression, on the other hand, correlate well with parent-ratings of child self-esteem, hopelessness, loneliness, et cetera, but poorly with child ratings of these constructs (Kazdin, 1989b, 1990).

These findings do not necessarily imply that the child or parent is reporting inaccurately (Kazdin, 1990); other reasons for informant differences are situational specificity of behavior (e.g., the parent only sees a subsample of the child's behavior) and differences in construct measured (e.g., parent-report is dependent on behavior, while child-report reflects internal experience as well as behavior). In fact studies indicate that both child- and parent-reports of depression are valid (Kazdin, 1990). In any event, current research argues for the use of multiple informants from multiple settings and integration of this information with clinical interview in making a diagnosis and formulations (Kaslow and Racusin, 1990; Kazdin, 1987, 1990).

Clinician-Administered

Unstructured Interviews. In addition to structured diagnostic information, the data obtained in the unstructured clinical interview with the family can be relevant in understanding the characteristics and etiology of the child's depression. The development of the depressive symptomatology should be carefully analyzed, with particular attention to stressors and other events coinciding with the emergence of depressive symptoms. Co-occurrence of a stressful event with onset of depressive symptoms may suggest diagnoses ranging from a normal reaction to an Adjustment Disorder to a Mood Disorder. Family psychiatric history, especially for mood disorders, should also be carefully covered in the interview; incidence of Bipolar or Major Depressive Disorder may suggest a genetic risk and possible role for medication.

The clinician's observations are also crucial in the interview. Depressed children often appear fatigued, irritated, bored, or sad in interview, although they will on rare occasions respond well to the stimulation and support of the clinical setting. Clinical observations that are discrepant with parent- or child-report suggest the need for caution in making a diagnosis of depression.

Interview Schedule for Children.   The Interview Schedule for Children (ISC; Kovacs, 1978, 1981, 1985) is a semistructured clinical interview designed to assess mental status, behavioral observations, developmental milestones, symptoms of depression, conduct disorders, and other behavior problems in children age 8–17. Both parent and child are interviewed; duration, onset, and severity are investigated for most symptoms. The ISC is designed to be administered by trained interviewers, and diagnoses are assigned based on consensus of a group of professionals. Psychometric properties are reported to be good (Kaslow and Racusin, 1990). The ISC is primarily a research scale (Petti, 1989) and is infrequently used in clinical settings.

Bellevue Index of Depression.   The Bellevue Index of Depression (BID; Petti, 1985), a forty-item scale of depression, is designed to quantify the clinician's impressions of depressive symptoms in children age 6–12. Interviews with the parents and child are used for the basis of the clinician's ratings. Each item is rated on a 4- (0–3) point scale of severity and a 4- (1–4) point scale of duration. Fifty-two sample questions assist the clinician in the gathering of information for the clinician-rated items; the questions ask about the severity and duration of each symptom. The items of the BID cluster into ten groups: dysphoric mood, self-deprecatory ideation, aggressive behavior, sleep disturbance, change in school performance, diminished socialization, change in attitude toward school, somatic complaints, loss of energy, and unusual change in appetite/weight.

The BID has been shortened and changed somewhat to yield a revised version (BID-R; Kazdin et al., 1983). The BID-R has twenty-six items. For each item, severity is measured on a 1 (not at all) to 5 (very much) scale, and duration is rated on a 1 (new) to 3 (always) scale. Three BID-R scores can be obtained based on child and/or parent interviews: severity (sum of severity items), duration (sum of duration items), and total (sum of severity and duration items)(Kazdin et al., 1983; Kazdin, Rodgers, and Colbus, 1986). BID-R scores have been found to correlate with CDI scores within informant (i.e., child CDI with child BID-R; parent CDI with parent BID-R)(Kazdin, 1989b).

Children's Depression Rating Scale.   The Children's Depression Rating Scale (CDRS; Poznanski, Cook, and Carroll, 1979; Poznanski, Freeman, and Mokros, 1985; Poznanski et al., 1984) is a fifteen-item clinician-completed depression rating scale for children age 6–12. The CDRS is similar to the Hamilton Rating Scale for Depression. Each item is rated by the clinician on a 1–5 scale of severity based on data about the child's behavior during the past month, gathered from multiple interview sources (usually parents and child) and observation of the child's behavior.

A revised version of the CDRS (CDRS-R; Poznanski et al., 1985) includes seventeen items about verbalizations of depressed feelings, depressed feelings observed by clinician, irritability, weeping, appetite, sleep, fatigue, hypoactivity, physical complaints, self-esteem, sense of guilt, morbid ideation, suicidal ideation, anhedonia, social withdrawal, tempo of speech, and academic functioning; fourteen items are rated on a 1–7 severity scale, while three are rated on a 1–5 severity scale. Scores can be obtained for number of positive symptoms (items with a score of 3 or higher) and total depression severity (sum of all seventeen items). Total scores greater than 40 are indicative of probable depression (Mokros and Poznanski, 1992; Poznanski et al., 1985). Psychometric properties for the scale are reported to be good (Kaslow and Racusin, 1990), although further study of this instrument is needed.

Children's Affective Rating Scale. The Children's Affective Rating Scale (CARS; McKnew et al., 1979) is a three-item (mood/behavior, verbal expression, and fantasy) scale measuring clinical impressions of depression in children age 5–15 (McKnew et al., 1979). Based on observation and interview, each item is rated on a 10-point scale, with verbal descriptors used to anchor the "low," "moderate," and "high" ranges on the scale. Interrater reliability and validity are reported to be adequate (McKnew et al., 1979). The CARS has seen very little research or clinical use, so its psychometric properties and clinical utility are not well established. It may have value as a very brief rating scale, but it should be used with caution if at all.

Child-Report

The largest body of syndrome-specific assessment instruments for depression are based on the self-report of the child. Virtually all of these tests contain questions asking the child about the presence and/or severity of depressive symptoms. The scales differ in their length, format, and targeted symptomatology. Some are designed to assess depressive symptoms only, while others assess associated features of depression such as hopelessness and loneliness. All suffer from the disadvantages of self-report questionnaires, particularly when the respondent is a child: social desirability, difficulty understanding questions, lack of insight into problem, biased self-view, and limited vocabulary (Finch et al., 1990; Kazdin, 1990). Nevertheless, self-report measures have a major advantage: They allow the direct questioning of the child about internal states, which otherwise can only be inferred by outsiders. Studies indicate that children may be more accurate reporters of their internal experiences than observers are (Kazdin, 1990), while observers may be more objective sources of information about external behaviors. A caveat to be considered in the use of observer-report instruments, on the other hand, is the effect of observers' psychopathology and/or observational skill on their report of the child's behavior (Kazdin, 1990). All of these factors must be considered when a self-report instrument is administered to a depressed child, and the use of another reporter of the child's behavior is advisable. Hence, several of these tests include parent or teacher forms.

Children's Depression Inventory. The Children's Depression Inventory (CDI; Kovacs, 1992) is the most widely used measure of depression in children (Kazdin, 1990). A downward extension of the Beck Depression Inventory, the CDI contains twenty-seven items measuring cognitive, affective, behavioral, and social symptoms of depression in children age 6–17. Each item consists of three statements, one representing nondepressed symptomatology, one representing moderately depressed symptomatology, and one representing severely depressed symptomatology. The child chooses the one of the three statements that best describes him or her during the past 2 weeks. Endorsing the nondepressed statement receives a score of 0; the moderately depressed statement is scored 1; the severely depressed statement is scored 2. Items are added to give a total score and five subscale scores (Negative Mood, Interpersonal Problems, Ineffectiveness, Anhedonia, Negative Self-Esteem). Raw scores can be converted to T-scores based on normative samples divided by age and sex (Kovacs, 1992). Although T-scores are now available to assist with CDI interpretation, in the past interpretation has often been done based on cutoff raw scores of 12 to 19 (Fristad et al., 1991). Scores at or above the cutoff presumably indicate clinical levels of depression. The most common cutoff score is probably 19, with children scoring at or above this level classified as clinically depressed (Smucker et al., 1986). Answers to individual items may also be clinically relevant, such as item 9, which asks about suicidal ideation and intent.

The CDI has good psychometric properties, with the possible exception of discriminant validity in clinical samples. Internal consistency reliability is high, and test-retest reliability is moderate. Construct and criterion validity studies show that the CDI relates to self-esteem, hopelessness, cognitive processing, and depression as measured by other instruments (Kazdin, 1989b, 1990; Kovacs, 1992). However, it does not typically differentiate clinically referred depressed children from other clinical subgroups, especially anxious children (Kazdin, 1990; Kovacs, 1992), although some studies do find differences in CDI scores between depressed and anxious children (e.g., Hodges, 1990). In addition, the CDI was not designed to reflect DSM-IV symptomatology and hence may not have acceptable power in identifying DSM-IV depressed children; in one study, only 31.6% of children with a Major Depressive Disorder diagnosis scored at or above the CDI cutoff of 19 (Kazdin, 1989b). Therefore, the CDI should be considered as a self-report measure of depression-anxiety, with the items face-valid for depression. Combined with other scales from multiple informants, it can contribute significantly to the assessment of a child's depression-related distress.

Some authors use a parent-completed version of the CDI (Fristad et al., 1991; Kazdin, 1989b; Kendall et al., 1990) to gather information from multiple informants. Studies have found relatively low agreement between child and parent CDI scores, with parents tending to give higher scores (Fristad et al., 1991; Kazdin, 1989b). Other studies with different instruments show parents giving lower depression scores than children (Kaslow and Racusin, 1990). A child cutoff score of 17 for the 67th percentile, for example, corresponded to a parent score of 24 in one study (Kazdin, 1989b). As with child scores, parent

CDI scores do not identify DSM-IV diagnosed depressed children very well (Fristad et al., 1991; Kazdin, 1989b). In fact, child CDI scores may be more predictive of depression than parent CDI scores (Fristad et al., 1991).

Children's Depression Scale. The Children's Depression Scale (CDS; Lang and Tisher, 1978; Tisher, Lang-Takac, & Lang, 1992) is a sixty-six–item measure of depressive symptoms and positive affects in children age 9–16. Each item is printed on a card; the cards are read to the child and placed by the child into one of five categories—very wrong (assigned a value of 1), wrong (2), don't know/not sure (3), right (4), and very right (assigned a value of 5). The card response format presumably encourages accurate responding on the part of the child, although a paper-and-pencil form is also available (Petti, 1989). Next to the CDI, the CDS may be the most used measure of child depression (Mokros and Poznanski, 1992).

CDS items cluster into two broad scales (48-item Depression scale and 18 item Positive affective experience scale) and six specific subscales (Affective Response, Social Problems, Self-Esteem, Preoccupation with Own Sickness or Death, Guilt, and Pleasure/Enjoyment). Scale and subscale scores are sums of item scores, with higher scores reflecting more depression. Based on literature review, clinically depressed samples score in the 165 to 190 range on the Depression scale, while normal controls score in the 120 to 140 range (Tisher et al., 1992). Other clinical groups score between these ranges (Tisher et al., 1992). Like the CDI, there is a parent version of the CDS (which uses pencil and paper instead of pictures). The reported relationships between child and parent CDS scores are small (Tisher et al., 1992; Mokros & Poznanski, 1992).

Although the CDS has not been subjected to the quantity of research scrutiny that has accompanied the CDI, it has seen use in numerous studies (Tisher et al., 1992). Internal consistency appears to be good. Test-retest reliability was adequate in one study, but additional test-retest information is needed (Tisher et al., 1992). Norms are reported for several nonclinical samples in various studies (Tisher et al., 1992), but representative normative samples have not been gathered. Factor analysis has not supported the subscales, which were derived on an *a priori* basis, but some evidence does exist that the depression and positive affective experience scales are not simply opposites of each other (Kazdin, 1990; Tisher et al., 1992). Studies have also found a significant relationship between CDS scores and other measures of depression (Kazdin, 1989b; Tisher et al., 1992). Discriminant validity (ability to differentiate between depressed and other groups) is reported to be better than that of the CDI (Tisher et al., 1992), although additional study is needed (Finch et al., 1990). The CDS is useful because of its broad range of items, its novel response format, and its inclusion of a positive experience scale. However, some drawbacks (uncertain psychometrics, lack of empirical verification for subscales, time and difficulty to administer, weak norms) limit its utility for general clinical use.

Finch et al. (1990) suggest that the CDS is more a measure of negative affect in general than of depressive symptomatology in particular. In this respect, CDS scores can be interpreted in the same manner as CDI scores—as a measure of anxiety-depression and general upset (Kazdin, 1990).

Depression Self Rating Scale.   The Depression Self Rating Scale (DSRS; Birleson, 1981; Birleson et al., 1987) is an eighteen-item self-report measure of depression for children age 7–14. Each item is a depressive symptom that the child rates on a 3-point (0–2) scale of frequency (most of the time, sometimes, never) based on the experiences of the past week (sometimes the past 2 weeks are used; Asarnow, Carlson, and Guthrie, 1987). Item scores are added to give a total depression score; scores of 13 or 14 and higher indicate depression (Birleson, 1981; Birleson et al., 1987). Reliability and validity for the DSRS are reported to be adequate (Birleson, 1981; Finch et al., 1990; Kaslow and Racusin, 1990; Petti, 1989), although little research has been done on its psychometric properties. This fact, combined with the lack of scale norms, limits the scale's clinical utility. Modified versions of the DSRS with additional items have been used but have not yet been adequately studied (Asarnow and Carlson, 1985; Kaslow and Racusin, 1990).

Center for Epidemiological Studies—Depression Scale for Children (CES-DC).   The CES-DC (Weissman, Orvaschel, and Padian, 1980) is a twenty-item self-report scale modeled after the adult version of the CES-D. Items are rated on a 0 (not at all) to 3 (a lot) scale based on the frequency with which the child experienced each depressive symptom in the past week. The sum of the items yields a total depression score. The CES-DC's focus on frequency as opposed to intensity of depressive symptoms differentiates it from other self-report depression scales. Hence, high scores on the CES-DC indicate high frequency of depressive symptomatology but do not necessarily relate to severity of symptoms. For example, correlations between CES-DC total scores (measuring frequency of depressive symptoms) and CDI total scores (measuring intensity of depressive symptoms) were found to be only 0.44 (Weissman et al., 1980). Finch et al. (1990) summarize studies indicating questionable test-retest reliability and discriminant validity for the CES-DC. They suggest that it not be used clinically without further research.

Reynolds Adolescent Depression Scale.   The Reynolds Adolescent Depression Scale (RADS; Reynolds and Coats, 1986; Reynolds, 1987) is a thirty-item measure of depression in adolescents. Each item is rated on a 4-point scale, and item scores are summed to give a total score. Normative data are available for a large sample of adolescents between ages 13 and 18 (Reynolds, 1987). Psychometric properties are quite good (Finch et al., 1990), with good test-retest reliability and excellent internal consistency. RADS scores correlate highly with other measures of depression and related constructs, suggesting good validity as well (Finch et al., 1990; Reynolds, 1987). The utility of the RADS is tempered by its somewhat limited age range, particularly at the lower end.

Reynolds Child Depression Scale.   The Reynolds Child Depression Scale (RCDS; Reynolds, 1989; Reynolds and Graves, 1989) is a thirty-item measure of depression in children in grades 3–6 similar to the RADS. Items are intended to correspond roughly to DSM-III-R criteria for Major Depressive Disorder and Dysthymic Disorder. The first twenty-nine items are scored on a 4-point frequency ("almost never" to "all the time") scale, while the thirtieth item is a list of five faces ranging from sad to happy (scored on a 1 to 5 point scale). The sum of the items gives a depression score. Internal consistency, test-retest reliability, and criterion validity (using other depression scales and interview as criteria) are reported to be good, and norms exist based on a relatively large normative sample (Reynolds, 1989; Reynolds and Graves, 1989).

Depression Adjective Checklist.   Forms H and I of the Children's Version of the Depression Adjective Checklist (C-DACL; Sokoloff and Lubin, 1983) are thirty-four–item lists of adjectives that pertain to depressed mood or its absence. Internal consistency reliability and validity are reported to be good (Sokoloff and Lubin, 1983). The C-DACL has low test-retest reliability, which is consistent with the authors' contention that the version used in their study is a state measure as opposed to a trait measure. A trait measure of the C-DACL exists (differing from the state measure only by changing the time frame from "how you feel today" to "how you generally feel"), although its psychometric properties are not well established. Over all, the C-DACL has not received enough research or clinical attention to justify its use in the clinical setting.

Modified Zung.   The Modified Zung (Lefkowitz and Tesiny, 1980) is a sixteen-item yes-no self-report measure of depressive symptoms derived from the adult version of the Zung scale (Kaslow and Racusin, 1990; Kazdin, 1990). It yields a total depression score for children in fourth and fifth grades. Reliability is reported to be adequate (Kaslow and Racusin, 1990), although the scale has not been sufficiently researched to merit its use in the clinical setting.

Preschool Symptoms Self-Report.   The Preschool Symptom Self-Report (PRESS; Martini, Strayhorn, and Puig-Antich, 1990), a twenty-five–item self-report measure of depression in children age 3–5, has the youngest age range for a self-report measure of depression. Each PRESS item consists of two pictures, one illustrating a symptom of depression and the other showing the absence of the symptom. Each picture is described by a caption that is read aloud by the examiner, followed by the question, "Which one is most like you?" Total PRESS score is the number of symptom pictures (e.g., depicting a depressive symptom) chosen by the child. Separate male and female forms exist, differing only in the sex of the main character in the pictures. A parent/teacher version of the PRESS exists as well (Martini et al., 1990). The psychometric properties of the PRESS have received relatively little attention, with one study finding adequate test-retest and internal consistency reliability; reliability does not appear to be affected by the child's age (Martini et al., 1990). Correlations between child, parent, and teacher ratings on the PRESS were essentially zero (Martini et al., 1990). More research is needed on this instrument before its clinical use can be endorsed.

Children's Attributional Style Questionnaire.   The Children's Attributional Style Questionnaire (CASQ or KASTAN; Benfield, Palmer et al., 1988; Bodiford et al., 1988; Kaslow, Tannenbaum, and Seligman, 1978; Seligman and Peterson, 1986) is a forty-eight–item measure of the attributional style of children in third through sixth grades (Kazdin, 1990). Based on the reformulated learned helplessness theory of Abramson et al. (1978), it does not assess depression by itself, but rather attributional biases thought to be related to the development of depressive symptoms. The CASQ consists of a number of descriptions of events. For each event the child chooses one of two possible causes. Three attributional dimensions are assessed by the CASQ (internal-external, global-specific, and stable-unstable) for two valences of outcome (good and bad). The CASQ yields six subscales (Good Internality, Good Stability, Good Globality, Bad Internality, Bad Stability, and Bad Globality), two composites (Positive and Negative), and a Depressive Attribution score (Positive minus Negative)(Kaslow et al., 1978; Bodiford et al., 1988). Internal, global, and stable attributions are believed to be related to the development of depressive symptoms in the case of bad outcomes (Abramson et al., 1978). The CASQ has been predominantly used as a research instrument, although it could be clinically useful in identifying target attributions for cognitive-behavioral therapy.

Hopelessness Scale for Children. The Hopelessness Scale for Children (Kazdin et al., 1986) is a seventeen-item true-false scale measuring negative future expectations in children age 6–13. Children receive 1 point for each item they endorse in the "hopeless" direction. Items appear to cluster into two factors: negative expectations/giving up and unhappiness/negative expectations. Like the CASQ, the Hopelessness Scale does not measure depression, but rather an associated feature: future expectations and hopelessness. Higher scores reflect greater hopelessness and correlate with depression, suicidal ideation, low self-esteem, poor social skills, poor school performance, and CDI scores (Kazdin, 1989a, 1989b; Kazdin et al., 1986).

Children's Negative Cognitive Error Questionnaire (CNCEQ). The CNCEQ, (Leitenberg, Yost, and Carroll-Wilson, 1986) is a twenty-four–item measure of cognitive processing errors based on Beck's (1976) theory of depression. For each item the child is presented with a situation and a statement about the situation that reflects one of Beck's cognitive errors. Using a 1–5 scale, the child rates the degree to which the statement reflects his or her thoughts about or perceptions of the situation. The scale is designed to be completed by children in fourth through eighth grades (Leitenberg et al., 1986). The psychometric properties of the scale appear to be adequate, and data based on a large sample of 4th-, 6th-, and 8th-graders has been published (Leitenberg et al., 1986).

Loneliness Questionnaire. The Loneliness Questionnaire (Asher, Hymel, and Renshaw, 1984; Asher and Wheeler, 1985) is a twenty-four–item measure of loneliness at school for children in third through sixth grade. Items assess popularity, difficulty making friends, and social isolation at school. Children rate each item on a 5-point scale of degree to which the item is true of them (e.g., always true, true most of the time, true sometimes, hardly ever true, not true at all). Eight of the items are "filler" items and are not used in scoring. Research has not yet demonstrated clinical utility or clear relationships between this scale and other depression scales.

Other Measures.   Many other instruments are potentially useful in the measurement of depressive symptoms and associated features (Kazdin, 1990). A multitude of additional specific depression measures exist, for example, but many of these have been inadequately researched and have unknown psychometric properties (see Kaslow and Racusin, 1990, and Kazdin, 1990, for reviews). In addition, measures of features associated with depression may also be helpful, such as stress (e.g., Life Events Checklist; Johnson and McCutcheon, 1980), reinforcement (e.g., Adolescent Reinforcement Survey Schedule; Holmes et al., 1987), social support (e.g., the Social Support Questionnaire; Sarason et al., 1983), social skills (e.g., Matson Evaluation of Social Skills with Youngsters; Matson, Rotatori, and Helsel, 1983), maladaptive thoughts (e.g., Automatic Thoughts Questionnaire; Hollon and Kendall, 1980), self-esteem (e.g., Piers-Harris Self-Concept Scale for Children; Piers, 1984) and family environment (e.g., the Family Environment Scale; Moos and Moos, 1981). Ultimately the decision whether to administer these additional instruments will depend on the characteristics of the child, the etiology of the depression, and the orientation of therapy.

Parent-Report

As previously noted, the CDI, CDS, and PRESS have parent forms that are identical to the child forms but that use parental response instead of self-report. These modified child self-report inventories have not been extensively studied.

Other-Report

Peer Nomination Inventory of Depression (PNID).   The PNID (Lefkowitz and Tesiny, 1980) is a twenty-item measure of depression (14 items), happiness (4 items), and popularity (2 items) in the classroom situation. It can be used with children who are in approximately fourth or fifth grade who know each other in a social situation (usually the classroom). Each child nominates a peer(s) for each of the twenty items, based on which person in the group is best described by the item. Each child's PNID score is the number of nominations he or she receives on the depression items divided by the number of children in the class. Subscales of happiness and popularity can also be derived based on their respective items (Lefkowitz and Tesiny, 1980).

The PNID has good internal consistency, test-retest reliability, and interrater reliability (Kaslow and Racusin, 1990; Kazdin, 1990). Validity studies show only moderate to low correlations with self- and teacher-report of depression (Kazdin, 1990; Lefkowitz and Tesiny, 1980, 1985). However, this is typical for ratings from different informants, and construct validity of the PNID appears to be good (Kazdin, 1990). Norms for third through fifth grade are available (Lefkowitz and Tesiny, 1985).

☐   TREATMENT OPTIONS

Treatment options for depression in early and middle childhood are outlined in Table 5.4.

Medication

The effects of medication on childhood depression are variable. Furthermore, studies of antidepressant treatment effects in children tend to produce much

TABLE 5.4   Treatment Options for Depression in Early and Middle Childhood

MEDICATION

Tricyclic antidepressants
Prozac (emerging use; anecdotal reports)

PSYCHOTHERAPY

Cognitive-behavioral interventions

    Psychoeducation of the child—examples of linkage between thoughts, feelings, and behaviors
    Self-monitoring
    Challenging automatic thoughts
    Cognitive restructuring
    Self-reinforcement
    Activity scheduling
    Realistic goal setting
    Behavioral exposure
    Relaxation training
    Social-skills training
    Cognitive-affective modeling
    Anticipatory coping
    Problem solving
    Self-talk

Play therapy
Group therapy

FAMILY INTERVENTIONS

Family therapy
Parent psychotherapy

Note: This outline of options summarizes major treatments covered in the text. Specific treatments are often combined into an intervention package. Refer to the text for additional descriptions of each treatment. This table is not necessarily an exhaustive list of all treatments available.

weaker results than do studies of adults. This lack of clear findings contrasts with the abundance of biological theories for childhood depression.

The most obvious potential medications for the treatment of childhood depression are the tricyclic antidepressants, which include imipramine (Tofranil), desipramine (Norpramin), amitriptyline (Elavil), and nortriptyline (Pamelor) (Rancurello, 1985). In open, uncontrolled trials, 50–100% of children and 30–40% of adolescents were reported to respond positively to tricyclics (Pliszka, 1991; Rancurello, 1985), although the results of controlled, blind treatment studies are mixed (Jensen, Ryan, and Prien, 1992; Pliszka, 1991; Rancurello, 1985; Ryan, 1992). This discrepancy in findings may be the result of as many as 60% of children and adolescents improving on placebo (Pliszka, 1991). Rancurello (1985) reports that dysphoria, anhedonia, and suicidal ideation improve on tricyclics, but his conclusions are apparently based on a review of only one or two studies. Ryan (1992) summarizes studies indicating a plasma level–dependent response of imipramine, but other studies reviewed by Ryan (1992) show no difference of imipramine over placebo. Similar mixed or negative imipramine results have been found with adolescents, and studies with prozac have also not yet provided convincing results (Ryan, 1992).

At present the data on the efficacy of tricyclics for childhood depression are so tentative that Pliszka (1991) writes, "The data do not allow one to conclude that antidepressants are clearly effective in either childhood or adolescent affective disorder" (p. 317). Kazdin (1989a), however, disagrees: "Current results have suggested clear therapeutic effects, particularly for imipramine, when plasma levels fall within a specified range. . . . Studies of adolescents do not provide parallel support" (p. 156). Angold (1988) suggests that there probably exists a group of tricyclic-responsive children, but that there is currently no way to identify them. In light of the current state of disagreement over the efficacy of tricyclics for depressed children, Jensen et al.'s (1992) point of view is likely to best represent the state of knowledge about the treatment of childhood depression with tricyclics: "All in all, the available data do not yet provide evidence for the efficacy of TCAs in children and adolescents with major depression, but further studies will be needed before one can conclude with certainty that they are ineffective" (p. 35). Hence, while numerous explanations have been offered for the current discrepancies in tricyclic research, more research in this area is clearly needed. Uncertainty about the effects of the tricyclics, combined with knowledge of their side effects in children, argues for caution in using them to treat depression in children (Pliszka, 1991; Rancurello, 1985; Simeon, 1989).

Even more than with the tricyclics, the effects of monoamine oxidase inhibitors (MAOI) on depression in children are not known. The few child studies that exist have such questionable methodology as to render them essentially useless (Rancurello, 1985). Furthermore, use of the MAOIs requires dietary restrictions, with extreme physical consequences for violating these restrictions. Hence, use of the MAOI's with children, who may not understand the importance of the dietary restrictions, should be done with great care (Rancurello, 1985; Ryan, 1992).

The emergence of selective serotonin reuptake inhibitor (SSRI) medications as the treatment of choice for depressed adults may be occurring for children as well. However, use of SSRIs in child populations is far less common than for adults, and placebo-controlled outcome studies remain to be seen. Some psychiatrists prescribe Prozac for childhood depression, with anecdotal reports of positive results.

Psychotherapy

Cognitive-Behavioral Interventions

Cognitive-behavioral therapy for depression in children follows directly from theories of the cognitive-behavioral etiology of depression (Beck, 1976; Lewinsohn, 1974; Rehm, 1977). These theories posit that depression results from maladaptive and distorted cognitions, schemas, and perceptions (Schrodt, 1992). In other words, depressed children tend to see themselves and their lives more negatively than do nondepressed children (Schrodt, 1992). These negative interpretations reinforce the child's self-view as inadequate and hopeless. Ultimately, sadness and despair result from this negative self- and world-view. When future events occur, they are interpreted in line with the child's negative bias, creating a cycle of depression.

Cognitive-behavioral therapies seek to change children's distorted cognitions with a variety of techniques. First, a firm therapeutic alliance must be established, since the remainder of therapy will involve challenges to the children's way of thinking. If children do not accept the therapist, they are very unlikely to accept the therapist's challenges to their cognitions, particularly because many children do not want to be in therapy in the first place. During this initial period, problems, goals, and a therapeutic contract are agreed upon, giving the children a sense of what will happen in therapy and when (Schrodt, 1992). Often cognitive-behavioral therapy will be time-limited, intensifying the need for a clear sense of agenda. Following these preliminary tasks, cognitive-behavioral interventions are undertaken in therapy. These interventions take many forms, but the most common ones are (Lewinsohn and Rohde, 1993; Schrodt, 1992; Stark et al., 1991):

- Psychoeducation
- Self-monitoring
- Challenging automatic thoughts
- Cognitive restructuring
- Self-reinforcement
- Activity scheduling
- Realistic goal setting
- Behavioral exposure
- Relaxation training

- Social-skills training
- Cognitive-affective modeling
- Anticipatory coping
- Problem solving
- Self-talk

Psychoeducational interventions involve teaching the child the tenets of the cognitive-behavioral theories of depression. Specifically, the child learns that distorting incoming information can lead to the thoughts and feelings characteristic of depression. This can be particularly difficult to explain to young children, who may have problems monitoring what they are thinking. Furthermore, young children tend to find lengthy psychological explanations boring and fail to attend to them. Hence, cognitive-behavioral principles usually must be acted out for younger children, for example in doll or puppet play.

One such technique involves the therapist taking a puppet that adopts cognitive distortions similar to those of the child. The distortions are presented in play such that the child sees that they are not realistic and cause the puppet to behave maladaptively. Through another puppet the therapist or child can point out the depressed puppet's problems. The depressed puppet may resist change but eventually see the more adaptive point of view. Stories can also be used for the psychoeducation of young children. In these stories the main character may have a cognitive distortion that creates problems that are only solved when he changes the way he thinks.

For older children, psychoeducation can be more direct. Older children can be taught about demographics, symptoms, causes, and effects of depression. Depression theories and treatment rationales can be spelled out more clearly to these children. Examples can be provided, such as pointing out the child's cognitive errors and showing how they lead to depressive symptoms. Defining such cognitive distortions as personalization, catastrophizing, overgeneralization, and minimization (Beck, 1976; Schrodt, 1992) also enhances the process of monitoring and correcting thoughts. In addition to these in-therapy techniques, numerous books exist to assist with psychoeducation related to depression (Dennison, 1989).

Many children respond to game-like ways of teaching the premises of cognitive-behavioral therapy (Dennison, 1989). Stark et al. (1992), for example, suggest several games to teach children how thoughts and affects are related. In Emotional Vocabulary the players pick cards with names of emotions. The players describe how the emotion feels, state the situation in which they last felt the emotion, and then state what a person who is experiencing the emotion might be thinking or doing. In Emotional Charades, one player acts out an emotion while another player tries to guess what the emotion is. When the emotion is correctly named, the second player states the situation in which he or she last felt the emotion and what his or her thoughts were at that time. Stark et al. (1992) and Dennison (1989) suggest other games, all of which have as their goal increasing children's awareness of what they are thinking and feeling.

It is often a good idea to involve parents in the psychoeducation, since they may be called on to facilitate the child's improvement at home. Parents may encourage the child to complete therapy homework assignments. They may also help to point out cognitive distortions to the child, provided that this does not create problems for the child or the family. Therefore, parents should have a firm sense of the goals and tenets of therapy.

The therapist must take care not to be overly preachy or evaluative during psychoeducation. Rather, psychoeducation should take the form of mutual discussion between the therapist and the child, with the goals of therapy always in mind. The tone of the session should be enjoyable, interesting, and engaging. A strong therapeutic alliance is also important at this time, since the child is being asked to admit problems and the necessity of change. Some children may be threatened by this and reject the notion outright.

Psychoeducation is often combined with homework assignments to apply what is learned in therapy. One such intervention is *self-monitoring* the monitoring of automatic negative thoughts, behaviors, and emotions (Stark et al., 1991). Initially the child is asked to track simple behaviors and emotions, such as the times when he or she is sad or happy. The target thought/emotion is then attached to the monitoring of other related phenomena, such as the situation in which the emotion occurred and the thoughts that accompanied the emotion (Kazdin, 1989a). Situation, thought, and emotion are then recorded for discussion at the next therapy session. This is done using a three-column worksheet, with the situation in the first column, the emotion in the second column, and the thought in the third column. In cases where the child does not have time to write in narrative form, tick marks can be used to track the occurrence and timing of thoughts, feelings, and situations (Stark et al., 1991).

Monitoring thoughts and emotions may initially occur within therapy. The therapist helps the child trace the automatic thoughts underlying feelings such as frustration, sadness, and inadequacy. These thoughts and feelings are then recorded, during the therapy session, just as they would be at home. The use of self-monitoring in therapy gives the therapist a chance to observe the child and make corrections or changes in the procedure. The child may then implement self-monitoring at home, with instructions to record the self-monitoring data as soon as possible after the target thought/emotion.

Self-monitoring encourages children to gain insight into their feelings and the thoughts that underlie them. In some cases, this insight alone and the increased feeling of self-control are beneficial. In other cases this information must be used in therapy to challenge maladaptive thoughts and to show how these thoughts lead to negative affect. Based on the self-monitoring diary, children are encouraged to change their patterns of behavior to maximize situations and thoughts leading to positive affect.

Much of the focus in cognitive-behavioral therapy is on the identification of maladaptive, automatic thoughts that underlie negative emotion (Schrodt, 1992). Children will tend to focus on problems (this went wrong, that went wrong; I don't like this or that) or excuses (this was the fault of something besides me; I can't help it), and it is the task of the therapist to redirect them to the thoughts that underlie their negative feelings. Identifying thoughts, however, is not sufficient. Children must be shown how these thoughts lead to unhappiness and behavior problems. Taking the children slowly through specific scenarios that happened in the past week can be particularly instructive.

After children see how the automatic thoughts lead to unhappiness, the task turns to *challenging,* or changing, the automatic *thoughts.* Schrodt (1992) suggests that children initially be encouraged to think of their thoughts as hypotheses as opposed to conclusions. Another alternative is to show children that they choose their thoughts freely and that they are not required to hold the automatic thoughts. Both of these strategies loosen children's allegiance to their thought patterns, by allowing at least the acknowledgement of alternative thoughts. Early in therapy the goal is not to abandon the automatic thoughts, but rather to admit that other thoughts are possible. If the therapist moves too quickly, the children may defensively cling to the maladaptive thoughts and reject any change.

Once children are willing to accept the possibility of alternative thoughts, techniques can be employed to test the reality of the automatic thoughts. First, the children can learn to use evidence to discount negative automatic thoughts. The therapist begins this process by asking for evidence that the automatic thought is true (Stark et al., 1991). Then, the children are asked to provide evidence that the thought is *not* true. If they are unable to give disconfirming evidence, the therapist does it for them. An example is the thought that "I can never pass a spelling test, no matter how hard I try." Children might provide evidence in favor of this, such as times when they studied and still failed. Then they are asked to provide disconfirming evidence. Perhaps they did not really study very hard; perhaps they have passed other spelling tests when they did study; or perhaps they have found that when they study, they do better on spelling tests.

Next, the therapist and children test the evidence for alternative thoughts. For example, if the automatic thought is "If I don't pass the spelling test, I'm a complete failure", then an alternative could be "If I don't pass the spelling test, I can try harder the next time and improve my grade" or "If I don't pass the spelling test, I'll have to try harder, but I can still be good at other things." The generation of alternative thoughts may be difficult for depressed children because it violates their world-view and introduces an unfamiliar world-view into their life. The therapist may initially provide extensive assistance in this process. Later the child gradually assumes responsibility for generating alternative explanations and thoughts.

Cognitive restructuring techniques encourage depressed children to interpret situations in alternative ways (Meichenbaum, 1977). Reframing, for example, involves taking a different point of view to make a situation seem less catastrophic, less significant, or even positive. A child may reframe an upcoming difficult experience not as a threat of failure but as a challenge to succeed. Taking the SAT test, for instance, could be seen as an opportunity to gain experience with standardized tests as opposed to the only chance for a college education. Likewise, children can be taught to see past negative experiences as less significant. For example, losing a tennis match may be seen as an opportunity to identify weaknesses. Then the identified weaknesses can be addressed in tennis practice. Reframing can work well even with young children, since the therapist can suggest the reframe and all that the child must do is accept it.

Another variant of cognitive restructuring is *decatastrophizing*. Decatastrophizing occurs when the child perceives a negative event accurately as opposed to magnifying its threat and significance. For example, a child who loses a tennis match may catastrophize the experience by assuming that he will be kicked off the team for the loss and will be abandoned by his friends. Decatastrophizing this situation would involve noting that it is unlikely that either of these scenarios would happen. Related to decatastrophizing is the "What If?" intervention described by Stark et al. (1991). This intervention accepts that the event feared by the child will occur and asks what the aftermath will be. Depressed children often overestimate the extent to which a negative event will lead to catastrophe. Realistic discussion of the aftermath often reveals that the outcome is not likely to be as negative as the child feared and that the child's emotional response is exaggerated.

Numerous other ways exist to change the way that an event is perceived by a child. All of these cognitive restructuring techniques involve the suggestion of an alternative frame of reference or an alternative explanation of the event. When the underlying cognitions of the child are challenged, the event can be seen as less threatening. Despite its intuitive appeal, however, cognitive restructuring is a delicate and potentially risky therapeutic maneuver. If it is done too abruptly, children may believe that their feelings are being discounted and that the therapist does not understand them. In therapy, cognitive restructuring should be done only after a thorough examination of the child's defenses. Once the child is open to considering other ways of conceptualizing a situation, a more direct cognitive restructuring approach can be adopted.

Self-reinforcement is "the process of presenting rewards to oneself contingent upon successful performance of a desired behavior" (Stark et al., 1991, p. 186). In other words, the therapist and child identify possible rewards and target behaviors for the child. Then a single target behavior and a single reward are chosen and paired in a contingency. Upon completing the target behavior, the child gives himself or herself the reward.

Despite the simplicity of this process, depressed children are at risk to fail at almost every stage of the self-reinforcement procedure. As a result of their anhedonia, depressed children often have considerable trouble identifying rewards, usually stating that nothing is fun or rewarding. The therapist may circumvent this problem by asking them what was fun in the past. Alternatively, the therapist may create a hierarchy of events in the order of liked least to liked most. Even if depressed children believe that everything is bad, they are likely to believe that some things are worse than others; the ordering of things along this parameter shows that some things are desired relative to others. In the case of very impaired children the parents may suggest rewards.

Once a group of rewards is chosen, the therapist must ensure that the children have access to the rewards so that they do not have the disappointment of performing the target behavior without a reward. The system should involve rewards that are immediate, contingent only on the target behavior, and meaningful to the children. In general, involving the parents at this stage is important in the selection of rewards and in the implementation of a realistic plan (Stark et al., 1991).

In addition to having problems identifying rewards, depressed children may choose unrealistic target behaviors. Essentially, they set themselves up to fail. In such a case the therapist should encourage the child to select behaviors that are relatively objective and, at first, easily attainable.

After target behaviors and rewards are identified, the therapist and child should practice the self-reinforcement system in therapy (Stark et al., 1991). Following external success with a simple target behavior and a simple reinforcer, the self-reinforcement system can be modified to include more difficult behaviors and more potent reinforcers. As with other interventions, monitoring is integral to self-reinforcement, and the child should be encouraged to use some record-keeping system that can be brought into therapy for discussion and modification.

Activity scheduling requires the structuring of the child's day so that purposeful or pleasant activity is built into each day (Kazdin, 1989a; Lewinsohn and Rohde, 1993; Stark et al., 1991). Planned activities should involve interesting stimuli and removal from social withdrawal. Initially the child may resist this intervention and complain that the activity is aversive. This response is typical and reflects the hopeless resistance characteristic of depression. However, if the activity is inherently purposeful, interesting, or pleasant, the child usually comes to a positive acceptance and anticipation of it.

Activity scheduling begins with an assessment of the typical behaviors in which the child engages each day. These behaviors are identified as "pleasant," "unpleasant," or "neutral." In addition to assessing behaviors, "empty time" (time the child does not use productively or time that is not normally scheduled) is also monitored. Then a baseline measure of behaviors and empty time is made over a 1-week period. Next the child identifies positive events that are not currently a part of the schedule. Such events should be relatively easy to gain access to, somewhat frequent, and acceptable to parents. Depressed children will often select unreasonable activities (e.g., going to Disney World) or will say that no activity is desirable. In these cases, activities may have to be selected for them. A scale such as the Pleasant Events Schedule (MacPhillamy and Lewinsohn, 1982) may be helpful in the selection of activities to schedule. After pleasant activities are identified, the children's daily schedule is altered to reduce the frequency of empty time and to increase the frequency of pleasant or productive activities.

It is initially very important to schedule activities rigidly, so that the children can anticipate their occurrence. Rigid scheduling also reduces the chances of children's scheming to avoid the activities. Parents are typically involved, and many scheduled activities require some effort on their part. Examples of scheduled activities are going to the zoo, getting a book from the library, going to the museum, attending a movie, fishing, taking a walk, and sitting on the porch. Activities must reflect children's current level of functioning. For example, a child who has not left his room for 10 days might be scheduled to sit on the porch or to take a walk around the block. A chronically ill child may be wheeled around the hospital unit or to the hospital gift shop.

Activity scheduling injects structure into children's lives and gives them a sense of anticipating positive events. Furthermore, activities increase the chance of reinforcement and pleasant experiences. Activity scheduling is an excellent intervention for severely impaired children who resist or do not respond to any other intervention.

Realistic goal setting is another cognitive-behavioral intervention. Depressed children sometimes experience multiple failures because their goals and ideals are simply too high for them to meet. If unrealistic goals are contributing to negative self-evaluation and negative affect, altering the children's goals and ideals may result in improved affect. This may be accomplished by encouraging the children to engage in activities that are nonevaluative, amenable to internally set goals, or unique (e.g., not engaged in by a sibling and thus not allowing social comparison). Alternatively, clear, realistic goals may be imposed by powerful adults in the children's environment, with overt rewards for meeting these goals. Tasks that are too difficult for the children should be discouraged or broken down into manageable steps, with each step existing as its own goal and with its own reward (Schrodt, 1992).

Behavioral exposure is a cognitive-behavioral technique that can be used with depressed children who refrain from engaging in numerous behaviors because of their fear of failure. Behavioral exposure involves prescribing homework assignments in which children engage in progressively increasing amounts of the feared behavior. For example, a depressed child who will not play with peers because she feels inferior may be given an initial homework assignment to say "Hi" to one peer each day of the week. The next week the assignment may be increased to saying one sentence to one peer each day. The assignments could progress until the child is playing with peers.

In addition to reducing the self-defeating withdrawal and paralysis of depression, behavioral exposure gives children a chance to try out techniques practiced in therapy. Furthermore, the results of the behavioral exposure are often discrepant with the children's catastrophic expectations. They can then be used to assist with cognitive restructuring. Finally, as children engage feared situations without catastrophe, their confidence grows and self-esteem improves.

The obvious risk with behavioral exposure is failure of children in the task or an extremely aversive environmental response. To reduce this risk, children can be coached in therapy, with role playing and reinforcement for desired behavior. In addition, the behavioral task should initially be as innocuous and nonthreatening as possible.

Relaxation training teaches depressed children to use imagery and concentration to achieve somatic and cognitive relaxation. The relaxation presumably increases children's sense of control and well-being, resulting in affective improvement. Studies of the efficacy of relaxation training in reducing depressive symptoms have been promising (Field et al., 1992).

Social-skills training aims to increase the frequency of positive social interactions for depressed children, since social withdrawal and lack of social reinforcement are two features commonly associated with depression (Kazdin, 1989a). Most social-skills training programs teach basic cognitive restructuring, social skills, and interpersonal problem solving in order to increase depressed children's ability to interact positively with peers (Kazdin, 1989a; Lewinsohn and Rohde, 1993; Liddle and Spence, 1990).

Liddle and Spence (1990), for example, used an eight-session social-skills training program consisting of the following components: The first session taught the children the rationale and background of the program. In session two, children were taught the cognitive-behavioral techniques of self-talk and self-praise, as well as how to use these techniques to challenge and reduce negative thoughts. Session three was devoted to problem-solving training, while session four involved teaching and practicing of the principles of nonverbal communication. Session five was devoted to direct teaching of how to begin, join, and end conversations with peers. The final three sessions involved the application of the skills taught in the first five sessions to specific problems. Modeling, rehearsal, and discussion were used to hone the children's skills.

Liddle and Spence's (1990) social-skills training exemplifies many of the components of such programs, although their program is more circumscribed and time-limited than is typically indicated for a clinically depressed child. This may explain their failure to find their program to be more effective than no treatment. Other social-skills training programs are presented as part of a much larger depression treatment package and involve the children's parents in order to encourage practice and reinforcement at home.

In *cognitive-affective modeling* the therapist models adaptive thoughts and affects in the context of therapy. Stark et al. (1991), for example, suggest that the therapist verbalize adaptive thoughts related to problematic situations that the children may face. This may take the form of telling a story about a similar event that happened to the therapist (understanding that self-disclosure should be cautiously used in therapy) and how the therapist dealt adaptively with the event.

The therapist can also use process interpretations of the therapeutic interaction for cognitive-affective modeling. For example, congruent with their world-view, depressed children often make their lives seem hopeless or catastrophic in therapy. The therapist may point out this inclination to see things as being hopeless. The therapist may then state that he or she does not see things as hopeless, using adaptive schemas and thoughts to reinterpret the situation. The focus of therapy can then turn to an analysis of the child's hopelessness and how the therapist interprets the child's situation more positively. The therapist's point of view provides cognitive modeling for the child.

Affective modeling is similar to cognitive modeling, but it involves the overall demeanor and presentation of the therapist. A therapist who conveys confidence that a child can be helped and who has a positive view of the child's future communicates to the child that there is hope and expectation that the child will improve. Children derive comfort from the appearance that someone is in control and positively inclined toward them. This is especially salient for depressed children, who feel alone, helpless, and out of control. The modeling of hope and confidence by the therapist offers such children an initial confidence and an eventual example of adaptive thinking.

Anticipatory coping is an important tool in assisting depressed children who are facing severe stresses. Many children anticipate stresses with denial and avoidance, resulting in shock and a lack of preparation when the stress occurs. With no preparation for the stress, the chances of children responding maladaptively are very high. Such maladaptive responses include decompensation, inappropriate behavior, emotional upset, and additional depression. Some preparation may assist children in understanding stress when it occurs, in reducing false beliefs about stressors, and in adopting coping strategies for minimizing the effects of stress.

Anticipatory coping usually consists of exposure to a lower level of the feared situation or the development of a plan for coping with the stress. The former intervention is typically administered in the form of systematic or *in vivo* desensitization. The latter intervention usually takes the form of talking about the future stressor and developing coping strategies for dealing with the stressor. The strategies are then practiced extensively and used when the stressor occurs. Anticipatory coping may be done more subtly by talking with children about what they expect from a stressor and how they plan to deal with it. Maladaptive beliefs or denial can be gently challenged by requests for more elaboration. When the stress occurs, the children are then more prepared to understand and respond to it.

An example of anticipatory coping occurs frequently in chronically ill children, who face major stresses on a daily basis. Such children have numerous fears about the hospital: physical exams, IVs, surgery, separation from parents, and adapting to a new environment. Exposing the children to these situations prior to their occurrence reduces the children's unrealistic beliefs and catastrophic fears about them. Likewise, talking to an older child about the process of recovering from a surgical procedure may reduce the shock or uncertainty that they may feel.

Anticipatory coping can also be used as a means to prevent the recurrence of depression in children following termination of psychotherapy (Lewinsohn and Rohde, 1993). Children are reminded of the techniques that they used to reduce their depression, and future problems are anticipated. Then applications of the techniques to future problems are practiced.

Problem solving is the teaching of a semistructured procedure for managing problems when they arise. Depressed children often rigidly adopt a defeatist attitude with regard to problems or respond to problems without thinking. Either strategy is likely to lead to failure and a confirmation of their depressive belief systems, creating a self-fulfilling prophecy. Numerous problem-solving intervention packages exist, some of which apply to general problems and others that apply to specific types of problems. Despite some differences, most problem-solving interventions teach a variant of a five-step package including identification of the problem, generation of alternative solutions, evaluation of outcomes for each solution, choice of a solution, and evaluation of the outcome. In therapy, direct teaching, modeling, coaching, role playing, and practice in situations of increasing difficulty are used to teach the problem-solving package. Reinforcement and self-monitoring are used to motivate the depressed children.

Self-talk interventions are incorporated in most of the cognitive-behavioral techniques described above. These interventions train children to say certain words or phrases to themselves. These self-talk phrases assist children in identifying maladaptive cognitions and in implementing cognitive-behavioral techniques. For example, children may mentally recite the steps of problem solving when faced with a difficult problem. At another time they may say a phrase such as "I can get over this just fine" at a time when they feel like they are facing a catastrophe.

Most cognitive-behavioral techniques share some overlap and are incorporated into treatment packages (e.g., Lewinsohn et al., 1990). However, despite the excitement over cognitive-behavioral treatments, research investigation of their efficacy is in its infancy. The few projects that have been done suggest that cognitive-behavioral interventions with children are effective (Lewinsohn et al., 1990), but the studies have numerous flaws and some discrepant data exist (Kazdin, 1989a).

Play Therapy

Psychodynamic play therapy for depression is based on the assumption that the depression is the result of an internal, often unconscious conflict, probably related to parenting and attachment. Impaired parent–child interactions can communicate a sense of nonacceptance and worthlessness to children, particularly when these interactions involve neglect or abuse. Many depressed children have internalized a view of themselves as unworthy of nurturance and inferior to others. Other children may harbor a latent anger toward their parents, that is threatening and so turned inward.

Psychodynamic play therapy aims to elicit these conflicts and emotions in the relatively nondirective, accepting, interpretive world of play therapy. By playing out conflicts and emotions, children can relieve the stress of having them unresolved and avoided. Dealing with the conflicts also allows children to gain insight into how the conflicts affect their behavior (Kaslow and Racusin, 1990). Acceptance and warmth communicated by the therapist allow children to adopt an attitude of self-acceptance that is needed to combat the negative self-view characteristic of depression, particularly as painful conflicts and emotions emerge.

Typically, play therapy with a depressed child is initially nondirective, although the therapist may need to engage an extremely withdrawn child. As the child plays, themes emerge, particularly in play involving interaction between characters. The therapist can facilitate the emergence of conflicts, emotions, and maladaptive cognitions by playing along with the child and conveying acceptance of what the child is doing. Eventually, interpretive statements describing the child's feelings and thoughts in play therapy will assist the child in understanding and accepting the issues driving his or her behavior. Maladaptive thoughts, negative affects, and interpersonal (particularly nurturing) relationships are key targets for interpretation. The delivery of these interpretations while maintaining a warm, accepting, and nondirective attitude is vital in helping the child to develop a healthy self-concept.

No controlled studies have systematically evaluated the efficacy of play therapy for depression. It is sometimes combined with behavioral and cognitive-behavioral techniques to add a psychodynamic component, as well as to assist in evaluating children's cognitive-affective status. For very young children, play therapy is often the modality of choice, since very young children often do not respond to cognitive-behavioral techniques.

Group Therapy

Many cognitive-behavioral interventions are delivered completely or partially in group settings, since the structured, didactic presentation of cognitive-behavioral interventions is amenable to groups. Cognitive-behavioral groups may or may not attend to group dynamics and the social interactions of group members. Social skills training, for example, is well suited to groups, and the interactions of group members are used in training group members. Psychoeducation, on the other hand, neither requires nor typically generates much group interaction.

Other forms of group therapy are designed specifically to focus on the interaction of group members, as opposed to being a byproduct of a cognitive-behavioral intervention. These group therapies are particularly relevant to depressed children who have social interaction deficits. Baxter and Kennedy (1992) point out several advantages of unstructured, interactional groups for depressed children: First, the groups allow children to see that some of their peers have the same feelings that they do, reducing feelings of being strange, isolated, or inferior. Second, the groups encourage expression of feelings and thoughts because group members model expression for each other, because there is some group peer pressure to express, and because group members can express feelings as a way of eliciting support from other group members. Third, the groups allow depressed children to see the impact of their depressive behavior on others. This experience increases insight and may improve social skills.

Baxter and Kennedy (1992) recommend separating groups by gender and age, so that the children have roughly the same cognitive ability, interests, and maturational level. For young children (age 6–12), groups are typically structured around play and other activities. Children at these ages have difficulty engaging in discussion alone, although discussion sometimes follows logically from the activities. The activities chosen generally facilitate the discussion of feelings or self-disclosure of other data in a nonthreatening, fun way (Dennison, 1989). In more psychodynamically oriented groups the therapist may be nondirective, making only interpretive statements. Behavioral groups resemble social-skills training, with a focus on learning and practicing adaptive social behaviors (Baxter & Kennedy, 1992). Adolescent groups rely more on discussion, with activities or topics used only as a springboard for beginning social interaction. The therapist in discussion-oriented groups acts as interpreter of the group process and attempts to help group members gain insight into their depressive cognitions and affects. Over all, the specific behavior of the group therapist depends on whether a psychodynamic or cognitive-behavioral approach is taken (Baxter and Kennedy, 1992). The social interaction of the group facilitates individual change and acts as a laboratory for the development of social skills.

Family Interventions

Inclusion of the family in the treatment of a depressed child may occur to facilitate a behavioral or cognitive-behavioral intervention (e.g., Blechman et al., 1989). Alternatively, family therapy may be the major treatment modality. Parents have a significant impact on the depressed child's behavior by virtue of their role as nurturant figures, providers of reinforcement and punishment, and models of adaptive behavior. Hence, enlisting the parents' aid is important, if not vital, to the success of intervention for childhood depression.

Unfortunately, many parents of depressed children have substantial problems themselves, which may in part be responsible for the development of the child's depression in the first place (Blechman et al., 1989). In these cases the parents are, at best, well-intentioned but imperfect therapy partners. At worst, parents can be saboteurs of therapeutic progress. In cases where the parents have significant problems, family therapy and/or individual therapy for one or both parents may be warranted. Hence, the therapist should be alert for significant problems in the family of the depressed child.

References

Abramson, L. Y., Seligman, M. E. P., and Teasdale, J. D. (1978). Learned helplessness in humans: Critique and reformulation. *Journal of Abnormal Psychology, 87,* 49–74.

Achenbach, T. M. (1991a). *Manual for the Child Behavior Checklist/4–18 and 1991 profile.* Burlington: University of Vermont Department of Psychiatry.

_____ . (1991b). *Manual for the Teacher's Report Form and 1991 profile.* Burlington: University of Vermont Department of Psychiatry.

_____ . (1991c). *Manual for the Youth Self-Report and 1991 profile.* Burlington: University of Vermont Department of Psychiatry.

Achenbach, T. M., McConaughy, S. H., and Howell, C. T. (1987). Child/adolescent behavioral and emotional problems: Implications of cross-informant correlations for situational specificity. *Psychological Bulletin, 101,* 213–232.

American Psychiatric Association. (1994). *Diagnostic and statistical manual of mental disorders* (4th ed.). Washington, DC: Author.

Anderson, J. C., Williams, S., McGee, R., and Silva, P. A. (1987). DSM-III disorders in preadolescent children: Prevalence in a large sample from the general population. *Archives of General Psychiatry, 44,* 69–76.

Angold, A. (1988). Childhood and adolescent depression II: Research in clinical populations. *British Journal of Psychiatry, 153,* 476–492.

Anthony, J., and Scott, P. (1960). Manic-depressive psychosis in childhood. *Child Psychology and Psychiatry, 1,* 53–72.

Arana, G. W., Baldessarini, R. J., and Ornsteen, M. (1985). The dexamethasone suppression test for diagnosis and prognosis in psychiatry: Commentary and review. *Archives of General Psychiatry, 42,* 1193–1204.

Asarnow, J. R., and Carlson, G. A. (1985). Depression self-rating scale: Utility with child psychiatric inpatients. *Journal of Consulting and Clinical Psychology, 53,* 491–499.

Asarnow, J. R., Carlson, G. A., and Guthrie, D. (1987). Coping strategies, self-perceptions, hopelessness, and perceived family environments in depressed and suicidal children. *Journal of Consulting and Clinical Psychology, 55,* 361–366.

Asher, S. R., Hymel, S., and Renshaw, P. D. (1984). Loneliness in children. *Child Development, 55,* 1456–1464.

Asher, S. R., and Wheeler, V. A. (1985). Children's loneliness: A comparison of rejected and neglected peer status. *Journal of Consulting and Clinical Psychology, 53,* 500–505.

Ball, J. D., Archer, R. P., Gordon, R. A., and French, J. (1991). Rorschach depression indices with children and adolescents: Concurrent validity findings. *Journal of Personality Assessment, 57,* 465–476.

Baxter, R. F., and Kennedy, J. F. (1992). Group therapy of depression. In M. Shafii and S. L. Shafii (Eds.), *Clinical guide to depression in children and adolescents* (pp. 177–195). Washington, DC: American Psychiatric Press.

Beardslee, W. R., Bemporad, J., Keller, M. B., and Klerman, G. L. (1983). Children of parents with major affective disorder: A review. *American Journal of Psychiatry, 140,* 825–832.

Beck, A. T. (1976). Cognitive therapy and the emotional disorders. New York: International Universities Press.

Benfield, C. Y., Palmer, D. J., Pfefferbaum, B., and Stowe, M. L. (1988). A comparison of depressed and nondepressed disturbed children on measures of attributional style, hopelessness, life stress, and temperament. *Journal of Abnormal Child Psychology, 16,* 397–410.

Birleson, P. (1981). The validity of depressive disorder in childhood and the development of a self-rating scale: A research project. *Journal of Child Psychology and Psychiatry, 22,* 73–88.

Birleson, P., Hudson, I., Gray-Buchanan, D., and Wolff, S. (1987). Clinical evaluation of a self-rating scale for depressive disorder in childhood (Depression Self-Rating Scale). *Journal of Child Psychology and Psychiatry, 28,* 43–60.

Blechman, E. A., Tryon, A. S., Ruff, M. H., and McEnroe M. J. (1989). Family skills training and childhood depression. In C. E. Schaefer and J. M. Briesmeister (Eds.), *Handbook of parent training: Parents as co-therapists for children's behavior problems* (pp. 203–222). New York: Wiley.

Bodiford, C. A., Eisenstadt, T. H., Johnson, J. H., and Bradlyn, A. S. (1988). Comparison of learned helpless cognitions and behavior in children with high and low scores on the Children's Depression Inventory. *Journal of Clinical Child Psychology, 17,* 152–158.

Brown, R., Kocsis, J. H., Caroff, S., Amsterdam, J., Winokur, A., Stokes, P. E., and Frazer, A. (1985). Differences in nocturnal melatonin secretion between melancholic depressed patients and control subjects. *American Journal of Psychiatry, 142,* 811–816.

Burgin, D. (1986). Depression in children and adolescents. *Psychopathology, 19* (Suppl. 2), 148–155.

Casat, C. D., Arana, G. W., and Powell, K. (1989). The DST in children and adolescents with major depressive disorder. *American Journal of Psychiatry, 146,* 503–507.

Cavallo, A., Holt, K. G., Hejazi, M. S., Richards, G. E., and Myer, W. J. (1987). Melatonin circadian rhythm in childhood depression. *Journal of the American Academy of Child and Adolescent Psychiatry, 26,* 395–399.

Cytryn, L., and McKnew, D. H. (1972). Proposed classification of childhood depression. *American Journal of Psychiatry, 129,* 149–155.

Dennison, S. T. (1989). *Twelve counseling programs for children at risk.* Springfield, IL: Thomas.

Derogatis, L. R. (1983). *SCL-90-R administration, scoring, & procedures manual—II.* Towson, MD: Clinical Psychometric Research.

Edelsohn, G., Ialongo, N., Werthamer-Larsson, L., Crockett, L., and Kellam, S. (1992). Self-reported depressive symptoms in first-grade children: Developmentally transient phenomena? *Journal of the American Academy of Child and Adolescent Psychiatry, 31,* 282–290.

Exner, J. E. (1986). *The Rorschach: A comprehensive system* (vol. 1, 2d ed.). New York: Wiley.

Field, T., Morrow, C., Valdeon, C., Larson, S., Kuhn, C., and Schanberg, S. (1992). Massage reduces anxiety in child and adolescent psychiatric patients. *Journal of the American Academy of Child and Adolescent Psychiatry, 31,* 125–131.

Finch, A. J., Jr., Casat, C. D., and Carey, M. P. (1990). Depression in children and adolescents. In S.B. Morgan & T.M. Okwumabua (Eds.), *Child and adolescent disorders: Developmental and health psychology perspectives* (pp. 135–173). Hillsdale, NJ: Erlbaum.

Fristad, M. A., Weller, R. A., Weller, E. B., Teare, M., and Preskorn, S. H. (1991). Comparison of the parent and child versions of the Children's Depression Inventory (CDI). *Annals of Clinical Psychiatry, 3,* 341–346.

Gershon, E. S., Targum, S. D., Kessler, L. R., Mazure, C. M., and Bunney, W. E., Jr. (1977). Genetic studies and biologic strategies in the affective disorders. *Progress in Medical Genetics, 2,* 101–164.

Glaser, K. (1968). Masked depression in children and adolescents. In S. Chess and A. Thomas (Eds.), *Annual progress in child psychiatry and child development* (vol. 1, pp. 345–355). New York: Brunner/Mazel.

Hammen, C., Burge, D., and Adrian, C. (1991). Timing of mother and child depression in a longitudinal study of children at risk. *Journal of Consulting and Clinical Psychology, 59,* 341–345.

Harris, F. C., and Ammerman, R. T. (1986). Depression and suicide in children and adolescents. *Education and Treatment of Children, 9,* 334–343.

Hodges, K. K. (1990). Depression and anxiety in children: A comparison of self-report questionnaires to clinical interview. *Psychological Assessment, 2,* 376–381.

Hollon, S. P., and Kendall, P. C. (1980). Cognitive self-statements in depression: Development of an automatic thoughts questionnaire. *Cognitive Therapy and Research, 4,* 383–395.

Holmes, G. R., Heckel, R. V., Chestnut, E., Harris, N., and Cautela, J. (1987). Factor analysis of the Adolescent Reinforcement Survey Schedule (ARSS) with college freshmen. *Journal of Clinical Psychology, 43,* 386–390.

Jensen, P. S., Ryan, N. D., and Prien, R. (1992). Psychopharmacology of child and adolescent major depression: Present status and future directions. *Journal of Child and Adolescent Psychopharmacology, 2,* 31–45.

Johnson, J. H., and McCutcheon, S. M. (1980). Assessing life stress in older children and adolescents: Preliminary findings with the Life Events Checklist. In I. G. Sarason and C. D. Spielberger (Eds.), *Stress and anxiety* (vol. 7, pp. 111–125). Washington, DC: Hemisphere.

Kashani, J. H., Carlson, G. A., Beck, N. C., Hoeper, E. W., Corcoran, C. M., McAllister, J. A., Fallahi, C., Rosenberg, T. K., and Reid, J. C. (1987). Depression, depressive symptoms, and depressed mood among a community sample of adolescents. *American Journal of Psychiatry, 144,* 931–934.

Kashani, J. H., Holcomb, W. R., and Orvaschel, H. (1986). Depression and depressive symptomatology in preschool children from the general population. *American Journal of Psychiatry, 143,* 1138–1143.

Kashani, J. H., McGee, R. O., Clarkson, S. E., Anderson, J. C., Walton, L. A., Williams, S., Silva, P. A., Robins, A. J., Cytryn, L., and McKnew, D. H. (1983). Depression in a sample of 9-year-old children. *Archives of General Psychiatry, 40,* 1217–1223.

Kashani, J. H., and Ray, J. S. (1983). Depressive symptoms among preschool-age children. *Child Psychiatry and Human Development, 13,* 233–238.

Kashani, J. H., and Schmid, L. S. (1992). Epidemiology and etiology of depressive disorders. In M. Shafii & S.L. Shafii (Eds.), *Clinical guide to depression in children and adolescents* (pp. 43–64). Washington, DC: American Psychiatric Press.

Kashani, J. H., and Sherman, D. D. (1988). Childhood depression: Epidemiology, etiological models, and treatment implications. *Integrative Psychiatry, 6,* 1–21.

Kaslow, N. J., and Racusin, G. R. (1990). Childhood depression: Current status and future directions. In A. S. Bellack, M. Hersen, and A. E. Kazdin (Eds.), *International handbook of behavior modification and therapy* (2d ed., pp. 223–243). New York: Plenum.

Kaslow, N. J., Rehm, L. P., Pollack, S. L., and Siegel, A. W. (1990). Depression and perception of family functioning in children and their parents. *American Journal of Family Therapy, 18,* 227–235.

Kaslow, N. J., Tannenbaum, R. L., and Seligman, M. E. P. (1978). *The KASTAN: A children's attributional style questionnaire.* Unpublished manuscript, University of Pennsylvania.

Kazdin, A. E. (1987). Assessment of childhood depression: Current issues and strategies. *Behavioral Assessment, 9,* 291–319.

———. (1989a). Childhood depression. In E. J. Mash and R. A. Barkley (Eds.), *Treatment of childhood disorders* (pp. 135–166). New York: Guilford Press.

———. (1989b). Identifying depression in children: A comparison of alternative selection criteria. *Journal of Abnormal Child Psychology, 17,* 437–454.

———. (1990). Assessment of childhood depression. In A.M. LaGreca (Ed.), *Through the eyes of the child: Obtaining self-reports from children and adolescents* (pp. 189–233). Boston: Allyn & Bacon.

Kazdin, A. E., French, N. H., Unis, A. S., and Esveldt-Dawson, K. (1983). Assessment of childhood depression: Correspondence of child and parent ratings. *Journal of the American Academy of Child Psychiatry, 22,* 157–164.

Kazdin, A. E., Rodgers, A., and Colbus, D. (1986). The Hopelessness Scale for Children: Psychometric characteristics and concurrent validity. *Journal of Consulting and Clinical Psychology, 54,* 241–245.

Keller, M. B., and Wunder, J. (1990). Bipolar disorder in childhood. In M. Hersen and C. G. Last (Eds.), *Handbook of child and adult psychopathology* (pp. 69–81). New York: Pergamon Press.

Kendall, P. C., Stark, K. D., and Adam, T. (1990). Cognitive deficit or cognitive distortion in childhood depression. *Journal of Abnormal Child Psychology, 18,* 255–270.

Khan, A. U. (1987). Biochemical profile of depressed adolescents. *Journal of the American Academy of Child and Adolescent Psychiatry, 26,* 873–878.

Kotsopoulos, S. (1989). Phenomenology of anxiety and depressive disorders in children and adolescents. *Psychiatric Clinics of North America, 12,* 803–814.

Kovacs, M. (1978). *Interview schedule for children (ISC)* (10th rev.). Pittsburgh, PA: University of Pittsburgh School of Medicine.

_____ . (1981). Rating scales to assess depression in school-aged children. *Acta Paedopsychiatrica, 46,* 305–315.

_____ . (1985). The Interview Schedule for Children. *Psychopharmacology Bulletin, 21,* 991–994.

_____ . (1992). *Children's Depression Inventory (CDI) manual.* North Tonawanda, NY: Multi-Health Systems.

Kovacs, M., Feinberg, T. L., Crouse-Novak, M. A., Paulauskas, S. L., and Finkelstein, R. (1984a). Depressive disorders in childhood: I. A longitudinal prospective study of characteristics and recovery. *Archives of General Psychiatry, 41,* 229–237.

_____ . (1984b). Depressive disorders in childhood: II. A longitudinal study of the risk for a subsequent major depression. *Archives of General Psychiatry, 41,* 643–649.

Kronenberger, W. G. (1990). The effects of perceived social, marital, and familial environments on the psychological adjustment of mothers of children with spina bifida. Doctoral Dissertation, Duke University.

Lachar, D. (1982). *Personality Inventory for Children (PIC) revised format manual supplement.* Los Angeles: Western Psychological Services.

Lang, M., and Tisher, M. (1978). *Children's Depression Scale.* Victoria, Australia: Australian Council for Educational Research.

Leenaars, A. A., and Wenckstern, S. (1991). Suicide in the school-age child and adolescent. In A. A. Leenaars (Ed.), *Life span perspectives of suicide* (pp. 95–107). New York: Plenum.

Lefkowitz, M. M., and Tesiny, E. P. (1980) Assessment of childhood depression. *Journal of Consulting and Clinical Psychology, 48,* 43–50.

_____ . (1985). Depression in children: Prevalence and correlates. *Journal of Consulting and Clinical Psychology, 53,* 647–656.

Leitenberg, H., Yost, L. W., and Carroll-Wilson, M. (1986). Negative cognitive errors in children: Questionnaire development, normative data, and comparisons between children with and without self-reported symptoms of depression, low self-esteem, and evaluation anxiety. *Journal of Consulting and Clinical Psychology, 54,* 528–536.

Lewinsohn, P. M. (1974). Clinical and theoretical aspects of depression. In K. S. Calhoun, H. E. Adams, and K. M. Mitchell (Eds.), *Innovative treatment methods of psychopathology* (pp. 63–120). New York: Wiley.

Lewinsohn, P. M., Clarke, G. N., Hops, H., and Andrews, J. (1990). Cognitive-behavioral treatment for depressed adolescents. *Behavior Therapy, 25,* 385–401.

Lewinsohn, P. M., and Rohde, P. (1993). The cognitive-behavioral treatment of depression in adolescents: Research and suggestions. *Clinical Psychologist, 46,* 177–183.

Liddle, B., and Spence, S. H. (1990). Cognitive-behaviour therapy with depressed primary school children: A cautionary note. *Behavioural Psychotherapy, 18,* 85–102.

MacPhillamy, D. J., and Lewinsohn, P. M. (1982). The Pleasant Events Schedule: Studies on reliability, validity, and scale intercorrelation. *Journal of Consulting and Clinical Psychology, 50,* 363–380.

Mahler, M. (1961). On sadness and grief in infancy and childhood. *Psychoanalytic Study of the Child, 16,* 332.

Martini, D. R., Strayhorn, J. M., and Puig-Antich, J. (1990). A symptom self-report measure for preschool children. *Journal of the American Academy of Child and Adolescent Psychiatry, 29,* 594–600.

Matson, J. L., Rotatori, A. F., and Helsel, W. J. (1983). Development of a rating scale to measure social skills in children: The Matson Evaluation of Social Skills with Youngsters (MESSY). *Behavior Research and Therapy, 21,* 335–340.

McCauley, E., Carlson, G. A., and Calderon, R. (1991). The role of somatic complaints in the diagnosis of depression in children and adolescents. *Journal of the American Academy of Child and Adolescent Psychiatry, 30,* 631–635.

McKnew, D. H., Jr., Cytryn, L., Efron, A. M., Gershon, E. S., and Bunney, W. E., Jr. (1979). Offspring of patients with affective disorders. *British Journal of Psychiatry, 134,* 148–152.

Meichenbaum, D. (1977). *Cognitive-behavior modification: An integrative approach.* New York: Plenum.

Meyer, R. G. and Deitsch, S. (1996). *The clinician's handbook* (4th ed.). Boston: Allyn & Bacon.

Mokros, H. B., and Poznanski, E. O. (1992). Standardized approaches to clinical assessment of depression. In M. Shafii and S. L. Shafii (Eds.), *Clinical guide to depression in children and adolescents* (pp. 129–155). Washington, DC: American Psychiatric Press.

Moos, R. H., and Moos, B. S. (1981). *Family Environment Scale manual.* Palo Alto, CA: Consulting Psychologists Press.

Myers, K., McCauley, E., Calderon, R., Mitchell, J., Burke, P., and Schloredt, K. (1991a). Risks for suicidality in major depressive disorder. *Journal of the American Academy of Child and Adolescent Psychiatry, 30,* 86–94.

Myers, K., McCauley, E., Calderon, R., and Treder, R. (1991b). The 3-year longitudinal course of suicidality and predictive factors for subsequent suicidality in youths with major depressive disorder. *Journal of the American Academy of Child and Adolescent Psychiatry, 30,* 804–810.

Pataki, C. S., and Carlson, G. A. (1990). Major depression in childhood. In M. Hersen and C. G. Last (Eds.), *Handbook of child and adult psychopathology* (pp. 35–50). New York: Pergamon Press.

_____ . (1992). Bipolar disorders: Clinical manifestations, differential diagnosis, and treatment. In M. Shafii and S. L. Shafii (Eds.), *Clinical guide to depression in children and adolescents* (pp. 269–294). Washington, DC: American Psychiatric Press.

Petti, T. A. (1985). Scales of potential use in the psychopharmacological treatment of depressed children and adolescents. *Psychopharmacology Bulletin, 21,* 951–955.

Petti, T. A. (1989). Depression. In T. H. Ollendick and M. Hersen (Eds.), *Handbook of child psychopathology* (2d ed., pp. 229–246). New York: Plenum.

Pfeffer, C. R. (1992). Relationship between depression and suicidal behavior. In M. Shafii and S. L. Shafii (Eds.), *Clinical guide to depression in children and adolescents* (pp. 115–127). Washington, DC: American Psychiatric Press.

Piers, E. V. (1984). *Piers-Harris Children's Self-Concept Scale Revised manual 1984*. Los Angeles: Western Psychological Services.

Pliszka, S. R. (1991). Antidepressants in the treatment of child and adolescent psychopathology. *Journal of Clinical Child Psychology, 20,* 313–320.

Poznanski, E. O., Cook, S. C., and Carroll, B. J. (1979). A depression rating scale for children. *Pediatrics, 64,* 442–450.

Poznanski, E. O., Freeman, L. N., and Mokros, H. B. (1985). Children's Depression Rating Scale—Revised. *Psychopharmacology Bulletin, 21,* 979–989.

Poznanski, E. O., Grossman, J. A., Buchsbaum, Y., Banegas, M., Freeman, L., and Gibbons, R. (1984). Preliminary studies of the reliability and validity of the Children's Depression Rating Scale. *Journal of the American Academy of Child Psychiatry, 23,* 191–197.

Rancurello, M. D. (1985). Clinical applications of antidepressant drugs in childhood behavioral and emotional disorders. *Psychiatric Annals, 15,* 88–100.

Rehm, L. P. (1977). A self-control model of depression. *Behavior Therapy, 8,* 787–804.

Reynolds, W. M. (1987). *Assessment of depression in adolescents: Manual for the Reynolds Adolescent Depression Scale (RADS)*. Odessa, FL: Psychological Assessment Resources.

———. (1989). *Reynolds Child Depression Scale: Professional manual*. Odessa, FL: Psychological Assessment Resources.

Reynolds, W. M., and Coats, K. I. (1986). A comparison of cognitive-behavioral therapy and relaxation training for the treatment of depression in adolescents. *Journal of Consulting and Clinical Psychology, 54,* 653–660.

Reynolds, W. M., and Graves, A. (1989). Reliability of children's reports of depressive symptomatology. *Journal of Abnormal Child Psychology, 17,* 647–655.

Rosenthal, N. E., Sack, D. A., Skwerer, R. G., Jacobsen, F. M., and Wehr, T. A. (1989). Phototherapy for seasonal affective disorder. In N. E. Rosenthal and M. C. Blehar (Eds.), *Seasonal affective disorders and phototherapy* (pp. 273–294). New York: Guilford Press.

Ryan, N. D. (1992). The pharmacologic treatment of child and adolescent depression. *Pediatric Psychopharmacology, 15,* 29–40.

Sarason, I. G., Levine, H. M., Basham, R. B., and Sarason, B. R. (1983). Assessing social support: The Social Support Questionnaire. *Journal of Personality and Social Psychology, 44,* 127–139.

Schildkraut, J. J. (1965). The catecholamine hypothesis of affective disorders. *American Journal of Psychiatry, 122,* 509–522.

Schrodt, G. R. (1992). Cognitive therapy of depression. In M. Shafii and S. L. Shafii (Eds.), *Clinical guide to depression in children and adolescents* (pp. 197–217). Washington, DC: American Psychiatric Press.

Seligman, M. E. P. (1975). *Helplessness: On depression, development and death*. San Francisco: Freeman.

Seligman, M., Kaslow, N., Alloy, L., Peterson, C., Tannenbaum, R., and Abramson, L. (1984). Attributional style and depressive symptoms among children. *Journal of Abnormal Psychology, 93,* 235–238.

Seligman, M. E. P., and Peterson, C. (1986). A learned helplessness perspective on childhood depression: Theory and research. In M. Rutter, C. E. Izard, and P. B. Read (Eds.), *Depression in young people: Developmental and clinical perspectives* (pp. 223–249). New York: Guilford Press.

Shafii, M., and Shafii, S. L. (1992). Clinical manifestations and developmental psychopathology of depression. In M. Shafii and S. L. Shafii (Eds.), *Clinical guide to depression in children and adolescents* (pp. 3–42). Washington, DC: American Psychiatric Press.

Simeon, J. G. (1989). Depressive disorders in children and adolescents. *Psychiatric Journal of the University of Ottawa, 14,* 356–361.

Smith, K., and Crawford, S. (1986). Suicidal behavior among "normal" high school students. *Suicide and Life-Threatening Behavior, 16,* 313–325.

Smucker, M. R., Craighead, W. E., Craighead, L. W., and Green, B. J. (1986). Normative and reliability data for the Children's Depression Inventory. *Journal of Abnormal Child Psychology, 14,* 25–39.

Sokoloff, M. R., and Lubin, B. (1983). Depressive mood in adolescent, emotionally disturbed females: Reliability and validity of an adjective checklist (C-DACL). *Journal of Abnormal Child Psychology, 11,* 531–536.

Sonis, W. A. (1989). Seasonal affective disorder of childhood and adolescence: A review. In N. E. Rosenthal and M. C. Blehar (Eds.), *Seasonal affective disorders and phototherapy* (pp. 46–84). New York: Guilford Press.

_____ (1992). Chronobiology of seasonal mood disorders. In M. Shafii and S. L. Shafii (Eds.), *Clinical guide to depression in children and adolescents* (pp. 89–114). Washington, DC: American Psychiatric Press.

Spitz, R. A. (1945). Hospitalism. *Psychoanalytic Study of the Child, 1,* 53–74.

_____ . (1946). Anaclitic depression: An inquiry into the genesis of psychiatric conditions in early childhood, II. *Psychoanalytic Study of the Child, 2,* 313–342.

_____ . (1965). *The first year of life.* New York: International Universities Press.

Stark, K. D., Rouse, L. W., and Livingston, R. (1991). Treatment of depression during childhood and adolescence: Cognitive-behavioral procedures for the individual and family. In P. C. Kendall (Ed.), *Child and adolescent therapy: Cognitive-behavioral procedures* (pp. 165–206). New York: Guilford Press.

Strober, M. (1992). Bipolar disorders: Natural history, genetic studies, and follow-up. In M. Shafii and S. L. Shafii (Eds.), *Clinical guide to depression in children and adolescents* (pp. 251–268). Washington, DC: American Psychiatric Press.

Teichman, Y. (1989). Childhood depression: A family perspective. *Israel Journal of Psychiatry and Related Sciences, 26,* 46–57.

Tisher, M., Lang-Takac, E., and Lang, M. (1992). The Children's Depression Scale: Review of Australian and overseas experience. *Australian Journal of Psychology, 44,* 27–35.

Tsuang, M. T. (1978). Genetic counseling for psychiatric patients and their families. *American Journal of Psychiatry, 135,* 1465–1475.

Weinberg, W. A., and Brumback, R. A. (1976). Mania in childhood: Case studies and literature review. *American Journal of Diseases in Childhood, 130,* 380–385.

Weissman, M. M., Gammon, G. D., John, K., Merikangas, K. R., Warner, W. V., Prusoff, B. A., and Sholomaskas, D. (1987). Children of depressed parents: Increased psychopathology and early onset of major depression. *Archives of General Psychiatry, 44,* 847–853.

Weissman, M. M., Orvaschel, H., and Padian, N. (1980). Children's symptom and social functioning self-report scales: Comparison of mother's and children's reports. *Journal of Nervous and Mental Disease, 168,* 736–740.

Weller, E. B., and Weller, R. A. (1988). Neuroendocrine changes in affectively ill children and adolescents. *Endocrinology Metabolism Clinics of North America, 17,* 41–54.

Weller, R. A., Weller, E. B., Fristad, M. A., and Bowes, J. M. (1991). Depression in recently bereaved prepubertal children. *American Journal of Psychiatry, 148,* 1536–1541.

Yaylayan, S., Weller, E. B., and Weller, R. A. (1992). Neurobiology of depression. In M. Shafii and S. L. Shafii (Eds.), *Clinical guide to depression in children and adolescents* (pp. 65–88). Washington, DC: American Psychiatric Press.

CHAPTER 6

Anxiety Disorders

Anxiety disorders of childhood and adolescence appear under two sections of DSM-IV: "Disorders Usually First Diagnosed in Infancy, Childhood, or Adolescence" and "Anxiety Disorders." Only Separation Anxiety Disorder (SAD) appears in the childhood disorders section, where it is grouped with the "Other Disorders of Infancy, Childhood, or Adolescence." The other anxiety disorders may be diagnosed in adults as well as in children; they fall in the "Anxiety Disorders" section of DSM-IV.

The DSM-IV has consolidated certain anxiety disorders that were previously separated by developmentally different features. Overanxious Disorder from DSM-III-R has been subsumed into the DSM-IV Generalized Anxiety Disorder (GAD) category. Likewise, Avoidant Disorder of Childhood or Adolescence was eliminated as a diagnosis in DSM-IV. Most children who formerly received this diagnosis will be diagnosed with Social Phobia in DSM-IV (Bernstein and Borchardt, 1991; Francis, Last, and Strauss, 1992). In order to simplify the presentation of current anxiety disorder diagnoses, descriptions of pre-DSM-IV research pertaining to Overanxious Disorder and Avoidant Disorder diagnoses will use the DSM-IV diagnostic names (GAD and Social Phobia, respectively) for the remainder of this chapter.

■ Separation Anxiety Disorder

□ CLINICAL DESCRIPTION

Diagnostic Considerations

Anxiety over separation from primary caregivers is a normal phenomenon, especially from the ages of 6 months through 5 years. However, when anxiety over separation is excessive and causes significant problems in daily functioning, the presence of Separation Anxiety Disorder (SAD) should be evaluated. The essential feature of SAD is excessive anxiety when the child is separated from a major attachment figure. This anxiety may approach a panic level and impairment may be severe if the child refuses to engage in independent functioning. Anxiety is relieved when the child is in the presence of attachment figures. While separated, the child may experience worries about injury, illness, harm, or other circumstances preventing reunion. He or she may resist engagement in other activities, such as school, social interaction, play, or even sleep. Nightmares and somatic complaints are other commonly seen diagnostic criteria. Onset is required before age 18, but onset after age 10 is unusual.

Normal childhood development includes a period when separation from attachment figures causes an anxiety reaction. In fact, the lack of *any* observable reaction to separation from a caretaker could indicate a Reactive Attachment Disorder. Diagnosis of SAD, therefore, requires consideration of the child's age and developmental level.

The terms "school phobia" or "school refusal" are often used to indicate the school-avoidance feature of SAD, but they do not exist as independent diagnoses. Rather, school refusal is usually an associated feature of a constellation of separation anxiety problems as opposed to a stand-alone problem. In rare cases, school refusal may be diagnosed separately as Specific or Social Phobia when separation anxiety is not also present.

SAD is probably the most common childhood anxiety disorder, with a prevalence as high as 4% (American Psychiatric Association, 1994). SAD is more unusual in adolescents. Bowen, Offord, and Boyle (1990) found that 2.4% of adolescents in an epidemiological study conducted in Ontario, Canada, were diagnosable with SAD. In their community adolescent sample, Kashani and Orvaschel (1988) found SAD to be the least common Anxiety Disorder. Among children and adolescents presenting for treatment at an outpatient anxiety disorders clinic, separation anxiety was the most common primary diagnosis, making up 33% of the sample (Last, Strauss, and Francis, 1987). Cantwell and Baker (1987) report a high prevalence of SAD and Social Phobia (10%) in children receiving treatment for communication disorders.

Appearance and Features

The appearance of SAD (see Table 6.1) varies substantially by age (Francis, Last, and Strauss, 1987). Preschool children often express vague fears and general distress upon separation from caretakers. Because some separation distress is normal at the preschool age, distress qualifying for SAD diagnosis must be profound. A typical preschool response to parental separation may include some crying, social withdrawal, and attempt to follow the parent. However, the preschooler can often eventually be engaged (usually within 5–10 minutes but almost always within an hour or two) in an appealing activity with appropriate support. On the other hand, extremely long or severe temper tantrums, excessive crying and sobbing, persistent social withdrawal, and paralyzing fear responses are typical of the preschool SAD child. In some cases the child's response is so extreme that it causes physiological distress such as difficulty breathing, hyperventilation, or vomiting. Younger children tend to have more

TABLE 6.1   Appearance and Features of Separation Anxiety Disorder

COMMON FEATURES

Extended show of distress upon real or threatened separation from primary care-
    givers (tantrums, crying, freezing, somatic complaints, social withdrawal)
Fear of harm or permanent separation from caretaker
Fear of getting lost, death, kidnapping, assault
Lower socio-economic status
Onset before age 10
School refusal

OCCASIONAL FEATURES

Somatic symptoms of distress
Nightmares with separation theme
Refusal to sleep alone
Whiny, clinging, or demanding behavior when not receiving caretaker attention

Note: The features listed above are often seen but are not universal. Some features may be
diagnostically relevant or required, while others may not be required for diagnosis. "Common"
features are typical of the disorder; "occasional" features appear frequently but are not necessarily
seen in a majority of cases.

gastrointestinal complaints, while older children experience more cardiovas-
cular symptomatology (Koplewicz, 1989). Livingston, Taylor, and Crawford
(1988) report that, among psychiatrically hospitalized children, those with separation anxiety had increased somatic complaints, typically abdominal pain and
palpitations.

At home, preschool children may resist sleeping alone in bed or in a room.
They may sneak into the bed of a parent or sibling at night or may sleep outside a family member's room. In some cases these sleeping patterns persist for
years. Separation reactions are seen most often in new daycare or babysitting
situations that involve rapid and prolonged separation from the caretaker and
familiar others. Hence, children who rarely experience these situations may
not manifest SAD until school ages.

At early school ages, children with SAD experience more defined separation fears. Themes of getting lost are typical, and fears of specific dangers such
as illness, death, kidnapping, and assault are extremely common. School-age
children also frequently worry about unrealistic harm to attachment figures. If
separation anxiety has not been noticed prior to school ages, it is almost always noticed at children's entry to school at age 5 or 6. Frequent illness complaints, missed school days, visits to the school nurse, calls home during the
school day, crying in class, social withdrawal, and manipulative behavior to
avoid school are all suggestive of SAD. Last, Francis et al. (1987) noted that
approximately 75% of children meeting criteria for SAD exhibit school refusal
or avoidance.

At later school ages and during adolescence, children may conceal separation anxiety or may refine their manipulative behavior to avoid school. Somatic complaints and manipulation of parental guilt are often combined to avoid school. In extreme cases these complaints may develop into a Somatoform Disorder. At home, children with SAD may maintain excessive proximity to the parent and express the belief that parents need them for physical or emotional protection. Such behavior can lead to impaired peer relationships secondary to social withdrawal. However, many children who develop SAD do not appear to have interpersonal difficulties and are generally well liked (Last, 1989a).

Families of children with SAD are often described as close-knit and caring (Kaplan and Sadock, 1988), but these adjectives often suggest enmeshed relationships. In many cases children with SAD appear to be overly attached to their caretakers. Whiny, demanding behavior is common, particularly when the caretaker's attention is diverted from children with SAD. Often, however, children with SAD appear shy and compliant at home.

In some cases children with SAD perceive stress or emotional distress in their parent and try to support the parent with their presence and dependency. Parents who are experiencing extreme stress may inadvertently encourage separation anxiety by leaning on their children too strongly for support. Similarly, children with SAD may be fearful for depressed parents, who may not have the motivation to encourage appropriate independence in their child. Unhappy or depressed parents may experience secondary emotional gain from the increased presence of their child. For example, in one case a depressed divorced mother permitted her child to miss school frequently, admitting that she felt better when her child was home.

Symptoms of SAD tend to vary considerably with time. Cantwell and Baker (1990) observed a high rate of recovery and a low rate of stability of SAD over a 4- to 5-year period for children receiving treatment at a speech and language clinic. A stressful event or social problem may cause recurrence of SAD symptoms in a child who had not shown symptoms for months or years. However, if the environmental contingencies maintaining SAD are unchanged, SAD can become entrenched and persistent.

Etiology

SAD can develop in a number of ways. In some cases a recent stressor involving separation or danger is responsible for onset of SAD. The child seeks proximity to the caretaker in order to prevent a recurrence of the stressor and to decrease feelings of anxiety.

In other cases, familial and behavioral causes appear to be responsible for SAD. Attachment theorists suggest that SAD may develop because of a child's insecure attachment with the primary caretaker. The child feels that he or she must constantly be vigilant or else the fragile attachment will be broken, resulting in loss of the caretaker. Bowlby's (1973) attachment theory strongly influences this etiological hypothesis. Infants who do not experience a sensitive, responsive, and available mother fail to develop a firm base of security and trust, leading to anxiety and SAD.

Other family-based etiological theories suggest that SAD develops out of enmeshed relationships between parent and child. Enmeshment prevents children from developing an independent, confident view of themselves, and it fosters excessive dependence on the parent. Such children need the presence of the parent for their psychological integrity, and they feel disloyal and vulnerable without the presence of the parent. Often the parent or the family system derives some benefit from the enmeshed relationship as well. For example, a depressed parent may rely on the constant presence of the child for social support. Alternatively, the child's "disorder" may deflect attention from problems in the relationship between the parents.

Behavioral theories focus on the reinforcing results of having SAD. SAD may gain children increased access to the parent and allow them to avoid situations of stress and failure, such as school and social relationships. Hence, children develop separation anxiety because reinforcements associated with the presence of the parent outweigh the reinforcements associated with the absence of the parent. This presence/absence reinforcement ratio is sufficiently large that the children will engage in extreme behaviors and psychological reactions in order to retain it. Attention to secondary gain for SAD symptoms is important in understanding the underlying behavioral etiology of SAD.

Cognitive and social learning theories of SAD explain the disorder based on the child's observations of an anxious or needy parent. Some parents unwittingly model separation anxiety by appearing anxious or concerned when their child is separated from them. This scenario is likely to emerge if a parent has experienced a stressful situation involving potential separation from the child, such as childhood chronic illness or loss of the child in a divorce. The child notices the parent's anxiety and becomes anxious as well, modeling the parent's separation anxiety.

Support for a genetic basis of SAD has received preliminary investigation, with equivocal results. Mothers of children with separation anxiety did not have an increased history of the disorder (Last, Phillips, and Statfeld, 1987). However, another study found that 83% of mothers of children with SAD or GAD had a lifetime history of anxiety disorders. Further, 57% of these mothers were concurrently presenting for an Anxiety Disorder (Last et al., 1987). In addition, it has been suggested that a relationship between SAD and Panic Disorder may suggest a similar genetic etiology for the disorders (see Casat [1988] for a review).

ASSESSMENT PATTERNS

A sample assessment battery for SAD is shown in Table 6.2.

Broad Assessment Strategies

Anxiety has both internal (thoughts, emotions, fears) and external components (shaking, whining, facial expressions, body posture). Hence, both child self-

TABLE 6.2 Sample Assessment Battery for Separation Anxiety Disorder

PSYCHOLOGICAL

Thematic Apperception Test

BEHAVIORAL

Child Behavior Checklist
Teacher's Report Form

FAMILY

Family Environment Scale

SYNDROME-SPECIFIC

Fear Survey Schedule for Children—Revised

Note: Assessment instruments are intended to supplement (not substitute for) a good clinical interview and, when possible, a structured diagnostic interview.

report and observer-report are likely to be important in the assessment of childhood anxiety (Strauss, 1993). Inconsistencies in child- and observer-reports of anxiety phenomena may suggest denial or lack of insight on the part of the child or an exaggeration by the observer.

Cognitive Assessment

Clinician-Administered. Separation anxiety disorder occurs in children of all intellectual ability levels (Mattison, 1992). Hence, cognitive instruments are not useful for identifying or diagnosing SAD (Husain and Cantwell, 1991). Cognitive assessment may be warranted if the SAD appears to be due to a lack of understanding (e.g., cognitive deficiency or deficit) on the part of the child. If the child is found to have a cognitive deficit, treatment for SAD will probably have to include very basic teaching and behavioral components.

Psychological Assessment

Clinician-Administered. The Rorschach and TAT are sometimes used to assess SAD (Samuels and Sikorsky, 1990), although characteristic response patterns of SAD children have not been extensively investigated. Content themes of danger, harm, loss, and anxiety are expected in projective testing. These themes coincide with the beliefs and tension that a SAD child may experience.

Because most children with SAD are of pre-adolescent age, broad assessment instruments that involve extensive reading (e.g., MMPI) or child self-report generally cannot be used. However, broad structured and semistructured clinical interviews for children, such as the DICA-R, DISC, CAS, and K-SADS, include extensive anxiety sections and may be helpful in probing child-report of anxiety symptoms.

Behavioral Assessment

Parent-Report. The value of parent-report checklists for evaluating what amounts to an internal, experiential state such as anxiety has been questioned. Nevertheless, internal states are frequently reflected in external behaviors that are observed by parents. Hence, parent-report checklists can provide insight into the effects of internal anxiety on the external behavior of the child.

SAD children can be expected to elevate the Anxious-Depressed, Somatic Complaints, Withdrawn, Social Problems, and Internalizing scales of the CBCL. Because the Anxious-Depressed subscale includes a mix of anxiety and depression items, individual items should be examined to see if children are showing primarily anxious or primarily depressed symptoms. Higher scores on the Somatic Complaints scale often indicate the use of somatic problems to maintain proximity to the parent, while the Withdrawn and Social Problems scales can indicate the extent to which SAD is harming social relationships. Elevations of the Thought Problems scale typically indicate the presence of obsessional thought processes, possibly surrounding separation fears. Elevations of the Externalizing subscales are less common in SAD children; if these are seen, they could indicate the presence of aggressive or coercive behavior to maintain proximity to the parent. One CBCL item pertains specifically to school avoidance, while several other items describe shyness/withdrawal that could indicate separation anxiety.

As with the CBCL, SAD children elevate subscales measuring anxiety and somatic problems on the MCBC and CPRS. Elevations of the Inhibition and Somatization scales on the MCBC are typical, and the Sleep Disturbance subscale can indicate the extent to which anxiety problems are reflected in sleep. The CPRS is less sensitive to anxiety issues, but the Anxiety and Psychosomatic scales can indicate SAD-related symptomatology. The MCBC and CPRS-93 each contain several items pertaining directly to symptoms of separation anxiety and school avoidance; the CPRS-48 contains one item asking about separation anxiety.

Teacher-Report. Teachers often see a different set of behaviors than do parents, so their input is valuable. On the TRF the Somatic Problems scale is elevated for SAD children who use somatic complaints to avoid school activities or to gain special attention. Anxiety scales of the TRF (Anxious-Depressed) and the CTRS (Anxious-Passive on the CTRS-39, Emotional-Overindulgent on the CTRS-39, and Inattentive-Passive on the CTRS-28) may or may not be elevated, depending on the extent to which the children are able to control their anxiety at school. Perhaps most important are scales that reflect children's social functioning at school, such as the Withdrawal and Social Problems scales of the TRF. The Anxious-Passive (CTRS-39), Asocial (CTRS-39), and Inattentive-Passive (CTRS-28) scales of the CTRS may also indicate social problems resulting from separation anxiety.

Like the CBCL, the TRF contains several items asking about school avoidance and separation anxiety behavior. Furthermore, the TRF items are more anxiety-specific than are the CTRS items. The CTRS-28 and CTRS-39 items, on the other hand, tap combined anxiety/depression symptoms (crying, withdrawal) without asking about specific anxiety-diagnostic criteria. Over all, the TRF appears to have broader and more appropriate coverage of school problems that are likely to be manifested by SAD children.

Family Assessment

Parent-Report. Separation anxiety frequently occurs in close-knit, caring, and/or enmeshed families. The FES may provide an evaluation of these and other aspects of family functioning. Typical SAD families would show a pattern of relatively high scores on the Cohesion and Control scales and comparatively low scores on the Independence and Active-Recreational Orientation scales. High Supportive factor scores might indicate that the family wishes to portray themselves as "perfect" and free of problems in interpersonal functioning. Typically the FES must be completed by a parent, since the child is too young to complete the scale. Child report on the FES can be useful with children over the age of 13.

Syndrome-Specific Tests

Clinician-Administered

Interview and Rating Measures. In conducting the clinical interview with a child with suspected SAD, particular attention should be paid to separation behavior and to the child's behavior in the presence of the clinician. In severe cases the child may not permit separation from attachment figures. If separation is attempted, the child may cry, scream, tantrum, or appear extremely anxious. The child may refuse to talk to the clinician without the parent present; some children will not talk at all. Less severe SAD cases will merely show mild discomfort with the separation. Some children with mild SAD are content to separate from the parent and talk to the clinician because they know that their parent is nearby. Compliance and interaction usually improve as children become more familiar with the clinician.

A useful anxiety-focused semistructured clinical interview is the Anxiety Disorders Interview Schedule for Children—Child and Parent versions (ADIS-C and ADIS-P) (Silverman and Nelles, 1988). The ADIS-C and ADIS-P allow for systematic data collection and assessment of DSM-III-R anxiety diagnoses in children age 6–18. ADIS-C/ADIS-P items ask about anxiety symptoms, cues, intensity, avoidance, and precipitating events. In addition to the DSM-III-R diagnosis, ADIS-C/ADIS-P data provide an extensive overview of children's symptoms. Reliability of the interview appears to be good (Silverman and Nelles, 1988).

In addition to the ADIS, other clinician-rated scales and interviews exist for the anxiety disorders, but these have received little attention or empirical support (Bernstein, 1990). The Children's Anxiety Evaluation Form (CAEF; Hoehn-Saric, Maisami, and Wiegand, 1987), for example, is a semistructured interview that assesses anxiety symptoms based on the self-report of children age 7–17. Results of a small clinical sample provide preliminary support for the CAEF (Hoehn-Saric et al., 1987).

Physiological Measures.   Physiological anxiety measures are rarely used in the child clinical situation, although they may be helpful in some cases. Furthermore, the relationship between physiological states and subjective reports of anxiety is variable within and between children (Strauss, 1993). Preliminary data suggest that child and adolescent physiological anxiety patterns are similar to those of adults. Generally, anxiety-disordered individuals show higher absolute values of response (heart rate, blood pressure) to an acute stressor and a slower than normal speed of return to baseline values while the stress is maintained (Strauss, 1993).

Child-Report

Five commonly used self-report instruments for the assessment of childhood anxiety are the Children's Manifest Anxiety Scale—Revised (RCMAS; Reynolds and Richmond, 1978), the State-Trait Anxiety Inventory for Children (STAIC; Spielberger et al., 1973), the Fear Survey Schedule for Children—Revised (FSSC-R; Ollendick, 1983), the Children's Depression Inventory (CDI; Kovacs, 1992), and the Visual Analogue Scale for Anxiety—Revised (Bernstein, Garfinkel, and August, 1986). Although none of these scales is designed specifically for the measurement of SAD, scale scores can indicate the extent and types of fears/anxieties being experienced by the child. In using these scales, it is important to remember that high scores on any of the scales are as likely to be indicative of another anxiety disorder as they are to be indicative of SAD. In fact, the overall item content of the scales appears to be more representative of GAD than of a more specific anxiety disorder diagnosis.

The RCMAS (Reynolds and Richmond, 1978) is a thirty-seven–item (eight of which form a lie scale) yes-no scale that assesses the general state of anxiety across a variety of situations. It produces a total score and three factor-analytically derived subscales: Worry/Oversensitivity, Physiological, and Concentration. The Worry/Oversensitivity factor appears best able to discriminate children with and without anxiety, using a cutting T-score of 60 (Mattison, 1992). Psychometric properties are reported to be good (Reynolds and Richmond, 1978; Mattison, 1992), although some items overlap with symptoms of depression. Hence, the degree to which the RCMAS discriminates between anxiety and depression is suspect, particularly given the strong co-occurrence of anxious and depressive symptoms in children. Nonetheless, it has seen wide use in assessing anxiety in children and adolescents.

The State-Trait Anxiety Inventory for Children (STAIC; Spielberger et al., 1973) is composed of two 20-item subscales that assess anxiety-state (situational symptoms or transitory anxiety) and anxiety-trait (generalized anxiety across a variety of situations). The extent to which children can successfully differentiate between transitory and stable anxiety, however, is suspect (Johnson and Melamed, 1979). The STAIC has been shown to successfully discriminate anxiety-disordered children with and without major depression from each other and from children free of anxiety. It does not appear useful, however, in discriminating among anxiety disorders (Mattison, 1992).

The Fear Survey Schedule for Children—Revised (FSSC-R; Ollendick, 1983) is an eighty-item scale that asks children to rate their fear of a variety of objects and events on a 3-point scale. It has been found useful in differentiating among anxiety disordered children (King, Gullone and Tonge, 1991; Last et al., 1989) and has been utilized for clinical classification at an anxiety disorder clinic (Francis et al., 1992). The FSSC-R has been extensively researched; factor analyses indicate five item clusters, and extensive normative data are available (Ollendick, Matson, and Helsel, 1985). The FSSC-R can provide data concerning not only the types of fears that the child has, but also the degree of fear relative to comparison samples.

Another widely used instrument in the assessment of children with anxiety disorders is the Children's Depression Inventory (CDI; Kovacs, 1992). The CDI consists of twenty-seven depression-related items that are administered to children age 6–17. Items are added to give a total score and five subscale scores (Negative Mood, Interpersonal Problems, Ineffectiveness, Anhedonia, Negative Self-Esteem). Raw scores can be converted to T-scores based on normative samples divided by age and sex (Kovacs, 1992). The CDI has good psychometric properties, with the possible exception of discriminant validity in clinical samples. It is used in anxiety disorder diagnosis due to symptom overlap between anxiety and depression in children (Bernstein, 1990).

The Visual Analogue Scale for Anxiety—Revised (Bernstein, Garfinkel, and August, 1986) is a self-report instrument on which children are instructed to indicate their experience of anxiety in various situations by choosing one "face" from a set of expressions ranging from "steady" to "jittery/nervous."

TREATMENT OPTIONS

Treatment options for SAD are outlined in Table 6.3.

Behavioral Interventions

Numerous behavior therapy methods apply to children with SAD (Werry and Wollersheim, 1991). In vivo desensitization consists of graduated exposure to separation from the parent while the child maintains a response incompatible with anxiety, such as relaxation, distraction, or engagement in activity. For

TABLE 6.3   Treatment Options for Separation Anxiety Disorder

---

BEHAVIORAL INTERVENTIONS

In vivo desensitization
Flooding/implosive therapy
Contingency management (operant conditioning)
Modeling

PSYCHOTHERAPY

Cognitive-behavioral interventions
    Self-monitoring
    Self-talk
    Distraction
    Self-reinforcement
    Relaxation techniques

Psychodynamic psychotherapy

FAMILY INTERVENTIONS

Family therapy

MEDICATION

Benzodiazepines
Tricyclic antidepressants

REFERRAL TO AUTHORITIES

Regular communication with school

Note: This outline of options summarizes major treatments covered in the text. Specific treatments are often combined into an intervention package. Refer to the text for additional descriptions of each treatment. This table is not necessarily an exhaustive list of all treatments available.

example, the initial goal may be for the child to visit the school after hours, with the parent in another room or out of the building. Next, the child may be driven by the parent to attend a half day of school. A third step could be attending a full day of school with a phone call home allowed at lunchtime. Final steps would involve the elimination of the phone call and riding the bus to school. Throughout the process the child and teacher are given strategies to reduce anxiety. For example, the child may be taught relaxation strategies, and problem situations are anticipated and practiced.

Success of an *in vivo* desensitization plan often depends on a firm set of rules: The child may go to the nurse's office if feeling faint, upset, or sick. The child may not call the parent or have any parental contact during the day (except for that allowed by the treatment plan). The child may not engage in social interaction or favored activity while in the nurse's office. Complaining and whining are ignored at school and at home. The child is dropped off at school every morning regardless of manipulation or complaints.

Last (1988) provides a case study of *in vivo* desensitization of a child with SAD. In this case the therapist and child developed two fear and behavior hierarchies: one for school avoidance and another for all separation situations. In weekly outpatient sessions and daily homework assignments (and with frequent telephone contact with the therapist for the first 2 weeks of treatment) the 10-year-old-child worked through his hierarchy for school avoidance. A contact at his school was used to keep the school apprised of treatment plans, to make it less likely that the child would attempt to "cheat" on assignments and to provide an on-location source of additional reinforcement and support. After 6 weeks of treatment and school attendance at the half-day level, work on the second hierarchy began. Treatment was successfully completed in 3 months, and progress was verified as maintained through more than a year's followup.

Flooding and *implosive therapy* involve continuous actual or exaggerated exposure to the object or situation that elicits anxiety (e.g., attendance at school and separation from caretaker) until the child's anxiety level decreases. Flooding, which is more often used with children, involves actual or imagined exposure to the anxiety-provoking situation. Implosive therapy uses imagined exposure to the situation. For example, a common flooding treatment for the SAD child is to force the child to go to school for a full day regardless of complaints or attempts to resist separation from the parent. Unlike desensitization, there is no gradual exposure to separation; separation from the caretaker is sudden and complete.

Flooding tends to be extremely effective in school avoidance situations because most schools have resources (e.g., nurse's office, ability to contact parent) to accommodate the child if an adverse reaction should occur. Although implosion and flooding can be effective treatments, they should be used cautiously with children, who may have a more limited ability than do adults to tolerate extreme anxiety.

Operant conditioning or *contingency management* methods identify and modify the rewards and secondary gain that maintain SAD. Such interventions begin with a thorough evaluation of the positive reinforcement and negative reinforcement the child receives for displaying separation anxiety. Common positive reinforcers are increased access to pleasant activities with the parent (e.g., staying home from school and playing games with mom), increased control over environment (e.g., access to preferred foods because the child is "sick"), and parental attention and positive interaction with the parent (e.g., the message that the child is "a good little girl" who stays with her parent). Common negative reinforcers are avoidance of negative peer interactions, avoidance of the fear that something will happen to the parent, avoidance of failure and work at school, avoidance of having to achieve independence and separation, and avoidance of general anxiety at being separated from the parent. Existing reinforcers of the SAD behavior must be eliminated, and new reinforcers of behavior that is incompatible with SAD are identified and implemented. For example, if the child stays home from school, the parent might be instructed to confine the child to bed with only schoolwork (no TV or other social interaction with the parent). Rewards may be set up for each day that the child attends school. The efficacy of contingency management is often enhanced when it is combined with desensitization (Meyer, 1993).

Social learning treatments, such as *modeling*, can also be effective components in the management of SAD. Typical modeling techniques used for SAD are participant modeling (usually most effective), use of live models, and symbolic modeling (Husain and Kashani, 1992). In live model and participant modeling techniques, another person demonstrates successful separation from the caretaker. The model should show initial difficulty with separation, followed by gradual mastery. In participant modeling the child repeats the modeled behavior after the model has demonstrated it. In symbolic modeling the child watches a videotape of another child successfully performing the desired separation. Alternatively, the therapist may describe the child successfully separating from the caretaker. In general, greater similarity between the model, the situation, and the child produces better results.

Behavior-modification techniques have produced generally positive results for focused problems such as SAD (Thyer, 1991). However, the choice of which behavioral treatment is most effective or appropriate for a particular child remains the clinical decision of the therapist. A multimodal approach involving modeling, contingency management, and *in vivo* desensitization is likely to be effective for most children.

Psychotherapy

Cognitive-behavioral treatment methods, which teach children to identify anxiety cues and to apply specific coping responses, have seen application in SAD, as well as in other anxiety disorders (Werry and Wollersheim, 1991). These treatments begin with self-monitoring tasks, such as keeping a diary of anxiety-provoking situations and cues. Based on self-monitoring, children learn to identify cues that lead to anxiety in future situations, such as separation from the caretaker. Next, the children are taught coping skills they can use in separation situations. Examples of coping skills include positive self-talk, distraction, self-reinforcement, and progressive muscle relaxation. Finally, the children apply the coping skills to the separation event. This general approach has received some clinical and research support (Ollendick, Hagopian, and Huntzinger, 1991). Cantwell and Baker (1989) note, however, that cognitive techniques are reported in the literature predominantly as case studies and have rarely been systematically studied. Furthermore, cognitive-behavioral treatments may be difficult with young or resistant SAD children.

Kendall (1994) applied a 16-week cognitive-behavioral regimen to children diagnosed with primary SAD, Overanxious Disorder (GAD in DSM-IV), or Avoidant Disorder (Social Phobia in DSM-IV). The intervention included several components: recognizing somatic reactions and anxious feelings, becoming aware of anxiety-related cognitions, developing a coping plan (self-talk and problem solving), evaluating coping responses, and applying self-reinforcement for adaptive behavior. Education in each of the cognitive-behavioral techniques was the focus of the first eight sessions, and skill practice using both imaginal and *in vivo* exposure was the focus for the remaining eight. The participants used a treatment workbook throughout. In-session and extrasession activities reinforced use of the skills. Measurements taken at completion and at 1-year followup indicated that treatment was beneficial compared to controls.

The *psychodynamic treatment* perspective hypothesizes that separation anxiety is a defense mechanism that keeps intrapsychic conflict out of awareness. In order to treat children's separation anxiety, the therapist must identify and give them insight into the conflicts underlying it. In many cases this involves dealing with parental relationships and ambivalence about separation from the parent. Psychodynamic treatment uses the therapeutic relationship and the children's insight into unconscious conflicts as the mechanism of change. Typical therapeutic modalities for psychoanalytic and psychodynamic therapy are discussion of issues, play therapy, and storytelling (Meyer, 1993). There is disagreement about the effectiveness of psychoanalytic and psychodynamic therapy for SAD, and the outcome research for these therapies is sparse (Kaplan and Sadock, 1988; Husain and Cantwell, 1991; Cantwell and Baker, 1989; Thyer, 1991).

Family Interventions

Parent Intervention and Training

Because the children's anxiety is centered on their relationship with the primary caretaker, parents are often involved in the treatment of SAD. Education of the parents about the etiology, symptoms, and treatment of SAD is often a good introduction to any intervention. This education can motivate parents to change their behaviors and to support behavioral and family interventions. Parents should also be educated about the role of their behaviors and environmental stresses in evoking SAD symptoms in their child.

Family Therapy

In some cases of SAD the parent interview may indicate that the parent is overreliant on the child and is reinforcing the child for the clinging behavior (Meyer, 1993). A focus in family therapy on boundaries and roles of family members may indicate systemic characteristics that are maintaining SAD (Bernstein, 1990). Restoration of appropriate family roles, reinforcement of child–parental boundaries, and reinstatement of the proper family hierarchy may then become targets of therapy (Meyer, 1993).

Medication

Differing opinions exist about the appropriateness and efficacy of psychophar-macological treatments for SAD. One view is that, due to its lack of systematic study with children, pharmacotherapy is not recommended as a first-choice intervention. Rather, it may prove a useful adjunct to behavioral therapy when the child's experience of anxiety prevents engagement in other treatments (Thyer, 1991). Another view is that pharmacotherapy should be immediately initiated in order to facilitate achievement of normal separation behavior (Kaplan and Sadock, 1988). Later, medication can be reduced once the adaptive separation behavior is in place. This latter view has particular merit in cases where the anxiety is so severe that the child cannot engage in even basic therapeutic techniques.

Some tricyclic antidepressants and benzodiazepines have been used with children with SAD (Sylvester and Kruesi, 1994). In particular, imipramine has shown promising results, although it may not be as widely effective as once thought (Klein, Koplewicz, and Kanner, 1992). Alprazolam and imipramine have been used for children with anxiety-related school refusal, and a host of other benzodiazepines have seen use for general anxiety as a result of care-taker separation (Sylvester and Kruesi, 1994). More research is needed in this area.

Referral to Authorities

While it is unlikely that SAD children will need a referral to legal authorities, excessive school refusal will sometimes result in legal action taken by the school. In these cases, coordination of the efforts of clinician and school is even more important than usual. Direct communication between the clinician and school is important in cases of parent or family pathology, since the parent may distort information. When mental health professionals, family members, school officials and the courts maintain open communication and cooperate with one another, the child is most expediently and best served (Bernstein, 1990).

Specific Phobia

CLINICAL DESCRIPTION

Diagnostic Considerations

Childhood fears arise normally and are often spontaneously outgrown (Beeghly, 1986). However, phobic anxiety differs from these normal fear responses in a number of ways: First, the child's fear is far out of proportion to the actual danger posed by the object. Second, the child's fear is extreme, sometimes resulting in an anxious outburst or excessive avoidance of certain situations.

Third, the child's fear has a significant negative impact on daily functioning. Fourth, the child's fear is resistant to attempts to extinguish it. Although these characteristics may apply, to a certain extent, to many childhood fears, when they are severe and occur together, a phobia is likely.

The essential feature of Specific Phobia is an irrational fear of an object or situation that almost invariably produces an immediate anxiety response. In children this response may be expressed by crying, immobilization, clinging to an adult, aggressive avoidance, or tantrums. In order to reduce anxiety, the phobic stimulus is consciously avoided (more typical in adolescents) or endured with intense upset (more typical in children), resulting in significant interference with the child's normal routine or with social activities or relationships. The child may not be aware that this phobic reaction is a problem or is out of normal proportion to the stimulus, although such awareness is typical of adolescents. Specific Phobia does not include phobias covered in Panic Disorder or Social Phobia.

Typically, physiological, psychological, and behavioral signs of anxiety occur in the presence of the phobic stimulus. Anticipatory anxiety is likely if children expect to confront the phobic stimulus, and children soon learn to avoid the source of their fear. The impact of such avoidance on daily life will depend upon the rate of normal contact with the phobic stimulus, but some functional impairment is necessary for a diagnosis. Obviously, uncommon contact will result in relatively little impairment (e.g., fear of elephants will not impair a city-dwelling child except in zoo or circus environments), but fear of an object or situation with which there is much contact can become quite debilitating.

Phobias are a common anxiety disorder in children. However, they generally go untreated due to the ease with which the phobic stimulus may be avoided (American Psychiatric Association, 1994). Using a 6-month duration criterion, occurrence estimates of 5–12% have been found in various studies that cross all age levels (Kaplan and Sadock 1988). Prevalence studies of Specific Phobia in child populations, however, are sparse. The Isle of Wight study (Rutter, Tizard, and Whitmore, 1970) reported that 0.7% of children age 10–11 had clinically detectable phobias. A study of 792 11-year-old children taken from New Zealand's general population found a 2.4% rate of Specific Phobia (Anderson et al., 1987) as identified by measures taken from the child, parent, and/or teacher. This rate dropped to 0% when more than one source was required to make the diagnosis. Among children and adolescents presenting for clinical treatment of Overanxious Disorder, Strauss et al. (1988) found a rate of 50% for Specific Phobia.

Appearance and Features

Typical phobic stimuli vary by age. Animal phobias are most common in childhood, while blood-injury phobias emerge as most common in adolescence. Children with phobias show varying responses when confronted with the phobic object. Most children cringe, grimace, and attempt to distance themselves from the object. Persistence of the presence of the phobic object may cause crying, shaking, immobilization, and an attempt to get caretakers to intervene. (Appearance and features of Specific Phobia are listed in Table 6.4.)

Often children are reluctant to admit phobias to peers, and they may also keep phobias from adults. Phobias are sometimes seen by other children as a sign of weakness, and teasing with the phobic object sometimes occurs. Parents may or may not be willing to tolerate the phobia. Intolerant parents may attempt their own flooding intervention with the child, with varying results. If done poorly (especially if the child is flooded with a particularly threatening stimulus, such as a growling, snapping dog), flooding can result in intensified fear. Overly tolerant parents may indulge the child's phobia, giving secondary gain of attention or avoidance of negative activities. Some parents acknowledge having the same phobia as their child has.

Despite the discomfort of the phobia, phobic children are often reluctant to follow through with treatment for their phobia. There are several reasons for this: First, the children frequently will not admit that the phobia is a problem. Second, they generally choose avoidance of the phobic object over treatment. Third, because most phobia treatments involve exposure to the feared object, children fear the treatment.

Etiology

Biological factors are not significantly supported in the development of phobias, although a genetic predisposition may be present. Relatives of children with phobias have a greater likelihood of having phobias themselves. Furthermore, the type of feared stimulus may run in families. For example, if one member of a family has an animal phobia, the other family members are more likely to have animal phobias than other phobias (American Psychiatric Association, 1994). On the other hand, this familial concordance could reflect the impact of learning and observation that some stimuli are to be feared.

TABLE 6.4	Appearance and Features of Specific Phobia (formerly Simple Phobia)

COMMON FEATURES

Intense anxiety in presence of feared object or situation, manifest as crying, immobilization, clinging, aggressive avoidance, or tantrums
Avoidance of feared object or situation

OCCASIONAL FEATURES

Denial of Phobia

Note: The features listed above are often seen but are not universal. Some features may be diagnostically relevant or required, while others may not be required for diagnosis. "Common" features are typical of the disorder; "occasional" features appear frequently but are not necessarily seen in a majority of cases.

Behavioral theories of phobias currently have the most research and clinical support. Both classical conditioning and operant conditioning provide explanations for the development of phobias. In classical (Pavlovian) conditioning of a phobia, a natural fear response (unconditioned response) to a natural fear elicitor (unconditioned stimulus) is paired with a formerly neutral situation or object (conditioned stimulus). For example, a child who is painfully bitten (natural fear elicitor or unconditioned stimulus) has a reflexive fear response (natural fear response or unconditioned response) to the presence of a dog (formerly neutral, conditioned stimulus) who bit him. The next time that the child encounters a dog, the pairing of dog—bite/pain—fear is shortened to dog—fear, and the child shows a fear response to the dog even though there is no bite. The fear response persists across time and different dogs, and in the absence of the presence of the natural fear elicitor (bite). Actual experience may not be necessary for this conditioning if the child has the opportunity to observe another person receiving negative consequences from a stimulus object. In other words, a phobia may be conditioned by observation as opposed to personal experience.

In operant conditioning, environmental contingencies account for the development and maintenance of a phobic reaction. Simply stated, the child is rewarded for the phobic behavior. Rewards may take the form of social attention, avoidance of an unpleasant activity, or caretaking behavior. For example, a child who expresses a fear of dogs may be rewarded by the elimination of a chore (e.g., taking out the trash, which the child fears will put him in proximity to a dog) and the sympathy of his parents. The phobia persists because it is rewarded.

Mowrer's (1939) Two-Factor Theory weds the two conditioning paradigms (classical and operant) and attempts to explain acquisition of the phobic avoidance behavior. Phobic behavior is rewarded because it allows the child to avoid exposure to the feared stimulus and to prevent a classically conditioned anxiety response to the phobic stimulus. Hence, the reward (operant conditioning) is avoidance of unpleasant anxiety. The phobic stimulus produces anxiety because it has been associated, through classical conditioning, with the anxiety response. Mowrer's theory explains why individuals do not give up their phobias after repeated evidence that no harm comes to them when they are in the presence of the phobic object. They are constantly reinforced for the phobia by avoiding the anxiety associated with the phobic object. Because of this constant reinforcement, the behavior persists. Hence, phobias persist because they reduce anxiety, regardless of whether the anxiety is justified based on the individuals' experience.

The psychoanalytic view of phobias suggests that phobias develop due to a failure of the normal repression defense against the conflict of an unresolved Oedipal situation. Oedipal urges and conflicts are displaced onto an object or situation, which may or may not have symbolic meaning. Avoidance of the displacement object or situation keeps the original conflict out of conscious awareness.

Alternatively, the child may use the defense mechanisms of denial and reaction formation to adopt a counterphobic attitude toward a feared object. A counterphobic attitude is one in which the child, rather than experiencing anxiety as a passive victim, attempts to confront and master the feared situation (Fenichel, 1945). Such an individual rushes to participate in fear-provoking situations (e.g., dangerous activity such as rock climbing). Behaviors such as childhood play involving reenactment of a feared situation may employ the additional defense of identification with the aggressor in the adoption of a counterphobic attitude (Kaplan and Sadock, 1988).

ASSESSMENT PATTERNS

A sample assessment battery for Specific Phobia is shown in Table 6.5.

Broad Assessment Strategies

Psychological Assessment

Clinician-Administered. MMPI/MMPI-A profiles of adolescents with Specific Phobia are frequently unremarkable, because of the encapsulated nature of a Specific Phobia. However, if the phobia coexists with another mental disorder or significant personality problem, the MMPI profile will reflect the other disorder. The F scale of a phobic adolescent may be mildly elevated, reflecting the expression of concern and unique reactions to the phobic fear. A mild elevation on the K scale suggests an attempt to compartmentalize the anxiety into a discrete phobia; adolescents with an elevated K may be unwilling to admit that their phobia is a problem. Scales 2, 3, and 7 may show minor elevations as a result of anxiety, dissatisfaction, and somatic upset, especially if contact with the phobic stimulus cannot be avoided. In rare cases, scales 6 and 8 may become elevated if the adolescent fears a loss of control because of contact with the phobic stimulus. Clinical elevations on any MMPI/MMPI-A scale should be examined carefully, as they may indicate the presence of other psychopathology in addition to the phobia.

TABLE 6.5   Sample Assessment Battery for Specific Phobia (formerly Simple Phobia)

BEHAVIORAL

Child Behavior Checklist
Youth Self Report

SYNDROME-SPECIFIC

Revised Children's Manifest Anxiety Scale
Fear Survey Schedule for Children—Revised

Note: Assessment instruments are intended to supplement (not substitute for) a good clinical interview and, when possible, a structured diagnostic interview.

Projective personality tests such as the TAT and Rorschach are not often used in the diagnosis of Specific Phobia. Rather, direct questioning of the phobic child and parents generally leads to identification of the phobic object and relevant behavioral contingencies. However, if the phobia is suspected to be symptomatic of a more significant disorder (e.g., schizophrenia), projective testing may be helpful. On the TAT, phobic children may or may not give remarkable stories. Themes involving the phobic object are not necessarily present, although they do occur in numerous cases. Many phobic children tell TAT stories involving feared situations such as burglary, death, and kidnapping. Outcomes may be negative or avoided by the main character (e.g., escape from the dangerous situation). Analysis of the content of Rorschach responses may indicate the degree to which children inject the phobia into their interpretation of ambiguous stimuli. For example, a child with a blood phobia who repeatedly sees blood on the Rorschach may allow her phobia to affect her interpretations of many events in her life.

The interview of the phobic child is often facilitated by a structured format, such as that adopted by the DICA-R, K-SADS, or CAS. These interviews probe the child's phobias in addition to screening for the presence of other disorders. Unstructured followup questions can then address the behavioral contingencies, environmental characteristics, and historical events that are contributing to the phobia. Unfortunately, structured interviews are usually too unwieldy for routine clinical use in phobic cases; hence, unstructured interviews are more often used.

Behavioral Assessment

Parent-Report.   Parents are often excellent sources of information about a child's phobia and the circumstances surrounding it. Subscale scores on the CBCL can be deceptive for phobic children, since the CBCL's one phobia item alone will not cause a major elevation on any subscale. Hence, a child with a circumscribed Specific Phobia would not show elevations on CBCL scales. However, the CBCL can be an important instrument for detecting the child's other behavioral problems. Phobic children may elevate the Anxious/Depressed scale if they have additional anxiety symptoms. Other CBCL configurations may suggest additional behavioral problems in the child. Analysis of the single phobia item on the CBCL can indicate the intensity and stimulus of the phobia. Similar issues apply to the TRF and YSR.

Neither the MCBC nor the Conners scales include Specific Phobia items. Hence, while these scales may be used to evaluate the child's overall anxiety or other behavioral problems, they are not good instruments for Specific Phobia per se.

Syndrome-Specific Tests

Clinician-Administered

As noted, perhaps the most useful component of the clinical evaluation of the phobic child is the interview. Topics to be covered in an unstructured interview include the diagnostic criteria, typical features, and possible etiological factors of the phobia. The Anxiety Disorders Interview Schedule for Children (ADIS-C) is a useful structured interview for assessing phobias and related anxiety problems (see description in the SAD section of this chapter).

In addition to interview techniques, the child's fear can sometimes be evaluated by behavioral observation. Occasionally the child will demonstrate the fear response when the feared object is mentioned by the clinician. In other cases the child's response may be elicited by pictures of the feared object, which can then lead to discussions about the nature of the fear.

Child-Report

The Revised Children's Manifest Anxiety Scale (RCMAS), State-Trait Anxiety Inventory for Children (STAIC), and Children's Depression Inventory (CDI) (described in the SAD section of this chapter) can be useful for measuring general anxiety and distress in the phobic child. Phobic children who are in little distress (usually because they can avoid the phobic stimulus) may not give high scores on these scales. As a group, however, phobic children give higher RCMAS and CDI scores than do normal controls, although their scores are lower than those of children with Posttraumatic Stress Disorder (Saigh, 1989a). A high Lie scale on the RCMAS may indicate the child's reluctance to admit faults and, therefore, a tendency to minimize phobic symptoms. The Fear Survey Schedule for Children—Revised (FSSC-R) may also assist with the identification of the type and variety of objects feared by phobic children.

Some instruments have been designed to evaluate certain specific phobias, such as fear of tests. One such assessment device is the Test Anxiety Inventory (TAI) (Spielberger, 1980), a twenty-item scale developed to measure differences in test anxiety. Each TAI item is scored on a 4-point Likert scale. The TAI has been used in clinical settings for pretreatment and posttreatment assessment.

Evaluation of the cognitive underpinnings of the phobic behavior may be assisted by the use of the Children's Anxious Self-Statement Questionnaire (CASSQ; Kendall and Ronan, 1989). The CASSQ asks about the child's anxiety-related self-statements. It yields two subscales: Negative Self-focused Attention and Positive Self-Concept and Expectations.

TREATMENT OPTIONS

Treatment options for Specific Phobia are outlined in Table 6.6.

Behavioral Interventions

The use of behavior therapies for specific phobias appears to be the most effective and most researched treatment approach (Husain and Kashani, 1992; Meyer, 1993; Strauss and Francis, 1989). Specifically, desensitization appears to be the treatment of choice for most childhood phobias. Desensitization pairs gradual

TABLE 6.6   Treatment Options for Specific Phobia (formerly Simple Phobia)

BEHAVIORAL INTERVENTIONS

In vivo desensitization
Systematic desensitization
Flooding/implosive therapy
Modeling

PSYCHOTHERAPY

Cognitive-behavioral interventions
    Self-monitoring
    Self-talk
    Role playing

FAMILY INTERVENTIONS

Family therapy

MEDICATION

Benzodiazepines
Other medications (propranolol)

Note: This outline of options summarizes major treatments covered in the text. Specific treatments are often combined into an intervention package. Refer to the text for additional descriptions of each treatment. This table is not necessarily an exhaustive list of all treatments available.

exposure to the phobic stimulus with a relaxed internal state. Systematic desensitization exposes the child to *imagined* stimuli, while in vivo desensitization exposes the child to *actual* stimuli. Desensitization begins with the identification of a hierarchy of anxiety-provoking situations related to the phobic stimulus. For example, if a child or adolescent is afraid of dogs, such a hierarchy might include, in order of increasing anxiety, looking at a picture of a dog, walking down a street where dogs can be seen behind fences, approaching a dog who is on a leash, and petting a dog. Next, the child is given strategies for coping with exposure to the phobic stimulus, such as relaxation training and self-talk. Examples of relaxation training include progressive muscle relaxation, hypnosis, or even tranquilizing drugs in difficult cases. Through exposure to increasingly intense levels of the phobic situation (and concomitant use of coping techniques), the phobic response can be eliminated. Desensitization may be more effective when combined with modeling techniques (Strauss and Francis, 1989), which use actors to demonstrate the child's achievement of each treatment goal. Modeling techniques have the greatest effectiveness when live models similar to the child are used.

Two behavioral methods that employ more intensive exposure to the phobic stimulus are flooding and implosive therapy. These therapy techniques expose the child to the full intensity of the feared stimulus until the fear diminishes. The exposure may be carried out *in vivo* or it may be accomplished imaginally (implosive therapy). *In vivo* flooding is the preferred method, as the impact of implosive therapy will necessarily depend on such variables as capacity for imagination and willingness to comply with an anxiety-provoking technique (Meyer, 1993).

Typically, desensitization and flooding are accompanied by contingency-management techniques to reward the child for exposure to the phobic stimulus. For example, goals may be set for each therapy session. The child's attainment of the therapy goal gains him or her a privilege or other reward from the parents. Social reinforcement can also be used as a reward for attaining therapy goals. In addition to providing rewards for goal attainment, it is essential to identify and remove any factors that are reinforcing or maintaining the phobic behavior. Typically, these factors involve increased attention, avoidance of a negative event, or changes in family structure. Attention must be given to these potential interfering factors in the initial assessment, with appropriate steps taken prior to intervention.

Over all, *in vivo* desensitization appears to be the most effective treatment for phobias in children, although several things can be done to increase the probability of success. First, the use of cognitive-behavioral components such as self-talk can be quite helpful during the desensitization process. Second, use of modeling can also enhance the therapy. Finally, it is important to build in rewards for attainment of goals and to remove any secondary gain for the phobia.

Psychotherapy

Cognitive-behavioral approaches have been used to reduce anxiety and avoidance in some phobic children. The most promising of these include the use of self-statements that reflect coping and competency (Strauss and Francis, 1989).

Assessment and treatment of a child's dental phobia using such an approach was conducted by Nelson (1981), whose cognitive-behavioral intervention began with an examination of the child's thoughts, feelings, and behavior while she imagined a dental visit. This examination indicated that her self-statements and images were contributing to her high level of anxiety and avoidant behavior. Based on these results, a four-step self-statement treatment program was designed. First, the therapist modeled coping statements to reduce fear and increase self-efficacy (cognitive modeling). Second, the child verbalized the statements under the therapist's guidance (external guidance). Third, the child verbalized them by herself (overt self-guidance). Finally, the child role played the target scenario while verbalizing the coping statements to herself (covert self-guidance).

Cognitive-behavioral techniques can provide children with coping strategies to use when confronting a phobic stimulus. Furthermore, they can help children to understand their cognitive responses and the contribution of thoughts to the anxiety problem. However, purely cognitive methods are rarely used for the treatment of Specific Phobia in children. Rather, cognitive techniques are often used to augment desensitization interventions. The effectiveness of cognitive interventions, alone and in combination with behavioral techniques, warrants further study.

Family Interventions

Family therapy may help the phobic child actively confront the phobic situation by mobilizing family support and motivation for the phobia treatment. Alternatively, family therapy may be necessary if the child's phobia is serving a role in the family system. For example, a child who has a phobia of dogs may be deflecting his parents' attention from the trouble in their own marital relationship. On the other hand, the child's fear of dogs may allow him to have an enmeshed relationship with his "concerned" mother. If such a family component is suspected, family therapy must precede behavioral treatment of the phobia. Failure to address family issues first could result in the family sabotaging the behavioral intervention.

Medication

Treating Specific Phobias with the use of medications is not well documented in the literature, but severe cases may warrant therapeutic drug trials in conjunction with behavior therapy (Kaplan and Sadock, 1988). Propranolol may reduce the child's anxious mood, but it is not curative for phobia. Additionally, it is contraindicated if evidence of asthma or congestive heart failure is present (Meyer, 1993). Diazepam, clonazepam, and alprazolam can also be used for general anxiety symptoms, such as those resulting from a Specific Phobia (Sylvester and Kruesi, 1994).

■ Social Phobia

□ CLINICAL DESCRIPTION

Diagnostic Considerations

Prior to DSM-IV, fears leading to avoidance in social situations were diagnosed in two categories, based on age: Social Phobia (adults) and Avoidant Disorder of Childhood or Adolescence (children). This developmental separation has been intensely debated, culminating in a combined DSM-IV diagnosis of Social Phobia that applies across the age span (Bernstein and Borchardt, 1991; Francis et al., 1992). The DSM-IV Social Phobia diagnosis retains the key aspects of the Avoidant Disorder diagnosis (avoidance of social situations, with some capacity for social relationships) while adding the more "phobic" flavor (e.g., emphasis on fear, anxiety) of the adult Social Phobia diagnosis. Because of diagnostic nomenclature differences between DSM editions, pre–DSM-IV studies of Social Phobia in children typically use the descriptors "Avoidant Disorder" or "avoidant behavior" rather than "Social Phobia" or "socially phobic behavior." These two diagnoses will be considered as essentially the same for the purposes of this section.

In Social Phobia, anxiety is focused on a specific type of situation: contact with unfamiliar people or negative social appraisal. Because of this anxiety there is excessive shrinking from unfamiliar social contact, which is sufficiently severe to interfere with social relationships. The children may seem socially withdrawn, embarrassed, and timid in the company of unfamiliar people, but they may not realize that the fear is unreasonable. Requests to interact in even a minor way with strangers bring on anxiety in the form of shaking, hiding, immobilization, or clinging to familiar others. If social anxiety is severe, children may become inarticulate and even mute. In contrast, contact with familiar people is welcome and desired, indicating that the children can achieve normal social relationships. To warrant the diagnosis of Social Phobia, the avoidant behavior must have been present for at least 6 months.

Social Phobia differs from normal "quietness" and separation anxiety. Children or adolescents who are socially reticent but not socially phobic are slow to warm up to strangers but eventually do respond. "Shy" or "quiet" children do not suffer severe impairment in peer interaction; children with Social Phobia, on the other hand, virtually never "warm up." In addition, Social Phobia differs from SAD, because SAD-based anxiety is experienced as a result of separation from caretakers, regardless of the presence of others. The children clearly identify (verbally or behaviorally) the loss of their caretaker as the anxiety-provoking event. In Social Phobia, anxiety results from contact with people who are unfamiliar, and the children identify the presence of unfamiliar people as the anxiety-provoking event. Hence, SAD children are often comfortable in social situations at home with their parents, while socially phobic children usually fear and avoid social situations in their home.

Although social withdrawal is typical of other DSM-IV disorders (e.g., Major Depressive Disorder), the social withdrawal of Social Phobia tends to be longer lasting (parents can often date it back to childhood), focused (e.g., not accompanied by other depressive symptoms), and specific to unfamiliar people. Furthermore, some shy and withdrawn children are clearly not socially anxious or are merely uninterested in any social relationships. This presentation may be more consistent with depression or schizoid features.

Across the life span, prevalence rates for Social Phobia are estimated at 3–13% (American Psychiatric Association, 1994), but childhood prevalence has not received much specific attention. Social Phobia rarely occurs alone and frequently coexists with another anxiety disorder (American Psychiatric Association, 1994; Kashani and Orvaschel, 1988). In a clinical sample of children and adolescents, for example, 27.3% of those diagnosed with GAD and 4.5% of those having SAD also received a Social Phobia diagnosis (Bernstein and Borchardt, 1991); overlap with Major Depressive Disorder is also common (Last, Francis, et al., 1987). Social phobia can be more frequently seen in children than in adults, especially if children formerly meeting criteria for Avoidant Disorder are shifted to the Social Phobia category.

Appearance and Features

(Appearances and features of Social Phobia are listed in Table 6.7.) At a subclinical level, the hallmark of Social Phobia—social withdrawal resulting in little interaction with peers and possible refusal to speak in school—has been found in 2–10% of the normal school-age population and in 10–20% of the normal preschool population (Morris, Kratochwill, and Aldridge, 1988). Some degree of "shyness" in children is common, and even symptoms of excessive shyness are not unusual.

Shyness anxiety symptoms differ in type by age of the child, and the symptoms experience an overall decline with increasing age (Orvaschel and Weissman, 1986). Stranger fear at approximately 6–8 months of age is developmentally normal. This fear of strangers abates somewhat by toddler age, when additional abilities expand the responses in the child's social repertoire. In some cases, however, considerable stranger anxiety may be maintained into school ages. With the onset of school attendance, fear of social evaluation tends to replace simple fear of strangers (Campbell, 1986).

Because social contact and the emergence of evaluation fears increase dra-

TABLE 6.7   Appearance and Features of Social Phobia

COMMON FEATURES

Anxiety upon contact with unfamiliar people
Fear of negative social appraisal
Socially withdrawn, embarrassed, or timid appearance
Social skills deficits
Attempt to avoid or escape social situations
Attachment to a few familiar people
Easily embarrassed
Unassertive

OCCASIONAL FEATURES

Refusal to speak in social situations
School avoidance
Somatic complaints
Low self-esteem, lack of self-confidence
Perfectionism
Overly sensitive to criticism

Note: The features listed above are often seen but are not universal. Some features may be diagnostically relevant or required, while others may not be required for diagnosis. "Common" features are typical of the disorder; "occasional" features appear frequently but are not necessarily seen in a majority of cases.

matically in the early school years, the onset of Social Phobia in children is often at ages 5–7. Unlike developmentally normal social anxiety, the intensity and persistence of Social Phobia symptoms are markedly greater than the developmental norm. Toddlers and preschool children may hide behind adults or may attempt to physically leave social situations. Older children may remain in the social situation but are silent and removed.

Coaxing them to engage in social interaction is typically unsuccessful with socially phobic children. Young children may respond to such coaxing with increased anxiety, crying, and additional withdrawal. Older children may become oppositional, embarrassed, or silent, appearing to resent the intrusion on their withdrawal. When children are forced or coaxed to engage in social activity, they are clearly anxious and unhappy throughout the interaction, failing to experience the sense of involvement with the other children.

In the clinic, children with Social Phobia usually present as unassertive, withdrawn, anxious, and lacking in self-confidence (Last, 1989a). They demonstrate a high degree of inhibition in social or recreational activities, preventing them from the experience of normal social interaction. In school-age children and adolescents, social inhibition is often the result of fears of embarrassment. Frequently children with Social Phobia are perfectionistic and self-condemning, and they may be quite well-behaved at home (Bernstein, 1990; Husain and Cantwell, 1991). They are sometimes described as overly sensitive to criticism and evaluation, expecting rejection from their peers. Low self-esteem and feelings of alienation and inferiority are common. Because of their lack of social experience, impairment in social functioning and social skills is often severe. In adolescence a delay or inhibition in psychosexual development may occur, accompanied by inappropriate social, sexual, and aggressive activities.

The clinical course of Social Phobia is variable. Some children (probably a minority) enjoy spontaneous recovery, which is more likely to occur after a positive social experience with peers (Husain and Cantwell, 1991). Other children experience ongoing feelings of isolation and depression due to their failure to form friendships and social bonds outside the family (American Psychiatric Association, 1994). Some residual or full-blown symptoms of the disorder often persist into adulthood, with exacerbations or remissions based on the degree and type of stress in the environment (American Psychiatric Association, 1994; Last, 1989b).

Etiology

There has been some speculation but little research about the etiology of Social Phobia in children. One potential pathway of development is lack of early experience in developing social relationships, leading to poor social skills and social failures. Out of these difficulties, anxiety develops. Several conditions could act as catalysts in preventing crucial early social experiences: isolated family, losses of significant others, chronic medical illness, family moves, insecure attachments, and profound differences from the majority culture (e.g., speaking a foreign language).

Temperamental differences such as shyness or timidity are also possible contributing factors in the development of Social Phobia (Husain and Cantwell, 1991). Therefore, it is usually wise to ask the parents questions about the children's early temperament. Children with a Social Phobia are sometimes described as having been hypersensitive or withdrawn as infants. When this is the case, a temperamental-biological explanation should be considered. In addition to temperamental features, developmental disorders can predispose children to the emergence of Social Phobia by interfering with language and speech development (American Psychiatric Association, 1994). Because speech is a critical social-communication modality, children who fail to develop adequate speech are at risk for social stresses and resulting anxiety.

Behaviorally, parents may intentionally or unwittingly reinforce socially phobic behavior by giving it attention or other secondary gain. For example, the socially phobic child may be perceived by the parent as vulnerable, leading to increased nurturant behavior. Alternatively, a parent who overdoes the (usually appropriate) "don't talk to strangers" rule may scare the child or communicate that avoidant behavior will be rewarded. Notably, parents of children suspected of having Social Phobia are less likely to refer them for clinical attention than are teachers, who can observe their discomfort among peers in the school setting (Last, 1989a).

A second behavioral explanation for the development of Social Phobia cites the role of internal reinforcement for withdrawn behavior. Internally, the child's experience of anxiety is paired with the presence of unfamiliar people, perhaps as a result of early negative experiences or a lack of social confidence. The child feels inferior or threatened by the presence of others and avoids interaction in order to reduce anxiety. Withdrawal, then, is negatively reinforced by a reduction in feelings of anxiety, insecurity, and inferiority.

Biological theories of Social Phobia have received some attention, but empirical data are preliminary. Support for the presence of familial patterns is accumulating (American Psychiatric Association, 1994), although the extent to which this reflects genetic or environmental influences has yet to be determined. There is some evidence that mothers of children with anxiety disorders such as Social Phobia experience anxiety disorders at a rate higher than the general population (Bernstein and Borchardt, 1991).

☐   ASSESSMENT PATTERNS

A sample assessment battery for Social Phobia is shown in Table 6.8.

Broad Assessment Strategies

Cognitive Assessment

Clinician-Administered.   Although Social Phobia occurs in children of all intellectual ability levels, selective use of cognitive instruments may provide use-

TABLE 6.8   Sample Assessment Battery for Social Phobia

PSYCHOLOGICAL

Piers-Harris Self-Concept Scale

BEHAVIORAL

Child Behavior Checklist
Teacher's Report Form

FAMILY

Family Environment Scale

SYNDROME-SPECIFIC

Fear Survey Schedule for Children—Revised

Note: Assessment instruments are intended to supplement (not substitute for) a good clinical interview and, when possible, a structured diagnostic interview.

ful clinical data. Global or focal cognitive deficits may explain the failure of some children to develop appropriate social skills. Such deficits may be reflected in overall IQ scores (global deficits) or scores on subtests measuring practical knowledge, social judgment/reasoning, social knowledge, and social-temporal sequencing (e.g., the Comprehension and Picture Arrangement subtests of the Wechsler instruments). When cognitive deficits are found, their impact on the child's failure to learn social skills must be considered. Simply exposing a delayed child to age-appropriate social interaction may not be therapeutic.

Additionally, Cantwell and Baker (1987) have found that communication skills are frequently impaired in the presence of Social Phobia. Intelligence and achievement testing that evaluates various aspects of communication skills may be warranted given the relationship of Social Phobia and communication difficulties. Children with co-occurring communication problems and Social Phobia show deficits on WISC-III Verbal Comprehension factor and subscale (Vocabulary, Comprehension, Information, Similarities) scores. On the WJ-R and WIAT, such children may have difficulty with reading and written language subtests.

Psychological Assessment

Clinician-Administered. Although not widely used for the diagnosis of Social Phobia, projective tests may provide insight into children's beliefs and conflicts regarding social relationships. On the TAT, stories involving character relationships may indicate children's expectations of social relationships and orientation to a social viewpoint. Some children with Social Phobia tell TAT stories with impoverished or underdeveloped social relationships, while others focus on the danger or risks of relationships. The former story type suggests avoidance or lack of awareness of social relationships; the latter story type suggests anxiety about relationship problems.

On the Rorschach, children with Social Phobia often give few human and many animal responses. In some cases, human contents are associated with negative themes or poor form quality. A large number of conservative, pure form responses suggests defensiveness about internal experience, which may also lead children to avoid the risks of social evaluation. Special scores and poor form quality may indicate that children are having difficulties with adopting a conventional perception of the world, perhaps because of isolation from social consensus experiences.

Child-Report. In some cases, Social Phobia can be linked to children's feelings of low self-esteem. Whether such self-esteem problems are a cause or a result of social phobia, they are important to consider in designing a treatment plan. Administration of the PHSCS may indicate self-esteem problems that are contributing to the anxiety, withdrawal, and evaluation fears common in Social Phobia. On this instrument, children with Social Phobia may show particularly low (e.g., low self-esteem) scores on the Anxiety and Popularity scales, reflecting a lack of social self-esteem and dissatisfaction over social anxiety. A general depression of all scales and the total score is not unexpected.

Behavioral Assessment

Parent-Report. Both the MCBC and CBCL include several items that relate to the Social Phobia diagnosis. For the most part, these items fall into two groups: those that ask about shyness and withdrawal and those that ask about attachment behavior toward familiar and unfamiliar people. The CPRS-48 has no items relating directly to Social Phobia, and the CPRS-93 has only a few items that relate tangentially to Social Phobia symptoms. Over all, then, the MCBC and CBCL may be more appropriate measures for a child with Social Phobia.

On the MCBC a child with Social Phobia will typically elevate the Inhibition scale, with a possible secondary elevation of the Somatization or Depression scale. The Externalizing factor and subscale scores are not usually elevated. Of the ten MCBC Sociability scale items, nine can be interpreted by the parent as pertaining to the child's behavior in the presence of familiar adults. Hence, high scores on the MCBC Sociability subscale (indicating appropriate, positive social behavior) are possible if the parent answers the items as they pertain to the child's behavior *with the parent*. Low Sociability scores indicate either that the child is not sociable around the parent or that the parent has answered the questions as they pertain to the child's behavior in the presence of peers.

On the CBCL, children with Social Phobia are expected to elevate the Withdrawn and Social Problems scales, with possible secondary elevations of the Anxious/Depressed and Somatic Complaints scales. More unusual are elevations of the Externalizing factor and subscales. Like the MCBC, the CBCL contains scales measuring socially competent behaviors, and similar considerations for interpretation apply. Specifically, social competence scale elevations are likely to be affected by the extent to which behaviors are reported as they are seen in the presence of the parent or in the presence of peers.

Teacher-Report. Teachers can be extremely valuable sources of information on the behavior of a child with Social Phobia. Because they see the child regularly in a large social situation, teachers are often better informed about the child's peer relationship behaviors than are the parents. Hence, administration of a teacher-report behavioral measure is important in assessing a child with Social Phobia.

As with the CPRS, the CTRS includes few items pertaining specifically to Social Phobia symptoms. The CTRS-28 includes one or two items remotely related to social anxiety and no Social Phobia item; the CTRS-39, on the other hand, includes two items that assess shyness/withdrawal and a few other items that may relate to anxiety. Over all, neither CTRS scale assesses Social Phobia and related anxiety problems comprehensively.

The TRF contains many of the same anxiety items as the CBCL and is therefore a reasonably good measure of Social Phobia and related constructs. Expected scale patterns on the TRF mirror those on the CBCL. Of the teacher-report behavioral measures, then, the TRF appears to be the test of choice for assessing Social Phobia.

Family Assessment

Parent-Report. Children with Social Phobia show dramatically different behaviors depending on whether they are in the peer or family environment. The FES can provide structured information about the family environment to assist with the understanding of the child's differing peer and family behaviors. Families with relatively high scores on the Cohesion and Control scales and comparatively low scores on the Independence and Active-Recreational Orientation scales may have problems with enmeshment and a lack of independence of family members. When this is the case, the child may fear separation from the family and see the peer situation as threatening relative to the overprotective family.

Syndrome-Specific Tests

Clinician-Administered

In addition to structured interviewing with the Anxiety Disorders Interview Schedule for Children (ADIS-C; see description in the SAD section of this chapter), many characteristics of children's withdrawal and social anxiety can be confirmed by unstructured behavioral observation. In conducting the clinical interview with a child, particular attention should be paid to the behaviors of the parents and child during separation. Social Phobia is usually readily recognized through the child's verbal and physical behavior in the interview. The child often insists on having a parent present during the interview. The child may not speak at all and may hide from the interviewer (Last, 1989a). Overall, the child's social behavior indicates avoidance, wariness, withdrawal, and anxiety toward the interviewer.

Occasionally a child with Social Phobia may appear at ease with the interviewer, even from the beginning of the interview. Children who have this presentation may fear groups more than individual situations, and/or they may fear peers more than adults. Their positive response to the interview situation, then, may be a result of the individual contact with a nonthreatening adult. Avoidant, withdrawn behavior may be more likely when they are in groups of peers.

Samuels and Sikorsky (1990) have developed a diagnostic interview and a checklist of behavioral attributes for use by mental health professionals of various backgrounds who assess school-age children. Their behavioral criteria for Social Phobia and Avoidant Disorder are isolation, withdrawal, avoidance, and anxiety. They also cite the inability to form/maintain relationships, depression, somatic complaints, and inhibited speech skills as associated features of Social Phobia.

Child-Report

Anxiety-specific tests such as the Fear Survey Schedule for Children—Revised (FSSC-R), Revised Children's Manifest Anxiety Scale (RCMAS), the Children's Anxious Self-Statement Questionnaire (CASSQ), and the State-Trait Anxiety Inventory for Children (STAIC) can be helpful in evaluating the breadth and intensity of children's anxious feelings, cognitions, and behavior (see descriptions earlier in this chapter). However, none of these tests specifically assesses Social Phobia. Rather, elevated scores on these tests could indicate the presence of significant distress or a co-occurring anxiety disorder. The Social Anxiety Scale for Children (SASC; LaGreca et al., 1988; LaGreca and Stone, 1993) measures social avoidance, fear of evaluation, and general social distress. Hence, it may be helpful in evaluating these components of Social Phobia.

TREATMENT OPTIONS

Behavioral Interventions

Reinforcement and Modeling Techniques

Behavioral strategies dominate the treatment of children with Social Phobia (see Table 6.9). Furthermore, in light of the interpersonal nature of this disorder, treatment approaches that emphasize social experience and social-skills building are seeing increasing use.

Positive reinforcement, symbolic modeling, and shaping are common be-

TABLE 6.9 Treatment Options for Social Phobia

BEHAVIORAL INTERVENTIONS

Reinforcement techniques
Symbolic modeling
Shaping
School-based interventions
    Reinforcement of social interaction during school
    Seating near familiar friends at school
    Assignment of peer "buddy" to facilitate interaction
    Avoidance of socially embarrassing activities
Social-skills interventions

PSYCHOTHERAPY

Cognitive-behavioral interventions
    Self-monitoring
    Self-talk
Play therapy

FAMILY INTERVENTIONS

Family therapy

Note: This outline of options summarizes major treatments covered in the text. Specific treatments are often combined into an intervention package. Refer to the text for additional descriptions of each treatment. This table is not necessarily an exhaustive list of all treatments available.

havioral treatments for Social Phobia (Morris et al., 1988). Positive reinforcement techniques reward the child for increased interactions with peers. Typically, a hierarchy of social goals is developed, beginning with very modest goals (e.g., stand or sit next to another child) and moving to more complex ones (start a conversation, play a game). Reinforcers are identified and paired with goal attainment. A monitor in the child's environment (usually a parent or teacher) records attainment of each goal and dispenses rewards.

Symbolic modeling uses training films that show peer models engaging in appropriate social behaviors. Review or discussion may follow the films to clarify the expected behaviors or to anticipate potential problems. Shaping techniques can be added to a symbolic modeling intervention by having the child gradually approximate the desired behavior of the model. Role-playing techniques can be used to facilitate the shaping process, allowing the child to practice the modeled behavior in a safe situation with the therapist.

While some studies have shown promising results using behavioral methods, the long-term maintenance effects of behavioral treatments are suspect (McBurnett, Hobbs, and Lahey, 1989). Hence, careful followup attention to the child's continued social interactions and use of social skills is important in any behavioral treatment. In addition, behavioral techniques are unlikely to be effective without *in vivo* application of the techniques. With such followup attention and *in vivo* application, modeling and reinforcement techniques are likely to have short- and long-term effectiveness in the treatment of Social Phobia (Carlson, Figueroa, and Lahey, 1986; Husain and Cantwell, 1991).

School-Based Behavioral Interventions

In addition to home- and office-based interventions, the school setting offers numerous opportunities for the application of behavioral techniques to promote the child's social interaction and engagement. Therapist enlistment of teachers' cooperation opens up avenues for using teacher–child interaction and child-peer interaction that will improve social skills and provide the basis for positive learning experiences. Among the types of strategies that might be employed are reinforcement of social interaction during classroom instruction, development with the child of a hierarchical list of preferred reinforcers that can be earned through specific social behaviors in the school setting, seating placement near others whom the child likes and away from anyone who may tease or bully the child, assignment of a more socially skilled "buddy" who will engage the child and involve him or her in group activities, and avoidance of placing the child in socially embarrassing or frightening situations (Blanco and Bogacki, 1988).

Social-Skills Interventions

To address potential social-skills deficits in children with Social Phobia, a variety of modified social-skills training interventions have been developed (e.g., Francis and Ollendick, 1988). These typically involve education and practice to teach children social skills in a structured way. A typical social-skills intervention program involves five major steps. First, children learn the content and principle behind a social skill. Second, the children learn to identify situations in which the skill can be applied. Third, they learn to perform the skill. Fourth, the children practice the skill in a mock social situation. Finally, the children implement the skill *in vivo* and notice the response of the social environment. Social skills that are typically taught include smiling, starting a conversation, saying hi, saying goodbye, seeking out proximity to others, reading social cues to approach or end interaction, and group entry behavior.

Since social-skills training provides both education and practice, it overcomes deficits in both knowledge and implementation of social-skills. Koplewicz (1989) recommends group social skills therapy as the treatment of choice for children with Social Phobia. The group situation facilitates learning by providing immediate opportunities for social interaction and by allowing the children to learn from each other's behavior.

Psychotherapy

Cognitive-Behavioral Techniques

Treatment that combines behavioral training with cognitive psychotherapy techniques can be especially helpful for avoidant children who experience high levels of anticipatory anxiety. Cognitive-behavioral intervention may be essential if children's anxiety precludes the implementation of even the simplest behavioral goals. In these cases the children must gain some control over their anxiety before adequate performance of behavioral homework assignments can be expected.

Some of the most promising of the cognitive-behavioral interventions for social anxiety involve the use of self-monitoring and self-statements that reflect coping and competency (Strauss and Francis, 1989). Cognitive-behavioral interventions begin with assessment and self-monitoring techniques. For example, the therapist might sample the child's thoughts, feelings, and behavior at intervals while the child imagines a recent unsuccessful social interaction. Alternatively, the child might record an actual experience in a diary. Underlying beliefs and self-statements are identified and linked to feelings and behaviors. The child's beliefs are then challenged, and alternative beliefs are suggested. The alternative beliefs are then tested with *in vivo* homework assignments. To reduce the stress of *in vivo* experiences, the child is taught alternative self-statements that are related to positive thoughts and less anxiety. In some cases, additional skills, such as relaxation and written plans for coping with social stress, are used.

Play Therapy

Nondirective (Axlinian) play therapy may be effective for younger children with Social Phobia whose home environments are fairly restrictive. The success of developing a relationship with the therapist gives children a positive social experience. Based on this experience, they may overcome social inhibition and increase self-confidence and assertiveness in other social situations (Husain and Cantwell, 1991; Husain and Kashani, 1992). Furthermore, the development of independent, self-directed behavior emerges from the nondirective environment, which requires that the children take the lead in social interaction.

Family Therapy

When parents or other family members consciously or unconsciously reinforce the child's dependence and isolation, family therapy may be indicated (Husain and Cantwell, 1991). In addition, if the child's avoidant symptoms seem to be serving a role in the family environment, structural family issues may need to be addressed prior to behavioral interventions. If such family influences are ignored, the family may be subtly resistant to behavioral interventions.

In family therapy for Social Phobia, the therapist receives data from a variety of sources: home observations provided by the family members, differing interpretations within the family, and in-session observation of family interactions. Bringing this material to the attention of the family, integrating the viewpoints of family members, and facilitating communication within the family ideally help the family to remove support for the child's symptoms and to remove barriers to treatment (Bernstein, 1990). For example, the therapist may explain how the child is using avoidant behavior to retain control in the family relationship or to avoid independent roles and behaviors (Kaplan and Sadock, 1988).

In some cases, reinforcement of the child's dependence and isolation may signal an underlying depression or other psychopathology in the parent (Husain and Cantwell, 1991). When this is the case, the parent should be evaluated and treated for the problem prior to the parent's involvement in interventions.

Medication

The efficacy of pharmacological agents in the treatment of Social Phobia is debatable, and some authors contend that they are not the treatment of choice (Thyer, 1991). Husain and Cantwell (1991) maintain that antianxiety or sedative medications are seldom indicated for Social Phobia, in contrast to treatment for SAD. Such medications may reinforce passivity and withdrawal, undermining the attainment of mastery and social interaction. However, use of some medication may be indicated when children's symptoms are so severe that they cannot adhere to even the most modest behavioral recommendations.

Proponents of medication use note that alprazolam has achieved positive results in a single-blind, uncontrolled investigation of children with Social Phobia and/or GAD (Simeon and Ferguson, 1987). Medications such as imipramine, diazepam, and clonazepam are used for the treatment of anxiety symptoms in general (Sylvester and Kruesi, 1994); the extent to which these medications are effective in the specific case of Social Phobia remains to be seen.

Obsessive-Compulsive Disorder

CLINICAL DESCRIPTION

Diagnostic Considerations

Obsessive-Compulsive Disorder (OCD) in children is quite similar to its presentation in adults. In each case, obsessions, compulsions, or both are present. *Obsessions* are defined as persistent thoughts, ideas, images, or impulses that are considered inappropriate and intrusive and that create marked distress or anxiety. *Compulsions* are repetitive behaviors or mental acts engaged in for the purpose of reducing or preventing distress or anxiety. These behaviors are not engaged in for any pleasurable or satisfying benefits they may produce. The requirement that the obsessions and compulsions be ego-dystonic is relaxed for children, but children often recognize their excessive nature. Often children are able to suppress these behaviors when away from the home, only to return to the behaviors when back at home. The symptoms of OCD must significantly interfere with normal functioning due to either the distress experienced or the time involved in completing compulsive acts (American Psychiatric Association, 1994).

Repetitive thoughts are characteristic of numerous disorders in addition to OCD, and the presence of such thoughts during the course of another mental disorder does not necessarily indicate that a diagnosis of OCD is appropriate. For example, the other anxiety disorders, mood disorders, phobias, Anorexia Nervosa, Bulimia Nervosa, Tourette's Syndrome, Mental Retardation, pervasive developmental disorders, brain damage syndromes and Schizophrenia share features with OCD and must be carefully considered in diagnosis (Leonard, Swedo, and Rapoport, 1991; Swedo and Rapoport, 1988). In general, OCD differs from other mental disorders in several ways:

1. The obsessions or compulsions are ego-dystonic (unlike repeated thoughts in the mood disorders or anorexia).

2. The obsessions or compulsions are not specific to the content of another anxiety disorder (e.g., separation, phobia).

3. The obsessions or compulsions are understood to be excessive or unrealistic (unlike delusions or psychosis), although this may not be true for children.

4. The obsessions or compulsions are not rigidly tied to a single feared stimulus (unlike a phobia).

5. The obsessions or compulsions are related to beliefs and do not appear to offer anxiety relief (unlike the stereotypical behaviors seen in Mental Retardation and the pervasive developmental disorders; also unlike the reflexive behaviors of tics).

It should be noted, however, that Major Depressive Disorders, other anxiety disorders, and especially anorexia and Tourette's Syndrome co-occur with some frequency in OCD children (Leonard, Swedo, and Rapoport, 1991). In fact, OCD may co-occur with other psychological disorders more often than it occurs alone. In a large prospective study of childhood OCD, 74% of 70 children and adolescents presenting with a primary diagnosis of OCD met criteria for other psychiatric diagnoses as well. The diagnoses most frequently seen were depression (39%), developmental disabilities (24%), Specific Phobia (17%), GAD (16%), Oppositional Defiant Disorder (11%), and Attention-Deficit/Hyperactivity Disorder (10%) (Leonard, Swedo, & Rapoport, 1991).

Empirical work indicates that one-third to one-half of adult OCD cases experience onset by age 15 (Rapoport, 1988). Lifetime prevalence of OCD is estimated to be 2.5% (American Psychiatric Association, 1994). Onset age for adult OCD may be earlier for males than for females, with a typical male onset age in the 6–15-year-old range and a typical female onset age in the 20–29-year-old range (American Psychiatric Association, 1994). Onset age for childhood OCD also shows the pattern of earlier onset for boys (age 9) than for girls (age 12), with boys having OCD approximately twice as often as girls during childhood (Leonard, Swedo, and Rapoport, 1991). In one epidemiological study, approximately 0.3% of the general child and adolescent population were found to have OCD symptomatology, and 1% of child psychiatric inpatients had OCD (Flament et al., 1990; Rapoport, 1988). However, these estimates may be low because children with OCD often conceal their symptoms.

Appearance and Features

Many children hide their obsessive-compulsive symptoms (see Table 6.10) because the symptoms frequently involve "internal," thought-based activity. There is sometimes indirect evidence for OCD when the child seems distracted, has difficulty concentrating, and has difficulty with activities because of a lack of task-focus. Symptoms may reach dramatic proportions before coming to the attention of parents (e.g., skin breakdown from a handwashing ritual). Signs that OCD should be considered include unproductive hours spent on homework, retracing over words, excessive erasures, unexplained increases in utility bills or laundry, very fast depletion of cleaning supplies, stopped-up toilets, requests that family members repeat phrases, unreasonably high requests for reassurance, a preoccupying fear of harm coming to the child or to others, long bedtime rituals, fear of leaving the home, hoarding of useless objects, or peculiar patterns of sitting or walking (Leonard, Swedo, and Rapoport, 1991).

The most frequent compulsions seen in children and adolescents with OCD are washing, repeating, checking, touching, counting, arranging, hoarding, and scrupulosity (Kaplan and Sadock, 1988; Leonard, Swedo, and Rapoport, 1991). Common obsessions are contamination, danger, doubts, disorder, guilt for imagined negligence, aggressive thoughts, and sexual thoughts. Onset of OCD is sometimes acute, and children can occasionally recall when they first began to experience OCD symptoms (Rapoport, 1988). Symptoms commonly change over time, such as when cleaning rituals give way to repeating or checking (Leonard, Swedo, and Rapoport, 1991; Swedo and Rapoport, 1988).

The course of OCD is variable. Some children report that their obsessions and compulsions subside during certain periods of time, while others report that they are continuous. Stress and boredom may be related to exacerbation of symptoms; distraction is sometimes effective in preventing obsessions and compulsions. About

TABLE 6.10   Appearance and Features of Obsessive-Compulsive Disorder

COMMON FEATURES

Persistent, automatic, intrusive thoughts, images, or impulses
Repetitive behaviors
Cleaning, repeating, checking
Hiding of disorder as long as possible

OCCASIONAL FEATURES

Difficulty concentrating
Lack of productive or purposeful activity
Sudden onset
Missing household items, rearranged items, or overuse of items

Note: The features listed above are often seen but are not universal. Some features may be diagnostically relevant or required, while others may not be required for diagnosis. "Common" features are typical of the disorder; "occasional" features appear frequently but are not necessarily seen in a majority of cases.

15% of people with OCD show a progressively declining course (American Psychiatric Association, 1994). Suicide is a risk for OCD children and should be investigated in interview (Kaplan and Sadock, 1988; Kearney and Silverman, 1990).

Etiology

Three groups of theories have received the most attention in OCD etiology: biological, behavioral, and psychodynamic. Biological theories identify neurotransmitters and genetics as primary in the explanation of OCD; these theories have received the most attention to date. A serotonin hypothesis of OCD is based on clinical response to the serotonin reuptake inhibitors. Neuroanatomical studies using CAT and PET scans have found some abnormalities in some patients with OCD. The involvement of abnormalities of basal ganglia is supported by the association of OCD and Sydenham's Chorea in some children, the presence of obsessive-compulsive symptoms in Tourette's syndrome, and OCD's association with postencephalitic Parkinson's disease (Leonard, Swedo, and Rapoport, 1991). Also, approximately 20% of first-degree relatives of OCD patients meet OCD diagnostic criteria, though the symptom pictures often differ (Leonard, Swedo, and Rapoport, 1991). Twin studies also support a genetic hypothesis (American Psychiatric Association, 1994).

Psychodynamic theories emphasize the role of obsessions and compulsions as defenses to deflect anxiety arising from internal conflicts. Because the conflicts are too threatening to experience directly, the child represses the actual content of the internal conflict. In its place emerge thoughts and compulsions to behavior that may be symbolically related to the original intrapsychic conflict but deflect attention from the original conflict. For example, a child with Oedipal urges toward her father may develop obsessions of sex with a boy next door. Ultimately, psychodynamic theories stress the importance of uncovering the underlying conflict and resolving it. Without the repressed conflict the obsessions and compulsions have no reason to continue.

Behavioral theories explain the presence of obsessions and compulsions by stressing the anxiety relief that the person gets from engaging in them. Holding back an obsession, for example, creates feelings of anxiety and stress in the child. The anxiety relief from giving in to the obsession is reinforcing, causing the child to give in to the obsession at a later time for anxiety relief. While this model explains the maintenance of OCD, it does not address questions about its emergence.

ASSESSMENT PATTERNS

A sample assessment battery for OCD is shown in Table 6.11.

Broad Assessment Strategies

Cognitive Assessment

OCD does not seem to cluster in the upper ranges of intellectual functioning, as was previously widely believed. Rather, OCD has been found in persons of

TABLE 6.11   Sample Assessment Battery for Obsessive-Compulsive Disorder

PSYCHOLOGICAL

Thematic Apperception Test
Rorschach

BEHAVIORAL

Child Behavior Checklist

SYNDROME-SPECIFIC

Maudsley Obsessional-Compulsive Inventory
Children's Yale-Brown Obsessive-Compulsive Scale

Note: Assessment instruments are intended to supplement (not substitute for) a good clinical interview and, when possible, a structured diagnostic interview.

varying intellectual abilities (American Psychiatric Association, 1994). Children with OCD tend to have an average distribution of intelligence (Husain and Kashani, 1992). Consequently, intelligence and achievement testing scores do not provide material that can be used to support or rule out an OCD diagnosis. Occasionally, severe OCD symptoms can interfere with processing speed, attention, and concentration on intelligence tests. This interference is usually easily observed behaviorally, and it may result in lower scores on the Wechsler Arithmetic, Digit Span, Coding, and Symbol Search tests. Interference with motor speed may also affect any timed cognitive test, such as the Wechsler performance subtests.

Psychological Assessment

Clinician-Administered. Although little empirical research is available as to characteristic MMPI-A profiles of OCD adolescents, a combination of scales 7, 8, and 2 would be expected. The 7-8 combination is more benign than is the 8-7 code type, which indicates possible deteriorating personality function. The 2-7/7-2 profiles generally indicate depression over the individual's level of functioning and possible social withdrawal. The 2-7-8 code type represents a self-analytic person who may feel some loss of cognitive control, with a sense of catastrophe and hopelessness. The high point 7 profile is not often encountered, but when seen supports an obsessive-compulsive diagnosis. High scale 7 scores more generally reflect obsessions than compulsions (Meyer, 1993).

On projective tests, OCD symptoms are usually manifest in overelaborated, perfectionistic, minute, detailed, or repetitive responses. On the TAT, OCD children often tell elaborate, detailed stories, giving names to characters and providing detailed descriptions of irrelevant story details. Some hesitation or lack of coherence in the story lines could indicate that the obsessions are interfering with the child's storytelling thought process. Repetitive themes may be present and should be analyzed for connections with the reported obsessions or compulsions. In other cases the stories may be stereotypical and devoid of emotion. For many OCD children, the "tired hand" rule applies to the TAT: If the clinician's hand is tired of writing down all of the child's story details and elaborate themes, consider the OCD diagnosis (this is not entirely facetious, although it has not been empirically studied).

The Rorschach responses of children with OCD may indicate doubt as to the content of the percept, with the children modifying the response immediately or during the inquiry. Small details of the blot may be used for responses, with the whole ignored. Alternatively, they may exclude small details of the blot in the response in an attempt to have the blot more closely fit their response. Descriptions of the blot may be elaborate and detailed, although this detail may not result in increased determinant complexity. A large number of responses is typical, with many W or Dd responses, a high F+ percentage, and many edge details (Meyer, 1993).

Behavioral Assessment

Parent-Report.   The CBCL includes several items relevant to the assessment of OCD. For the most part, these items cluster on the Thought Problems subscale. Hence, OCD children almost always have elevated Thought Problems scores on the CBCL. When interpreting the CBCL profile, it is important to be clear that the elevated Thought Problems score does not refer to thought problems in the psychotic sense. Rather, it tends to be more of an obsessive-compulsive-unconventional thought scale. In addition to the Thought Problems scale, the Attention Problems scale includes several items (e.g., poor concentration) that are either directly or tangentially related to OCD symptoms. Hence, this scale is also often elevated in OCD children. Again, it is important to be clear as to the meaning of an elevated Attention Problems scale for an OCD child. In such an instance the Attention Problems scale probably reflects obsessive-compulsive thought processes as opposed to a fundamental attention-deficit.

The pattern of elevations of the other CBCL subscales may indicate characteristics of the OCD and related problems. Elevations of the Somatic Problems and Anxious/Depressed scales, for example, are not uncommon in OCD children and reflect somatization and general upset, respectively. The Withdrawal and Social Problems scales may indicate social difficulties secondary to the OCD.

Unlike the CBCL, the MCBC and Conners' scales have fewer items related to OCD symptoms. Hence, these scales are less often used for OCD assessment, although they may be useful for assessment of co-occurring problems.

Teacher- and Self-Report.   Like the CBCL, the TRF and YSR contain several items measuring OCD symptoms and related problems. Furthermore, administration of these checklists may identify symptoms of which the parent is unaware. The extent to which OCD symptoms are apparent in the child's classroom behavior may be probed with the TRF. More importantly, the self-report YSR taps internal experience and personal appraisal of the symptoms. Because of the internal nature of obsessions, the YSR can be a valuable component of assessment, although its utility is diminished because it cannot be administered to children less than 11 years of age. Profile patterns and interpretation of the TRF and YSR mirror those for the CBCL.

Syndrome-Specific Tests

Clinician-Administered

In addition to structured interview information gathered with the Anxiety Disorders Interview Schedule for Children (ADIS-C; see description in SAD section of this chapter), a clinician rating scale can be used to document children's OCD symptoms. The Children's Yale-Brown Obsessive-Compulsive Scale (CY-BOCS; Goodman, Rasmussen, and Price, 1988; Jensen, 1990) is a clinician rating scale that assesses the severity of both obsessive and compulsive symptoms. For each symptom the following categories are assessed: amount of time consumed per day, amount of distress, interference with normal functioning, effort required to resist the symptom, and the amount of control the individual has over symptoms. The adult version of this clinician rating scale has been shown to be valid and reliable (Goodman et al., 1988; Jensen, 1990).

Child-Report

The Maudsley Obsessional-Compulsive Inventory (MOCI; Hodgson and Rachman, 1977) is specifically designed for use in evaluating the cognitive and behavioral aspects of OCD. It is made up of thirty items scored true or false and yields a total score as well as scores for Washing, Checking, Slowness, and Doubting. The MOCI has been found to be useful both in assessing treatment effects and in discriminating between OCD-disordered individuals and those not having the disorder (McCarthy and Foa, 1988; Rachman and Hodgson, 1980).

Several other OCD-specific self-report tests for children exist. For example, the Leyton Obsessional Inventory—Child Version (LOI-CV) is a downward age extension of an adult version of the scale (Berg, Rapoport, and Flament, 1986). The LOI-CV has seen some clinical use with OCD children, and it may provide information to guide treatment (Wolff and Wolff, 1991). The Compulsive Activity Checklist has been suggested as another childhood OCD measure (McCarthy and Foa, 1988).

In addition to OCD-specific tests, it may be helpful to give a more general anxiety test to assess the presence of other anxiety symptoms. Several general anxiety tests were described earlier in the chapter (e.g., the Revised Children's Manifest Anxiety Scale, State-Trait Anxiety Inventory for Children). In addition, the Children's Depression Inventory may be helpful in identifying the presence of co-occurring depressive symptoms.

TREATMENT OPTIONS

Treatment options for OCD are outlined in Table 6.12.

Behavioral Interventions

Perhaps more than for any other disorder, the child's cooperation is essential for effective behavior therapy for OCD. Eliciting anxiety-provoking private events is required for treatment to be effective, and such private behavior cannot be externally verified. Thus, the child's accurate self-report of internal events is critical for success. These requirements are less crucial for external compulsive behavior, which can be monitored by observation. If the child appears unmotivated or unable to report private experience honestly, behavioral techniques may not be appropriate (Foa and Steketee, 1989).

Application of learning theory has thus far resulted in two overriding behavioral approaches to treating OCD: exposure procedures and response prevention. *Exposure procedures,* such as desensitization, flooding, and satiation, expose the child gradually or completely/rapidly to obsessions, to compulsions, or to the situations that are associated with the obsessions or

TABLE 6.12   Treatment Options for Obsessive-Compulsive Disorder

BEHAVIORAL INTERVENTIONS

Exposure therapies
In vivo desensitization
Systematic desensitization
Flooding/implosive therapy
Satiation

Response prevention

PSYCHOTHERAPY

Cognitive-behavioral interventions

FAMILY INTERVENTIONS

Family therapy

MEDICATION

INPATIENT HOSPITALIZATION

Note: This outline of options summarizes major treatments covered in the text. Specific treatments are often combined into an intervention package. Refer to the text for additional descriptions of each treatment. This table is not necessarily an exhaustive list of all treatments available.

compulsions.. This exposure presumably reduces the anxiety associated with the obsession, compulsion, or trigger situation by pairing relaxation (or lack of negative outcome) with the anxiety-provoking symptom or situation. For example, a child with cleanliness obsessions may be asked to cover himself with dirt.

Satiation techniques expose the child to high levels of the obsession or compulsive behavior in an attempt to make the behavior aversive or to tire the processes driving the behavior. They also bring the "uncontrollable" urges under control by "prescribing the symptom." For example, a child may be asked to perform the obsession or compulsion repeatedly until she can do so no more because of boredom or fatigue. The pairing of the symptom with control, monotony, and fatigue encourages the child to discontinue it.

Some individuals can be exposed to their obsessions only in fantasy, such as committing murder or their house burning down. Nonetheless, where possible the actual anxiety-provoking stimulus should be used in treatment as this produces better results than imaginal exposure (Foa and Steketee, 1989). Additionally, exposure must take place until habituation has occurred and OCD symptoms have diminished.

Response prevention through blocking or punishing approaches has also been used to reduce the number of obsessive thoughts or the performance of compulsive behaviors. Response prevention techniques include thought stopping, covert sensitization and aversion therapy. Response prevention typically begins by limiting the child to a single performance of a compulsive act or obsessive thought, and then eventually completely extinguishing its performance. The limiting can be done by the self-control of the patient, alteration of the environment (e.g., not giving a hand washer private access to the bathroom), physical restraint (having a hand washer wear gloves or restraints to prevent washing), or administration of a punishment whenever the event occurs.

Exposure and response prevention have been employed singly with some success. However, when used in combination, the results have proven superior to either single method (Foa and Steketee, 1989). Descriptions of combined behavioral treatments for OCD are presented in McCarthy and Foa (1988) and Emmelkamp, Kloek, and Blaauw (1992).

Psychotherapy

Insight therapies have historically met with infrequent success in OCD treatment (Husain and Kashani, 1992; Rapoport, 1988). However, cognitive techniques have been incorporated successfully into behavioral programs (e.g., thought stopping). Kearney and Silverman (1990), for example, describe a case study in which cognitive therapy was systematically alternated with the behavioral technique of response prevention in treatment of an adolescent with obsessions and two compulsions. The cognitive therapy consisted of identifying irrational and obsessional thoughts and examining more realistic alternatives. Evaluation of treatment response indicated that cognitive therapy was more helpful in treating the compulsion closest to the obsessive thinking, and treatment gains were equivalent for the two therapeutic techniques. Cognitive therapy techniques are rarely used alone in the treatment of OCD, because some method of application of specific behavioral techniques appears to be crucial for success.

Family Interventions

If a child's OCD has a major impact on family life, the family may also require treatment to adapt to the stress of the child's symptoms or to the changes as the child's symptoms abate. Alternatively, family members may act as co-therapists in the implementation of behavioral techniques at home. Finally, families may benefit from education about the nature and treatment of OCD in children. The overriding consideration in these family scenarios is the importance of the family in changing and/or maintaining the behavior of the child. To the extent that this family power can be harnessed and channeled in a positive (e.g., discouraging symptoms) direction by the therapist, therapy is more likely to be effective.

In some cases, formal family therapy may be required to intervene in maladaptive family dynamics that have evolved in response to the child's aberrant behavior. Family members' overinvolvement with the OCD child and a reluctance to change family structure to accommodate symptom change can interfere with treatment (Leonard, Swedo, and Rapoport, 1991).

Lenane (1991) describes an approach to joining with such families: An initial assessment must be made about the extent of each family member's collusion with the OCD child. Positive reframing of that collusion as their best attempt to help the child is often required, as those living with the child may otherwise feel attacked and guilty for their contribution to the problem. This may be particularly true if any other family members have exhibited obsessive-compulsive traits themselves. Complete and accurate understanding of how each family member participates in the OCD is also important. Once the therapist has joined with the family, structural and strategic family therapy techniques can then be used to change family interactions and family hierarchy. For example, a child who is enmeshed with his mother could be given a homework assignment to do something with his father every day for 1 hour. Alternatively, the family could be told that the boy may make complaints about his OCD only to the disengaged father.

Medication

Pharmacological Interventions

A number of pharmacological interventions have been tried with OCD, with varying success. In addition to the benzodiazepines, the cyclic antidepressant clomipramine appears to offer greatest promise for OCD treatment (Husain and Kashani, 1992; Leonard, Swedo, and Rapoport, 1991). In a double-blind study, clomipramine showed a clear superiority over desipramine in reducing OCD symptomatology (Leonard, Swedo, Rapoport, et al., 1991). Interestingly, the findings of the study supported the view that clomipramine's antiobsessional effect is independent of its anxiolytic or depressant action (Leonard, Swedo, Rapoport, et al., 1991). Clomipramine's effectiveness has in some cases "worn off" over time, so it should not be considered a complete solution for child OCD (Rapoport, 1988). Fluoxetine may be an emerging alternative medication for the treatment of OCD (Sylvester and Kruesi, 1994).

Psychosurgery

Psychosurgery (specifically, bimedial leukotomies to produce lesions in the thalamofrontal connections) has not been used as a treatment modality with children or adolescents having OCD but it has been studied in the adult population (Jensen, 1990). It has had some traditional support in cases of severe OCD that has not responded to other treatments (Kaplan and Sadock, 1988; Meyer, 1993). Given the severity of this treatment, it is unlikely that it will see any use in the child population.

Combination Treatments

A recent review (Abel, 1993) concludes that the most efficacious treatment for OCD may be a combination of exposure with response prevention and pharmacotherapy. Each of these two OCD treatments affects different symptomatology. Exposure with response prevention is more effective over all and seems to have the greatest effect on alleviating compulsive rituals. Clomipramine, on the other hand, has greater overall effect among individuals experiencing obsessions only and among those with comorbid depression. Used in combination, then, there is the opportunity for a greater reduction in both obsessive and compulsive symptoms. Additionally, such combination might also serve to increase compliance by providing quicker symptom relief.

Inpatient Hospitalization

In extreme or dangerous cases of OCD, therapy is conducted on an inpatient basis. The inpatient setting provides a structured environment in which the child receives constant monitoring and consistent behavior management by staff. At times such close supervision and constant monitoring cannot be carried out in the home, particularly if the home environment is chaotic, the child's symptoms are functionally debilitating, and the child resists outpatient treatment. When these characteristics occur in the child's OCD, inpatient hospitalization may be appropriate. Inpatient treatment of OCD usually involves a more intensive implementation of the traditional behavioral and medical therapies.

■ Posttraumatic Stress Disorder

☐ CLINICAL DESCRIPTION

Diagnostic Considerations

The essential feature of Posttraumatic Stress Disorder (PTSD) is development of intrusive and avoidant symptoms following exposure to a traumatic event. A "traumatic event" is defined by two criteria: First, the event involves a threat to the physical integrity (including death, injury, or other physical harm) of self or others. The person need not be present at the event if it involved a family member or close friend, although some personal experience (at least witnessing the event) appears to be required if the event involved a less familiar person. Second, the experience of the event includes intense fear, terror, helplessness, disorganized behavior, or agitated behavior (the latter two criteria apply only to children).

PTSD's characteristic symptoms fall into three categories: intrusive reexperiences of the event, avoidance of experiences related to the event, and physiological arousal. Intrusive reexperiences include memories of the event (in children this may be through repetitive play or reenactment), dreams or nightmares related to the event, reliving part or all of the experience, and psychological or physiological upset in response to cues related to the event. Avoidance symptoms include avoidance of thoughts connected with the experience, avoidance of activities and social interaction connected with the experience, amnesia for part of the trauma, reduced interest in activities, feeling of detachment, flat or constricted affect, and sense of shortened future. Physiological arousal symptoms include difficulty sleeping, irritability, diminished concentration, hypervigilance, and exaggerated startle response.

PTSD symptoms are essentially the same for children and adults, with some provisions for children to have less defined cognitive symptoms and more behavioral symptoms. For example, children's memories may be expressed in play. PTSD has been established to occur in children at various ages, including ages 6–9 (Saigh, 1989a), ages 9–13 (Saigh, 1989b), and with adolescents (Saigh, 1988).

PTSD symptomatology must have been present for at least 1 month for the PTSD diagnosis to be made (American Psychiatric Association, 1994). If the event is more recent than 1 month or the duration of symptoms is less than 1 month, a diagnosis of Acute Stress Disorder should be considered. The Acute Stress Disorder diagnosis requires fewer intrusive and avoidant symptoms, and it must be of 2 days to 4 weeks duration; symptoms must develop within 4 weeks of the traumatic event.

Lifetime prevalence of PTSD is estimated at 1.2% for women and 0.5% for men (Kaplan and Sadock, 1988), or approximately 1% for adults (Pynoos, 1990). Although no such data are available for children, children are exposed to traumatic situations, such as natural disasters, domestic violence, abuse, neglect, gunshot injury, war, death of a loved one, and chronic illness. In a psychiatric inpatient sample, 20.7% of sexually abused, 6.9% of physically abused and 10.3% of nonabused psychiatric cases met criteria for PTSD (Deblinger et al., 1989).

Appearance and Features

Children with PTSD typically present with a mix of intrusive and avoidant symptoms (see Table 6.13). Perhaps the most common intrusive symptom seen is nightmares, the content of which the child sometimes cannot remember. However, avoidant symptoms are more prominently seen in the clinic or hospital situation, probably because the clinic environment is safe and different from the environment in which the traumatic event occurred. Often children with PTSD resist attempts to talk about the situation, or they give a flat, "newspaper" account of what happened. They may appear withdrawn and cautious, and obvious signs of adult-type grief (e.g., crying) may be infrequent. Very young children may show no reaction or a muted reaction to the death of a loved one because of their limited comprehension. They often have limited understanding of the permanence of death, believing that the loved one has gone bodily to a different place and may return.

The child's avoidance may break down at times of exposure to traumatic memories or at times when distraction is absent, such as nighttime, sleep, return to the site of the trauma, experience of additional stresses, or return to a place where there are cues to trigger intrusions. In addition, the child often will have more intrusive symptoms when in the presence of familiar people who are identified as caretakers. Hence, the clinician may hear that the child is "totally different" at home than in the hospital or office. Familiarity with the clinician, familiarity with the hospital, and the presence of toys related to the trauma can facilitate the emergence of intrusive themes in the therapy situation.

TABLE 6.13   Appearance and Features of Posttraumatic Stress Disorder

---

COMMON FEATURES

Intrusions: nightmares, unbidden thoughts, intrusive emotions, tenseness, exaggerated startle, agitation, disorganized behavior
Avoidance/denial: avoidance of stimuli associated with the event, emotional numbness, flat appearance, refusal to discuss event
Recent traumatic event

OCCASIONAL FEATURES

Calm, avoidant presentation when in a safe environment that allows cognitive avoidance

---

Note: The features listed above are often seen but are not universal. Some features may be diagnostically relevant or required, while others may not be required for diagnosis. "Common" features are typical of the disorder; "occasional" features appear frequently but are not necessarily seen in a majority of cases.

Although children with PTSD show many similarities in behavior, there are some differences in presentation based on the child's premorbid personality and the type of trauma experienced. Bernstein and Borchardt (1991), for example, note symptomatic differences based on acute versus chronic exposure to trauma. For children exposed to a single violent event, temporal proximity to the event is correlated with severity of symptoms. Disturbances of concentration and sleep are typical of severe reactions to the single traumatic event, while moderate reactions to the event are characterized by emotional constriction, occasional intrusions, and avoidance of reminders of the trauma. Exposure to multiple or chronic traumatic experiences (e.g., childhood physical and sexual abuse) causes greater disruption of normal development, adoption of a guarded attitude, and more profound effects on self-esteem and long-term emotional stability (Bernstein and Borchardt, 1991).

Symptom differences have also been observed among children and adolescents having acute (4 months or less) versus chronic (8 months or more) duration of PTSD symptoms (Famularo, Kinscherff, and Fenton, 1990). Those in the acute duration group primarily experience nightmares, distress upon real or symbolic exposure to the trauma situation, difficulty falling asleep, an exaggerated startle response, hypervigilance and generalized agitation/anxiety. The chronic duration group, on the other hand, experiences detachment/estrangement from others, restricted range of affect, sadness/unhappiness, thinking that life would be hard, and dissociative episodes (Famularo et al., 1990).

Deblinger et al. (1989) found that the symptom pictures of PTSD in sexually, physically, and nonabused individuals differed across subject categories. Reexperiencing phenomena and inappropriate sexual behaviors were significantly more prevalent among the sexually abused children than in the other two groups. Also, sexually and physically abused individuals exhibited more symptoms of avoidance/dissociation than did the nonabused children.

Etiology

PTSD and Acute Stress Disorder are unique among the anxiety disorders in that they require the occurrence of a specific type of external event (an abnormal and serious stressor) for diagnosis. Typically, the more severe the stressor, the greater the number of people who will develop PTSD and the greater the severity of PTSD symptomatology (Kaplan and Sadock, 1988). Obviously, then, etiological theories must have the traumatic stressor as their linchpin. Where the theories differ is in the role of predisposing factors and in the explanation of how the traumatic event causes PTSD.

Biological theories posit that a premorbid tendency to excessive autonomic reaction exists in those who eventually develop PTSD. Biological theories also hypothesize that PTSD symptoms are reflections of biological changes caused by the traumatic experience. A recent hypothesis suggests that endogenous opioids are released when the trauma is relived and intervening symptoms are the result of opioid withdrawal; another hypothesis suggests that PTSD patients demonstrate increased release of catecholamine neurotransmitters while reexperiencing the traumatic event. Sleep EEG studies point to similarities between PTSD and Major Depressive Disorder, since there is increased REM latency and stage 4 sleep in many cases of both disorders (Kaplan and Sadock, 1988). While these results are suggestive, they are preliminary at best.

Several theorists have proposed cognitive-psychodynamic models for the development of PTSD in response to a traumatic stressor (e.g., Horowitz, 1986; Roth and Lebowitz, 1988; Straker, Moosa, and Sanctuaries Counselling Team, 1988; Watson et al., 1988). These models suggest that people have mental structures, called schemas, that allow them to make sense out of incoming information in their daily experiences. A schema is a structure that anticipates relationships or rules involving experiences that people have. Stated differently, a schema is a belief about the way the person and the world operate. While some of these schemas are value-neutral (e.g., how to behave in an unfamiliar restaurant), others are extremely important and form the core of an individual's identity (e.g., the sense of a just world; the sense of having reasonable control over what happens to one).

Traumatic experiences are so damaging and out of the normal sphere of human experience that they violate the expectations and emotions inherent in these identity-core schemas. Thus, the individual who experiences a traumatic event is faced with discrepant cognitive structures: the memory of the event and the schemas that the event violated. In order to achieve cognitive stability, the individual must resolve the discrepancy between the memories and the schemas; the memory must be accounted for by changes in the schemas. This resolution can happen only by processing the memory of the traumatic event and modifying the schemas, so that the traumatic memory can be understood based on the new core schemas. The ultimate goal is to change the schemas so that they account for the event while still making sense based on the remainder of the individual's experience. Essentially, the individual is trying to understand the meaning of the event, but meaning can only be achieved with a modification or clarification of basic core schemas that the traumatic event has violated. This is done by "dosing" with the traumatic memory so that the memory is processed on the one hand, but the emotional upset caused by constantly dwelling on the memory is avoided.

The initial processing of the memory is painful and difficult because it causes a questioning of basic schemas; if this initial processing reaches a certain level of difficulty, it takes the form of intrusive symptoms of PTSD. Likewise, the individual attempts to contain the effects of the memory so as to not be overwhelmed with upset; this containment of memory comes in the form of avoidance and denial. The individual cycles between avoidance/denial and intrusion as a way of processing the memory while not allowing it to overwhelm him or her (this process is referred to as "working through" the trauma). This processing continues until the memory and the core schemas are reconciled. Ideally, the memory and the schema become integrated so that the individual can access both without feeling that there is a discrepancy between them. Until this happens, however, the traumatic event remains in "active memory," threatening to emerge and affect the individual's thoughts or behaviors without warning (Horowitz, 1986). PTSD occurs when the amplitude of the swings between intrusion and denial become excessive and significantly interfere with functioning over a relatively long and consistent period of time.

ASSESSMENT PATTERNS

A sample assessment battery for PTSD is shown in Table 6.14.

Broad Assessment Strategies

Cognitive Assessment

Clinician-Administered.   Traumatic events happen to children of all intellectual ability levels. However, PTSD presumably affects attention/concentration more than it affects "crystallized" intelligence tasks (e.g., vocabulary, basic knowledge). Thus, administration of a Wechsler scale may indicate the extent to which certain abilities have been temporarily affected by PTSD symptoms. Low scores on Digit Span, Arithmetic, Coding, and Symbol Search could indicate attention, concentration, and processing speed deficits secondary to PTSD symptoms.

Psychological Assessment

Clinician-Administered.   Several MMPI/MMPI-A code types can be expected in adolescents with PTSD, with the F-2-8 code type probably the most common. This code type indicates a feeling of dissatisfaction, alienation, loss of control, and unique experiences. Another expected code type is the 7-2, which

TABLE 6.14   Sample Assessment Battery for Posttraumatic Stress Disorder

PSYCHOLOGICAL

Thematic Apperception Test

BEHAVIORAL

Child Behavior Checklist

SYNDROME-SPECIFIC

Children's PTSD Inventory
Revised Children's Manifest Anxiety Scale
Fear Survey Schedule for Children—Revised

Note: Assessment instruments are intended to supplement (not substitute for) a good clinical interview and, when possible, a structured diagnostic interview.

may indicate social distancing and distress (Meyer, 1993). An elevation on scale 9 can indicate that the PTSD is characterized by components of agitation, pressure for action, and avoidance of introspection. Elevations of scales 4 and 6 are present in individuals who are angry, alienated, and suspicious as a result of their traumatic experience.

Projective personality tests such as the TAT and Rorschach may reveal intrusive themes or rigid denial structures. Intrusive themes may be represented by violent content and many color and shading responses on the Rorschach. Denial structures will be manifest in brief, unelaborated TAT stories and Rorschach protocols with high lambda and low R scores. The plot of TAT stories can be analyzed to see the schemas of the child. For example, a child who consistently has authority figures behaving illegally and immorally may hold a schema that authorities are untrustworthy and dangerous.

Behavioral Assessment

Parent-Report. Behavior checklists are of limited use in assessing the symptomatology of PTSD, but they may be helpful in identifying associated features or co-occurring problems. On the CBCL, children with PTSD typically elevate the Anxious/Depressed, Thought Problems, and Attention Problems scales. Social withdrawal is often present in PTSD, leading to elevation of the CBCL Withdrawal scale. The MCBC and CTRS are of very limited use in PTSD diagnosis because they contain few items related to PTSD.

Syndrome-Specific Tests

Clinician-Administered

As a starting point in PTSD assessment the Anxiety Disorders Interview Schedule for Children (ADIS-C; see description in the SAD section of this chapter) may be helpful in documenting children's anxiety symptomatology. Alternatively, the clinician-rated Children's PTSD Inventory can be used to assist with PTSD diagnosis using DSM-III criteria (Saigh, 1987). It is made up of four groups of items dichotomously scored according to presence or absence of symptoms. Field trials demonstrated an 85% classification rate of children diagnosed with PTSD.

Child-Report

Revised Children's Manifest Anxiety Scale (RCMAS) and Children's Depression Inventory (CDI) scores are elevated in children with PTSD (Saigh, 1988, 1989a, 1989b), and they may provide information about general levels of anxiety and depression, respectively. The Fear Survey Schedule for Children—Revised (FSSC-R) may be useful in assessing specific fears arising as a result of PTSD. Analysis of such fears can suggest targets for treatment, as well as topics for discussion in therapy.

□   TREATMENT OPTIONS

PTSD can have a long-term impact on functioning, so early treatment is imperative (Eth, 1990). Generally, the principal aim in PTSD treatment techniques is integration of the trauma and its meaning into the individual's enduring schema of the world (Straker et al., 1988). Reenactment in a safe environment is typically a necessary part of this process (Cantwell and Baker, 1989). (Treatment options are outlined in Table 6.15.)

Behavioral Interventions

Systematic desensitization to traumatic stimuli, implosion and flooding therapy are behavioral methods that can be used to treat children and adolescents suffering from PTSD (Cantwell and Baker, 1989). Such methods extinguish the conditioned arousal state, as explained by Mowrer's Two Factor Theory (see description under Specific Phobia). Without therapy the high levels of emotional reactance experienced in the traumatic situation and the lack of habituation to its stimuli due to avoidance combine to prevent the expected extinction of the anxiety state over time (Straker et al., 1988).

Psychotherapy

As noted earlier, the goal of psychotherapy for PTSD is to achieve an integration of the memory of the traumatic event with the individual's existing schemas. Psychotherapy methods designed to achieve this goal tend to have several components in common. First, they involve the systematic opening up (e.g., remembering) of memories and closing (e.g., removing from the individual's immediate awareness) of the traumatic memories. "Opening" and "closing" occur based on the degree to which the individual can re-experience the memories without being overwhelmed. Second, memories of the trauma are processed in detail. Often PTSD patients will tell quick, unelaborated stories of their traumatic experience. PTSD-focused psychotherapy asks for detailed explanations of what happened, how the person felt, what they were thinking, and what they expected to happen next. This assists with the re-experiencing

TABLE 6.15   Treatment Options for Posttraumatic Stress Disorder

BEHAVIORAL INTERVENTIONS

Desensitization

PSYCHOTHERAPY

Trauma-focused therapy (see Doyle and Bauer, 1989, for example)

Note: This outline of options summarizes major treatments covered in the text. Specific treatments are often combined into an intervention package. Refer to the text for additional descriptions of each treatment. This table is not necessarily an exhaustive list of all treatments available.

of the trauma. Third, PTSD-focused therapies attempt to change the individual's cognitive-affective interpretation of the memories based on careful processing in the safe therapeutic environment. The person is able to change from being a participant in the memories to also being an observer of the memories. The observer role allows the person to control and access the memory without being overwhelmed. Finally, PTSD-focused therapies help the person to make sense out of the memory and to integrate it into his or her world-view.

An example of systematic and comprehensive treatment of severely traumatized children is described in Doyle and Bauer (1989). Using their treatment model as a guide, a seven-step child treatment plan for child PTSD might proceed as follows:

1. Establishment of the therapeutic relationship—before any stress-related therapy work is initiated, the therapist establishes a relationship with the child through activity, play, or talk. The therapist is less directive and does not force the discussion of stressful topics.

2. Education on the stress recovery process—this psychoeducational step involves an explanation of the progression of therapy and the rationale behind the need for working through the traumatic experience.

3. Management and reduction of stress—this step takes different forms in different programs, but, in general, involves the identification of stress and teaching of strategies to manage stress when it arises. Techniques can be used in or out of therapy.

4. Articulation of affect—this step involves discussion of feelings related to the trauma and its aftermath, as well as current emotions.

5. Reexperience of the trauma—verbal or play methods are used to recreate the trauma in the safe therapeutic environment.

6. Cognitive transformation—the child's interpretation of the trauma and its aftermath are processed with the therapist.

7. Integration of the experience—the child makes sense of the trauma in light of his or her existing schemas.

Medication

The pharmacologic treatment of PTSD in children and adolescents has not been extensively studied (Cantwell and Baker, 1989; Gittelman and Koplewicz, 1986). However, medications might be used to manage specific anxiety symptoms when they arise. For example, tricyclic antidepressants (imipramine) and antihistamines (diphenhydramine, hydroxyzine) may be used to manage some of the depressive and sleep symptoms arising from PTSD (Sylvester & Kruesi, 1994). Benzodiazepines such as diazepam and alprazolam may also be useful with general anxiety symptoms (Sylvester and Kruesi, 1994). Finally, propranolol and clonadine have shown promise in PTSD treatment (Sylvester and Kruesi, 1994). In general, however, psychopharmacological treatment for childhood PTSD is at an early stage.

■ GENERALIZED ANXIETY DISORDER

☐ CLINICAL DESCRIPTION

Diagnostic Considerations

Prior to DSM-IV, Generalized Anxiety Disorder (GAD) was described along developmental lines in the separate classifications of Overanxious Disorder and GAD. Often the prognosis for Overanxious Disorder was anecdotally described as potentially developing into GAD (Husain and Kashani, 1992; Last, 1989b), and differential diagnosis between the two anxiety disorders was primarily age-based. The decision to combine the disorders has been made with the publication of DSM-IV, essentially making childhood GAD the current diagnosis for the former Overanxious Disorder.

Criteria for childhood GAD include excessive worry and anxiety about a number of activities or events, difficulty controlling the worry, and a variety of worry-related symptoms such as restlessness, tiring easily, difficulty in maintaining concentration, irritability, body tension, and disturbed sleep. The frequency, intensity, and duration of GAD worries sets them apart from normal levels of anxiety. The child with GAD reports experiencing multiple worries in numerous situations, without precipitating circumstances. In addition, children with GAD report difficulties controlling their worries and that their worries interfere with daily activity. GAD differs from other anxiety disorders because it involves multiple topics of worry that cannot be traced to a single issue (such as separation from parent or an acute stressor) or other disorder (such as depression). Furthermore, GAD worries tend to be about everyday or real-world problems as opposed to obsessions or delusional worries.

Strauss et al. (1988) found that other disorders often co-occur with GAD. In a 5–11-year-old group, SAD was found in 70% of GAD-diagnosed children, and Attention-Deficit Hyperactivity Disorder had an occurrence rate of 35%. Among GAD children age 12–19, a major depressive episode was found 47% of the time, and Specific Phobia was present in 41% of the sample. These percentages, however, may be inflated somewhat by failure to apply the exclusionary criteria of DSM-IV.

Lifetime prevalence of GAD is estimated to be 5% (American Psychiatric Association, 1994). However, at an anxiety disorders clinic, GAD was diagnosed in 52% of all children and adolescents presenting for treatment (Husain and Cantwell, 1991). In another sample of children referred to an anxiety clinic, mean age of presentation of children having the principal diagnosis of GAD was 13.4 years, with boys and girls equivalently represented (Last, Hersen, Kazdin, Finkelstein, et al., 1987). GAD was diagnosed in both pre- and postpubertal children at about the same rate. It is notable that only Whites presented with this disorder since 35% of children referred to this clinic were Black (Last, Hersen, Kazdin, Finkelstein, et al., 1987). Also, unlike other anxiety Disorders, GAD occurs primarily in upper-middle class children (Last, Francis, et al., 1987). Clinical speculation (to be taken cautiously) states that GAD is most commonly found in the oldest children in small families in upper socioeconomic levels where there exists overemphasis on achievement (Beeghly, 1986; Samuels and Sikorsky, 1990).

Appearance and Features

Appearance and features of GAD are listed in Table 16.6. Younger children commonly report anxiety in more circumscribed situations than do older children (e.g., in the presence of a particular person). Anxiety topics and concerns with evaluation appear to generalize to more people and situations with increasing age, perhaps reflecting the children's growing social sphere and cognitive ability. Typical topics of GAD worries range from the mundane (school performance, performance in sports or the arts, being on time, animals, the environment, rejection by peers) to the unusual (nuclear war, natural disasters, being condemned for sins, being raped or killed).

GAD children seem unable to relax. They carry around a constant level of generalized tension, which is sometimes apparent in motor restlessness (e.g., constant movement, nail biting, or knuckle popping), emotional reactivity (crying), and vulnerability to stress. They may exhibit an exaggerated emotional response to demanding or unpleasant circumstances such as illness (Husain and Cantwell, 1991). Somatic complaints are often present in the form of stomachaches, headaches, or a general malaise (Last, 1989b), but these decrease with increasing age.

Parents often describe their child with GAD as "a nervous wreck" and "a worry wart." Many children with GAD have a pseudomature appearance, with

---

TABLE 6.16   Appearance and Features of Generalized Anxiety Disorder

COMMON FEATURES

Excessive worry about multiple topics
Worry not cued by specific stimuli
Restlessness, irritability, difficulty concentrating, tension, sleep problems, and
    hyperarousal
Overly serious presentation
Perfectionism/overachievement
Constant seeking of reassurance

OCCASIONAL FEATURES

Somatic complaints
Self-conscious
School avoidance

Note: The features listed above are often seen but are not universal. Some features may be diagnostically relevant or required, while others may not be required for diagnosis. "Common" features are typical of the disorder; "occasional" features appear frequently but are not necessarily seen in a majority of cases.

a speaking style and interests that better fit grown-ups. Often they experience greater comfort in the company of adults than peers. Perfectionistic tendencies, conformity, and self-consciousness are commonly present. To counter self-doubts, children with GAD may repeatedly seek reassurances and approval. Because they tend to be hardworking and conforming, GAD children rarely come to clinical attention at the request of school personnel (American Psychiatric Association, 1994; Last, 1989a, 1989b).

Frequently the children have endured the disorder for years before coming to clinical attention. Because of somatic complaints, they may have been seen by numerous health care providers and endured many diagnostic tests (Last, 1989b). School phobia is a common complication of GAD since children having the GAD symptomatology of self-consciousness, overconcern about competence, and worry learn to avoid school and the evaluation it represents. Additionally, children and adolescents with GAD routinely refuse to engage in age-appropriate activities if performance plays a part (Last, 1989a).

Children having mild GAD may continue to function at a fairly high level while enduring symptoms such as difficulty falling asleep due to worries, problems interacting with peers, and some interference with academic performance. Those having severe GAD, on the other hand, may experience heightened anxiety in most areas of functioning, major depression, and suicidal ideation. GAD may persist through the life cycle if left untreated (American Psychiatric Association, 1994).

Etiology

Very little is known about the etiology of GAD. Evidence of a familial association and response to some anxiolytic medication could indicate a biological component such as physiological tenseness or hypersensitivity (American Psychiatric Association, 1994; Last, 1989a). Behavioral theories, on the other hand, suggest that GAD may develop out of experiences in which the child was surprised (punished) by unexpected occurrences. Expected worries, on the other hand, did not occur and were therefore reinforced (e.g., the feared situation did not come to pass if the child worried). Hence, the child learned that worry was related to a lack of negative outcomes, while avoidance or lack of worry was related to surprise, negative outcomes. Cognitive theories of the etiology of GAD suggest that GAD develops out of multiple negative experiences, which are internalized by the child into a view of the world as an unfriendly, worrisome place. Over all, no etiological theory for childhood GAD has received much empirical attention or support.

ASSESSMENT PATTERNS

A sample assessment battery for GAD is shown in Table 6.17.

TABLE 6.17   Sample Assessment Battery for Generalized Anxiety Disorder

PSYCHOLOGICAL

Thematic Apperception Test
Piers-Harris Self-Concept Scale

BEHAVIORAL

Child Behavior Checklist

SYNDROME-SPECIFIC

Revised Children's Manifest Anxiety Scale
Fear Survey Schedule for Children—Revised

Note: Assessment instruments are intended to supplement (not substitute for) a good clinical interview and, when possible, a structured diagnostic interview.

Broad Assessment Strategies

Psychological Assessment

Clinician-Administered.   MMPI/MMPI-A scores for adolescents with GAD are likely to show elevations on scales 2, 3, and 7. These scales reflect the anxiety, somatization, and dissatisfaction typical of adolescents with GAD. Given the potential for chronic hyperarousal, scale 9 should also be relatively high. A high F scale is expected if GAD worries and somatic complaints are unusual or lead to unusual ideas and sensations (Meyer, 1993). High scale 0 may reflect social anxiety and social withdrawal as a result of performance fears. Scales 4 and 6 are likely to be moderate to low because of the perfectionism and conformity common in GAD adolescents.

The worries and concerns of GAD children will often affect their projective testing results. Negative outcomes and worried characters, for example, are often seen on the TAT, reflecting the children's generalized worries. The progression of the plots in the TAT stories may be helpful in understanding the expectations of GAD children about the progression of social interactions and life events.

Child-Report.   PHSCS scores of GAD children are expected to be low, reflecting fears, worries, perfectionism, and critical self-evaluation. Low scores on the PHSCS should probably be followed up by a careful assessment for depressive symptomatology co-occurring with the GAD.

Behavioral Assessment

Parent-Report.   The CBCL includes numerous items relating to fears and worries. Parent response to these items may indicate the extent to which a child suffers from GAD and the content of GAD worries. The fears and worries of GAD tend to elevate the Anxious/Depressed and Thought Problems scales of the CBCL. The Somatic Complaints score can be used to assess the degree to which GAD symptoms are associated with somatization. Additional elevations on the Withdrawal and Social Problems scales could indicate difficulties with social interaction, which may result from GAD. Elevations on the Attention Problems scale suggest that GAD is interfering with concentration and task focus. Alternatively, such an elevation could indicate the presence of a co-occurring attention deficit.

Less useful in the diagnosis of GAD are the MCBC and Conners scales, which have few items relating to GAD symptoms. On the MCBC, GAD children elevate the Inhibition and Somatization scale. Similar elevations of CPRS Anxiety/Anxious-Shy and Psychosomatic scales would be expected from children with GAD.

Syndrome-Specific Tests

Clinician-Administered

Because children with GAD report a variety of worries, they may appear to qualify for one of several anxiety disorder diagnoses. Use of the Anxiety Disorders Interview Schedule for Children (ADIS-C; see description in the SAD section of this chapter) may assist with differential diagnosis. Furthermore, the ADIS-C allows systematic evaluation of a variety of anxiety symptoms that may be creating problems for the child.

Child-Report

General anxiety disorders tests can be helpful in investigating the extent and severity of GAD worries. The Revised Children's Manifest Anxiety Scale, State-Trait Anxiety Inventory, Children's Anxious Self-Statement Questionnaire, and Fear Survey Schedule for Children—Revised (FSSC-R) were described earlier in this chapter. The FSSC-R in particular has been found to reliably discriminate among GAD, SAD, and Social Phobia in children and adolescents in an anxiety disorders clinic (Last et al., 1989). One of its factors, Fear of Failure and Criticism, is particularly likely to be elevated in children with GAD. If depression is suspected, the CDI may be useful, as there is some co-occurrence of GAD and depression.

TREATMENT OPTIONS

Treatment options for GAD are outlined in Table 6.18.

Behavioral Interventions

Generally, a treatment package for GAD combines behavioral and cognitive components in such a way as to treat the behavioral, physiological, and cognitive aspects of the disorder (Last, 1989a). Such a treatment package typically incorporates the following: relaxation techniques (e.g., progressive muscle relax-

TABLE 6.18   Treatment Options for Generalized Anxiety Disorder

BEHAVIORAL INTERVENTIONS

Relaxation techniques
In vivo desensitization
Reinforcement techniques
Social-skills training

PSYCHOTHERAPY

Cognitive-behavioral interventions
   Self-talk
   Cognitive restructuring
   Self-monitoring
   Modification of maladaptive thoughts

FAMILY INTERVENTIONS

Family therapy

MEDICATION

Benzodiazepines
Tricyclic antidepressants

Note: This outline of options summarizes major treatments covered in the text. Specific treatments are often combined into an intervention package. Refer to the text for additional descriptions of each treatment. This table is not necessarily an exhaustive list of all treatments available.

ation, visual imagery), positive self-statements, *in vivo* exposure to evaluative situations, a home-based token economy system or other reinforcement schedule that rewards the absence of worrying or anxious behavior, and cognitive control in which coping strategies are employed to achieve a state of relaxation (Husain and Kashani, 1992; Thyer, 1991). Social skills training may be applied at a later phase in treatment of GAD to address social performance fears. Such training is often achieved in a group setting and strongly resembles social-skills training for Social Phobia.

Psychotherapy

In addition to the cognitive components embedded in the behavioral treatments just described, cognitive therapy is a common treatment component for GAD in older children. Cognitive restructuring, for example, attempts to change the child's negative interpretations and worries about neutral events by challenging the child to provide alternative interpretations. These alternative interpretations are typically less anxiety provoking. Self-talk can also be used to alter the child's worry-based thought processes and negative interpretations of events.

Kane and Kendall (1989) describe a treatment program in which four children ranging in age from 9–13 were treated for GAD using a variety of cognitive-behavioral techniques. The program taught the children to recognize anxious feelings and accompanying somatic reactions. Next, the children investigated the cognitions underlying these feelings. Finally, the negative cognitions were modified so that they were more realistic and positive. The children rewarded themselves for successful *in vivo* use of the new cognitions and reframed interpretations of events. Additionally incorporated into this treatment program were the behavioral techniques of modeling, in vivo exposure to the evaluative situations that they had come to avoid, role playing, relaxation methods, and contingent reinforcement.

In the absence of comparative studies, little can be said about the efficacy of different cognitive and behavioral approaches. However, the use of psychodynamic or nonspecific therapies in isolation (e.g., play or supportive treatment without concomitant behavior therapy) does not seem indicated with GAD children. Rather, cognitive and behavioral therapeutic techniques tailored to the individual child's experience of GAD hold greater promise (Thyer, 1991).

Family Interventions

Family psychoeducation is warranted if it seems likely that parental expectations of the child's performance or parental worries have contributed to the child's anxiety. In this case an explanation of GAD and the impact of the family (through stress, modeling, and reinforcement) on GAD symptoms can be helpful. Adjunct therapy for family members is indicated if the parental psychopathology (especially anxiety) contributes to and escalates the anxiety experienced by the child. Family resistance to change based on psychoeducation may indicate the need for more intensive family therapy.

Medication

Benzodiazepines and tricyclic antidepressants have proven useful in the treatment of anxiety symptoms such as those experienced in GAD. Also, sedating medications such as antihistamines (diphenhydramine, hydroxyzine) may be effective in short-term treatment of GAD anxiety occurring with insomnia (Sylvester and Kruesi, 1994). Although successfully used in adults with GAD, long-term use of benzodiazepines in children and adolescents is not recommended due to inhibition of secretion of growth hormone and unwelcome side effects (Thyer, 1991). Medication is probably best used for GAD when it is combined with cognitive and behavioral therapy.

■ References

Abel, J. L. (1993). Exposure with response prevention and serotonergic antidepressants in the treatment of obsessive compulsive disorder: A review and implications for interdisciplinary treatment. *Behavior Research and Therapy, 31,* 463–478.

American Psychiatric Association. (1994). *Diagnostic and statistical manual of mental disorders* (4th ed.). Washington, DC: Author.

Anderson, J. C., Williams, S., McGee, R., and Silva, P. A. (1987). DSM-III disorders in pre-adolescent children. *Archives of General Psychiatry, 44,* 69–76.

Beeghly, J. H. (1986). Anxiety and anxiety disorder in childhood. *New Directions for Mental Health Services, 32,* 57–80.

Berg, C. J., Rapoport, J. L., & Flament, M. (1986). The Leyton Obsessional Inventory—child version. *Journal of the American Academy of Child Psychiatry, 25,* 85–91.

Bernstein, G. A. (1990). Anxiety disorders. In B. D. Garfinkel, G. A. Carlson, and E. B. Weller (Eds.), *Psychiatric disorders in children and adolescents* (pp. 64–83). Philadelphia: Saunders.

Bernstein, G. A., and Borchardt, C. M. (1991). Anxiety disorders of childhood and adolescence: A critical review. *Journal of the American Academy of Child and Adolescent Psychiatry, 30,* 519–532.

Bernstein, G. A., Garfinkel, B. D., and August, G. J. (1986). Visual analogue scale for anxiety, revised. *Scientific proceedings for the annual meeting* (vol. 2). American Academy of Child and Adolescent Psychiatry.

Blanco, R. F., and Bogacki, D. F. (1988). *Prescriptions for children with learning and adjustment problems: A consultant's desk reference* (3d ed.). Springfield, IL: Thomas.

Bowen, R. C., Offord, D. R., and Boyle, M. H. (1990). The prevalence of overanxious disorder and separation anxiety disorder: Results from the Ontario Child Health Study. *Journal of the American Academy of Child and Adolescent Psychiatry, 29,* 753–758.

Bowlby, J. (1973). *Attachment and loss: II. Separation.* New York: Basic Books.

Campbell, S. B. (1986). Developmental issues in childhood anxiety. In R. Gittelman (Ed.), *Anxiety disorders of childhood* (pp. 24–57). New York: Guilford Press.

Cantwell, D. P., and Baker, L. (1987). The prevalence of anxiety in children with communication disorders. *Journal of Anxiety Disorders, 1,* 239–248.

_____ . (1989). Anxiety disorders. In L. K. G. Hsu & M. Hersen (Eds.), *Recent developments in adolescent psychiatry* (pp. 162–199). New York: Wiley.

_____ . (1990). Stability and natural history of DSM-III childhood diagnoses. In S. Chess and M. E. Hertzig (Eds.), *Annual progress in child psychiatry and child development, 1990* (pp. 311–332). New York: Brunner/Mazel.

Carlson, C. L., Figueroa, R. G., and Lahey, B. B. (1986). Behavior therapy for childhood anxiety disorders. In R. Gittelman (Ed.), *Anxiety disorders of childhood* (pp. 204–232). New York: Guilford Press.

Casat, C. D. (1988). Childhood anxiety disorders: A review of the possible relationship to adult panic disorder and agoraphobia. *Journal of Anxiety Disorders, 2,* 51–60.

Deblinger, E., McLeer, S. V., Atkins, M. S., Ralphe, D., and Foa, E. (1989). Posttraumatic stress in sexually abused, physically abused, and nonabused children. *Child Abuse and Neglect, 13,* 403–408.

Doyle, J. S., and Bauer, S. K. (1989). Posttraumatic stress disorder in children: Its identification and treatment in a residential setting for emotionally disturbed youth. *Journal of Traumatic Stress, 2,* 275–288.

Emmelkamp, P. M. G., Kloek, J., and Blaauw, E. (1992). Obsessive-compulsive disorders. In P. H. Wilson (Ed.), *Principles and practice of relapse prevention* (pp. 213–234). New York: Guilford Press.

Eth, S. (1990). Posttraumatic stress disorder in childhood. In M. Hersen and C. G.

Last (Eds.), *Handbook of child and adult psychopathology: A longitudinal perspective,* (pp. 263–274). New York: Pergamon Press.

Famularo, R., Kinscherff, R., and Fenton, T. (1990). Symptom differences in acute and chronic presentation of childhood posttraumatic stress disorder. *Child Abuse and Neglect, 14,* 439–444.

Fenichel, O. (1945). *The psychoanalytic theory of neurosis.* New York: Norton.

Flament, M. F., Rapoport, J. L., Berg, C. Z., Sceery, W., Whitaker, A., Davies, M., Kalikow, K., and Shaffer, D. (1990). Obsessive-compulsive disorder in adolescence: An epidemiological study. In S. Chess and M. E. Hertzig (Eds.), *Annual progress in child psychiatry. and child development, 1989* (pp. 499–515). New York: Brunner/Mazel.

Foa, E., and Steketee, G. (1989). Obsessive-compulsive disorder. In C. Lindemann (Ed.), *Handbook of phobia therapy* (pp. 181–206). Northvale, NJ: Aronson.

Francis, G., Last, C. G., and Strauss, C. C. (1987). Expression of separation anxiety disorder: The roles of age and gender. *Child Psychiatry and Human Development, 18,* 82–89.

Francis, G., Last, C. G., and Strauss, C. C. (1992). Avoidant disorder and social phobia in children and adolescents. *Journal of the American Academy of Child and Adolescent Psychiatry, 31,* 1086–1089.

Francis, G., and Ollendick, T. H. (1988). Social withdrawal. In M. Hersen and C. G. Last (Eds.), *Child behavior therapy casebook* (pp. 31–41). New York: Plenum Press.

Gittelman, R., and Koplewicz, H. S. (1986). Pharmacotherapy of childhood anxiety disorders. In R. Gittelman (Ed.), *Anxiety disorders of childhood* (pp. 188–203). New York: Guilford Press.

Goodman, W., Rasmussen, S., and Price, L. (1988). *Children's Yale-Brown obsessive-compulsive scale (CY-BOCS).* New Haven, CT: Clinical Neuroscience Research Unit, Connecticut Mental Health Center.

Hodgson, R. J., and Rachman, S. (1977). Obsessive compulsive complaints. *Behavior Research and Therapy, 15,* 389–395.

Hoehn-Saric, E., Maisami, M., and Wiegand, D. (1987). Measurement of anxiety in children and adolescents using semistructured interviews. *Journal of the American Academy of Child and Adolescent Psychiatry, 26,* 541–545.

Horowitz, M. J. (1986). *Stress response syndromes.* Northvale, NJ: Aronson.

Husain, S. A., and Cantwell, D. P. (1991). *Fundamentals of child and adolescent psychopathology.* Washington, DC: American Psychiatric Press.

Husain, S. A., and Kashani, J. H. (1992). *Anxiety disorders in children and adolescents.* Washington, DC: American Psychiatric Press.

Jensen, J. B. (1990). Obsessive-compulsive disorder in children and adolescents. In B. D. Garfinkel, G. A. Carlson, and E. B. Weller (Eds.), *Psychiatric disorders in children and adolescents* (pp. 84–105). Philadelphia: Saunders.

Johnson, S. B., and Melamed, B. G. (1979). Assessment and treatment of children's fears. In B. B. Lahey and A. E. Kazdin (Eds.), *Advances in clinical child psychology* (vol. 2, pp. 108–139). New York: Plenum Press.

Kane, M. T., and Kendall, P. C. (1989). Anxiety disorders in children: A multiple-baseline evaluations of a cognitive-behavioral treatment. *Behavior Therapy, 20,* 499–508.

Kaplan, H. I., and Sadock, B. J. (1988). *Synopsis of psychiatry: Behavioral sciences clinical psychiatry* (5th ed.). Baltimore, MD: Williams & Wilkins.

Kashani, J. H., and Orvaschel, H. (1988). Anxiety disorders in mid-adolescence: A community sample. *American Journal of Psychiatry, 145,* 960–964.

Kearney, C. A., and Silverman, W. K. (1990). Treatment of an adolescent with obsessive-compulsive disorder by alternating response prevention and cognitive therapy: An empirical analysis. *Journal of Behavior Therapy and Experimental Psychiatry, 21,* 39–47.

Kendall, P. C. (1994). Treating anxiety disorders in children: Results of a randomized clinical trial. *Journal of Consulting and Clinical Psychology, 62,* 100–110.

Kendall, P. C., and Ronan, K. R. (1989). *The children's anxious self-statement questionnaire (CASSQ).* Available from the first author, Psychology Department, Temple University, Philadelphia, PA 19122.

King, N. J., Gullone, E., and Tonge, B. J. (1991). Childhood fears and anxiety disorders. *Behaviour-Change, 8,* 124–135.

Klein, R. G., Koplewicz, H. S., and Kanner, A. (1992). Imipramine treatment of children with separation anxiety disorder. *Journal of the American Academy of Child and Adolescent Psychiatry, 31,* 21–28.

Koplewicz, H. S. (1989). Childhood phobias. In C. Lindemann (Ed.), *Handbook of phobia therapy* (pp. 147–151). Northvale, NJ: Aronson.

Kovacs, M. (1992). *Children's Depression Inventory (CDI) manual.* North Tonawanda, NY: Multi-Health Systems.

LaGreca, A. M., Dandes, S. K., Wick, P., Shaw, K., and Stone, W. L. (1988). Development of the Social Anxiety Scale for Children: Reliability and current validity. *Journal of Clinical Child Psychology, 17,* 84–91.

LaGreca, A. M., and Stone, W. L. (1993). Social Anxiety Scale for Children—Revised: Factor structure and concurrent validity. *Journal of Clinical Child Psychology, 22,* 17–27.

Last, C. G. (1988). Separation anxiety. In M. Hersen and C. G. Last (Eds.), *Child behavior therapy casebook* (pp. 11–17). New York: Plenum.

_____ . (1989a). Anxiety disorders. In T. H. Ollendick and M. Hersen (Eds.), *Handbook of child psychopathology* (2d ed., pp. 219–227). New York: Plenum Press.

_____ . (1989b). Anxiety disorders of childhood or adolescence. In C. G. Last and M. Hersen (Eds.), *Handbook of child psychiatric diagnosis* (pp. 156–169). New York: Wiley.

Last, C. G., Francis, G., Hersen, M., Kazdin, A. E., and Strauss, C. C. (1987). Separation anxiety and school phobia: A comparison using DSM-III criteria. *American Journal of Psychiatry, 144,* 653–657.

Last, C. G., Francis, G., and Strauss, C. C. (1989). Assessing fears in anxiety-disordered children with the Revised Fear Survey Schedule for Children (FSSC-R). *Journal of Clinical Child Psychology, 18,* 137–141.

Last, C. G., Hersen, M., Kazdin, A. E., Finkelstein, R., and Strauss, C. C. (1987). Comparison of DSM-III separation anxiety and overanxious disorders: Demographic characteristics and patterns of comorbidity. *Journal of the American Academy of Child and Adolescent Psychiatry, 26,* 527–531.

Last, C. G., Hersen, M., Kazdin, A. E., Francis, G., and Grubb, H. J. (1987). Psychiatric illness in the mothers of anxious children. *American Journal of Psychiatry, 144,* 1580–1583.

Last, C. G., Phillips, J. E., and Statfeld, A. (1987). Childhood anxiety disorders in mothers and their children. *Child Psychiatry and Human Development, 18,* 103–112.

Last, C. G., Strauss, C. C., and Francis, G. (1987). Comorbidity among childhood anxiety disorders. *Journal of Nervous and Mental Diseases, 175,* 726–730.

Lenane, M. C. (1991). Family therapy for children with obsessive-compulsive disorder.

In M. T. Pato and J. Zohar (Eds.), *Current treatments of obsessive-compulsive disorder* (pp. 103–113). Washington, DC: American Psychiatric Press, Inc.

Leonard, H. L., Swedo, S. E., & Rapoport, J. L. (1991). Diagnosis and treatment of obsessive-compulsive disorder in children and adolescents. In M. T. Pato & J. Zohar (Eds.), *Current treatments of obsessive-compulsive disorder* (pp. 87–102). Washington, DC: American Psychiatric Press.

Leonard, H. L., Swedo, S. E., Rapoport, J. L., Koby, E. V., Lenane, M. C., Cheslow, D. L., and Hamburger, S. D. (1991). Treatment of obsessive-compulsive disorder with clomipramine and desipramine in children and adolescents: A double-blind crossover comparison. In S. Chess and M. E. Hertzig (Eds.), *Annual progress in child psychiatry and child development, 1990* (pp. 467–480). New York: Brunner/Mazel.

Livingston, R., Taylor, J. L., and Crawford, S. L. (1988). A study of somatic complaints and psychiatric diagnosis in children. *Journal of the American Academy of Child and Adolescent Psychiatry, 27,* 185–187.

Mattison, R. E. (1992). Anxiety disorders. In S. R. Hooper, G. W. Hynd, and R. E. Mattison (Eds.), *Child psychopathology: Diagnostic criteria and clinical assessment* (pp. 179–202). Hillsdale, NJ: Erlbaum.

McBurnett, K., Hobbs, S. A., and Lahey, B. B. (1989). Behavioral treatment. In T. H. Ollendick and M. Hersen (Eds.), *Handbook of child psychopathology* (2d ed., pp. 439–471). New York: Plenum.

McCarthy, P. R., and Foa, E. B. (1988). Obsessive-compulsive disorder. In M. Hersen and C. G. Last (Eds.), *Child behavior therapy casebook* (pp. 55–69). New York: Plenum Press.

Meyer, R. G. (1993). *The clinician's handbook,* (3d ed.). Boston: Allyn & Bacon.

Morris, R. J., Kratochwill, T. R., and Aldridge, K. (1988). Fears and phobias. In J. C. Witt, S. N. Elliott & F. M. Gresham (Eds.), *Handbook of behavior therapy in education* (pp. 679–717). New York: Plenum.

Mowrer, O. H. (1939). A stimulus-response analysis of anxiety and its role as a reinforcing agent. *Psychological Review, 46,* 553–565.

Nelson, W. M., III (1981). A cognitive-behavioral treatment for disproportionate dental anxiety and pain: A case study. *Journal of Clinical Child Psychology, 10,* 79–82.

Ollendick, T. H. (1983). Reliability and validity of the Revised Fear Survey Schedule for Children (FSSC-R). *Behavior Research and Therapy, 21,* 685–692.

Ollendick, T. H., Hagopian, L. P., and Huntzinger, R. M. (1991). Cognitive-behavior therapy with nighttime fearful children. *Journal of Behavior Therapy and Experimental Psychiatry, 22,* 113–121.

Ollendick, T. H., Matson, J. L., and Helsel, W. J. (1985). Fears in children and adolescents: Normative data. *Behavior Research and Therapy, 23,* 465–467.

Orvaschel, H. (1989). Diagnostic interviews for children and adolescents. In C. G. Last and M. Hersen (Eds.), *Handbook of child psychiatric diagnosis* (pp. 483–495). New York: Wiley.

Orvaschel, H., and Weissman, M. M. (1986). Epidemiology of anxiety disorders in children: A review. In R. Gittelman (Ed.), *Anxiety disorders of childhood* (pp. 58–72). New York: Guilford Press.

Pynoos, R. S. (1990). Posttraumatic stress disorder in children and adolescents. In B. D. Garfinkel, G. A. Carlson, and E. B. Weller (Eds.), *Psychiatric disorders in children and adolescents* (pp. 48–63). Philadelphia: Saunders.

Rachman, S. and Hodgson, R.J. (1980). *Obsessions and compulsions.* Englewood Cliffs, NJ: Prentice-Hall.

Rapoport, J. L. (1988). Childhood obsessive-compulsive disorder. In S. Chess, A. Thomas, and M. E. Hertzig (Eds.), *Annual progress in child psychiatry and child development, 1987* (pp. 437–445). New York: Brunner/Mazel.

Reynolds, C. R., and Richmond, B. O. (1978). What I think and feel: A revised measure of children's manifest anxiety. *Journal of Abnormal Child Psychology, 6,* 271–280.

Roth, S., and Lebowitz, L. (1988). The experience of sexual trauma. *Journal of Traumatic Stress, 1,* 79–105.

Rutter, M., Tizard, J., and Whitmore, S. (1970). *Education, health and behavior.* London: Longman.

Saigh, P. A. (1987). The development and validation of the Children's Posttraumatic Stress Disorders Inventory. Paper presented at the meeting of the Association for the Advancement of Behavior Therapy, Boston.

_____ . (1988). The validity of the DSM-III Posttraumatic Stress Disorder classification as applied to adolescents. *Professional School Psychology, 3,* 283–290.

_____ . (1989a). A comparative analysis of the affective and behavioral symptomology of traumatized and nontraumatized children. *Journal of School Psychology, 27,* 247–255.

_____ . (1989b). The validity of the DSM-III Posttraumatic Stress Disorder classification as applied to children. *Journal of Abnormal Psychology, 98,* 189–192.

Samuels, S. K., and Sikorsky, S. (1990). *Clinical evaluations of school-aged children: A structured approach to the diagnosis of child and adolescent mental disorders.* Sarasota, FL: Professional Resource Exchange.

Silverman, W. K., and Nelles, W. B. (1988). The anxiety disorders interview schedule for children. *Journal of the American Academy of Child and Adolescent Psychiatry, 27,* 772–778.

Simeon, J. G., and Ferguson, H. B. (1987). Alprazolam effects in children with anxiety disorders. *Canadian Journal of Psychiatry, 32,* 570–574.

Spielberger, C. D. (1980). *Test anxiety inventory.* Palo Alto, CA: Consulting Psychologists Press.

Spielberger, C. D., Edwards, C. D., Lushene, R. E., Montouri, J., and Platzek, D. (1973). *Preliminary manual for the State-Trait Anxiety Inventory for Children.* Palo Alto, CA: Consulting Psychologists Press.

Straker, G., Moosa, F., and Sanctuaries Counselling Team. (1988). Posttraumatic stress disorder: A reaction to state-supported child abuse and neglect. *Child Abuse and Neglect, 12,* 383–395.

Strauss, C. C. (1993). Anxiety disorders. In T. H. Ollendick and M. Hersen (Eds.), *Handbook of child and adolescent assessment* (pp. 239–250). Boston: Allyn & Bacon.

Strauss, C. C., and Francis, G. (1989). Phobic disorders. In C. G. Last and M. Hersen (Eds.), *Handbook of child psychiatric diagnosis* (pp. 170–190). New York: Wiley.

Strauss, C. C., Lease, C. A., Last, C. G., and Francis, G. (1988). Overanxious disorder: An examination of developmental differences. *Journal of Abnormal Child Psychology, 16,* 433–443.

Swedo, S. E., and Rapoport, J. L. (1988). Obsessive compulsive disorder in childhood. In M. Hersen and C. G. Last (Eds.), *Handbook of child and adult psychopathology: A longitudinal perspective* (pp. 211–219). New York: Pergamon Press.

Sylvester, C. E., and Kruesi, M. J. P. (1994). Child and adolescent psychopharmacotherapy: Progress and pitfalls. *Psychiatric Annals, 24,* 83–90.

Thyer, B. A. (1991). Diagnosis and treatment of child and adolescent anxiety disorders. *Behavior Modification, 15,* 310–325.

Watson, C. G., Kucala, T., Manifold, V., Juba, M., and Vassar, P. (1988). The relationship of posttraumatic stress disorder to adolescent illegal activities, drinking, and employment. *Journal of Clinical Psychology, 44,* 592–598.

Werry, J. S., and Wollersheim, J. P. (1991). Behavior therapy with children and adolescents: A twenty-year overview. In S. Chess and M. E. Hertzig (Eds.), *Annual progress in child psychiatry and child development, 1990* (pp. 413–447). New York: Brunner/Mazel.

Wolff, R. P., and Wolff, L. S. (1991). Assessment and treatment of obsessive-compulsive disorder in children. *Behavior Modification, 15,* 372–393.

CHAPTER 7

Eating Disorders

Eating disorders are classified in two areas in DSM-IV, based on age of onset. Pica, Rumination Disorder, and Feeding Disorder of Infancy or Early Childhood are grouped with other child disorders under the subcategory "Feeding and Eating Disorders of Infancy or Early Childhood". Anorexia Nervosa and Bulimia Nervosa are not classified in the childhood disorders, but rather fall under the title "Eating Disorders." In DSM-III-R, Anorexia Nervosa, Bulimia Nervosa, Pica, and Rumination Disorder had all been classified as Eating Disorders under the larger rubric of "Disorders Usually First Evident in Infancy, Childhood, or Adolescence." The separation of anorexia and bulimia from the other eating disorders reflects the large difference in onset age between anorexia/bulimia and the other eating disorders. Feeding Disorder of Infancy or Early Childhood (FDI) is a new diagnosis in DSM-IV.

Obesity, which is frequently treated with psychological and behavioral interventions, is not classified as a mental disorder in DSM-IV because "it has not been established that it is consistently associated with a psychological or behavioral syndrome" (American Psychiatric Association, 1994, p. 539). The exclusion of obesity for this reason is surprising, since a major cause of obesity, overeating, is obviously a discrete, identifiable behavior. Furthermore, behavioral modification programs are among the most effective treatments for obesity. When obesity is the result of identifiable psychological factors, it should be coded under the category of Psychological Factors Affecting Medical Condition.

Children with eating disorders often first come to the attention of pediatricians because of the adverse medical effects of these disorders. Very few of these children (i.e., 8% of anorexics [Mickalide and Anderson, 1985]) are self-referred to psychology clinics; most are referred by pediatricians (Mickalide and Anderson, 1985). In the unlikely event that a child presents for therapy and has not been evaluated by a pediatrician for medical effects of the eating disorder, such an evaluation should be recommended.

Anorexia Nervosa

CLINICAL DESCRIPTION

Diagnostic Considerations

According to DSM-IV, the essential features of Anorexia Nervosa are a failure to maintain body weight at or above the minimal level for age and height; fear of weight gain or being overweight; disturbance of body image; and, in females, absence of at least three consecutive expected menstrual cycles (amenorrhea). Anorexia occurs in 0.5% to 1% of females, with the highest prevalence between ages 14 and 19 (American Psychiatric Association, 1994; Weltzin et al., 1993). It is considerably more rare in adolescent boys, with an estimated 10–20 anorexic girls for every anorexic boy and an estimated incidence rate of 0.02% for males (American Psychiatric Association, 1994; Weltzin et al., 1993).

Diagnostically, Anorexia Nervosa differs from Bulimia Nervosa in several areas: First, bulimia always involves binge eating, while one major subtype of anorexia does not involve this feature. Second, bulimia involves clear attempts to prevent weight gain, usually purging, in which the person uses vomiting or laxatives to remove food from the digestive tract before it can be absorbed into the bloodstream. No such provision is necessary for the anorexia diagnosis. In DSM-IV the Anorexia Nervosa diagnosis precludes the Bulimia Nervosa diagnosis, unless the bulimia occurs outside of episodes of anorexia. For example, an adolescent who was diagnosed with and subsequently recovered from anorexia may later be diagnosed with bulimia.

Two major subgroups of anorexics can be identified based on the presence of associated binge eating or purging behavior: "Restricting type" (or "restricting anorexics": no binge or purge episodes; only restricted food intake) and "Binge-Eating/Purging type" (or "bulimic anorexics": anorexics with binge or purge behavior [American Psychiatric Association, 1994; Mickalide and Anderson, 1985]). In the past, bulimic anorexics typically received both the anorexia and the bulimia diagnoses. However, in DSM-IV, they receive only the Anorexia Nervosa, Binge-Eating/Purging type, diagnosis, unless they develop bulimia outside of the anorexic episodes. Some evidence exists that anorexics of the binge/purge subtype have higher rates of outpatient therapy utilization, impulsivity, premorbid behavior problems, family dysfunction, and psychopathology than do restricting anorexics (Mickalide and Anderson, 1985; Weltzin et al., 1993).

Appearance and Features

The most obvious feature of anorexia (and the reason for most anorexia referrals) is low body weight. During a clinical interview, however, the intense fear of gaining weight and distorted body image generally become apparent. Anorexics are so preoccupied with weight and food that they will often talk about them in great detail during the interview. They frequently harbor the fear that if they lose control of their hunger they will binge until they become fat. Intensifying this fear is the fact that their "comfort zone" of body size is in the extremely thin range. Hence, they may regard even normal weights as "fat" (Appearance and features of anorexia are listed in Table 7.1.)

Anorexics typically achieve their weight loss with a combination of reduction of total food intake, ingestion of low calorie foods, and excessive exercising. Most patients experience intense feelings of hunger that they must keep in check with their exercise regimen or abnormal eating habits. When they do eat, they restrict themselves to foods such as lettuce and diet cola. Exercise such as walking or running may take place several times a day, and some anorexics work out on machines that increase upper body strength. Thus, despite their appearance of frailty and weakness, anorexics can be surprisingly strong. They may resort to laxatives and vomiting to maintain their low body weight in the face of food consumption, in which case they receive the Binge-Eating/Purging specification.

Anorexia occurs primarily in middle and upper socioeconomic class women during early to middle adolescence (Bruch, Czyzewski, and Suhr, 1988; Agras, 1987). Onset before age 11 and after age 22 is unusual. Denial of the illness and

TABLE 7.1   Appearance and Features of Anorexia Nervosa

COMMON FEATURES

Low body weight
Weight loss
Distorted body image
Fear of weight gain
Preoccupation with weight and food
Fear of loss of control
Knowledge of food and nutritional principles
Excessive exercising
Perfectionism
Family enmeshment
Onset between ages 11 and 22 years
Female

OCCASIONAL FEATURES

Mid–upper SES
Good achievement/high IQ
Good verbal skills
Depression/low self-esteem

Note: The features listed above are often seen but are not universal. Some features may be diagnostically relevant or required, while others may not be required for diagnosis. "Common" features are typical of the disorder; "occasional" features appear frequently but are not necessarily seen in a majority of cases.

enjoyment in losing weight is commonly seen along with unusual behaviors concerning food. As previously noted, approximately 1 in every 100–250 females develops this disorder, with mortality rates of 5–15%. Anorexia is rare in males (approximately 5–10% of anorexia cases, [Golden and Sacker, 1984]), and there is disagreement over whether male anorexics differ significantly from female anorexics. Three research reports of male anorexics (Burns and Crisp, 1984; Robinson and Holden, 1986; Oyebode, Boodhoo, and Schapira, 1988) conclude that many of the clinical features and outcomes of male anorexics resemble those of female anorexics, although mortality may be greater for females.

Because of its rarity in males, anorexia has been studied almost exclusively in females. Girls with anorexia are often perfectionistic achievers, usually reflected in excellent school achievement and high IQ scores. Hence, they frequently present as verbally skilled, insightful, and competent. This verbal skill and insight appear incongruous in the context of their self-starvation. Intent on fulfilling their perfectionistic tendencies, anorexic girls are often passively controlling and stubborn. Their fixation on weight loss and perfectionistic achievement may be only two representations of compulsive behavior throughout their life. In fact, anorexics can, at times, resemble women with obsessions or compulsions (Weltzin et al., 1993). Their shy, introverted presentation belies their strength of will to maintain their maladaptive behaviors.

Underlying this perfectionistic and controlling behavior is often a combination of depressive symptoms and low self-esteem; between 20–90% of anorexic girls show symptoms of depression (Weltzin et al., 1993). Because of the frequency of underlying depression, anorexics may be at risk for a major depressive episode or, in severe cases, self-injurious behavior when their fasting defenses are removed in hospitalization or therapy.

Within the family the anorexic may be a model child in all areas but eating, which may generate considerable family concern. This concern may even reach absurd proportions, with family members carefully tracking the anorexic's every bite of food and loss of weight. Many anorexic families have been described as overly "enmeshed," with weak boundaries between members who speak, feel, and think for each other. In such families the parents are typically very controlling individuals who use a mixture of control and caring to bind the family together (Golden and Sacker, 1984). Struggling for independence from her family, the anorexic may use the disorder as the only independent statement that she can make within the family's enmeshed confines. Hence, control is often an issue in these families.

Etiology

Theories of the etiology of anorexia fall into the typical areas of biology and psychology/environment, with no etiological theory yet receiving confirmatory support. Most likely, anorexia results from different causes for different children, and a combination of biological, psychological, and environmental factors is responsible for its emergence.

Biological theories of the etiology of anorexia have focused on the role of serotonin, a neurotransmitter, in regulating food intake. Because serotonin levels affect such functions as appetite and mood, it has been hypothesized that changes or dysfunctions in the brain serotonergic system could disrupt eating behavior and cause anorexia. Specifically, increased levels of serotonin in certain brain pathways inhibit eating behavior and may result in behavioral symptoms (compulsive behavior, inhibition, rigidity) typical of anorexics. In support of this theory, anorexics have been found to have increased levels of a serotonin metabolite in their cerebrospinal fluid (Weltzin et al., 1993). However, elevated serotonin levels could be either a cause or an effect of anorexia, and no direct serotonin-anorexia causal link has yet been found.

Psychological theories of anorexia have centered on family dysfunction as causally significant in the development and maintenance of anorexia. Family theorists (i.e., Minuchin, 1974) have hypothesized that one role that an anorexic may have in the family is to deflect attention and pressure from a conflicted marital subsystem by making the child's eating behavior the focus of family interaction. As the family channels its attention and energy into concern and monitoring of the anorexic, issues of conflict, unhappiness, and division are lessened. Furthermore, family agreement congeals over the drama and importance of "helping" the anorexic. The resulting appearance of solidarity takes the form of interaction that is fixated on the anorexic child. Relationships between other family members, especially within the parental subsystem, are minimized, which can be a relief for a tense, conflicted family.

Other family theories focus on overprotectiveness, perfectionism, and rigidity as the cause of the anorexic's behavior. In one scenario the anorexic child is burdened and controlled by expectations and rebels in the specific area of food and eating. In another case the rigid control over eating may reflect rigid control in all areas of life, which is in turn taught by a family that demands complete compliance and perfection. A third dynamic may occur in a child who fears maturity and independence from an enmeshed family system. She avoids the pressures of growing up by refusing to eat, and thus (presumably) remaining small and dependent on parents. For girls in particular, anorexia slows (or halts) the development of sex characteristics such as breast development, pubic hair, and the menstrual cycle. These sex characteristics, which reflect the maturing process of adolescence, may be threatening to an adolescent who wishes to remain in a childlike role.

Recently the role of societal and environmental factors in the development of anorexia has been more apparent. Obesity is often a source of prejudice and derision in American society, and thinness is particularly valued in adolescent girls and young women. Models and dancers, who depend on a lithe, delicate appearance, may be most at risk for these pressures, but the pressure of social acceptance is profound for all adolescents. A child who suddenly receives compliments for weight loss and constantly discusses dieting with her friends is given the message that "thin is in." When this message is taken to the extreme, anorexia becomes a major risk.

ASSESSMENT PATTERNS

A sample assessment battery for Anorexia Nervosa is shown in Table 7.2.

Broad Assessment Strategies

Cognitive Assessment

Clinician-Administered. WISC-III IQ scores of anorexics may be expected to be in the High Average range or higher, with Verbal IQ (VIQ) scores generally exceeding Performance IQ (PIQ) scores. This verbal-performance difference often reflects the anorexic's overachievement in school-based tasks, especially when elevations are seen on Information, Vocabulary, and Arithmetic subtests. Particularly capable, rigid, controlled anorexics will elevate scales on the Freedom from Distractibility index (Arithmetic and Digit Span), reflecting their ability to focus and concentrate. Processing Speed index scores (Symbol Search and Coding) are variable; some anorexics achieve very high scores as a result of motivation and concentration, while others receive low scores because of slow, perfectionistic writing and checking behavior. Observation of the anorexic's test-taking behavior and verbal responses may reveal some of the obsessive and/or perfectionistic tendencies; subtests requiring open-ended answers (such as the Vocabulary and Comprehension subtests) often provide the most salient data in this area. Over all, the WISC-III can be a valuable tool in identifying the anorexic's cognitive style and the effects of this style on adaptive behavior.

As with IQ testing, anorexics' scores on measures of academic achievement such as the WJ-R and WIAT frequently meet or exceed what would be

TABLE 7.2   Sample Assessment Battery for Anorexia Nervosa

PSYCHOLOGICAL

MMPI/MMPI-A

FAMILY

Family Environment Scale
FACES-III

SYNDROME-SPECIFIC

Eating Disorders Inventory
Eating Attitudes Test
Body Image Test

Note: Assessment instruments are intended to supplement (not substitute for) a good clinical interview and, when possible, a structured diagnostic interview.

expected, consistent with achievement orientation and perfectionism. While no achievement test score pattern is typical of anorexics, scales that tap achievement in more "basic" achievement areas (such as reading, spelling, and science) are more likely to be elevated than those that measure more "applied" achievement areas (such as oral expression or listening comprehension).

Psychological Assessment

Clinician-Administered.   In addition to the basic clinical interview, projective data can provide insight into issues that may be driving the anorexic's beliefs and behaviors. The perfectionism and denial characteristic of anorexia are sometimes shown by a low number of Rorschach responses (Wagner and Wagner, 1978). Likewise, a low number of human movement (M) responses could reflect a striving beyond resources, while a high proportion of major detail responses (D) to M responses may indicate a cognitive defensiveness or cautiousness. A large number of Dd responses, on the other hand, could be consistent with cognitive constriction and perfectionistic attention to detail. Defensiveness and cautiousness are also represented by high F and F+% records. Less common are color responses and sexual/anatomical responses, which may be an indication of emotional undercontrol, immaturity, and fears of sexual maturity.

On other clinician-administered tests of personality and environmental stress, anorexics have been found to have elevated scores across a variety of syndromes (i.e. somatic symptoms, anxiety, depression [Mickalide and Anderson, 1985]). For example, elevated scores have been found on the Diagnostic Interview for Borderlines (Gunderson, 1978). The general testing pattern is for anorexics to score in clinical ranges on tests of psychopathology, character pathology, and family stress; anorexics with binge/purge complications may have more stress and greater psychopathology than do restricting anorexics.

Because most anorexics are of adolescent age or higher, they may be administered adult tests of personality, such as the MMPI and the more current MMPI-A. On the MMPI, anorexics can be expected to show the 2-4-8 pattern typical of adolescent rebelliousness, distress, and family discord (Meyer, 1993). The perfectionism and obsessive features of anorexia will likely elevate scale 7. Scales 6 and 8 may be elevated by general psychopathology and character pathology as well (Small et al., 1981). To the extent that bodily concern, self-centeredness, and egocentricity are present, scales 1 and 3 will be elevated. Elevations on scale 9 are more typical of anorexics with binge/purge complications than of restricting anorexics (Piran et al., 1988). Denial of pathology, common in anorexics, may be manifest as elevations on scales L and K with a depression on the F scale, especially when adolescent norms are used (Gallucci, 1987). Other MMPI elevations, as well as the general shape of the profile, may provide insight into how the adolescent's individual personality contributes to symptoms.

Family Assessment

Child-Report. Because anorexia is often accompanied (or caused) by family pathology, an assessment of family functioning is generally desirable. Two self-report measures of family environment with considerable utility in these cases are the FES and the FACES-III. The enmeshment characteristic of anorexic families would likely be shown by elevated scores on the Cohesion, Moral-Religious Emphasis, Organization, and Control scales of the FES and depressed scores on the Independence and Active-Recreational Orientation scales. Repressed emotion may result in low Conflict and Expressiveness scores. Controlling factor scores are likely to be high, while scores on the Conflicted factor will be low. Very high Supportive factor scores (over 280) could reflect denial of problems, social desirability, and tendency to portray the family as perfect. On the FACES-III, anorexic families would be expected to score high on the Cohesion scale and low on the Adaptability scale, reflecting components of enmeshment and rigidity, respectively.

Syndrome-Specific Tests

Child-Report

Several tests have been developed to assess the specific eating behaviors and cognitions thought to underlie Anorexia Nervosa. The Eating Disorders Inventory (EDI; Garner, Olmstead, and Polivy, 1983) is a sixty-four–item self-report measure of psychological and behavioral traits common to anorexia and bulimia. Items are rated on a 6-point scale (always to never) of frequency or agreement. The EDI yields eight scales: Drive for Thinness (DT), Bulimia (B), Body Dissatisfaction (BD), Ineffectiveness (I), Perfectionism (P), Interpersonal Distrust (ID), Interoceptive Awareness (IA), and Maturity Fears (MF). Anorexics generally score higher than normals on all scales of the EDI, reflecting abnormal food, eating, and body image beliefs in addition to perfectionistic tendencies, emotional confusion, and problematic social relationships. Scores on the B scale may indicate whether the anorexia is of the Restricting or of the Binge-Eating/Purging type; the latter type generally elevates the B scale.

The Eating Attitudes Test (EAT; Garner and Garfinkel, 1979) is a forty-item inventory that gives a total score and 3 subscale scores: Dieting, Bulimia/Food Preoccupation, and Oral Control. Items, which are rated on a 1–6 scale of frequency, reflect anorexic thoughts and behaviors. Scoring is *not* a matter of simply summing items; certain items and ratings are weighted differently. Total scores as high as 59 are typical of anorexics, while scores of 16 are average for controls; a cutting score of 30 can be used to identify eating concerns typical of anorexics (Garner and Garfinkel, 1979). Anorexics elevate all subscales of the EAT, and binge/purge anorexics endorse many of the "bulimia" items. The EAT includes fewer cognitive and affective items than the EDI. Hence, while both the EAT and EDI provide diagnostically useful information for anorexics, the EDI is preferable in cases with a significant cognitive/affective component.

☐ TREATMENT OPTIONS

Treatment options for Anorexia Nervosa are outlined in Table 7.3.

Medical Evaluation/Hospitalization

First and foremost, anorexics must be closely evaluated and followed medically. Because many organic conditions may lead to weight loss, organic causes must be first ruled out before the Anorexia Nervosa diagnosis is made and psychological treatments are deemed appropriate. Once the Anorexia Nervosa diagnosis is made, treatment generally involves three components: (1) weight gain; (2) resolution of psychological, social, and behavioral abnormalities; and (3) weight maintenance.

TABLE 7.3   Treatment Options for Anorexia Nervosa

MEDICAL EVALUATION/HOSPITALIZATION

Physical exam
Tests to rule out other conditions
Enforced, monitored weight gain (1/4 to 1/2 pound/day)
    Enforced, monitored food intake
    Monitored electrolyte balance
    Monitored output

Restricted access to laxatives
Restricted access to exercise

BEHAVIORAL INTERVENTIONS

Reinforcers tied to weight gain

PSYCHOTHERAPY

Psychodynamic psychotherapy
Cognitive-behavioral interventions
Group therapy

FAMILY INTERVENTIONS

Family therapy (typically with systemic approach focused on boundaries within the
    family)

MEDICATIONS (usually for co-occurring diagnoses such as depression)

Note: This outline of options summarizes major treatments covered in the text. Specific treatments are often combined into an intervention package. Refer to the text for additional descriptions of each treatment. This table is not necessarily an exhaustive list of all treatments available.

Because of the potentially life-threatening weight loss and accompanying physical symptoms, hospitalization is often necessary to facilitate the attainment of the first two treatment goals (weight gain and psychotherapy). Medically, the hospitalized child should be evaluated for weight gain, food intake, electrolyte balance, output, and complications. Weight gain is usually targeted at one-quarter to one-half pound per day (Golden and Sacker, 1984). In addition, the hospital provides a tightly controlled environment that allows the management team to remove the child from the home/family environment, set behavioral contingencies, and restrict access to laxatives and exercise equipment. Psychopharmacological interventions may be tried during hospitalization to address the anorexia or associated psychological features (i.e. depression, anxiety); it is unusual, however, for these to cause a significant behavioral response in the absence of other intervention.

Behavioral Interventions

Behavioral modification is the cornerstone of intervention to correct anorexia. Once reinforcers and punishers are identified, these are tied to weight gain. A common strategy is to allow the child initial access to basic hospital amenities (TV, bathroom privileges, books, freedom to leave room, make-up, toiletries, telephone and clothes) with the understanding that she will retain these privileges for as long as she meets weight goals. Weight goals should be explicit and time of day for weighing should be constant from day to day. If the patient fails to meet weight goals, privileges are progressively removed with the understanding that they will be returned progressively on the first day of weight gain. It is possible in the first few days of hospitalization to find an anorexic in her room with no phone, no TV, only a hospital gown to wear, no make-up, and restricted access to the bathroom or to the unit outside the room! If behavioral interventions fail (which is rare) or the anorexic is too weak to respond, intravenous feeding may be necessary.

Psychotherapy

Although behavioral treatment often results in weight gain, in some cases it amounts to "curing the symptom." Psychosocial change must accompany the behavioral change if psychological adjustment is to be achieved and weight is to be maintained. Psychotherapy regimens use individual, family, and group interventions to achieve this goal.

Individual psychotherapy generally addresses common issues of anorexics such as ambivalence over dependency, denial of illness, fear of being overweight, need for perfectionism, and anger at family (Bruch, 1978). More psychodynamic approaches stress the need to access fears and emotions tied to these issues and to achieve resolution through insight. Cognitive-behavioral approaches, on the other hand, take a systematic approach by building a therapeutic relationship; identifying maladaptive thoughts, feelings, and behaviors; correcting maladaptive thoughts, practicing coping; boosting self-esteem with self-monitoring and self-statements; and teaching relaxation techniques (Sagardoy et al., 1989).

Group treatment for anorexia, while not as common as individual and family therapy, is receiving attention as a potentially important adjunct to these traditional therapies. A typical group (Hendren et al., 1987) may have five to eight members and meet weekly for an hour. Because of the similarity of many issues between anorexia and bulimia, anorexics and bulimics may be included in the same group. Group process may vary with the orientation of the therapist, from more task-oriented, cognitive-behavioral groups to more process-oriented, interpersonal groups. The group setting offers numerous advantages: In open groups, older members can model effective and honest working-through of issues, which may assist in challenging the denial of illness characteristic of anorexia. Additionally, the group acts as a source of support for its members, removing some of the stigma of having an eating disorder. Finally, the group offers a variety of viewpoints for discussion of issues, facilitating empathy and working-through of difficulties. Some encouraging preliminary data on group therapy for anorexia have been reported (Hendren et al., 1987).

Family Interventions

In developing a treatment plan for an anorexic child, it is important to remember that, in virtually all cases, anorexia affects the entire family. Patterns of family interaction established when the child had an eating disorder are unlikely to change easily. Hence, even if change is made in individual or inpatient therapy, the child is returning to an environment that, potentially, provokes the eating disorder behavior. To address this problem, family therapy is a frequent component of treatment for anorexia.

Family therapy for anorexia first involves an assessment of the family unit, family relationships, and family interaction patterns. This may be particularly enlightening if done during a meal in order to observe the family's response to the anorexic's refusal to eat. A frequently seen pattern is that of enmeshment, in which family relationships are too strong and boundaries too thin, resulting in members talking and feeling for each other and failing to allow individual development.

Overprotectiveness, rigidity, and overcontrol on the part of the parents are often seen, to which the children respond with subtle rebelliousness such as not eating. Coalitions between family members are not uncommon; for example, the anorexic may be enmeshed with the mother and other children against the father. The task of the family therapist in these cases is to identify enmeshed relationships and coalitions within the family. Family intervention is then aimed at giving members insight into these underlying dynamics and at changing the family's structure and behaviors (Minuchin, 1974).

Medication

While several medications have been suggested as potential treatments for anorexia, "results from double-blind trials do not find a 'magic bullet' drug that provides a significant remission of the anorexic symptom complex" (Weltzin et al., 1993, p. 222). For the most part, neuroleptic medications (chlorpromazine, pimozide, sulpiride) have been used to treat anorexic symptoms, with some success in individual cases. However, more controlled studies have reported limited success of these medications, prompting Weltzin et al. (1993) to contend that they should not be used in the routine treatment of anorexia. Antidepressant medications such as amitriptyline and fluoxetine have been used for anorexics with a depressed component.

Over all, understanding of medication for anorexia is in the experimental stage, but progress is being made in identifying medications that are related to weight gain in certain cases. Medication trials may be indicated for anorexics with severe symptoms, anorexics who are resistant to psychobehavioral interventions, and anorexics who have co-occurring diagnoses of depression and/ or anxiety.

■ Bulimia Nervosa

☐ CLINICAL DESCRIPTION

Diagnostic Considerations

Bulimia Nervosa has as its essential characteristic binge eating, in which the individual consumes a large amount of food with little perceived control over her eating behavior. Binge eating is followed by behaviors to prevent the individual from gaining weight as a result of the excessive consumption. Many bulimics follow a binge-purge cycle in which binge eating is followed by purging of the digestive system by vomiting or use of laxatives. In some cases, fasting or exercise is also used as a method of restricting weight gain in the face of massive caloric intake. According to DSM-IV, bulimics feel a lack of control over eating binges, average at least two bulimic episodes a week for at least 3 months, and exhibit overconcern with weight. It is not uncommon to encounter a patient with an eating disorder who does not binge frequently enough to be classified as bulimic according to DSM-IV criteria. These patients are technically classified as having Eating Disorder, NOS, although their testing patterns and treatment options are similar to those of bulimics.

Bulimia is more common than anorexia, although diagnostic uncertainty or misuse of the term *bulimia* results in different definitions being used. "Bulimic behavior," for example, is sometimes used to mean having *ever* binged or purged. Obviously, a single incident of this behavior is much more common than the bulimia diagnosis. Using these more lax definitions of bulimia, prevalence rates have been estimated at between 4% and 20% (Weltzin et al., 1993). On the other hand, using a more stringent DSM-IV definition, bulimia has a prevalence rate of 1–3% in females (American Psychiatric Association, 1994). Bulimia is much more common in females, who outnumber males by as much as 7 to 1 (Weltzin et al., 1993).

Diagnostic differences between bulimics and anorexics were noted in the consideration of anorexia. In DSM-III-R, there was significant overlap between bulimia and anorexia, but in DSM-IV, exclusionary criteria in the Bulimia Nervosa diagnosis have substantially reduced this overlap. Many bulimics who would have received diagnoses of *both* bulimia and anorexia will now only qualify for the Anorexia Nervosa, Binge-Eating/Purging type. Nevertheless, because of the shared binge-purge component in both disorders, evaluation for anorexia should include a component of evaluation for bulimia, and vice versa.

Appearance and Features

As with anorexics, bulimics tend to be females between the ages of 13 and 21. The binge episodes of bulimics usually involve the consumption of large amounts of calorie-rich foods. Binge eating is done in secret, and special efforts (e.g., hiding large quantities of food prior to a binge) may be taken to avoid detection. Bulimics feel out of control when on a binge and may go to great lengths to obtain food. Stealing food or money to buy food may occur on college campuses where shared rooms make access to others' food or money easier. Such antisocial behavior may be so out of character for the bulimic that she appears driven to eat at any cost.

Bulimia and anorexia share several similarities. Beyond the obvious fact that both involve eating behavior, both disorders are usually characterized by overconcern about weight, distortion of body image, and an unusual focus on food. Many theorists and clinicians have also implicated the family in the development and maintenance of bulimia, much the same as for anorexia. Like anorexia, bulimia generally occurs in adolescent-age females; male cases are rare.

Despite their shared characteristics, bulimia and anorexia have several differences. Many bulimics are of normal weight or are obese, whereas anorexics are, by definition, dangerously thin. Therefore, the weight fluctuations of bulimics who are not diagnosed as anorexic usually range from thin (but not anorexic) to significantly overweight. Anorexics tend to stay in one (unacceptably low) weight range. Because bulimics generally do not have the extreme weight loss of anorexics, bulimia is rarely life-threatening. However, bulimia is associated with a number of problematic medical conditions such as dental erosion, electrolyte imbalance, and dehydration. Bulimics do not typically have the rigid bodily control of anorexics; they may, in fact, complain of feeling out of control of their body at times (i.e., binges). Bulimics may be more extroverted than are anorexics, more aware of subjective distress, and more prone to acting-out behaviors as well (Agras, 1987; Rybicki, Lepkowsky, and Arndt, 1989). Features of Bulimia Nervosa are summarized in Table 7.4.

Etiology

Etiological theories of bulimia often resemble those for anorexia, probably because the two syndromes were often co-diagnosed prior to DSM-IV. Little has

TABLE 7.4   Appearance and Features of Bulimia Nervosa

COMMON FEATURES

Significant weight fluctuation
Binge eating
Purge episodes
Distorted body image
Preoccupation with food
Fear of loss of control
Knowledge of food
Extreme/atypical behaviors to obtain food
Physical complications: dental erosion; electrolyte imbalance
Family problems
Onset between ages 11 and 22 years
Female
Depression/low self-esteem/personality disorder

Note: The features listed above are often seen but are not universal. Some features may be diagnostically relevant or required, while others may not be required for diagnosis. "Common" features are typical of the disorder; "occasional" features appear frequently but are not necessarily seen in a majority of cases.

been written about the etiology of "pure" (normal weight) bulimia. Psychologically, bulimia may result from several factors. First, sensation seeking may cause some adolescents to gorge for the pleasure of eating. This gorging, however, must then be eliminated in order to avoid long-term weight consequences. The sensation-seeking theory of etiology also borrows from the concept of substance abuse in noting that bulimics have a compulsion to eat that resembles an addiction (Weltzin et al., 1993). In addition, bulimics may be vulnerable to other addictions, and addiction may run in the families of bulimics (Weltzin et al., 1993).

A second etiological theory suggests that the purging characteristic of bulimia may be a result of guilt over eating too much and fear of becoming fat. The bulimic succumbs to the compulsion to eat, but this temporary pleasure is followed by massive guilt, shame, and fear of being discovered. To avoid discovery and to allay guilt, the bulimic purges and disposes of any evidence of a binge.

Socially, bulimia may be learned by modeling others who engage in binge eating and purging. Since most bulimics binge in secret, purging is usually what is observed, or the cycle is discussed with friends. Girls in high school, for example, can learn binge eating as a way of staying thin. The knowledge that other girls are engaging in the behavior makes it more acceptable.

Biological theories of the cause of bulimia are in their infancy and currently borrow from theories of substance abuse disorders. In particular, endorphins and enkephalins have been suggested as neurotransmitters that are responsive to binges (Weltzin et al., 1993), and bulimics may binge for the pleasant feeling created by these neurotransmitters. These theories remain to be tested empirically.

☐   ASSESSMENT PATTERNS

A sample assessment battery for Bulimia Nervosa is shown in Table 7.5.

Broad Assessment Strategies

Cognitive Assessment

Clinician-Administered. Unlike anorexics, little has been written about the cognitive and achievement status of bulimics. Hence, the "typical" WISC-III score of a bulimic is difficult to anticipate. Nevertheless, testing with the WISC-III can indicate cognitive styles of problem solving that may be useful in therapy planning, in much the same way as with anorexics.

Psychological Assessment

Clinician-Administered. Bulimics tend to score higher on both general and specific pathology measures than do controls and higher than restricting anorexics as well. Measures used to assess the general psychopathology of bulimics include the MMPI (or MMPI-A) and SCL-90-R.

The bulimic MMPI pattern resembles that of the anorexic in reflecting elements of rebelliousness, distress, and family problems, but to a greater extent. In addition to elevations across all clinical scales (with the exception of scale

---

TABLE 7.5   Sample Assessment Battery for Bulimia Nervosa

PSYCHOLOGICAL

MMPI/MMPI-A
SCL-90-R

FAMILY

Family Environment Scale
FACES-III

SYNDROME-SPECIFIC

Eating Disorders Inventory
Compulsive Eating Scale
Bulimic Thoughts Questionnaire

Note: Assessment instruments are intended to supplement (not substitute for) a good clinical interview and, when possible, a structured diagnostic interview.

5), a 2-4-7-8 pattern has been found in bulimics (Rybicki et al., 1989); scales F, 1, 3, 6, 9, and 0 can be expected to be in the 60–70 range. Because the bulimic often feels more out of control than the anorexic, higher scores on scales 4 and 8 are to be expected. Furthermore, the general psychopathology and distress of bulimics contribute to significant elevations on scales 2, 4, 7, and 8, which may average as high as 70–80 in this group.

Child-Report. In keeping with the higher psychopathology scores on the MMPI, bulimics also show elevations on the Beck Depression Inventory (BDI; Rybicki et al., 1989; Williamson et al., 1990) and SCL-90-R. On the BDI, bulimics typically yield scores in the clinically depressed range, with studies finding mean raw scores on the BDI for bulimics of 16–22 as compared to 4–6 for controls (Rybicki et al., 1989; Williamson et al., 1990). These results are consistent with elevated MMPI scores on scales 2 and 7. The occurrence of general psychopathology in bulimics is also reflected in higher scores on the SCL-90-R and a related scale, the Hopkins Symptom Checklist, (Derogatis et al., 1974), although there is some indication that depression scores drop with treatment (Norman and Herzog, 1986). It should be noted that, although bulimics elevate scores on psychopathology scales, their depression scores may not be much higher than those of extremely obese individuals or compulsive overeaters (Williamson et al., 1990).

Family Assessment

Child-Report. The family problems suggested by high scale 4 scores on the MMPI can be assessed in more detail using the FES. On the FES, bulimics can be expected to show lower scores on scales identified as "Supportive" by Kronenberger and Thompson (1990): Cohesion, Expressiveness, Independence, Intellectual-Cultural Orientation, and Active-Recreational Orientation. Some empirical support exists for this hypothesis (Rybicki et al., 1989), especially for the Expressiveness and Active-Recreational scales. Bulimic families tend to be less expressive and to engage in fewer recreational, "leisure time" activities together. FES scales measuring Conflict and Control will be clinically useful in individual cases but show no clear pattern across bulimics as a group. This may be because bulimics distort these dimensions on self-report or because conflict/control issues are covert in many bulimic families.

Syndrome-Specific Tests

Child-Report

This group of tests focuses specifically on eating, body image, and/or food-related attitudes and behaviors. The rationale for the use of syndrome-specific measures is their more specific delineation of the critical problem of bulimia: eating behavior and the beliefs that motivate it. Self-report measures of eating behavior and eating attitudes include the Eating Attitudes Test (EAT; Garner and Garfinkel, 1979), the Eating Disorders Inventory (EDI; Garner et al., 1983), the Conroy-Healy Eating Questionnaire (CHEQ; Healy, Conroy, and Walsh, 1985), the Bulimia Test (BULIT; Smith and Thelen, 1984), the Compulsive Eating Scale (CES; Dunn and Odercin, 1981), the Bulimic Thoughts Questionnaire (BTQ; Phelan, 1987), and the Binge Scale (BS; Hawkins and Clement, 1980). These tests can be loosely grouped into two categories: bulimia-focused tests (tests that were developed to assess primarily bulimic and related symptomatology) and general eating problem tests (tests to assess a variety of eating problems, including bulimic symptoms).

Bulimia-Focused Tests. The CES, BTQ, CHEQ, BULIT, and BS measure eating cognitions and behaviors characteristic of bulimia such as binge eating, purging, and distorted self-image. The CHEQ and the BS are brief but relatively sensitive bulimic symptom scales. They tend to tap a single, "bulimic" trait, as shown in studies demonstrating high internal consistency (e.g., Welch and Hall, 1989). The BS consists of nineteen items, of which nine are added to give a total Binge score. BS scores correlate with dieting and self-image concerns and are unrelated to social desirability (Hawkins and Clement, 1980). Clinicians who are using the BS may want to administer only the 9 scored items. The CHEQ consists of thirteen items and produces reliable information about bulimic symptoms (Healy et al., 1985).

The CES, BTQ, and BULIT, on the other hand, are somewhat longer scales with several subcategories (e.g., factors or subscales) of items. The CES is a thirty-two–item scale, of which sixteen items are used in scoring (Dunn and Odercin, 1981). It yields a total score and three factor scores (Golden, Buzcek, and Robbins, 1986): Negative Affect (about eating behavior), Dietary Restraint, and Positive Affect (about eating behavior). Higher CES scores are related to less emotional stability and control as well as to greater suspiciousness, guilt, social desirability, and tension (Dunn and Odercin, 1981). The CES is highly related to DSM-III bulimic symptomatology (Golden et al., 1986). A total CES score of 59 or higher can be used as a clinical cutoff (Dunn and Odercin, 1981).

The BTQ assesses self statements in three areas: "self-schema" (actually more of a measure of body image), "self-efficacy" (perceived self-control over eating), and "salient beliefs" (maladaptive beliefs related to eating and craving for food). Phelan (1987) presents data suggesting that the BTQ discriminates between bulimics, normals, and, to a lesser extent, obese individuals; the BTQ can also be used to track treatment progress.

The BULIT is a thirty-six–item scale, consisting of thirty-two "original" items and 4 items which were added later. The thirty-two original items are added to give a BULIT total score. A factor analysis of the thirty-two items yielded five factor-analytically derived subscales: Binges (binging behavior and fear of binging), Feelings (emotions related to binges), Vomiting (purge-related vomiting), Food (food preferred during a binge), and Weight (weight gain or loss within a month's time). The BULIT correlates highly with the BS and EAT.

It also discriminates significantly between bulimic individuals and healthy controls (Smith and Thelen, 1984). Smith and Thelen (1984) suggest that a total cutoff score of 102 be used for classification of bulimics.

Bulimics score in the pathological direction relative to normals on the CES, BTQ, CHEQ, BULIT, and BS. Although all five scales do an adequate job of identifying bulimics, the BULIT may yield the best discrimination between bulimics and normals (Welch and Hall, 1989) and between bulimics and obese individuals (Williamson et al., 1990).

The Goldfarb Fear of Fat Scale (GFFS; Goldfarb, Dykens, and Gerrard, 1985) is a ten item self-report scale that assesses the fear of being overweight, a characteristic of anorexics and bulimics. Both anorexics and bulimics have higher GFFS scores than do normals, and GFFS scores are related to general psychological symptomatology in these groups. The Forbidden Food Survey (FFS; Ruggiero et al., 1988) is a forty-five–item self-report questionnaire that assesses emotional reactions to food types and caloric levels. Bulimics report more negative reactions to all of the food/calorie groups of the FFS and to foods of high and medium caloric levels from the grain, meat, and milk groups in particular. This negative reaction to food in general and to high calorie food in particular is consistent with a fear of binge eating, which typically involves high-calorie food.

General Eating Problem Tests.   Unlike the CES, CHEQ, BS, BTQ, and BULIT, the EAT and EDI assess cognitive, affective, and/or behavioral characteristics of eating disorders in general. Hence, they can be used with anorexics as well as bulimics. The EAT and EDI are described in detail in the anorexia assessment section. Bulimics show elevations on all of the EDI scales relative to normal subjects, with the largest differences occurring on the DT, B, I, ID, and IA scales (Gross et al., 1986). If the EDI is given to a bulimic or suspected bulimic patient, the B subscale, as a measure of bulimic symptoms, is an excellent substitute for the CHEQ or BS (Welch and Hall, 1989). Bulimics have also been found to score higher than normals on the Dieting, Bulimia, and total scores of the EAT (Gross et al., 1986).

The most useful syndrome-specific tests for bulimics appear to be the BULIT and EDI. The CHEQ and BS scales, although useful, are too narrow in scope and can easily be substituted for by the B subscale of the EDI. The CES and EAT overlap somewhat with the BULIT and EDI, but they lack some of the dimensions of the latter scale. Furthermore, the CES shares the narrow "bulimic" focus of the CHEQ and BS scales. Hence, an assessment for eating disordered behaviors and beliefs should begin with the EDI and, if a high B subscale score is found, bulimic behaviors and beliefs might be probed with the BULIT. If an interview is desired instead of a questionnaire/self-report measure, the Eating Disorders Examination (EDE; Wilson and Smith, 1989), a semistructured interview, might be used instead of or in conjunction with the EDI. The EDE may be particularly helpful in distinguishing bulimics from restrained, nonbulimic patients, who are concerned about food and dieting but do not binge-purge.

Body Image Tests. A final group of assessment instruments that may be relevant to the bulimic patient involve the measurement of body image and attitudes toward food (as opposed to eating behavior). Measurement of body image can be accomplished through the use of body satisfaction questionnaires, which ask patients to rate their satisfaction with shape and size of body parts (e.g., the Body Image Self-Evaluation Questionnaire [BISE; Lindholm and Wilson, 1988]), through the use of pictoral tests of body size (e.g., Williamson et al., 1990), and through the use of video image distortion, in which the patient alters her image on a video screen until it is an acceptable size. Bulimics show a predictable dissatisfaction with body image, but this dissatisfaction may be no greater than that of very diet-conscious ("restricting") nonbulimic people (Lindholm and Wilson, 1988). Distortion of body image is greater in bulimics than in compulsive overeaters or obese individuals (Williamson et al., 1990).

An important caveat regarding almost all of these measures of eating behavior, beliefs, and body image is their dependence on self-report. Their results may be distorted by social desirability, malingering, or simply by poor insight. Wilson (1987) suggests that multidimensional assessment (observation and self-report) is important in monitoring bulimic and related behaviors/beliefs.

TREATMENT OPTIONS

Treatment options for Bulima Nervosa are outlined in Table 7.6.

Medical Evaluation/Hospitalization

Although bulimia is not as immediately life-threatening as is anorexia, it can create numerous physiological problems. Therefore, a thorough medical examination is indicated. In many cases, regular medical supervision or check-ups are necessary as well. Hospitalization for bulimia is less frequent than for anorexia and usually occurs only in cases involving significant medical complications; severe weight loss; or uncontrollable, constant binge-purging. Yager (1985) recommends hospitalization if either of three conditions are met: (1) Outpatient treatment fails and symptoms are health-threatening, (2) medication is being tried to control the symptoms, or (3) the patient is suicidal. Inpatient treatment typically involves a behavior management plan, intensive cognitive-behavioral and/or psychodynamic psychotherapy (individual, group, and, sometimes, family), and occasionally medication.

Psychotherapy

Most treatment for bulimia involves outpatient individual, family, and/or group psychotherapy. Individual psychotherapy frequently makes use of cognitive-behavioral techniques, beginning with a self-monitoring period in which the patient keeps a journal of eating behaviors, thoughts, and feelings (e.g., Freeman, 1991). This is followed by the establishment of a pattern of regular eating

TABLE 7.6 Treatment Options for Bulimia Nervosa

MEDICAL EVALUATION/HOSPITALIZATION

Physical exam
Intervention to address physical complications
Restricted access to situations allowing binging or purging (e.g., vomiting in the
    bathroom, access to refrigerators or vending machines, access to laxatives)

PSYCHOTHERAPY

Cognitive-behavioral interventions
    Self-monitoring
    Establishing pattern of regular eating and control over food
    Psychoeducation
    Identification of maladaptive cognitions about food, eating, and body image
    Coping strategies to manage cognitions and urges related to binges (cognitive
        restructuring, thought stopping, substitution, problem solving, use of social
        support)
    Reinforcement for lack of binge-eating behavior
    Anticipation of future problems

Psychodynamic psychotherapy
Group therapy

FAMILY INTERVENTIONS

Family therapy (typically with systemic approach focused on boundaries within the
    family)

MEDICATIONS (usually for co-occurring diagnoses such as depression)

Note: This outline of options summarizes major treatments covered in the text. Specific treatments
are often combined into an intervention package. Refer to the text for additional descriptions of
each treatment. This table is not necessarily an exhaustive list of all treatments available.

and control over exposure to food. The middle stage of therapy involves the
use of psychoeducation to provide information about the nature of bulimia, its
detrimental physiological effects, and how it can be controlled. The patient is
encouraged to identify maladaptive cognitions involving body image, food,
and eating behavior both during therapy and as part of self-monitoring between therapy sessions. These cognitions can then be challenged and addressed
in therapy, initially by the therapist, but with responsibility shifting to the patient to correct the maladaptive cognitions. Coping strategies are taught to
manage cognitions or urges that could lead to binges; these include cognitive
restructuring, thought stopping, substitution, problem solving, and use of social support. Other psychoeducational components of cognitive-behavioral
therapy for bulimia include teaching methods of weight control (such as calorie restriction and structured eating behaviors) and teaching patients about
the hazards of binge-purge behavior (Freeman, 1991).

Contracts can be used to implement a self-reinforcement program that rewards non–binge-eating behavior. The patient is encouraged to continue self-monitoring and to practice techniques learned in therapy. Regular monitoring of the patient's progress using the EDI, SCL-90-R, BDI, or related inventories is recommended throughout therapy, and assessment results can be used to identify intervention targets or areas of improvement that can be reinforced. The final stage of cognitive-behavioral therapy for bulimia focuses on maintenance of the improved behavior and anticipation of future problems. Cognitive-behavioral therapy has been found to be generally effective in reducing bulimic symptomatology (Yager, 1985; Fairburn, 1985). It may be more effective than psychodynamic or nondirective therapy alone (Fairburn, 1985; Fairburn et al., 1986), although the most effective intervention probably involves the flexible use of both cognitive-behavioral and psychodynamic techniques.

Although psychodynamic psychotherapy for bulimia has not been systematically researched, the use of psychodynamic techniques in conjunction with cognitive-behavioral techniques is widely accepted. Psychodynamic techniques involve the exploration of the origins of the eating disorder (with a particular focus on the family); the factors maintaining the behavior; and developmental issues such as independence, intimacy, loneliness, maturing, the importance of physical appearance, and need for control. The goal of these techniques is to improve the insight of the patient into the dynamics driving the eating disorder so that these dynamics can be resolved and removed as motivations for maladaptive behavior. The therapeutic relationship and insight into personal issues are emphasized. Because cognitive-behavioral and psychodynamic interventions share the same goals (improved eating behavior, insight into motivating factors such as thoughts and feelings), they should be regarded as complementary and used together.

In addition to individual therapy, group therapy is widely used in the treatment of bulimia. Group therapies generally combine cognitive-behavioral, psychodynamic, psychoeducational, and process-interactional techniques to form an integrated treatment for bulimia. The cognitive-behavioral components are similar to those for individual psychotherapy, encouraging use of self-monitoring, behavioral (e.g., self-reinforcement), coping, and cognitive-restructuring techniques. Similarly, the psychodynamic group issues mirror those of individual therapy (independence, family issues), with the group acting as a forum for introducing and discussing such issues. Process-interactional techniques involve group activities such as role playing and psychodrama as well as use of group interaction to facilitate insight into members' motivations for maladaptive behavior. Group therapy has been shown to be effective in relieving symptoms in many bulimics (Yager, 1985; Sykes, Currie, and Gross, 1987), although a significant proportion do not benefit from group therapy. Yager (1985) suggests that patients first be tried in individual therapy before being placed in a group so that the appropriateness of group treatment can be evaluated.

Family Interventions

Family therapy for bulimics typically follows the same pattern and examines the same issues as family therapy for anorexics. Structural family interventions emphasize components of the family such as boundaries around family subsystems (e.g., the spousal subsystem), which are observed and corrected if boundaries are overly weak or overly strong. For example, the mother may be involved in a coalition with the bulimic daughter against the father, who rigidly controls the family system. The daughter's bulimic behavior gives her control in one area of her life (weight) and arouses the concern of the mother, who becomes more enmeshed with the daughter and avoids the role of parent-spouse (partner of the domineering husband). A structural intervention would seek to strengthen the spousal-parental relationship and create appropriate boundaries between the parents and child. Behavioral interventions can also be carried out in family therapy, such as the negotiation and implementation of eating contracts and reinforcement for appropriate eating behavior.

Medication

Yager (1985) summarized the data on pharmacological treatment of bulimia by stating that "some medications offer some promise for some patients" (p. 218). Fairburn's (1985) finding of equivocal results concerning the efficacy of antidepressants in reducing bulimic symptomatology is consistent with this view. Anticonvulsants (diphenylhydantoin) and antidepressants (monoamine oxidase inhibitors [MAOIs] and tricyclics such as imipramine) have been tried as medications for bulimia, usually with minimal results (Yager, 1985). In addition, MAOIs carry the increased risk of a need to restrict foods containing tyramine, which can be dangerous if eaten when the patient is taking an MAOI. If the bulimic binges on a tyramine-rich food (certain cheeses, red wine), an adverse, possibly severe reaction may result. Antidepressant medication may be effective in reducing depressive symptoms and therefore may have an indirect effect on bulimia by elevating mood and reducing need for binges.

■ Pica

□ CLINICAL DESCRIPTION

Diagnostic Considerations

Pica is characterized by "the persistent eating of nonnutritive substances" (American Psychiatric Association, 1994, p. 95). The two critical elements of Pica are found in the words "persistent" and "nonnutritive" in this definition. According to DSM-IV, the persistent behavior of Pica is manifest in repeated ingestion of the substance for 1 month. The nonnutritive items that are eaten typically include sand, dirt, clay (geophagia), starch (amylyphagia), ice (pagophagia), hair (trichophagia), gravel (lithophagia), grass/leaves (folio-phagia), feces (coprophagia), paint, plaster, string, cloth, paper, metal objects, glass, plastic, and cigarette butts (Feldman, 1986). Other items suggested as Pica targets may be food items (lettuce, tomato seeds, coffee grounds, insects, and butter) the child eats in inappropriately large quantities or in inappropri-ate form. The inclusion of these items as diagnostic of Pica is questionable, given their potential nutritive status.

The most common manifestation of Pica by far is in mentally retarded and autistic individuals. Prevalence rates as high as 30% in severely mentally re-tarded individuals and 60% in autistic groups have been reported (Feldman, 1986; Kinnell, 1985). Pica behavior also co-occurs with severe psychopathol-ogy such as schizophrenia. The frequency of Pica in severely retarded, autistic, and schizophrenic patients is large enough that the possibility of Pica should be assessed routinely in these individuals.

Appearance and Features

Pica is diagnosed most frequently in infants, young children, retarded indi-viduals, psychotic individuals, and, occasionally, in pregnant women. It is ex-tremely rare in normal adolescents and adults. The highest prevalence of Pica in otherwise normal children occurs between the ages of 1 and 6 years; onset age is typically 12 to 24 months (Feldman, 1986; Kinnell, 1985). Before age 1, children often do not have sufficient mobility to come in contact with a large amount of nonnutritive substances; tolerance for Pica decreases predictably with the child's entrance to school at age 6. It is important to note that most very young children will mouth or occasionally eat nonnutritive substances. However, based on parental and sensory feedback, they quickly learn what not to eat. Pica involves the repeated eating of a nonnutritive substance.

In addition to age differences in Pica prevalence, evidence also exists that the incidence of Pica is higher in Blacks than in Whites, higher in behaviorally disordered children, and higher in low SES groups (Feldman, 1986). Sex differ-ences in Pica have not been consistently documented (Marchi and Cohen, 1990). (Appearance and features of Pica are summarized in Table 7.7.)

Because of American views of Pica as unusual or pathological, individuals with Pica often hide their disorder, making the diagnosis of Pica difficult. Indi-viduals with Pica usually come to the attention of a pediatrician because of the physical consequences of the disorder. They are then referred to a psychologist or psychiatrist for treatment of the behavioral component. Parents may not be distressed by Pica behaviors, feeling that their child will "grow out of it" (ad-mittedly, this is often the case) or attending to other, more global problems such as developmental delay. Hence, parents may not report Pica behaviors in the course of a diagnostic interview, unless directly asked.

Etiology

Several factors have been hypothesized to account for Pica. First, nutritional factors such as deficiencies in vital substances (e.g., iron) have been suggested

TABLE 7.7   Appearance and Features of Pica

COMMON FEATURES

Infant/toddler age or mentally retarded
Onset before age 2 years
Ingestion of nonnutritive substances

OCCASIONAL FEATURES

Lower SES
Other behavior problems

Note: The features listed above are often seen but are not universal. Some features may be diagnostically relevant or required, while others may not be required for diagnosis. "Common" features are typical of the disorder; "occasional" features appear frequently but are not necessarily seen in a majority of cases.

as the motivators behind the compulsive eating behavior. This explanation has been buoyed by case studies of subjects whose Pica abated following nutritional supplements (Feldman, 1986). However, Pica behavior often does not change with a change of diet, and the nonnutritive substance ingested in Pica often does not contain the nutrients that the patient lacks. An alternative hypothesis suggests that Pica causes nutritional deficiency by impairing gastrointestinal functioning and substituting for nutritive foods.

A second group of factors hypothesized to account for Pica is psychological. Psychoanalytic views stress the emergence of Pica in individuals who are fixed at the oral phase of development, seeking gratification through oral stimulation. Social-learning theories suggest modeling as a factor accounting for the adoption of the unusual eating behavior. Preliminary evidence for this view comes from studies indicating that children with pets (who presumably eat nonnutritive substances at a greater rate than do humans) and with siblings diagnosed with Pica are more prone to having Pica (Feldman, 1986). Psychodynamic views focus on Pica as a response to intrapsychic and/or environmental stress; they cite as support studies indicating the higher incidence of Pica in children who are separated from a parent or who are suffering from child abuse/neglect (Prince, 1989). Other psychological explanations of Pica emphasize the maladaptive feeding relationship between mother and infant and the use of Pica as an aggressive or self-injurious behavior.

A third group of explanations of Pica stresses the role of cultural factors in its development. Earth eating (geophagia) in some societies, for example, is believed to promote physical well-being. The incidence of geophagia is believed to be higher in Africa because of cultural acceptance and cultural beliefs in some tribes (Prince, 1989). In much of U.S. society, on the other hand, Pica is associated with shame and humiliation; hence, the Pica is often hidden and is difficult to diagnose or detect.

☐   ## ASSESSMENT PATTERNS

A sample assessment battery for Pica is shown in Table 7.8.

Broad Assessment Strategies

Cognitive Assessment

Clinician-Administered—IQ Testing. An often critical component in assessing Pica is the determination of the child's level of intellectual functioning. Because children with Pica (especially older children) often are intellectually or developmentally delayed, they are routinely given tests of intellectual ability and adaptive behavior. To the extent that a child shows deviant scores on these tests, a significant component of the Pica may be assumed to be low intellectual and adaptive functioning. For children who do not show deviant scores, other arenas (e.g., family environment) must be investigated as possible contributors to the Pica (which is not to imply that these arenas will not contribute to the behavior of a retarded child as well).

Infants up to 42 months can be tested with the Bayley-II, while older children (age 2 and older) are often assessed with the SB:FE or one of the Wechsler scales (WPPSI-R for children age 3–7 or WISC-III for children age 6–17). Because many children with Pica are mentally retarded, selection of the appropriate intelligence test is crucial. In general, it is wise to use the Bayley with children under the age of 3½ years and for severely retarded children under age 6. Even though Bayley norms will not apply to those children between ages 3½ and 6, age equivalents and norms relative to 3½-year-olds can be obtained. The WPPSI-R and SB:FE have floor effects below age 6, and the SB:FE is a poor test for retarded children under the age of 3½. For children over the age of 6, the WPPSI-R, SB:FE, and, at older ages, the WISC-III should be used.

As noted, children with Pica often score in the low ranges on these intelligence tests. An intellectual assessment of children with Pica is also important to determine underlying causes of the disorder as well as the extent to which

---

TABLE 7.8   Sample Assessment Battery for Pica

COGNITIVE

Bayley-II or Wechsler Scale
Vineland Adaptive Behavior Scales

BEHAVIORAL

Child Behavior Checklist

Note: Assessment instruments are intended to supplement (not substitute for) a good clinical interview and, when possible, a structured diagnostic interview.

psychoeducational interventions (i.e., didactically teaching the child what to eat) can be used.

Clinician-Administered—Adaptive Functioning. Tests of adaptive functioning such as the Vineland Adaptive Behavior Scales (VABS) provide useful estimates of the child's ability to meet the basic demands of the environment (including self-care, independent functioning, and socially responsible behavior), and they are required for a diagnosis of mental retardation. Severely retarded children for whom Pica is one of a constellation of maladaptive and/or self-injurious behaviors do poorly on these scales. As with the intellectual assessment scales, the adaptive behavior scales indicate the extent to which the child can be expected to participate without assistance in such basic behaviors as self-care and eating.

Behavioral Assessment

Parent-Report. Because most children with Pica are young and/or retarded, self-report tests have little if any use in the assessment of Pica. Parent-report tests, on the other hand, can be quite useful. Items pertaining to Pica can be found on some major child behavior checklists (e.g., CBCL) and can be used as indicators that such behaviors should be probed in a clinical interview. As previously noted, the hypothesis of Pica should always be considered in mentally retarded, autistic, and psychotic individuals.

Family Assessment

Parent-Report. Because Pica occasionally occurs as a result of lax parental supervision or a stressful family environment (Minde, 1988), attention should be given to assessing family dynamics and major stresses in the environment. In addition to direct observation, family assessment measures such as the FES may be useful in identifying difficulties in the family that may contribute to the child's condition. Although no systematic research has investigated FES scores of families of children with Pica, high Conflict, low Cohesion, low Expressiveness, and low Independence scores would be expected in abusive families in which a child has Pica. Low FES Supportive factor scores and high FES Conflicted factor scores characterize these families as well.

Syndrome-Specific Tests

Clinician-Administered

Interviewing the parent and observing behavioral contingencies may reveal subtle reinforcement for the deviant eating behavior. For example, a child may receive attention or self-stimulation or be released from some negative situation (e.g., early termination of time-out) in response to eating nonnutritive substances. A standard behavioral assessment of Pica should involve asking the parent or other observer to relate the specific antecedents and consequences of the behavior, as well as the context in which it occurs; alternatively, the child's behavior could be directly viewed by the examiner and coded for behavioral contingencies.

☐   ## TREATMENT OPTIONS

Treatment options for Pica are outlined in Table 7.9.

Medical Evaluation/Hospitalization

As with other disorders, assessment of the total situation of the child with Pica will guide the choice of intervention. All children with Pica should be referred to a physician for evaluation if they have not already been evaluated. Based on nutritive screening studies, the physician may prescribe nutritional supplements, which may have some effect on the Pica behavior. However, as noted before, in the great majority of cases, such supplements do little to mitigate the behavior. In addition to assessing nutritive status, the physician should evalu-

TABLE 7.9   Treatment Options for Pica

MEDICAL EVALUATION/HOSPITALIZATION

Physical exam
Nutritive studies
Blood/tissue toxicity studies

BEHAVIORAL INTERVENTIONS

Differential reinforcement of other behavior
Overcorrection
Time-out following pica behavior
Restriction of access to situations in which pica behavior occurs
Aversive techniques (use with caution)

PSYCHOTHERAPY

Nutritional education
Play therapy

FAMILY INTERVENTIONS

Family therapy (typically with systemic approach focused on the role of pica in maintaining family structure)

Note: This outline of options summarizes major treatments covered in the text. Specific treatments are often combined into an intervention package. Refer to the text for additional descriptions of each treatment. This table is not necessarily an exhaustive list of all treatments available.

ate the child for other negative effects of the Pica such as parasites, lead poisoning, anemia, and bowel problems.

In cases of severe or life-threatening Pica, hospitalization may be necessary for evaluation and intervention. Interventions for hospitalized children with Pica generally mirror outpatient interventions (see the following section), although the former are delivered with greater supervision, intensity, and duration. Use of medication to treat Pica is unusual, unless Pica is associated with a condition that is commonly treated with medication.

Behavioral Interventions

Following the physical examination, psychotherapy should address the relevant psychological and social contributors to the Pica behavior. The available interventions in these areas may be curtailed by the child's age and level of functioning. For mentally retarded and very young children, behavioral interventions and changes in environment have been found to be the most effective interventions.

A common behavioral intervention is differential reinforcement of other behavior (DRO; Kalfus et al., 1987) in which the caretaker rewards the child (e.g., with verbal praise and physical affection) for every time period (e.g., 30 seconds) in which behavior other than Pica has occurred. DRO has the advantage of teaching positive substitute behaviors to children with Pica. In addition, many therapists and parents prefer the "positive" tenor of the DRO intervention. However, DRO requires almost constant attention to the child's behavior in addition to the energy to deliver reinforcement repeatedly. Many parents simply cannot sustain this effort over long time periods. In addition to DRO of specific, small time periods, tangible reinforcers such as food and stars can be used to reward long periods during which Pica does not occur.

Overcorrection is also used to treat Pica. In this intervention the caretaker reprimands the child, removes the substance from the child's mouth, cleans the child's mouth (or has the child clean the mouth, for example, by brushing teeth), and has the child clean the surroundings of nonnutritive substances. While overcorrection deals directly with the Pica behavior, it can lead to caretaker–child battles and negative affect toward the caretaker.

More aversive behavioral techniques have been suggested for mentally retarded children with intractable Pica. Time-out and physical restraint, for example, may be used to remove behavior and/or access to reinforcers. Two other aversive techniques that have been used are exposure to aromatic ammonia following Pica behavior and spray (in the face) with a water mist following Pica behavior. Water mist treatment may be the more effective and less ethically problematic of these two treatments (Rojahn, McGonigle, Curcio, & Dixon, 1987). These more severe aversive conditioning procedures should generally be used only with retarded children after other behavioral techniques have failed.

Regardless of the behavioral intervention implemented, the child's Pica behavior should be carefully operationalized and assessed at baseline and during intervention. Although all the preceding behavioral treatments have been found to be effective in curtailing Pica, a "package" involving multiple behavioral treatments may be the most effective option; aversive techniques are rarely needed or used (Paniagua, Braverman, and Capriotti, 1986).

Psychotherapy

For higher-functioning older children, nutritional education, play therapy, and traditional forms of "talking" psychotherapy are available as treatment options. The nutritional education may take the form of teaching the child about the hazards of eating nonnutritive substances and the benefits of eating healthy food. Play and psychotherapy may address life stresses, attitudes toward eating, and controlling compulsive behavior. For children facing significant environmental stresses, simple attention to behavioral contingencies may not be sufficient to reduce the Pica behavior (Minde, 1988). Play and psychotherapy can give children a chance to act or talk out their beliefs, fears, and coping strategies. With a reduction in appraised stress is expected to come a reduction in Pica behavior, which acts as a defense mechanism to deflect attention from the stress.

Family Interventions

If the assessment indicates that family dynamics are contributing to the child's problems, family therapy and/or parent behavior training may be effective. These interventions typically involve training the parents in behavioral techniques (see previous sections), encouraging closer supervision of the child, enriching the environment, and reducing stress. Psychodynamic/systems family therapy may address the role of the child's Pica in maintaining family dynamics and structure.

■ Rumination Disorder

□ CLINICAL DESCRIPTION

Diagnostic Considerations

Rumination Disorder is characterized in DSM-IV as "repeated regurgitation and rechewing of food" (American Psychiatric Association, 1994, p. 98), without an explanatory medical problem, for at least 1 month. There must have been a period of normal functioning prior to the rumination. No age criteria are specified in the diagnostic requirements, although the typical age of onset for Rumination Disorder is between 3 and 12 months. However, in mentally retarded or severely developmentally disabled children, the disorder can begin much later in life.

Appearance and Features

Appearance and features of Rumination Disorder are listed in Table 7.10. The rumination is often associated with facial expressions and behavior indicating that the child derives pleasure, satisfaction, and relaxation from the rumination activity. At any rate, the food is brought up into the mouth without any sign of nausea or disgust. The rumination behavior typically follows the adoption of a characteristic position of arching the back with the head held back and making sucking movements with the tongue. Occasionally children will stick fingers or other objects into their mouth to initiate the rumination activity. Food brought up from the stomach may be either spit out, drooled, chewed, or reswallowed. Rumintion Disorder is a serious condition, with a mortality rate as high as 25% (American Psychiatric Association, 1994).

The distinction between non-retarded infants who develop Rumination Disorder and mentally retarded children with Rumination Disorder has led some authors (e.g., Mayes et al., 1988) to speculate that there are two or more subtypes of the disorder. Mayes et al. (1988) review data suggesting that two subtypes of Rumination Disorder exist: "Psychogenic Rumination," a disorder characterized by onset during infancy and normal developmental functioning in the vast majority of cases; and "Self-Stimulating Rumination," characterized by onset at any age (including infancy and adulthood) and occurring exclusively in mentally retarded individuals. Two other types of rumination have been suggested (LaRocca and Della-Fera, 1986): an "Adult Rumination" type that occurs in otherwise normal adults and may be the remnant of untreated childhood rumination, and a "Bulimic" type that co-occurs with Bulimia Nervosa. The existence of these latter two types, however, has received little recognition and will not be considered further. The Psychogenic/Self-Stimulating subtypes of Rumination Disorder, on the other hand, have different

TABLE 7.10   Appearance and Features of Rumination Disorder

COMMON FEATURES

Reported regurgitation
Weight loss/insufficient weight gain
Onset between 3 and 12 months, unless mentally retarded
Expression of pleasure/relaxation during rumination

OCCASIONAL FEATURES

Mental retardation/developmental disability
Sticking things into the mouth (to cause regurgitation)
Disturbed parent–child relationships (Psychogenic Rumination)

Note: The features listed above are often seen but are not universal. Some features may be diagnostically relevant or required, while others may not be required for diagnosis. "Common" features are typical of the disorder; "occasional" features appear frequently but are not necessarily seen in a majority of cases.

implications for the etiology and understanding of the disorder and therefore will be described separately.

Etiology

Psychogenic Rumination Disorder

Psychogenic Rumination Disorder represents the classic presentation of Rumination Disorder, with onset between age 3 to 12 months and typical rumination symptoms. Major etiological theories of this disorder emphasize the role of the Rumination Disorder in the environment of the infant. Psychodynamic theories focus on the caretaker–infant relationship. They suggest that the caretaker interacts with the child in an immature or mechanical way, bringing little satisfaction to the child in the course of the interaction. The infant responds to this deprivation by developing difficulties with oral and feeding needs. Eventually, significant feeding problems, such as recurrent vomiting, may occur. As these problems develop, the infant may discover that it is pleasurable to rechew the regurgitated food. The regurgitation and rechewing then become a behavior pattern that provides the neglected infant with some pleasure and satisfaction, replacing that lost in the parent–infant relationship.

Research concerning psychodynamic theories of the development of Rumination Disorder has found disturbed mother–child relationships in some infants with the disorder. Familial problems such as maternal psychiatric disorder, neglect, and family stress have been cited in case studies of children with Rumination Disorder (Mayes et al., 1988). However, studies with larger samples do not always find extremely disturbed mother–child relationships (Sauvage et al., 1985), and certainly not all children with impaired mother–child relationships develop Rumination Disorder.

Learning theories of the etiology of Rumination Disorder emphasize the role of the rumination in bringing attention to the infant. The disorder emerges from one or several incidents in which the infant regurgitates food (because of some physiological reason) and receives attention from parents; eventually the regurgitation of food occurs for the purpose of attention and is reinforced by parental attention. Learning theories have received more attention in the context of treatment for Rumination Disorder as opposed to etiology.

Self-Stimulating Rumination

This second subtype of Rumination Disorder occurs exclusively in mentally retarded individuals. It is assumed to be associated with cognitive rather than social factors. Age of onset of this type of rumination is much more variable than that for Psychogenic Rumination, with a range from infancy through early adulthood (Mayes et al., 1988). In general, Self-Stimulating Rumination occurs in individuals who are considered to be severely impaired, even relative to the mentally retarded group.

Unlike Psychogenic Rumination, Self-Stimulating Rumination is generally not the result of impaired parenting or unmet emotional needs, although this may occasionally be the case. More often, this type of rumination is created and maintained by environmental contingencies or by a need for self-stimulation. The self-stimulation hypothesis is particularly relevant because these children's impaired cognitive abilities may restrict them from using many of the usual internal and external sources of gratification. Deprived of these gratification sources, they revert to the simple sensory-motor gratification of rumination.

ASSESSMENT PATTERNS

Medical Examination

Assessment of Rumination Disorder must begin with a thorough medical examination to rule out any of numerous possible physical causes, including gastrointestinal (e.g., pyloric stenosis), metabolic (e.g., electrolyte abnormalities), and central nervous system (e.g., hydrocephalus) abnormalities (Mestre, Resnick, and Berman, 1983). This assessment is often done during a period of inpatient hospitalization and reflects the potential seriousness of the rumination behavior. Rumination Disorder can be fatal, with a mortality rate of as high as 25% (American Psychiatric Association, 1994). Because of the physiological consequences of rumination, the child should be closely followed by a pediatrician even after physical causes have been ruled out.

Broad Assessment Strategies

A sample assessment battery for Rumination Disorder is shown in Table 7.11.

Cognitive Assessment

Clinician-Administered. As with Pica, it is important to determine the child's level of cognitive functioning in the evaluation of Rumination Disorder. The

TABLE 7.11 Sample Assessment Battery for Rumination Disorder

COGNITIVE

Bayley-II or Wechsler Scale
Vineland Adaptive Behavior Scales

FAMILY

Family Environment Scale
FACES-III

Note: Assessment instruments are intended to supplement (not substitute for) a good clinical interview and, when possible, a structured diagnostic interview.

major intelligence tests (Bayley-II, SB:FE, WPPSI-R, and WISC-III) are applied to Rumination Disorder in the same way they are applied to Pica. Short forms or subtests of these instruments can be used as confirmatory data when the level of cognitive functioning appears to be obvious. For example, a child who is obviously retarded may be given only the Vocabulary subtest of the WPPSI-R as confirmation of cognitive deficit—although short forms must be used with caution.

Children who score in the Low Average range or higher (IQ of 80+) are likely to have a Psychogenic Rumination Disorder, suggesting that psychosocial factors should be extensively evaluated in followup testing. On the other hand, children in the Borderline range or below (less than 80 IQ) are more likely to have a Self-Stimulating Rumination Disorder. For this latter group of children, intellectual deficit and self-stimulation must be considered in addition to any psychosocial contributors to the disorder.

Family Assessment

Parent-Report.   Assessment of the parents and caretakers of ruminating children may be of importance, particularly in the case of Psychogenic Rumination with a suspected caretaking component. Unfortunately, no data have been systematically collected on the parents of ruminating children, and one should not necessarily expect parents to appear abnormal on instruments such as the MMPI. Sauvage et al. (1985), for example, report that no specific caretaker personality type appears to be associated with rumination. However, because rumination may involve a caretaking component, administration of psychopathology and family environment tests (such as the FES) may be valuable in planning treatment. Scales reflecting caretaking and interpersonal/relationship difficulties (scales 4, 6, and 8 on the MMPI; Cohesion, Expressiveness, and Conflict on the FES) should be examined carefully for elevations.

Syndrome-Specific Tests

Clinician-Administered

Because virtually all children with Rumination Disorder are very young or mentally retarded, little can be gathered by verbal self-report methods. Thus, assessment tends to be focused on the children's interaction with their environment, and observational strategies are emphasized. Following the ruling out of physical causes, in infants the feeding interaction between mother and child should be closely observed. As noted earlier, infants with Rumination Disorder may appear tense and stiff when fed and will follow meals with a characteristic arching of the back and head that leads into rumination behavior. Distress during rumination is generally not observed. Other mother–child interactions should be observed as well, as an impaired mother–child relationship may suggest a dynamic driving the rumination behavior.

For both infants (Psychogenic Rumination) and older children (Self-Stimulating Rumination), a thorough analysis of the environment and behavioral sequence is critical to the understanding and treatment of the child. Attention should be paid to antecedent events that predict rumination, as well as to reinforcers, particularly attention, that follow the behavior. These antecedents and consequences of the rumination behavior are likely to become the major targets of a behavioral intervention.

TREATMENT OPTIONS

Treatments for Rumination Disorder (see Table 7.12) reflect the major features of the disorder. Because virtually all children with Rumination Disorder are cognitively limited by age or retardation, traditional individual psychotherapy is not an option. Furthermore, because medical causes for the behavior are ruled out in the process of formulating the diagnosis, medication is generally not used. When the disorder is treatable by medication because of a physical disorder (e.g., a digestive disorder), Rumination Disorder is not diagnosed. Hence, treatments for Rumination Disorder must rely on the child's environment and behavior to produce change. Two types of therapy that have these characteristics are family therapy and behavior therapy.

Family Interventions

Family interventions are based on the assumption that Rumination Disorder results from a disturbed family environment and/or maladaptive parent–infant

TABLE 7.12   Treatment Options for Rumination Disorder

FAMILY INTERVENTIONS

Parent–child relationship therapy
    Supervised, didactic sessions of regular, nonthreatening, supportive interactions
        between parent and child
    Education about child development and parenting techniques

Family therapy
Marital therapy

BEHAVIORAL INTERVENTIONS

Punishment techniques
Overcorrection
Extinction
Reinforcement of incompatible behaviors
Satiation techniques

Note: This outline of options summarizes major treatments covered in the text. Specific treatments are often combined into an intervention package. Refer to the text for additional descriptions of each treatment. This table is not necessarily an exhaustive list of all treatments available.

relationship. Two family therapy techniques have been recommended for children with Rumination Disorder—parent–child relationship therapy and family/marital therapy.

Parent–Child Relationship Therapy

This type of therapy emphasizes the need for the infant to have a warm, stimulating environment and a supportive relationship with the parent. Parents are provided support and guidance by the staff and are encouraged to modify their behavior to meet the infant's emotional and bonding needs. In particular, regular, nonthreatening, supportive interactions are encouraged, at first under supervision and later at home. This intervention is often combined with parenting skills training, which involves education about child development and parenting techniques, in addition to attention to the parents' adjustment problems.

Family/Marital Therapy

Traditional family or marital therapy for parents of ruminating children seeks to address familial problems that drive maladaptive and nonnurturing interactions between parents and children. The role of the child and of the rumination behavior in the family system may be assessed. Then suggestions are made to modify the system to make it incompatible with the rumination behavior. In addition, work may be performed to keep marital problems within the spousal subsystem and thus insulate the infant from parental conflicts that may result in less nurturing behavior.

Both parent–child and family-marital therapy for Rumination Disorder have been criticized for resulting in slow progress and placing high demands on staff (Starin and Fuqua, 1987; Tierney and Jackson, 1984). Furthermore, their effectiveness is not known, because studies cited in their support are either case studies or suffer from major methodological weaknesses. It must be noted, however, that the current (admittedly weak) outcome literature concerning these interventions is generally favorable. Because Rumination Disorder almost always involves some relationship issues (if not etiologically, then as a consequence of the disorder), family-based interventions are often combined with other interventions into a treatment package.

Behavioral Interventions

These interventions focus only on the rumination behavior of the child and attempt to decrease it through punishment techniques, overcorrection, extinction, differential reinforcement, satiation, and/or a combination of techniques. No assumptions are made about etiology or relationship issues.

Punishment Techniques

Despite numerous legal and ethical issues, punishment is a frequently used technique to decrease rumination behavior. All punishment techniques involve early identification of rumination behavior followed by the administration of a noxious stimulus. Generally, the noxious stimulus is administered during rumination precursor behaviors such as lip smacking, back arching, sticking a finger in the throat, or the appearance of small amounts of regurgitated food. Punishment techniques differ by the nature of the noxious stimulus.

Electric shock is frequently used in research studies of the effects of punishment on Self-Stimulating Rumination. Shock is used less often for Psychogenic Rumination. Studies of the effect of shock punishment on rumination indicate that shock is a very effective treatment, resulting in rapid decreases in rumination behaviors to near-zero levels (Starin and Fuqua, 1987). While apparently very effective, shock treatment has a number of drawbacks, including a need for the patient to be in contact with a shocking device (often resulting in limited mobility), occasional failure to maintain treatment gains at followup, and ethical concerns about the use of shock treatment. For these reasons, shock treatment is usually reserved for extreme, dangerous, or multiple-failure cases.

A second group of widely used noxious stimuli is noxious tastes such as tabasco sauce or lemon juice. In this treatment a small quantity of the liquid is squirted into the person's mouth upon the appearance of rumination behavior. Noxious tastes have been effective in reducing rumination behavior, although generally not as quickly or completely as shock treatments. One drawback to the use of these substances is the possibility that they may irritate the mouth and surrounding area. Furthermore, if the patient is surprised by the noxious taste, a risk exists of aspirating the lemon/tabasco juice and ruminated material into the lungs. Although other noxious stimuli (such as pinching) have been used to reduce rumination behavior, shock and noxious taste substances have been the most effectively and widely used.

Overcorrection

Overcorrection for rumination involves responses in which the patient restores the environment to its previous state and practices desired responses. Specifically, the patient is made to clean the vomit, change clothes, and repeatedly practice appropriate forms of vomiting (bending over a toilet many times). An oral hygiene component can be added as well, with the patient brushing teeth several times and gargling with an oral antiseptic. Overcorrection for Self-Stimulating Rumination has been shown to be effective and is often combined with other techniques. Overcorrection is usually not used for Psychogenic Rumination.

Extinction

This technique involves withholding the reinforcement that is maintaining the rumination behavior. Identification of the reinforcement is the crux of this method and usually requires careful behavioral assessment. In addition, a cooperative and controlled environment is required. Because the reinforcer most frequently identified is attention, extinction techniques often involve ignoring the behavior or withdrawal of social interaction. While extinction represents a useful adjunct to other techniques, it is likely to be only moderately effective if used alone, because it does not address the self-stimulating motivation for much rumination behavior.

Differential Reinforcement of Other Behavior (DRO)

DRO and Differential Reinforcement of Incompatible Behavior (DRI) share the characteristic of providing the patient with substitute responses for rumination. Most DRO protocols involve the provision of a reinforcer when the rumination behavior has not occurred for a specified period of time. It is assumed that this will result in an increase in nonrumination responses, which are reinforced. Although this technique is often effective in reducing rumination behavior, problems can arise with patients who exhibit such high levels of rumination that it is difficult to catch them not ruminating for any significant period of time. In addition, it is not always desirable to reward the behaviors in which the subject engages between ruminations; these intermittent behaviors may be undesirable or maladaptive themselves.

DRI involves reinforcing behaviors that do not occur concurrently with rumination and that eventually replace rumination. Behaviors selected for DRI include toy play and talking. Like DRO, DRI has been shown to be moderately effective in reducing rumination behavior.

Satiation Treatments

These treatments involve feeding the patient large quantities of food, possibly resulting in sufficient esophageal stimulation to reduce the need to ruminate (although it is not known why this technique works). Studies using satiation report some reductions in rumination, although the ability of this technique to consistently produce favorable outcomes is questionable.

Combination Treatments

These are by far the most common treatments for both Psychogenic and Self-Stimulating Rumination Disorder and involve the combination of multiple treatments previously described into a single treatment package. For example, Parent–child and family therapy can be combined with overcorrection and DRI techniques. Because of their multidimensional approach, these packages are likely to have the greatest efficacy in reducing rumination behavior.

■   Feeding Disorder of Infancy or Early Childhood

☐   CLINICAL DESCRIPTION

Diagnostic Considerations

Feeding Disorder of Infancy or Early Childhood (FDI), a new diagnosis in DSM-IV, resembles the medical diagnosis of nonorganic failure-to-thrive (NOFT).

NOFT is a disorder in which infants and toddlers fail to grow physically and to develop socially (Tibbits-Kleber and Howell, 1985; Green, 1989; Kelley and Heffer, 1990). FDI is characterized by a failure to eat adequately, stagnant weight or weight loss, and onset prior to age 6. Because the FDI diagnosis is a new one, little research has been performed on the DSM-IV-defined FDI diagnosis *per se.*

In the absence of specific FDI research, existing knowledge about related syndromes must be integrated with the small database on FDI. Two disorders that are particularly relevant in the understanding of FDI are Reactive Attachment Disorder of Infancy or Early Childhood (RAD) and NOFT. RAD is described elsewhere in this book, and the interaction between RAD and FDI is expanded upon in that section. Briefly, RAD is often associated with feeding disorders such as FDI, because the RAD disorder of parent–child interaction is often played out at mealtimes.

NOFT, which has been an established medical syndrome for some time, has the following characteristics (Tibbits-Kleber and Howell, 1985; Green, 1989; Kelley and Heffer, 1990):

1. Weight below third percentile for age
2. Normal head circumference
3. Malnourished or emaciated appearance
4. Weight loss or failure to gain weight
5. Abnormal social development (often unresponsive or unusually responsive to social stimuli)
6. Delayed achievement of physical developmental milestones
7. Not due to organic causes (Some cases of failure-to-thrive (FTT) are due to physiological problems. These cases are classified as organic failure-to-thrive and are not attributed to psychological factors.)

Appearance and Features

Because of the overlap between children with FDI and those with RAD, FDI children often have similar presentations (see Table 7.13) to those with RAD. Thus, many of the appearance and features of RAD children apply to those with FDI.

It is no surprise that FDI characteristics are most apparent during feeding. Some parents are not sensitive to their children's feeding rhythm and feed them too quickly or too slowly, provoking a negative response from the children. This response leads to parental frustration and to a worsening of the abnormal feeding interaction. Other parents misjudge infant cues of satiety, mistakenly thinking that their children are hungry when they are not. This can lead to over- or underfeeding, which causes the infant to associate feeding with unpleasantness (Fischhoff, 1989). In some cases the child has a bona fide medical problem (e.g., reflux) that creates an initial problem with the feeding

TABLE 7.13   Appearance and Features of Feeding Disorder of Infancy

COMMON FEATURES

Failure to eat adequately
No change or loss of weight
Onset prior to age 6
Conflictual or maladaptive feeding behavior

OCCASIONAL FEATURES

Failure to attach or indiscriminate attachment
Grossly abnormal/negative care (abuse, neglect, separation from caretaker)
Family conflict/family stress
Lack of stimulation from environment
Impaired social relationships
Lethargy
Resistance to being held
Lack of interest in social environment or excessive interest in strangers
Ambivalent or disinterested attitude of parent toward child
Failure of parent to respond to social cues of child
Developmental (especially language) delay
Parental psychopathology: insecurity, depression, dependence
Parental stress: marital distress, social isolation
Lack of parenting knowledge

Note: The features listed above are often seen but are not universal. Some features may be diagnostically relevant or required, while others may not be required for diagnosis. "Common" features are typical of the disorder; "occasional" features appear frequently but are not necessarily seen in a majority of cases.

interaction. However, even after this medical problem is corrected, the history of maladaptive feeding interaction remains and can affect feeding and attachment behavior.

In other cases, family characteristics interfere with the feeding. Family conflict, for example, may emerge when the family gathers to eat, creating a tense or loud atmosphere that is not conducive to relaxed infant feeding. Other children may demand much of the parents' attention, distracting them from the infant's cues and preventing parent–infant interaction during feeding. Any of these situations may lead to an association of feeding with discomfort and distress, causing the infant to be fussy and avoidant at mealtime.

The course of FDI can be serious. Malnutrition, growth deformity, and developmental delays are a significant risk. For infants in this category, immediate medical intervention is essential. Cognitive delay or impairment occurs in many FDI cases (Hufton and Oates, 1977).

Etiology

Like NOFT, FDI may be caused by maladaptive parent-child relationships in many cases. These maladaptive relationships may result in a lack of stimulation for the child, which could cause growth deficits by way of neuroendocrinological mechanisms (Tibbits-Kleber and Howell, 1985). In addition, maladaptive parent–child relationships often become manifest at mealtimes, resulting in abnormal feeding behavior by the FDI child. Parents and FDI children frequently engage in power struggles over food, and mealtime is often a time of anxiety and conflict. The resultant failure of the child to ingest adequate nutrition causes the growth deficit characteristic of FDI (Kelley and Heffer, 1990; Hathaway, 1989; Green, 1989).

In some cases, child factors such as difficult temperament or illness can begin a negative interaction that leads to increasing feeding problems. Even when these precipitating factors are later cured or mitigated (as when reflux is corrected pharmacologically or surgically), the negative parent–child feeding interaction remains.

In other cases, parental psychopathology, low intellectual functioning, or inability to change behavior leads to maladaptive parent behavior at feeding times. Some parents are unable to read their child's cues. Others express their anger or frustration at the child by "forcing" him or her to eat. Parents with borderline intellectual or social functioning may simply not know how to feed the child. Bad advice from parents, friends, or quasi-professionals may also result in poor parental feeding behavior.

ASSESSMENT PATTERNS

A sample assessment battery for FDI is shown in Table 7.14.

Broad Assessment Strategies

Cognitive Assessment

Clinician-Administered. Because of the risk of malnutrition, lack of stimulation, and developmental delay, sensory, motor, and cognitive assessment should be considered for children with FDI. Tests such as the Bayley-II may indicate intellectual and motor deficits. The Vineland Adaptive Behavior Scales (VABS)

TABLE 7.14 Sample Assessment Battery for Feeding Disorder of Infancy

COGNITIVE

Vineland Adaptive Behavior Scales

FAMILY

Family Environment Scale
Parent MMPI (when possible)

Note: Assessment instruments are intended to supplement (not substitute for) a good clinical interview and, when possible, a structured diagnostic interview.

can provide insights into the infant's development of adaptive behavior. Overall, it is important to track these children cognitively because of the long-term intellectual risks of malnutrition.

Family Assessment

Parent-Report. Formal psychological assessment may be helpful in understanding parental contributions to the dynamics underlying maladaptive FDI family interactions. Mothers of NOFT children have been the target of study, and the results of this research can be applied to FDI mothers. No assessment research exists on fathers of NOFT or FDI children.

Maternal defensiveness and denial may appear on the MMPI-2 as an elevated L (for low SES mothers) or K (for higher SES mothers). Additional elevations for distressed FDI mothers can be expected on scales 2 and 7, reflecting emotional upset and/or depression. An elevated scale 4 indicates troubles in the current family or family of origin and should be followed up by a Dyadic Adjustment Scale and FES (see following discussion). Difficulties with empathy and nurturance may be manifest in a 4-5 code type for women. Scales 3 and 0 indicate the mother's social presentation; mothers with a high 3 and low 0 are likely to be selfish and needy/dependent in relationships. They may be unable to give their infant sufficient stimulation because they themselves are in need of attention and validation from others. Mothers with a low 3 and high 0 may be reclusive, introverted, and avoidant of any social relationships. Elevations on scales 6 and 8 suggest a more pathological process underlying the FDI, with suspiciousness, anger, attributional biases, and lack of cognitive control driving the maladaptive parent–child interaction. Empirical research is needed to identify "typical" MMPI-2 patterns for FDI mothers.

Contrary to clinical observation, mothers of FDI/NOFT children tend to score in the same ranges as do other mothers on measures of self-esteem (Benoit, Zeanah, and Barton, 1989). It is possible, however, that this finding reflects defensiveness or denial on the part of the mothers. If defensiveness is suspected, the mother should be administered an MMPI-2, using the preceding interpretation guidelines.

Assessment of the marital relationships of FDI mothers often reveals troubled marriages. FDI mothers report significantly lower marital satisfaction on the Dyadic Adjustment Scale (Spanier, 1976). In one study, 36% of partners of mothers of NOFT children were substance abusers, a value three times as high as that for controls (Benoit et al., 1989). Similar problems can be expected to become apparent on the FES, with some FDI mothers elevating the Conflict and Control subscales in conjunction with deficits on Cohesion, Active-Recreational Orientation, and Intellectual-Cultural Orientation. Defensive mothers, on the other hand, may report high Cohesion and low Conflict. Assessment of the marital and family environment may suggest potential sources of difficulty and sources of intervention for these FDI families.

Because of marital/family difficulties, FDI mothers often look for support outside of their families. Measures of social support such as the Social Support

Questionnaire (Sarason et al., 1983) can provide some insight into the constellation of social support experienced by the FDI mother. FDI/NOFT mothers report less social support from within the family but more social support from nonfamily sources (Benoit et al., 1989).

Syndrome-Specific Tests

Clinician-Administered

The evaluation of the family of a child with FDI should take into account the risk of RAD and related problems. Hence, the clinician should routinely evaluate FDI children and families for RAD. If RAD is found to be present in a child with FDI, evaluation and treatment options must include methods to address the attachment disorder.

TREATMENT OPTIONS

Options for treatment of FDI are outlined in Table 7.15.

Medical Evaluation/Hospitalization

Initial treatment attention must be paid to the medical needs of the FDI child. Many of these children are undernourished or neglected and require immediate medical attention. Medical treatment typically consists of measures to increase nourishment and body weight, which may range from regular feeding to placement of a G-tube. If the infant thrives in the hospital environment after failing to gain weight at home (and this is often the case within the first 2 weeks), intervention with parents is essential prior to hospital discharge to prevent a recurrence of the weight loss and other feeding problems.

Behavioral Interventions

Behavioral treatments are typically used to address the feeding problems of FDI children. A typical behavioral plan for feeding problems begins with a careful observation and analysis of mealtime, ideally with videotape of the interaction. These observations are then used to identify problem behaviors of the child, antecedents of these problem behaviors, and consequences of these problem behaviors.

Typically, the feeding problem behaviors of the FDI child involve pushing food (or utensils) away from the mouth, refusal to open the mouth, throwing food (or utensils or dishes), spitting food out, screaming, squirming, turning the head away from food, trying to get out of the chair, or failure to attend to the food. Initial maladaptive parental responses are things such as criticism, screaming at the child, stuffing food into the child's mouth, giving the child increased attention during food refusal, distracting the child from the meal with a toy, looking exasperated, feeding the child too quickly, or not allowing the child to choose the type of food to be eaten next. Behavior techniques to

TABLE 7.15 Treatment Options for Feeding Disorder of Infancy

MEDICAL EVALUATION/HOSPITALIZATION

Evaluation for physical causes
Enforced, monitored feeding or G-tube placement

BEHAVIORAL INTERVENTIONS

Allow the child to play with the food to reduce aversion to the presence of food
Do not force the child to eat; do not use utensils to force food into the child's mouth
Do not allow "grazing"
Ignore resistant or oppositional behavior
Praise eating behaviors
Reduce distractions during mealtimes as much as possible
Allow toddlers to feed themselves
Do not allow access to desserts or snacks until the child has eaten the food required
   for the meal
Model eating behavior during the child's meals; allow the child to eat in the presence
   of other people who are eating

FAMILY INTERVENTIONS

Family therapy
Marital therapy
Parent Psychotherapy

HOME MONITORING AND PROTECTIVE REMOVAL

Temporary separation of parent and child
Home visits by social worker
"Parental holiday" while child is hospitalized

Note: This outline of options summarizes major treatments covered in the text. Specific treatments are often combined into an intervention package. Refer to the text for additional descriptions of each treatment. This table is not necessarily an exhaustive list of all treatments available.

address these problems teach the caretaker to reduce consequences that may be reinforcing to the child. Several specific guidelines are often followed:

1. For children who have an aversion to the presence or texture of food, allow them to handle and play with the food before asking them to eat it. This will increase their familiarity with food and desensitize them to its presence.

2. Encourage, but do not force, the child to eat. *Never* force a utensil into the child's mouth.

3. Do not allow the child to "graze" during the day. "Grazing" involves nibbling at snacks throughout the day so that the child is not hungry at mealtimes. In infants, this usually occurs when the infant is allowed to have a

milk-filled bottle at all times. A typical feeding day for an FDI child involves three meals and two to four snacks, which must be eaten at certain, discrete times. If the child does not eat at snack or mealtime, the food is removed until the next feeding.

4. Ignore resistant or oppositional behavior during mealtimes. This ignoring should be done by looking away and remaining silent for 5 seconds. If the child persists in the negative behavior, ignoring should continue until the behavior stops.

5. Praise eating behavior, even for small bites or attempts.

6. Unless absolutely necessary, do not use toys or other attention-getting devices to reward the child during mealtime. These often distract the child from the meal interaction.

7. Allow toddlers to take more responsibility for the feeding interaction. This can be accomplished by letting them feed themselves and choose the order in which they eat food from their plate. Finger food is often appealing to toddlers.

8. Do not place desserts or other snacks on the child's plate until the child has eaten the food required for the meal.

9. Allow the child to eat in the presence of other people who are eating, unless this is too distracting to the child.

10. Remove toys and other distractions from the feeding area.

Family Interventions

Marital and family techniques to address FDI are virtually identical to those that address RAD. Family contributions to the FDI problem (stress, conflict, need for additional knowledge) are identified using assessment techniques outlined here and are addressed in family or marital psychotherapy. The goal is to provide a positive feeding interaction for the child without stress or conflict.

Home Monitoring and Protective Removal

Some severe cases of FDI warrant more extreme interventions, such as temporary separation of parent and child, required home visits by a social worker, or even removal of the infant from the parents' care. This decision is usually made based on a combination of four factors: the severity of abuse/neglect, medical status of the child, willingness of the parent to change through psychological intervention, and psychological stability of the parent.

In some cases of hospitalized FDI children who are refusing to eat, a "parental holiday" may be suggested as a way to break the cycle of negative parent–child interactions at mealtimes. This "holiday" serves several purposes: First, it allows the parents to be away from the stressful situation of hostile interaction with their child. A reduction of stress often results in more parental patience and tolerance. Second, the holiday allows greater control of feeding interactions, which are usually conducted by a nurse, psychologist, or feeding specialist in the absence of the parent. Third, the time spent away from the parent may result in a weakening of the child's association of the parent with certain adversarial mealtime behaviors. Ideally, when the parent is returned to the mealtime interaction (typically after 1–3 days), the cycle of adversarial interaction has been broken.

Many parents are, understandably, vehemently opposed to separation from their child in the form of a parental holiday. They see that their child is "sick" enough to be in the hospital and want to be there to support and monitor the child. Also, parents are often given the message that their child's FDI is their fault; thus, they regard the holiday as a further sign of their failure and possibly as the precursor to permanent separation. Hence, the parental holiday must be suggested with tact, understanding, and support. Parents should be given a chance to express their concerns. Ideally, a trusted doctor or nurse should be present or should make the suggestion of a holiday. Finally, the rationale for the holiday should be explained, with reassurance that the parents are not being blamed for the problem.

■ References

Agras, W. (1987). *Eating disorders*. New York: Pergamon.

American Psychiatric Association. (1994). *Diagnostic and statistical manual of mental disorders* (4th ed.). Washington, DC: Author.

Benoit, D., Zeanah, C. H., and Barton, M. L. (1989). Maternal attachment disturbances in failure to thrive. *Infant Mental Health Journal, 10*, 185–202.

Bruch, H. (1978). *The golden cage: The enigma of anorexia nervosa*. Cambridge, MA: Harvard University Press.

———. (1985). Twenty years of eating disorders. In D. M. Garner and P. E. Garfinkel (Eds.), *Handbook of psychotherapy for anorexia nervosa and bulimia* (pp. 7–18). New York: Guilford Press.

Bruch, H., Czyzewski, D., and Suhr, M. (1988). *Conversations with anorexics*. New York: Basic Books.

Burns, T., and Crisp, A. H. (1984). Outcome of anorexia nervosa in males. *British Journal of Psychiatry, 145*, 319–325.

Derogatis, L. R., Lipman, R. S., Rickels, K., Uhlenhuth, E. H., and Covi, L. (1974). The Hopkins Symptom Checklist (HSCL): A self-report symptom inventory. *Behavioral Science, 19*, 1–15.

Dunn, P., and Odercin, P. (1981). Personality variables related to compulsive eating in college women. *Journal of Clinical Psychology, 37*, 43–49.

Fairburn, C. G. (1985). The management of bulimia nervosa. *Journal of Psychiatric Research, 19*, 465–472.

Fairburn, C. G., Kirk, J., O'Connor, M., and Cooper, P. J. (1986). A comparison of two psychological treatments for bulimia nervosa. *Behavior Research and Therapy, 24*, 629–643.

Feldman, M. D. (1986). Pica: Current perspectives. *Psychosomatics, 27*, 519–523.

Fischhoff, J. (1989). Reactive attachment disorder of infancy. *Treatments of psychiatric disorders: A task force report of the American Psychiatric Association* (pp. 734–746). Washington, DC: American Psychiatric Association.

Freeman, C. P. (1991). A practical guide to the treatment of bulimia nervosa. *Journal of Psychosomatic Research, 35,* 41–49.

Gallucci, N. (1987). The influence of elevated F scales on the validity of adolescent MMPI profiles. *Journal of Personality Assessment, 51,* 133–139.

Garner, D. M., and Garfinkel, P. E. (1979). The Eating Attitudes Test: An index of the symptoms of anorexia nervosa. *Psychological Medicine, 9,* 273–279.

Garner, D. M., Olmstead, M. P., and Polivy, J. (1983). Development and validation of a multidimensional eating disorder inventory for anorexia nervosa and bulimia. *International Journal of Eating Disorders, 2,* 15–34.

Golden, B. R., Buzcek, T., and Robbins, S. B. (1986). Parameters of bulimia: Examining the Compulsive Eating Scale. *Measurement and Evaluation in Counseling and Development, 19,* 84–92.

Golden, N., and Sacker, I. M. (1984). An overview of the etiology, diagnosis, and management of anorexia nervosa. *Clinical Pediatrics, 23,* 209–214.

Goldfarb, L. A., Dykens, E. M., and Gerrard, M. (1985). The Goldfarb Fear of Fat Scale. *Journal of Personality Assessment, 49,* 329–332.

Green, W. H. (1989). Reactive attachment disorder of infancy or early childhood. In H. I. Kaplan and B. J. Sadock (Eds.), *Comprehensive textbook of psychiatry* (vol. 2, 5th ed., pp. 1894–1903). Baltimore, MD: Williams & Wilkins.

Gross, J., Rosen, J. C., Leitenberg, H., and Willmuth, M. E. (1986). Validity of the Eating Attitudes Test and the Eating Disorders Inventory in bulimia nervosa. *Journal of Consulting and Clinical Psychology, 54,* 875–876.

Gunderson, J. G. (1978). *Diagnostic interview for borderlines.* Belmont, MA: McLean Hospital.

Hathaway, P. (1989). Failure to thrive: Knowledge for social workers. *Health and Social Work,* 122–126.

Hawkins, R. C., and Clement, P. E. (1980). Development and construct validation of a self-report measure of binge eating tendencies. *Addictive Behaviors, 5,* 219–226.

Healy, K., Conroy, R. M., and Walsh, N. (1985). The prevalence of binge eating and bulimia in 1063 college students. *Journal of Psychiatric Research, 19,* 161–166.

Hendren, R. L., Atkins, D. M., Sumner, C. R., and Barber, J. K. (1987). Model for the group treatment of eating disorders. *International Journal of Group Psychotherapy, 37,* 589–602.

Hufton, I. W., and Oates, K. (1977). Nonorganic failure to thrive: A long-term follow-up. *Pediatrics, 59,* 73–77.

Kalfus, G. R., Fisher-Gross, S., Marvullo, M. A., and Nau, P. A. (1987). Outpatient treatment of pica in a developmentally delayed child. *Child and Family Behavior Therapy, 9,* 49–63.

Kelley, M. L., and Heffer, R. W. (1990). Eating disorders: Food refusal and failure to thrive. In A. M. Gross and R. S. Drabman (Eds.), *Handbook of clinical behavioral pediatrics* (pp. 111–127). New York: Plenum.

Kinnell, H. G. (1985). Pica as a feature of autism. *British Journal of Psychiatry, 147,* 80–82.

Kronenberger, W. G., and Thompson, R. J., Jr. (1990). Dimensions of family functioning in families with chronically ill children: A higher order factor analysis of the Family Environment Scale. *Journal of Clinical Child Psychology, 19,* 380–388.

LaRocca, F. E. F., and Della-Fera, M. A. (1986). Rumination: Its significance in adults with bulimia nervosa. *Psychosomatics, 27,* 209–212.

Lindholm, L., and Wilson, G. T. (1988). Body image assessment in patients with bulimia nervosa and normal controls. *International Journal of Eating Disorders, 7,* 527–539.

Marchi, M., and Cohen, P. (1990). Early childhood eating behaviors and adolescent eating disorders. *Journal of the American Academy of Child and Adolescent Psychiatry, 29,* 112–117.

Mayes, S. D., Humphrey, F. J., Handford, A., and Mitchell, J. F. (1988). Rumination disorder: Differential diagnosis. *Journal of the American Academy of Child and Adolescent Psychiatry, 27,* 300–302.

Mestre, J. R., Resnick, R. J., and Berman, W. F. (1983). Behavior modification in the treatment of rumination. *Clinical Pediatrics, 83,* 488–491.

Meyer, R. G. (1993). *The clinician's handbook* (3d ed.). Boston: Allyn & Bacon.

Mickalide, A. D., and Anderson, A. E. (1985). Subgroups of anorexia nervosa and bulimia: Validity and utility. *Journal of Psychiatric Research, 19,* 121–128.

Minde, K. (1988). Behavioral abnormalities commonly seen in infancy. *Canadian Journal of Psychiatry, 33,* 741–747.

Minuchin, S. (1974). *Families and family therapy.* Cambridge, MA: Harvard University Press.

Norman, D. K., and Herzog, D. B. (1986). A 3-year outcome study of normal-weight bulimia: Assessment of psychosocial functioning and eating attitudes. *Psychiatry Research, 19,* 199–205.

Oyebode, F., Boodhoo, J. A., and Schapira, K. (1988). Anorexia nervosa in males: Clinical features and outcome. *International Journal of Eating Disorders, 7,* 121–124.

Paniagua, F. A., Braverman, C., and Capriotti, R. M. (1986). Use of a treatment package in the management of a profoundly retarded girl's pica and self-stimulation. *American Journal of Mental Deficiency, 90,* 550–557.

Phelan, P. W. (1987). Cognitive correlates of bulimia: The Bulimic Thoughts Questionnaire. *International Journal of Eating Disorders, 6,* 593–607.

Piran, N., Lerner, P., Garfinkel, P. E., Kennedy, S. H., and Brouillette, C. (1988). Personality disorders in anorexic patients. *International Journal of Eating Disorders, 7,* 589–599.

Prince, I. (1989). Pica and geophagia in cross-cultural perspective. *Transcultural Psychiatric Research Review, 26,* 167–197.

Robinson, P. H., and Holden, N. L. (1986). Bulimia nervosa in the male: A report of nine cases. *Psychological Medicine, 16,* 795–803.

Rojahn, J., McGonigle, J. J., Curcio, C., and Dixon, M. J. (1987). Suppression of pica by water mist and aromatic ammonia. *Behavioral Modification, 11,* 65–74.

Ruggiero, L., Williamson, D., Davis, C. J., Schlundt, D. G., and Carey, M. P. (1988). Forbidden Food Survey: Measure of bulimics' anticipated emotional reactions to specific foods. *Addictive Behaviors, 13,* 267–274.

Rybicki, D. J., Lepkowsky, C. M., and Arndt, S. (1989). An empirical assessment of bulimic patients using multiple measures. *Addictive Behaviors, 14,* 249–260.

Sagardoy, R. C., Ashton, A. F., Mateos, J. L. A., Perez, C. B., and Carrasco, J. S. D. (1989). *Psychotherapy and Psychosomatics, 52,* 133–139.

Sarason, I. G., Levine, H. M., Basham, R. B., and Sarason, B. R. (1983). Assessing social support: The Social Support Questionnaire. *Journal of Personality and Social Psychology, 44,* 127–139.

Sauvage, D., Leddet, I., Hameury, L., and Barthelemy, C. (1985). Infantile rumination: Diagnosis and follow-up study of twenty cases. *Journal of the American Academy of Child Psychiatry, 24,* 197–203.

Small, A., Madero, J., Gross, H., Teagno, L., Leib, J., and Ebert, M. (1981). A comparative analysis of primary anorexics and schizophrenics on the MMPI. *Journal of Clinical Psychology, 37,* 773–776

Smith, M. C., and Thelen, M. H. (1984). Development and validation of a test for bulimia. *Journal of Consulting and Clinical Psychology, 52,* 863–872.

Spanier, G. B. (1976). Measuring dyadic adjustment: New scales for assessing the quality of marriage and similar dyads. *Journal of Marriage and the Family, 38,* 15–28.

Starin, S. P., and Fuqua, R. W. (1987). Rumination and vomiting in the developmentally disabled: A critical review of the behavioral, medical, and psychiatric treatment research. *Research in Developmental Disabilities, 8,* 575–605.

Sykes, D. K., Currie, K. O., and Gross, M. (1987). The use of group therapy in the treatment of bulimia. *International Journal of Psychosomatics, 34,* 7–10.

Tibbits-Kleber, A. L., and Howell, R. J. (1985). Reactive attachment disorder of infancy (RAD). *Journal of Clinical Child Psychology, 14,* 304–310.

Tierney, D., and Jackson, H. J. (1984). Psychosocial treatments of rumination disorder: A review of the literature. *Australia and New Zealand Journal of Developmental Disabilities, 10,* 81–112.

Wagner, E., and Wagner, C. (1978). *The interpretation of psychological test data.* Springfield, IL: Thomas.

Welch, G., and Hall, A. (1989). The reliability and discriminant validity of three potential measures of bulimic behaviors. *Journal of Psychiatric Research, 23,* 125–133.

Weltzin, T. E., Starzynski, J., Santelli, R., and Kaye, W. H. (1993). Anorexia and bulimia nervosa. In R. T. Ammerman, C. G. Last, and M. Hersen (Eds.), *Handbook of prescriptive treatments for children and adolescents* (pp. 214–239). Boston: Allyn & Bacon.

Williamson, D. A., Prather, R. C., McKenzie, S. J., and Blouin, D. C. (1990). Behavioral assessment procedures can differentiate bulimia nervosa, compulsive overeater, obese, and normal subjects. *Behavioral Assessment, 12,* 239–252.

Wilson, G. T. (1987). Assessing treatment outcome in bulimia nervosa: A methodological note. *International Journal of Eating Disorders, 6,* 339–348.

Wilson, G. T., and Smith, D. (1989). Assessment of bulimia nervosa: An evaluation of the Eating Disorders Examination. *International Journal of Eating Disorders, 8,* 173–179.

Yager, J. (1985). The outpatient treatment of bulimia. *Bulletin of the Meninger Clinic, 49,* 203–226.

CHAPTER 8

Somatoform Disorders

■   **Somatoform Disorders**

☐   CLINICAL DESCRIPTION

Diagnostic Considerations and Features

Children frequently complain of aches, pains, and various other physical symptoms that cannot be definitively linked to a physical condition. These functional somatic complaints occur in as many as 20% of children who present to pediatric clinics with physical symptoms (Walker, McLaughlin, and Greene, 1988; Robinson, Greene, and Walker, 1988). When an organic cause is not found for the symptoms, the diagnostic focus often moves to the psychological realm, with a search for stressors or behavior problems that might explain the condition. The vast majority of functional somatic complaints disappear spontaneously or are "cured" with a general antibiotic or other placebo drug. Some functional somatic complaints, however, persist and develop into significant psychological problems. These psychological disorders of persistent, pervasive physical complaints are categorized as "somatoform disorders."

Somatoform disorders are characterized by physical symptoms suggesting an illness or other organic problem when careful physical examination reveals no physical cause for the symptoms. In the absence of a physical cause, psychological factors are assumed to be producing the symptomatology. However, the presence of a known stressor (or other psychological factor) is *required* only for the diagnosis of Conversion Disorder. Pain Disorder requires that psychological factors have an important role, but these factors do not need to be specified.

Children will sometimes intentionally fake medical symptoms in order to adopt the sick role, to gain a reward (such as attention), or to avoid some unpleasant event (such as school). When symptoms are intentionally produced, a somatoform disorder is not diagnosed. The somatoform diagnosis is reserved only for symptoms that are unintentional or not consciously produced.

The intentional production of symptoms, while not a somatoform disorder *per se*, can have deleterious psychosocial and physical consequences. Thus, such behavior should be carefully assessed and followed. Intentionally produced physical symptoms may be an attempted escape from a dangerous environment (e.g., abuse) or may signal a state of desperation or upset in the child. For these reasons a careful psychological and social evaluation of the child and the child's environment is warranted. Often, it is found that the parents are subtly reinforcing the child's illness behavior, inducing its maintenance; the prime reinforcers in this case are attention and nurturance.

Feigning illness to avoid school is also common in children. Factors such as lack of structure, inconsistent parenting, inappropriate academic expectations within the family, and child psychological problems should be investigated when such absences are frequent and regular. Treatment for illness-related school phobic behavior begins by addressing the problems parents may have in sending children to school. This is followed by insistence that the children attend school regardless of their reported physical condition. If the children claim that their illness is debilitating, they may remain in the nurse's office *at school*. In cases when abuse/neglect is suspected as the cause of the faking, appropriate social services should be called to investigate and modify the children's environment.

If a reward for illness behavior can clearly be identified, the disorder falls under the category of Malingering. Occasionally, however, children will intentionally produce symptoms for no apparent reinforcement. Such voluntary adoption of a sick role without an associated reward is categorized as Factitious Disorder. Children with Factitious Disorder seem to have a self-concept consistent with the sick role, and they will produce symptoms to place themselves in this role. Often such children have recently had an illness or have observed someone with an illness, and this past experience with illness may be responsible for the motivation and inclination to intentionally produce symptoms.

Regardless of whether symptoms are believed to be intentionally or unintentionally produced, significant physical complaints or symptoms should be taken very seriously. Most children with somatoform disorders have had numerous medical tests to rule out plausible physical causes. It is extremely important that these tests be conducted carefully and exhaustively. Studies have found that as many as 27–46% of children diagnosed with one type of somatoform disorder (Conversion Disorder) actually had a physical disease (Lehmkuhl, Blanz, Lehmkuhl et al., 1989). Although the accuracy of somatoform disorder diagnosis appears to be increasing (American Psychiatric Association, 1994), caution must still be exercised with regard to the rule-out of physical causes. In the unlikely event that a child presents with symptoms of a somatoform disorder *without* a prior physical examination, a physical examination should be ordered before any psychological intervention.

Although careful medical examination is necessary prior to making a diagnosis of a somatoform disorder, the exam may have the unfortunate effect of legitimizing the physical nature of the symptoms or of terrifying the child into thinking that he or she has a major illness. Because the symptoms are not intentionally produced and seem to have been taken very seriously by the medical establishment, most children and their parents are extremely reluctant to accept the diagnosis of a somatoform disorder. They assume that physical monitoring and physical treatment will stop, so if any undiagnosed physical illness is actually present, it will develop unchecked. Furthermore, most children and parents have difficulty understanding the difference between a somatoform disorder and a Factitious/Malingering disorder. Hence, a statement that the symptoms have no physical cause is often interpreted as an accusation that the child is intentionally producing the symptoms. Such a perceived accusation may cause defensiveness in both parent and child, further complicating psychological assessment and treatment. For these reasons, somatoform disorders should be diagnosed and explained by a team of experienced professionals. (Appearance and features of somatoform disorders are listed in Table 8.1.)

Etiology

Some theorists hypothesize that somatoform disorders develop as coping mechanisms against intrapsychic or environmental stress. Psychodynamic theories cite the role of somatization defenses in "converting" psychological con-

TABLE 8.1   Appearance and Features of Somatoform Disorders

COMMON FEATURES

Physical symptoms without physical basis
Not intentional
Recent stressor
Defensiveness about psychological explanations for symptom
Age range 6 and older
Failure of lab tests to support physical complaints
Presence of an illness model
Secondary gain
Past history of somatic complaints
Focus on somatic sensations ("body scanning")
Family dysfunction
Family focus on illness issues

OCCASIONAL FEATURES

School rejection/teasing
Covert/subtle parental support for symptom
La belle indifférence
Presentation with neurological complaint

Note: The features listed above are often seen but are not universal. Some features may be diagnostically relevant or required, while others may not be required for diagnosis. "Common" features are typical of the disorder; "occasional" features appear frequently but are not necessarily seen in a majority of cases.

flict into physical symptoms. Instead of experiencing uncomfortable thoughts and feelings, individuals develop physical symptoms that occupy their attention. Unhappiness over parents' divorce, for example, becomes transformed into an inability to walk. The inability to walk serves as an outlet for the conflict over experiencing parental divorce.

The defense mechanism involved in this psychodynamic principle is *somatization*. Somatization is a primitive coping mechanism that occurs in cases of overwhelming stress and insufficient or maladaptive coping resources. In cases of moderate stress or adequate resources, children tend to engage in more adaptive coping, such as problem solving, seeking social support, or distraction. However, high stress and inadequate resources can lead to a feeling of being trapped and out of control. At these times, more adaptive coping fails to work, and children are left with primitive, defensive coping responses such as somatization.

Other theorists have emphasized learning paradigms to explain somatoform disorders. Social learning theories, for example, stress the importance of imitation in the development of a somatoform disorder. Children who observe their parents or siblings having gastric pains, for example, may scan their own abdominal sensations for anything resembling a pain. Upon finding a possible pain sensation, they may then model the behavior of the other family member. Some evidence exists for this theoretical view: Children with conversion symptoms are often found to have a family member with a similar symptom (Volkmar, Poll, and Lewis, 1984; Lehmkuhl et al., 1988). In addition, somatoform disorders sometimes mimic previous physical disorders that a child no longer has.

Classical conditioning paradigms may also explain the emergence of a somatoform disorder. According to these paradigms, a child experiences a stressful event that results in normal, stress-related physiological changes that produce temporary physical discomfort (Selye, 1956). Over time, sensations of physical discomfort become associated with stress. Hence, whenever stress occurs, the child reports significant physical discomfort, even if the actual physical changes are minimal or absent. More severe or prolonged stresses create greater feelings of discomfort such that traumatic or chronic stress could produce a somatoform disorder.

Finally, family theorists cite the role of the somatoform disorder in the family system. Some families, for example, structure their interactions around somatic topics. Children raised in these environments "scan" their bodies for problems, which then become the topic of family attention. Sufficient attention to a problem can make it the focus of attention, to the point that the child believes that she is sick.

Other families use the somatic symptoms of the child as an excuse to avoid difficult issues, particularly conflict. These families invest all of their energy into concern over the "sick" child, leaving no energy or time for family conflict. Furthermore, the presence of a sick child can allow the family to adopt the role of a "family of an ill youngster." This role can be a source of family activity and can distract the family from other issues that may lead to conflict. In particular, the integrity of the marital subsystem may be violated by the sick child, leaving the parents no time for spousal activities such as romance, fun, and sex.

Over all, family theories postulate that the child's illness performs a role in the family system. Consequently, the family is unlikely to give up this role easily, since doing so would require systemic change. The etiological goal of the clinician is to identify the role of the symptom in the family and to identify the effect of removing this role.

Six types of somatoform disorders are recognized in DSM-IV: Conversion Disorder, Pain Disorder, Somatization Disorder, Hypochondriasis, Body Dysmorphic Disorder, and Undifferentiated Somatoform Disorder. Conversion Disorder is the most common somatoform disorder in children and adolescents, followed by Pain Disorder. These two disorders will be covered in more detail.

Conversion Disorder

CLINICAL DESCRIPTION

Diagnostic Considerations

Conversion Disorder is the most common and most commonly studied somatoform disorder in children, although its exact incidence in the childhood population is unknown (Regan and Regan, 1989). According to DSM-IV, the hallmark of Conversion Disorder is "one or more symptoms or deficits affecting voluntary motor or sensory function that suggest a neurological or other general medical condition" (American Psychiatric Association, 1994, p. 457), in the absence of sufficient physiological cause. Usually conversion symptoms are manifest by a loss of sensory or motor functioning. The conversion symptoms must affect the person's daily functioning or must cause distress. In addition, known psychological stressors must precede the development or exacerbation of the conversion symptoms. It is important to note that when symptoms are limited to pain, Conversion Disorder is *not* diagnosed. These latter conditions typically are diagnosed in the Pain Disorder or Somatoform Disorder NOS category.

Conversion Disorder is extremely rare before age 6 and may peak at age 11–13 in childhood (Grattan-Smith, Fairley, and Procopis, 1988). Estimates of adult prevalence are in the 1–3% range (American Psychiatric Association, 1994). The disorder may be more common in girls (Lehmkuhl et al., 1989), although the data for this should be considered preliminary. Most Conversion Disorders present as apparent neurological abnormalities. Possible seizures and walking/gait problems seem to be most common, although limb paralysis and sensory-loss symptoms (usually visual or auditory disturbances) are seen as well.

Appearance and Features

Siegel and Barthel (1986) found eight features to occur with some regularity in Conversion Disorder:

1. Findings inconsistent with physical and laboratory evaluation (found in all cases and required for a Conversion Disorder diagnosis)
2. Identifiable stress (89% of cases)
3. Presence of a model for the conversion symptoms (66% of cases)
4. Family dysfunction (56% of cases)
5. Family communication that avoids resolving stress and conflict by focusing on illness issues (44% of cases)
6. Secondary gain for the symptom (41% of cases)
7. Past history of somatic complaints (33% of cases)
8. La belle indifférence (30% of cases)

Interestingly, Siegel and Barthel (1986) were unable to identify any cases in which the symptom was symbolically related to the stressor or conflict that caused it. Major and associated features of Conversion Disorder are described in detail in the following discussion.

Stress

Because Conversion Disorder is assumed to result from some psychosocial stressor, several studies have investigated the nature of the stressors underlying it. Most stressors that have been associated with Conversion Disorder appear to fall into two categories: school/peer and family (Leslie, 1988). Examples of these stressors are separation from parent, academic failure, peer relationship problems, chronic parental discord, and parental unemployment (Lehmkuhl et al., 1989; Volkmar et al., 1984).

Despite the hypothesis that Conversion Disorders arise in order to protect the individual from a catastrophic internal conflict or stress, stressors preceding the development of Conversion Disorder are not always catastrophic or traumatic. In fact, children and adolescents with Conversion Disorder show no greater prevalence or severity of stressors than do children with other DSM-IV disorders (Lehmkuhl et al., 1989). However, as many as 90% of children with a Conversion Disorder have some family, peer, or school stress (Siegel and Barthel, 1986). Relatively common school stressors such as teasing by peers and poor academic performance are often cited as responsible for the development of a Conversion Disorder. Because problems with peers or academic achievement may occur in as many as 50% of cases of Conversion Disorder (Thomson and Sills, 1988; Leslie, 1988), the school should be routinely considered as a potential source of the stress underlying the disorder. In addition, because of the possibility of a stressful family situation, the family environment should routinely be assessed. Common stresses seen in the families of children with Conversion Disorder are parental discord, parental divorce (Volkmar et al., 1984), sexual abuse (Leslie, 1988; Volkmar et al., 1984), and psychiatric impairment of a parent (Lehmkuhl et al., 1989).

Family Issues

The role of some families in cases of Conversion Disorder is so strong that they are referred to as "conversion families" (Seltzer, 1985). Although not all families of children with Conversion Disorder create the children's problem, family issues must be attended to in the understanding and treatment of a Conversion Disorder. Family issues can cause or maintain Conversion Disorder in several ways: First, the family may be the source of the precipitating stressor, such as family conflict, loss of a family member, abuse, or neglect. Second, the illness behavior may serve an important role in organizing family life. Third, the illness of a family member may provide a model for the child's Conversion Disorder.

Several types of family units have been described as "typical" of families of children with Conversion Disorders (Grattan-Smith et al., 1988; Seltzer, 1985). The first type, "anxious families," has a preoccupation with disease and disease processes. Communication between family members often turns to topics of illness, pain, and even death. In many cases, these families have had unfortunate medical histories marked with serious illnesses in relatives and friends. In other cases, serious illness is not seen in family and friends, but the family concerns itself excessively with trivial and everyday physical symptoms. In the extreme, this illness-interaction process becomes a shared experience of family members, fostering bonding and communication at the price of excessive somatic focus. The tacit communication between members of these families is that serious physical disorders are imminent and disabling. Combined with high levels of stress and hyperattention to bodily symptoms, this attitude could lead to a mistaken belief that some bodily function has been lost.

A second type of family, the "chaotic family," is characterized by a lack of organization, rules, and responsibilities (Seltzer, 1985). Children in these families fear being lost in the chaos. Therefore, they are highly reinforced by any event that brings attention or focuses the family. Their somatic complaints bind the family's attention in a single area, bringing some organization to family life. In addition, because it is more difficult to garner social support in a chaotic environment, these children are less able to depend on family members at times of stress. This lack of social support, normally a vital coping resource, makes the children more likely to use primitive coping behaviors such as somatization.

A third type of family, the "compensating family," is characterized by a desire to appear normal or ideal. This desire is brought on by a fear that the family is vulnerable to conflict, lack of support, and even disintegration (Seltzer, 1985). Such families appear at first to be mutually supportive, normal, and well adapted; they will go to great lengths to convince the medical team that this is the case. Further investigation, however, reveals defensiveness about family problems and rigid resistance to any type of change. The rigid controls in these families often take the form of authoritarian parenting or strict moral values. Dissent from family unity is not tolerated, which hampers the children's development of feelings of independence. Transitions characteristic of independence (beginning school, changing schools, entering peer groups, puberty, adolescent issues) are particularly problematic and may be the precipitating incident for the development of the Conversion Disorder.

Compensating families acknowledge their feelings, but they address or deflect attention from strong feelings with the use of somatic complaints. Conflict is particularly poorly managed. The family usually denies conflict, avoiding potentially conflictual topics by focusing on the "sick" child. Because they have little experience in managing conflict, children who are raised in Compensating Families have considerable difficulty managing conflict in social situations. Their underdeveloped conflict resolution skills place them at a particular disadvantage in the school situation, in which conflict arises regularly. Hence, they are vulnerable to overreaction to conflictual events or to conflict avoidance and passivity; either situation may lead to social rejection and further use of somatization defenses.

Presence of an Illness Model

Another common characteristic of children with a Conversion Disorder is the presence of an illness model. According to social learning theory, people are more likely to engage in a behavior if they observe another person receiving reinforcement for the behavior. In addition, people will imitate models whom they admire or who are powerful or competent. Hence, children who observe siblings, parents, or friends engaging in actual illness behavior may be more prone to exhibit this behavior themselves. However, if a child's imitation of illness behavior is intentional or conscious, it is not diagnosed as Conversion Disorder but falls in the Factitious Disorder or Malingering category.

Studies report that illness models are found in 44–66% of Conversion Disorder cases (Thomson and Sills, 1988; Siegel and Barthel, 1986; Steinhausen et al., 1989; Grattan-Smith et al., 1988). Furthermore, evidence exists that children with Conversion Disorder are more likely to have a physically ill parent than are children with other psychiatric disorders (Steinhausen et al., 1989). Children tend to develop illness symptoms very similar to those of the illness model, with occasional variations (Volkmar et al., 1984).

Of course, only a very small proportion of children with an illness model develop a Conversion Disorder. It appears that the presence of an illness model acts in conjunction with other factors in the development of a Conversion Disorder.

La Belle Indifférence

"La belle indifférence" is a condition in which a person appears emotionally unconcerned with the loss of function in a Conversion Disorder. Hypothetically, la belle indifférence results from a denial of the stress the patient is managing by using somatization defenses. This denial of problems manifests itself in a blasé attitude toward one's physical condition and life situation. Patients with la belle indifférence may appear calm, accepting, and even happy in the face of overwhelming functional impairments. This incongruity gives la belle indifférence a dramatic appearance.

Despite widespread case studies and theoretical speculation, la belle indifférence appears to be the exception rather than the rule in cases of somatoform disorder in children (Regan and Regan, 1989), occurring in only 19–30% of cases (Grattan-Smith et al., 1989; Siegel and Barthel, 1986), although one study reports la belle indifférence in 50% of their somatoform disorder sample (Volkmar et al., 1984). In fact, rather than being unconcerned with their disorder, evidence exists that many children with somatoform disorder are distressed by their condition and suffer deficits in self-esteem and general happiness (Robinson et al., 1988; Kronenberger, Laite, and LaClave, in press). Furthermore, children with actual physical disease may display an emotional unconcern as a defense mechanism. Hence, the presence of la belle indifférence does not always imply functional impairment. It is probably best thought of as characteristic of rigid denial defenses exhibited by children with Conversion Disorder or actual physical illness.

Secondary Gain

The issue of secondary gain can be a valuable source of diagnostic data or a source of error in the diagnosis of Conversion Disorder. First, secondary gain does *not* necessarily rule out the diagnosis of Conversion Disorder. Clinicians sometimes assume that secondary gain implies that the symptoms are intentional. Although intentional symptoms would force the rule-out of Conversion Disorder in favor of Factitious Disorder or Malingering, secondary gain does not always imply intentionally produced symptoms. In the case of true Conversion Disorder with secondary gain, the child is either consciously unaware of the secondary gain or acknowledges secondary gain but denies any connection between the gain and the symptoms.

Secondary gain is common in Conversion Disorder, occurring in as many as 40–50% of cases (Siegel and Barthel, 1986). Therefore, it should routinely be assessed in cases of suspected Conversion Disorder. Because the child is often not aware of the existence or significance of secondary gain, the clinician must take the lead in the search for possible sources of gain. In many cases, secondary gain is related to avoidance of a stressful situation such as peer conflict, teasing at school, growing up, and family conflict. In other cases the secondary gain comes from increased attention or more positive social interactions.

It is not always clear whether secondary gain has an etiological or maintaining role in Conversion Disorder. Regardless of the role of the gain, the child will be more reluctant to give up the conversion symptom as long as the gain persists. Hence, identification of the source of secondary gain suggests one facet of intervention to remove the conversion symptoms: Removal of secondary gain for the symptom heightens the chances for therapeutic success.

Two points are important to remember when secondary gain is identified: First, the presence of secondary gain does not guarantee the presence of a Conversion Disorder. Many children with bona fide physical diseases receive considerable secondary gain in the form of attention, gifts, and special treatment. This does not imply that their disease is any less real. Second, removal of the secondary gain is not necessarily sufficient to cause removal of the conversion symptom. If children believe that they have loss of function, the disorder may persist even in the face of uncomfortable conditions.

Etiology

Etiological factors in the development of Conversion Disorder mirror those for somatoform disorders in general. However, the diagnostic stipulation of a causal stress underscores the assumption that the Conversion Disorder is at least in part the result of a stressful situation.

☐ ASSESSMENT PATTERNS

A sample assessment battery for Conversion Disorder is shown in Table 8.2.

Broad Assessment Strategies

Cognitive Assessment

Clinician-Administered. Although little research exists concerning the intelligence of children with Conversion Disorder, some studies (i.e., Brooksbank, 1984) report that as a group they have at least average intelligence. The diagnostic utility of an intelligence test for Conversion Disorder is questionable, although it may provide some insight into the nature of school stressors. If academic pressures are suspected as stressors, an individual intelligence (WISC-III) and achievement (WJ-R) test should be administered. If achievement is commensurate with intelligence and grade placement, academic pressures are less likely to be playing a role in the etiology of the disorder. It is possible, however, that the child is doing fine in school but has a distorted view of his or her performance. If intelligence is low and achievement is well below grade placement, the child may be in a class that is too advanced and may be experi-

TABLE 8.2   Sample Assessment Battery for Conversion Disorder

PSYCHOLOGICAL

MMPI/MMPI-A
Piers-Harris Self-Concept Scale
Children's Depression Inventory

FAMILY

Family Environment Scale
FACES-III

Note: Assessment instruments are intended to supplement (not substitute for) a good clinical interview and, when possible, a structured diagnostic interview.

encing academic failure as a stressor; in this case, academic stressors should be further probed.

Psychological Assessment

Clinician-Administered. Because somatoform disorders are not intentionally produced, face-valid data-gathering methods are of limited use in discovering underlying psychological factors. Furthermore, the children's responses to interview questions often are distorted by their defenses and lack of insight. Hence, the MMPI and MMPI-A are particularly valuable tools in the assessment of somatoform disorders. The MMPI provides information on personality dynamics and defenses that may not be understood or readily admitted by the child.

In the case of the MMPI, a "conversion *V*" (scales 1 and 3 elevated with scale 2 relatively low) would be expected from an adolescent with a Conversion Disorder. Such an MMPI profile is typical of a somatically focused child who lacks insight and is likely to deny psychological problems. If scales 2 and 7 are very low (less than 40–45 T-score), la belle indifférence is likely to be present. Elevations on scales 6 and 8 should be carefully examined, because they may be indicative of distorted thought processes underlying or contributing to the somatization problem. On the validity scales, elevations on L or K may show some defensiveness, denial, or lack of insight into psychological processes. It is important to note that many adults and adolescents with actual physical problems will show the conversion *V* profile, because of the many somatic items on scales 1 and 3. There is no foolproof way to distinguish patients with actual physical illness from those with Conversion Disorder based on MMPI profiles alone. However, when scales 1 and 3 exceed T-scores of 80, the likelihood of a diagnosis of Conversion or other somatoform disorder becomes much greater.

Child-Report. In addition to the MMPI, several self-report scales may assist in the understanding of the adolescent with a Conversion Disorder. Low scores on the Offer Self-Image Questionnaire (OSIQ; Garrick, Ostrov, and Offer, 1988), a 130-item self-report scale of adolescent self-image, have been found to be related to somatic symptomatology. Of the twelve OSIQ scales, Impulse Control, Emotional Tone, Body and Self-Image, Social Relations, Morals, Family Relations, Mastery of the External World, Vocational Educational Goals, Psychopathology, and Superior Adjustment were related to somatic symptoms in boys. Lower self-image scores on all of these scales were related to more somatic symptoms. Only Impulse Control, Emotional Tone, Body and Self-Image, and Psychopathology were related to somatic symptoms in girls. For both sexes, Emotional Tone was most highly related to somatic symptoms, indicating that children who reported more emotional distress had more somatic symptoms. Hence, children with Conversion Disorder would be expected to have low scores on the OSIQ and particularly on the Emotional Tone scale (Garrick et al., 1988).

Two other scales, the Self-Esteem Inventory (a six-item measure of general self-esteem) and the Index of Peer Social Comparison (a five-item measure of self-concept in popularity, school performance, and athletic ability) have been found to be related to functional somatic complaints in adolescents (Robinson et al., 1988). Adolescents with functional somatic complaints reported lower general and peer-social self-esteem on these measures, as compared to adolescents without a physical illness. Hence, adolescents with Conversion Disorder as a group score lower than do healthy adolescents on self-image and self-esteem scales.

Less is known about the self-reports of latency age children with Conversion Disorder. Only one study (Kronenberger et al., in press) has used self-report scales with preadolescent children diagnosed with a somatoform disorder (primarily Conversion Disorder). On the Children's Depression Inventory (Kovacs, 1992) and the Piers-Harris Self-Concept Scale (Piers, 1984), children with somatoform disorder scored lower on Behavioral Self-Esteem than did physically ill children with no psychiatric diagnosis. On the other hand, children with somatoform disorder scored higher on Behavioral Self-Esteem than did physically ill children with a diagnosis of depression. However, most other self-report scales did not differentiate somatoform and normal children. Children with somatoform disorder averaged a CDI total score of 7, while depressed children averaged a CDI score of nearly 10, and no diagnosis children averaged a CDI score of only 5. On the Piers-Harris, children with somatoform disorders averaged T-scores in the 54–58 range, while depressed children scored largely in the 48–52 range and no diagnosis children scored in the 58–63 range.

Based on their findings, Kronenberger et al. (in press) draw several conclusions about the self-report of children with somatoform disorders: First, children with somatoform disorder show a wide range of self-esteem scores on the Piers-Harris; some have a belle indifférence level of very high esteem, while some are clearly in distress with low self-esteem. Over all, somatoform disorder children show slightly lower self-esteem than do other children with a physical illness. Second, children with somatoform disorders rarely appear depressed on the CDI, although their CDI scores may be slightly higher on average than those of children with no psychiatric diagnosis. Over all, the value of the CDI and Piers-Harris is in the assessment of co-occurring depression, belle indifférence, or distress in the child with Conversion Disorder.

Family Assessment

Clinician-Administered. Because of the potential role of the family in the development and maintenance of Conversion Disorder, careful assessment of the family environment is warranted. Much can be learned by simply observing the interactions of the family and determining the extent to which the family can be classified into one of the "conversion family" types. Anxious-somatic families, for example, will appear to be fixated on medical topics, death, and illness. They may also impress the interviewer with their knowledge of medical topics, relating an extensive family history of illness. Chaotic families, on the other hand, appear confusing almost from the start, with multiple care-takers, hard-to-reach parents, and lack of family information impeding the assessment process. Compensating families openly or passively resist the Conversion Disorder diagnosis and demonstrate hypercompetence in all areas except expressed emotion.

Child-Report/Parent-Report. Family observations can be supplemented by results from several self-report family assessment measures. On the FACES-III the conversion family would be expected to score extremely high or extremely low on both Cohesion and Adaptability subscales. Extremely high Cohesion scores are characteristic of an enmeshed family that does not allow for individual development or expression of emotion. Adolescents in enmeshed families may adopt Conversion Disorders to deflect attention from family problems or to resist the increased independence of growing up. Extremely low Cohesion scores are characteristic of a disengaged family, in which family members share little mutual concern or emotional bonding. The Conversion Disorder in this case may attract attention or bring the family together over a single issue. Extremely high Adaptability scores indicate a chaotic family, in which rules and responsibilities change constantly and are routinely unclear. The function of the Conversion Disorder in the chaotic family may be to focus the attention of the family and to impose some structure on the chaos. Finally, extremely low Adaptability scores are characteristic of rigid families who control the behavior of members with extensive, unyielding rules. The Conversion Disorder in this type of family may be a sign of rebellion.

On the FES the conversion family would be expected to score low on the Expressiveness and Conflict subscales, reflecting the family's discomfort with psychological insight and expressed emotion. Scores on the Cohesion subscale may be high or low, depending on whether the family is enmeshed or disengaged, respectively. Likewise, scores on the Organization and Control subscales may be high or low, depending on the level of rigidity or chaos in the family system. In some conversion families, Supportive and Conflicted factor scores are low, showing the low level of expressed negative emotion but also the low level of overall support for individual members of the family. On the other hand, the Supportive factor may be artificially high in compensating families, reflecting a denial of problems and claim of perfection. In the case of both the FACES-III and the FES, no typical family profile exists because there are numerous types of conversion families. The value of family assessment lies in the identification of the type of conversion family for aid in treatment planning.

TREATMENT OPTIONS

Medical Evaluation/Hospitalization

Children with Conversion Disorder often come to the attention of psychological personnel when they are in a pediatric hospital. The children have generally been hospitalized under the care of a medical service (often neurology or pulmonology), which has run numerous inconclusive or negative tests. Once the medical service arrives at the conclusion that the children's problems are partly or wholly the result of psychological factors, they consult the psychologist, psychiatrist, or social worker for a psychological evaluation. If the evaluation is consistent with the Conversion Disorder diagnosis, therapy often begins at the hospital. Children whose symptoms partially or completely remit prior to discharge are often referred for followup outpatient therapy; children with more severe or persistent symptomatology may need to be referred for intensive inpatient psychiatric treatment (Kronenberger et al., 1991). Some evidence exists that children with somatoform disorders are referred for inpatient psychiatric treatment at least as often as those with depressive disorders (Kronenberger et al., 1991).

Numerous treatments have been suggested for Conversion Disorder, and no one preferred treatment exists. Regan and Regan (1989) list as possible treatments "psychotherapy, . . . reassurance, suggestion, placebos, hypnosis, tranquilizers, biofeedback, reward management, relaxation techniques, behavior modification, faradic stimulation, . . . and family therapy" (p. 351).

Psychotherapy

Psychotherapeutic techniques use insight, teaching, and the therapeutic relationship to assist children in changing their physical and psychological condition. These techniques are one of the most widely used approaches to managing Conversion Disorder, although their efficacy when used alone is suspect. Outpatient psychotherapy is recommended for 30–70% of children with Conversion Disorder (Kronenberger et al., 1991; Kotsopoulos and Snow, 1986; Goodyer and Mitchell, 1989), usually as part of a treatment package. Some tentative evidence exists that outpatient psychotherapy alone may be less effective than inpatient treatment (Kotsopoulos and Snow, 1986). Furthermore, families often fail to follow through on the recommendation to enter psychotherapy.

Play Therapy

Perhaps the most well-known and historically significant psychotherapeutic technique for Conversion Disorder in adults is psychoanalysis. Traditional psychoanalysis, however, is generally not feasible with children because of their limited insight, limited personal history, and limited verbal abilities. Psychodynamic play therapy, on the other hand, allows children to express and process internal conflicts in a supportive and secure atmosphere. Young children respond particularly well to play therapy techniques because of their nonthreatening and nonconfrontative quality. Confrontational techniques often fail with children, who respond to them with intensified illness behavior and denial.

Play therapy for children with Conversion Disorder should be structured only in terms of the available play items, which should focus on factors that are hypothesized to maintain the Conversion Disorder. Within these parameters, however, play should be as nondirective as possible to allow the child to feel secure in displaying stresses and concerns in a nonjudgmental atmosphere. Toys which should be available are a play medical kit (with stethoscope, syringes, tubing, bandages, etc.), house and family figures, peer figures, and puppets. Children who have difficulty beginning play with the therapist are usually easily engaged in the care of a "sick" puppet or "family" member. Themes of attention for symptoms, family conflict, peer conflict, and rejection should be carefully monitored and eventually interpreted for the children. Theoretically, it is believed that the children relieve some of the tension from inner conflicts and stresses through the play, removing the underlying cause of the conversion symptom.

Psychodynamic Psychotherapy

For older children and adolescents, psychotherapeutic discussion of stresses involving school, peers, and family can be helpful. It is not unusual for children to resist discussion of stressful issues, especially if they see psychotherapy as an acknowledgment that their problem is psychological. Once a therapeutic bond of trust is formed, however, children with Conversion Disorder often seem relieved to have someone with whom to discuss their problems. Progress in this case is made with a combination of support, acceptance, emotional working-through of inner conflicts, and active problem solving to reduce external stress. In the case of peer stress, role playing and social skills training are two techniques that can increase perceptions of efficacy and decrease perceptions of threat.

Hypnotic Techniques

Hypnotic states, relaxed states, and suggestion are commonly used for the management of Conversion Disorders. Because Conversion Disorder is assumed to result from an unintentional psychological-somatic process, altered states of consciousness may offer a means of controlling the symptom by accessing the psychological process that is maintaining it. The use of hypnotherapy varies widely based on the training and theoretical orientation of the clinician (LaClave et al., 1992). Hypnotherapy is recommended for as many as 50% of Conversion Disorder cases in some settings (Kronenberger et al., 1991).

Hypnotherapy for Conversion Disorder can take several forms. In all cases, hypnotic induction is performed, followed by deepening into the hypnotic state. Once the child is in the hypnotic state, suggestions of relaxation and symptom removal may be made to relieve the conversion symptom (Olness and Gardner, 1988). Suggestions are often metaphorical rather than direct. For example, a child who cannot bend an arm may receive the suggestion to imagine the arm as a hinge that bends freely. Because it is important that children feel some control over the symptom removal, they are often taught self-hypnosis, which they practice between hypnotherapy sessions.

In many cases, self-hypnosis is not entirely effective, in particular when secondary gain, internal conflict, or external stress hinder children's motivation to overcome the problem. In these cases, other treatment components or an additional abreaction/catharsis component must be added to the hypnotherapy (Gross, 1983). Hypnotic abreaction/catharsis occurs when children are hypnotically regressed to the time of the stressors. They then reexperience the behaviors, sensations, cognitions, and emotions connected with the stressful event. By reexperiencing and mastering the stressful event, they may achieve a sense of insight, completion, and control (Gross, 1983). This technique has some risks, however, because it involves the reexperiencing of what obviously was a psychologically harmful event. Thus, abreaction/catharsis should be performed carefully by a trained hypnotherapist.

Other techniques, such as relaxation and suggestion, share many characteristics with hypnosis. Because relaxation is assumed to be incompatible with feelings of tension and stress, stress- and anxiety-based conversion symptoms may be reduced when children are in a relaxed state. In addition, the teaching of relaxation techniques may increase children's feeling of control over their body. Suggestion involves administering a treatment such as hypnotherapy, relaxation, or placebo while giving the children verbal and nonverbal cues that the treatment will cure the conversion symptom.

Because of a lack of controlled outcome studies, the effectiveness of hypnotherapeutic techniques in relieving conversion symptomatology is not known. Case studies (e.g., Gross, 1983; Olness and Gardner, 1988) indicate that some children do respond to hypnotherapy and related techniques, but many other children show no response to these interventions. The appropriateness of hypnotherapy for any individual case probably depends on factors such as hypnotizability, resistance to hypnosis, and secondary gain for symptoms.

Behavioral Interventions

Behavioral treatments for Conversion Disorder are based on the assumption that the conversion symptom is reinforced by contingencies in the children's environment. Hence, all behavioral treatments for Conversion Disorder begin with an assessment of the secondary gain that the children are receiving for the conversion symptom. This gain is best assessed in two ways: First, the children and families should be asked what the child can no longer do because of the conversion symptom. Initial answers to this question are often limited to descriptions of the functional loss (e.g., "I can't bend my leg") and must be probed to gather information regarding what activities (e.g., "I can't go to gym class") have been lost because of the symptom. Regardless of whether children and families attach positive or negative valence to the lost activity, any change must be considered as a possible reinforcer for the symptoms. A second way of assessing secondary gain is to ask how the children's environments have changed since the emergence of the conversion symptoms. Factors such as attention, change in family roles, and tangible reinforcement should be considered.

Once possible sources of secondary gain are identified, these sources are modified or removed. Provisions are made for the children to engage in as many activities as possible, given their functional loss. A child with difficulty walking, for example, can be provided with crutches, a walker, or a wheelchair in order to attend school. Normal activities and chores are resumed, and positive reinforcement is given for behavior characteristic of a lessening of the conversion symptom. A critical component of this treatment package is a lack of attention for the conversion symptom. If children complain about the symptom, they may be given a brief supportive response that expresses understanding and a belief in their ability to manage normal behavior in spite of the conversion symptom. The conversion symptom is not allowed to be used as an excuse for avoiding an activity, whenever possible.

Family Interventions

Some involvement of the family is common in the treatment of Conversion Disorder. Family members may be participants in a behavioral plan, or they may be brought into formal family therapy. Seltzer (1985) observed fifteen families of children with Conversion Disorder and concluded that the families functioned as "illness units" that created and perpetuated the conversion symptom in the children. Each family had a typical pattern of illness behavior involving certain organ systems through which somatic symptoms were expressed. Furthermore, families considered the ill children to be functioning well socially, intellectually, and emotionally. Families resisted psychological explanations of the conversion symptom. Family interactions indicated that the conversion families had very high expectations for the children, causing high levels of control and enmeshment. Underlying these expectations and enmeshment, however, was a fundamental feeling of fear that the families might not be "normal." To maintain the appearance of normalcy and control, strong emotion was avoided and usually expressed through somatic complaints.

Selzer (1985) suggests that family therapy is needed to address the problems of many conversion families. Such therapy typically aims to increase family insight into interaction patterns such as enmeshed interactions and avoidance of conflict. Structural aspects of the family system must be attended to as well: Boundaries should be clear between the child subsystem and the parental subsystem, and individual family members should have some measure of independence. Communication between family members should be direct and honest. Finally, the role of the child's illness in the family must be understood, and changes in the family system must occur.

Many of Minuchin's (1974) techniques to modify family structure can be applied to the family of a child with a Conversion Disorder. One technique, manipulating space, involves moving family members to different locations in the room in order to represent physically the boundaries that should exist in the family system. For example, in one conversion family the mother was sitting on the couch with the children and the father was sitting alone in the corner. To weaken the enmeshed mother–child subsystem and strengthen the disengaged parental subsystem, the family was made to move so that mother and father were together on the couch, with the children in separate chairs. In a second technique, family members are forbidden to talk about each other; comments about a family member must be directed to that member, who then responds to the statement. Family members may not answer a question directed to another family member, as when a parent answers a question directed to a child. This technique disrupts enmeshed interaction patterns in which family members think and feel for each other. A third family restructuring technique involves the therapist pointing out and probing differences that the family attempts to avoid. This forces an unfamiliar interaction and allows processing of unstated issues that have a profound impact on the system's interaction. In a fourth technique the therapist joins with a family member in a coalition. This strengthens the position of that family member and changes his or her position in the family hierarchy. For example, if mother and the children are enmeshed and in control of the family, the therapist might join with the father, elevating his status and assuring his centrality in family interaction. Several related techniques may be helpful in assessing and restructuring the conversion family system (Minuchin, 1974).

Multidimensional Techniques

In practice it is rare to see only one type of technique used to treat a child with a Conversion Disorder. Most clinicians combine two or more types of techniques based on the characteristics of the individual case. Most treatment packages for children with Conversion Disorder include a behavioral component and a psychotherapeutic component. If the family system is felt to have maladaptive qualities that are contributing to the disorder, a family therapy component is indicated. Two specific multidimensional approaches will be described in detail to illustrate these techniques.

Medical Multidimensional Approach

In a medical multidimensional approach the mental health clinician works closely with the medical team, often on a pediatric unit, to address the somatic symptoms. The first step to this approach involves a meeting with the parents, child, primary physician, and mental health clinician. At this meeting the family is told that the treatment team believes there is a psychological component to the child's physical symptoms. The family is assured of the continued involvement of the medical team, and the role of the psychologist is defined as a member of the medical team that is treating the child. By keeping the medical team involved with the child, it is hoped that both child and family will be less defensive and more amenable to change.

In the second step, physical and psychological interventions are performed concurrently. Some physical interventions, such as physical therapy and monitoring of medical condition, are continued. The presence of continued physical intervention prevents children from feeling abandoned by the medical team and gives them a way to "save face." Often children believe that they actually had an illness and that the physical therapy "cured" them of it. Physical therapy also gives children a sense of competence and ability to overcome the impairment. In addition to continued physical intervention, psychotherapeutic techniques are initiated with the child, and parents are trained in behavioral techniques. Parents are especially encouraged to avoid attention for physical symptoms, to reward independent behavior, and to treat the child as though he or she were not ill.

Schulman's Coping Approach

Another multidimensional technique for managing Conversion Disorders, the "coping approach" was suggested by Schulman (1988). The coping approach involves ten components:

1. Review existing medical evidence with the physician and family.

2. Continue medical care and tracking of the patient's condition in case future medical tests are warranted.

3. Review with the family previous treatments that have been effective in relieving the somatic symptoms.

4. Review with the family the extent to which the child has altered or eliminated normal life activities.

5. Tell the family that since everything has been tried with no significant effects, the most reasonable course of action is for the child to return to a normal schedule (i.e., school, living at home, etc.). Essentially, the rationale here is that since nothing more can be done, the child should learn to function as normally as possible with the conversion problem. Families are usually very resistant at this step and may be expected to offer numerous reasons for not being able to carry out this recommendation.

6. Discuss with the family that there are many children who, despite actual physical illness, participate in normal life activities. The family may be provided with examples of good coping on the part of these physically ill children. This step addresses some of the family concerns raised in Step 5.

7. Point out that difficulty with coping is understandable, but a failure to *attempt* to cope is unreasonable and self-defeating. The child must leave the hospital environment eventually.

8. Working with the medical team and the family, set up rules of illness behavior. First, the child is to avoid somatic complaints such as verbal complaining, grimacing, and body contortions; the parents will ignore these complaints. Second, every few days for a brief period of time the child is permitted to describe to the parents any somatic concerns that he or she has. The parents will relay these concerns to the medical team. This is important for the continued monitoring of the child's medical condition. Third, a gradual return to normal daily function is planned by the staff and parents, and the parents are to carry out this plan without deviation.

9. Help parents to see how their child's somatic problems have affected their own lives, and plan a return to normal life for the parents. At this point the therapist must be careful to observe any parental/family dynamics that will jeopardize the therapeutic plan; family therapy may be warranted if the symptom is likely to be maintained by the family system.

10. Discuss with the child any problems the child anticipates with the plan, and suggest ways to cope with the return to normal life. Resistance on the part of the child may suggest the need for individual psychotherapy (Schulman, 1988).

Schulman's (1988) treatment package combines behavioral and cognitive-behavioral interventions with the possibility of psychotherapeutic and family therapy interventions to arrive at a comprehensive approach to managing Conversion Disorder. He provides several examples of the implementation of this approach and reports no cases of symptom substitution (Schulman, 1988).

APPROACHES TO OTHER SOMATOFORM DISORDERS

Although research and theory on Somatoform Disorders in children have been largely confined to Conversion Disorders, other types of somatoform disorders are seen in children. The assessment and treatment of these disorders is managed in much the same way as a Conversion Disorder. Any differences in assessment or treatment will be noted.

Pain Disorder

CLINICAL DESCRIPTION

Probably the most common of the "other" somatoform disorders is Pain Disorder. Pain Disorder is characterized by complaints of pain in the absence of a somatic explanation for the pain or for its intensity. Like a Conversion Disorder, the pain must either cause distress or interfere with daily functioning. Furthermore, evidence of a role for psychological factors in the development of the pain symptoms is required, although the factors need not be specified. Pain Disorder can and often does co-occur with actual physical problems; when this is the case, "Pain Disorder Associated with Both Psychological Factors and a General Medical Condition" is diagnosed. This diagnosis requires that the reported intensity of pain or impairment clearly exceeds what would be expected from the physical problem. Therefore, determining the intensity of the pain and the extent of functional impairment is often critical to this diagnosis. Pain Disorders that do not co-occur with actual physical problems are coded as "Pain Disorder Associated with Psychological Factors."

Pain Disorder can have broad effects on functioning. Children with Pain Disorder often miss school and other activities. Many are shuttled from doctor to doctor in an attempt to find the cause of the disorder. Family concern and family conflict may be concurrent with or may result from the child's pain complaints. Pain may interfere with the child's concentration and cause irratibility or sadness. These factors may contribute to social isolation and low self-esteem in some children. DSM-IV reports that Pain Disorder is "relatively common" (American Psychiatric Association, 1994, p. 460), but prevalence in children is not known.

ASSESSMENT PATTERNS

A sample assessment battery for Pain Disorder is shown in Table 8.3.

Broad Assessment Strategies

The broad assessment strategies for Conversion Disorder apply to Pain Disorder as well. Like Conversion Disorder, Pain Disorder is frequently accompanied by some apparent decrease in functioning. Perhaps the only difference in assessment that may be anticipated would be higher scores for children with Pain Disorder on scales of depression such as the CDI and MMPI scale 2. These higher depression scores would reflect the anxiety, irritation, and hopelessness that many of these children feel when the medical establishment is unable to cure their pain.

TABLE 8.3   Sample Assessment Battery for Pain Disorder

PSYCHOLOGICAL

MMPI/MMPI-A
Piers-Harris Self-Concept Scale
Children's Depression Inventory

FAMILY

Family Environment Scale
FACES-III

SYNDROME-SPECIFIC

Body outline for shading of pain areas
Visual pain intensity scale (Pain Thermometer; Oucher)
Verbal pain intensity scale (1–10 rating)
McGill Pain Questionnaire

Note: Assessment instruments are intended to supplement (not substitute for) a good clinical interview and, when possible, a structured diagnostic interview.

Syndrome-Specific Tests

Child-Report

It is often helpful to administer the child with Pain Disorder a self-report measure of pain (see Katz, Varni, and Jay [1984] and Savedra and Tesler (1989) for a review of specific measures of pain). Many aspects of pain can be assessed, but three of the most commonly assessed pain components are location (where is the pain?), intensity (how badly does the pain hurt?), and quality (what does the pain feel like?). Having the child shade in the painful area on a body outline can provide the clinician with an estimate of the localization of the pain. Use of different colored crayons to represent different severity levels of pain can add a severity dimension to the body outline shading task (Savedra and Tesler, 1989).

Many unidimensional self-report measures of pain intensity exist as well. These measures can be divided into visual scales, verbal scales, and numerical scales. Visual pain intensity scales use pictures to anchor the pain scale. Often these pictures are of faces (Beyer, 1984; McGrath, DeVeber, and Hearn, 1985), although other objects such as ladders (Jeans and Johnston, 1985) and thermometers (Katz et al., 1982) are sometimes used as well. The Oucher scale (Beyer, 1984) and nine face scale (McGrath et al., 1985), for example, present the child with several pictures of faces with expressions ranging from happy to pain/cry; the children point to the face that best characterizes their pain. The Pain Ladder (Jeans and Johnston, 1985), on the other hand, asks the child to point to the place on a ladder that typifies their pain. The bottom of the ladder is classified as no pain, while the top is classified as pain that is as bad as it can be. The Pain Thermometer (Katz et al., 1985) asks children to point to the place on a thermometer that represents their level of pain. Higher temperatures represent greater pain. More simple visual pain scales consist simply of a line with one end signifying extreme pain and the other end signifying no pain; children make a mark along the length of the line that characterizes their pain (Savedra and Tesler, 1989). Line scales can be scored by using a ruler to measure millimeters from the "no pain" beginning of the line. Many of these visual pain intensity scales include a numerical scale in addition to the visual component, and all of the intensity scales yield numerical scores. The visual scales have the advantage of requiring less verbal ability in the child.

Verbal scales rely exclusively on verbal descriptions of the pain, which are usually anchored to a numerical value. Savedra and Tesler (1989), for example, describe a scale used by McGrath and Unruh (1987) to assess children's pain. This scale consists of six verbal statements ranging from "no pain" to "pain— I can't ignore it but I can do my usual activities" to "pain—such that I can't do anything." Children choose one of the six statements, which are coded on a 0 (no pain) to 5 (extreme pain) scale for scoring (Savedra and Tesler, 1989). Other verbal pain intensity scales use only a numerical scale to characterize pain.

Asking children to rate their pain on a scale of 1–10 is an example of such a pain scale.

In addition to location and intensity, the quality (subjective sense or "feel") of the pain may be assessed. For example, pain may be described as "shooting," "dull," "sharp," "pressured," or "hot." The McGill Pain Questionnaire (Melzack, 1975) is one questionnaire designed to assess pain quality issues.

Other-Report

Children's pain can also be assessed by behavior rating scales such as the Observational Scale of Behavioral Distress (OSBD; Jay and Elliott, 1984). Such scales require no effort on the part of the child and eliminate self-report bias. However, they do not tap the subjective component of pain and thus should be regarded as incomplete or supplementary measures. When a child is suspected of significant self-report bias, a pain behavior rating scale such as the OSBD may be considered.

Despite the availability of numerous pain assessment scales, little formal pain assessment research has been done with children with Pain Disorder. Regarding pain location, no typical pattern of assessment results is seen. Some children will vary the pain location (a red flag for the diagnosis of Pain Disorder), while others will be consistent. Clinical experience suggests that children with Pain Disorder generally report very high levels of pain intensity, which can at times seem outrageous. One child, for example, after being asked to rate his pain on a scale of 1 to 10, groaned and said, "20." As for location, no typical result can be stated for assessment of pain quality in Pain Disorder. Although the value of pain assessment in the differential diagnosis of Pain Disorder is unclear, routine pain assessment is recommended in order to track treatment efficacy and to assist the child with self-monitoring of improvement of symptoms.

TREATMENT OPTIONS

Because Conversion Disorder and Pain Disorder share in common components such as somatic focus and secondary gain, most treatments for Conversion Disorder are appropriate for Pain Disorder with minimal modifications (see Table 8.4). Play therapy, behavior modification, hypnotherapy, family therapy, and multidimensional techniques are all widely used.

In addition to these techniques, the teaching and modeling of coping with pain may help these children. Such a coping-skills approach begins with an assessment of the level of pain, using one of the standardized pain instruments. Next comes an evaluation of the child's coping strategies, using an interview, parent-report, observation, and possibly a coping scale such as the KIDCOPE (Spirito, Stark, and Williams, 1988). The effectiveness of individual coping strategies is likely to vary from one child to another, making individual

TABLE 8.4   Treatment Options for Somatoform Disorders

MEDICAL EVALUATION/HOSPITALIZATION

PSYCHOTHERAPY

Play therapy
Psychodynamic psychotherapy
Hypnotic techniques
Coping-skills training to manage pain components

BEHAVIORAL INTERVENTIONS

Removal of secondary gain
Reinforcement for "healthy" behavior
Resumption of normal activity
Reduction of attention for somatic symptoms

FAMILY INTERVENTIONS

Family therapy

MULTIDIMENSIONAL TECHNIQUES

Medical-multidimensional approach
    Multidisciplinary meeting to inform family that a psychological dimension is being
       investigated
    Clear, continued involvement of medical team
    Concurrent implementation of physical (medical) and psychological interventions
    Resumption of normal activity

Coping approach (see Schulman, 1988)

Note: This outline of options summarizes major treatments covered in the text. Specific treatments
are often combined into an intervention package. Refer to the text for additional descriptions of
each treatment. This table is not necessarily an exhaustive list of all treatments available.

assessment very important. Coping strategies that are ineffective in managing
pain are discouraged, and more effective coping strategies are taught. For example, the child is encouraged to purposefully use strategies such as distraction, social support, problem solving, and information seeking to attempt to
manage the pain. Coping strategies are practiced, and a live model or videotape can be used to teach the use of the strategies. The effectiveness of these
strategies is tested by readministering a standardized pain measure and looking for decreases in reported pain. Because the effectiveness of the coping-
skills approach is dependent on the child's motivation, resistance on the part
of the child may necessitate the use of other interventions before the coping-
skills approach can be effective.

Hypochondriasis, Somatization Disorder, and Undifferentiated Somatoform Disorder

CLINICAL DESCRIPTION

This subgroup of Somatoform Disorders shares in common the belief that something is physically wrong with the person, in the absence of any physical findings. In the case of Hypochondriasis, the person believes (or fears) that he or she has some serious, specific disease. This belief persists despite medical evidence to the contrary. Although Hypochondriasis can occur in children, it is relatively rare, with age at onset usually in early adulthood. In many cases, apparent childhood Hypochondriasis may actually be the result of the child's response to a *parent's* fear that the child is ill.

Unlike Hypochondriasis, Somatization Disorder involves recurrent, multiple physical symptoms, typically without the belief that one has some specific disease. A diagnosis of Somatization Disorder requires at least eight of a large number of possible physical symptoms in four areas: pain symptoms (at least four) gastrointestinal symptoms (at least two), sexual symptoms (at least one), and neurological symptoms (at least one). The large number and variety of physical symptoms are often the most clinically striking feature of this syndrome. Symptoms may change or abate, but the child generally has some set of physical complaints virtually all of the time for several years. Somatization Disorder typically occurs in females between the ages of 10 and 20, and it is often related to some environmental stressor, intrapsychic conflict, or anxiety. Little research exists on this disorder in children, and it is relatively rare (less than 1% prevalence) in adults as well (American Psychiatric Association, 1994).

Undifferentiated Somatoform Disorder is diagnosed for children with one or more physical complaints that last at least 6 months, affect daily functioning or cause distress, and do not have a physical explanation. Because the symptom pattern cannot fit that of another somatoform disorder, pain and neurological complaints rarely fit this diagnosis. Children with single long-lasting physical complaints of other types will often receive the Undifferentiated Somatoform Disorder diagnosis. In addition, most children who do not have enough symptoms to qualify for the Somatization Disorder diagnosis receive the Undifferentiated Somatoform Disorder diagnosis. Hence, the Undifferentiated Somatoform Disorder category encompasses a rather heterogeneous and diverse group of clinical presentations, ranging from children with unexplained fatigue to children who nearly meet the Somatization Disorder diagnostic criteria.

Body Dysmorphic Disorder

CLINICAL DESCRIPTION

This final somatoform disorder is characterized by an excessive focus on an imagined physical defect. The target of focus may be an actual physical problem, but the person's concern and distress is out of proportion to the problem. The person's concern must cause significant distress or problems in daily functioning. Facial flaws are the most common targets of this concern, although other body parts may be targets as well. As may be expected, appearance-related preoccupations are exceedingly common in adolescence, but the point at which one of these preoccupations becomes a Body Dysmorphic Disorder is unclear. DSM-IV suggests that the amount of lost time and loss of daily functioning resulting from the symptoms should be used in distinguishing between appearance concerns and a Body Dysmorphic Disorder. Virtually no research evidence exists on the diagnosis, course, or treatment of this disorder in children.

Individuals with Body Dysmorphic Disorder often change their behavior patterns because of the symptoms. They may spend hours examining the "defect" in front of a mirror. Alternatively, they may avoid mirrors in order to reduce distress over the imagined problem. Social withdrawal and impaired social interactions are risks in children who are embarrassed about their imagined defect.

Clinical experience suggests that Body Dysmorphic Disorder is not necessarily stress-related, although it often can be tied to some internal belief system, low self-esteem, or past experience. Family or peer modeling may play a role in its development, as when a family preoccupation with nose size leads to the child's belief that he or she has a large nose. Secondary gain is rarely present but should be ruled out in an interview.

Because secondary gain is not often a factor in the development of Body Dysmorphic Disorder, behavioral treatments would appear to be contraindicated in most cases, with family and individual psychotherapy being the treatments of choice. It is important to reiterate that little is known about this disorder in children.

References

American Psychiatric Association. (1994). *Diagnostic and statistical manual of mental disorders* (4th ed.). Washington, DC: Author.

Beyer, J. E. (1984). *The Oucher: A user's manual and technical report.* Charlottesville: University of Virginia Alumni Patent Foundation.

Brooksbank, D. J. (1984). Management of conversion reaction in five adolescent girls. *Journal of Adolescence, 7,* 359–376.

Garrick, T., Ostrov, E., and Offer, D. (1988). Physical symptoms and self-image in a group of normal adolescents. *Psychosomatics, 29,* 73–80.

Goodyer, I. M., and Mitchell, C. (1989). Somatic emotional disorders in childhood and adolescence. *Journal of Psychosomatic Research, 33,* 681–688.

Grattan-Smith, P., Fairley, M., and Procopis, P. (1988). Clinical features of conversion disorder. *Archives of Disease in Childhood, 63,* 408–414.

Gross, M. (1983). Hypnoanalysis in conversion reaction. *Medical Hypnoanalysis,* 160–165.

Jay, S. M., and Elliott, C. (1984). Behavioral observation scales for measuring children's distress: The effects of increased methodological rigor. *Journal of Consulting and Clinical Psychology, 52,* 1106–1107.

Jeans, M. E., and Johnston, C. C. (1985). Pain in children: Assessment and management. In Lipton, S., and Miles, J. (Eds.), *Persistent pain: Modern methods of treatment* (vol. 5, pp. 111–127). London: Grune & Stratton.

Katz, E. R., Sharp, B., Kellerman, J., Marston, A., Hirschman, J., and Siegel, S. E. (1982). Beta-Endorphin immunoreactivity and acute behavioral distress in children with leukemia. *Journal of Nervous and Mental Disease, 170,* 72–77.

Katz, E. R., Varni, J. W., and Jay, S. M. (1984). Behavioral assessment and management of pain. In M. Hersen, R. Eisler, and P. Miller (Eds.), *Progress in behavior modification* (vol. 18, pp. 163–193). New York: Academic Press.

Kotsopoulos, S., and Snow, B. (1986). Conversion disorders in children: A study of clinical outcome. *Psychiatric Journal of the University of Ottawa, 11,* 134–139.

Kovacs, M. (1992). *Children's Depression Inventory manual.* North Tonawanda, NY: Multi-Health Systems.

Kronenberger, W. G., Laite, G., and LaClave, L. (1991). *Somatoform disorders in pediatric populations: Self-perceptions and recommendations.* Paper presented at the Indiana University Department of Psychiatry Grand Rounds Series.

———. (in press). Somatoform disorders in pediatric populations: Self-perceptions and recommendations. *Psychosomatics.*

LaClave, L., Kronenberger, W. G., Baker, E., and Morrow, C. (1993). Use of hypnosis following training in a psychiatry residency and psychology internship program. *International Journal of Clinical and Experimental Hypnosis, 41,* 265–271.

Lehmkuhl, G., Blanz, B., Lehmkuhl, U., and Braun-Scharm, H. (1989). Conversion disorder (DSM-III 300.11): Symptomatology and course in childhood and adolescence. *European Archives of Psychiatry and Neurological Sciences, 238,* 155–160.

Leslie, S. A. (1988). Diagnosis and treatment of hysterical conversion reactions. *Archives of Disease in Childhood, 63,* 506–511.

McGrath, P. A., DeVeber, L. L., and Hearn, M. T. (1985). Multidimensional pain assessment in children. In Fields, H. L., Dubner, R., and Cervero, F. (Eds.), *Advances in pain research and therapy* (vol. 9, pp. 387–393). New York: Raven Press.

McGrath, P. J., and Unruh, A. M. (1987). *Pain in children and adolescents.* New York: Elsevier.

Melzack, R. (1975). The McGill Pain Questionnaire: Major properties and scoring methods. *Pain, 1,* 277–299.

Minuchin, S. (1974). *Families and family therapy.* Cambridge, MA: Harvard University Press.

Moos, R. H., and Moos, B. S. (1981). *Family Environment Scale manual.* Palo Alto, CA: Consulting Psychologists Press.

Olness, K., and Gardner, G. G. (1988). *Hypnosis and hypnotherapy with children* (2d edition). Philadelphia: Grune & Stratton.

Piers, E. V. (1984). *Piers-Harris Children's Self-Concept Scale Revised manual 1984.* Los Angeles: Western Psychological Services.

Regan, J. J., and Regan, W. M. (1989). Somatoform disorders. In C. G. Last and M. Hersen (eds.), *Handbook of child psychiatric diagnosis* (pp. 343–355). New York: Wiley.

Robinson, D. P., Greene, J. W., and Walker, L. S. (1988). Functional somatic complaints in adolescents: Relationship to negative life events, self-concept, and family characteristics. *Journal of Pediatrics, 113,* 588–593.

Savedra, M. C., and Tesler, M. D. (1989). Assessing children's and adolescents' pain. *Pediatrician, 16,* 24–29.

Schulman, J. L. (1988). Use of a coping approach in the management of children with conversion reactions. *Journal of the American Academy of Child and Adolescent Psychiatry, 27,* 785–788.

Seltzer, W. J. (1985). Conversion disorder in childhood and adolescence: A familial/cultural approach. Part I. *Family Systems Medicine, 3,* 261–280.

Selye, H. (1956). *The stress of life.* New York: McGraw-Hill.

Siegel, M., and Barthel, R. P. (1986). Conversion disorders on a child psychiatry consultation service. *Psychosomatics, 27,* 201–204.

Spirito, A., Stark, L. J., and Williams, C. (1988). Development of a brief coping checklist for use with pediatric populations. *Journal of Pediatric Psychology, 13,* 555–574.

Steinhausen, H. C., Aster, M., Pfeiffer, E., and Gobel, D. (1989). Comparative studies of conversion disorders in childhood and adolescence. *Journal of Child Psychology and Psychiatry and Allied Disciplines, 30,* 615–621.

Thomson, A. P. J., and Sills, J. A. (1988). Diagnosis of functional illness presenting with gait disorder. *Archives of Disease in Childhood, 63,* 148–153.

Volkmar, F. R., Poll, J., and Lewis, M. (1984). Conversion reactions in childhood and adolescence. *Journal of the American Academy of Child Psychiatry, 23,* 424–430.

Walker, L. S., McLaughlin, F. J., and Greene, J. W. (1988). Functional illness and family functioning: A comparison of healthy and somaticizing adolescents. *Family Process, 27,* 317–320.

CHAPTER 9

Schizophrenia

■ Schizophrenia and Psychosis

□ CLINICAL DESCRIPTION

Diagnostic Considerations

As with the mood disorders, the diagnostic criteria for schizophrenia in children are essentially the same as for adults. These criteria include some combination of delusions, hallucinations, incoherence, disorganized behavior, and negative symptoms such as flat affect. Symptoms must be of sufficient severity to result in a significant decrease in adaptive functioning. Depending on the predominant symptoms, children are diagnosed into one of five types of schizophrenia: Catatonic (predominantly motor disturbance), Disorganized (predominantly disorganized behavior and affect disturbance), Paranoid (predominantly delusions without the symptoms of the other subtypes), Undifferentiated (schizophrenic symptoms that do not meet criteria for the first three categories), and Residual (residual symptoms but no active delusions, hallucinations, disorganized speech, disorganized behavior, or negative symptoms). Most schizophrenic children and young adolescents fall into the Paranoid and Undifferentiated subtypes (McClellan and Werry, 1992).

The diagnostic separation of schizophrenia and autism is a relatively new phenomenon, first occurring in DSM-III. Before 1980, childhood schizophrenia and autism were grouped together under the title "childhood schizophrenia." This grouping occurred in spite of the fact that the symptom pictures of the two disorders are different and that there is little overlap between cases (Kolvin, Berney, and Yoeli, 1990). Unfortunately, this older classification scheme has persisted, so that the term "childhood schizophrenia" is sometimes used mistakenly to refer to autism. Research prior to 1980 (and some research following 1980) frequently combined schizophrenic and autistic children, obscuring the symptom picture and empirical correlates of each of these disorders. Recent research suggests that, although some autistic children develop schizophrenic features, the diagnostic separation of the two disorders is a good idea

(Kolvin et al., 1990; McClellan and Werry, 1992). Schizophrenia should be diagnosed in a child with a pervasive developmental disorder (such as autism) only if hallucinations or delusions are prominent during a period of 1 month or more (American Psychiatric Association, 1994).

There has been a paucity of studies of the prevalence of schizophrenia in preadolescent children. Authors universally agree, however, that schizophrenia is rare in children and that its prevalence increases throughout adolescence and into adulthood. As of 1990, fewer than 200 cases of preadolescent schizophrenia had been the subject of clinical or scholarly articles (Kolvin et al., 1990). Consistent with this rarity, prevalence estimates of childhood schizophrenia have been in the range of 0.03% of the child population (Kolvin et al., 1990). Schizophrenia is fifty times as rare before the age of 15 than after the age of 15 (Kolvin et al., 1990). There is consensus that schizophrenia before age 10–12 is extremely rare. Hence, in preadolescent children, schizophrenia should be diagnosed cautiously and only after ruling out more likely explanations such as organic causes, drugs, attention-seeking behavior, and oppositionality.

Although schizophrenia is quite rare in preadolescent children, "schizophrenic-like" behaviors or symptoms are more common. These behaviors are unusual, incoherent, or lack reality testing, but they do not have the pervasive and long-lasting quality of schizophrenia. Children under extreme stress will sometimes decompensate into incoherence, delusions, hallucinations, and disorganized or catatonic behavior. A child who has lost both parents in a traumatic accident may, for example, construct a delusion that she is being pursued by an imaginary villain. This delusion may be accompanied by hallucinations and incoherent behavior. In most cases, such a pattern of symptoms and behavior reflects the disorganizing and traumatic effects of a stressor on the child. When provided with structure and support, traumatized children lose these symptoms within days or a couple of weeks. Children who display this symptom pattern (for a period of 1 day to 1 month) are diagnosed as having a Brief Psychotic Disorder with Marked Stressors. If no stressors are identified, the diagnosis Brief Psychotic Disorder without Marked Stressors is made (American Psychiatric Association, 1994).

When the child shows psychotic behavior for 1 to 6 months, a diagnosis of Schizophreniform Disorder may be made. This diagnosis acknowledges the presence of schizophrenic symptoms that do not meet the schizophrenia criterion of lasting longer than 6 months (American Psychiatric Association, 1994). Schizophreniform Disorder may represent a number of conditions, ranging from the development of schizophrenia to a behaviorally caused cluster of strange behavior that is currently reinforced by the child's environment.

Another presentation that resembles schizophrenia occurs when a child is drawn into someone else's delusion, usually held by a caretaker or other person with whom the child has bonded. This condition is diagnosed as Shared Psychotic Disorder or Folie à Deux (American Psychiatric Association, 1994). Parents have considerable influence over the ways in which their children perceive and interpret the world. A child who is repeatedly exposed to a parent's delusion may come to believe it because of allegiance to the parent as well as because of "evidence" presented by the parent. In most cases these children do not show evidence of hallucinations, bizarre behavior, or grossly inappropriate affect, and they do not develop delusions other than the one that is believed by the parent. However, they tenaciously hold to their delusion as long as they remain with the parent. Separation of the child from the parent generally results in the disappearance of the delusion, although the child may initially be resistant to giving up the delusion. Bonding with other adults often helps the child reach this goal.

Most instances of "psychotic" symptomatology seen by clinicians are isolated symptoms that arise in children for a variety of reasons unrelated to schizophrenia. Children in general tend to have looser control over their behavior than do adults, particularly when they have an "externalizing" problem such as ADHD, Conduct Disorder, or Oppositional-Defiant Disorder. A child with externalizing tendencies who is sufficiently upset may engage in behaviors that would be considered psychotic in adults. Such behaviors as screaming incoherently, falling to the ground, flailing around, and making bizarre statements may be symptoms of an externalizing behavior problem as opposed to schizophrenia. When this is the case, the apparently "psychotic" behaviors tend to follow environmental restrictions or frustrations, to occur only when provoked, to occur as a single symptom (not as a cluster of psychotic symptoms), and to disappear when the provoking situation is removed.

Some symptoms that would be considered psychotic at adult ages are normal at younger ages. It is not at all uncommon, for example, for children under the age of 6 or 7 to have an imaginary friend. Thus, it is a challenge to differentiate normal childhood fantasies from schizophrenic hallucinations at these early ages. One factor that may differentiate fantasies from hallucinations is the degree to which children retain contact with their environment. For example, a normal child who is playing with imaginary superhero friends is usually responsive to adults and treats his imaginary "friends" differently from his actual child friends (e.g., he does not ask if the imaginary friend can sleep over). In addition, older children can often directly tell an adult that they know that their fantasy world really does not exist. On the other hand, a vivid perception and the insistence in an older child that the fantasy is *actually* present are more typical of hallucinations. However, acknowledged child hallucinations are much less suggestive of psychosis than are hallucinations in an adult (Kemph, 1987; McClellan and Werry, 1992).

Childhood fears can also take on a delusion-like appearance, when in fact these are developmentally normal. A persistent belief that a "robber" is under the bed, for example, is developmentally appropriate for a 4-year-old. A similar fear in an adult may be considered a hallucination or delusion.

Finally, autistic children can at times display behaviors that resemble schizophrenic symptoms. For example, social withdrawal, bizarre movements, and unusual verbalizations are common to both schizophrenia and autism. However, there are major differences between schizophrenia and autism. Perhaps the largest difference is that the onset of childhood schizophrenia tends to occur relatively late in the childhood years (8–12 years, with increasing rates in adolescence), while that of autism occurs relatively early in the childhood years (Watkins, Asarnow, and Tanguay, 1988). In fact, schizophrenia is virtually absent before age 6, while autism is almost always noticed or diagnosed before age 6 (American Psychiatric Association, 1994; Gelfand, Jenson, and Drew, 1988; Watkins et al., 1988). In a combined sample of autistic and schizophrenic children, for example, Watkins et al. (1988) found that 83% of the children had symptom onset either before age 2 years, 7 months or after age 8 years, 11 months. All children with onset before age 9 received a diagnosis of a pervasive developmental disorder.

In addition to differences in age of onset, schizophrenic and autistic children show differences in other symptoms. First, virtually all autistic children show a pervasive lack of social responsiveness, while schizophrenic children are usually socially responsive, even if their responses are sometimes unusual (Gelfand et al., 1988). Second, autistic children tend to display early language deficits at a higher rate than do schizophrenic children, although a high percentage of schizophrenic children also have language deficits (Watkins et al., 1988). Third, autistic children often display echolalia, which is extremely rare in schizophrenic children (Watkins et al., 1988). Fourth, autistic children tend to have greater resistance to change, over- or underresponsivity to stimuli, and self-injurious behaviors than schizophrenic children have (Kolvin et al., 1990; Watkins et al., 1988). Fifth, the majority of autistic children are mentally retarded, while only a minority of schizophrenic children score in mentally retarded ranges on IQ tests (Gelfand et al., 1988; Kolvin et al., 1990). Sixth, autistic children have fewer delusions and hallucinations than do schizophrenic children (Gelfand et al., 1988). Although the differential diagnosis of autism and schizophrenia is relatively straightforward, the disorders do co-occur in a minority of cases (Watkins et al., 1988). In order for a dual schizophrenia-autism diagnosis to be made, the child must have significant hallucinations or delusions for a period of 1 month or more (American Psychiatric Association, 1994).

Appearance and Features

Genuine childhood schizophrenia almost never occurs before age 6, and it is very rare before age 9 (McClellan and Werry, 1992; Watkins et al., 1988). Onset of the schizophrenia is usually slow and chronic (80–94% of cases; Asarnow and Ben-Meir, 1988; Kolvin et al., 1990). Younger children often present with unusual verbalizations, unusual behaviors, and unusual beliefs. In older children and adolescents, delusions and hallucinations are more prominent, occurring in approximately half of cases (Kolvin et al., 1990). Loose/impaired association is seen in approximately half of schizophrenic children, while flat or constricted affect occurs in 60% of cases (Kolvin et al., 1990). (Appearance and features of childhood schizophrenia are listed in Table 9.1.)

Children with schizophrenia may follow several developmental paths. A minority have autistic features during infancy and toddlerhood, developing schizophrenia in the latency or adolescence period (Watkins et al., 1988). Other

TABLE 9.1   Appearance and Features of Schizophrenia in Childhood

COMMON FEATURES

Onset after age 9
Slow, chronic onset
Unusual verbalizations, behaviors, and beliefs (younger children)
Delusions (adolescents)
Primarily internal auditory hallucinations
Disorganized thought
Flat or constricted affect
Premorbid social withdrawal, personality oddities, cognitive delays
Peer rejection

OCCASIONAL FEATURES

Loose association
Deficits in preschool social and language functioning
Self-injurious behavior
Behavior dangerous to others
Guarded, suspicious social attitude

Note: The features listed above are often seen but are not universal. Some features may be diagnostically relevant or required, while others may not be required for diagnosis. "Common" features are typical of the disorder; "occasional" features appear frequently but are not necessarily seen in a majority of cases.

children show deficits in social and language functioning during the toddler and preschool years (Asarnow and Ben-Meir, 1988; McDaniel, 1986; Watkins et al., 1988). Asarnow and Ben-Meir (1988), for example, found that schizophrenic children had poorer premorbid adjustment than depressed children, particularly in the areas of IQ and social functioning. McClellan and Werry (1992) report that 54–90% of schizophrenic children have poor premorbid functioning, characterized by social withdrawal, personality oddities, cognitive delays, and sensory-motor abnormalities.

After age 6, more classic schizophrenic symptoms such as thought disorder (incoherence, loose associations, poverty of content), inappropriate affect, and hallucinations may begin to emerge, although these are rare before age 8 or 9. Development of classic symptoms often follows a progression from an unusual affective appearance (e.g., stoic looking, flat affect) to social isolation and social adjustment problems and, eventually, to the emergence of disorders of thought and perception (Fish, 1986; McClellan and Werry, 1992). Thought disorder, inappropriate affect, and hallucinations become more prevalent after age 9 (Watkins et al., 1988), and in late adolescence, symptoms such as delusions, catatonia, and poverty of thinking may emerge (McClellan and Werry, 1992).

The duration and severity of schizophrenic symptoms vary widely from child to child. Some children have a relatively constant presentation of social withdrawal, inappropriate affect, and delusions. Others cycle between periods of more florid symptoms (hallucinations, bizarre behaviors, and thought disorder) and periods of relative calm (although rarely normal behavior). The florid periods in these children can range from 1 week to 3 months, while the remission periods can range from 3 months to several years. Generally, "positive" symptoms such as hallucinations, delusions, and thought disorganization are more likely to change with cycles, while "negative" symptoms such as apathy and withdrawal persist to a certain extent even in remission periods. Other children exhibit symptoms only in certain environments (e.g., in large crowds) or only when stressed. Because of these differences in symptom duration, type, and severity, careful attention to these issues should occur in the initial interview.

Perceptual Features: Hallucinations

Hallucinations in children differ somewhat from those of adolescents and adults. Differentiating between normal fantasy and abnormal hallucinations in children is sometimes extremely difficult (Garralda, 1984b). In addition, preschool children may tend to report more "internal" (within the self) as opposed to "external" (outside the self) hallucinations. Surprisingly, Kemph (1987) found hallucinations to be more common in young psychotic children than in older psychotic children. Two-thirds of psychotic children age 6–11 reported hallucinations, compared to 32–48% of older psychotic children reporting hallucinations. This result is in contrast to contentions by others (e.g., Kolvin et al., 1990) that hallucinations may become more prominent as the schizophrenic child ages.

In the preadolescent age group, hallucinations are most often auditory or auditory/visual. The identity of the voice may be known or unknown. Usually the voice is telling the child to do something (command hallucinations) or is calling the child names. More rare are visual and olfactory hallucinations (Del Beccaro, Burke, and McCauley, 1988; Kemph, 1987).

Hallucinations can be persistent in some children and transient in others. For example, Garralda (1984a) found that 69% of a sample of hallucinating children had hallucinations over a decade later. Likewise, Del Beccaro et al. (1988) found 52% of their sample of hallucinating children to still have hallucinations 2–6 years later. The mean duration of the hallucinations in the Del Beccaro study (1988) was 3 years, 4 months. The relationship between hallucinations and other behavioral problems is unclear, although Del Beccaro et al. (1988) report that children with hallucinations have significant additional problems in the areas of somatization and schizoid behavior.

Behavioral Features

In addition to disorders of perception, schizophrenic children display clear disorders of behavior. They may injure themselves, others, or animals for bizarre reasons or for no reason at all (Fish, 1986). At times their verbalizations range from meaningless to bizarre. Because of their undercontrolled behavior and poor judgment, older schizophrenic children and adolescents can possibly be dangerous, injuring people or animals without regard to the effects of their behavior. Evidence exists that the death rate of schizophrenic children and adolescents is 5–10%, far higher than in the normal population (McClellan and Werry, 1992). These children are at increased risk for violent behaviors such as suicide or homicide.

Social Features

Socially, schizophrenic children are often isolated or teased by peers, who cannot understand their behavior. Some schizophrenic children respond to peer rejection with further withdrawal and adoption of a guarded, suspicious attitude toward others. Social communication may be minimal and hindered by absent or inappropriate facial expressions. Their poor judgment and low insight may lead to behaviors that peers find inappropriate and selfish. Unfortunately, isolation and rejection put the schizophrenic child even more at risk for the development of psychotic symptoms because of a lack of social support, modeling, or peer encouragement of appropriate behaviors (Fish, 1986).

Long-Term Features

The prognosis for schizophrenic children is generally poor, although a dearth of longitudinal research restricts what is known about long-term prospects. Younger age of onset (especially before 10 years of age) is associated with greater severity and chronicity, as are slow onset, poor premorbid functioning, and low intelligence (Kolvin et al., 1990; Werry and McClellan, 1992). There is controversy over the importance of family environment for long-term prognosis. Some authors stress the importance of family characteristics such as expressed emotion, while others find that family environmental components are not important for prognosis (Kolvin et al., 1990).

In mid- to late adolescence, childhood schizophrenia evolves to closely resemble schizophrenia in the adult form. Disorders of thought, perception, communication, and social relationships become more evident as the child gains cognitive capacity and the ability to engage in concrete or formal operational thinking. At age 15 and above, conceptualizations of adult schizophrenia apply to the behavior and dynamics of the adolescent (see Meyer, 1993).

Etiology

Unlike adult schizophrenia, childhood schizophrenia has been the subject of very little etiological research. Hence, comments about the etiology of childhood schizophrenia are predominantly speculative. Because childhood schizophrenia resembles adult schizophrenia and because it is sometimes responsive to medication, biological causes have been proposed for schizophrenia in childhood. However, despite sporadic reports of neurological impairment, abnormal EEG, and soft signs in schizophrenic children, there is little direct evidence of a neurological cause (Kolvin et al., 1990).

The effectiveness of medications that block the neurotransmitters dopamine and serotonin has also been taken as evidence that childhood schizophrenia has a biological cause. However, these medications vary in effectiveness from child to child and tend to affect positive symptoms (hallucinations, delusions, motor behavior) more than negative symptoms (withdrawal). Hence, the fact that they may produce some desired effects in some children does not mean that they are acting on the cause of schizophrenia in all children. Over all, biological theories need more empirical verification to be accepted as valid etiological theories for childhood schizophrenia.

In addition to biological theories, family theories have been advanced to account for the development of childhood schizophrenia. Various components of family environment, such as open, extreme expression of hostility ("expressed emotion") and the presence of a parent who gives the child messages of both acceptance and rejection at the same time ("double bind") have been proposed as factors in schizophrenia development or recurrence. Like the biological theories, however, these have received only weak and sporadic support (Gelfand et al., 1988).

Perhaps the ripest area of speculation is a "diathesis-stress" model of the development of childhood schizophrenia. According to this model, the child has a biological propensity or weakness ("diathesis") to develop schizophrenia. This diathesis must be activated by an environment that is characterized by stress or contingencies that encourage the emergence of schizophrenic behavior. For example, a child with a family history of schizophrenia may carry a genetic, anatomical, or biochemical propensity to engage in some unusual behavior and unusual thinking. Stress in the environment may result in an increase in disorganization of the child's behavior and thinking. When these thoughts and behaviors emerge, they may be "encouraged" by the environment through reinforcing attention or the withdrawal of an aversive stimulus (e.g., less teasing by peers, who are driven away by the strange behavior). This results in more abnormal behavior, more stress, and more activation of the propensity to behave and think strangely. As this dynamic develops, it may have neurobiological effects on the brain, modifying the body's propensity to engage in schizophrenic behavior. Eventually the behavioral, environmental, and biological factors combine to favor the emergence of schizophrenia.

Despite its intuitive appeal, the diathesis-stress model of childhood schizophrenia needs additional empirical support. Nevertheless, the biological and diathesis-stress theories are the most widely accepted explanations for the development of childhood schizophrenia. Hence, the clinician should attend to both biological and environmental issues in evaluating children for etiological factors related to the emergence of schizophrenia.

ASSESSMENT PATTERNS

Before initiating interview and testing, it is important to remember that true schizophrenia is rare in children below the age of 12. Hence, assessment (see

Table 9.2) often seeks to rule out schizophrenia and to determine which of the related, nonschizophrenic disorders the child is exhibiting. Most children below the age of 12 who present with bizarre or unusual behavior will *not* be diagnosed schizophrenic. In fact, because of the low base rate of childhood schizophrenia (before age 12), the clinician should be very cautious when diagnosing it, even if the referral question suggests that the child may be schizophrenic.

Broad Assessment Strategies

Cognitive Assessment

Clinician-Administered. Because schizophrenia frequently affects the quality of thought, researchers have hypothesized that IQ testing results of schizophrenics may differ systematically from those of nonschizophrenics. Specifically, it is not unreasonable to expect a drop in IQ scores following schizophrenia onset (Fish, 1986; Kolvin et al., 1990). However, research data in this area are contradictory. Some studies find lower IQ scores in schizophrenic samples relative to healthy and depressed control groups (Asarnow and Ben-Meir, 1988). Other studies report no difference between schizophrenic children and controls (Asarnow and Ben-Meir, 1988; Kolvin et al., 1990). Unfortunately, studies vary by the definition of schizophrenia used and the extent to which children were medicated. Hence, the relationship between IQ and schizophrenia is not entirely clear.

Studies typically find mean WISC-R VIQ, PIQ, and FIQ scores in the 85–95 range for schizophrenic samples, with no VIQ-PIQ difference (Asarnow and Ben-Meir, 1988; Caplan Foy et al., 1990; Caplan, Perdue et al., 1990). Intuitively, WISC-R scales requiring association and higher-order thinking, such as Simi-

---

TABLE 9.2   Sample Assessment Battery for Schizophrenia in Childhood

PERSONALITY

Rorschach
Thematic Apperception Test
Sentence-completion tests

BEHAVIORAL

Child Behavior Checklist

SYNDROME-SPECIFIC

Schizophrenia Symptom Rating Scale

Note: Assessment instruments are intended to supplement (not substitute for) a good clinical interview and, when possible, a structured diagnostic interview.

larities and Comprehension, would be expected to be impaired in schizophrenic children. In addition, tests that are more responsive to social problem solving, such as Comprehension and Picture Arrangement, may be hypothesized to be lower for schizophrenic children. These hypotheses have not been extensively investigated, although Fish (1986) suggests that a drop of 2–9 scaled score points on the Comprehension subtest in several years is typical of a schizophrenic child. Evidence also exists that schizophrenic children score lower on measures of attention/concentration, such as the Freedom from Distractibility factor (FFD) on the WISC-R and WISC-III, than on other clusters of subtests.

In addition to differences in IQ between schizophrenic and normal children, studies indicate that certain IQ measures relate to schizophrenic symptomatology. WISC-R FIQ, VIQ, and FFD, for example, correlate negatively with the number of loose associations, but PIQ is not related to loose associations (Caplan, Foy, et al., 1990; Caplan, Perdue, et al., 1990). In addition, IQ scores have been found to be negatively related to negative symptoms of schizophrenia, such as social withdrawal and flat affect (Bettes and Walker, 1987). Surprisingly, IQ scores have not been found to be related to illogical thinking (Caplan Foy, et al., 1990; Caplan, Perdue, et al., 1990).

Psychological Assessment

Clinician-Administered.   Projective testing data can be a great help in evaluating a child with suspected schizophrenia. Projective tests present stimuli in a less structured form, which often elicits disorganized or unusual responses from schizophrenics. Furthermore, repetitive thought-behavior patterns may emerge in projective testing. Analysis of these thematic patterns allows the clinician to generate hypotheses about the nature of the thought disorder affecting the child. Thus, projective testing can provide the clinician with a view of the child's thought and perceptual processes. Hypotheses regarding these internal processes can then be integrated with behavioral data reported by parents and other adults.

Organized, coherent, appropriate responses to projective testing are usually not consistent with a thought disorder. However, schizophrenia should not be ruled out based on projective testing data alone. Some genuinely schizophrenic children can maintain an organized presentation throughout projective testing, particularly if they are not stressed by the experience. Other children fluctuate between different degrees of thought disorder. On a "good" day, these children may do fine on projectives, while on a "bad" day, they may give a plethora of strange responses. In general, however, a discrepancy between behavioral data indicating schizophrenia and projective data suggesting appropriate thought should act as a red flag to slow the diagnosis of schizophrenia. Over all, projective testing can allow the clinician to evaluate thought and perceptual processes in more detail than can be gained by behavioral observation or structured self-report.

Perhaps the most common projective test for schizophrenic children is the

Rorschach. Schizophrenic children give varying numbers of responses to the ten cards. A high proportion of F responses ("high" in this context means more than 1 S.D. above the mean; see Exner [1986] for norms by age) combined with a low number of total responses ("low" in this context means more than 1 S.D. below the mean) may be suggestive of a child who is rigidly maintaining cognitive control by constricting the content and process of thought and perception. Very few responses may also be suggestive of a depressive component, particularly if the child appears flat or withdrawn. On the other hand, many responses and few F responses could indicate cognitive loosening, impulsivity, and an inability to control cognitive content and process.

Perceptual distortion may be manifest by several Rorschach indices. Low numbers of popular (P) responses indicate an inability to perceive even the most blatant and mundane interpretation of a visual stimulus. However, many schizophrenic children are able to identify several popular responses. In fact, a total lack of popular responses is more likely to suggest either malingering, misunderstanding of the task, or extreme stress. More diagnostic is the form quality of the child's responses, reflected in the F+%, X+%, and X–% indices of the Rorschach. An X+% (the proportion of responses with good or ordinary form quality) of 80% with a standard deviation of 10% is typical of nonclinical children at different ages (Exner, 1986). Exner (1986) states that X+% scores of less than 60% indicate markedly unconventional perceptions that probably affect adjustment. However, clinical observations suggest that a 50% value could be used as a more conservative indicator. When a low X+% is coupled with an X-% (the proportion of responses with poor form quality) of 30% or higher, the child is distorting perceptions significantly, probably impairing adjustment. Such a pattern is consistent with schizophrenic perception and thinking, although it should NOT be the major basis for a diagnosis. Alternative explanations for X+%<60% and X–%>30% include misunderstanding of the task, oppositionality, low IQ, anxiety, and depression.

It should be noted that there is a major difference between poor form quality (coded as "–") and unusual form quality (coded as "u"). Poor form quality reflects true distortions in perception. Unusual form quality, on the other hand, reflects unusual perceptions that, by and large, are not distorted. Hence, a record with many unusual form quality responses may indicate a child with unique, but not distorted, ways of perceiving ambiguous stimuli. Children with high numbers of unusual form quality responses and low numbers of poor form quality responses tend to have low X+% scores *and* low X–% scores. In some cases a child who is malingering schizophrenia will give large numbers of unusual form quality responses. This response pattern indicates that the child is attempting to malinger by giving strange responses. However, the child has intact reality testing, which is guiding the selection of responses and conforming to the appearance of the blot.

Exner (1986) notes several other areas in which disordered thinking affects Rorschach scores. Perhaps the most obvious of these is the special score coding for Rorschach answers. Special scores are assigned to answers that reflect unusual ways of identifying Rorschach responses. In most cases these unusual responses consist of strange statements that are assumed to reflect a breakdown in the thinking or perceptual process. Because these breakdowns can occur as a result of a thought disorder, special scores can indicate the presence of schizophrenic distortion of thought. Six "critical" special scores receive attention as possible indicators of schizophrenic thinking (Exner, 1986): Deviant Verbalizations (neologisms or redundancies), Deviant Responses (inappropriate phrases, irrelevant phrases, or circumstantial responses), Incongruous Combinations (combination of inappropriate images into a single whole, such as a snake with six legs), Contaminations (two impressions fused into one, such as a bat-fly to refer to a single space on the blot), Fabulized Combinations (an implausible relationship between two details, such as a frog driving a truck), and Inappropriate Logic (strained reasoning used to justify an answer). While young (age 6 and under) children average as many as six of these responses, older children and adults average only one to three. More than eight critical special score responses, however, is unusual at any age. More than four such responses would be considered high for a child over the age of 12.

In addition to the six critical special scores, Exner (1986) reports that human movement answers with poor or no form quality (M– answers) are typical of schizophrenic adults. The extent to which this observation corresponds to schizophrenic children, however, is unknown. More than one M– answer is extremely unusual in nonschizophrenics.

Other Rorschach scores that are sometimes seen in schizophrenic children are low numbers of human content responses and high numbers of imaginary (parenthesized) human responses. Absent or distorted human content responses may suggest few, poor, or unusual social relationships. A preponderance of chromatic color responses can indicate an emotional or impulsive component to the schizophrenia. On the other hand, achromatic color or shading responses may be driven by a depressed or painful component. Finally, unusual content, fantasy content, and a large number of morbid responses can provide some insight into the bizarre thought content of the child.

Over all, the responses of the schizophrenic child to the Rorschach have an unusual quality. Verbalizations may be bizarre, contents may be unusual or perseverative, and form quality may be poor. Analysis of the characteristics of Rorschach responses provides insight into the child's cognitive processing and cognitive contents. It must be remembered throughout the interpretation process, however, that some unusual verbalizations or distortions are normal for young children. Use of the standardized Exner (1986) system can allow the clinician to compare a child to normative samples of nonreferred peers. These comparisons are vital in determining if a Rorschach protocol reflects unusual responses or merely age-appropriate responses. Furthermore, despite its utility in the assessment of the schizophrenic child, the Rorschach should be used only as a hypothesis-generating device following extensive interviewing and behavioral data gathering.

In addition to the Rorschach, the TAT can provide information concerning the schizophrenic child's thought and perceptual processes. TAT stories provide the clinician with a sense of the child's scripts for interpreting the events of daily life. For children over age 6 or so, scripts involve a plausible progression of events that occur in a story-like form. They indicate the child's expectations of how events occur in the world, usually based on past experience or recollections of stories told by others. At the most basic level a script involves an initial scene followed by an event. Based on the event, an outcome occurs. This outcome may then become an event that leads to yet another outcome, and so on. "Characters" in the script are things that act or produce change in the story; they are usually people, animals, or objects.

The characters and events in the child's stories often reflect some aspect of the child's fantasy or reality life. Thus, they indicate the child's internalized structures for interpreting reality. The schizophrenic child's scripts may be rambling, purposeless, confused, or disjointed. This presentation reflects a disorganization of thought and the basic building blocks for interpreting events (scripts). Other schizophrenic children tell markedly impoverished stories or simply describe the TAT cards. This constriction of thought occurs as a defense against disorganization produced when thought is allowed to flow freely. Less common is the schizophrenic child who tells stories that are linear and purposeful, but with bizarre themes. Children who show this latter pattern are more likely to be traumatized, malingering, or to have overly active fantasy lives.

As with the Rorschach, the TAT is valuable as a hypothesis generator and as a source of added information in the assessment of the schizophrenic child. However, it should never be used alone, independent of behavioral/interview assessment techniques. Bizarre or disjointed TAT stories can reflect conditions other than schizophrenia, such as brain damage, mental retardation, depression, or oppositionality. Furthermore, the clinician must adopt a developmental view when interpreting TAT stories. Children under the age of 6 will often tell brief, stereotypical, or disjointed stories. Such stories in a 13-year-old would be considered indicative of depression, oppositionality, mental retardation, or schizophrenia. Between the ages of 6 and 12, children acquire improved verbal and storytelling skills, and their repertoire of scripts increases. Hence, TAT stories improve greatly between these ages.

Many other projective techniques are used to assess children with suspected schizophrenia. The most popular of these techniques are sentence completion tests and drawing tests. Schizophrenic children's responses to sentence completion tests reflect their disorder of thought and perception. For example, the schizophrenic child may perseverate on an unusual or bizarre theme in all sentence completion responses. In other cases, responses may not logically follow the theme of the beginning of the sentence. Very impaired children may make up their own sentence and ignore the beginning of the sentence given to them to complete. Analysis of children's responses on the sentence completion test can indicate specific problems with organization of thought as well as specific thought contents.

Projective drawing techniques range from self-portraits, to drawings of the family, to open-ended drawings of anything. The drawings of schizophrenic children may reflect disorganization, attention problems, or bizarre thought/

perceptual processes. Some schizophrenic children leave critical elements off of drawings (e.g., body without a head), while others make drawings with strange or painful themes (e.g., a graphic drawing of a killing or suicide). Drawings can sometimes serve as a starting or connection point for therapy, with the child explaining the drawing to the therapist. Child and therapist can then explore thoughts and feelings related to the drawing.

Behavioral Assessment

Parent-Report. In order to obtain a complete picture of the behavior of the schizophrenic child, administration of a broad-band behavior problem rating scale is usually warranted. The Child Behavior Checklist (CBCL) has been used in several studies to assess the behaviors of schizophrenic children. Del Beccaro et al. (1988), for example, found that children with hallucinations scored higher on most CBCL scales than did psychiatric controls. Scales with the highest elevations were the Hostile-Withdrawn, Aggressive, Delinquent, Hyperactive, and Immature scales. In addition, the Schizoid and Somatic Complaints scales differentiated the two groups. All scale scores were 69 or higher for the hallucinating group.

The CBCL has been revised since the Del Beccaro study, and the new subscales have not been extensively studied with schizophrenic children. However, a general elevation of subscales in the 70+ range is to be expected, with varying patterns for different types of problems in the individual child. In particular, the Thought Problems, Somatic Complaints, and Withdrawn subscales are likely to be elevated in a child showing classic schizophrenic symptoms. Specific CBCL findings can be probed in a later clinical interview.

Syndrome-Specific Tests

Clinician-Administered

Unstructured Interview. A detailed history of the child's development, family history of psychiatric disorders, and specifics of the "schizophrenic" behaviors are crucial for the accurate diagnosis and effective treatment of schizophrenia in childhood. Many behaviors and syndromes may appear schizophrenic, when in fact the child has a very different problem (see preceding Clinical Description section). These schizophrenic-like syndromes should be ruled out, especially in pre-adolescent children. Medical history of neurological injury or insult (e.g., exposure to toxic substances, traumatic head injury, or epilepsy) may suggest an organic condition that should be evaluated by a neurologist.

In addition to developmental history, careful consideration of family history of psychiatric disorders is important. A strong family history of schizophrenia may suggest a genetic component or propensity to develop schizophrenic symptoms; family history of mood disorders may also suggest a genetic risk. Alternatively, chronic exposure to the bizarre or abusive behavior of a severely mentally ill parent may create stress and modeling effects that account for the emergence of schizophrenic behavior in the child.

Kiddie Formal Thought Disorder Rating Scale.   The K-FTDS (Caplan et al., 1989) is an observer-rating scale of four types of thought disorder derived from DSM-III: illogical thinking, loose association, incoherence, and poverty of content of speech. It is administered by playing the Kiddie Formal Thought Disorder Story Game (Caplan et al., 1989) with the child and then coding the child's answers to the game. The Kiddie Formal Thought Disorder Story Game is a 20–25 minute technique that consists of three parts: In the first part the child listens to an audiotaped story and then must repeat it and answer questions based on it. In the second part the child is asked to make up a story based on one of four topics. The third part is identical to the first part. Responses to the game are typically videotaped for later coding by trained coders (Caplan, Perdue, et al., 1990).

The child's responses to the three parts of the story game are coded into the four thought disorder categories based on operational definitions and examples for each category. Illogical thinking is defined as inappropriate statements, inappropriate reasoning, or contradictory ideas within the same statement. Loose association is defined as changes in the topic of communication without transition or reason for doing so. Incoherence is defined as jumbled syntax or meaning in a statement. Finally, poverty of content of speech is coded when the child does not elaborate on the topic of conversation for at least two statements (Caplan et al., 1989; Caplan, Foy, et al., 1990; Caplan, Perdue, et al., 1990). Scores for each category are the number of times each category occurs during the story game, divided by the total number of utterances during the game. A total score can be derived by summing the category scores.

Interrater reliability for the K-FTDS is reported to be good (Caplan, Perdue, et al., 1990). Incoherence and poverty of content scale scores are typically very low, even in schizophrenic samples (Caplan et al., 1989; Caplan, Foy, et al., 1990; Caplan, Perdue, et al., 1990). However, illogical thinking, loose association, and total scores discriminate between schizophrenic and normal samples (Caplan et al., 1989; Caplan, Foy, et al., 1990; Caplan, Perdue, et al., 1990). Raw scores for schizophrenic samples on these scales are 0.27, 0.04, and 0.31, respectively. Furthermore, younger schizophrenic children score higher on illogical thinking and loose association than do older schizophrenic children (Caplan, Perdue, et al., 1990).

Clinically, the K-FTDS has limited utility because its coding procedure can be time-consuming. In addition, more studies are needed in order to demonstrate discriminant validity between schizophrenics and children with other psychiatric disorders. Nevertheless, the K-FTDS has value because of its standardized presentation and quantified scoring. Using the Kiddie Formal Thought Disorders Story Game with informal scoring during the game may allow clinical use of the K-FTDS. However, interrater reliability and standardization are likely to suffer with this informal use.

DSM-III Schizophrenia Symptom Rating Scale. Watkins et al. (1988) developed the SRS simply by listing DSM-III symptoms of schizophrenia, with a rating scale of 0 (not true), 1 (somewhat true), and 2 (very true) for each item. Although they had clinicians rate children based on review of records, the SRS could conceivably be administered to a parent or teacher. Watkins et al. (1988) reported high interrater reliability for the SRS, although their technique for computing interrater reliability is inadequately described. The SRS has not been used with parents and needs to be updated to reflect the current DSM-IV criteria. Furthermore, norms, reliability, and validity are unknown. However, an updated SRS would be simple for any clinician to develop and may provide a structure for interviewing a parent about a child's symptoms. Because it requires minimal clinical time and effort, the SRS could be useful in spite of its numerous drawbacks.

TREATMENT OPTIONS

Treatment options for schizophrenic children (see Table 9.3) have received little research attention. This lack of knowledge is probably a result of several factors: the general lack of research and empirical knowledge about childhood schizophrenia, the rarity of true childhood schizophrenia, a reluctance to use neuroleptic medication with children because of side effects, and concern that psychotic children cannot benefit from verbally or cognitively oriented psychotherapy. Despite the lack of empirical knowledge, schizophrenic children

TABLE 9.3 Treatment Options for Schizophrenia in Childhood

BEHAVIORAL INTERVENTIONS

Reinforcement of incompatible behavior or lack of "schizophrenic" behavior
Elimination of access to antecedent situations (e.g., stressors) that are associated with schizophrenic behavior

MEDICATION

Neuroleptics

PSYCHOTHERAPY

Play therapy

FAMILY INTERVENTIONS

Family therapy

INPATIENT HOSPITALIZATION

Note: This outline of options summarizes major treatments covered in the text. Specific treatments are often combined into an intervention package. Refer to the text for additional descriptions of each treatment. This table is not necessarily an exhaustive list of all treatments available.

are a reality, and they require treatment. Inpatient milieu therapy, behavioral therapy, and pharmacotherapy have emerged as the most common treatment approaches for childhood schizophrenia.

Behavioral Interventions

Behavioral treatments conceptualize schizophrenic behavior as a response that occurs because it is reinforced or elicited by the environment. Internal schizophrenic thoughts or perceptual processes are largely ignored. Rather, behavioral interventions target the external, behavioral manifestations of internal processes.

Behavior therapy for schizophrenia begins with a detailed analysis of the child's schizophrenic behaviors. First, the behaviors are listed, operationally defined, and broken down into molecular parts. For example, if the child is making strange statements, the word "strange" is operationally defined as including certain themes or components. Examples are gathered, until the therapist and parents are in agreement as to exactly what constitutes a strange statement.

Next, the antecedents and consequences of the behavior are investigated. The therapist, parent, and (sometimes) child discuss what typically happens before and after each of the target schizophrenic behaviors. In many cases it is wise to have the parent keep a diary of occurrences of the behavior, antecedents, and consequences for a week or so. This diary technique may identify antecedents and consequences of which the parent was unaware.

Once antecedents and consequences are identified, baseline monitoring can begin. This monitoring consists simply of tracking the number of occurrences of the target behavior over time, before intervention occurs. Usually only one or two circumscribed schizophrenic behaviors are chosen for monitoring.

Following baseline monitoring, an intervention is designed and implemented. This intervention involves a manipulation of antecedents and consequences in order to discourage the occurrence of the target behavior. For example, consequences are modified by rewarding the nonoccurrence of the behavior or by rewarding the occurrence of behaviors that are incompatible with the target behavior. Typically, reinforcement is delivered on a fixed-interval schedule, in which the child is rewarded if the behavior does not occur for a certain period of time (usually a day or half-day).

The implementation of the intervention occurs concurrently with continued monitoring of the target behavior. If the target behavior responds to the intervention, the intervention may continue unchanged. On the other hand, if the target behavior does not respond to intervention, the intervention may be modified in order to have a greater effect. For example, antecedents may be modified, such as keeping the child out of situations in which the psychotic behavior occurs.

When a criterion level is reached for the target behavior, the intervention is faded by increasing the intervals between reinforcement, reducing the amount of reinforcement, or implementing a variable interval or variable ratio scheme, with the interval/ratio gradually increasing. A new target behavior is then selected, and the process begins again.

Examples of target schizophrenic behaviors are inappropriate affect, reports of hallucinations, random babbling, and odd behavior. For example, a child who laughs at random or inappropriate times may be put on a behavioral plan that begins with monitoring of the inappropriate laughter. Following the monitoring period, the child is then instructed about when laughter is and is not appropriate. A reinforcer (i.e., 5 extra minutes of TV time) is then given for each instance of appropriate laughter, with punishment (i.e., 5 fewer minutes of TV) for inappropriate laughter.

Behavioral techniques have the advantages of being straightforward, easy to teach to parents, and easy to evaluate for efficacy. However, they ignore the subjective, cognitive components of schizophrenia, which are a major part of the disorder. Furthermore, some schizophrenic children report having little control over their behavior during a psychotic episode. Therefore, they have little ability to purposefully respond to a reinforcement schedule.

Over all, behavioral techniques are most likely to be effective for children who have more of a behavioral than a thought disorder, for children who exhibit schizophrenic behaviors for attention, and for schizophrenic children whose symptoms have an oppositional-defiant quality. Behavioral therapy can also be a useful adjunct to medication by encouraging the emergence of appropriate behaviors at a time when the medication is causing a reduction in negative behaviors. More-impaired children may not respond as well to behavioral techniques alone and may require a medication component.

Medication

The use of medication with schizophrenic children is controversial because of a lack of adequate research and the potential negative side effects of neuroleptic medication. There are no double-blind, random-assignment medication studies with schizophrenic children and few such studies with adolescents. Furthermore, it is suspected that neuroleptics do not work as well with schizophrenic children as with adults (McClellan and Werry, 1992; McDaniel, 1986). Nevertheless, McClellan and Werry (1992) state that "the only specific treatment of documented efficacy in schizophrenia is antipsychotic (neuroleptic) medication" (p. 137). Furthermore, clinical experience and case study support the use of neuroleptics with some child schizophrenics. Hence, the "documented" efficacy of medication derives from case studies with children and empirical studies with adults. It is assumed that adult data apply to children. Other than neuroleptics, other types of medication have not been shown to be effective in controlling schizophrenic symptoms in children (McDaniel, 1986).

McClellan and Werry (1992) state that "there is no evidence to suggest that any one neuroleptic is superior in the treatment of schizophrenia" (p. 139). Hence, a variety of neuroleptics are used. Haloperidol (Haldol) and thioridazine (Mellaril) are perhaps the most popular of such medications. The choice of medication appears to depend on the type of symptoms, the response of the individual child, and the extent of side effects.

The primary effect of neuroleptics in child schizophrenics is the decrease of positive symptoms such as hallucinations, delusions, hyperactivity, and disorganized thought. Negative symptoms, such as flatness and withdrawal, do not respond as well to neuroleptic medication (McDaniel, 1986).

The largest drawback to the use of medication with childhood schizophrenics is the potential for severe side effects. Side effects vary somewhat from one neuroleptic to another, but certain effects are common: Fatigue, akathisia (constant movement), tardive dyskinesia, and cognitive clouding are a few of the more common effects (McClellan and Werry, 1992). Ultimately, the decision to use medication with a childhood schizophrenic involves a weighing of the benefits and risks. In general, failure of psychological interventions, more impairment, longer duration, and more dangerous behavior are characteristics that are likely to argue in favor of using medication.

Psychotherapy

A variety of psychotherapeutic interventions have been attempted with schizophrenic children, with varying success from child to child. Play therapy, for example, allows the schizophrenic child to play in an unstructured, accepting therapy situation (Axline, 1969; Gelfand et al., 1988). The therapist acts as a facilitator for the child's growth and as a source of acceptance. The rationale for play therapy is the belief that schizophrenic children have not internalized an acceptance of themselves as worthwhile, valuable persons. By playing in a nondirective, accepting atmosphere, they have a chance to explore themselves and to have their sense of self validated by the therapist. Play therapy may be effective for psychotic children who have been neglected, rejected, or traumatized. However, the utility of play therapy for the majority of schizophrenic children has not been established.

Family Interventions

Family therapy focuses on the role of the child's schizophrenic symptoms within the family system and the role of family conflict in exacerbating schizophrenic symptoms. In some cases the child's symptoms may deflect attention from other family issues. Alternatively, the symptoms may serve the psychological needs of one or more family members. For example, a schizophrenic child may serve the needs of a mother who has an intense need to care for a dependent person. The child's symptoms may bring the child attention from the mother and preserve the family system by allowing mother to retain her caretaking role. On the other hand, family conflict may create distress within a vulnerable child, resulting in disorganization of thought and bizarre behavior. Family therapy attempts to change the family system so that the child's symptoms no longer are needed to preserve the integrity of the system. In addition, the behavior of the family is modified in order to reduce the child's distress and psychotic behavior. Family therapy probably applies to a proportion of cases of childhood schizophrenia, but it rarely addresses all of the key issues and symptoms of the childhood schizophrenic.

Inpatient Hospitalization

Children with severe schizophrenic symptoms sometimes require hospitalization to stabilize their behavior and return them to a minimally adaptive level of functioning. Usually these children have exhibited a worsening of symptoms despite efforts at behavioral or psychopharmacological treatment. In other cases, children are hospitalized because their psychotic symptoms render them unmanageable or dangerous in the home environment. For children with milder psychotic symptoms, every effort should be made to avoid hospitalization, so that they do not receive the message that they are very sick. Hospitalization may also expose children to negative peer behavior models. Children with milder symptoms can often be managed with outpatient therapy or medication.

Inpatient treatment generally involves the use of intense milieu behavioral therapy combined with trials of medications to determine the most beneficial medication and dose. Behavior therapy is usually administered by the unit staff, who follow a behavior plan devised by a mental health professional. This plan typically involves the allocation of privileges and access to favored activities based on compliance with target behaviors. In many cases the target behaviors consist of compliance, behavioral control, and positive interaction with peers. Although these targets are not psychotic symptoms *per se*, they presumably encourage more appropriate behavior that is inconsistent with psychotic behavior.

In addition to behavior therapy in the context of the unit milieu, inpatient placements generally include components of individual, group, or family therapy. The effectiveness of these interventions in addressing schizophrenic symptoms is unclear, but they can be valuable for postdischarge planning. For example, the child can be prepared in individual therapy for difficulties that are likely to be encountered following discharge. Likewise, parents can be educated, and family changes can be encouraged to prevent schizophrenic behavior at home.

Over all, inpatient placements can provide the intensive, consistent environment necessary to regulate persistent, severe, and bizarre schizophrenic behavior. However, the effectiveness of an inpatient placement is only as good as its ability to produce lasting change in the child's behavior once the child is returned to the home environment. Hence, work with parents and outpatient follow are critical to the efficacy of inpatient therapy for schizophrenic children.

References

American Psychiatric Association. (1994). *Diagnostic and statistical manual of mental disorders* (4th ed.). Washington, DC: Author.

Asarnow, J. R., and Ben-Meir, S. (1988). Children with schizophrenia spectrum and depressive disorders: A comparative study of premorbid adjustment, onset pattern and severity of impairment. *Journal of Child Psychology and Psychiatry, 29,* 477–488.

Axline, V. M. (1969). *Play therapy.* New York: Ballantine.

Bettes, B. A., and Walker, E. (1987). Positive and negative symptoms in psychotic and other psychiatrically disturbed children. *Journal of Child Psychology and Psychiatry, 28,* 555–568.

Caplan, R., Foy, J. G., Asarnow, R. F., and Sherman, T. (1990). Information processing deficits of schizophrenic children with formal thought disorder. *Psychiatry Research, 31,* 169–177.

Caplan, R., Guthrie, D., Fish, B., Tanguay, P. E., and David-Lando, G. (1989). The Kiddie Formal Thought Disorder Scale (K-FTDS): Clinical assessment, reliability, and validity. *Journal of the American Academy of Child Psychiatry, 28,* 408–416.

Caplan, R., Perdue, S., Tanguay, P. E., and Fish, B. (1990). Formal thought disorder in childhood onset schizophrenia and schizotypal personality disorder. *Journal of Child Psychology and Psychiatry, 31,* 1103–1114.

Del Beccaro, M. A., Burke, P., and McCauley, E. (1988). Hallucinations in children: A follow-up study. *Journal of the American Academy of Child and Adolescent Psychiatry, 27,* 462–465.

Exner, J. E. (1986). *The Rorschach: A Comprehensive System I. Basic Foundations* (2d ed.). New York: Wiley.

Fish, B. (1986). Antecedents of an acute schizophrenic break. *Journal of the American Academy of Child Psychiatry, 25,* 595–600.

Garralda, M.E. (1984a). Hallucinations in children with conduct and emotional disorders: II. The follow-up study. *Psychological Medicine, 14,* 597–604.

———— . (1984b). Psychotic children with hallucinations. *British Journal of Psychiatry, 145,* 74–77.

Gelfand, D. M., Jenson, W. R., and Drew, C. J. (1988). *Understanding child behavior disorders* (2d ed.). New York: Harcourt Brace Jovanovich.

Kemph, J. P. (1987). Hallucinations in psychotic children. *Journal of the American Academy of Child and Adolescent Psychiatry, 26,* 556–559.

Kolvin, I., Berney, T. P., and Yoeli, J. (1990). Schizophrenia in childhood. In M. Hersen and C. G. Last (Eds.), *Handbook of child and adult psychopathology: A longitudinal perspective* (pp. 99–113). New York: Pergamon Press.

McClellan, J. M., and Werry, J. S. (1992). Schizophrenia. *Pediatric Psychopharmacology, 15,* 131–148

McDaniel, K. D. (1986). Pharmacologic treatment of psychiatric and neuro-developmental disorders in children and adolescents (Part 2). *Clinical Pediatrics, 25,* 143–146.

Meyer, R. G. (1993). *The Clinician's Handbook* (3d ed.). Boston: Allyn & Bacon.

Watkins, J. M., Asarnow, R. F., and Tanguay, P. E. (1988). Symptom development in childhood onset schizophrenia. *Journal of Child Psychology and Psychiatry, 29,* 865–878.

Werry, J. S., and McClellan, J. M. (1992). Predicting outcome in child and adolescent (early onset) schizophrenia and bipolar disorder. *Journal of the American Academy of Child and Adolescent Psychiatry, 31,* 147–150.

CHAPTER 10

Pervasive Developmental Disorders

The pervasive developmental disorders (PDDs) have been the subject of considerable debate and confusion in the mental health, education, and medical communities. This unsettled state of affairs is represented, to a certain extent, in the current research and diagnostic classification systems for the PDDs. For example, several sets of diagnostic criteria exist for "autism," and clinicians often use undefined terms such as "mild autism" and "high-functioning autism" to describe children who have some symptoms of autism but do not meet all of the criteria for diagnosis. Hence, clinicians working with PDD-diagnosed children must understand that the knowledge base for these disorders is currently evolving, with some disagreement on issues of diagnosis, assessment, and treatment.

Clinicians should also be sensitive to the sometimes dramatic effects of labeling a child as having "autism" or another PDD. Such diagnoses should be made with caution and only following evaluation by medical, mental health, and educational (usually speech-language and teaching) specialists. Furthermore, children with PDD diagnoses should be monitored regularly for progress that may indicate their readiness to adopt more adaptive social roles.

In DSM-III-R, pervasive developmental disorders (PDDs) were coded on Axis II with mental retardation (MR) and specific developmental disorders (SDD). DSM-IV, however, places PDDs on Axis I. Furthermore, several new PDD subtypes were added, such that DSM-IV contains five categories of PDDs: Autistic Disorder, Rett's Disorder, Childhood Disintegrative Disorder (CDD), Asperger's Disorder, and PDD Not Otherwise Specified (PDDNOS). Formerly, only Autistic Disorder and PDDNOS were coded under the PDD category. The identification of three new disorders (Rett's, CDD, and Asperger's) is a major change in DSM-IV.

Rett's Disorder, Childhood Disintegrative Disorder, and Asperger's Disorder

CLINICAL DESCRIPTION

Like autism, the three new, "nonautistic" PDDs are characterized by serious communication problems and social deficits. Rett's Disorder emerges following normal prenatal and early infant (e.g., the first few months) development. After about age 5 months, however, the infant experiences slowed head growth, loss of purposeful hand movement, the emergence of stereotypical movement, loss of interest in social interaction, poor coordination, slow movement, and language delay. Slowed head growth may persist until as late as age 4, while a decline in hand movement skills may persist until age 2½. Little recovery of these pervasive losses occurs throughout the life span, and the disorder has an appearance of progressive decline in the early years.

Children with Rett's resemble autistic children somewhat in their language and social delays. However, they may eventually acquire greater levels of social interaction, and they may show more motoric problems than autistic children. In some children with Rett's, the loss of hand movement and social involvement reflects a noticeable loss of previous skills, in contrast to the autistic child's typical failure to develop social orientation from infancy. Rett's Disorder is extremely rare, and research data are sparse (American Psychiatric Association, 1994).

CDD emerges following normal infant and early toddler development (age 2 or older). In the late toddler–early preschool years, CDD children lose some of their early skills in the language, social, play, adaptive functioning, and motor areas. This "disintegration" in functioning is accompanied by social and communication deficits or by odd behaviors that appear autistic. Unlike autistic children, however, CDD children have at least 2 years of normal development. Furthermore, their social-communication-behavior deficits need not be as severe as those of autistic children, and deficits in only two of the three (social, communication, or behavior) areas are required for diagnosis. Many children who were previously classified as "late" or "childhood" onset autism are diagnosed CDD in DSM-IV. Because many children diagnosed with Rett's Disorder and Autistic Disorder will also meet the milder CDD criteria, CDD can only be diagnosed when Rett's and Autistic Disorder are ruled out. Like Rett's Disorder, CDD is rare (American Psychiatric Association, 1994).

The last of the "new" PDDs, Asperger's Disorder, is characterized by social and behavioral deficits *without* significant language, cognitive, or adaptive functioning deficits. Typical social deficits of the Asperger's child are lack of empathy, lack of social interest, and impaired social nonverbal interaction (e.g., lack of eye contact). Typical behavioral deficits involve the presence of a restricted range of stereotyped behaviors, interests, or routines. Children diagnosed with Asperger's Disorder appear to be socially unresponsive and withdrawn, with limited interests and activities. Their problems cause significant impairment in daily functioning, particularly in the social arena. However, their language, performance in school, and testing data all suggest no major problems with intellectual ability, language, or adaptive behavior. Like CDD, Asperger's Disorder can only be diagnosed when Autistic Disorder and Rett's Disorder are ruled out.

PDDNOS is diagnosed when a child shows considerable, pervasive, "autistic-like" impairment in social, communication, or behavioral skills but does not meet criteria for any specific PDD diagnosis. Prior to DSM-IV, many children with CDD, Rett's, and Asperger's Disorder were diagnosed PDDNOS. The delineation of these new categories, therefore, has reduced the number of children who qualify for PDDNOS.

While Rett's Disorder and Asperger's Disorder have received some attention in the past, their failure to be included in DSM nomenclature significantly reduced the attention and study they received (Kolvin, Berney, and Yoeli, 1990; Ornitz, 1989). CDD and PDDNOS also have received little attention, and what attention they have received has been as a result of studies of children with "atypical autism," "childhood-onset autism," or "autistic features." Most of the literature, empirical studies, and treatment of PDDs have been with the syndrome of autism. Fortunately, much of the autistic treatment literature can be applied (with some appropriate modifications to accommodate symptom differences) to the other PDDs. As the literature grows about other PDDs, specific assessment and treatment models may emerge. Until then, Autistic Disorder must be used as a model from which assessment and treatments for the other disorders are derived.

Autistic Disorder

CLINICAL DESCRIPTION

Diagnostic Considerations

Unlike the other PDDs, Autistic Disorder (or autism) has received considerable clinical and research attention. Autism has been defined in numerous ways by clinicians and researchers. The DSM-IV definition of Autistic Disorder focuses on three major areas: impairment in social interaction; impairment in communication; and restricted or stereotyped activities, interests, and behaviors. Social interaction impairment is characterized by lack of appropriate nonverbal social behavior (e.g., eye contact), lack of peer relationships, and lack of socio-emotional empathy or reciprocity. Communication impairment is shown by language delay, stereotyped/inappropriate use of language, inability to initiate or sustain conversation, and markedly reduced imaginative play. Examples of restricted interests and behaviors are distress at change in routine, stereotyped motor behavior, focus on odd objects, and extreme interest in a circumscribed activity. Onset age for autism has been changed in each of the last three DSMs. In DSM-IV, age of onset is placed at 3 years or younger.

Other criteria for autism are occasionally used, but the differences between autism definitions are largely in the amount of emphasis put on particular symptoms. Nevertheless, disagreement over an autism diagnosis can result from the use of different definition systems (Morgan, 1988). For example, the definition held by the National Society for Autistic Children requires onset prior to 30 months of age. It also emphasizes disturbances of developmental rate (e.g., emergence of some developmental behaviors before expected and others after expected) and abnormal responses to sensory stimuli (i.e., hypo- or hyperresponsivity) to a greater extent than does DSM-IV (Ritvo and Freeman, 1978). Numerous authors use the National Society's definition as opposed to that of DSM-IV, resulting in some diagnostic discrepancy in the autism area (Freeman et al., 1978).

In addition to differing definitions, the diagnosis of autism is further complicated by conditions that consist of autistic-appearing features that have not been defined as autism *per se* (Ornitz, 1989). DSM-IV has taken a step toward diagnostic improvement by clarifying the differences between Autistic Disorder, Rett's Disorder, CDD, and Asperger's Disorder. However, some confusion about "autistic-like" disorders continues to exist. Wolff and Chick (1980), for example, describe a schizoid personality of childhood, which has many of the features of autism but seems to be a milder form of the disorder (Ornitz, 1989). In addition, the diagnosis "childhood schizophrenia" has in the past been used as a synonym for autism, presumably as a result of the belief that autism represented a precursor for later schizophrenia. Given this multiplicity of definitions, synonyms, and variants of autism, the use of the DSM-IV PDD categories is not only parsimonious but less confusing.

Once the diagnosis of autism is considered, perhaps the most important co-occurring or differential diagnoses to be investigated are organic brain dysfunction and mental retardation. Children with brain dysfunction or brain injury can engage in bizarre or stereotyped behaviors and have communication deficits similar to those of autistic children. For this reason, it is important that an autistic-appearing child be referred to a neurologist for a CT scan or EEG analysis. A child with brain dysfunction can be co-diagnosed with autism if he or she also meets diagnostic criteria for autism. However, many brain-damaged children will not meet the social interaction criteria for the autism diagnosis.

Mental retardation is a second condition that frequently co-occurs with autism, perhaps in more than 75% of cases of autism (Morgan, 1990; Ornitz, 1989). However, the bulk of mentally retarded children are *not* autistic, despite the fact that they may show some autistic behaviors. One characteristic that frequently differentiates autistic and mentally retarded children is appearance. Autistic children tend to have fewer physical anomalies and to be more attractive than mentally retarded children (Morgan, 1990). A second difference is that autistic children tend to have better motor coordination than mentally retarded children. Third, autistic children usually do not show the uniformly delayed development seen in mentally retarded children. Instead, autistic children often develop isolated abilities at or before normative ages. Finally, mentally retarded children often show social interest and development of relationships, while autistic children do not.

There is a growing realization that autistic features are more common in children than was once believed. However, the prevalence of the full-blown Autistic Disorder depends on the definition used to define the disorder (Ornitz, 1989). Using the early, more rigorous definitions of autism, only 1 in 10,000 children would be diagnosed with the disorder (Morgan, 1990). However, using more modern definitions (Ritvo and Freeman, 1978), autism affects 4–5 out of every 10,000 children, and there are 3–4 autistic males for every autistic female (Morgan, 1990; Lotter, 1966; Ornitz, 1989; Wing et al., 1976).

Little agreement exists on subtyping of autistic children. Authors do agree, however, that autistic children form a somewhat heterogeneous group. Newsom and Rincover (1989) suggest that autistic children can be divided into subgroups based on intelligence. Autistic children who are severely and profoundly retarded typically have negative outcomes, with little growth in intelligence, modest communication skills, and lifelong problems with social interaction (Morgan, 1990). As many as 60–75% of autistic children may face this outcome, especially without intensive intervention (Morgan, 1990; Newsom and Rincover, 1989). They typically can learn, at most, self-care skills, following instructions, simple social conventions, and very basic communication. Independent living is often not a reasonable goal for severely retarded autistic children, and intervention programs should be geared toward the modest gains that they are capable of making. Failure to develop communicative language by age 5 and failure to achieve normal toy play are both associated with particularly poor prognosis (Morgan, 1990; Ornitz and Ritvo, 1976).

A second group of autistic children identified by Newsom and Rincover (1989) is those who score in mildly retarded or higher ranges on intelligence tests. These children have considerably more potential than those in the former group, and some of them will achieve a nearly normal level of functioning, especially if they develop communicative language before age 5 (Morgan, 1990). In general, these children tend to be easier to teach basic self-care and communication skills. Thus, the emphasis (and hard work) is on teaching them higher-level skills that are needed for normal functioning in society. Such goals as social skills, average vocabulary and grammar, and independent living may be encouraged in this latter group of autistic children.

Because of their higher potential, mildly retarded to normal-intelligence autistic children have a wider range of outcomes. If early intervention is neglected or if the child is in an impoverished environment, outcome may resemble that of the moderately to severely retarded group. On the other hand, intensive, early intervention may result in impressive gains in functioning. However, autistic children rarely achieve a completely normal level of functioning. High functioning autistic children tend to retain some elements of shyness, introversion, poor social judgment, and impaired empathy (Ornitz and Ritvo, 1976).

Other categorizations of autistic children, such as schizoid personality of childhood and childhood schizophrenia, are often ill-defined and outdated. A more promising subtyping characterization is the hypothesis that "autism occurs along a continuum of severity" (Ornitz, 1989, p. 248). Different points along this continuum refer to greater or lesser degrees of autistic symptoms. While this characterization does not delineate discrete subtypes of autistic children, it does suggest that autistic children form a heterogeneous group and that each child's variant of the disorder should be identified based on number and type of symptoms.

Appearance and Features

Despite disagreement over the relative importance of specific diagnostic criteria, common features of autistic appearance and behavior (see Table 10.1) are well agreed upon. Controversy arises when authors designate some symptoms as more important than others, or when authors attempt to group symptoms into meaningful categories.

The earliest conceptualizations of autism by Kanner (1943) emphasized five features of the disorder: (1) inability to relate to social stimuli, (2) need for sameness and order in the environment, (3) failure to use language to communicate, (4) fascination with objects, and (5) potential for normal cognitive development. The latter characteristic has been abandoned, but the first four persist in modern definitions of autism. In DSM-IV the three categories of autistic symptoms are impairment in (1) reciprocal social interaction, (2) communication, and (3) repertoire of activities and interests. Ornitz and Ritvo (1976) emphasize five symptom categories: disturbances of (1) perception, (2) developmental rate, (3) relating to people and objects, (4) speech and language, and (5) motility.

The following description of autistic features lists the basic features of autism without judging their relative importance. Not all autistic children will have all of these features, and the manifestation of the features may occur at varying degrees of severity:

Impaired Social Interaction.   One feature of autism is impaired social interaction (American Psychiatric Association, 1994; Ornitz and Ritvo, 1976). Autistic children often have poor or absent eye contact and do not orient to a person who is interacting with them. When picked up or touched, their response is unusual, ranging from ignoring to actively resisting the social contact. They may stiffen when held by a parent or pull away from physical contact as though it were an aversive stimulus. Reciprocal social interaction with these children is extremely difficult to initiate and maintain. They often show no interest in their social environment, will not abide by the rules of social "games," and do not initiate their own social interactions. When they do show an interest in a person, the interest may be unusual, such as fascination over a body part or a piece of clothing. Over- or underreaction to social interactions is the general rule for these children.

The almost absent social orientation of autistic children is also reflected in behaviors suggesting that they have little ability to sympathize with another's feelings or to understand what another person may be thinking. Autistic chil-

TABLE 10.1   Appearance and Features of Autistic Disorder

COMMON FEATURES

Impaired social interaction: poor eye contact, failure to orient to a speaker, discomfort with physical touching, lack of interest in social interaction, refusal/inability to follow social rules, lack of imitation, lack of empathy
Impaired/absent peer relationships
Impaired communication: language delay, echolalia, pronoun reversal
Unusual or inappropriate tonal quality of speech (flatness, sing-song)
Impaired use of objects: stereotyped use of objects, focus on one quality of an object (e.g., touch), resistance to novel use of objects
Disturbance of motor behavior: arm flapping, hand waving, head banging, whirling, rocking, swaying, scratching, toe walking
Attachment to routine
Hyper- and/or hyporesponsivity to sensory input
Repetitive, stereotypic play without imagination or fantasy
Inappropriate or flat affect
Self-stimulating behavior
Disturbances of developmental rate
Mental retardation
Onset before age 3

OCCASIONAL FEATURES

Negative/impaired relationship with caretakers
Unusual attachment behavior toward caretakers
One or two extremely well-developed, narrow, encapsulated abilities
Seizures

Note: The features listed above are often seen but are not universal. Some features may be diagnostically relevant or required, while others may not be required for diagnosis. "Common" features are typical of the disorder; "occasional" features appear frequently but are not necessarily seen in a majority of cases.

dren sometimes ignore the distress of others. They may act in ways that provoke anger or upset in other children, apparently oblivious that their actions will have that effect. Similarly, they show a blunted or absent response to the affection of others. Attention and praise often have a limited impact on them, and they rarely seek reassurance or comfort from others.

A lack of imitation and unresponsiveness to social reinforcement make autistic children extremely difficult to teach. Much of a child's learning is dependent upon imitation and social shaping of behavior. These venues are, at least initially, not available to the autistic child. Because of their detached, oblivious social behavior, they rarely have friendships among peers, and they may alienate or upset their caretakers.

On the other hand, some autistic children do show attachments to their caretakers or other familiar people, although the attachment may be demonstrated in unusual ways. For example, the child may engage in a favorite ritual when reunited with a parent. Alternatively, the child may ignore a caretaker until the caretaker leaves and then throw a tantrum. Newsom and Rincover (1989) report that as many as half of autistic children cuddle when held by a caretaker and show a social smile.

Impaired Communication.   Autistic children almost always have problems with communication, beginning with a delay in the acquisition of communicative language skills. In the worst cases of autism, this begins as total mutism (roughly 1 in 4 autistic children is mute [Morgan, 1990]), and the best outcome is use of simple words and signs/gestures. About half of autistic children speak very little and use only primitive gestures to communicate (Newsom and Rincover, 1989).

Often, however, the child verbalizes in an abnormal way. For example, the child may vocalize syllables that initially have no meaning but are eventually recognized by the parent to reflect internal states or needs. At later ages, phrases may be used by the child that have completely different meaning to the child than their meaning in the language. For example, a child may say, "The train is leaving" when he wants to go for a ride in the car. Other children engage in echolalia, repeating phrases that they hear without modifying the information to convey any measure of communication. Another unusual characteristic of the speech of autistic children is pronoun reversal, which occurs when the autistic child substitutes "you" for "me" and "me" for "you." For example, if the child is thirsty, she may say, "You want a drink of water."

When speech occurs, it may be accompanied by odd inflections (e.g., total flatness or sing-song, meaningless tonal quality) and unusual or absent expressive mannerisms (such as a lack of facial expression). Verbal and nonverbal communication modes may not be congruent, as when a child monotonously states that he is very happy or intensely angry. Likewise, a child may attempt to indicate an object without pointing, an action that even mentally retarded children very easily learn. These impairments in simple communication and language make social interaction with autistic children difficult and at times uncomfortable.

Impaired Use of Objects.   Autistic children tend to relate to objects in unusual ways. Stereotyped, rigid, or self-stimulating behaviors in relation to objects are common. For example, a child may carefully feel the texture of a surface for an hour, repeatedly stroking and patting it. Autistic children also frequently spin or twirl objects, leading to the inclusion of a spinning top in some assessments of autism (Schopler et al., 1980). Repetitive, ritualistic play with objects is common, and the children may become extremely distressed if they are encouraged to play with an object in a novel way. For example, autistic children may become preoccupied with parts of objects, showing excruciating attention to simple details. However, they may ignore major details, such as the child who plays with the tail of a stuffed animal but ignores the head. Creative, imaginative play with objects, seen in normal 3-year-olds, is often absent in autistic children. Autistic children can become very attached to unusual objects, such as a potato chip bag, while ignoring objects that typically elicit attachment behaviors, such as blankets and stuffed animals. The features described here, along with autistic children's preference for their environments to be structured, have been interpreted by some authors to indicate autistic children's need for a rigid sameness in the environment (Ornitz, 1989), as well as control over idiosyncratic details.

Disturbances of Motor Behavior.   Autistic children frequently engage in a number of unusual, purposeless motor behaviors. For example, an autistic child may flap his arm for no apparent reason or may repeatedly wave his hands in front of his face for hours. Self-destructive behaviors may also be exhibited, as when a child bangs her head against the wall for hours or scratches part of the body until it bleeds. Whirling, rocking, and swaying behaviors also are common, as is walking up on the toes. These motor behaviors are intermittent and may occur without any significant change in the environment. Some authors also note that observation of a spinning top tends to elicit motility disturbances (Ornitz and Ritvo, 1976). At other times, the child may remain motionless for an abnormal period of time, without any apparent sensory input or other reason for doing so. The stereotyped, intense, unpredictable, repetitive nature of autistic children's behavior has caused some authors to suggest that the behavior is performed in order for the child to receive vestibular or proprioceptive input (Ornitz, 1989).

Attachment to Routines.   Autistic children show a pathological attachment to even the finest detail of routines, and they may become extremely agitated or upset if deviations occur. This is likely related to their general resistance to any environmental change (Schopler et al., 1980). Even meaningless details may be extremely important to the autistic child, such as the cup that is used for drink at breakfast each morning or the steps in getting ready for school or daycare.

Problems with Sensory Input and Responsiveness.   Hyper- and hyporeactivity to sensory stimuli are common in autistic children, although the stimuli that elicit them are unpredictable. Knowledge of what stimuli normal children find preferable or aversive is often of little help in identifying what stimuli a particular autistic child will relate to. Loud sounds sometimes elicit no response from the autistic child, while certain quiet sounds may cause extreme distress. Hence, an autistic child who has loudly banged on a can may wail and cover his ears at the sounds of two pieces of paper rubbing together.

   In the tactile area, young autistic children seem to prefer smooth surfaces and textures, avoiding rough-textured objects and foods (Ornitz, 1989). This tactile hyperresponsivity sometimes results in significant feeding problems, as the child refuses all textured, solid food in favor of milk and baby food. In extreme cases this can cause failure-to-thrive and dangerous weight loss. Also in the tactile arena, painful stimuli may elicit no response, while simple tactile stimuli, such as the touch of an adult, may result in extreme agitation.

Sensory input may be focused on irrelevant details of objects, as when a child repeatedly feels the texture of a book page but shows no interest in the words or pictures on the page. In other cases, sensory input may be overly focused on minute details; for example, a child may notice the briefcase of a stranger but pay no attention to the new person. Autistic children will also often try to create their own sensory stimuli, sometimes in bizarre ways. For example, the child may repeatedly scratch a surface with her ear close to it.

Strangely, it is often difficult to predict what auditory, tactile, or visual stimuli autistic children will ignore and what stimuli they will find aversive. Such stimuli tend to differ from child to child and from time to time within the same child, although there is some within-child constancy. However, several authors note that autistic children in general tend to prefer proximal (touch, taste, smell) sensory stimulation over distal (hearing, seeing) sensory stimulation (Ornitz and Ritvo, 1976; Schopler et al., 1976). Hence, they will often engage in extensive, inappropriate touching, smelling, and mouthing of objects.

Unusual Play.   Unusual play is manifest in several other characteristics of autism, but it deserves individual mention because it is often reported by parents of autistic children. The play of autistic children is often repetitive, stereotypic, and lacking in creativity. Imaginative play is frequently absent, and coordinated play with other children is rarely observed.

Inappropriate Affect.   The emotional displays and responses of autistic children are often blunted, absent, inappropriate, or overly intense (Schopler et al., 1980). For example, a child may show no reaction to pain or to separation from a caretaker but become vehemently angry if the floor is vacuumed. Emotional responses to the upset of others are also often blunted or absent.

Self-Stimulating Behavior.   The self-stimulating behaviors of autistic children include rocking, head banging, kicking, arm waving, and self-injurious behavior. The purpose of these behaviors is apparently to provide sensory input, although the need for this input is unclear.

Disturbances of Developmental Rate.   Another feature of autism is disturbances of developmental rate (Ornitz and Ritvo, 1976). Unlike mentally retarded children, who achieve developmental milestones at a uniformly delayed rate, autistic children achieve some milestones early, others on time, and others very late. The affected developmental milestones tend to vary from child to child, although motor development is usually normal or only slightly delayed (Newsom and Rincover, 1989). For example, an autistic child may say a first word early in development but then not use language for communication until age 4 or 5. The achievement of some developmental milestones at or before appropriate ages, combined with the often normal or attractive appearance of autistic children, caused some authors (Kanner, 1943) to speculate that autistic children have normal intelligence but have difficulty expressing it. A substantial body of research, however, suggests that this is not the case (Ornitz, 1989).

Intellectual Functioning.   As many as 75–80% of autistic children are mentally retarded, scoring below 70 on tests of intellectual functioning. In many cases, autistic children refuse to cooperate sufficiently to be tested; this almost always reflects low functioning rather than oppositionality (Morgan, 1990). Combined with severe delays in adaptive communication, self-care, and judgment skills, these intellectual deficits are pervasive and have a major impact on the child's development. Occasionally an autistic child will show normal development or even extraordinary skills in a very defined area, such as computation, memory, or music. However, this talent is typically well encapsulated and should not be used as an indicator of general intelligence.

Considerable confusion has resulted from the early definitions of autism, which included potential for normal intelligence as a major feature (Morgan, 1990). This feature is not present in any modern definitions. In fact, it is now assumed that a diagnosis of autism almost always connotes some cognitive impairments.

Associated Neurological Problems.   There is a high rate of comorbidity of autism and seizure disorders, particularly at later ages (Ornitz and Ritvo, 1976). As many as 25% of autistic children may develop seizures, usually in adolescence (Ornitz, 1989; Ornitz and Ritvo, 1976). Childhood seizures typically indicate poorer outcome for the autistic child (Morgan, 1990).

Age of Onset.   Most parents report noticing autistic symptoms in their child before the age of 2½ years, even if they do not bring the child to professional attention until much later (Ornitz, 1989). Onset before age 3 is diagnostically required, and many authors believe that "autism is probably present at birth" (Ornitz and Ritvo, 1976, p. 610). Before 18 months, parents may notice that their child responds strangely to being held (rigid or limp), does not respond to social or other stimulation, has a delayed social smile, vocalizes rarely, and cries little. Nevertheless, the full autistic syndrome is typically *not* noted by parents before age 18 months (Ornitz and Ritvo, 1976). After 18 months, developmental delays become much more obvious. Children who clearly have onset of autistic symptomatology after age 3 are diagnosed with Rett's Disorder, CDD, or PDDNOS.

Etiology

Family Theories

Historically, family theories of etiology were used to explain the emergence of autism. Parents of autistic children were described as aloof, intelligent, cold, perfectionistic, achievement-oriented, and wealthy (Morgan, 1990; Ornitz and Ritvo, 1976). Presumably these characteristics suggested that the parents (particularly the mother) were cold and unresponsive to the children's needs. The children, with their needs ignored and in an uncomfortable state, internalized an image of the environment as hostile and withdrew into their own world.

Initial evidence for this explanation was anecdotal and based on selective clinical observations. Followup empirical studies have not supported this character- ization of parents of autistic children. No significant differences have been found between parents of autistic children and control parents (Morgan, 1990; Ornitz, 1989). Other family etiology theories, which postulated parental hostility, re- jection, and disturbed family dynamics, have also not received empirical sup- port (Ornitz and Ritvo, 1976). However, there is some evidence that having a child with autism may contribute to family stress and parental problems (Ornitz and Ritvo, 1976).

Biological Theories

With the fall of family etiology theories has come the rise of biological theories of autism. These theories postulate that autism is the result of a genetic-neuro- logical-physiological defect that causes the symptoms of the disorder. Twin studies support a genetic basis for the disorder, with monozygotic twins show- ing higher concordance rates than dizygotic twins. Furthermore, autism cuts across geography, culture, and racial populations, suggesting a biological cause as opposed to a cultural one (Ornitz & Ritvo, 1976).

Additional support for the biological theory comes from neurological and physiological studies. These studies find an abnormally large number of neu- rologic soft signs in children with autism, with 40–75% of children showing soft signs (Ornitz and Ritvo, 1976). EEG, sleep and REM studies have been contradictory and inconclusive. However, many autistic children are found to have abnormal EEG, and a significant minority develop seizures (Morgan, 1990). A host of biochemical studies have suggested some possible abnormality of serotonin or dopamine levels in autistic children, although this finding awaits further support (Newsom and Rincover, 1989; Ornitz and Ritvo, 1976).

Despite its intuitive appeal, the biological theory of autism has only sug- gestive research support at this point. Furthermore, results of several studies are inconsistent with the biological theory. Ornitz and Ritvo (1976) reviewed studies that indicate no increased incidence for schizophrenia or autism in the parents and siblings of children with autism, although some contradictory data exist. Furthermore, gene/chromosome studies have not isolated a genetic lo- cus of the disorder. Attempts to connect autism and specific genetic disorders (such as phenylketonuria and Fragile X) have explained only a fraction of au- tism cases (Ornitz, 1989).

Rather than research support, the biological theory appears to be currently supported by logical arguments. First, it is argued that such a pervasive, se- vere, stereotyped behavioral disorder must have a biological cause because environmental conditions alone could not account for it in such a large num- ber of children across different cultures. Second, the repudiation of the family theory of autism is often used as evidence that the biological theory must ap- ply. Obviously, though, these two theories are not the only two possible ones. Third, the problems managing the disorder using psychological therapies prior to the 1970s suggested that the disorder involved some biological cause that could not be changed with psychotherapy alone. Fourth, because autistic features emerge at a young age, the possibility of environmental influence is reduced. Finally, suggestive research evidence is taken as an indication that a biological cause exists but that current studies are too crude to identify it. Although several of these arguments are outdated, circular, or just plain wrong, the biological theory remains a leading candidate for the explanation of autism. However, it has not been conclusively supported to date.

Behavioral Theories

The major competitor with the biological theory is the behavioral explanation of autism (Lovaas, 1979). According to this theory, autism is not a disease but a cluster of behaviors that occasionally co-occur in children. Although this co-occurrence is greater than chance, it is not sufficiently high to define a homogeneous group of children. Rather, autistic children form a heterogeneous group. Thus, the best conceptualization of "autism" in any one child requires a look at specific behaviors as opposed to a disease entity.

Behaviorists argue that autism develops because autistic children do not find social stimuli to be reinforcing. As an infant the typical child learns that social stimuli (e.g., interaction, praise, imitation) are rewarding by pairing them with intrinsic reinforcers such as food, comfort, and warmth. For various reasons (biological predisposition, environmental contingencies, parental behavior), this pairing does not occur in autistic children, resulting in a lack of social interaction or interest in the child. This lack of social interest then leads to severe problems because the children do not learn from their environment how to behave like socialized human beings. The problems grow progressively larger as the children continue to fail to learn through observation of and interaction with the social environment. Finally, the children's behaviors appear bizarre because of their continuing divergence with "typical" human behaviors, which can only be learned in a social context through modeling and social reinforcement (Lovaas, 1979).

Support for the behavioral view has come largely from studies indicating that autistic children do not find their social environment to be reinforcing. When autistic children are taught to attend to their social environments, behavior change occurs. Behavioral interventions have brought about dramatic changes in the behavior of autistic children (Lovaas, 1979). Behavioral studies have been criticized because they tend to focus only on higher functioning autistic children. Furthermore, behavioral theories have difficulty explaining children who do not respond to behavior therapy.

ASSESSMENT PATTERNS

Assessment of a child suspected to be autistic should include medical, mental health, and educational personnel. Frequently the child's primary care physician is already involved and coordinating the medical side of a diagnostic assessment. Educationally, teachers and speech-language pathologists may be enlisted from the school system to assess the child and to implement recommendations.

The mental health component of the assessment of a child suspected to have autism consists of at least three parts: a specific test of autistic symptomatology, an intelligence test, and a test of adaptive functioning. The intelligence and adaptive functioning tests are intended to give a view of the child's cognitive functioning and ability to function in the environment. These tests are also required to make a diagnosis of mental retardation. Syndrome-specific tests are helpful in making the initial autism diagnosis and in identifying the autistic features present in a specific child (see Table 10.2).

Broad Assessment Strategies

Cognitive Assessment

Clinician-Administered—IQ Testing. Because 75–80% of autistic children are mentally retarded (Morgan, 1990; Ornitz, 1989; Ornitz and Ritvo, 1976), intelligence testing should be a routine part of the assessment of the autistic child. In addition, IQ scores of less than 70 are generally negative prognostic indicators for future development (Morgan, 1990). Three-fourths of mentally retarded autistic children will have IQ less than 50 (Morgan, 1990), indicating that 50–60% of all autistic children are in this very low-functioning group.

Parents often express surprise when told that their autistic child is mentally retarded. Rather than mental retardation, parents usually attribute the child's poor performance to emotional problems, withdrawal, inattentiveness, or refusal to complete items that the child is capable of doing (Morgan, 1990). However, there is no evidence that apparent mental retardation in the autistic child is caused by these problems (Morgan, 1990; Ornitz, 1989; Ornitz and

TABLE 10.2	Sample Assessment Battery for Autistic Disorder

COGNITIVE

Intelligence test (Bayley-II, SB:FE, or Wechsler scale)
Vineland Adaptive Behavior Scale

BEHAVIORAL

Child Behavior Checklist

SYNDROME-SPECIFIC

E-2 Scale
Childhood Autism Rating Scale (if possible)

Note: Assessment instruments are intended to supplement (not substitute for) a good clinical interview and, when possible, a structured diagnostic interview.

Ritvo, 1976). In fact, the refusal of the child to participate in testing is indicative of later mental retardation (Morgan, 1990; Ornitz and Ritvo, 1976).

The selection of a scale to use in assessing the autistic child is often crucial in obtaining valid data. If significant mental retardation is suspected (IQ below 55), the newly revised Bayley-II should be used, or, for older children, the SB:FE. Given the heavy reliance of the SB:FE on verbal communication, the Bayley-II may be more appropriate for low-functioning, young autistic children. For older (age 8 or above) children with suspected higher IQs (above 55), the WISC-III can be used.

While overall low IQ is to be expected in the autistic child, isolated areas of good performance are occasionally found. Areas that involve rote responses or little use of communicative language (such as WISC-III Digit Span) are most likely to be discrepant with otherwise low scores. On the other hand, subtests that rely on verbal communication, reasoning, and expression (such as WISC-III Vocabulary and Comprehension) are likely to be uniformly low.

Clinician-Administered—Adaptive Functioning. In addition to IQ testing, a test of adaptive behavior is both useful in understanding the functioning of the autistic child and essential in making a diagnosis of mental retardation. The Vineland Adaptive Behavior Scales (VABS) are particularly useful in the assessment of the autistic child. Information from the VABS should be used in combination with the child's IQ scores to form a profile of cognitive and adaptive strengths and weaknesses. Autistic children give a variety of scores on the VABS, but, as with IQ testing, composite scores tend to be below 70. Communication and Socialization scores are virtually always extremely low, and Daily Living Skills are frequently significantly below average as well. Motor Skills scores are variable and may be average for some autistic children.

VABS scores are essential in making residential, schooling, and training recommendations for autistic children. It should never be assumed that an autistic child with low IQ has poor adaptive functioning, without first administering a VABS or other adaptive functioning test.

Syndrome-Specific Tests

Tests of autistic symptomatology vary considerably in form, standardization, and psychometric properties. At the unstructured end of this range is a simple reading of DSM-IV symptoms to the parent. Endorsement of the requisite number of symptoms in each area is taken as indicative of autism. If numerous symptoms are endorsed but diagnostic criteria are not met, a diagnosis of PDDNOS is probably warranted. It is usually wise to observe/interact with the child alone (if the child will tolerate it), as well as to observe parent–child interaction. These observations may provide some insight into the validity of the parent's report of the child's symptoms. Several more structured tests, such as the E-2, BOS, BRIAAC, ABC, and CARS, have also been developed to standardize the assessment of autism. These tests can be extremely helpful in more difficult diagnostic cases, although none of them uses strict DSM-IV criteria for autism diagnosis.

Clinician-Administered

Autism Behavior Checklist.   The Autism Behavior Checklist (ABC; Krug, Arick, and Almond, 1980) is a fifty-seven–item rating scale of autistic children's behaviors. Initial scale development and norms were based on the ratings of 1049 professionals, although the final format of the scale potentially can be applied to parent ratings. Each item is rated for presence/absence, with 1–4 points assigned to symptom presence based on an empirically derived weighting scheme. Items are added to give five scales (sensory, relating, body and object use, language, and social self-help) and a total score. Summary scores can be compared to normative groups by age and diagnosis. Autistic groups receive average total scores of 78, while other diagnostic groups average 45 (Krug et al., 1980).

The ABC is part of the Autism Screening Instrument for Educational Planning (ASIEP), which includes tests of vocal behavior, interaction skills, educational skills, and novel learning skills (Krug et al., 1980; Teal and Wiebe, 1986). The ABC appears to be the most diagnostically useful of the ASIEP tests (Teal and Wiebe, 1986), and it is certainly the most widely researched (Morgan, 1988). The ABC was extensively developed, using items and information from existing autism scales combined with feedback from numerous clinical experts. It has good reliability and content validity (Krug et al., 1980; Teal and Wiebe, 1986), although discriminant validity needs more extensive study (Morgan, 1988). Unfortunately, little has been written on its potential use with parent groups. As a parent-completed checklist, the ABC could have clinical utility and diagnostic usefulness, but it remains primarily an instrument for professional raters. As a professional rating instrument, its utility is limited by the requirement that the rater be very familiar with the behavior of the child.

Behavior Observation Scale for Autism.   The Behavior Observation Scale for Autism (BOS; Freeman et al., 1978) is a second measure developed specifically for the measurement of autistic symptoms. The BOS consists of a list of sixty-seven behaviors that are coded based on observation of the autistic child in a standardized setting. The behavioral items were selected based on Ritvo and Freeman's (1978) definition of autism. Observations are made during nine intervals of 3 minutes each, and each behavior is scored on a 0–3 scale of frequency for each interval. Standardized stimuli (a top, noises, lights, and tactile stimuli) are presented at the beginning of the middle seven intervals. Freeman et al. (1978) have identified BOS behaviors that are predictive of autism, and they note that different behaviors may be indicative of autism at different ages.

Unfortunately, Freeman et al. (1978) do not provide extensive information on summary scoring or norms for the BOS, although they suggest that these are forthcoming. Freeman et al. (1980) factor-analyzed BOS scores, but their results have not been used widely to create summary scales. Morgan (1990) also notes a lack of information concerning test-retest and internal consistency reliability. Interrater reliability and validity appear to be good (Morgan, 1990), and the list of BOS behaviors is a helpful summary of behaviors that can be casually observed by the clinician during a clinical interview of the child. Nevertheless, length of administration, as well as the lack of norms, cutoff scores, and summary scores, severely limits the clinical utility of the formally administered BOS.

Behavior Rating Instrument for Autistic and Atypical Children. Like the BOS, the Behavior Rating Instrument for Autistic and Atypical Children (BRIAAC; Ruttenberg, Dratman et al., 1966; Wenar and Ruttenberg, 1976) relies on observer ratings of autistic children's behaviors. Children are rated on eight scales of development (Relationship to an Adult, Communication, Drive for Mastery, Vocalization and Expressive Speech, Sound and Speech Reception, Social Responsiveness, Body Movement, and Psychobiological Development). Each scale gives a score up to 10, and scales can be added to give a total score (Wenar and Ruttenberg, 1976).

The BRIAAC is primarily based on Kanner's (1943) conservative definition of autism, which may not apply to all DSM-IV cases. It appears to have good internal consistency, interrater reliability, and validity, although some problems may exist with differential validity (Morgan, 1988, 1990). Because the BRIAAC is relatively easy to rate, score, and interpret, it can be easily applied in the clinical setting. However, it requires some familiarity with the child's daily functioning and does not have good norms.

Childhood Autism Rating Scale. The Childhood Autism Rating Scale (CARS; Schopler et al., 1980) is an observer rating scale consisting of fifteen "scales," each of which is a general area of autistic symptomatology: impairment in human relationships, imitation, inappropriate affect, bizarre use of body movement and persistence of stereotypes, peculiarities in relating to nonhuman objects, resistance to environmental change, peculiarities of visual responsiveness, peculiarities of auditory responsiveness, near receptor responsiveness, anxiety reaction, verbal communication, nonverbal communication, activity level, intellectual functioning, and general impressions. Each area is rated on a 1 (normal) to 4 (severely abnormal) scale based on the child's age and developmentally appropriate behavior. Observations and ratings are made during a structured diagnostic session.

Three types of scores are obtained from the CARS: First, the scale raw scores can be interpreted to find particular problem areas. Second, the scales can be added to give a total score between 15 and 60. Third, the number of scales with scores of 3 or greater can be counted. Schopler et al. (1980) suggest using a criterion for severe autism of total score greater than 36 and five or more scales rated 3 or higher. Children with total scores of less than 30 are considered nonautistic, while those with scores greater than 29 who do not meet autistic criteria are considered "mildly to moderately autistic" (Schopler et al., 1980, p. 97).

The CARS was not developed according to any one set of diagnostic criteria, but instead incorporates items from numerous diagnostic systems of autism (Morgan, 1988; Schopler et al., 1980). Reliability and validity are good to excellent, and developmental considerations increase the utility of the scale. Teal and Wiebe (1986) found that the CARS had higher discriminant validity than the E-2 and the ASIEP. Morgan (1988) reports that "when all measures of reliability and validity are considered for the [ABC, E-2, BRIAAC, CARS, and BOS], the CARS clearly emerges as the strongest scale in terms of demonstrated psychometric properties (p. 149)." Norms are available for the CARS based on large samples, and the scale is relatively easy to learn and give. However, it must be administered by a trained evaluator and its administration is time-consuming. These latter characteristics limit its use to only the most critical diagnostic cases, well-funded specialty clinics, or research projects.

Parent-Report

Diagnostic Checklist for Behavior-Disturbed Children, Form E-2.   The Diagnostic Checklist for Behavior-Disturbed Children, Form E-2 (E-2; Rimland, 1971) consists of eighty parent-completed questions assessing behaviors in several areas: social interaction, speech/language, motor skills, intelligence, reaction to stimuli, medical history, family environment, and physiological data.

The E-2 is a revision of an earlier questionnaire (the E-1) that was developed as part of Rimland's (1964) *Infantile Autism* book. The E-1 posed questions about the child's development through age 7, which was later considered by Rimland (1971) to be too old. Hence, the E-2 was developed as a measure of behavior through age 5, and it replaced form E-1 within 2 years (Rimland, 1971). Both the E-1 and the E-2 are intended to differentiate autistic children from children with other "psychotic" disorders, depending heavily on Kanner's (1943) conceptualization of autism.

Each symptom of autism on the E-2 that is endorsed by the parent is assigned a positive point, while each question answered in the nonautistic direction is given a negative point. Some questions can yield either positive or negative points depending on the answer, while other questions give only positive points. Positive and negative points are added to give a total score. Hence, a score of +15 would indicate a child whose parent endorsed fifteen more autistic items than nonautistic items. E-2 scores of +20 or higher are considered indicative of autism. The +20 criterion seems to reflect agreement with the more strict Kanner (1943) criteria of autism as opposed to DSM-IV. Hence, some children with legitimate DSM-IV autism diagnoses may not elevate E-2 sufficiently to meet the +20 criterion. In addition to the total score, E-2 responses can be divided into behavior and speech scores (Rimland, 1971), although little has been done with these specific scores.

Rimland (1971) has accumulated a large database to support the validity of the E-2. He has found that, using the E-2 +20 criterion score, only 10% of children with suspected autism, psychosis, or a related severe behavior problem are actually diagnosed as autistic. Teal and Wiebe (1986) found that E-2 scores correctly classified 85% of autistic children and 95% of retarded children. Thus, the E-2 has considerable validity support, although it has some drawbacks as well. Reliability of the E-2 has not been extensively studied, and reliance on Kanner's (1943) criteria may be too strict (Morgan, 1988, 1990; Teal and Wiebe, 1986). Nevertheless, the E-2 has clinical utility, since it is relatively "cheap" to obtain (parents can complete it in the waiting room) and provides easily interpreted data.

Over all, the CARS appears to have the best psychometric properties and most utility of the clinician-rated autism scales, and the E-2 appears to be the best of the parent-rated autism scales. A combination of parent-rating and clinician observation appears to be the most useful way to proceed with the autism assessment (Teal and Wiebe, 1986). However, the time-consuming nature of some clinician-rated scales severely limits their utility, usually resulting in the use of unstructured clinician observation of the behavior of the autistic child.

TREATMENT OPTIONS

Because 75–80% of autistic children are mentally retarded or have severe social communication deficits, traditional "talking" psychotherapies are infrequently used with them. In the case of the 1–10% or so of autistic children who do attain relatively normal functioning, play therapy, psychodynamic psychotherapy, cognitive-behavioral therapy, or family therapy may be warranted (Ornitz, 1989; Ornitz and Ritvo, 1976). However, these cases are rare enough that they are virtually ignored by the clinical and research literature. The predominant therapies currently used with autistic children require only basic communication with the child and rely on the environment, the parents, or psychopharmacology to alter the child's behavior (see Table 10.3).

Family Interventions

Parent Intervention

Traditional family therapy is rarely done in cases of autism, because of the autistic child's limited capacity to benefit from socially-based interventions. However, autism does have effects on the family and parents. Furthermore, the parents are vital to the success of behavioral therapies for autism. Hence, attention must be given to family issues and to the adjustment of parents. This is often accomplished by a combination of psychoeducation, support, and recommendations presented to the parents.

When the autistic child spends extensive time in the home environment, parents are a critical component of the treatment package for autism. Hence, parent intervention is a part of virtually all autism treatments with psychological or behavioral components. Parent training must begin with the understanding that the parents of an autistic child face enormous stresses: loss (of the idealized healthy child), guilt, fear, sadness, concern over the future, strain

TABLE 10.3   Treatment Options for Autistic Disorder

FAMILY INTERVENTIONS

Parent psychotherapy
    Education about autism and its effects on parent stress and emotions
    Parenting stress management

BEHAVIORAL INTERVENTIONS

Reduce interfering and dangerous behavior
    Time-out
    Differential reinforcement of other behaviors
    Positive practice
    Ignoring
    Punishment techniques

Teach learning readiness skills
    Learning that adults are sources of reinforcement
    Attending to the adult
    Learning to comply with requests
    Imitation
    Adaptive use of language

Teach social behaviors
Teach pivotal skills

MEDICATION (for control of specific symptoms)

Note: This outline of options summarizes major treatments covered in the text. Specific treatments are often combined into an intervention package. Refer to the text for additional descriptions of each treatment. This table is not necessarily an exhaustive list of all treatments available.

of the child on the family environment, and effort in caring for the autistic child (Newsom and Rincover, 1989). Many coping strategies are used by parents to deal with these stresses, but two of the most dangerous and most common are wishful thinking and denial. Parents who engage in denial and wishful thinking have difficulty coming to terms with the reality that their child is autistic. They may point out behaviors that lead them to believe that the child is not mentally retarded or that the child has advanced intelligence. They may believe that their child will "grow out" of the disorder or that a miracle cure exists. The sensitive clinician listens to the beliefs of the parents and investigates their claims without confronting them in a way that raises their defensiveness.

Most parents have misconceptions of autism based on outdated books and errors in the media. One common misconception, for example, is that the autistic child constructs an elaborate inner reality in which he or she "lives" in withdrawal from the real world. Related to this is the belief that the autistic child has high intelligence but simply cannot express it. Other misconceptions are that autism is caused by a cold family and that autism is always accompanied by phenomenal abilities in certain specific mental areas.

With these background issues in mind, the clinician first must inform and educate the parents. Morgan (1990) recommends that both parents be seen together. This prevents undue stress on the parent who must educate the other parent and reduces the risk of miscommunication and misinformation. However, the informing session should be limited only to parents and possibly another major caretaker, if one exists. Too many people in the session, especially children, who are at a different cognitive level, can be overwhelming and cause confusion. The parents should be informed about the child's condition as directly, completely, realistically, and sensitively as possible. They should be informed about the child's current level of functioning, strengths/weaknesses, and prognosis, with appropriate caution that nobody has all of the answers. Results of formal testing can be helpful in organizing the presentation to the parents, who should be provided with a sketch of their child's cognitive, adaptive, social, motor, and behavioral functioning.

The clinician must also be prepared in this initial session to gently dispel myths held by the parents about their child's condition. Morgan (1990) recommends that parents be directly told that their child's condition is not their fault. He suggests using a biological explanation of autism, but this is risky (and possibly inaccurate) since the etiology of autism is still unknown. It is probably sufficient to say that the etiology of autism is unknown, that it may involve a biological contributor, and that the parents are part of the solution, not part of the problem. Parents should also be honestly told about their child's intelligence, and inaccurate beliefs about their child's intelligence should be gently corrected with the use of articles and research data. In addition, parents are generally most concerned with two issues: treatment and prognosis. They should be told that these are related issues (prognosis depends in part on treatment), and they should be informed of the most likely outcomes. At the very least, parents should understand that autism is pervasive, chronic, and debilitating. However, they should also understand that, regardless of anticipated prognosis and severity, intensive intervention should be implemented to help the child as much as possible. Finally, parents should be given an opportunity to ask questions and express feelings in this initial session (Morgan, 1990). These questions and feelings can be diagnostic of future problems for the parents and for the implementation of behavioral plans.

The questions of the parents can lead to a behavioral intervention beginning with psychoeducation (Newsom and Rincover, 1989). Parents should be provided with descriptions of autism, as well as descriptions of treatments. In many cases, simply understanding autism will help the parents' adjustment and will improve parenting behavior. Common treatments to be taught include special education, behavior modification, and joining support groups. Parents should also be warned about the stress of the autistic child on them and on the family. For example, the needs of the other children in the family may intensify as the autistic child receives increasing attention. Stress management, family therapy, or individual therapy may be warranted if the situation becomes unbearable (Newsom and Rincover, 1989).

Behavioral Interventions

Special Considerations for Autistic Children

Behavioral modification has been called "the most promising treatment for autistic persons" (Lovaas, 1987, p. 3) and "the only intervention which has been empirically demonstrated to offer help for autistic children" (Lovaas, 1974, p. 111). Morgan (1990) states that "there is little doubt that treatment based on behavioral principles has been much more effective with autistic children than any other approach" (p. 31). Furthermore, some startling findings have been reported from behavioral treatment programs for autism (Lovaas, 1987). Behavioral treatment is likely to be most effective when it is started at a young age (before age 4) with a child whose IQ is at least 50. However, behavioral techniques produce change in almost all autistic children.

Behavioral modification with autistic children is based on the simple behavioral principles that behavior followed by a reinforcer is more likely to recur, while behavior followed by punishment is less likely to recur. This simple tenet becomes much more complex when one considers that autistic children tend not to respond to secondary or social reinforcers (Lovaas, Schreibman, and Koegel, 1974). Secondary reinforcers are things that have no rewarding qualities in and of themselves but come to be paired with more basic rewards and thus acquire rewarding qualities through association. Money, praise, and social interaction, for example, are secondary reinforcers. Primary reinforcers, on the other hand, have basic biological rewarding properties and thus do not have to be learned. Food and electric shock are examples of a primary reinforcer and a primary punisher, respectively.

A second complicating factor in behavioral modification with autistic children is that they have deficits in observation and imitation. Speech, language, social interaction, and most other complex tasks are learned through the social learning modalities of observation and imitation. A related complicating factor is the communication deficit of the autistic child. This deficit hinders verbal explanation of the behavioral plan, which further slows learning and generalization of the learned behavior.

With these issues in mind, behavior modification for the autistic child begins with the psychoeducation of the parents and other authorities about autism and behavior modification. Following this teaching, a target behavior is selected. In addition to the usual rule that the behavior be circumscribed and operationally defined, target behaviors for autistic children must be very basic, taking into account their developmental delay and intellectual status. Common target behaviors for autistic children are learning to imitate, making simple sounds, learning simple signs for communication, learning basic self-care skills, and stopping self-injurious behavior.

Newsom and Rincover (1989) suggest that autistic children be divided into two groups for the purposes of behavior modification. The first group of children functions in the severely/profoundly mentally retarded range (roughly corresponding to IQ < 40). Because the prognosis for these children is so poor, their behavioral goals should be more modest: basic self-care skills, compliance with basic commands, basic social interaction behaviors, and reduction of harmful behaviors. While it is important not to set goals too low, goals set too high will only frustrate and disappoint the parent, staff, and child.

The second group of children, those with IQ > 40, have a better prognosis, particularly if IQ is greater than 60 or 70. These children will begin with the same objectives as those with IQ < 40, but they should be pushed to develop verbal language, social interaction, and other "normal behaviors," according to Newsom and Rincover (1989). However, despite their greater potential, their acquisition of basic skills is painstakingly slow and requires special techniques (e.g., use of primary as opposed to secondary reinforcers).

Techniques for Reduction of Interfering and Dangerous Behavior

Regardless of which IQ group the child falls into, the first behaviors chosen for intervention are behaviors that are dangerous or that interfere with the learning of appropriate behaviors (Lovaas, 1987; Lovaas et al., 1974; Morgan, 1990). These are typically self-stimulating or self-injurious behaviors such as spinning, twirling, head banging, rocking, self-scratching, and self-hitting. The cause of such behavior is unknown, but it is usually reinforced by attention and sensory feedback (Lovaas et al., 1974).

Morgan (1990), Lovaas et al. (1974), and Lovaas (1987) suggest five interventions that have been used to address these behaviors. First, *time-out* is sometimes tried as an initial intervention. However, time-out is unsuccessful for many low-functioning autistic children because they do not mind separation from social contact. In higher functioning autistic children, the time-out intervention may be sufficiently aversive to produce behavior change. The evaluation of whether time-out is effective is based on change in the children's behavior over a 1–2-week period of pairing time-out with self-stimulating or self-injurious behaviors. Time-out periods for autistic children may last from 5–10 minutes, with additional minutes given for noncompliance during time-out.

A second intervention, *differential reinforcement of other behaviors,* can be used to modify behaviors, as long as the reinforcer is powerful and salient. As previously noted, secondary reinforcers tend not to have an effect on the autistic child's behavior, at least initially. Primary reinforcers such as food (M&Ms are a favorite reinforcer for autistic children), on the other hand, can sometimes encourage a desirable behavior. The behavior to be rewarded must be one that can substitute for or is incompatible with the undesirable behavior.

A third behavioral technique for autistic children, *positive practice,* involves repeatedly performing ("practicing") behaviors that are incompatible with the response. For example, a child who is head banging could repeatedly be required to hold his head absolutely still. Positive practice, however, is a huge strain on caretakers, who must usually force the autistic child to engage in the practice behavior. Furthermore, because of the child's communication deficit, it is sometimes unclear whether he understands the goal of the intervention.

Because positive practice can lead to physical battles, emotional upset, and possibly injury, it is rarely recommended.

Ignoring is a fourth technique for managing autistic behavior. Lovaas et al. (1974) present convincing data showing that ignoring self-stimulating behavior results in a reduction of such behavior. Unfortunately, it is difficult to identify the children who will respond to ignoring and those who will not. A basic rule is that if attention seeking is involved, ignoring *may* work. However, ignoring is contraindicated if children are hurting themselves, hurting others, or destroying property.

Finally, direct *punishment* is the most effective way to reduce self-stimulating or self-injurious behaviors (Lovaas et al., 1974). As with reinforcement, however, primary punishers must often be used because most secondary punishers have no meaning to the autistic child. The most commonly used primary punisher for such behaviors is electric shock. Use of contingent electric shock typically results in rapid elimination of the problem behavior, but it is unacceptable to most parents and poses ethical problems. The generally accepted use of electric shock for autistic children is in situations where the behavior is dangerous and when other interventions have been ineffective. Even in these cases, such procedures are best used only under supervision of the guardian and a human rights committee (Morgan, 1990). An alternative punishment is to say "no" loudly, paired with a mild slap on the thigh (Lovaas, 1987). While not as effective as shock, this technique does result in behavior change. The risk of such a technique is that an angry or upset parent could use it inappropriately, indiscriminately, or with too much force. Hence, this less objectionable punishment must be carefully used as well.

In sum, the first step in behavior modification of the autistic child is the identification of behaviors that are dangerous or will interfere with future learning of new behaviors. These behaviors are then paired with primary reinforcers or punishers such that their occurrence is decreased. Following accomplishment of this goal, the child is then taught basic skills that form the building blocks for later learning. Among such skills are communication, attention, observation, imitation, compliance, and self-care. Again, these must be initially paired with primary reinforcers.

Teaching Learning Readiness Skills

Lovaas et al. (1974) and Newsom and Rincover (1989) summarize several procedures for teaching autistic children the basic building blocks for later learning. One such skill is *learning that adults are sources of contingent reward and punishment*. This may be accomplished by having the adult simply give the child a piece of candy whenever the child seeks proximity or basic interaction with the adult.

Another learning readiness skill is *attending to the adult*. Autistic children often do not observe or make eye contact with adults, which prevents them from further learning. Eye contact is encouraged by giving the child a piece of candy when the child happens to look at the adult. For children with extremely low initial frequencies of eye contact, an attractive object may be held in front of the adult while the adult makes an orienting request (e.g., saying "look!"), causing the child to look at the adult. The candy is then administered. Later the object is still held and the orienting request is made, but the child must look at the adult's eyes to receive the reward. Finally, the object is gradually faded (e.g., moved a greater distance from the adult or exposed for a shorter duration) but the orienting request continues, and the child must make eye contact in response to the request alone. The attention response is then generalized to other people by allowing them to dispense the reinforcement. Newsom and Rincover (1989) also describe negative reinforcement procedures (e.g., holding the child's head until eye contact occurs) and punishment procedures (e.g., repeatedly turning the child's head to face the adult if the child fails to attend on his own) to achieve the attention goal. However, these procedures may cause the adult to be paired with an aversive situation and should be used very cautiously if at all.

Like attention, *compliance* is a very basic concept that must be taught to autistic children. Autistic children should first be taught to comply with very simple, single-step commands (sit, wait, come here) before they are asked to comply with more extensive requests. Newsom and Rincover (1989) and Lovaas (1987) suggest several ways to teach compliance: First, during 10-minute practice sessions the child is asked to comply with a simple command about twice a minute. Compliance is rewarded with praise and a piece of candy. Noncompliance is ignored. In the case of a child who cannot perform the behavior even once, he or she may be physically guided through the behavior, or successive approximations may be rewarded. A second strategy is based on the assumption that noncompliance and escalation are an attempt to escape the situation. Hence, the child is not allowed to escape (which would reward the noncompliance if it were allowed to occur) until he or she complies. Instead of escape, the prompts and commands continue to occur during the noncompliance and escalation. A third strategy, for particularly resistant children, is the administration of a punishment during noncompliance. This last strategy is difficult to implement, since electric shock is generally considered too severe for the situation. Newsom and Rincover (1989) and Lovaas (1987) suggest a loud, startling reprimand as a punisher. However, the reprimand could soon lose its punishing status as the child habituates to it. Over all, reinforcement is most effective, but it requires considerable practice and patience.

A fourth learning readiness skill is *imitation*. Like attention and compliance, imitation is taught at a very basic level by pairing it with primary reinforcers. Initial behaviors to be imitated are simple gestures, which are immediately rewarded with a piece of candy and praise. Most autistic children, however, will either not spontaneously imitate or will only imitate randomly and sporadically. Two strategies to address this problem are to physically help the child imitate and to reward successive approximations to the behavior that the child is imitating. The adult must vary the gesture to be imitated, or the child will simply learn to perform a single gesture and not to imitate what is seen. Once simple imitation is learned, more complex imitation can be undertaken.

Finally, *language* is an extremely important learning skill, particularly when the goal is achievement of a near-normal level of functioning. Lovaas et al. (1974) describe a procedure in which language can be shaped in mute or near-mute autistic children. First, the child is reinforced with candy for any vocal utterance. Second, the child is reinforced only when the vocalizations follow the speech of the therapist. Third, the child is reinforced only when the vocalizations approximate the sound of the therapist. Fourth, the child is taught an increasing number of phonemes and to combine these phonemes into words. Once words are learned, the child is taught to use the words to label objects. Next, comprehension (as opposed to simply pairing words and objects) is encouraged by teaching the child to generalize the use of words. Finally, the use of sentences is taught by gradually encouraging the child to combine words in simple and meaningful ways (Lovaas et al., 1974).

Teaching Social Behaviors

Learning readiness skills can also be seen as very basic social behaviors. Building on these simple learned behaviors, behavior therapies for autism expand the rudimentary behaviors of the autistic child into approximations of appropriate social behaviors. Several social behaviors and concepts can be taught to the autistic child: proximity seeking, social reinforcement, modeling, affect, and play. In all cases the desired behavior is operationally defined and paired with a more basic (usually primary) reinforcer until the child is regularly performing it. If a child has trouble with initial trials, modeling or physically guiding the child through the behavior may be used. Eventually, as the child learns the more basic principles of social interaction, these are used to teach more complex principles, such as conversation. These more complex principles must be initially broken down into simple parts before growing into approximations of the ultimate goal (e.g., conversation of one sentence, then two, then three, and so on).

For example, social reinforcement is taught to the autistic child by pairing the social reinforcement with a more basic reinforcer. Initially, social reinforcers such as praise, social affection, and proximity have little or no value to the autistic child. However, primary reinforcers, such as food, fulfillment of needs/wants, and access to favored activities, have considerable meaning to the child. The first step in teaching social reinforcement, then, is to identify a social stimulus that is to be rewarding (e.g., a single praise word, such as "good"; or proximity to peers). Next, a primary reinforcer is identified, such that it can be easily paired with the social stimulus. Finally, a response of the child must be chosen (e.g., standing within 5 feet of a peer, or coming over to an adult when the word "good" is said). Then, the social stimulus and primary reinforcer are paired in discrimination trials. That is, multiple events are allowed to happen in the child's environment, but the child is reinforced only after responding to the social stimulus (Lovaas, 1987; Newsom and Rincover, 1989).

For example, a child may be taught to come to the adult within several seconds after the word "good" is said. If the child does, she is given a piece of candy. To improve peer relationships, the child may be required to interact with a peer before an adult will give her access to a favored object or activity (Newsom and Rincover, 1989). Such trials must be repeatedly practiced for extended periods of time, and even then a lack of generalization and extinction are realistic risks. The risk of these problems may be lowered, however, by introducing multiple social stimuli (e.g., multiple adults saying "good") or by gradually reducing the reinforcement ratio (e.g., from every response to every fifth, every tenth, and so on) once the child has learned the basic principle.

Teaching Pivotal Skills

Schreibman and Pierce (1993) advocate a somewhat different behavioral treatment approach to autism. They believe that autistic children should be taught behaviors that may affect a wide range of other behaviors ("pivotal" behaviors), as opposed to learning specific behaviors one at a time. They propose techniques for teaching autistic children two pivotal skills: motivation and responsivity to multiple cues. Presumably, once these skills are learned, the child will be in a position to learn a variety of other adaptive behaviors.

Schreibman and Pierce's (1993) intervention program avoids the use of food reinforcers as motivators. Rather, motivation is taught with techniques such as allowing the child to have greater control over the environment, giving the child access to favored toys, reinforcing (with praise and access to favored activity) very simple approximations of the target behavior, and repeatedly testing and rewarding the child for performance of overlearned tasks (to give success experiences).

Responsivity to multiple cues involves attending to more than one characteristic of the environment at a time. Schreibman and Pierce (1993) teach children to use multiple cues by giving trial problems in which two or more aspects of an object must be considered in order to solve the problem. For example, a child may be asked to pick the red cup from an array of a red pencil, a green cup, and a red cup. Both "red" and "cup" must be considered to solve the problem correctly. Correct responses are reinforced. Presumably, the child learns to attend to multiple aspects of situations, improving functioning in the complex social environment.

Schreibman and Pierce's (1993) program includes other components such as parent behavior training and training the child in self-management (selecting a behavior, monitoring it, and giving self-reinforcement when goals are met). Their program is appealing because it devotes constant attention to the generalization of learning and the application of behavioral learning to actual functioning in the environment. Because the program relies more on internal and/or social motivation, however, it may not be appropriate for low-functioning children or for children who have few reinforcers besides food. Nevertheless, the program has potential for higher-functioning autistic children and for children who have progressed through the early stages of behavioral management.

Evaluation of Behavioral Interventions for Autism

Ivar Lovaas is perhaps the staunchest supporter of behavior therapy for autistic children, and his research/clinical programs have produced impressive results. Working with all but the most profoundly retarded autistic children, Lovaas has presented results from an intensive program that showed that 47% of his autistic sample achieved "normal" (IQ > 90, placement in normal first-grade class) intellectual and educational functioning. IQ scores for Lovaas's treatment group were, on average, 30 points higher than those of controls (Lovaas, 1987).

If there is a downside to Lovaas's program, it is its time-consuming, expensive, and intensive nature. Lovaas (1987) estimates that his program costs $40,000 per child, but he notes that the cost of lifelong institutionalization is in the millions of dollars per child. Children are identified before age 3½ or 4, and they are given 40 hours per week of intensive therapy by trained therapists for at least 2 years. Parents are also trained and expected to work intensively with their children. Children must also be enrolled in preschools with teachers willing to implement the behavioral program (Lovaas, 1987).

Lovaas's program resembles a "typical" behavioral program. Initially, self-stimulating, dangerous, and disruptive behaviors are reduced to prepare the child for learning. Next, the child is taught compliance, imitation, and simple play. Following the learning of these basic skills, the child is taught communication and interactive play. Finally, emotional expression, basic academic skills, and observational learning are taught to the child. Techniques used to promote learning are ignoring, time-out, shaping, reinforcement of alternate behavior, and aversive stimuli.

Although they are time-consuming and expensive, behavioral techniques are currently the basic treatment of choice for autism. In many cases the intervention is too intensive and time-consuming for parents to manage alone, and the child must be placed in an institution to obtain comprehensive behavioral treatment. This is best accomplished by placing the child in the least restrictive environment that results in the least family disruption. Day-treatment programs may be effective for higher-functioning autistic children, but a full-time residential placement may be necessary for more severely retarded, dangerous, or disruptive autistic children. Regardless of what type of program is chosen, an intensive behavioral focus is extremely important, particularly for the younger child. Autistic "warehouses," which simply monitor the children and keep them out of trouble, result in more negative outcomes. In general, psychiatric hospitalization is warranted only in the case of acute, severe behavioral problems or medication management problems. Most psychiatric hospitals cannot provide the years of treatment needed for the autistic child.

Medication

Medication is commonly used with autistic children, although it is rarely prescribed for the autistic symptoms *per se*. There is no current evidence that any specific medication consistently removes the core symptoms of autism (Ornitz, 1989). Rather, medication is usually prescribed for associated features of autism, such as dangerous behavior, psychotic behavior, aggressiveness, hyperactivity, sleep disturbance, and lack of behavioral control. Ornitz and Ritvo (1976), for example, state that "psychotropic medications do not alter the natural history or course of autism. However, they are useful adjuncts to treatment on a symptomatic level. The target symptoms amenable to medication . . . are not specific to autism" (p. 618). They suggest that medication only be used for autism when behavioral interventions have failed (Ornitz and Ritvo, 1976).

The medications most commonly used with autistic children are sedatives or tranquilizers. These medications are generally used for purposes of calming overly active, aggressive, self-injurious, or "out-of-control" children. Major tranquilizers (such as haloperidol [Haldol] and thioridazine [Mellaril]; Morgan, 1990) are frequently prescribed for aggressive-active autistic children, although some authors (e.g., Ornitz, 1989) have noted negative side effects, little benefit, and, hence, little utility for these medications. Ornitz (1989) cautions that 25% of autistic children prescribed neuroleptics could develop tardive dyskinesia. Furthermore, although occasional studies indicated some hope for major tranquilizers and sedatives, more recent, better-designed studies have not borne out this hope (Ornitz, 1989). Conventional sedatives and stimulants rarely have a positive effect on symptoms (Ornitz, 1989), and some early excitement over fenfluramine (which appears to reduce some of the motor disturbances in some autistic children) has died down with more recent treatment study failures (Ornitz, 1989). The current medications with the most promise for helping autistic children are haloperidol and fenfluramine, which may assist in controlling hyperactivity and stereotypic behavior in a minority of children (Morgan, 1990). These medications have sufficient research and clinical support to be considered in the treatment of the autistic child. However, no medication has a significant effect on the primary autistic symptoms (Morgan, 1990; Ornitz, 1989; Ornitz and Ritvo, 1976).

Over all, it appears that medication may be effective with some autistic children, and haloperidol or fenfluramine should be strongly considered for children with extremely disruptive or dangerous behaviors. However, at the present time medication should not be routinely considered for all autistic children. Medication should be considered only in cases of extreme behavior problems that have not responded to behavioral techniques.

References

American Psychiatric Association. (1994). *Diagnostic and statistical manual of mental disorders* (4th ed.). Washington, DC: Author.

Bayley, N. (1993). *Bayley scales of infant development: Second edition*. San Antonio, TX: Psychological Corporation.

Freeman, B. J., Ritvo, E. R., Guthrie, D., Schroth, P., and Ball, J. (1978). The Behavior

Observation Scale for Autism: Initial methodology, data analysis, and preliminary findings on 89 children. *Journal of the American Academy of Child Psychiatry, 17,* 576–588.

Freeman, B. J., Schroth, P., Ritvo, E., Guthrie, D., and Wake, L. (1980). The Behavior Observation Scale for Autism (BOS): Initial results of factor analysis. *Journal of Autism and Developmental Disorders, 10,* 343–346.

Kanner, L. (1943). Autistic disturbances of affective contact. *Nervous Child, 2,* 217–250.

Kolvin, I., Berney, T. P., and Yoeli, J. (1990). Schizophrenia in childhood. In M. Hersen and C.G. Last (Eds.), *Handbook of child and adult psychopathology: A longitudinal perspective* (pp. 99–113). New York: Pergamon Press.

Krug, D. A., Arick, J., and Almond, P. (1980). Behavior checklist for identifying severely handicapped individuals with high levels of autistic behavior. *Journal of Child Psychology and Psychiatry, 21,* 221–229.

Lotter, V. (1966). Epidemiology of autistic conditions in young children: I. Prevalence. *Social Psychiatry, 1,* 124–137.

Lovaas, O. I. (1979). Contrasting illness and behavioral models for the treatment of autistic children: A historical perspective. *Journal of Autism and Developmental Disorders, 9,* 315–323.

_____ . (1987). Behavioral treatment and normal educational and intellectual functioning in young autistic children. *Journal of Consulting and Clinical Psychology, 55,* 3–9.

Lovaas, O. I., Schreibman, L., and Koegel, R. L. (1974). A behavior modification approach to the treatment of autistic children. *Journal of Autism and Childhood Schizophrenia, 4,* 111–129.

Morgan, S. B. (1988). Diagnostic assessment of autism: A review of objective scales. *Journal of Psychoeducational Assessment, 6,* 139–151.

_____ . (1990). Early childhood autism: Current perspectives on definition, assessment, and treatment. In S. B. Morgan and T. M. Okwumabua (Eds.), *Child and adolescent disorders: Developmental and health psychology perspectives* (pp. 3–45). Hillsdale, NJ: Erlbaum.

Newsom, C., and Rincover, A. (1989). Autism. In E. J. Mash and R. A. Barkley (Eds.), *Treatment of childhood disorders* (pp. 286–346). New York: Guilford Press.

Ornitz, E. M. (1989). Autism. In C. G. Last and M. Hersen (Eds.), *Handbook of child psychiatric diagnosis* (pp. 233–278). New York: Wiley.

Ornitz, E. M., and Ritvo, E. R. (1976). The syndrome of autism: A critical review. *American Journal of Psychiatry, 133,* 609–621.

Rimland, B. (1964). *Infantile autism.* New York: Appleton-Century-Crofts.

_____ . (1971). The differentiation of childhood psychoses: An analysis of checklists for 2218 psychotic children. *Journal of Autism and Childhood Schizophrenia, 1,* 161–174.

Ritvo, E., and Freeman, B. J. (1978). Current research on the syndrome of autism. *Journal of Autism and Childhood Schizophrenia, 8,* 162–167.

Ruttenberg, B. A., Dratman, M. L., Fraknoi, J., and Wenar, C. (1966). An instrument for evaluating autistic children. *Journal of the American Academy of Child Psychiatry, 5,* 453–478.

Schopler, E., Reichler, R. J., DeVellis, R. F., and Daly, K. (1980). Toward objective classification of childhood autism: Childhood Autism Rating Scale (CARS). *Journal of Autism and Developmental Disorders, 10,* 91–103.

Schreibman, L., and Pierce, K. (1993). Achieving greater generalization of treatment effects in children with autism: Pivotal response training and self-management. *Clinical Psychologist, 46,* 184–191.

Teal, M. B., and Wiebe, M. J. (1986). A validity analysis of selected instruments used to assess autism. *Journal of Autism and Developmental Disorders, 16,* 485–494.

Wenar, C., and Ruttenberg, B. A. (1976). The use of BRIAAC for evaluating therapeutic effectiveness. *Journal of Autism and Childhood Schizophrenia, 6,* 175–191.

Wing, L., Yeates, S. R., Brierley, L. M., and Gould, J. (1976). The prevalence of early childhood autism: Comparison of administrative and epidemiological studies. *Psychological Medicine, 6,* 89–100.

Wolff, S., and Chick, J. (1980). Schizoid personality in childhood: A controlled follow-up study. *Psychological Medicine, 10,* 85–100.

CHAPTER 11

Learning, Motor Skills, and Communication Disorders

DSM-III-R grouped disorders characterized by specific, developmental deficits under the general title of "Specific Developmental Disorders." Such disorders involved focal deficits in areas such as reading, language, and coordination, and they were coded on Axis II. The general Specific Developmental Disorder grouping was eliminated in DSM-IV, but the individual disorders remain as diagnoses that are now coded on Axis I. The former Specific Developmental Disorders now occur under three areas in DSM-IV: motor-skills disorder (Developmental Coordination Disorder), communication disorders (Expressive Language Disorder, Mixed Receptive-Expressive Language Disorder, Phonological Disorder, and Stuttering), and learning disorders (Reading Disorder, Mathematics Disorder, and Disorder of Written Expression).

■ Motor Skills Disorder

□ CLINICAL DESCRIPTION

Only one motor-skills disorder is identified in DSM-IV, and there is no provision for a "not otherwise specified" category. Developmental Coordination Disorder is assigned to children who perform substantially below their expected level on daily tasks that involve coordinated movement. The "expected level" of coordination depends on the child's chronological age and intelligence. DSM-IV does not provide extensive criteria on how to judge a person's coordination level, although factors such as developmental milestones, handwriting, and sports are suggested as factors for judgment. Developmental Coordination Disorder can only be diagnosed when the coordination problem "significantly" affects the child's daily activities.

□ ASSESSMENT PATTERNS

Assessment of the child with a motor-skills disorder requires, at a minimum, measures of IQ and motor skills. Assessment of IQ is relatively straightforward and can be accomplished with a Wechsler scale for children over age 3. Assessment of motor skills, on the other hand, is less well defined. Because DSM-IV does not require the administration of a standardized motor-skills test, the documentation of a motor-skills deficit may be accomplished by interviewing the parent and observing the child's movement on fine and gross motor tasks. Asking the child to walk, stand on one leg, skip, hop, jump, walk with eyes closed, handle objects of various sizes, and write something are all examples of tasks that can indicate coordination problems.

If a more standardized measure of motor ability is desired, the McCarthy Scales of Children's Abilities (McCarthy, 1972), a standardized, normed measure of cognitive abilities in children aged 2½ to 8½ years, may be very useful. The McCarthy provides *both* an overall estimate of cognitive ability *and* measures of motor coordination. Hence, it can be used to obtain the baseline level of intelligence and the degree of motor coordination in a single assessment. Because the McCarthy is standardized and provides normative data, children's normative motoric ability relative to other abilities can readily be obtained. Children who score substantially lower on the Motor Scale of the McCarthy relative to the Verbal Scale, Perceptual-Performance Scale, Quantitative Scale, and Memory Scale are likely to have a Developmental Coordination Disorder. The number of standard score points that represents "substantially lower" performance is left to the clinician. A 10–15 point difference is likely to be meaningful.

If the clinician is unable to test the child or prefers parental interview data, the VABS includes a Motor Skills scale that may indicate the presence of coordination problems. Regardless of what method is used to indicate the coordination deficit, the deficit must be manifest in daily living for the Developmental Coordination Disorder to be diagnosed.

TREATMENT OPTIONS

Treatment of a child with Developmental Coordination Disorder requires extensive consultation and referral to other professionals. First, the child should be evaluated by a pediatrician for possible organic contributors to the coordination problem. Referrals to physical therapists, occupational therapists, or to physicians specializing in motor deficits are also indicated. In addition to making appropriate referrals, the mental health clinician's role in the process is to recommend daily activities that can enhance coordination learning and to monitor any ill effects of the coordination problem on psychological-emotional functioning.

Communication Disorders

CLINICAL DESCRIPTION

Three of the four DSM-IV "Communication Disorders" were previously classified as "Language and Speech Disorders" in DSM-III-R. The fourth communication disorder, Stuttering, was previously grouped in the "Speech Disorders

Not Otherwise Classified" area. In all cases the communication disorders involve deficits in the oral production and/or comprehension ability. These deficits must be of sufficient severity to interfere with daily functioning. For the expressive or receptive language disorders, standardized test data are required. The communication disorders cannot be diagnosed when the symptoms are exclusively a result of a pervasive developmental disorder, mental retardation, impoverished environment, or a physical condition.

Expressive Language Disorder (ELD) involves deficits in the expression of language. These deficits must be documented by expressive language test scores that are substantially lower than scores on tests of nonverbal intelligence *and* receptive language. The magnitude of discrepancy required for diagnosis is not specified. Children with ELD have a variety of presentations. Some have a restricted vocabulary when talking, using overly simple words for their age. Other children with ELD manifest deficits in grammar, misusing sentence structure, word placement, or tense when they express themselves orally. A final common presentation of ELD is word-finding difficulty. Children with this latter difficulty speak haltingly because they cannot seem to find the words to express their thoughts. When the missing words are provided for the child, the child recognizes them. Often the child is able to use simple language without word-finding difficulty, but more complex words are lost. Estimates of the prevalence of ELD are in the 3–5% range (American Psychiatric Association, 1994).

Mixed Receptive-Expressive Language Disorder (MLD) is diagnosed when the child's receptive *and* expressive language abilities are delayed. As with ELD, MLD requires administration of expressive language, receptive language, and nonverbal intelligence tests. Scores in the expressive and receptive language areas must be lower than the nonverbal intelligence score. Again, the magnitude of the difference is not specified in DSM-IV. Children with MLD resemble those with ELD in their oral-verbal presentation. However, superimposed on the expressive language deficits are problems in the understanding of vocabulary and/or sentence structure or syntax. Hence, the child's comprehension lags as well as language production. MLD is less common than ELD, with estimated prevalence of less than 3% (American Psychiatric Association, 1994).

Phonological Disorder (PD) is diagnosed in children who do not articulate appropriate sounds for their age. Unlike ELD and MLD, a standardized test is not required for diagnosis. Children with PD may be unable to produce certain speech sounds, although a more common presentation is the slurring or substitution of sounds. For example, the child may use the "f" sound instead of the correct "th" sound, saying "free" instead of "three." It is important to note the distinction between PD, which is a disorder of sound *production*, and some types of reading disorders, which are disorders of sound (phonological) *recognition or awareness*. Children with PD may or may not have problems with phonological awareness; conversely, children with deficits in phonological awareness may have no difficulty with sound production. Hence, clinicians should carefully evaluate if a phonological problem is one of awareness and/

or production. If a PD *is* associated with a deficit in phonological awareness, dyslexia (reading disorder) is a risk. PD is rare in older children, although it may affect as many as 3% of children under age 7 (American Psychiatric Association, 1994).

Finally, Stuttering is characterized by halting speech in which words and sounds are repeated, prolonged, or separated many times throughout the oral speech pattern. Children who stutter sometimes try to avoid their problem by interrupting the speech of difficult words or by substituting other words in the place of words they have trouble pronouncing. They may have difficulty finding the word they want to say, although more often they know what they want to say but have trouble saying it.

Stuttering is often embarrassing to children and misunderstood by adults, who may take it as a sign of developmental delay or retardation. Stuttering may disappear in certain situations, such as when singing or talking to a doll. Teasing and embarrassment are common, and social withdrawal is a significant risk. Estimated prevalence in children under age 12 is 1%, decreasing with age.

ASSESSMENT PATTERNS

The symptoms of stuttering and phonological disorder are readily observed, and the observations of the clinician should be corroborated with the parent to ensure that the child's behavior at the clinic also occurs in the environment. DSM-IV can be used as a starting point for symptom-based questions to discuss with the parents.

Although intellectual assessment is *required* only for ELD and MLD, it is generally wise to obtain IQ and specific cognitive information on any child with a communication disorder. These data can assist the clinician in ruling out or confirming the effects of other cognitive factors on the language problem. One of the Wechsler intelligence scales or the SB:FE is usually most appropriate for the cognitive assessment. Most children with communication disorders will score in the low average to normal ranges on overall measures of IQ, although the distribution spans from mentally deficient to very superior.

The Wechsler Performance IQ or SB:FE Abstract/Visual Reasoning Area Scores can be used as the measure of "nonverbal intelligence" for diagnosis of ELD and MLD. Specific verbal subtest scores can be examined to document deficits in expressive and receptive language ability. On the Wechsler scales, children with ELD and MLD may be expected to have lower scores on subtests that call for extensive use of expressive language, such as Vocabulary and Comprehension. Information and Similarities, which call for less expression, may be slightly higher. Furthermore, the ELD/MLD child typically has a higher Performance than Verbal IQ. The SB:FE Vocabulary, Comprehension, and Absurdities subtests use receptive language (e.g., pointing to pictures) items for lower age ranges and expressive language (e.g., oral expression) for higher age ranges. Hence, their interpretation varies based on the age of the child. For children older than 6, these three tests primarily reflect expressive language and are likely to be affected in the child with ELD or MLD.

Although the Wechsler and SB:FE tests contain some verbal items, additional testing may help with the specific documentation of expressive and receptive language deficits. The Test of Auditory Comprehension of Language—Revised (TACL-R; Carrow-Woolfolk, 1985) and Peabody Picture Vocabulary Test—Revised (PPVT-R; Dunn and Dunn, 1981) are individually administered, standardized, normed measures of receptive vocabulary that are commonly used. For both tests the child is shown a group of pictures and asked to point to the picture that best fits a word or sentence. No verbal response is required. The PPVT-R and TACL-R test the child's ability to comprehend verbally presented information and to match this information with visual stimuli. Because they require no verbal production, they are relatively "pure" measures of receptive vocabulary. Both tests provide an overall receptive vocabulary score using a mean of 100 and a standard deviation of 15. The TACL-R provides additional scores for Word Classes and Relations (mostly simple nouns, verbs, adjectives, and some word relations represented in pictoral form), Grammatical Morphemes (short sentences in which a grammatical concept is represented in the picture), and Elaborated Sentences (more complex sentence themes shown on the picture). Children with ELD typically score in average ranges on the PPVT-R and TACL-R. Children with MLD show deficits on the PPVT-R and TACL-R that are consistent with their expressive language deficits but discrepant with their nonverbal ability.

In many cases, expressive vocabulary deficits are adequately documented with the Vocabulary and Comprehension subtests of the Wechsler scales. However, clinicians desiring a more detailed view of expressive vocabulary may wish to give an expressive vocabulary test such as the Expressive One-Word Picture Vocabulary Test (EOWPVT; Gardner, 1990). The EOWPVT presents the child with a picture, and the child must name the subject depicted. Virtually all pictures can be identified with a single word. The EOWPVT is advantageous for assessing children who have problems understanding verbal questions (such as those used on the Wechsler Vocabulary subtest) and children with word-finding difficulties.

Achievement tests can also provide cues about communication deficits and are a valuable part of a testing battery for a possible communication disorder. In addition to assisting in the understanding of the Communication Disorder *per se*, an achievement test can help identify other problems, particularly in the learning area. Many items of the Knowledge subtests of the WJ-R call for the use of expressive language in response to pictures. The child's responses to these items can be used as additional data concerning the presence of a MLD or ELD. Likewise, the WIAT Oral Expression and Listening Comprehension subtests measure complex components of expressive language and receptive language, respectively. The WJ-R Word Attack supplemental subtest is an enormous help in identifying children with PD who also have problems with phonological awareness (and therefore risk for reading disorder).

Over all, then, the child with ELD may be expected to show low scores on the Wechsler Vocabulary and Comprehension subtests, the EOWPVT, and the WIAT Oral Expression test, and *higher* scores on the PPVT-R, TACL-R, and

WIAT Listening Comprehension and Performance IQ. The child with MLD will show low scores on all of these tests *except* Performance IQ. Some discrepancy in this testing pattern may be expected, but the overall impression is one of expressive and/or receptive language deficit.

Because communication disorders can be stressful and frustrating to children and families, administration of the Child Behavior Checklist and Family Environment Scale is warranted to rule out associated child or family problems. Problematic scores on either of these scales suggest that assessment and treatment may need to focus on other Axis I disorders as well.

TREATMENT OPTIONS

Children with communication disorders should be evaluated by medical, speech, hearing, and educational personnel in addition to the mental health clinician. Therefore, the first intervention is often to seek consultation and assistance from professionals in these areas. Speech and language therapy is often necessary for children with Phonological Disorder or Stuttering. Special educational interventions, enrichment programs, and tutoring are indicated for children with ELD and MLD. The case management of the actual communication disorder treatment frequently occurs in the speech/language or educational setting.

Long-term involvement of the mental health clinician with a child with a communication disorder usually occurs only when the child has a concurrent behavioral-emotional disorder. In some cases, behavioral-emotional problems are related to the child's difficulty with communication. In other cases the child's behavior problems co-occur with the communication disorder but do not appear to be causally related to it. Treatment for co-occurring or associated behavior problems sometimes must be modified to accommodate the child's communication problem.

Learning Disorders

CLINICAL DESCRIPTION

Diagnostic Considerations

DSM-IV recognizes three specific learning disorders, and it allows for a "Not Otherwise Specified" designation for other disorders of learning. Reading (Reading Disorder), mathematics (Mathematics Disorder), and writing (Disorder of Written Expression) areas are given their own diagnostic categories. In each case the skill in question (i.e., reading, math, or writing) must be tested by an individually administered, standardized test of achievement in that area. The score obtained on that test must be substantially lower than the score that would be expected given the person's age, education, and intelligence. Typically, this "expected" score is obtained from an IQ test like a Wechsler scale.

The IQ–achievement discrepancy is diagnostic of a learning disorder. Furthermore, the deficit must be manifest in the child's daily activities. If an achievement area other than reading, math, or writing is affected, the disorder is diagnosed as Learning Disorder Not Otherwise Specified.

The DSM-IV diagnosis "learning disorders" is somewhat synonymous with the more widely used category of "learning disabilities". The term *learning disability* is much more widely recognized than the term *learning disorder*, perhaps because learning disability terminology has been used more often in clinical, research, educational, and political circles than has DSM terminology. Hence, most of what is known about learning disorders is inferred from learning disability research. Because of this fact, the remainder of this chapter will use learning disability terminology and learning disability research, although statements about learning disabilities may be assumed to apply directly to the DSM-IV learning disorders. The abbreviation "LD" will be used to refer to the learning disabilities designation.

The first issue to be considered in any discussion of LD is its definition. Definitional problems appear to have arisen for at least four reasons: First, LD has been used at times as a label to explain any learning problem or, in some cases, behavioral problem in children. As the LD label became fashionable, it has been seen by some schools as a more acceptable label than "behavior problem" or mentally retarded. This unfortunate use of the LD terminology to satisfy the needs of politically correct speech has confused the use of the LD diagnosis by teachers. Second, people without proper training, including the popular media, have advanced definitions of learning disability that distorted the truth. For example, dyslexia has become a very popular "self-diagnosis" for people with reading or writing difficulty. Third, legal definitions of LD have varied with court decisions, changes in laws, and use of the definition to control state funding for programs. Fourth, DSM-IV definitions of learning disorders are sufficiently vague as to allow multiple interpretations.

This definitional and diagnostic confusion has resulted in multiple definitions of LD in the legal, mental health, and educational arenas. Legally, the most widely accepted definition occurs in Public Law 94-142 (Education for All Handicapped Children). This law defines a learning disability as a disorder in written or spoken language that results in an imperfect ability to listen, think, read, write, spell, or do math. Children who have learning problems as a result of visual problems, hearing problems, MR, motor problems, or environmental deprivation cannot be classified LD under this law. Additional clarification is made on a regular basis by the U.S. Department of Education as well as by specific state educational agencies.

Psychologically, the major issue in LD definition is the exact nature of what is meant by a "discrepancy" between IQ and achievement testing. DSM-IV defines "substantially below" as a difference of more than 2 standard deviations between the intelligence and achievement test scores. However, DSM-IV also states that a 1–2 standard deviation difference may be used for LD diagnosis in certain situations. Sattler (1990) describes several methods that have been used to define learning disability on the basis of psychological testing:

1. LD may be defined as low achievement regardless of level of intelligence. This definition, however, is inappropriate because it classifies most mentally retarded children as LD. Furthermore, children could be classified LD if they were achieving commensurate with their intelligence. Contrary to this definition, there is almost universal agreement that LD children should be achieving below expectations and that mentally retarded children should not be classified as LD.

2. LD may be defined as a discrepancy between verbal and performance IQ scores. This definition is also inappropriate, since it says nothing about children's school achievement. LD is an achievement-based disorder.

3. LD may be defined as school performance significantly below age or grade level. Thus, a child who is in the fifth grade but is only achieving at a second-grade level would be classified as LD. A major issue within this definition is the number of years discrepancy that can result in the LD diagnosis. Some clinicians use a fixed 2 year criterion, but this criterion is extremely difficult to meet at the lower grades and easier at the higher grades. Thus, Sattler (1990) recommends using a discrepancy of 1 year for grades 1 and 2, 1½ years for grades 3 and 4, 2 years for grades 5–8, and 3 years for grades 9–12.

4. LD may be defined as a difference in standard scores between an IQ and an achievement test, with the assumption being that the IQ test measures "ability" as opposed to achievement. Usually 1 standard deviation (15 points for the commonly used IQ and achievement tests) is used as the criterion for a significant difference. It is wise to add another criterion to this classification method: The achievement score must be below a certain value. Without this criterion a child with very high achievement (e.g., score of 130) but even higher IQ (e.g., score of 150) could be classified LD even though the child is undoubtedly doing very well in school. Thompson and Kronenberger (1990), for example, used the 20th percentile as a cutoff for the achievement score of LD children. Another suggested criterion is an achievement test score of at least 1 standard deviation below the mean (standard score of 85 or lower) or an achievement test score below the normal range (89 or lower). There is no agreement on the exact value of this LD achievement cutoff score.

Another problem with this criterion is the selection of what IQ score is to be used as the comparison IQ score. The Full Scale IQ score is probably most often used, and it is probably the most reasonable score to use when the discrepancy between Verbal and Performance IQ is not significant. However, if there is a significant difference between Performance and Verbal IQ scores, the selection of the comparison IQ is unclear. Some clinicians continue to take the Full Scale IQ, although this score has little meaning when there is a significant VIQ–PIQ difference (Sattler, 1990). Other clinicians select the higher of the two (VIQ or PIQ) scores as most representative of the child's "highest potential." However, especially in the case of PIQ, the degree to which this potential should be expected to be reflected in schoolwork is unclear. Finally, some clinicians select the VIQ if there is a discrepancy, reasoning that verbal skills relate most closely to potential to learn in school. Unfortunately, the only recommendation that can be made here is that clinical flexibility in the selection of comparison IQ score is very important. In a majority of cases this flexibility will lead to the selection of the FIQ score if there is no VIQ–PIQ discrepancy and to the selection of the VIQ score if there is such a discrepancy.

5. LD may be classified as a statistically significant difference between IQ and achievement scores. Unfortunately, this criterion requires considerable calculation or, at the very least, extensive use of tables to determine if a statistically significant difference exists (Sattler, 1990).

Sattler (1990) also lists expectancy formulas and regression equations as methods to determine LD. However, these require the use of formulas and computations that, except in a tiny fraction of cases, are not justified because of the time and sophistication they demand. For the most part, methods 4 and 5 yield identical results. It must also be remembered that the use of standardized IQ and achievement tests restricts the behaviors that are sampled to the items within these tests. If the child's LD area is not sufficiently sampled on an achievement test, the results will be misleading.

Prevalence

The prevalence of LDs varies considerably based on the criteria used, but estimates are in the range of 1–5% (Gelfand, Jenson, and Drew, 1988; U.S. Department of Education, 1987). Estimates by the U.S. Department of Education set LD prevalence at 5% based on legal definitions (U.S. Department of Education, 1987). Children with LD also appear to be at risk for behavioral problems in both the internalizing (depression, withdrawal, anxiety) and externalizing (aggression, hyperactivity) areas, although their risk is less than that of mentally retarded children (Thompson and Kronenberger, 1990).

Appearance and Features

Because numerous categories of LDs exist, the appearance and features of a child with an LD (see Table 11.1) vary depending on specific diagnosis. In addition to the DSM-IV diagnoses, several subtyping systems of learning disabilities have been proposed, each of which has a unique appearance and features. Forness (1990), for example, empirically classified LD subtypes into five categories: Non-LD Pattern (children who underachieve in school or relative to grade but not relative to IQ), Production Deficits (children with difficulty retrieving information or translating cognition into verbal or nonverbal production), Verbal Organization Disorders (deficits in understanding or use of language), Nonverbal Organization Disorders (poor visuospatial achievement), and Global Disorders (deficits across a range of achievement areas). While these categories have the strength of being empirically derived, they lack clinical acceptance and use in educational settings.

Sattler (1990), on the other hand, focuses on subtypes in a specific achievement area, reading. Reading disability, also known as dyslexia, may be mani-

TABLE 11.1   Appearance and Features of Learning Disorders

COMMON FEATURES

Discrepancy between intelligence and achievement/performance in a specific area
Variability depending on area of deficiency

OCCASIONAL FEATURES

Risk of behavior problems, especially in situations requiring use of the impaired
 skill

Note: The features listed above are often seen but are not universal. Some features may be
diagnostically relevant or required, while others may not be required for diagnosis. "Common"
features are typical of the disorder; "occasional" features appear frequently but are not necessarily
seen in a majority of cases.

fest as any of a number of problems. First, *auditory-linguistic dyslexia* is characterized by deficits in auditory short-term memory, sound blending, sound discrimination, spelling, and sequencing. Children with these problems have
difficulty matching symbols with sounds; hence, they confuse sounds, omit
sounds, blend sounds poorly, and make errors with symbol-sound association. They tend to have lower Verbal than Performance IQ (Sattler, 1990). A
second category of reading disability is *visual-spatial dyslexia*. Children with
this dyslexia subtype have difficulty with visual memory, visual discrimination, visual analysis and synthesis, letter/word reversal, and sequencing of
letters. They do worse on performance, perceptual-organizational subtests than
on verbal-linguistic subtests (Sattler, 1990). Third, *mixed dyslexia* involves both
auditory-linguistic and visual-spatial problems (Sattler, 1990).

Surface dyslexia involves the inability to recognize whole words. However,
surface dyslexics retain, for the most part, the ability to sound out words
phonologically. Hence, they must rely on sounding out words to learn their
meaning. Finally, *phonological dyslexics* recognize whole words but have trouble
sounding them out phonologically. These two latter groups rely on sound reading and sight reading, respectively.

In addition to these classification schemes, learning disabilities can be
broadly classified into behavior problems, perceptual problems, and information processing problems (Gelfand et al., 1988). Behavior problem LDs occur
when the child's behavior interferes with the learning process, creating a learning deficit. The most common of these is Attention-Deficit Hyperactivity Disorder with an associated LD. Perceptual problem LDs involve problems in
visual perception and auditory perception. These perception problems are *not*
sensory difficulties but rather difficulties in discrimination, identification, association, sequential ordering, and perception. Finally, information processing
LDs reflect problems in one or more cognitive processing areas: short-term
memory, long-term memory, attention problems, organization and categoriza-
tion of verbal or nonverbal material, and self-motivation deficits (Gelfand et

al., 1988). The three broad areas and multiple subtypes of LDs are not mutually exclusive and, in fact, often overlap.

Over all, subtyping of LDs can assist in the identification, communication, and remediation of a child's learning problem. In the case of a reading disability, the Sattler (1990) and Gelfand et al. (1988) subtypes may be helpful. Other disabilities tend to fall into DSM-IV or Gelfand et al. (1988) subtypes. Numerous other subtyping systems exist in the neuropsychological and educational specialty fields. These have in common the detailed identification and description of the basic deficit and effects of the learning problem.

Etiology

The causes of LDs have been the source of much speculation but little empirical research support. A minority of LDs can be traced to specific neurological damage, injury, or an extremely impoverished environment; these causes are technically excluded in the legal definition of PL 94-142, but not in DSM-IV. However, most LD children do not have a discrete event or environment that accounts for their problems. Speculation about the cause of LD has focused on three biological explanations (developmental lag, neurological cause, and genetic factors) and one psychological explanation (environmental factors) (Gelfand et al., 1988; Sattler, 1990).

Biological Theories

Developmental lag theories state that some children with LD have learning problems because their neurological development is progressing more slowly than that of their peers. This is a reasonable assumption, since most human traits show variability, with a fraction of humans falling at the very low and the very high end of a frequency distribution. Neurological development, then, could be one of those normally distributed human traits, and LD children could be those children in the lower tail of the distribution. Research support for this position comes from studies suggesting that LD children have neurological immaturities and immaturities in other psychological testing (Gelfand et al., 1988; Sattler, 1990). According to developmental lag theories, LD children will eventually catch up to their peers in many abilities, although evidence suggests that they may never reach their peers' level in others, such as reading (Gelfand et al., 1988; Sattler, 1990). Hence, the label "developmentally delayed" implies a developmental lag theory. The clinician should use such a label with caution, since it may imply to the parent that the child will catch up with other children and become relatively normal. While this is a possibility, it can rarely be forecasted with much certainty.

Neurological theories state that LD is a reflection of structural damage or improper development of the nervous system. Such problems could occur during the prenatal or neonatal period, as the nervous system is developing. Alternatively, head injury, lack of oxygen, seizures, alterations in blood flow, exposure to toxins, and nutrition all may contribute to these structural-neurological problems. These events or problems may be small enough not to be noticed or to be downplayed by the physician, child, and parent. Rational support for this theory comes from proponents who reason that since all behavior is the result of neurological-physiological processes, LD must result from such processes. Empirical support comes from studies indicating EEG abnormalities in some LD children. Furthermore, brain damage is often associated with reading disability (Gelfand et al., 1988; Sattler, 1990). While these results support neurological etiology, few LD children have confirmed neurological cause for the disorder.

Genetic theories suggest that LDs are genetically determined, with genetic traits manifesting themselves in the neuroanatomy and neurophysiology of the child. These structural-physiological characteristics, in turn, are manifest as an LD. Support for the genetic theory is found in studies that show that LDs run in families and that LD concordance rates are higher for identical than for fraternal twins (Gelfand et al., 1988). However, most of these studies are poorly designed (Sattler, 1990), calling their results into question. Furthermore, the high rates of LDs within families could reflect family environment as much as genetics. In addition, identical twins share a prenatal environment that could account as much as genetics for their LD. Nevertheless, parents often adopt a genetic explanation for their child's learning disability, suggesting that the child is "just like me." Such parent-child similarity could reflect family environment as much as genetics. Hence, genetic theories have received weak and tentative support but need further research.

Psychological Theories

Psychological theories of LDs propose that environmental factors affect the behavior, motivation, and thought processes of the child in a way that interferes with learning. For example, the family may devalue education, or educational success may not be rewarded (or may be punished out of control issues or jealousy) in the family. Alternatively, the child may live in an impoverished environment, resulting in a delay in cognitive development. Extreme stress may interfere with attention, memory, and motivation. Sattler (1990) summarizes research support showing that environmental factors such as SES, family size, school, parental education, family conflict, and motivation are related to academic performance. Furthermore, children with LDs have more behavioral problems (Sattler, 1990; Thompson and Kronenberger, 1990), perhaps contributing to or causing the learning disability.

ASSESSMENT PATTERNS

A sample assessment battery for LDs is shown in Table 11.2.

Broad Assessment Strategies

Cognitive Assessment

Clinician Administered—IQ Testing. Diagnosing LD requires, at the very least, an intelligence and an achievement test. More specific tests, including

TABLE 11.2 Sample Assessment Battery for Learning Disorders

COGNITIVE

Intelligence test (Bayley-II, SB:FE, or Wechsler scale)
Achievement test (WIAT or WJ-R)

BEHAVIORAL

Child Behavior Checklist
Missouri Child Behavior Checklist
Conners Parent Rating Scale
Teacher-Report Form
Conners Teacher Rating Scale
Youth Self-Report

Note: Assessment instruments are intended to supplement (not substitute for) a good clinical interview and, when possible, a structured diagnostic interview.

neuropsychological testing, may be helpful in complex and severe cases. First, however, administration of an individual, standardized intelligence test is essential in the diagnosis of LD. Because most children being evaluated for LD are over the age of 4, the Wechsler instruments (WPPSI-R, WISC-III) are usually the tests of choice.

Although WISC-III/WPPSI-R scores should never be used alone to diagnose LD (Sattler, 1990), LD children do show characteristic patterns on subscales of the Wechsler scales. Sattler (1990) reviewed studies and rank-ordered WISC-R subscales from easiest to most difficult for LD children: Picture Completion, Picture Arrangement, Block Design, Object Assembly, Similarities, Comprehension, Vocabulary, Coding, Digit Span, Arithmetic, Information. Of note is that the easiest four subtests all form the Perceptual-Organization (PO) factor of the WISC-III and that two of the hardest three subtests form the Freedom from Distractibility (FFD) factor of the WISC-III. In addition, the most difficult four subtests form the so-called "ACID" (Arithmetic-Coding-Information-Digit Span) profile of subscales. Low scores on the ACID profile are considered as "typical" of the LD child. Finally, the Verbal Comprehension (VC) subtests (Similarities, Comprehension, Vocabulary, and Information) are generally in the middle of the range.

By definition, LD children usually score in the average (90–109) range on Full Scale IQ. LD children also tend to have higher PO (or Performance) IQ scores than VC (or Verbal) IQ scores. The FFD Index score tends to be the lowest. Clinically, it appears that the Processing Speed (PS) score often falls between the FFD and VC scores for LD children, although this remains to be researched. As noted, LD children often show an ACID profile, meaning that their Arithmetic (A), Coding (C), Information (I), and Digit Span (D) scores are their lowest. WPPSI-R patterns vary somewhat from WISC-III patterns, because of differences in content and subtests. Freedom from distractibility (which does *not* emerge as a WPPSI-R factor, unlike the WISC-III; Sattler, 1990) may be cautiously inferred from the Sentences, Arithmetic, and Animal House subtests of the WPPSI-R.

The Wechsler scales can be valuable adjuncts in delineating the specific nature of an LD. Auditory-linguistic dyslexics, for example, score higher on Performance IQ than on Verbal IQ. Visual-spatial dyslexics, on the other hand, score higher on Verbal IQ than on Performance IQ. Visual-spatial dyslexics also have particularly weak scores on Coding and Symbol Search. Likewise, a low FFD score in the context of a low PO score is suggestive of a perceptual LD. Low FFD coupled with low Processing Speed and low Verbal scores would be indicative of a form of information processing LD. More specific LD problems may be inferred from subtest scores. For example, low scores on Digit Span, Coding, and Picture Arrangement could indicate a sequential processing deficit.

Occasionally it is necessary to use a test other than one of the Wechsler scales for an LD child. The SB:FE is often the substitute test of choice. Interpretation strategies for this and other substitute tests are found in Sattler (1990).

Clinician-Administered—Achievement Testing. In addition to the intelligence test, an individually administered achievement test is typically required in order to make the LD diagnosis. Unlike with intelligence testing, there is no consensus as to the best achievement test for an LD assessment. This lack of consensus is understandable, considering that the choice of an achievement test should depend somewhat on the child's reported learning problems. Ideally, the achievement test chosen will have several subtests assessing the child's problem area, such that analysis of these subtest scores will not only indicate the presence of a problem but also tell something about the nature of the problem. Failure to find an achievement–intelligence discrepancy could indicate that the achievement test did not tap the child's reported problem area.

Two excellent global achievement tests for an LD evaluation are the WJ-R and the WIAT. The WJ-R has several advantages in the assessment of an LD child. First, it covers an extremely wide age range, from age 2½ to adulthood. Hence, children just beginning school and even children in preschool can be tested using the WJ-R, with little fear of floor effects. However, preschool testing of achievement differs from achievement testing of a child who is of school age. In particular, the preschool child does not have formal school experiences that can be tested for retention and learning. Hence, achievement must be inferred based on acquisition of preschool achievement activities. For example, the preschool items of the Dictation subtest involve copying marks (resembling letters) and staying within lines when using a pencil. The extent to which these skills will be predictive of later spelling and punctuation Dictation items may vary from child to child. One would not want to draw strong conclusions about future spelling ability based on copying and staying within lines, even though these skills are somewhat correlated. In other words, an assumption is made that the "preschool" WJ-R items reflect basic processes that are predictive of later achievement. However, since the child has not yet undergone formal schooling, performance on these items does not directly reflect ability to learn in the school environment.

A second advantage of the WJ-R is the extensive body of scores it yields. In addition to standard scores, the WJ-R gives age-equivalent, grade-equivalent, percentile, confidence-interval, and Relative Mastery Index (RMI) scores. The RMI is a measure of the percent of mastery of a topic obtained by the tested child when the average child would score a 90%. For example, an RMI of 95 on Calculation indicates that, when the average child has achieved a 90% mastery level of Calculation, the tested child is likely to show 95% mastery of Calculation. The RMI can be useful in predicting how much of an achievement area the LD child is likely to have learned when his or her classmates are considered to have mastered it at a 90% mastery rate.

A third advantage of the WJ-R is the use of subtests within the cluster areas to identify specific problems within learning areas. For example, within the Reading cluster, the Letter-Word Identification subtest (LWI) evaluates identification and pronunciation of words, while the Reading Comprehension (RC) subtest measures comprehension of word clusters (sentences and paragraphs). A child who does well on LWI but poorly on RC may have more of a comprehension than a word-identification problem. Supplementary subtests can be extremely helpful in a more specific analysis of problems. The Word Attack (WA) subtest, for instance, is a supplementary reading subtest that asks the child to read unfamiliar "nonsense" words. Because the WA "words" are unfamiliar, the child must read them phonetically; "sight" or recognition reading is of no help on WA. Hence, a low score on WA coupled with a high score on LWI (which consists of familiar words that can be read based either on recognition or pronunciation) could indicate that the child is reading adequately by sight but has poor phonetic reading skills.

Like the WJ-R, the WIAT is an excellent test for the assessment of ability–achievement discrepancy, although its age range is substantially smaller than that of the WJ-R (age 5 years to 19 years, 11 months). LD children tend to score low on one or more of the WIAT clusters, relative to their Full Scale IQ score. Unlike the WJ-R, the WIAT includes no supplementary subtests. A useful feature of the WIAT is its ability to be used as a brief screening test by eliminating some of the more lengthy and complex subtests.

Choosing between the WJ-R and the WIAT in the assessment of the LD child can be done on the basis of several considerations. Both tests allow the fine-grained analysis of subtests to probe deficits within broad achievement areas, such as reading. Similarly, both tests give extensive standard scores, confidence intervals, and percentiles based on excellent standardization samples. However, the WJ-R provides more extensive age-equivalent, grade-equivalent, and RMI information than the WIAT. In addition, the WJ-R has a wider age range and, thus, a wider range of items than does the WIAT. Thus, for very young children, very impaired children, and very bright children, the WJ-R may be the test of choice.

On the other hand, the WIAT is designed to allow analysis of very specific abilities within each subtest. Furthermore, the WIAT was co-normed with the

WISC-III, so WIAT scores can be directly linked to WISC-III scores. In other words, a "predicted" score for each WIAT area can be calculated from the WISC-III IQ score, and the statistical significance of the IQ–achievement difference can be calculated. Hence, in addition to using a 15 point discrepancy for LD diagnosis, the clinician could calculate whether the IQ–achievement difference is statistically significant.

Within cluster areas there are advantages to each of these achievement tests as well. For example, the supplementary WA subtest on the WJ-R allows the testing of phonetic reading ability; there is no similar subtest on the WIAT. Furthermore, the Knowledge subtests on the WJ-R (Science, Social Studies, and Humanities) tap school achievement areas that are not covered by the WIAT. On the other hand, the Oral Expression and Listening Comprehension subtests on the WIAT do not have counterparts on the WJ-R Achievement Tests (there are, however, counterparts to these subtests in the WJ-R Cognitive Battery). Hence, selection of the appropriate achievement test for the LD child requires the integration of the referral question with what is known about these major achievement tests. For example, a child with a suspected reading disability may be administered the WJ-R, including the supplementary reading tests. On the other hand, a child with language comprehension deficits may give more pertinent data on the WIAT, with its capacity to differentiate reading and listening comprehension.

In addition to the WJ-R and WIAT, several other achievement tests exist that have good psychometric properties and clinical usefulness. The *Kaufman Test of Educational Achievement* (K-TEA; *Kaufman and Kaufman,* 1985) and the *Peabody Individual Achievement Test—Revised* (PIAT-R; Markwardt, 1989) are widely used tests in LD assessments. Like the WJ-R and the WIAT, the K-TEA and PIAT-R include measures of reading, mathematics, and written language. Their subtests vary slightly but not substantially from ones included in the WJ-R and WIAT. Like the WIAT, the K-TEA has the advantage of identifying very specific academic areas for intervention, and a brief form is available (Kaufman and Ishikuma, 1993).

Most other broad achievement tests should be used with caution or for screening purposes only. For example, the extensively used *Wide Range Achievement Test—Revised* (WRAT-R; Jastak and Wilkinson, 1984) has received severe criticism for its norms and psychometric properties. Kaufman and Ishikuma (1993), for example, state that "the WRAT-R should not be used for any reason" (p. 203) and that "results from the WRAT-R are misleading and confusing" (p. 203). Hence, the clinician evaluating a child for LD should use one of the four established tests described here whenever possible. Most local and state departments of education will provide a list of "acceptable" achievement tests on request; clinicians who are doing extensive work for the schools will likely want to verify that their achievement test is consistent with the goals of the department of education.

In some cases, assessment of a very specific achievement area is all that is called for in an evaluation. When this is the case, a more specific achievement test may be used. The *Sequential Assessment of Mathematics Inventories* (SAMI;

Reisman, 1985) and the *Woodcock Reading Mastery Test—Revised* (WRMT-R; Woodcock, 1987) are examples of good tests focused in the mathematics and reading areas, respectively. Specific tests such as these can provide a briefer but more in-depth view of a focused achievement area. However, many poorly designed, poorly standardized, and poorly normed tests exist in this "specific achievement test" area, and often such tests yield information that is less useful than information obtained with the WJ-R or WIAT. Hence, these tests should be used warily.

Integration of Intelligence and Achievement Tests.   Once intelligence and achievement testing data are obtained, the clinician must integrate them into a formulation about the existence and nature of a learning disability. Several steps can facilitate this process:

   1. *Selecting a comparison IQ score.* First, the IQ score to be used for the basis of comparison must be selected. If there is no VIQ–PIQ difference, it is usually wisest to use the FIQ score. This score tends to be the most reliable measure on the test (Wechsler, 1991). However, if there is a significant VIQ–PIQ discrepancy, the FIQ loses meaning. In this case, either the VIQ or PIQ should be chosen as the comparison score. Because the VIQ tends to be the most similar to and the most correlated with achievement, this score will often be the one chosen. However, in some cases the examiner may wish to choose the PIQ for comparison purposes. Such a situation may occur when a child has verbal production difficulties. WISC-III index (factor) scores are not typically used for purposes of comparison. However, use of the Verbal Comprehension index score may be warranted if Freedom from Distractibility problems (reflected in the Arithmetic subtest on VIQ) confound the VIQ.

   If the comparison IQ is less than 70, LD cannot be diagnosed. Analysis of scores may proceed in this case, but the child should not be diagnosed LD.

   2. *Identification of normative achievement deficits.* Following selection of the IQ score, *normative achievement deficits* are identified. These deficits occur in achievement cluster areas (e.g., reading, math, written language, language, knowledge) relative to norms. Typically, a cutoff score of 85 is used for a "deficit," although scores of 90 and 80 are also used. A compromise may be to designate scores between 80 and 89 as "mild deficits" while scores below 80 are designated as "severe deficits."

   3. *Identification of intelligence–achievement discrepancies.* Next, the selected IQ score is matched to the achievement cluster area scores. Numerous ways exist to calculate "significant" discrepancies, but the most parsimonious way is to use a discrepancy of 15 or more points (IQ greater than achievement) as the criterion of significance for an intelligence–achievement discrepancy. Areas that are *both* normative achievement deficits (see Step 2) and intelligence–achievement discrepancies are consideredLDs.

   In some cases a clinician may want to use specific achievement subtest (as opposed to composite achievement cluster) scores to identify an intelligence–

achievement discrepancy. This analysis may be done, but because of the lower reliability of individual subtests relative to cluster scores, conclusions will be more tentative.

4. *Analysis of subtest scores within the LD area.* Once the LD area is identified, subtest scores and items within the LD area may be examined to analyze in detail the nature of the LD deficit. Subtest scores differing by 15 or more points are generally considered to be discrepant, although the reliabilities of the subtests must be considered in choosing a cutoff for discrepancy. Statistical significance may be calculated if necessary, although the 15-point criterion is usually sufficient for the major achievement tests.

5. *Explanation of residual deficits and discrepancies.* Some achievement areas will meet the criterion for a normative achievement deficit or an intelligence–achievement discrepancy but not both. These achievement areas are not typically considered areas of learning disability. Normative achievement deficits that are not intelligence–achievement discrepancies occur when children are achieving below their peers but in line with expectations based on IQ. Such children have low IQ and similar achievement. On the other hand, intelligence-achievement discrepancies that are not normative achievement deficits typically occur when high-IQ children are achieving at age-appropriate levels. Hence, achievement is not a "problem" relative to peers, but it does not meet expectations based on the individual children's IQ. Explanation to parents of the differences between LD and these residual problems is essential.

Behavioral Assessment

Parent-Report/Other Report. Substantial evidence exists that children with learning problems are at risk for behavioral problems (Thompson and Kronenberger, 1990). There are three possible explanations for this finding: First, behavioral problems, such as ADHD, may interfere with the child's ability to learn. Second, the child's learning problems may lead to frustration, boredom, and low self-esteem that result in behavioral problems. Third, some other factor, such as neurological damage, may cause both learning and behavioral problems. Often there is interplay between all three of these explanations, which have reciprocal, interactive, and dynamic effects on the child.

A common referral question is the effect of a child's behavior on his or her LD. Essentially, this question asks if the disability is behavioral or cognitive. The answer is usually yes to both questions, which then leads to the question of the relative importance of cognitive and behavioral factors. Assessment of the degree and type of behavior problems can help with this determination. Children with severe behavior problems in the attention, hyperactivity, thought problems, and disobedience areas are likely to have a strong behavioral component to their problems.

Because of the risk and importance of behavior problems, children with suspected LD should be routinely assessed for behavior problems. Parents may complete a checklist such as the CBCL or MCBC as a screening device. Teacher-report can be gathered with the TRF or the CTRS. The CBCL, MCBC, TRF, and CTRS have proven utility with LD children.

There is no "typical" pattern of behavior problems for LD children, although many of them show symptoms of ADHD. Any significant elevation found with behavioral problem testing can be further probed with syndrome-specific test batteries described in other chapters. If a behavior problem is found, knowing the time of its emergence (especially if it predated or postdated learning problems) can be extremely helpful in evaluating the etiology of the LD and behavior problem.

TREATMENT OPTIONS

Treatment options for LD are outlined in Table 11.3. The most common treatment for children with LD is special educational planning. This planning may range from regular class placement with tutoring to placement in LD classes for the problem academic areas. The goal of most clinicians and schools is to place the child in the "least restrictive environment," which typically means the environment that resembles as closely as possible that of non-LD children. Many LD children, for example, attend regular classes but are given additional time in "resource rooms" where they have access to more structured learning with smaller student-to-teacher ratios (often individual instruction).

Some children who do not meet exact criteria for LD diagnosis may nevertheless show skills or achievement deficiencies that can be remediated at school. These should also be identified by the clinician and presented to the school. Many schools are willing to accommodate (within reason) to the learning needs of individual students, even if a formal LD cannot be diagnosed.

The mental health clinician is rarely involved with the details of these special educational services, although the clinician holds a powerful position as

TABLE 11.3   Treatment Options for Learning Disorders

SPECIAL EDUCATIONAL PLANNING (referral to school experts)

Resource room
Access to tutor
Teaching at a different pace or using different modalities (e.g., talking as opposed to writing)
Clinician–school collaboration

CO-OCCURRING BEHAVIOR PROBLEMS

Address using techniques specific for each behavior problem

Note: This outline of options summarizes major treatments covered in the text. Specific treatments are often combined into an intervention package. Refer to the text for additional descriptions of each treatment. This table is not necessarily an exhaustive list of all treatments available.

advocate for these services in appropriate cases. It is important to remember that the final decision belongs to the school and not to the clinician. Hence, a collaborative relationship with the school is essential. Often the communication of findings and recommendations is easily accomplished by mail and phone, but if disagreement exists between the clinician, school, and parents, a meeting may be necessary. Such a meeting may enlighten the clinician about other issues (such as parental embarrassment or school finances) that enter the decision making process. In such complex cases a school counselor or school psychologist can be an excellent liaison between the parents, clinician, and school.

In many cases, behavior problems of the LD child are as much of a concern as the LD itself. When a behavior problem is identified, the contribution of the LD to the problem must constantly be considered. Nevertheless, intervention for the behavior problem often follows the same procedures as for non-LD children with a similar behavior problem.

■ References

American Psychiatric Association. (1994). *Diagnostic and statistical manual of mental disorders* (4th ed.). Washington, DC: Author.

Carrow-Woolfolk, E. (1985). *Test for auditory comprehension of language* (rev.). Allen, TX: DLM Teaching Resources.

Dunn, L. M., and Dunn, L. M. (1981). *Peabody picture vocabulary test—revised.* Circle Pines, MN: American Guidance Service.

Forness, S. R. (1990). Subtyping in learning disabilities: Introduction to the issues. In H. L. Swanson and B. Keogh (Eds.), *Learning disabilities: Theoretical and research issues* (pp. 195–200). Hillsdale, NJ: Erlbaum.

Gardner, M. F. (1990). *Expressive one-word picture vocabulary test—revised.* Los Angeles: Western Psychological Services.

Gelfand, D. M., Jenson, W. R., and Drew, C. J. (1988). *Understanding child behavior disorders* (2d ed.). New York: Harcourt Brace Jovanovich.

Jastak, S., and Wilkinson, G. S. (1984). *Wide range achievement test—revised.* Wilmington, DE: Jastak Associates.

Kaufman, A. S., and Ishikuma, T. (1993). Intellectual and achievement testing. In T. H. Ollendick and M. Hersen (Eds.), *Handbook of child and adolescent assessment* (pp. 192–207). Needham Heights, MA: Allyn & Bacon.

Kaufman, A. S., and Kaufman, N. L. (1985). *Manual for the Kaufman Test of Educational Achievement (K-TEA) Comprehensive Form.* Circle Pines, MN: American Guidance Service.

Markwardt, F. C. (1989). *Manual for the Peabody Individual Achievement Test—Revised (PIAT-R).* Circle Pines, MN: American Guidance Service.

McCarthy, D. A. (1972). *Manual for the McCarthy Scales of Children's Abilities.* San Antonio, TX: Psychological Corporation.

Reisman, F. T. (1985). *Sequential assessment of mathematics inventories.* San Antonio, TX: Psychological Corporation.

Sattler, J. M. (1990). *Assessment of children* (3d ed.). San Diego, CA: Author.

Thompson, R. J., Jr., and Kronenberger, W. G. (1990). Behavior problems in children with learning problems. In H. L. Swanson and B. Keogh (Eds.), *Learning disabilities: Theoretical and research issues* (pp. 155–174). Hillsdale, NJ: Erlbaum.

U.S. Department of Education. (1987). *Ninth annual report to Congress.* Washington, DC: Author.

Wechsler, D. (1991). *Manual for the Wechsler Intelligence Scale for Children—Third Edition.* San Antonio, TX: Psychological Corporation.

Woodcock, R. W. (1987). *Manual for Woodcock Reading Mastery Tests—Revised (WRMT-R).* Circle Pines, MN: American Guidance Service.

CHAPTER 12

Mental Retardation

■ **Mental Retardation**

□ CLINICAL DESCRIPTION

Diagnostic Considerations

Excluding the personality disorders, mental retardation (MR) is the only other diagnosis that can be made on DSM-IV Axis II. The rationale for placing MR on Axis II is to ensure "that consideration will be given to the possible presence of . . . Mental Retardation that might otherwise be overlooked when attention is directed to the usually more florid Axis I disorders" (American Psychiatric Association, 1994, p. 26). Formerly, the "specific developmental disorders" (now learning, motor, and communication disorders) and pervasive developmental disorders were also coded on Axis II with MR. However, the specific developmental disorders and pervasive developmental disorders have undergone substantial changes in DSM-IV, including removal from the Axis II category. In contrast, the MR diagnosis has changed little.

Outside of professional circles it is widely believed that MR is diagnosed based only on intelligence testing information. In fact, a diagnosis of MR requires significant deficits not only in intellectual functioning, but also in adaptive functioning. DSM-IV identifies eleven areas of adaptive functioning (communication, self-care, home living, social skills, use of community resources, self-direction, academic skills, work, leisure, health, and safety) and requires deficits in two of them in order to make the MR diagnosis. Hence, it is not possible for a person who functions well in society to be diagnosed as mentally retarded. This DSM-IV definition of MR is very similar to the other widely accepted definition of MR, which has been proposed by the American Association on Mental Deficiency (Grossman, 1983).

For the MR diagnosis to be met, the individual must have an IQ (presumably Full Scale IQ, although DSM-IV encourages flexibility in cases of significant ability scatter) of 70 or lower on an *individually* administered IQ test. Less rigorous (and less valid) group IQ tests cannot and should not be used for diagnosing MR. When it is not possible to obtain an IQ measure (e.g., because the child is uncooperative or cannot do the test at all), a diagnosis of Mental Retardation, Severity Unspecified, is made.

Unlike the IQ criterion, no specific score or type of adaptive functioning test is required for the MR diagnosis. Hence, the clinician could presumably make the diagnosis based on clinical impression of level of adaptive functioning. However, because several tests of adaptive functioning exist, it is wise to use a standardized, normed measure of adaptive functioning. A cutting score of 70 on two adaptive functioning subscales (each representing one of the DSM-IV adaptive functioning areas) would meet the adaptive functioning criterion, although a case could be made for meeting this criterion if several critical subscale (e.g., communication, daily living) scores were close to 70 *and* the overall adaptive functioning score was less than 70. In addition to the standardized normed measures of adaptive behavior, tables of representative adaptive behavior for different ages and degrees of MR have been published in several sources (Sattler, 1990; Gelfand, Jenson, and Drew, 1988).

Mental retardation is a relatively common disorder. Estimates of prevalence are usually in the 1–3% range (Gelfand et al, 1988; Grossman, 1983), although a 1% prevalence rate seems to be more widely accepted (Aman, Hammer, and Rojahn, 1993). Prevalence estimates of 3% appear to mistakenly not take adaptive functioning into account (Aman et al., 1993). The majority of MR children fall into the upper (IQ of 40–70) ranges of MR intellectual functioning; approximately 50–85% of MR children fall into the 55–70 IQ range, while another 10–30% fall into the 40–55 range (American Psychiatric Association, 1994; Baroff, 1986).

Within the MR category, DSM-IV subtypes exist based on severity of the IQ deficit. *Mild* MR is diagnosed when IQ scores range from approximately 50–70; *moderate* MR is diagnosed for IQ scores from approximately 35–55; *severe* MR is diagnosed when IQ falls between 20 and 40; and *profound* MR is diagnosed for children with IQ below 25. The overlap in the IQ scores is deliberate and allows the clinician some discretion in classifying "borderline" cases. The decision about which category to diagnose in these borderline cases depends on validity concerns about testing, level of adaptive functioning, behavioral observations during testing, and global clinical impression. For example, a child with an IQ of 53 who had an outlying low score on a subtest that she did not seem to understand (thus artificially lowering her overall IQ score) may be diagnosed as mild MR, especially if adaptive functioning is in the 55–70 range.

The IQ subtypes delineated in DSM-IV are matched by a system of subtypes used by educators. The educational subtypes of MR provide labels to each IQ range based on the expected academic achievement of the MR child (Gelfand et al., 1988). The "educable" category roughly corresponds to the mild MR category; the "trainable" category corresponds to the moderate and severe categories; and the "custodial" category is reserved for children with profound retardation.

Appearance and Features

The appearance and associated behavioral features of mentally retarded children (see Table 12.1) vary so widely that it is difficult to characterize a "typical" presentation. Hence, it is important to note that the MR diagnosis is a heterogeneous one with regard to the physical appearance and behavioral features of the child. Some MR children are quiet, polite, confident, and compliant; others are aggressive, oppositional, anxious, and hostile. Some MR children are extremely sociable, while others may be withdrawn. Over all, however, there appears to be a somewhat elevated risk of behavior problems in the MR population. Significant problems with aggressive behavior, self-injurious behavior, stereotypic behavior, overactivity, and language disorders are reported in MR populations (Aman et al., 1993; Jacobson, 1982). These behaviors may occur at greater frequencies in more intellectually impaired and older groups.

The MR group, in fact, shares little in common beyond poor intellectual and adaptive functioning. Intellectually, MR children tend to be concrete, to have poor problem solving, to have delayed verbal skills, and to do poorly in novel situations. Developmentally, MR children show significant delays in the achievement of intellectual, social, and motor milestones. They typically talk later than do average children, and their vocabulary grows more slowly. Socially, they are typically responsive, attached, and oriented to interaction, but social understanding and social skills are often poor. Mentally retarded children often violate basic social conventions and exhibit unusual behavior in social situations. Mild to Moderate MR children may be taught some adaptive behaviors, but they typically require more practice and guidance than do average children.

TABLE 12.1   Appearance and Features of Mental Retardation

COMMON FEATURES

Significantly below average cognitive functioning
Significantly below average adaptive functioning
Developmental delay
Socially responsive
Risk of behavior problems (Axis I)
Need for special education
Need for structured caretaking environment throughout life

OCCASIONAL FEATURES

Neurological involvement
Unusual appearance/soft signs

Note: The features listed above are often seen but are not universal. Some features may be diagnostically relevant or required, while others may not be required for diagnosis. "Common" features are typical of the disorder; "occasional" features appear frequently but are not necessarily seen in a majority of cases.

As with behavior, the appearance of the mentally retarded child can vary from unusual to completely normal. A large subgroup of mentally retarded children, however, has clearly unusual physical appearances characterized by neurological soft signs, unusual facial features, and poor motor coordination. Neurological soft signs and unusual appearance are typically associated with a biological cause. Examples of unusual appearance include webbed digits, small head, eyefolds, flat nose, large and protruding ears, short stature, and protruding tongue. More normal appearance tends to be (but is not always) associated with psychosocial causes.

Etiology

Unlike other psychological disorders, there is little debate about the causes of MR. When debate does occur, it usually centers on the role of the environment in the MR of a particular child. Mental retardation can result from numerous factors that can loosely be grouped into biological and psychological categories.

Biological Theories

At least five broad biological causes can be identified for MR, accounting for approximately 15–25% of total cases (Grossman, 1983; Gelfand et al., 1988):

1. *Infection/intoxication.* Certain infections (e.g., meningitis) can attack or have effects on the child's developing nervous system, causing permanent damage that is reflected in MR. Toxic substances can have similar effects. These effects are particularly pronounced at earlier ages. In these cases the child is not born with an inclination toward MR but "acquires" the condition as a result of infection or poisoning.

2. *Metabolic disorders.* These disorders (such as phenylketonuria (PKU)) are characterized by the body's inability to correctly metabolize or eliminate chemicals, resulting in a toxic internal biochemical environment for the child. This toxic environment causes neurological damage and MR. In some cases the child is born with normal functioning, but the metabolic disorder poses a future risk. Hence, control of the disorder can reduce or prevent MR.

3. *Genetic factors.* These factors are often the cause of metabolic disorders, and they can be traced to the genes or chromosomes of the child. The genetic abnormality is reflected in neuroanatomical or neurophysiological abnormality, which functionally appears as MR. The most well known of these factors involves a third chromosome 21 (Down's syndrome).

4. *Prenatal factors.* Because much of the child's neurological development occurs before birth, a host of prenatal factors (including infection, nutrition, and impaired biological development) can affect the child's neurological integrity and functional status. In these cases the child is born with a condition that is likely to result in MR. Microcephaly and spina bifida are two such conditions.

5. *Injury or trauma.* These factors include birth difficulties (lack of oxygen during birth, premature birth, traumatic injury during birth) and later physical injury (closed head injury, lack of oxygen) that have neurological effects functionally manifest as MR.

Psychological Theories

In addition to biological causes, MR can result from psychological environmental causes. The most widely accepted psychological cause of MR is environmental deprivation. Infants placed in environmentally deprived situations (typically characterized by unchanging sensory stimulation, lack of social contact, and, possibly, restricted movement) are at significant risk for MR. Typically, this takes the form of parental neglect and lack of social stimulation.

In all but the most extreme biological cases, however, MR results from an interaction of biological and psychological factors. The most widely accepted theory at this point is that genetics and biology set a range of intellectual levels that can be achieved by the child. Where the child falls within this range is dependent on environmental factors. In the case of some biological conditions this range is small and low; in other cases the range is quite large.

ASSESSMENT PATTERNS

Children with MR are usually identified in one of four ways: First, some children have medical or environmental conditions that are associated with risk of MR. These conditions are recognized by a physician or agency who then refers the child for assessment. Second, some children referred for behavior problems are noticed by the clinician to be intellectually or developmentally delayed. Third, parents sometimes become concerned when their children do not meet developmental milestones at appropriate ages. They bring the child to a pediatrician, who then refers for assessment. Finally, higher-functioning MR children may not be identified until they reach school age. They are singled out when they fail at age-appropriate academic tasks. In all four scenarios there is some concern about the child's present and future ability to meet developmentally appropriate intellectual-achievement expectations. Hence, whenever developmental-intellectual delays present in a referral, the clinician must be aware of the possibility of an MR diagnosis. Conversely, a large number of children referred for developmental testing will not receive the MR diagnosis.

Before testing begins, the clinician must attend to problems that may be associated with or mask as MR. First, the child should be evaluated by a physician to rule out biomedical conditions such as lead poisoning, infection, and genetic disorder. Second, the clinician should attend to the hearing and vision capacity of the child. In some cases, sensory deficits can mask as MR because the child does not perceive the environment accurately, leading to learning deficits and inappropriate behaviors. Any other factors felt to account for the MR should be thoroughly investigated by the clinician or another professional.

There are three basic components to psychological assessment of MR: cognitive testing, adaptive functioning, and associated behavior problems (see Table 12.2).

TABLE 12.2 Sample Assessment Battery for Mental Retardation

COGNITIVE

Intelligence test (Bayley-II, SB:FE, or Wechsler scale)
Vineland Adaptive Behavior Scales

BEHAVIORAL

Child Behavior Checklist
Teacher's Report Form
Conners Teacher Rating Scale

Note: Assessment instruments are intended to supplement (not substitute for) a good clinical interview and, when possible, a structured diagnostic interview.

Broad Assessment Strategies

Cognitive Assessment

Clinician-Administered—IQ Testing. The most critical component of cognitive testing for MR is the intelligence test, which is required for the MR diagnosis. The choice of intelligence test is crucial and should be made based on preliminary information obtained by the clinician. For children with estimated IQ levels of 50 and above the instruments of choice are the Wechsler intelligence scales. Children age 3–7 can be tested with the WPPSI-R; children between the ages of 6 and 17 can be tested with the WISC-III.

When testing with the Wechsler scales, the clinician must consider several issues. First, the Wechsler scales experience floor effects in the 40–50 IQ range; below these scores they simply give the floor IQ. Hence, they are not useful with children in the severe to profound range of MR. If the child fails to score more than 0 or 1 raw score point on the first three or four subtests of a Wechsler scale, the clinician should probably select a different intelligence test. Second, the floor for the Wechsler scales extends farther and is more valid as the MR child becomes older than the lower age range on the test. In other words, there are fewer "easy" items on the WISC-III for a 6-year-old than there are for a 12-year-old. Hence, a more valid result is obtained for the mentally retarded 12 year old. This problem can be easily handled in the 6-year-old age range, when the child can be given either the WPPSI-R or WISC-III. At test overlap ages, MR children should be given the "easier" (in the sense of having more items for younger mental ages) WPPSI-R rather than the "harder" WISC-III. Third, in addition to the overall Full Scale IQ, the Wechsler scales give Verbal and Performance IQ scores, Index or Factor scores, and subscale scores. Hence, it is possible to identify strengths and weaknesses in the profile, which may lead to hypotheses about the nature and treatment of the disorder.

In some cases, use of the Wechsler scales to assess intelligence is contraindicated in the MR child. For example, if a child's suspected IQ is less than 50, the Wechsler scales may not provide an accurate IQ. Furthermore, at the lower end of the age range for the WPPSI-R (age 3 years), an MR child may be able to complete few items, giving an unreliable indication of intelligence. In addition, a child may have trouble understanding the tasks of the Wechsler scales, or the examiner may want a second measure of IQ because of validity concerns with a previously administered Wechsler scale. For children with these issues, one of two intelligence tests are usually substituted for the Wechsler scale: the SB:FE or Bayley-II.

The SB:FE can be administered to children age 2 years to 24 years. Because of this extensive age range, it includes items that may be in the developmental range for severely and profoundly retarded children over the age of 6. Hence, for children above age 6 who are suspected of being severely or profoundly retarded, the SB-IV is the test of choice. In this age range it can give IQ scores as low as 36. However, for children under age 6 the SB:FE has floor effects comparable to those of the WPPSI-R. These floor effects become extreme at age 3 years, 6 months, rendering the test meaningless for MR children below this age. For children under 3½ years, the lowest SB:FE IQ that can be obtained is a 66, and at age 2, the lowest IQ is 95 (Sattler, 1990).

In addition to floor effect problems at young ages, the SB:FE has psychometric and practical problems. First, it uses a mean of 100 and standard deviation of 16 for composite (IQ) scores. This convention is confusing, since most other intelligence scales use a standard deviation of 15 for IQ. Second, different subtests are given at different ages, impairing comparability across ages. Third, the SB:FE has not received the factorial and empirical support that the Wechsler scales have. Fourth, the SB:FE is difficult to give and can be extremely time-consuming in some cases. Fifth, the subscale and composite scale scores on the SB:FE have not received as much attention as have Wechsler subscale scores, making them more difficult to interpret. Nevertheless, the SB:FE is the test of choice for severely MR children over age 6, although the Wechsler scales are stronger for mildly to moderately MR children over age 3½.

For MR children under age 3½, the test of choice is the Bayley-II. The Bayley-II yields a Mental Developmental Index (MDI) and a Psychomotor Developmental Index (PDI), as well as a Behavior Rating Index, which is less relevant to MR. The MDI can be used as an approximation of IQ, although IQ at very young ages is minimally predictive of IQ at later ages. Nevertheless, the MDI and PDI of the Bayley-II average 3 standard deviations below the mean for Down's syndrome children, showing the utility of the Bayley-II for MR children (Bayley, 1993). Like the Wechsler scales, the Bayley-II scores have a mean of 100 and standard deviation of 15.

For children at or below age 42 months, Bayley II scores reach a floor level at a standard score of 50. Hence, children with index scores that may be below 50 will receive a score of 50. In addition to being the test of choice for MR children under age 3½, the Bayley is the test of choice for older children who are so impaired that they cannot complete either the Wechsler or SB:FE scales. These children are usually severely retarded and below age 6 or profoundly retarded and over age 3½. In these cases, an MDI cannot be obtained (because the norm tables end at age 42 months), but a developmental age equivalent can be obtained from Table B.2 in the Bayley-II manual (Bayley, 1993). This developmental age can at least give some idea of level of functioning.

In addition to the three intelligence tests covered here, another good intelligence test for developmentally delayed or MR children is the *McCarthy Scales of Children's Abilities* (McCarthy, 1972). On the other hand, the *Kaufman Assessment Battery for Children* (K-ABC; Kaufman and Kaufman, 1983), which is an otherwise good test, should *not* be used to assess MR because of floor effects. For children with severe sensory handicaps, consult Sattler (1990) for testing procedures. Other intelligence tests have various problems including poor psychometrics, inadequate norming, questionable validity, outdated norms, and outdated items. Hence, these other tests should be used with caution in assessing the child with MR.

By diagnostic definition, the MR child scores a 70 or below on the intelligence tests. Special provision may need to be made for the SB:FE since it has a different standard deviation, and a cutting score of 68 can be used. With the Bayley, interpretation typically stops with the MDI, but the SB:FE and Wechsler scales should be interpreted for strengths and weaknesses. MR children generally show a uniform depression across subscales, but some children have areas of greater competence.

Cognitive testing can also include achievement and neuropsychological testing. Achievement testing is warranted if the child is placed in an academic setting and a baseline or followup measure of learning is desired. This is usually the case for most mildly and some moderately retarded children. Typically, achievement test scores for MR children mirror their IQ scores.

Clinician-Administered—Adaptive Functioning.   Intellectual functioning is only the first half of the MR diagnostic picture. Concurrent with intellectual testing, it is essential to assess the child's adaptive functioning. Adaptive functioning can be defined as the degree to which the child is personally independent and socially responsible, relative to age (Gelfand et al., 1988). It is typically correlated with intellectual functioning (Sattler, 1990). As with IQ, adaptive behavior scores must be considered relative to a child's age; what is expected of a child at age 5 will be very different from what is expected at age 15. A developmental, normative sense of adaptive behavior is therefore important.

Numerous informal measures of adaptive behavior exist, such as clinical impressions and lists of expected behaviors at various ages. Clinical impressions, while providing useful information, should not be the only basis for assessing adaptive behavior in an MR evaluation. At the very least, these impressions should be compared to tables that list examples of adaptive behaviors for children of various ages and various levels of functioning (see Gelfand et al., 1988; Sattler, 1990). For a diagnosis as important as MR, however, it is important to get a valid, standardized, normed assessment of the child's adaptive behavior. For this purpose, several adaptive behavior scales have been created. The most used of these standardized scales are the AAMD Adaptive Behavior Scale (ABS) and the Vineland Adaptive Behavior Scales (VABS).

The VABS assesses social competence and adaptive behavior in children age birth–19. All VABS scales can be scored relative to norms to give standard scores (m = 100; S.D. = 15). Over all, the VABS is the scale of choice for assessing adaptive behavior in MR children. MR children tend to score 70 or below on all subscales of the VABS.

The ABS (Nihira et al., 1974) is an adaptive behavior scale for individuals age 3–69. It is designed to be completed by staff in institutions. The ABS is briefer than the VABS (15–30 minutes) and can be given as a questionnaire or as an interview. Hence, it is less costly in terms of time and effort. The ABS has two parts, the first of which measures adaptive behavior and the second of which measures behavior problems. Part I of the ABS asks questions from ten domains (independent functioning, physical development, economic activity, language development, numbers/time, domestic activity, vocational activity, self-direction, responsibility, and socialization) that are combined to give a total score. This Adaptive Behavior total score is then assigned a percentile based on normative data. Subscale scores can also be obtained from the ten Part I domains, but the validity of these scores is weak.

In addition to the basic ABS, there is a school edition (ABS-SE; Lambert et al., 1981) that can be completed by parents and teachers. The ABS-SE resembles the ABS but does not have the domestic activity domain. Administration is identical to the ABS. The ABS-SE yields three adaptive behavior subscales (Personal Self-Sufficiency, Community Self-Sufficiency, Personal-Social Responsibility) and two behavior problem subscales (Social Adjustmen, and Personal Adjustment) in addition to a total score. Each domain can also be scored separately, and all scores can be converted to percentiles.

Sattler (1990) criticizes the psychometric properties of the ABS and ABS-SE, stating that, for the most part, they have questionable or unknown interrater reliability, test-retest reliability, and internal consistency reliability. Furthermore, the ABS norm groups consisted of institutionalized mentally retarded individuals. Thus, norms may not be applicable to children living in the home. Little is known about the ABS-SE norm group, which also consisted of mentally retarded children. The use of a mentally retarded norm group prevents comparison with average children and comparability with IQ scores. Nevertheless, the ABS has demonstrated clinical utility with institutionalized MR people and may have a place in those settings. The ABS-SE, on the other hand, has unknown validity, and Sattler (1990) recommends very cautious use. In general, the VABS is a more relevant measure in the assessment of the MR child in the outpatient setting.

In addition to the very widely used VABS and ABS, other adaptive behavior scales exist, such as the Adaptive Behavior Inventory for Children (ABIC; Mercer and Lewis, 1978) and the Scales of Independent Behavior (SIB; Bruininks et al., 1984). MR children score below 70 (2nd to 3rd percentile) on most adaptive behavior subscales and composite scores, relative to normal children. If MR children are used as the normative group, the adaptive behavior score is typically within 1 standard deviation of the MR norm group. Unlike autistic children, who occasionally elevate physical-motor adaptive behavior subscales,

MR children tend to uniformly depress all adaptive behavior subscales. When IQ and adaptive functioning scores are below 70 and the onset of the problem is before age 18, a diagnosis of MR is warranted.

Behavioral Assessment

Clinician-Administered.   A final area of routine assessment of the MR child is behavior problems, which often co-occur with MR. Initial impressions of behavior problems are usually gathered using unstructured parental interviews and observation of the child. Most of the widely used semistructured diagnostic interviews are inappropriate for MR children because they require self-report. In child MR populations, lack of insight, level of intellectual functioning, and related problems seriously compromise the value of self-report data. Hence, observer-report inventories, observer interviews, and clinician observation of the child generally form the primary basis of assessment of behavior problems.

Parent-Report/Other-Report.   A good approach to gathering parent-report of the MR child's behavior problems is to begin with a broad-band behavior rating scale. The Achenbach Child Behavior Checklists (CBCL and TRF) and Conners Rating Scales (CPRS and CTRS) include both parent and teacher response forms, and they yield scores for a variety of behavior problem areas. However, because they were developed for psychiatric and normal samples, their interpretation in MR populations is less well known.

There is no "typical" MR pattern on the broad-band behavior rating scales, although MR and developmentally disabled children tend to have elevated scores in general on measures of behavior problems (Thompson and Kronenberger, 1990). Based on estimated dual diagnosis (e.g., diagnosed with MR and another DSM diagnosis) rates of 15–30% (Aman et al., 1993), as many as one-third of MR children can be expected to score in clinical ranges on these tests. Scales that may show highest elevations in MR populations include measures of learning difficulty, hyperactivity, inhibition/withdrawal, and social problems.

Syndrome-Specific Tests

After general behavioral data are obtained from the clinical interview and the broad-band behavior scale, assessment may turn to more specific behaviors. The assessment of these behavior problems is guided by the child's co-occurring Axis I diagnoses and appropriate assessment strategies for them.

In addition to assessment of other Axis I behavior problems, delineation of MR-specific behavior problems can be helpful in treatment planning for the MR child. Several broad-band behavior rating scales exist for use with MR or other developmentally disabled adolescents and adults (Aman et al., 1993), such as the Reiss Screen for Maladaptive Behavior (Reiss, 1988) and the Prout-Strohmer Assessment System (Prout and Strohmer, 1989). The Aberrant Behavior Checklist (Aman et al., 1985) and the Emotional Disorders Rating Scale (Feinstein et al., 1988), on the other hand, apply to children as well as adolescents.

Numerous other MR-specific behavior scales exist, most of which include questions about common MR behaviors such as stereotypic and self-injurious behaviors (Aman and White, 1986). Although the exact composition of subscales varies from measure to measure, most MR-specific behavior scales assess both internalizing (depression, anxiety, withdrawal, somatization) and externalizing (hyperactivity, hostility, aggression) problems, as well as behaviors more typical of MR populations (stereotypic behaviors). In general, however, MR-specific scales are not as well normed and have weaker psychometric properties than behavior-rating scales developed for use in normal and psychiatrically disturbed children.

TREATMENT OPTIONS

(Treatment options for MR are outlined in Table 12.3.) Treatment for the MR child begins with the separation of intellectual-adaptive retardation problems from associated behavioral problems. This division roughly corresponds to the "intellectual-adaptive retardation" problems versus co-occurring DSM-IV Axis I diagnoses. Admittedly, this division is somewhat artificial, since the intellectual-adaptive retardation of MR individuals often contributes to their behavioral-emotional problems. Likewise, behavioral-emotional problems hinder the children's adaptive behaviors, resulting in further intellectual-adaptive retardation. However, the identification of behavioral-emotional components and co-occurring diagnoses allows the application of more specific treatment techniques to MR children.

Treatment of Behavioral-Emotional Disorders

Behavioral Interventions

When a co-occurring DSM-IV disorder (or related problem) is diagnosed in the MR child, an effort should be made to apply specific treatment techniques for that disorder to the MR child. In many cases the treatment requires some modification to accommodate to the MR child's lower level of cognitive functioning and understanding of the situation. In addition, MR children will often "learn" (e.g., respond to treatment) more slowly and may require more intensive, simple procedures (e.g., more learning trials, simpler contingencies). The extent to which treatment procedures will have to be modified depends on the age and severity of retardation of the child. Adolescent children with mild MR may be able to manage some limited cognitive techniques. Those with moderate MR probably will not respond to cognitive techniques, but they may respond easily to behavioral treatments. Mentally retarded children with severe or profound retardation require very basic behavioral techniques and very modest goals.

TABLE 12.3   Treatment Options for Mental Retardation

CO-OCCURRING BEHAVIOR PROBLEMS

(Address using techniques specific for each behavior problem, with modifications to
  account for intellectual problems)
  Reduce, simplify, or eliminate cognitive interventions
  Set modest goals
  Use concrete, immediate reinforcement
  Play therapy for modeling purposes

SPECIAL EDUCATION

Placement in special classes and vocational learning classrooms

BEHAVIORAL INTERVENTIONS

Teach basic adaptive skills in the language, social, and self-help areas
  Shaping
  Reinforcement contingencies
  Punishment techniques
  Realistic goals for adaptive functioning

Note: This outline of options summarizes major treatments covered in the text. Specific treatments
are often combined into an intervention package. Refer to the text for additional descriptions of
each treatment. This table is not necessarily an exhaustive list of all treatments available.

Usually the accommodation of disorder-specific treatment procedures to
the MR child requires extensive use of behavioral techniques (Aman et al.,
1993). Because these techniques require only a basic level of functioning and
little if any processing of internal cognition, they are suited to even the most
impaired child. However, the effectiveness of behavioral techniques depends
on the child's environment and on the ability of the people in that environment to adhere to contingencies. In some cases, if the child's behavior is severe
and the home environment's ability to manage the behavior is limited, inpatient hospitalization is required to create the behavioral-therapeutic milieu. If
behavior problems persist even after extensive attempts at behavior modification, institutionalization may have to be considered.

Psychotherapy

Traditional cognitive and psychodynamic psychotherapy are rarely used with
MR children, since their limited insight makes progress in the cognitive arena
difficult (Kendall and Braswell, 1993). Play therapy, on the other hand, may be
effective in some specific cases as a means of modeling social interaction and
other desired behaviors, as well as a teaching tool for basic living principles.
For example, the therapist–child relationship in play therapy may serve as a
prototypic authority relationship for the child. In another case, puppet play

can be used to teach sharing behavior or rules of social interaction. In general, however, play, cognitive, and psychodynamic therapies should not be used without concurrent behavioral interventions to address the child's behavior problems in the environment.

Medication

In addition to behavioral and play therapy, medication is also sometimes used to treat behavior problems in the MR child. Although there have been few well-controlled studies with MR populations, Aman et al. (1993) state that, at this time, it can be assumed that most psychotropic medications will work in the same way with MR as with non-MR populations. Perhaps the most common application of medication in the MR population is for behavior that could result in injury (to self or other) or destruction. Neuroleptics, such as haloperidol (Haldol) and thioridazine (Mellaril), are often used to reduce these "acting-out" behaviors. Methylphenidate (Ritalin) appears to be effective only in mildly and some moderately retarded hyperactive children (Aman et al., 1993).

Treatment of Intellectual-Adaptive Problems

Special Education

Intellectual-adaptive problems in MR children can be classified into two related categories: learning problems and adaptive behavior problems. Learning problems are difficulties that the MR child has in the intake, processing, and storage of information. Because these functions are vital for schooling, interventions to improve learning usually occur in the context of special education. Special educational programs use detailed teaching, motivational, and behavioral principles to teach MR children at a pace consistent with their ability.

Traditionally, MR children have been separated from their classmates and put in an environment designed to specifically address their problems (Gelfand et al., 1988). Recently, however, societal trends have acted to reduce this separation, as a result of the belief that MR children should be "mainstreamed" as much as possible. According to this philosophy, mildly MR children may often be placed in regular classes, with additional tutoring or use of a "resource room." Moderately, severely, and profoundly MR children, however, are rarely mainstreamed for academic classes, although their classroom environment is often connected to the regular school and resembles a "normal" classroom.

The trend toward normalizing the educational environments of MR children is based more on ethical principles than on research data. Ethically and legally, it is widely believed that children should be placed in the "least restrictive environment." That is, children should be placed in the most normal, least isolated, and least controlled therapeutic situation. For some MR children this means placement in all regular classes; for others, placement in one or two regular classes; and for others, placement in special classes or workshops, with contact with nonretarded children whenever possible. The research data about the benefits of mainstreaming are mixed and do not show clear advantages of separation or of mainstreaming (Gelfand et al., 1988). Over all, the best approach is to observe the adjustment of the individual child in each situation, with the understanding that children should be fully mainstreamed only if their functioning is in the mild MR range.

Behavioral Interventions

Adaptive behavior problems are difficulties that the MR child encounters in language, social interaction, self-help skills, and independence. Depending on the severity of MR, these skills may need to be taught at a very basic level. Interventions to develop adaptive behavior skills in MR children rely heavily on behavioral principles and, in some cases, resemble closely the interventions for childhood autism.

Behavioral techniques to teach adaptive behavior to the MR child begin with an assessment of what the child *can* do. Simple goals are then identified and broken down into discrete learning steps ("task analysis"; Sattler, 1990). For example, brushing the teeth involves knowing where to find a toothbrush, identification of the correct toothbrush, holding the toothbrush, using toothpaste, putting the toothbrush into the mouth, moving the toothbrush, brushing all teeth, brushing for a specified period of time, and performing all of these activities without direct supervision. Each learning step is demonstrated (at times by physically moving the child to perform the correct behavior) and reinforced repeatedly with praise or another reinforcer (candy is often used as a reinforcer, although presumably not for toothbrushing). Behaviors that interfere with learning of the target behavior may be ignored, punished, or redirected (Aman et al., 1993). Once several parts of the skill are learned, the child is required to perform larger chunks of the skill in order to be reinforced. After the whole skill is learned, reinforcement is gradually faded by administering it less often and with less intensity. Simple skills such as dressing and washing hands, as well as complex skills such as answering social questions and interacting with people, can be taught this way (Gelfand et al., 1988).

Four principles that must be remembered throughout behavioral intervention are: (1) goals must be kept modest, (2) behavior must be broken down into discrete steps, (3) learning is often slow, and (4) the behavioral plan must be consistently followed. Unfortunately, all four of these principles are often maddening to parents and to institutional staff. Parents may complain that the child's achievements are insignificant, that the plan is not working, or that the plan is too difficult to follow. The clinician must be sensitive to these complaints, since they may indicate that the plan will be spontaneously modified or dropped by the parents. Continued severe family stress may suggest that family therapy is warranted. If the plan is implemented in school or an institution, the greatest risk is inconsistent implementation by staff. All staff should be informed of the plan and given an opportunity for input. One staff member should be responsible for monitoring the plan and dealing with problems.

References

Aman, M. G., Hammer, D., and Rojahn, J. (1993). Mental Retardation. In T. H. Ollendick and M. Hersen (Eds.), *Handbook of child and adolescent assessment* (pp. 321–345). Needham Heights, MA: Allyn & Bacon.

Aman, M. G., Singh, N. N., Stewart, A. W., and Field, C. J. (1985). Psychometric characteristics of the Aberrant Behavior Checklist. *American Journal on Mental Deficiency, 89*, 492–502.

Aman, M. G., and White, A. J. (1986). Measures of drug change in mental retardation. In K. Gadow (Ed.), *Advances in learning and behavioral disabilities* (pp. 157–202). Greenwich, CT: JAI Press.

American Psychiatric Association. (1994). *Diagnostic and statistical manual of mental disorders* (4th ed.). Washington, DC: Author.

Bayley, N. (1993). *Bayley Scales of Infant Development: Second Edition.* San Antonio, TX: Psychological Corporation.

Baroff, G. S. (1986). *Mental retardation: Nature, cause, and management* (2d ed.). New York: Wiley.

Bruininks, R. H., Woodcock, R. W., Weatherman, R. F., and Hill, B. K. (1984). *Scales of independent behavior (SIB).* Allen, TX: DLM Teaching Resources.

Feinstein, C., Kaminer, Y., Barrett, R. B., and Tylenda, B. (1988). The assessment of mood and affect in developmentally disabled children and adolescents: The Emotional Disorders Rating Scale. *Research in Developmental Disabilities, 9*, 109–121.

Gelfand, D. M., Jenson, W. R., and Drew, C. J. (1988). *Understanding child behavior disorders* (2d ed.). New York: Harcourt Brace Jovanovich.

Grossman, H. J. (1983). *Classification in mental retardation.* Washington, DC: American Association on Mental Deficiency.

Jacobson, J. W. (1982). Problem behavior and psychiatric impairment in a developmentally disabled population. I: Behavior frequency. *Applied Research in Mental Retardation, 3*, 121–139.

Kaufman, A. S., and Kaufman, N. L. (1983). *K-ABC: Kaufman assessment battery for children.* Circle Pines, MN: American Guidance Service.

Kendall, P. C., and Braswell, L. (1993). *Cognitive-behavioral therapy for impulsive children* (2d ed.). New York: Guilford Press.

Lambert, N. M., Windmiller, M., Tharinger, D., and Cole, L. J. (1981). *AAMD adaptive behavior scale—school edition.* Monterey, CA: CTB/McGraw-Hill.

McCarthy, D. A. (1972). *Manual for the McCarthy Scales of Children's Abilities.* San Antonio, TX: Psychological Corporation.

Mercer, J. R., and Lewis, J. F. (1978). *System of multicultural pluralistic assessment.* San Antonio, TX: Psychological Corporation.

Nihira, K., Foster, R., Shellhaas, M., and Leland, H. (1974). *AAMD Adaptive Behavior Scale* (rev.). Washington, DC: American Association on Mental Deficiency.

Prout, H. T., and Strohmer, D. C. (1989). *Prout-Strohmer Personality Inventory manual.* Schenectady, NY: Genium.

Reiss, S. (1988). *Test manual for the Reiss Screen for Maladaptive Behavior.* Orland Park, IL: International Diagnostic Systems.

Sattler, J. M. (1990). *Assessment of children* (3d ed.). San Diego, CA: Author.

Thompson, R. J., Jr., and Kronenberger, W. G. (1990). Behavior problems in children with learning problems. In H. L. Swanson and B. Keogh (Eds.), *Learning disabilities: Theoretical and research issues* (pp. 155–174). Hillsdale, NJ: Erlbaum.

CHAPTER 13

Other Childhood Mental Disorders

The disorders described in this chapter share the quality of being relatively rarely diagnosed in standard outpatient clinical practice. However, mild versions of some of their symptoms are commonly seen in children: For example, tics (the hallmark of tic disorders) occur occasionally in many children. Occasional irritation at the caretaker following separation (which is either extreme or absent in Reactive Attachment Disorder) is also not unusual in toddlers. Refusal to talk is very common in young children in certain situations (although not to the extent required for the Selective Mutism diagnosis). Finally, most children experiment with behaviors that are stereotypically identified with the opposite sex, although gender identification with the opposite sex and distress over biological sex (required for diagnosis of Gender Identity Disorder) are almost always absent. Hence, these four categories of disorders—tic disorders, Reactive Attachment Disorder, Selective Mutism, and Gender Identity Disorder—are rare in outpatient practice, although mild versions of some of their individual symptoms are common.

■ Tic Disorders

☐ CLINICAL DESCRIPTION

Diagnostic Considerations

Few childhood disorders are as uncontrollable and as unusual in appearance as tic disorders. A tic is a "sudden, rapid, recurrent, nonrhythmic, stereotyped motor movement or vocalization" (American Psychiatric Association, 1994, p. 103). Although they may be suppressed for varying periods of time, tics are experienced as involuntary impulses. Examples of tics are eye blinking, grimacing, coughing, hitting self, vocalizations, and verbalizations. Because they feel involuntary and can appear unusual, they are often associated with distress or social difficulty for the child.

Three major types of tic disorders are identified in DSM-IV, all of which must begin before age 18 in order to be diagnosed. Tic disorders that begin in adulthood are classified as Tic Disorder, Not Otherwise Specified. Tourette's Disorder (also called Tourette's Syndrome, or TS) is an extreme form of tic disorder in which the child has several motor and at least one vocal tics. The tics must be frequent (defined in DSM-IV as occurring many times a day, nearly every day), and the disorder must be of long duration (defined in DSM-IV as lasting more than 1 year). Furthermore, characteristics of the tics, such as number, frequency, location, complexity, and severity, change over time. Chronic Motor or Vocal Tic Disorder (CTD) is less severe than TS in that it involves either motor or vocal tics, but not both. As with TS, these tics must be frequent, and the disorder must be of long duration. Some evidence indicates that CTD is a less severe form of TS caused by the same underlying disorder (Dulcan and Popper, 1991). The final DSM-IV tic disorder is Transient Tic Disorder (TTD), which is characterized by one or more motor or vocal tics. Unlike TS and CTD, however, TTD has a duration of less than 1 year.

The prevalence of tic disorders is estimated to be 3–5 in every 10,000 people (American Psychiatric Association, 1994; Ollendick and Ollendick, 1990). However, simple tics which do not qualify for diagnosis are much more common. It is estimated that 12–25% of children will display a tic at one time or another (Ollendick and Ollendick, 1990; Shapiro et al., 1978). Two diagnoses that share similarities with tic disorders are Stereotypy/Habit Disorder and Obsessive-Compulsive Disorder. In these disorders the person feels compelled to perform a behavior, but the behavior is ultimately voluntary. Tics, on the other hand, are involuntary and usually unwanted. Furthermore, compulsions and habits may be more regular, rhythmic, and anxiety-reducing than are tics.

Appearance and Features

Tics may be grouped into several categories based on their appearance (see Table 13.1): *Motor* tics are movements, while *vocal/phonic* tics involve words or sounds. *Simple* tics are usually brief and unelaborated, while *complex* tics are coordinated and longer-lasting. Examples of simple motor tics are shoulder shrugging, eye blinking, twitching, or head nodding. Complex motor tics involve elaborate movements such as facial gestures, hitting, and stomping feet. Simple vocal tics are typically manifest as coughing or grunting, while complex vocal tics consist of words. Examples of complex vocal tics are coprolalia (use of socially unacceptable words), echolalia (repeating what is heard), palilalia (repeating what one just said), saying words out of context, or screaming words (Kurlan, 1989; Ollendick and Ollendick, 1990). In addition to the motor/vocal and simple/complex tic categories, Kurlan (1989) describes the phenomenon of "sensory tics." Sensory tics are feelings of abnormal sensation (pressure, tickle, temperature) in the body. The person attempts to remove these "tics" by movements that themselves may appear as motor tics.

Tics can range from being barely noticeable to overt and embarrassing. Complex vocal tics, particularly coprolalia, can be both humiliating and dis-

TABLE 13.1   Appearance and Features of Tic Disorders

COMMON FEATURES

Involuntary, rapid movements or vocalizations
May be suppressed for a time
May be diverted into different (but similar) behaviors
Onset between ages 2 and 13
Tics occur many times a day
Tics can range from barely noticeable to obvious
Aggravated by stress, excitement, or fatigue
Child can anticipate the tic
Avoidance of social situations

OCCASIONAL FEATURES

Attempt to disguise tic into apparently normal activity
Social rejection
Attention problems
Obsessive-compulsive symptoms

Note: The features listed above are often seen but are not universal. Some features may be diagnostically relevant or required, while others may not be required for diagnosis. "Common" features are typical of the disorder; "occasional" features appear frequently but are not necessarily seen in a majority of cases.

ruptive, requiring special arrangements for children with this type of tic. Uninformed children and adults often mistake complex vocal tics for intentionally rude and disruptive behavior. Their responses, therefore, often consist of punishment and avoidance; children may ridicule and reject the child with the disorder. Although coprolalia is the component of TS most often dramatized or portrayed in the media, it only occurs in 10–30% of children with TS (American Psychiatric Association, 1994; Kurlan, 1989; Ollendick and Ollendick, 1990).

The frequency and intensity of tics vary with time. Onset of TS is typically between the ages of 2 and 13 years, with an average onset age of 7 years (American Psychiatric Association, 1994; Dulcan and Popper, 1991). TS begins with a single motor tic. Vocal and other motor tics may then emerge, change, and disappear. Tics generally increase in times of stress, major life change, emotional excitement, or fatigue (Dulcan and Popper, 1991). In many individuals, decreases in tic behavior occur during activities requiring attention and concentration, or during sleep (American Psychiatric Association, 1994; Brunn, 1984; Ollendick and Ollendick, 1990).

Children with tic disorders often report that they can anticipate tics and, usually, suppress them for a time. However, they have a subjective sense of the tics "building up" when they are suppressed, and they have a period of increased tic behavior following suppression. Children will also attempt to disguise tics by blending them into apparently normal motor or vocal activity. Because they can sometimes suppress or disguise tics, children with tic disorder expend considerable amounts of energy holding back tics in order to avoid attention or humiliation in public (Bronheim, 1991). When they then enter a safer situation, such as the home environment or nurse's office, they may let out the tics in a burst of activity. Unfortunately, the amount of energy required to withhold tics distracts these children from learning or social situations, causing further difficulties for them. In some cases the child will suppress tics during a clinical interview. Hence, the failure to observe tics during interview does not mean that tics are never present. Parents and other observers must be enlisted to provide an accurate view of the child's tic suppression/expression pattern.

Children with tic disorders may manifest a variety of other behavior problems, and the risk of associated problems increases with the severity of the disorder. Hence, TS children may be most at risk for associated problems. Two psychiatric disorders most often noted as co-occurring with TS and CTD are Attention-Deficit Hyperactivity Disorder (ADHD) and Obsessive-Compulsive Disorder (OCD)(Kurlan, 1989). Kurlan (1989), for example, reviews studies indicating that up to 50% of TS children show symptoms of OCD; a similar percentage has been reported for ADHD. This co-occurrence may be explained by genetic/physiological factors (Kurlan, 1989) or by the increased stress that these children endure. Tic disorders may also lead to social difficulties, such as peer rejection, low self-esteem, feelings of alienation, and isolation (Bronheim, 1991). The presence of OCD, ADHD, or social dysfunction in a child with a tic disorder requires modification of assessment expectations and treatment plans.

Etiology

Theories of the etiology of tic disorders tend to focus on TS or severe CTD. Hypotheses about the development of TTD and mild CTD have received little attention. Family, behavioral, and physiological factors have been implicated in the development of TS, with physiological factors receiving the most attention. Four major findings support the hypothesis that TS has a physiological or genetic etiology: First, children with tic disorders have a higher incidence of neurological symptoms, including soft signs and abnormal EEG patterns (Dulcan and Popper, 1991; Ollendick and Ollendick, 1990). Second, TS tends to occur in children who have a family member with a tic disorder, an obsessive-compulsive disorder, or ADHD (Kurlan, 1989). Kurlan (1989) and Pauls and Leckman (1986), for example, believe that an autosomal dominant gene causes TS, CTD, and OCD. Similarly, DSM-IV reports that vulnerability to TS is carried on an autosomal dominant gene. The expression of this gene is dependent on other physiological, genetic, and environmental factors. Third, some support exists for the theory that prenatal experiences are related to TS, possibly by affecting neural development. For example, mothers of children with TS report more life stress, nausea, and vomiting during pregnancy (Leckman et al., 1990).

A fourth finding in support of a physiological etiology for TS is the effectiveness of psychotropic medication in reducing tics (Kerbeshian and Burd,

1988; Ollendick and Ollendick, 1990). Psychopharmacological evidence suggests that problems in dopaminergic neurotransmission may underlie TS. Kurlan (1989) cites four findings that support the dopamine hypothesis of TS: (1) The most effective TS medications block dopamine transmission; (2) tics are exacerbated by medications that facilitate dopaminergic transmission; (3) reduced levels of a dopamine metabolite have been found in some studies of TS children (although other studies report conflicting results [Ollendick and Ollendick, 1990]); and (4) tics sometimes result from chronic treatment with dopamine antagonists, which sensitizes dopamine receptors.

Physiological theories of the etiology of TS and CTD appear to have received the most research support (Kurlan, 1989). However, familial and behavioral factors may contribute to the expression of the TS and CTD. In mild tic disorder cases, behavioral factors may be solely responsible for the development of tics (Matthews et al., 1985). Families of children with tic disorders, for example, tend to have poorer communication between child and parents (Matthews et al., 1985). However, this characteristic could be a result of a tic disorder as opposed to a cause of the disorder. Nevertheless, lack of family communication may impair the child's ability to cope with stress, resulting in a greater frequency and intensity of tics following stress. Alternatively, the child's tics may serve a role in the family system, such as deflecting attention away from a poor marital relationship (Prata and Masson, 1985).

Behavioral theories characterize tics as behaviors that are reinforced by the environment (Malatesta, 1990). Tics that are followed by reinforcing attention, for instance, are likely to recur. In a classical conditioning paradigm, the tic may be part of a reflexive fear response that becomes classically conditioned to a particular type of situation such as a social gathering. Eventually the social gathering becomes directly paired with the tic behaviors even in the absence of the feeling of fear. Despite the intuitive appeal of these behavioral theories, behavioral treatments for tic disorders have received more attention than have behavioral causes of tic disorders.

Finally, personality psychology theories suggest that certain personality traits (e.g., obsessive, perfectionistic tendencies; somatic focus; poor self-control) may be related to tics. These traits may be manifest in irresistible thoughts and attention to a particular bodily sensation or behavior. When the person gives in to these thoughts, a tic occurs.

ASSESSMENT PATTERNS

A sample assessment battery for tic disorders is shown in Table 13.2.

Broad Assessment Strategies

Cognitive Assessment

Clinician-Administered. Considerable attention has been focused on the neurological and neuropsychological status of children with tic disorders. Before

TABLE 13.2   Sample Assessment Battery for Tic Disorders

PERSONALITY

MMPI/MMPI-A
Piers-Harris Self-Concept Scale

BEHAVIORAL

Child Behavior Checklist

SYNDROME-SPECIFIC

Tourette Syndrome Global Scale
Yale Global Tic Severity Scale

Note: Assessment instruments are intended to supplement (not substitute for) a good clinical interview and, when possible, a structured diagnostic interview.

any psychological evaluation is undertaken, the child should be seen by a neurologist. EEG studies and investigation for possible side effects of medication are essential to rule out other explanations for the tics. In most cases, children with TS and CTD have already been seen by a physician. It is generally advisable to consult a physician on cases of TTD as well.

Psychological assessment of the child with a tic disorder usually includes IQ and achievement testing. Based on initial findings from these tests, additional neuropsychological testing may be ordered. On the WISC-R and WISC-III, children with TS generally score in normal ranges for Full Scale (FIQ), Performance (PIQ), and Verbal (VIQ) IQ (Bornstein, 1990; Bornstein et al., 1991; Bornstein and Yang, 1991; Dykens et al., 1990). Although some authors suggest that a VIQ–PIQ discrepancy may be common in TS children, recent data generally do not support this claim (Bornstein et al., 1991).

TS children with ADHD will score 10–15 IQ points lower than TS children without ADHD, placing their group IQ mean in the low average range (Dykens et al., 1990). Medication for TS does not appear to have a significant effect on IQ (Bornstein and Yang, 1991). TS children appear to have strengths in abstract thinking and verbal knowledge (Similarities, Comprehension, and Vocabulary subtests, and the Verbal Comprehension factor), accompanied by a weakness in processing speed (Coding subtest and Processing Speed factor) (Bornstein et al., 1991; Dykens et al., 1990). Weaknesses in attention, concentration, and processing speed are most common when TS is accompanied by ADHD. Very little research data are available concerning the assessment patterns of children with CTD or TTD. CTD children will often show assessment patterns similar to those of children with TS. Children with TTD, as a group, usually score in normal ranges.

TS children tend to show average achievement testing patterns on reading and written language tests, with deficits in mathematics (Bornstein, 1990; Bornstein et al., 1991; Bornstein and Yang, 1991; Dykens et al., 1990). As with

IQ, TS children with accompanying ADHD score lower than those without ADHD (Dykens et al., 1990), and there is no difference based on medication status (Bornstein and Yang, 1991).

On neuropsychological testing there appears to be a subgroup (20–50%) of TS children who show mild to moderate deficits on tests involving performance skills such as motor speed, perceptual organization, and visuographic skills (Bornstein, 1990; Bornstein and Baker, 1991; Bornstein et al., 1991). This impaired subgroup of TS children has more frequent and severe tic symptoms (Bornstein et al., 1991) as well as physiological abnormalities (Bornstein and Baker, 1991).

Psychological Assessment

Child-Report. Because children with TS and CTD tend to have co-occurring behavioral and psychological problems, personality and behavior problem testing is often warranted. Such testing should target social problems, depression, low self-esteem, and anxiety, which may contribute to or result from the tics. Adolescents, for example may be expected to show MMPI and MMPI-A patterns characteristic of depression (elevated scale 2), anxiety/rumination (elevated scales 7 and 8), or social maladjustment (elevated scales 4 and 0). The configuration of these scales suggests the relative importance of each of these problems.

Younger children may show deficits on scales of self-esteem, reflecting their unhappiness over the disorder. TS children tend to score lower on the PHSCS Behavior subscale than controls, indicating that they are unhappy with their behavior and have more behavior problems (Edell-Fisher and Motta, 1990). TS children also scored lower on the Tennessee Self-Concept Scale (TSCS; Fitts, 1965) than did controls (Edell-Fisher and Motta, 1990). Most evidence supports the hypothesis that TS children have specific behavioral self-esteem problems as opposed to a global self-esteem deficit (Edell-Fisher and Motta, 1990). Edell and Motta (1989) did not find tic severity to be correlated with global PHSCS self-esteem scores.

Behavioral Assessment

Parent-Report. On parent-completed behavioral checklists such as the CBCL or MCBC, children with tic disorders may be expected to show a range of results. The individual results for each child will indicate the extent of associated difficulties (Bornstein and Yang, 1991; Matthews et al., 1985; Ollendick and Ollendick, 1990). Behavior subscales reflecting overactivity, obsessive-compulsive problems, depression, and social functioning are the most likely to show elevations. On the CBCL, elevations of the Thought Problems subscale usually reflect the unusual, compulsive nature of the tics, as well as obsessive-compulsive tendencies that often accompany TS. Elevations on the CBCL Withdrawn, Anxious/Depressed, and Attention Problems subscales could indicate problems with social relationships, unhappiness, and attention, respectively. Such problems commonly result from the stress of having TS and from the response of peers to the tics. On the MCBC the Inhibition and Depression subscales are sometimes elevated in a TS child, reflecting social and self-esteem difficulties resulting from having a tic disorder. Extreme elevations on any behavior problem scales suggest a component of the disorder that should be addressed in addition to the tics.

Family Assessment

Child-Report/Parent-Report. Family assessment is often warranted in order to track the effects of the tic disorder on the family. Such assessment may also probe for family characteristics that affect the tic disorder, such as stress or abnormal boundaries. No typical pattern should be expected for families of children with tic disorders, with the possible exception of higher stress. Using the FACES-II (Olson, 1986), Matthews et al. (1985) found that TS families had lower Adaptability scores, reflecting less flexibility in the face of change. FES scores may also provide insight into the quality and type of family functioning. Problematic family issues indicate the need for family therapy in addition to modalities directed specifically at the tic disorder.

Syndrome-Specific Tests

Clinician-Administered

A major consideration in the evaluation of a child with a tic disorder is to ascertain the type, frequency, intensity, and severity of the tics. Although this information and other relevant data are typically gathered in an interview, several instruments specific to tic disorders provide a more in-depth assessment.

The Tourette Syndrome Global Scale (TSGS; Harcherik et al., 1984), for example, is completed by the clinician. It assesses behavior in two areas: the Motor and Phonic Tic Domain and the Social Functioning Domain. In the Motor and Phonic Tic Domain, tics are scored according to type (simple, complex, motor, phonic), frequency, and degree of disruption. Frequency and degree of disruption are scored on a 6-point scale (0–5), with higher scores indicating greater impairment. A total tic domain score is obtained by multiplying the Frequency by the Disruption score. The Social Functioning Domain of the TSGS consists of three areas (behavioral problems, motor restlessness, and level of school functioning), which are rated on a 0 to 25 scale, again with higher scores indicating greater impairment. Scores on the TSGS are related to behavioral and cognitive impairment (Bornstein et al., 1991; Ollendick and Ollendick, 1990).

Like the TSGS, the Yale Global Tic Severity Scale (YGTSS; Leckman et al., 1989) allows the clinician to rate the severity of tics along the dimensions of number, frequency, intensity, complexity, and interference. Each of these five dimensions is rated on a 6-point scale (0–5), with higher scores indicating greater problems. The YGTSS also includes items pertaining to the type of tics and global impairment as a result of tics. It appears to have good reliability and validity and is easy to administer (Leckman et al., 1989). Although other tic rating scales exist (e.g., Shapiro et al., 1989), the TSGS and YGTSS appear to be the briefest and most useful.

TREATMENT OPTIONS

The first step in the treatment of a tic disorder is deciding whether to treat at all. Very minor tics that do not meet DSM-IV criteria and some very mild forms of TTD may not need immediate treatment. For brief, minor tics, parents might be advised to continue discretely monitoring the tic but to reduce overt attention to it. If the tic persists or meets criteria for CTD or TS, the child can be brought back for treatment (Dulcan and Popper, 1991). The most widely used treatments for TS and CTD are behavioral and pharmacological, although family therapy and individual psychotherapy are helpful in some cases. (Treatment options for tic disorders are outlined in Table 13.3.)

Behavioral Interventions

Behavioral techniques that have been used to treat tics include psychoeducation, massed practice, self-monitoring, reinforcement, relaxation, environmental change, and habit reversal (Ollendick and Ollendick, 1990). Although each of

TABLE 13.3   Treatment Options for Tic DIsorders

BEHAVIORAL INTERVENTIONS

Psychoeducation
Massed practice
Self-monitoring
Reinforcement contingencies
Relaxation techniques
Environmental change
Habit reversal

MEDICATION

PSYCHOTHERAPY

Hypnotic techniques

FAMILY INTERVENTIONS

Family therapy

Note: This outline of options summarizes major treatments covered in the text. Specific treatments are often combined these techniques has produced individual successes, habit reversal appears to be the most promising (Ollendick & Ollendick, 1990).

Psychoeducation

A behavioral treatment commonly used for the tic disorders is psychoeducation (Dedmon, 1986; Fisher et al., 1986). This technique involves informing the child and family about the nature of tics as well as the negative impact that the tics can have on personal, familial, and social functioning. The aim of the psychoeducational intervention is to facilitate understanding of the tic behavior as uncontrollable and not as something to be punished. In more mild cases, families are informed of the common nature of transient tics and asked to return only if the tics intensify. By improving understanding of the tics, it is hoped that the negative collateral impacts of the tic can be minimized and that potentially reinforcing attention to the tic will decrease. Psychoeducation may be extended to other influential adults in the child's life, such as teachers and coaches.

Massed Practice

Massed practice (Turpin, 1983) is a technique that requires the child to produce tics voluntarily for an extended period of time. Following brief rest periods, more voluntary production of tics is performed. This practice is hypothesized to reduce tics by fatiguing muscles or by making the production of the tic aversive to the child. Despite early widespread use of this technique, outcome studies question its effectiveness (Turpin, 1983).

Self-Monitoring

Self-monitoring (Ollendick, 1981) consists simply of having the child record the frequency or intensity of the tics, usually using a wrist-counter or a notebook. Wrist-counters are a more expensive but more discreet recording method. Documentation of the tics is hypothesized to increase the child's awareness of them, leading to internal motivation to stop them. Additionally, the self-monitoring can be used as part of a treatment package to assess the effects of other interventions.

Reinforcement Techniques

Reinforcement techniques are the most commonly used treatment for tics (Ollendick and Ollendick, 1990). These interventions reward the child for the absence of the tic or for the production of a behavior that is incompatible with the tic. In some cases the tic behavior is ignored or punished, and extensive parent training is included in the behavior package (Malatesta, 1990). When parent training is used, parents are encouraged to reduce stresses in the family, increase support for the child, and reinforce positive, nontic behaviors (Malatesta, 1990). Reinforcement contingencies, particularly contingent attention, may be the most appropriate treatment for TTD and mild CTD. However, reinforcement tends to produce only short-term and situation-specific gains for TS (Dulcan and Popper, 1991; Ollendick and Ollendick, 1990).

Relaxation Techniques

Relaxation techniques attempt to address the anxiety and stress that underlie and exacerbate tics. Relaxation may also reduce tics by giving the child greater control over the muscle groups that produce tics. Furthermore, muscles in a state of relaxation may be less likely to contract and produce tics. Despite their intuitive appeal, relaxation techniques for tic disorders have not been extensively researched. Until more clinical and research data are available, these techniques are probably best used as adjuncts to other types of behavior therapy (Ollendick and Ollendick, 1990).

Environmental Change

Environmental change interventions seek to make the environment as non-threatening and accommodating as possible for the child with a tic disorder (Bronheim, 1991; Dedmon, 1986). Many of these interventions are applied in the school setting in order to reduce the stress of a setting that is social (has risk of embarrassment), structured (is difficult to escape), and anxiety-provoking (involves evaluation). Environmental change in the school is accomplished by modifying classroom rules, educating teachers, educating peers, and communicating understanding to the child. For example, the child may be allowed to leave the room periodically to "let out" tics. Alternatively, the child may be permitted to leave the room during traditionally "quiet" times, such as tests (Bronheim, 1991; Dedmon, 1986). Other environmental interventions target deficits associated with the tic disorder, such as a learning disability or attention deficit. Ideally, as environmental stress is reduced, tic frequency and associated problems decrease.

Habit Reversal

Habit reversal (Azrin and Nunn, 1973) is a promising treatment for the tic disorders. It consists of five components that address tics (Azrin & Nunn, 1973; Azrin and Peterson, 1990): awareness training, self-monitoring, relaxation training, competing response training, and contingency management (Azrin & Peterson, 1990).

Awareness Training/Self-Monitoring. The awareness training component of habit reversal teaches the child to monitor, describe, and anticipate tics. The child first records the incidence and timing of certain tics and describes the appearance of each tic in detail. This monitoring teaches the child to detect and anticipate the occurrence of tics. Self-monitoring is augmented by feedback from the therapist or significant others as to when the tic is occurring.

Finally, the child learns to identify situations in which the tics are more likely to occur or are more likely to be severe.

Relaxation Training.   Awareness training is performed concurrently with relaxation training and contingency management. The relaxation techniques involve the teaching of progressive muscle relaxation, breathing, imagery, and relaxing self-statements (Azrin and Peterson, 1990). Children are instructed to practice the relaxation at home, eventually applying the relaxation techniques whenever a tic is imminent (Azrin and Peterson, 1990).

Contingency Management.   The contingency management component of habit reversal typically involves favorable comments and attention given to the child's decrease in tics and implementation of the habit reversal program. In addition, Azrin and Peterson (1990) suggest the use of a "habit inconvenience review," in which the therapist and child discuss the embarrassment, inconveniences, and effort that were caused by the tics. This review reminds the child of the intrinsic rewards of reducing the tic behavior. Finally, tangible rewards are arranged with the parents for documented decreases in the tic behavior (Azrin and Peterson, 1990).

Competing Response Training.   The final component of habit reversal is competing response training, which consists of the practice of a competing response that prevents the tic from occurring (Azrin and Nunn, 1973; Azrin and Peterson, 1989, 1990). The competing response must be opposite to the tic movement, inconspicuous, and not distracting for the child (Azrin and Peterson, 1990). Azrin and Peterson (1990) suggest that most competing responses consist of the tensing of muscles that control movement opposite to the tic, although other responses are possible. For example, a child with a head shaking tic would tense the neck muscles that hold the head still; an eye blink tic would be controlled by a systematic, voluntary eye blink (Azrin and Peterson, 1989). One tic is initially identified as the competing response target. Then the child practices the competing response, applying it *in vivo* for 1 minute when the child anticipates the tic or has just exhibited the tic (Azrin and Peterson, 1990). The competing response prevents the tic and may act as a punisher for the urge or tendency to have a tic (Ollendick and Ollendick, 1990).

Critique of Habit Reversal.   The habit reversal method has received considerable, enthusiastic empirical support for children with transient tics and CTD (Azrin and Nunn, 1973; Azrin and Peterson, 1989, 1990; Ollendick and Ollendick, 1990; Turpin, 1983). Turpin (1983) summarizes Azrin's results reporting an 80% success rate at 18 month followup, and other authors report similar results (Ollendick and Ollendick, 1990). In the largest study of the effectiveness of habit reversal, Azrin and Peterson (1990) report an average reduction of 93% in tic frequency in ten TS children. Half of the children showed no tic symptoms either at the clinic or at home, and 20% had a complete remission in both environments. The average therapy time was twenty sessions, and the program was equally effective for motor and vocal tics (Azrin and Peterson, 1990). These and other similar results cause Azrin and Peterson (1990) to speculate that "the present findings of a large reduction or elimination of tics . . . by psychological procedures raises a question as to the prevailing view of Tourette disorder as being almost entirely neurological. . . . [(T)]he subjective urge to perform the tic was reported by the present subjects to have been greatly reduced or absent" (p. 316).

Medication

Pharmacological treatments are a standard intervention for TS (Ollendick and Ollendick, 1990), and they are occasionally used for TTD and CTD as well. Some disagreement exists over the extent to which medication should be used for TS, with some authors (e.g., Ollendick and Ollendick, 1990) suggesting that medication is an essential component of TS treatment, while others (e.g., Dulcan and Popper, 1991) recommend attempting psychosocial interventions first. Kerbeshian and Burd (1988) advise to treat with medication based on the severity of the tics, the extent to which tics interfere with normal functioning, and the existence of other conditions that need medication. Because most pharmacological treatments for the tic disorders are directed at TS, only TS medications will be covered here.

Numerous medications, predominantly neuroleptics, are used to treat TS. The most frequently used and most effective medication is haloperidol (Ollendick and Ollendick, 1990; Shapiro et al., 1989), although other medications, such as clonidine, pimozide, fluphenazine, sulpiride, flunarizine, and clonazepam, are also used to treat TS (Kerbeshian and Burd, 1988; Leckman et al., 1991; Micheli et al., 1990; Robertson, Schnieden, and Lees, 1990; Shapiro et al., 1989). Response rates to these medications are all more effective than response to placebo. Within medications, haloperidol is usually more effective than pimozide or clonidine for tics. However, considerations such as co-occurring conditions or side effects may argue against haloperidol use (Kerbeshian and Burd, 1988; Shapiro et al., 1989).

It is difficult to state the effectiveness rates for the various medications because "effectiveness" may be defined differently from study to study. Ollendick and Ollendick (1990) summarize studies indicating a 70–90% effectiveness rate for haloperidol, apparently indicating that it causes a reduction in tics in 70–90% of cases. Shapiro et al. (1989) report a 65% decrease in tics with haloperidol and a 60% decrease with pimozide. Other researchers report improvements using medications such as clonidine (Leckman et al., 1991), sulpiride (Robertson et al., 1990), and flunarizine (Micheli et al., 1990). Importantly, some TS children improve on placebo, although to a lesser extent than with medication (Leckman et al., 1991). One study reported a decrease of 43.4% in tics for the placebo group (Shapiro et al., 1989).

Over all, the literature appears to support haloperidol as a first line of pharmacological treatment for TS (Ollendick and Ollendick, 1990). Depending on side effects and other symptoms, however, other medications may be used

(Kerbeshian and Burd, 1988). Haloperidol, for example, is faster acting than clonidine but may cause more extrapyramidal side effects. Likewise, pimozide is associated with fewer sedating and extrapyramidal effects than haloperidol, but it has potential negative cardiac side effects. Clonidine may be more effective than haloperidol for cases of tic disorder and ADHD; in these cases, clonidine would be a first line of treatment (Kerbeshian and Burd, 1988). For combined tic and seizure disorders, on the other hand, clonazepam may be the medication of choice (Kerbeshian and Burd, 1988). In cases where tic disorders and other disorders co-occur, haloperidol and another psychotropic medication may be combined, provided that there are no negative interactions (Kerbeshian and Burd, 1988). Informed flexibility in medication is the general rule for TS, trying medications sequentially until an appropriate treatment is found.

Psychotherapy

Hypnotic Techniques

Hypnotherapy may be particularly promising for tic disorders because it emphasizes relaxation and control over bodily functioning (Young and Montano, 1988). Hypnotherapy with relaxation and mastery images is antithetical to the tic behavior as well as distracting and pleasant for the child. Children who are taught self-hypnotic techniques can learn to apply this intervention to tics *in vivo*. Some studies (Kohen and Botts, 1987; Young and Montano, 1988) report positive outcomes for hypnotherapy to address tic disorders. However, as with relaxation techniques, supporting data for hypnosis techniques are sparse. Hypnotherapy may also be used as a component of a behavioral treatment package, in order to address relaxation and mastery goals (Young and Montano, 1988).

Psychodynamic and Play Therapy

Individual psychotherapy or play therapy is typically not used as the major treatment for a tic disorder, unless psychological factors are clearly contributing to the disorder. For example, individual psychotherapy may be necessary for the child who is reluctant to give up the tic symptom or for the child for whom the tic has created other problems such as depression or social maladjustment. However, for initial intervention in a "pure" tic disorder, medication and behavioral interventions are typically tried first.

Family Interventions

Family therapy is rarely used as a first or only treatment for tic disorders, largely because of the success rates of behavioral and pharmacological therapy. However, the clinician must be prepared to use family therapy if significant family issues emerge in the assessment. Family therapy may also be necessary if the tic serves a role in the family system such that the family sabotages other interventions (Prata and Masson, 1985). The tic may also be a major stressor in the family, demanding therapeutic attention.

Selective Mutism

CLINICAL DESCRIPTION

Diagnostic Considerations

Selective Mutism is a relatively unusual but debilitating disorder in which a child does not speak in one or more common situations such as school. This refusal to speak is not the result of a language or vocal deficit, but rather seems to be at least partially under the control of the child. True Selective Mutism occurs in 0.3 to 0.8 of every 1000 children (Brown and Lloyd, 1975; Labbe and Williamson, 1984; Silver, 1989), although lesser forms of mutism such as reluctant speech are much more common (Labbe and Williamson, 1984).

The diagnostic criteria for Selective Mutism in DSM-IV are relatively straightforward: First, the child must show a refusal to speak in one or more social situations. School is suggested as one such situation, probably because Selective Mutism, when it is seen, often occurs at school. Importantly, the child must speak in other situations. Hence, a child who never speaks in any situation would technically not qualify for the Selective Mutism diagnosis. Second, the child must not have a communication disorder that would remove the ability to comprehend or produce speech. This criterion eliminates physical causes for the mutism and inability to speak because of severe cognitive impairment. However, it does not exclude children who have language delays but can still understand language and speak. Third, the mutism must last at least 1 month (which cannot be the first month of school) and must interfere with social or educational functioning. Finally, the mutism cannot be a result of a lack of knowledge of the spoken language.

Several authors have attempted to identify subtypes of Selective Mutism that can be useful in clinical description or treatment of the disorder. For example, selectively mute children may be divided into compliant versus noncompliant types (Lesser-Katz, 1988). Compliant mute children are passive, fearful, insecure, and exhibit dependent behavior with one or more adults. They react to new situations with immobility and stranger anxiety, preventing them from speaking. However, at home they may be oppositional and aggressive. Noncompliant mute children are passive-aggressive, actively avoidant, and hostile-withdrawn. With adults, they are often manipulative, aggressive, stubborn, defiant, and oppositional, perhaps as a result of anger toward parents. They use their mutism and withdrawal to communicate rejection of peers and adults, defiantly resisting any attempts to be engaged.

Similar to the compliant-noncompliant subtyping is the grouping of selectively mute children based on level of anxiety. Mute children with speech-related anxiety are afraid to speak in social situations; they resemble compliant mutes. Mute children who lack speech-related anxiety are defiant and manipulative in withholding speech. They appear relaxed and comfortable in social situations, resembling defiant mutes (Reed, 1963; Laybourne, 1989).

A second subtyping system places Selective Mutism in the context of other speech-withholding behaviors. Labbe and Williamson (1984) suggest that Selective Mutism is an extreme version of speech-reduced behavior. A more moderate problem is that of "Reluctant Speech." Unlike the selectively mute child, who shows complete absence of speech in certain situations, the child with Reluctant Speech shows dramatically reduced, but not absent, speech (Brown and Doll, 1988). Selective Mutism may be associated with more language delays and family pathology than is Reluctant Speech, although both fall along the speech-reduced continuum (Carr and Afnan, 1989; Wilkins, 1985).

A third subtyping of mutism is the traumatic/elective distinction (Silver, 1989). Traumatic mutism follows a significant psychological or physical stressor, such as diagnosis of a chronic illness or death of a parent. The mutism in this case is often complete, with no speech in any situation. Technically, this problem would not meet DSM-IV Selective Mutism criteria, which state that the child speaks in some situations. Furthermore, traumatic mutism rarely lasts a full month. Rather, traumatic mutism is more likely to be temporary and to spontaneously disappear (Silver, 1989). Nontraumatic elective mutism has no apparent precipitating incident and is much more common.

A fourth subtyping of Selective Mutism groups children into symbiotic, passive-aggressive, reactive, and speech-phobic groups (Hayden, 1980). Symbiotic mutism is the most common and is characterized by an enmeshed relationship with the primary caretaker. The caretaker is often domineering and jealous of the child's other relationships, isolating the child by appearing to meet all of the child's needs. The other parent is generally disengaged and isolated from the caretaker–child relationship. Symbiotic mutes initially appear shy and clinging, but further observation reveals that they are manipulative and controlling (Hayden, 1980; Silver, 1989). Children with passive-aggressive mutism, the next most common type, use silence to show defiance and hostility. They tend to engage in aggressive and antisocial behaviors and are the targets of blame and rejection in their families (Hayden, 1980; Silver, 1989). Reactive mutism is somewhat similar to traumatic mutism. It occurs in response to a single traumatic stressor or a chronically stressful environment. Children with reactive mutism often have associated difficulties such as depression, social withdrawal, or PTSD (Hayden, 1980; Silver, 1989). The least frequent subtype is speech-phobic mutism, characterized by a fear of hearing one's own voice. These children sometimes exhibit compulsive or ritualistic behaviors.

Appearance and Features

(Appearance and features of Selective Mutism are listed in Table 13.4.) Selective mutism is generally first noticed in children between the ages of 3 and 5

TABLE 13.4   Appearance and Features of Selective Mutism

COMMON FEATURES

Refusal/inability to speak in one or more common situations
Adequate motor and language development to allow speech
Onset between 3 and 5 years of age
Usually speak to a small circle of family members
Use of gestures or whispering to communicate
Socially anxious, shy, timid
Clingy, protests separation from parent

OCCASIONAL FEATURES

Use of mutism to manipulate the environment
Use of mutism to get attention or to express anger
Developmental language disorders

Note: The features listed above are often seen but are not universal. Some features may be diagnostically relevant or required, while others may not be required for diagnosis. "Common" features are typical of the disorder; "occasional" features appear frequently but are not necessarily seen in a majority of cases.

(Shvartzman et al., 1990; Weininger, 1987). Parents may initially regard it as simple shyness, but the magnitude of the behavior becomes apparent when the child begins attending school. Many selectively mute children are referred based on muteness at school. It is not unusual for children to be initially quiet and reserved when they begin kindergarten or first grade. Some children are even completely silent for the first few days of school. However, selectively mute children continue this silent behavior for weeks, despite attempts by teachers and other children to encourage them to speak (Laybourne, 1989).

Children with Selective Mutism often speak normally at home and with a small circle of close relatives and friends (Dulcan and Popper, 1991; Laybourne, 1989; Silver, 1989). However, they are silent in certain situations, such as when they are with teachers, strange children, or unfamiliar adults. Although speech in these "mute" situations is not present, the child may still attempt to communicate using other means. Gestures, brief vocalizations, or whispering to a familiar person are common ways in which selectively mute children attempt to communicate (Laybourne, 1989; Silver, 1989). In extremely rare cases the child may be mute in all situations. These completely mute children do not meet DSM-IV Selective Mutism criteria and may be experiencing a transient reaction to trauma.

The presentation of Selective Mutism often gives the impression that these children are being controlling or dependent, causing several authors (Afnan and Carr, 1989; Brown and Doll, 1988; Lesser-Katz, 1988; Weininger, 1987) to speculate that they have additional social or behavioral problems. Brown and Doll (1988), for example, cite literature indicating that most selectively mute children have social difficulties manifested in either passively controlling or dependent behavior. They may also appear socially anxious and insecure, fearing separation from familiar others and clinging to parents (Dulcan & Popper, 1991; Lesser-Katz, 1988; Wilkins, 1985). With peers, they are often anxious, submissive, timid, and they are often rejected or neglected by their peer group. Depression, manipulative behavior, and developmental language disorders have also been reported as occurring with above average frequency in selective mutes (Afnan and Carr, 1989; Weininger, 1987; Wilkins, 1985).

Etiology

Theories of the etiology of Selective Mutism usually implicate the family or behavioral contingencies in the development and maintenance of the mute behavior. The family, and particularly the mother, has been emphasized in etiological explanations of the symbiotic and passive-aggressive subtypes of Selective Mutism (Atoynatan, 1986; Lesser-Katz, 1988).

Family conflict and marital disharmony have been cited as common to selectively mute children (Atoynatan, 1986). In many cases this disharmony results in the formation of a coalition by one parent and the child against the other parent. Mothers of selectively mute children are described as lonely, anxious, deprived, or depressed, with a resentment toward the father and a desire to be enmeshed with the child (Atoynatan, 1986; Dulcan and Popper, 1991; Lesser-Katz, 1988, Silver, 1989). They achieve this enmeshment by overprotecting the child and encouraging regression in the child. Sensing the needs and anxieties of the mother, the child rejects interaction with other people in order to maintain the symbiotic and enmeshed relationship. Speaking to others is, in effect, a rejection of the mother, and attempts to challenge this enmeshment are met with angry silence (Silver, 1989). Alternatively, the child may interpret the mother's anxiety and dependent behavior as a sign that the child is fundamentally flawed. Hence, the child fears separation from the mother because the child needs the mother for security (Atoynatan, 1986; Lesser-Katz, 1988). In other cases the child resents the maternal enmeshment and overprotectiveness and responds with silence as a means of defiance or control (Dulcan and Popper, 1991). Clearly, these explanations are somewhat stereotypical and do not apply to all Selective Mutism cases. Nevertheless, they may provide initial hypotheses for investigation in cases with a clear structural family component.

Psychodynamic explanations of the etiology of Selective Mutism overlap heavily with family theories, beginning with a focus on the mother–child relationship. Analytic theorists add to this model by hypothesizing that these children are silent because they fear that if they talk they will say something forbidden or nasty. Fearing the expression of these aggressive impulses, they choose to be silent. This withholding of speech reflects a fixation at the anal stage of development. The source of aggressive impulses and related fears is hypothesized to be the mother–child relationship and parental discipline of the expression of id impulses (Dulcan and Popper, 1991; Weininger, 1987).

A third group of theories of the etiology of Selective Mutism focuses on behavioral contingencies driving the mutism (Afnan and Carr, 1989; Carr and Afnan, 1989; Brown and Doll, 1988). Operant conditioning explanations conceptualize mutism as a behavior that is reinforced by attention and being kept home from school (Carr and Afnan, 1989; Brown and Doll, 1988). Classical conditioning suggests that the child has associated speech with some negative event, such as pain, humiliation, anxiety, or parental discipline for speaking. Failed social interactions could also lead to the development of mutism through this classical conditioning model. Thus, the child avoids speech in order to avoid the conditioned fear response that follows speech (Afnanand Carr, 1989; Carr and Afnan, 1989). Finally, social learning theories may explain the development of Selective Mutism in a child who is modeling the behavior of a quiet parent or sibling (Brown and Doll, 1988; Weininger, 1987).

A final explanation of the development of mutism pertains primarily to traumatic mutism, which often does not qualify for the formal Selective Mutism diagnosis. This explanation contends that the mutism represents the child's defensive response to a stressor. Abused children, for example, may use silence to remain inconspicuous or to express anger in a way that is less likely to lead to further abuse. The silence may also represent a shock response to a stressor for which there is no readily available coping mechanism. In some cases the trauma may be symbolically related to silence, as when a child who is repeatedly slapped in the face becomes mute (Dulcan and Popper, 1991; Silver, 1989).

ASSESSMENT PATTERNS

A sample assessment battery for Selective Mutism is shown in Table 13.5.

Broad Assessment Strategies

Children with Selective Mutism are often extremely difficult to assess because they refuse to communicate normally with the examiner. Techniques such as

TABLE 13.5   Sample Assessment Battery for Selective Mutism

COGNITIVE

Peabody Picture Vocabulary Test—Revised

BEHAVIORAL

Child Behavior Checklist

FAMILY

Family Environment Scale

Note: Assessment instruments are intended to supplement (not substitute for) a good clinical interview and, when possible, a structured diagnostic interview.

allowing the child to pantomime responses, whisper answers to another person, or say answers to a puppet may help at times. However, these techniques are time-consuming and violate the standardization of some tests.

Cognitive Assessment

Clinician-Administered. Many selectively mute children have cognitive and language skills in the normal ranges. However, a subgroup of cognitively delayed mute children does exist. As a whole group, then, selectively mute children may show a somewhat increased prevalence of cognitive or language deficit (Dulcan and Popper, 1991; Silver, 1989). Because of potential language and cognitive deficits, these children should routinely be administered a battery consisting of a major intelligence test such as the WISC-III, WPPSI-R, or SB:FE. In addition, a major achievement test such as the WJ-R or WIAT is recommended. A receptive vocabulary test such as the Peabody Picture Vocabulary Test—Revised (PPVT-R; Dunn and Dunn, 1981) may also be helpful because it does not require speech.

Although no systematic research exists on the IQ/achievement testing patterns of selectively mute children, average to somewhat below average scores on Full Scale and Verbal IQ would be expected. Children who score average or above on Full Scale and Verbal IQ are withholding speech without associated cognitive deficits. Language-based achievement tests such as reading and written language should also be analyzed to see if a language deficit pervades modalities other than speech. Expressive vocabulary subtests on the WISC-III and SB:FE (WPPSI-R vocabulary mixes expressive and receptive components) can be compared to the PPVT-R to see if the child has an expressive–receptive vocabulary discrepancy.

Psychological Assessment

Child-Report. In addition to cognitive testing, selectively mute children should be tested for psychological, behavioral, and social problems, since these appear to be risks associated with mutism (Dulcan and Popper, 1991). Some children may agree to complete self-report instruments such as the Children's Depression Inventory (CDI; Kovacs, 1992), but they are unlikely to cooperate with interview techniques.

Behavioral Assessment

Parent-Report. Parent-report behavior checklists such as the CBCL may be extremely helpful in identifying additional problems in the behavioral and social area. Depending on the subtype and dynamics of the individual child, different subscales of the CBCL may be elevated. Depressed, shy, and withdrawn children will elevate internalizing subscales, while more hostile and defiant children will elevate externalizing subscales (Carr and Afnan, 1989). Sociability is often low.

Family Assessment

Parent-Report. Based on theories implicating parental difficulties in the development of Selective Mutism, assessment of the parents, marriage, and family is often warranted. If an enmeshed mother–child relationship is present, mothers of selectively mute children may be expected to elevate scales 2, 3, 4, 8, and 0 on the MMPI, reflecting their depression, low self-esteem, alienation, anger, and need for a symbiotic relationship. The MMPI of fathers will vary depending on their desire to be involved in the family and their response to the mother's behavior. In any event, the MMPI can be a valuable tool in the identification of parental dynamics contributing to the mutism.

On the FES and FACES-III, families of selective mutes may be expected to show patterns characteristic of family conflict, enmeshment, and control. Elevations on FES Cohesion, Expressiveness, Conflict, Control, Conflicted, and Controlling scales/factors are likely to be coupled with a low score on Independence. On the FACES-III, high cohesion scores (enmeshment) and low adaptability scores (rigid) are typical. Family inventories should be given to both parents separately; differences in parental response may provide insight into family structure and differences in how the family is viewed. A mother who reports very high cohesion and a father who reports very low cohesion, for example, may indicate that the father is disengaged and the mother is enmeshed with the child. Likewise, scores on the Dyadic Adjustment Scale (DAS; Spanier, 1976) may suggest difficulties in the marriage or differences in how the marriage is perceived. DAS scores of less than 100 reflect poor marital adjustment in parents of selectively mute children.

TREATMENT OPTIONS

Treatment options for Selective Mutism are outlined in Table 13.6.

Behavioral Interventions

Behavior therapy is generally regarded as the most effective treatment for Selective Mutism (Brown and Doll, 1988). Other authors advocate the use of psychodynamic play therapy (Weininger, 1987) or family therapy (Furst, 1989) in certain cases. Given the current absence of controlled outcome studies, a flexible, multimodal approach emphasizing work with the parents and child appears to be the best option (Silver, 1989). Four types of behavior therapy have been suggested for children with Selective Mutism: stimulus fading, reinforcement contingencies, relaxation techniques, and shaping.

Stimulus Fading

Stimulus fading may be the most effective component of a behavior therapy package for Selective Mutism (Afnan and Carr, 1989; Carr and Afnan, 1989; Silver, 1989). In stimulus fading the child is taken by someone to whom the child will talk (e.g., the mother) to the situation in which the child is mute.

TABLE 13.6   Treatment Options for Selective Mutism

BEHAVIORAL INTERVENTIONS

Stimulus fading
Reinforcement contingencies
Relaxation techniques
Shaping

PSYCHOTHERAPY

Play therapy

FAMILY INTERVENTIONS

Family therapy

REFERRALS

Speech/language therapy

Note: This outline of options summarizes major treatments covered in the text. Specific treatments are often combined into an intervention package. Refer to the text for additional descriptions of each treatment. This table is not necessarily an exhaustive list of all treatments available.

Initially this situation is made as conducive as possible to talking, by removing any potential social stressors. For example, child and parent may visit the child's classroom after school, when only the child and parent will be present. The child is then encouraged to talk to the parent. Gradually other components of the environment are introduced, at a rate that does not stop the verbalizations of the child. The parent is used to support the introduction of these additional components. In the school example the teacher may gradually be introduced into the classroom, first hovering outside the doorway, then entering the room, then approaching parent and child, then sitting with the parent and child. The parent would introduce the teacher to the child and relay information between teacher and child (Afnan and Carr, 1989; Carr and Afnan, 1989; Laybourne, 1989; Silver, 1989).

Once the other components are introduced, the role of the parent is gradually faded, and the role of the other components are increased, again at a rate that does not significantly affect the child's verbalizations. To return to the school example, the parent would gradually stop relaying the teacher's questions to the child and the teacher would begin addressing the child directly. One or two children would then be added to the situation, and the child would be engaged by the group. The parent would then announce that she is moving to another area of the room. Following a period of being in the room but apart from the child, the parent would tell the child that she is leaving but will be back at a certain time. Finally, the situation is allowed to return to its normal state. This program must be implemented gradually, with returns to earlier stages if the child stops speaking. As few as 12 and as many as 180 sessions may be necessary to achieve the goal of speech in the normal situation (Afnan and Carr, 1989; Carr and Afnan, 1989; Laybourne, 1989; Silver, 1989).

Reinforcement Contingency

Stimulus fading is often combined with a second behavioral treatment, reinforcement contingency. A reinforcement contingency approach implements the simple principle of rewarding the child for speech behavior. Probably the most important part of this intervention is the selection of behaviors to reinforce. Initially, target behaviors must be relatively simple for the child to attain while requiring verbal response or an approximation of a verbal response, such as moving the lips (Laybourne, 1989; Mace and West, 1986). For example, an initial target might be a one-word response. The most common reinforcer is praise, although other reinforcers such as prizes have been used (Brown and Doll, 1988; Mace and West, 1986). Reinforcement contingencies have been reported to be effective in some cases (Brown and Doll, 1988; Mace and West, 1986), although they are probably best used as one component of a multidimensional behavioral program.

In some cases, peers are reinforced when the child speaks, creating an incentive for them to assist the child in speech. In one intervention, kindergarten classmates of a selectively mute girl were allowed to choose a prize each time the girl spoke to a member of the class (Brown and Doll, 1988). The children were reminded of the prizes before recess each day, and prizes were distributed after recess. In a 5–6-week period the girl's peer interactions increased, as did attempts by peers to engage her: "At various times, groups of children would gather about Amy and begin speaking to her, cheering when she would respond" (Brown and Doll, 1988, p. 114). Clearly, this intervention should be applied only to children who would benefit from the increased interaction; extremely shy or phobic children might find the attention aversive or overwhelming.

Relaxation Training

Some children are selectively mute because of anxiety over social interaction or speaking. For these children, relaxation techniques targeting the underlying anxiety may be the most effective approach to encouraging speech. Laybourne (1989) suggests that a systematic desensitization approach may be helpful for some children. In this approach the children create a hierarchy of anxiety-producing social situations. They are then taught a relaxation technique, such as progressive muscle relaxation. The anxiety-producing images are then gradually paired with the relaxed state, from least-anxiety-producing to most-anxiety-producing. The children practice this technique in therapy and at home. The ultimate aim of this intervention is to encourage the children to feel relaxed in social situations, facilitating speech.

Although relaxation techniques may be helpful for some children, they are unlikely to produce much benefit unless they are combined with *in vivo* practice. Furthermore, mute children may not be willing to engage in sufficient interaction with the therapist to allow the teaching of relaxation. Hence, this technique is best considered for selectively mute children who are so anxious that they cannot be helped by other techniques until their anxiety is managed.

Shaping

Shaping techniques underlie other components of behavior therapy and thus do not constitute a separate type of therapy *per se*. Shaping involves rewarding approximations of the target speaking behavior (Blake and Moss, 1967). For example, the child may be initially reinforced for moving the lips. Later, the behavior target is changed to movement of lips accompanied by a whispering speech. This target is then gradually increased in loudness until the child is speaking in an audible voice (e.g., Brown and Doll, 1988). The reinforcement may vary from praise to a more tangible reinforcer, such as candy.

Shaping is often necessary in order to achieve a positive outcome for selectively mute children. Expecting these children to speak loudly and normally with the implementation of a reinforcement contingency is simply unrealistic and may produce a failure experience that makes the child more resistant to intervention. Rewarding small increases in speech performance makes the intervention less aversive for the child and allows the therapist to teach proper speech behavior.

Behavior Treatment Packages

It is relatively rare to see any of the behavior techniques implemented alone. Rather, the techniques are combined into a treatment package that is tailored to fit individual needs. Children who respond well to praise, for example, should be given the reinforcement contingency of praise. In addition, a shaping component should be built into stimulus fading or reinforcement contingency conditions so that the child has achievable behavioral goals. Components should be added, deleted, or modified based on assessment of performance of the target behavior. As with all behavior interventions, the target behaviors should be observable and clearly defined; assessment of target behaviors is crucial to monitor change from baseline.

Psychotherapy

Psychodynamic Play Therapy

The use of play therapy as an intervention for Selective Mutism is based on three psychodynamic assumptions: first, that the mutism represents the child's response to internal conflicts; second, that the mutism reflects concerns about expression of feelings; and third, that feelings stemming from relationships with caretakers underlie the mutism. Play therapy aims to create an environment in which the child feels free to express feelings, manage conflicts, and gain insight into and control over the problem. Feelings and conflicts are initially acted out symbolically, with dolls and toys as facilitators. In early sessions the parent may need to be present in order for the child to engage in any activity at all. Later the therapist interprets the child's play and talks with the child about the conflicts and emotions. It is usually important for the parent to be absent in these later sessions in order for the child to freely address issues relating to the parent.

Lesser-Katz (1988) suggests that some children with Selective Mutism develop the disorder as a result of enmeshment with a lonely, deprived, and depressed mother. The mother overprotects the child, creating an insecure, sensitive, passive child. The child refuses to talk in order to protect the mother and to maintain loyalty and symbiosis with her. This loyalty and symbiosis are necessary for the child to feel secure, reflecting an extreme dependency on the mother. However, external influences (such as school) demand separation from the mother and development of independence. The child fears this separation and acts to regain the symbiosis by continuing to refuse to speak.

Lesser-Katz (1988) regards play as a way for children to express these difficult and threatening feelings without resorting to speech. Play becomes, for the children, an expression of unconscious fears, conflicts, and feelings regarding the relationship with the mother. The role of the therapist is to permissively allow the children to engage in the play of their choice. Through the symbolic modality of play the children can act out feelings of anger toward parents (for example, by having a baby lion attack a mother lion) and fear of separation from parents. The therapist's role is to provide acceptance and support for the children, validating their feelings and eventually interpreting the significance of the play situation. The children, seeing that their feelings are not "bad" or disastrous, begin to accept them and to communicate about them, allowing appropriate separation from the parents.

Weininger (1987) takes a similar approach, but for him the central issues are the child's fear of shouting inappropriately and desire to be taken care of. Both of these fears stem from anger toward parents and fear of separation from them. The mutism both prevents the possibility of an embarrassing outburst and increases caretaking behavior from parents. Again, play allows the child to symbolically express and resolve these feelings in the presence of a supportive therapist. The therapist provides acceptance, support, and, later, interpretation of the child's play themes.

Play therapy may also be an important technique in cases of traumatic mutism. Children with this subtype of Selective Mutism have encountered some stressful event in close proximity to the development of the mutism. Traumatically mute children use the mutism as a form of protective control over their thought and emotional state. By not allowing verbal interaction, they ward off conversations, thoughts, and feelings related to the event. These children often fear being overwhelmed with affects and stress if they talk about the traumatic event, and they see attempts to make them talk as dangerous to their well-being.

Play therapy allows the creation of a safe environment in which the topics and themes are under the children's control. As the children realize that they control the therapy environment, they can begin to process themes related to the trauma. These themes may be only superficially processed at first, with increasing depth as the children adjust to working through the painful event. Presumably, when the trauma is worked through and "mastered," the need for mutism disappears, along with the symptoms.

Family Interventions

Because of the role of the family in many cases of Selective Mutism, family therapy is often indicated to resolve family characteristics that are contributing to the mutism (Furst, 1989; Laybourne, 1989). In some cases the family dynamic is that of a mother who is enmeshed with the child against a disengaged father (Laybourne, 1989). At other times, family therapy is necessary to confront a family dynamic that rewards the child for mutism and resists change (Furst, 1989). Structural family therapy (Minuchin, 1974) aims to restructure family relationships by drawing an appropriate boundary between mother and child while engaging the father as a contributing family member. In order to achieve these structural goals, marital therapy may be necessary to strengthen the parents' relationship (Laybourne, 1989).

When the pathology of one parent appears to be maintaining the child's mutism and the parent subtly resists change, individual psychotherapy with the parent may be necessary. This therapy should target issues that prevent the parent from fostering independence and sociability in the child. In extreme cases, parents will stubbornly resist change and insist that there is not a problem until a parent–child separation is threatened (Atoynatan, 1986).

Referrals

Speech/Language Therapy

Some children with Selective Mutism engage in this behavior partly as a result of speech and language deficits (Dulcan and Popper, 1991). The child may be ashamed of speaking for fear of looking different or fear of saying something embarrassing. When testing indicates these deficits, a speech/language pathologist should be consulted to handle this component of therapy. The presence of language deficits, however, should not be thought of as precluding other psychological and behavioral treatments. The speech therapist and psychologist should consider themselves as collaborators working on two dimensions that are contributing to the mute behavior.

■ Gender Identity Disorder

□ CLINICAL DESCRIPTION

Diagnostic Considerations

Children develop a sense of gender identity (the awareness that one is a boy or girl) early in life, probably between the ages of 1 and 3 years (Zucker, 1989,

1990a; Coates, 1990). Gender identity is fundamental to the sense of self (Zucker, 1989), stable (Coates, 1990), emotionally meaningful, and value-laden (Zucker, 1990a), and it drives many types of behaviors, which are referred to as gender role behaviors (Coates, 1990). In most cases the gender identity of the child matches his or her biological sex. The DSM-IV diagnosis Gender Identity Disorder (GID) refers to cases in which the child's gender identity (or desired gender identity) does not match the biological sex. The diagnostic qualifier "in Children" is added to Gender Identity Disorder to specify that the GID is occurring in a child.

Diagnostically, the hallmark of GID is persistent discomfort or distress over biological sex and identification with the opposite sex. Identification with the opposite sex is usually manifest as desire to be (or insistence that one is) a member of the opposite sex, preoccupation with stereotypical activities or roles of the opposite sex, preference for peer interaction with the opposite sex, and strong preference for opposite-sex clothing. Distress over biological sex is shown by such behaviors as repudiation or disgust of the biological sex organ, sense of inappropriateness over one's sex, and aversion toward stereotypical activities/roles of the biological sex. The GID must cause distress or impairment in functioning in order to be diagnosed. GID behavior generally emerges in the preschool years (Bradley and Zucker, 1990). Its exact prevalence is not known, although the disorder is very uncommon and probably occurs in 0.001 to 0.01% of children (American Psychiatric Association, 1994; Dulcan and Popper, 1991).

The DSM-III-R gender identity diagnosis focused on the childhood emergence of the disorder, with the name Gender Identity Disorder of Childhood (American Psychiatric Association, 1987). DSM-IV places no age constraints on GID, allowing it to be applied to adults as well. However, childhood GID is assigned a unique code and diagnostic qualifier (GID in Children) in DSM-IV, separate from adolescent/adult GID.

The GID diagnosis occasionally comes under fire from those who regard it as psychiatric sanction for traditional gender roles. Critics contend that traditional gender roles are imposed on children whose interests would otherwise be androgenous and that GID represents the punishment for those who would transcend traditional roles. In addition, GID is criticized as a "homophobic" diagnosis assigned to boys who may be showing early signs of homosexuality. Although it is true that most GID boys become homosexual in adolescence and adulthood, only a fraction of adult homosexuals have GID in childhood. Finally, some clinicians see cross-gender behavior as an exploratory phase of childhood. These clinicians argue that most children grow out of cross-gender behavior without intervention and that parents should allow their children to engage in this exploration as a part of normal development. For these reasons, GID is sometimes attacked as an unfair diagnosis (Zucker, 1990b).

Despite potential misuses by those who cite GID as support for traditional gender roles, the GID diagnosis has value both as a behavioral descriptor and as a target for intervention (Zucker, 1990b). First, the diagnosis is not given to children who simply favor androgenous or opposite-gender activities. DSM-IV requires persistent cross-sex identification *and* persistent discomfort about one's biological sex. Boys who engage in traditional girl-role activities but do not have distress (or sense of inappropriateness) about their sex should not be diagnosed with GID. Likewise, girls who are "tomboys" typically do not express persistent and intense unhappiness with their sex. Furthermore, while tomboys may prefer boys' clothing, they can be persuaded under certain circumstances to dress in girls' clothing. Hence, the GID diagnosis need not be made for children with diverse or unusual interests.

Second, extensive cross-gender behavior and cross-gender identity in very young children is not normal (Zucker, 1989). It is true that children will, on some occasions, ask to dress like the parent of the opposite sex or will say that they are the sex of the opposite parent. However, in normal children such instances are not of the frequency, duration, and intensity seen in GID children. Intense and persistent cross-gender identity and behavior are atypical because children tend to form gender identity at a very early age.

Finally, some evidence exists that GID children are at risk for co-occurring psychopathology (Zucker, 1989, 1990b; Coates, 1990; Bates, Bentler, and Thompson, 1979; Coates and Person, 1985). They often have severely impaired peer relationships, characterized by frequent rejection (Zucker, 1989, 1990b; Coates, 1990). Hence, for whatever reasons, they are a group at risk for maladjustment. Zucker (1990b) also argues that GID children should be treated because they are at risk for adulthood conditions associated with societal prejudice and rejection, such as homosexuality and transsexualism. This final point, however, appears to be more of a value judgment than a valid reason for treating GID. Over all, however, there appear to be many valid reasons for diagnosing and considering treatment for GID, and it is likely to remain a DSM diagnosis for some time (Bradley et al., 1991).

Appearance and Features

(Appearance and features of GID are listed in Table 13.7.) Boys with GID show a pattern of preferences for female clothing, activities, and behavior. They often dress in girls' or women's clothing; prefer to play with dolls, seek out girls as playmates; adopt female motor behaviors/movements (swaying hips, droopy wrist, speaking in a high or soft voice); and favor female characters in movies, books, and on TV (American Psychiatric Association, 1994; Bradley and Zucker, 1990; Coates, 1990; Zucker, 1989; Doering et al., 1989). Often they pretend that they are girls or famous females and try to make themselves appear female by using cosmetics and jewelry. A fixation on female clothing may be seen as well (Coates, 1990; Zucker, 1989). These boys will state that they are or would like to be a girl (Coates, 1990; Zucker, 1989). They avoid traditional male behaviors and activities, such as rough-and-tumble play, all-boy play groups, and traditional male toys (Coates, 1990; Zucker, 1989; Doering et al., 1989). Less common is the stated desire to lose or cut off the penis. In some cases, desire to lose the penis is manifest by hiding the penis or sitting to urinate (Zucker, 1989). On very rare occasions, GID boys engage in self-mutilation (Coates, 1990).

Girls with GID are much less common than boys with GID, with five or six GID boys for every GID girl (Bradley and Zucker, 1990; American Psychiatric

TABLE 13.7   Appearance and Features of Gender Identity Disorder

COMMON FEATURES

Distress over biological sex
Desire to be a member of opposite sex
Impaired peer relationships, social rejection
Preference for clothing, activity, motor behavior, and fantasy play stereotypically
    associated with other sex
Avoidance of play with same-sex peers
More friendships with cross-sex peers
More common in boys

OCCASIONAL FEATURES

Internalizing symptoms (separation anxiety, depression, loneliness)
Homosexuality in adulthood

Note: The features listed above are often seen but are not universal. Some features may be diagnostically relevant or required, while others may not be required for diagnosis. "Common" features are typical of the disorder; "occasional" features appear frequently but are not necessarily seen in a majority of cases.

Association, 1994). Consequently, less is known about the presentation and clinical course of GID in females. GID girls express the desire to be a boy as well as dislike of being a girl. They may adopt behaviors (standing to urinate, insisting that they have a penis) that make this male identification apparent (Bradley & Zucker, 1990; Zucker, 1989). In addition, their behavior and activities are stereotypically male. For example, they seek out rough-and-tumble play with boys, prefer traditionally male toys, take a male role in fantasy or play, adopt male speech patterns, and avoid feminine clothing and activities (Bradley and Zucker, 1990; Zucker, 1989). Bradley and Zucker (1990) also note that GID girls throw extremely intense temper tantrums if forced to wear feminine clothing, and they socialize almost exclusively with boys throughout their childhood.

Two problematic features associated with GID are increased risk of psychopathology and negative peer relations. Zucker (1989) and Coates (1990) cite evidence indicating that GID boys have higher levels of general psychopathology. In particular, overcontrolled problems such as Separation Anxiety Disorder, clinginess, and depression have been reported as common for GID boys (Coates, 1990). These findings have led Coates (1990) to the conclusion that "extreme boyhood femininity occurs in the context of other behavioral disturbances and does not occur *de novo* in an otherwise normal boy" (p. 420). Other authors have supported this view (Coates and Person, 1985; Bates et al., 1979). Despite this evidence, controversy remains over the extent of associated psychopathology in GID boys (Zucker, 1989). The extent of associated psychopathology in GID girls is unknown, although GID girls may be less at risk for social problems and psychopathology than are GID boys (American Psychiatric Association, 1994).

Unlike the case of associated psychopathology, there is little argument that GID children, particularly boys, are at risk for poor peer relationships (Dulcan and Popper, 1991). Children, who can be exceedingly intolerant of differences in appearance and behavior, frequently single out GID boys for teasing, rejection, and ostracism (Zucker, 1990b). The rejection of the other children is generally based on their observation of the feminine speech and behavior of GID boys; taunts of "sissy" and "gay" are common (Coates, 1990). Same-sex friendships are difficult to establish because other children fear rejection by association and do not know how to interpret the unusual behavior (Coates, 1990). Some GID boys will form relationships with girls based on mutual interests. However, these relationships may be tenuous because the boy realizes that he is "different" despite having similar interests. Unless they find an accepting group of girls or similarly rejected boys, many of these boys are socially isolated by their teen years (Bradley and Zucker, 1990). Predictably, they often admit feelings of loneliness and rejection (Coates, 1990). Social rejection is often so severe that it may underlie some of the risk for psychopathology (Zucker, 1990b). The social relationships of GID girls have been less well studied, although they probably have fewer social problems than boys. Bradley and Zucker (1990) suggest that GID girls often find a relatively socially acceptable outlet for their interests in sports participation and adoption of a tomboy appearance. They may seek out same-sex peer groups that do not engage exclusively in traditional female interests.

Prospective research (i.e., Green, 1987) indicates that most, but not all, GID boys become homosexual adults (Zucker, 1989; Coates, 1990). Because sexual orientation is not a GID diagnostic criterion, it is incorrect to say that all GID boys are or will become homosexual. In addition, because there are many more homosexual men than GID boys, the GID-turned-homosexual group is only a very small subgroup of homosexual men. However, followup studies suggest that a significant proportion (probably greater than 50% and possibly in the 70–80% range (Bradley and Zucker, 1990; Coates, 1990; Zucker, 1989) of GID boys become bisexual or homosexual (Zucker, 1989). The pattern of development of sexual orientation for GID girls may be different than that for boys, with fewer GID girls becoming homosexual as adults. Girls who merely have traditionally male interests without GID generally develop more feminine interests at puberty (Dulcan and Popper, 1991). A disproportionate number of GID boys become transsexual as adults, although the risk of transsexuality is small even within the GID population (probably less than 5%; [Green, 1987; Zucker, 1989]).

Etiology

Most etiological theories focus on the development of GID in boys. The lack of research and theory pertaining to GID girls probably results from the rarity of the disorder for girls and the reliance of most theories on male-oriented psychoanalytic concepts.

Biological Theories

Biological theories of GID are based on animal studies that show that prenatal hormones have an effect on later sex-typed behavior such as aggressiveness, rough-and-tumble play, and mounting (Bradley and Zucker, 1990; Coates, 1990). However, most of these studies have induced stereotypic male behavior in genetic females, while GID occurs predominantly in boys. Furthermore, the value of generalizing from animal hormone studies to human functioning can be questioned. Certainly humans have shown much more plasticity in response to hormonal influences. Finally, hormonal disorders are rarely found in GID children, although this does not preclude the possibility that the hormonal influences occurred before birth. Hence, evidence for a biological explanation is speculative at present. Any biological influences that are found are likely to be predispositions that must be activated by environmental influences.

Psychological Theories

Psychodynamic/psychoanalytic theories of GID suggest that characteristics of the mother–child relationship (usually mother–son—these theories typically neglect daughters) encourage the development of GID. Stoller's (1968, 1975) "blissful symbiosis" theory, for example, attributes overly feminine behavior in many boys to an enmeshed relationship with the mother. The mother–son relationship is so intense that the boy is unable to separate himself from his mother's physical characteristics and behavior. Thus, the boy remains fixed at an early, "symbiotic" phase of development and identification with the mother. This identification includes the mother's gender identity.

Other authors agree with Stoller's central role of the mother but focus instead on separation as opposed to symbiosis. Coates (1990) contends that emotional or physical separation from the mother creates such anxiety in some boys that they adopt her beliefs, behaviors, and appearance in order to feel that she is present. This fantasy of maternal presence alters the self-view of the boy, who wants to be a girl and values females over males (Coates, 1990). Object relations theorists take a similar view of GID, suggesting that GID develops following parental loss (Bleiberg, Jackson, and Ross, 1986). Children who lose their mothers (physically or emotionally) at the time that they are attempting to gain a sense of self separate from their mother are vulnerable to considerable anxiety and a threat to their sense of self. To defend against these painful experiences, the child identifies extremely strongly with the mother, in some cases adopting her gender identity and behaviors. Adoption of the female role then becomes a part of the child's identity, particularly under stresses involving loss or deprivation (Bleiberg et al., 1986).

Behavioral Theories

Behavioral theories of GID have received much less attention than have psychodynamic theories, but they almost certainly have some role in explaining the etiology of GID. These theories hold that parents of GID children subtly reinforce cross-gender behaviors while ignoring or punishing same-gender behaviors. These parents may regard their son's dressing in the mother's clothing as "cute." They may also relish their child's exploration of cross-gender toys while ignoring more gender-congruent behavior. Other parents, wishing to expose their child to androgenous experiences, may unwittingly give the impression that they favor his playing with cross-sex toys by encouraging exposure to them. Gender-incongruent behavior in both children and adults is often regarded as "funny," and parents may laugh as their child behaves or acts in a silly, cross-gender way. This laughter may be highly reinforcing and lead to a repetition of the child's behavior. Less benign behavioral influences occur when parents force their child to dress or act like a member of the opposite sex, punishing same-sex behavior. In extreme cases, parents may give the child an opposite-sex nickname or buy only clothing typical of the opposite sex. Social-learning influences may arise if a child observes an opposite sex sibling receiving special attention for his or her behavior.

Family Theories

Theories of family influences on GID focus primarily on maternal psychopathology. They hold that mothers of boys with GID have psychopathology that affects their mothering, which in turn affects their son's identity development. For example, mothers of boys with GID report higher levels of depression and more often meet the criteria for Borderline Personality Disorder than do mothers of controls (Coates, 1990; Marantz and Coates, 1991). Depression may be present in as many as half of these mothers, and significant borderline pathology in as many as one-quarter (Coates, 1990). In addition, mothers of GID boys have been reported as having a strong "fear, anger, and devaluation of men. Mothers of GID boys frequently describe their sons as ... 'special, gentle, angelic, nonviolent, ... and sensitive' " (Coates, 1990, p. 423). In other words, the mothers' dislike of men is apparent, and they sometimes take pains to separate their sons from this image of men in general. Fathers are often the target of disparaging maternal remarks; many fathers are detached or absent from the family. Coates (1990) traces maternal devaluation of men to traumatic experiences with men.

Maternal psychopathology results in abnormal behavior on the part of the mother that communicates rejection of men and symbiosis with the son (Coates, 1990; Marantz and Coates, 1991). Marantz (Marantz and Coates, 1991) lists five types of maladaptive-symbiotic mother-son relationships: (1) dependent (on son), (2) difficulty separating (from son), (3) difficulty in differentiation of emotional states and boundaries, (4) intrusive control (of son), and (5) disapproving of (son's) relationships with others. This symbiotic behavior causes the son to take on characteristics of his mother, in order not to harm her and to win her favor. Furthermore, her rejection of stereotypically male roles and activities influences the types of activities that she reinforces and punishes for her son. It is likely, then, that a subgroup of GID mothers exhibits significant psychopathology that influences the development of their sons (Marantz and Coates, 1991).

It is important to note that not all cases of GID can be traced to maternal psychopathology. Certainly, other relatives and friends, as well as general societal messages, can have a profound influence on the gender identity of the child. Furthermore, theories emphasizing mothers are generally used only to explain the emergence of GID in boys. The development of GID in girls and in a subgroup of boys remains unexplained by maternal theories.

ASSESSMENT PATTERNS

A sample assessment battery for GID is shown in Table 13.8.

Broad Assessment Strategies

Cognitive Assessment

Clinician-Administered. Little research has been done to investigate the cognitive abilities of GID children. Rekers et al. (1991) report that their sample of twenty-nine gender-disturbed boys had a mean IQ of 108, with considerable variability within the sample (range of 72–141). Because matched controls were not used for comparison, it is not possible to say whether this IQ value is greater than average. No IQ subscale or achievement scores have been reported based on group or systematic research, and no data have been published regarding the cognitive status of GID girls. Based on the scant literature available, the IQ-achievement status of GID children as a group is expected to be average.

TABLE 13.8 Sample Assessment Battery for Gender Identity Disorder

PERSONALITY

Rorschach
Thematic Apperception Test

BEHAVIORAL

Child Behavior Checklist

FAMILY

Family Environment Scale

SYNDROME-SPECIFIC

Gender Behavior Inventory for Boys

Note: Assessment instruments are intended to supplement (not substitute for) a good clinical interview and, when possible, a structured diagnostic interview.

Psychological Assessment

Clinician-Administered.   The most striking diagnostic feature of children with GID is, of course, their behavior and gender attitudes. These are easily assessed with an interview and behavioral observations of the child at the office and *in vivo*. Younger children will often readily state their gender beliefs and preferences in interview. Older children, many of whom have endured teasing and isolation because of their preferences, may be more guarded.

In order to fully assess underlying beliefs and minimize defensiveness, projective tests may be used to supplement the observation and interview of GID children. On the Rorschach, GID boys often report seeing female figures such as ballerinas, cheerleaders, and female superheros (Coates, 1990). In addition, female clothing and other items related to female appearance are commonly identified. In more severe cases, gender confusion enters into the responses, as when a child transforms a response from one gender to another or combines gender in a percept (Coates, 1990).

Tuber and Coates (1989) report higher levels of two Rorschach special scores (confabulation and fabulized combination) in GID boys relative to controls. These special scores are sometimes categorized as thought-disordered responses. In addition, GID boys have been found to report more malevolent interactions between objects on the Rorschach (Tuber and Coates, 1989). Over all, the Rorschachs of GID boys are likely to be characterized by female and female-related percepts as well as occasional hostile and unusual responses. These responses should be carefully interpreted to provide a sense of the underlying thought and emotional processes. Rorschachs of GID girls have not been systematically studied but would be expected to be characterized by more stereotypically male responses.

Other projective tests such as the TAT and projective drawings are also occasionally used to reveal the personality dynamics of GID children. GID boys, for example, often draw female figures with female components emphasized (Coates, 1990). These drawings may provide an additional opportunity to discuss the child's preferences and beliefs.

Behavioral Assessment

Parent-Report.   Because GID children may be at risk for additional psychopathology, it is generally wise to administer a behavior problem checklist to the parents to screen for other difficulties. On the CBCL, GID boys often score in clinical ranges, especially for internalizing problems. Coates (1990), for example, reported that 84% of her sample of twenty-five GID boys scored in the clinical range. Most had symptoms of anxiety and depression, with half scoring in the clinical range on the depression factor. Two CBCL items have as their content behaving like the opposite sex or wishing to be of the opposite sex; these items can be used as an additional GID screen. CBCL results can also be used to assess the social functioning and social problems of the child.

Behavior problem scales related to social functioning (Withdrawn, Social Problems) and general internalizing problems (Anxiety/Depression) would be expected to be elevated for a GID child.

Family Assessment

Parent-Report. Assessment of parents of GID children has focused on the mothers of GID boys. Fathers are generally detached or absent, and mothers sometimes have enmeshed relationships with their GID sons. This feature suggests that assessment with the FES will indicate high Cohesion and Expressiveness scores, coupled with low Conflict and Independence scores. On the FACES-III, adaptability is likely to be reported as low, with these families showing controlling characteristics.

Coates (1990) suggests that many mothers of GID boys have significant psychopathology, including depression, borderline traits, fear/anger toward men, dependency, and low self-esteem. On the Beck Depression Inventory (Beck et al., 1961), mothers of boys with GID have been found to obtain scores averaging 15.8, with 46% falling in clinical ranges (Marantz and Coates, 1991); both of these values are greater than those obtained by controls. On the Diagnostic Interview for Borderlines (Gunderson, Kolb, and Austin, 1981), 25% of mothers of boys with GID obtained scores in the borderline range; their total, affect, psychosis, and interpersonal relations scores exceeded those of controls.

Although no systematic MMPI studies of mothers of GID children have been undertaken, some inferences can be made based on the observations of Coates (1990) and Marantz and Coates (1991). These mothers would be expected to show elevations on scales 2, 4, 6, 7, 8, and 0, reflecting their depression, low self-esteem, rejection of norms, anger, alienation from men or people in general, and poor or atypical social relationships. Their scale 5 score could indicate their own gender identification as well as passive-active tendencies in acting out this identification. Higher scale 5 may typify a more aggressive, openly defiant mother who clearly rejects the female gender role. A low scale 5 could reflect a more passive, nurturant mother who is in a symbiotic relationship with her son.

Syndrome-Specific Tests

Parent-Report

In addition to the general assessment instruments, several instruments have been developed to measure symptomatology specific to GID. The Gender Behavior Inventory for Boys (GBI; Bates, Bentler, and Thompson, 1973), for example, is a parent-report questionnaire that yields four factors: Extraversion, Feminine Behavior, Behavior Disturbance, and Mother's Boy. The fourth ("Mother's Boy") factor had relatively weak internal consistency and did not discriminate between normal and clinical samples. Thus, this six-item factor has been largely ignored. The remaining three factors, however, differentiate gender-disturbed from normal boys (Bates et al., 1973).

The Extraversion scale assesses friendliness and social/physical activity; the Feminine Behavior scale measures feminine and cross-gender behavior; the Behavior Disturbance scale contains diverse items relating to irritability, oppositionality, and emotional upset. Bates et al. (1973) found that gender-disturbed boys scored significantly higher on Feminine Behavior and Behavior Disturbance and lower on Extraversion than control boys. Similarly, Rekers and Morey (1989) reported that their sample of gender-disturbed boys scored significantly higher on Feminine Behavior and lower on Extraversion relative to norms. However, they found no difference for Behavior Disturbance. GBI Feminine Behavior and Extraversion scores have also been found to be related to the severity of gender disturbance (Rekers and Morey, 1989).

Clinician-Administered

A second GID-specific instrument was developed by Rekers, Kilgus, and Rosen (1991) for use in their study of the long-term effects of treatment of GID. This instrument asks professional raters to rate the gender behavior disturbance (defined as "maladaptive adoption of observable behaviors that are typically associated with the cross-sex role in conjunction with atypical avoidance of same-sex role behavior"; Rekers et al., 1991, p. 125) and gender identity disturbance (defined as "the desire to be a member of the opposite sex"; Rekers et al., 1991, p. 125) of a child on a 1 (extreme disturbance) to 5 (no disturbance) scale. Gender behavior disturbance and gender identity disturbance were found to be highly correlated (r = 0.72 [Rekers et al., 1991]). Gender-disturbed boys were found to average a gender behavior disturbance score of 3.17 (a value of 3 on this scale is assigned the descriptor "moderate gender behavior disturbance") and a gender identity score of 3.45 (a value of 3 on this scale is assigned the descriptor "gender identity confusion," while a value of 4 is designated "moderate cross-gender identification"). The Rekers et al. (1991) scale appears to have been specifically designed for that study alone. Therefore, its psychometric properties are unknown, norms are not available, and it should be used with caution in clinical settings.

☐ TREATMENT OPTIONS

Because GID is often associated with other types of psychopathology, a common initial question in therapy is what component of the psychopathology to address. In some children, mild gender dissatisfaction is merely a component associated with general dissatisfaction of self. For these children a focus on the underlying self-esteem issues may be more profitable than singling out the GID behaviors. For other children, however, the GID is clearly the most blatant and problematic behavior, and social isolation and psychopathology appear to be secondary to the GID. In these cases, the GID may be initially targeted, with the hope that the associated difficulties will abate when the GID is successfully treated. This section describes treatments for this latter group of children, in which GID is the major focus of treatment. Three types of treatment are commonly suggested for GID: behavior therapy, psychoanalytic/ psychodynamic therapy, and parent training/parent therapy (see Table 13.9).

Behavioral Interventions

Behavior therapy typically involves the use of attention reinforcement, self-monitoring, tangible reinforcement, or punishment to increase the frequency of same-gender behaviors and to decrease the frequency of cross-gender behaviors. Intervention targets are such behaviors as play with cross-sex toys, dressing in clothing of the opposite sex, fantasy/role playing of a member of the opposite sex, peer relationships, and motoric actions (Zucker, 1989, 1990b). Goal behaviors, consequently, are playing with same-sex toys, dressing in gender-appropriate clothing, establishment of same-sex relationships, and gender-appropriate mannerisms.

The crucial first step in behavior therapy for GID is the identification of the exact behaviors to be targeted. Parents are often distressed by their child's cross-sex behaviors and want all cross-sex behaviors to cease immediately. The tendency to target all cross-sex behaviors at once, however, can be overwhelming and confusing for the child. The targeting of a few clearly defined behaviors allows all parties involved to deal with a manageable group of contingencies. Clear definition of target behaviors prevents haggling over whether a specific behavior fits the "cross-sex" category or not.

TABLE 13.9   Treatment Options for Gender Identity Disorder

BEHAVIORAL INTERVENTIONS

Attention reinforcement
Self-monitoring
Reinforcement contingencies
Punishment techniques

PSYCHOTHERAPY

Play therapy

FAMILY INTERVENTIONS

Parent intervention/training
Family therapy

Note: This outline of options summarizes major treatments covered in the text. Specific treatments are often combined into an intervention package. Refer to the text for additional descriptions of each treatment. This table is not necessarily an exhaustive list of all treatments available.

Following the identification of target behaviors, a baseline level of behavior is identified. This baseline may either be a frequency count of cross-sex behaviors or a record of amount of time spent in cross-sex behaviors. The baseline record allows the parents to become familiar with behavior recording systems and, in some cases, increases the insight of the parents and the child into the magnitude of the problem. It also provides an initial data point from which to evaluate the effectiveness of future interventions.

Once specific behaviors are identified, they are matched with reinforcements, and, in some instances, punishments. A common intervention, for example, involves the use of attention as a reinforcer for appropriate behavior. Parents (and, in some cases, teachers, other caretakers, or even peers) are instructed to attend to same-sex behaviors and to ignore opposite sex behaviors (Zucker, 1990b). Another intervention involves the provision of tokens or other tangible primary or secondary reinforcers for appropriate behavior. This is often combined with a response cost intervention in which tokens are removed for inappropriate behavior. Finally, self-regulation has been suggested as an intervention that will promote generalization of same-sex behaviors to multiple contexts (Rekers and Varni, 1977). In this intervention the child is given a device, such as a wrist-counter and is taught to press it when engaging in a specific same-sex behavior. Initially the child is taught this self-monitoring behavior in a controlled setting such as a lab or office. The child is then instructed to continue this recording in the natural environment. The goal is to increase the counts of appropriate behavior during each week. This intervention has been reported to be very effective (Rekers and Varni, 1977; Zucker, 1990b), although it is highly dependent on the child's motivation.

Behavior therapy for GID has been reported to be effective both in the short and long term for reducing cross-gender behavior and increasing same-gender behavior (Rekers et al., 1991; Zucker, 1990b). Its effectiveness for changing the beliefs and affects associated with GID is less clear. Furthermore, most studies of behavior therapy effectiveness for GID are quite weak. Hence, only tentative conclusions can be drawn at this stage. For example, the extent to which behavioral improvements generalize to other contexts (especially those in which the reinforcer is absent) has not been studied. Despite these problems, however, behavior therapy has been one of the most extensively studied and supported interventions for GID.

Psychotherapy

Psychoanalytic/psychodynamic psychotherapy for GID has received at least as much attention as behavior therapy, but it suffers from a lack of published empirical research. Psychotherapy interventions usually target the early parent– (usually mother) child relationship and its effects on the child's current functioning. Specific themes addressed in psychoanalytic psychotherapy mirror those thought to be linked to the development of GID: symbiosis with the mother and overidentification with the mother following real or symbolic loss (Bleiberg et al., 1986; Coates, 1990). Loss causes separation anxiety in the child, which is alleviated by the adoption of the parent's behaviors. By behaving like the parent, the child can continue to feel attached to the parent. In order to abandon their GID behaviors, then, children must work through the loss of their attachment figure (Zucker, 1990b).

In preadolescent children, psychoanalytic therapy generally takes the form of psychoanalytic play therapy, in which the child is permitted to play out fantasies and concerns. The therapist, initially a nondirective partner in the play, gradually interprets the concerns and affects that the child manifests (Bleiberg et al., 1986). Interpretations usually focus on the fear of loss of the parent and anger toward caretakers. Another common theme to be interpreted is the fear of being different from the mother, leading to a withdrawal of her love and acceptance. This interpretation is particularly likely to arise when mothers reject and devalue men. Therapeutic interpretations, coupled with the nurturance and support of the therapeutic relationship, facilitate insight and working-through of anxiety provoking issues that underlie GID behavior.

Family Interventions

Parent Intervention and Training

The importance of including parents in the treatment of GID children has been underscored by several authors (Bradley and Zucker, 1990; Dulcan and Popper, 1991; Zucker, 1990b), largely because of the significant role that many parents have as identification and modeling figures for the child. The importance of a solid collaborative relationship with the parents cannot be overemphasized. Without such a relationship, parents will not accurately report on their child's behavior, and they may go so far as to sabotage a behavioral plan.

Once a therapeutic relationship is established with the parents, modification of parental attitudes and behaviors toward the child is important. Zucker (1990b) takes a directive approach, telling parents to discourage cross-sex behaviors such as cross-dressing, playing with cross-sex toys, playing with opposite-sex peers, and cross-sex mannerisms. Sex-appropriate or neutral activities such as playing with members of the same sex are encouraged. Parents are also encouraged to communicate to the child that they value him as a member of his own sex. In many cases a behavioral plan is arranged with parents to accomplish these goals.

Some parents are openly or passively resistant to these interventions, necessitating a focus on the issues of the couple, the family, or of the individual parent. Marital conflict, for example, may be played out in relationships with the children. The most common manifestation of this is for one parent to be enmeshed with the child while the other parent is disengaged from the family. The enmeshed relationship between the child and opposite-sex parent fosters and maintains the GID. The family system resists any change in this parent–child relationship because this would require a focus on and a change in the marital relationship. Hence, the crux of the issue is the marriage. In this case, marital therapy may be necessary to address the parents' problems before work on the child's GID can begin (Bradley and Zucker, 1990).

When only one parent is involved in the resistance to treatment, individual psychotherapy may be warranted. Such parental difficulties as depression, borderline personality disorder, and devaluation of men have been suggested as underlying GID. These long-standing problems are likely to interfere with suggestions of parent behavior change. Some parents may be deriving secondary psychological gain from their child's GID, as when a socially isolated mother enmeshes with her son and derives narcissistic pleasure from his imitation of her. Clinicians must be wary of parental psychopathology that could interfere with treatment; the initial focus of GID therapy may need to be on the problems of such parents.

Family Therapy

In some families the child's GID is a family affair. The initial signs that family therapy may be necessary are the presence of GID in more than one child, boundary difficulties between parents and children, or evidence that family life is organized around the GID of the child. When this is the case, structural interventions (e.g., Minuchin, 1974) to address family boundary issues and strategic interventions (Haley, 1976) to alter family behaviors are necessary components of treatment. Despite their insistence that they are committed to treatment, some families are unintentionally resistant to interventions because they fear the repercussions of a change in the family system. Discussion of the family structure and the role of the GID symptoms in family life can reveal the dynamics underlying the family's resistance. Restructuring the family is usually necessary in these cases.

■ Reactive Attachment Disorder

CLINICAL DESCRIPTION

Diagnostic Considerations

Reactive Attachment Disorder of Infancy or Early Childhood (RAD) refers to a disturbed pattern of attachment behavior seen in some infants and toddlers. This disturbed attachment behavior takes one of two forms: (1) failure to attach or positively respond to people or (2) indiscriminate attachment to multiple people, regardless of familiarity or caretaking function. Children with the former RAD presentation are classified as "inhibited type," while those with the latter RAD presentation are classified as "disinhibited type."

According to DSM-IV, RAD begins before the age of 5 and cannot be the result of mental retardation or a pervasive developmental disorder. In addition to abnormal social-attachment behavior, there must be some evidence of grossly abnormal or negative care, such as abuse, neglect, or multiple change of primary caregiver. It is presumed that this abnormal or negative care is responsible for the attachment disturbance. RAD is reportedly uncommon in the general population of infants and toddlers (American Psychiatric Association, 1994), although it is more common in certain situations (e.g., extended hospitalizations, parental neglect).

RAD overlaps substantially with the medical diagnosis of nonorganic failure-to-thrive (NOFT), a disorder in which infants and toddlers fail to grow physically and to develop socially. NOFT has several hallmarks (Tibbits-Kleber and Howell, 1985; Green, 1989; Kelley & Heffer, 1990):

- Weight below third percentile for age
- Normal head circumference
- Malnourished or emaciated appearance
- Weight loss or failure to gain weight
- Abnormal social development (often unresponsive or unusually responsive to social stimuli)
- Delayed achievement of physical developmental milestones
- Not due to organic causes

Some cases of failure-to-thrive (FTT) are due to physiological problems; these cases are classified as organic failure-to-thrive and are not attributed to psychological factors.

A new DSM-IV diagnosis, Feeding Disorder of Infancy or Early Childhood (FDI), is analogous to NOFT, and, therefore, is likely to co-occur with RAD. FDI is characterized by a failure to eat adequately, stagnant weight or weight loss, and onset prior to age 6. Because the FDI diagnosis is a new one, little research has been performed on the DSM-IV–defined FDI diagnosis *per se*. In the absence of specific FDI research, it must be assumed that NOFT research pertains to FDI cases. Hence, characteristics of FDI children will overlap substantially with those of RAD and NOFT children.

Like RAD, NOFT/FDI is thought to be caused by maladaptive parent–child relationships in many cases. These maladaptive relationships may result in a lack of stimulation for the child, which could cause growth deficits by way of neuroendocrinological mechanisms (Tibbits-Kleber and Howell, 1985). In addition, maladaptive parent–child relationships often become manifest at mealtimes, resulting in abnormal feeding behavior by the RAD child. Parents and RAD/NOFT/FDI children frequently engage in power struggles over food, and mealtime is often a time of anxiety and conflict. The resultant failure of the child to ingest adequate nutrition causes the growth deficit characteristic of NOFT (Kelley and Heffer, 1990; Hathaway, 1989; Green, 1989).

While little doubt exists that RAD and NOFT co-occur, some confusion apparently exists over the exact relationship between the two conditions. Some authors (e.g., Tibbits-Kleber and Howell, 1985) imply that RAD is merely the psychiatric component of NOFT, which is a purely physiologically defined (e.g., weight and size requirements) diagnosis. According to this definition, complete overlap exists between RAD and NOFT, which differ only in the type of symptoms to which they refer. Other authors see RAD as a "subset of nonorganic FTT" (Dulcan & Popper, 1991, p. 92), suggesting that some children with NOFT may not fit the diagnostic criteria of RAD. A final hypothesized relationship between RAD and NOFT conceptualizes NOFT as one manifestation of RAD, which may be manifest in other ways as well (Green, 1989). DSM-IV has taken a significant step toward simplifying matters by defining RAD and FDI as separate diagnoses. Hence, RAD children may or may not have an FDI. Likewise, FDI children may or may not exhibit RAD. The DSM-IV system appears to be the most accurate, allowing some flexibility in the application of the RAD diagnosis to children other than those with NOFT/FDI. Furthermore, no diagnostic requirement exists that children with RAD have a feeding or NOFT problem (American Psychiatric Association, 1994). Hence, while a diagnosis of NOFT/FDI is suggestive of RAD, it is neither necessary nor sufficient for the diagnosis.

Psychosocial dwarfism (or psychosocially determined short stature) is another medical diagnosis that may co-occur frequently with RAD (Green, 1989). This disorder generally emerges around age 2–3 and is characterized by a marked decrease in growth rate following an earlier period of approximately normal growth. Height is typically below the third percentile and bone growth is clearly stunted. Although the condition cannot be the result of malnutrition or other physical disorders, growth hormone levels are often found to be abnormally low or inconsistent. When children with psychosocial dwarfism are removed from their typical environment, growth returns to normal (see Green, 1989, for proposed diagnostic criteria for psychosocial dwarfism).

Like NOFT, psychosocial dwarfism is hypothesized to result from a maladaptive caretaker–child relationship such as that typically seen in RAD. Green (1989), for example, cites a "severely disturbed relationship between primary caretaker and child" (p. 1897) or child abuse as diagnostically important for the psychosocial dwarfism diagnosis. The effects of the parent–child relationship on stimulation and arousal adversely impact the endocrinological functioning of the child, including the regulation of growth hormone. Therefore, when this relationship is removed, hormone levels and growth return to normal (Green, 1989).

Appearance and Features

(Appearance and features of RAD are listed in Table 13.10.) Children with RAD often appear socially or developmentally delayed. For example, they may fail to smile in response to a playful person (at around 2 months), fail to engage in simple social games/play (at around 5 months), or fail to bond with a primary caretaker (at around 8 months)(Dulcan and Popper, 1991). Other characteristics of the RAD infant are lethargy, slow weight gain, weight loss, feeding problems, resistance to being held, poor visual tracking, lack of interest in the social environment, and verbal delays (American Psychiatric Association, 1994;

TABLE 13.10 Appearance and Features of Reactive Attachment Disorder

COMMON FEATURES

Failure to attach or indiscriminate attachment
Abnormal or negative care (abuse, neglect, separation from caretaker)
Nonorganic failure-to-thrive (weight loss, feeding problem)
Lack of stimulation from environment
Impaired social relationships
Lethargy
Resistance to being held
Lack of interest in social environment or excessive interest in strangers
Ambivalent or disinterested attitude of parent toward child
Failure of parent to respond to social cues of child

OCCASIONAL FEATURES

Developmental (especially language) delay
Parental psychopathology: insecurity, depression, dependence
Parental stress: marital distress, social isolation
Lack of parenting knowledge
Family conflict/family stress

Note: The features listed above are often seen but are not universal. Some features may be diagnostically relevant or required, while others may not be required for diagnosis. "Common" features are typical of the disorder; "occasional" features appear frequently but are not necessarily seen in a majority of cases.

Dulcan and Popper, 1991). RAD children with indiscriminate sociability display excessive interest and positive affect with strangers. They are often clingy, even with unfamiliar adults, and become immediately emotionally involved with new people. These infants and toddlers are often favorites in hospitals and institutions because they are extremely friendly and accepting of adults. However, their apparent "attachment" is fleeting because of their tendency to substitute one adult for another.

Because of the centrality of the parent-child relationship in the diagnosis and explanation of RAD, considerable attention has been devoted to identifying characteristics of families whose children develop RAD. Although no personality type can be attributed to *all* parents of RAD children, at least two subgroups of RAD parents can be identified. The first group are parents who are interested and invested in their child but who are physically or emotionally separated from their child because of circumstances beyond their control. Severe child illness, severe parent illness, traumatic or chronic stress, or extreme child behavior problems may result in these separations. Recovery from the effects of extended parent–child separation can take months or years, during which the child may exhibit RAD behavior. These parents are rarely described in the RAD literature, perhaps because their children tend to improve with minimal intervention.

The second group of RAD parents are those who have characteristics that interfere with appropriate parenting behavior and the formation of a parent–child relationship. Although little is known about fathers in this second group, the characteristics of mothers in this group are well documented. Many mothers of RAD children in this group are described as insecure, unhappy, dependent, and having low self-esteem (Tibbits-Kleber and Howell, 1985). Fischhoff (1989) suggests that the mother's psychological difficulties are, in most cases, the primary cause of RAD, minimizing the role of the child. He reviews literature that suggests that these mothers have had numerous stresses, both during their own development as well as during their child's pregnancy and infancy. In particular, these mothers frequently encounter social stresses such as marital distress, social isolation, and strained financial resources. These stresses may detract from their attention toward the child and may hinder their caretaking ability. In addition, Fischhoff (1989) describes these mothers as characterized by "low self-esteem, isolation, alienation, and deprivation" (p. 740).

Possibly most important, however, is the mother's attitude toward the child. Tibbits-Kleber and Howell (1985) suggest that RAD mothers often feel ambivalent toward their child and toward their mothering role, leading to difficulty interacting with the infant in a nurturing and supportive way. Furthermore, they may have a lack of knowledge about parenting that contributes to their unease about their role. Disagreement exists over whether a higher incidence of psychopathology exists in RAD mothers (Tibbits-Kleber and Howell, 1985; Fischhoff, 1989), although there is general agreement that they are often stressed, have low self-esteem, and are uncomfortable or careless about the mothering role. Interestingly, little is known about RAD fathers; the little clinical and research data that exist suggest that these fathers tend to be detached from or in conflict with the mother and infant. It is likely that mothers *and* fathers contribute to the development of RAD, although most attention has been on mothers.

Very little is known about infant characteristics that predate RAD, although it seems possible that these infants may tend to be temperamentally difficult. Combined with a vulnerable parent, this temperamental difficulty could lead to parental frustration, child distress, and maladaptive interactions characteristic of RAD. Once RAD has emerged, these infants appear developmentally delayed and may show behavioral and social disturbances (Tibbits-Kleber and Howell, 1985).

In addition to traits of the parent and child considered in isolation, certain aspects of the parent–child interaction are characteristic of RAD. Diagnostically relevant is the tendency of the child to show no special preference for the parent. In some cases this lack of child attachment follows from an almost complete absence of the parent or failure to assume a unique and important caretaking role. When the mother is present, she tends to place the child in an "interacting" position (i.e., a position that would lead to parent–child interaction, such as face-to-face, or in proximity) only infrequently. Furthermore, the parent may not notice or may be unresponsive toward the child's cues or bids for interaction, such as cries, vocalizations, or movement (Fischhoff, 1989).

Distress, delight, or interest on the part of the infant is ignored or minimized, and the parent's attempts to provide the child with stimulation are either ill-timed or altogether absent. Over all, the parent–child interaction seems, at best, out of sync or, at worst, neglectful; the parent appears either not to know or not to care what the child is feeling or communicating.

At no time is this pathological interaction more apparent than during feeding, perhaps because feeding represents a potential time of nurturance and satisfaction of the child's needs. Some parents are not sensitive to their children's feeding rhythm and feed them too quickly or too slowly, provoking a negative response from the children. This response leads to parental frustration and a continuation or worsening of the abnormal feeding interaction. Other parents misjudge infant cues of satiety, mistakenly thinking that their children are hungry or full when they are not. This can lead to over- or underfeeding, which causes the infant to associate feeding with unpleasantness (Fischhoff, 1989). In some cases the child has a bona fide medical problem (e.g., reflux) that creates an initial problem with the feeding interaction. However, even after this medical problem is corrected, the history of maladaptive feeding interaction remains and can affect feeding and attachment behavior.

In other cases, family characteristics interfere with the feeding. Family conflict, for example, may emerge when the family gathers to eat, creating a tense or loud atmosphere that is not conducive to relaxed infant feeding. Other children may demand much of the parents' attention, distracting them from the infant's cues and preventing parent–infant interaction during feeding. Any of these situations may lead to an association of feeding with discomfort and distress, causing the infant to be fussy and avoidant at mealtime.

The course of RAD is variable but can be serious. In cases of NOFT/FDI or other feeding difficulties, malnutrition, growth deformity, and developmental delays are significant risks. For infants in this category, immediate medical intervention is essential. Social deprivation can lead to difficulty forming positive attachments and to problematic social development. In severe cases, future behavior problems and personality disturbances characterized by relationship difficulties are a risk (Tibbits-Kleber and Howell, 1985). Cognitive delay or impairment can occur in severe RAD cases, particularly those characterized by co-occurring feeding disorders. Some studies report that as many as two-thirds of RAD children have a reading disorder (Hufton & Oates, 1977).

Etiology

Underlying the RAD diagnosis is the assumption that children need to emotionally "attach" to one or a few primary caretakers. Attachment is shown by recognition, preference, and positive emotional response to a caretaker, coupled with wariness of unfamiliar people. Bowlby (1952) hypothesized that this attachment was naturally selected through millennia of evolution, and numerous theorists have emphasized the importance of early attachment for later adjustment. Observations of cognitive, emotional, and social impairment in children who have been deprived of caretakers (Spitz, 1945) have convincingly shown the importance of interaction with a primary caretaker for normal development. Because attachment is thought to be a normal and adaptive behavior for the human species, deviations from this behavior are likely to be maladaptive.

RAD is associated with several environmental factors and medical presentations. Based on these factors and presentations, children with RAD can be classified into several overlapping groups. Each group can be considered a risk factor for the presence or development of RAD (Fischhoff, 1989):

1. Children who have been hospitalized repeatedly and/or extensively, either for medical or psychological problems ("hospitalism")
2. Children who have been placed in institutions and have received little attention from caretaking figures ("institutionalism")
3. Children from abusive or neglectful homes
4. Children who fail to develop normally because of maladaptive parent–child interactions and relationships such as conflict and double-binding (in this category are the diagnoses of NOFT and psychosocial dwarfism).

Hospitalism, institutionalism, abuse/neglect, and maladaptive interactions are thought to cause RAD because they are deviations in normal attachment between parent and child. In hospitals and institutions, infants have multiple caretakers, often spend less time with parents, and are not in a stable home environment. Hence, opportunities for a normal attachment relationship with a primary caretaker are lessened. These children sometimes indiscriminately attach to any caretaker, reflecting their experience of multiple adult caretakers, none of whom has a primary role. Children from abusive/neglectful homes, on the other hand, may form tenuous or ambivalent attachments (if any) to their unpredictable parents.

ASSESSMENT PATTERNS

A sample assessment battery for RAD is shown in Table 13.11.

Broad Assessment Strategies

Cognitive Assessment

Clinician-Administered.   Observations that RAD children may have cognitive delays suggest the need for sensory, motor, and cognitive assessment. Tests such as the Bayley-II may indicate intellectual and motor deficits. The Vineland Adaptive Behavior Scales (VABS) can provide insights into infants' development of adaptive behavior. Over all, it is important to track these infants cognitively because of the long-term intellectual risks of a lack of social-environmental stimulation.

TABLE 13.11 Sample Assessment Battery for Reactive Attachment Disorder

COGNITIVE

Vineland Adaptive Behavior Scales

BEHAVIORAL

Child Behavior Checklist

FAMILY

Family Environment Scale
Parent MMPI (when possible)

Note: Assessment instruments are intended to supplement (not substitute for) a good clinical interview and, when possible, a structured diagnostic interview.

Behavioral Assessment

Parent-Report.   Some indications exist that RAD children are at risk for long-term behavior problems such as externalizing problems and enuresis (Tibbits-Kleber and Howell, 1985). Hence, it may be warranted to track these children regularly with behavior problem checklists such as the MCBC or the CBCL.

Family Assessment

Parent-Report.   Formal psychological assessment may be helpful in understanding parental contributions to the dynamics underlying maladaptive RAD family interactions. Although little research addresses the assessment characteristics of mothers of RAD children, there is a body of research on mothers of NOFT children. NOFT research may be applied to RAD mothers, since NOFT and RAD overlap. Furthermore, NOFT research probably directly pertains to FDI cases, since FDI criteria so closely resemble those of NOFT. No assessment research exists on fathers of RAD or NOFT/FDI children.

Maternal defensiveness or denial may appear on the MMPI as an elevated L for low SES mothers or K for higher SES mothers. Additional elevations for distressed RAD mothers may be expected on scales 2 and 7, reflecting emotional upset or depression. An elevated scale 4 likely indicates troubles in the current family or family of origin and should be followed up by a Dyadic Adjustment Scale and FES. Difficulties with empathy and nurturance may be manifest in a 4-5 code type for women. Scales 3 and 0 indicate the mother's social presentation; mothers with a high 3 and low 0 are likely to be selfish and needy/dependent in relationships. They may be unable to give their infant sufficient stimulation because they themselves are in need of attention and validation from others. Mothers with a low 3 and high 0 may be reclusive, introverted, and avoidant of any social relationships. Elevations on scales 6 and 8 suggest a more pathological process underlying the RAD, with suspiciousness, anger, attributional biases, and lack of cognitive control driving the maladaptive parent–child interaction. Empirical research is needed to identify "typical" MMPI patterns for RAD mothers as well as RAD subgroups that may need different types of intervention. No research exists on the MMPI patterns of RAD fathers, but their presentation may be similar to that of RAD mothers.

Contrary to clinical observation, mothers of NOFT children tend to score in the same ranges as do other mothers on measures of self-esteem (Benoit, Zeanah, and Barton, 1989). It is possible, however, that this finding reflects defensiveness or denial on the part of the NOFT mothers. If defensiveness is suspected, the mother should be administered an MMPI, using the preceding interpretation guidelines.

Assessment of the marital relationships of NOFT mothers often reveals troubled marriages. NOFT mothers report significantly lower marital satisfaction on the Dyadic Adjustment Scale (Spanier, 1976). In one study, 36% of partners of mothers of NOFT children were substance abusers, a value 3 times as high as that for controls (Benoit et al., 1989). Similar problems may be expected on the FES, with some NOFT mothers elevating the Conflict and Control subscales in conjunction with deficits on Cohesion, Active-Recreational Orientation, and Intellectual-Cultural Orientation. Defensive mothers, on the other hand, may report high Cohesion and low Conflict. Assessment of the marital and family environment may suggest potential sources of difficulty and sources of intervention for these RAD families.

Because of marital and family difficulties, NOFT mothers often look for support outside of their families. Measures of social support such as the Social Support Questionnaire (Sarason et al., 1983) may provide some insight into the constellation of social support experienced by the NOFT mother. NOFT mothers report less social support from within the family but more social support from nonfamily sources (Benoit et al., 1989).

Assessment of NOFT fathers is also important, but much less is known about their personality characteristics. The role of the father in the family life and the status of the father–child relationship are important starting points in paternal assessment. Administration of the MMPI and FES to the father may provide some insight into his role in the family.

Syndrome-Specific Tests

Clinician-Administered

The evaluation of the family of a child with RAD should include careful observation by the clinician of parent–child and parent–parent interactions. The importance of first-hand observation cannot be overstated, because parents of RAD children may be unreliable reporters of their behavior and interactions (Fischhoff, 1989). Following is a list of items to be attended to in the observations of a RAD family. Although this list was compiled based on a review of

RAD literature and clinical observations of RAD families, no individual item should be considered exclusively representative of a RAD family (Dulcan and Popper, 1991; Fischhoff, 1989; Tibbits-Kleber and Howell, 1985):

CHARACTERISTICS OF THE PARENT(S)

- Lack of parenting confidence, low self-esteem, anxiety about parenting skill
- Lack of adequate observation of the child
- Lack of interest in the child (in hospitals and institutions, often manifest by infrequent or brief parental visits)
- Appearance of being under great stress, which appears to impact on caretaking ability
- Overt psychopathology
- Emotional lability
- Social awkwardness
- Attention to child's physical but not emotional needs
- Frustration/anger over feeding
- Overtly hostile/adversarial marital interaction
- One parent detached from family
- Lack of empathy for child
- Blaming child for problems
- Inappropriate expectations of child, relative to developmental level

CHARACTERISTICS OF THE PARENT–CHILD INTERACTION

- Lack of physical or emotional nurturance
- Inappropriate amount/timing of stimulation
- Inappropriate reactions to child's emotional behavior
- Failure to place infant in an interacting position
- Lack of communication between parent and infant (e.g., parent cannot or does not read infant's cues; infant may not attempt to engage parent)
- Adversarial feeding interaction (observation of the feeding interaction is often essential in the understanding of the RAD syndrome)
- Inconsistency in interaction, varying from pleasant/engaged to hostile to mutual disinterest
- Forced separation of parent and child because of illness or other problem

CHARACTERISTICS OF THE CHILD

- Developmental delay
- Feeding difficulty

- Thin, frail appearance
- Lack of eye contact, failure to engage socially, lack of attention to social environment
- Lethargic, inactive
- Resistance, withdrawing from nurturant tactile stimulation
- Fussy; easily upset
- In infants with indiscriminate sociability, smiling, reaching to be held by strangers; immediate change of preference for different caretakers

TREATMENT OPTIONS

Treatment options are outlined in Table 13.12.

Medical Evaluation/Hospitalization

Initial treatment attention must be paid to the medical needs of the RAD child. Many of these children are undernourished or neglected and require immediate medical attention. In fact, RAD children often present with medical problems in pediatric hospitals and are only later evaluated for RAD. Medical treatment typically consists of measures to increase nourishment and body weight, which may range from regular feeding to placement of a G-tube. If the infant thrives in the hospital environment after failing to gain weight at home (and this is often the case within the first 2 weeks), intervention with parents is essential prior to hospital discharge to prevent a recurrence of the weight loss and other feeding problems.

The provision of regular stimulation is a routine psychological intervention for RAD children. This increase in stimulation must be provided gradually to avoid overwhelming the child (Green, 1989). Placement of a mobile above the crib, coupled with frequent, regular social contact is usually beneficial. The social contact should include tactile, visual, and auditory stimulation, with extensive verbal stimulation. Ideally, this contact should occur with a small, consistent set of adults and one primary caretaker, in order to increase the possibility for attachment. Assignment of a small group of primary nurses and one or two parent figures (who make regular, extended visits) is often necessary to achieve this goal (Tibbits-Kleber and Howell, 1985).

Behavioral Interventions

Behavioral treatments are typically used with RAD children to address associated features of RAD, such as feeding problems. A typical behavioral plan for feeding problems begins with a careful observation and analysis of mealtime, ideally with videotape of the interaction. These observations are then used to identify problem behaviors of the child, antecedents of these problem behaviors, and their consequences.

TABLE 13.12   Treatment Options for Reactive Attachment Disorder

MEDICAL EVALUATION/HOSPITALIZATION

Evaluation for physical problems

Enforced, monitored feeding or G-tube placement if nutritional/growth status is a risk

Provision of regular stimulation and social interaction

Identification of one or two primary caretakers for the child; avoid multiple caretakers

BEHAVIORAL INTERVENTIONS (for children with at-risk nutritional or growth status)

Allow the child to play with the food to reduce aversion to the presence of food

Do not force the child to eat; do not use utensils to force food into the child's mouth

Do not allow "grazing"

Ignore resistant or oppositional behavior

Praise eating behaviors

Reduce distractions during mealtimes as much as possible

Allow toddlers to feed themselves

Do not allow access to desserts or snacks until the child has eaten the food required for the meal

Model eating behavior during the child's meals; allow the child to eat in the presence of other people who are eating

FAMILY INTERVENTIONS

Parent–child therapy
    Educating parents about treatment
    Modeling
    Support for parent

Family therapy

Marital therapy

Parent psychotherapy

HOME MONITORING AND PROTECTIVE REMOVAL

Temporary separation of parent and child

Home visits by social worker

"Parental holiday" while child is hospitalized

Note: This outline of options summarizes major treatments covered in the text. Because of the overlap of Reactive Attachment Disorder and Failure-to-Thrive, many of these interventions presume a concurrent problem with feeding and growth. Specific treatments are often combined into an intervention package. Refer to the text for additional descriptions of each treatment. This table is not necessarily an exhaustive list of all treatments available.

Typically, the feeding problem behaviors of the RAD child involve pushing food away from the mouth; refusal to open the mouth; throwing food, utensils, or dishes; spitting food out; screaming; squirming; turning the head away from food; trying to get out of the chair; failure to attend to the food; or failure to attend to the parent who is feeding the child. Initial maladaptive consequences are usually things such as criticism, screaming at the child, stuffing food or utensils into the child's mouth, giving the child increased attention during food refusal, distracting the child from the meal with a toy, looking exasperated, feeding the child too quickly, or not allowing the child to choose the type of food to be eaten next. In order to address these problems, behavior techniques teach the caretaker to reduce consequences that may be reinforcing or aversive to the child. Several specific guidelines are often followed:

- For children who have an aversion to the presence or texture of food, allow them to handle and play with the food before asking them to eat it. This will increase their familiarity with food and desensitize them to its presence.
- Encourage, but do not force, the child to eat. *Never* force a utensil into the child's mouth.
- Do not allow the child to "graze" during the day. Grazing involves nibbling at snacks throughout the day so that the child is not hungry at mealtimes. In infants this usually occurs when the infant is allowed to have a milk-filled bottle at all times. A typical feeding day for a NOFT child involves three meals and two to four snacks, which must be eaten at certain, discrete times. If the child does not eat at snack or mealtime, the food is removed until the next feeding.
- Ignore resistant or oppositional behavior during mealtimes. This ignoring should be done by looking away and remaining silent for 5 seconds. If the child persists in the negative behavior, ignoring should continue until the child stops.
- Praise eating behavior, even for small bites or attempts.
- Unless absolutely necessary, do not use toys or other attention-getting devices to reward the child during mealtime. These often distract the child from the meal interaction.
- Allow toddlers to take more responsibility for the feeding interaction. This may be accomplished by letting them feed themselves and choose the order in which they eat food from their plate. Finger food is often appealing to toddlers.
- Do not place desserts or other snacks on the child's plate until the child has eaten the food required for the meal.
- Allow the child to eat in the presence of other people who are eating, unless this is too distracting to the child.
- Remove toys and other distractions from the feeding area.

Family Interventions

If the parent is expected to be involved in the child's future care, intervention at the level of the parent–child relationship is necessary (Green, 1989). Such parent–child therapy begins with psychoeducation of the parent about interaction with children in general and about the needs and behaviors of RAD children in particular. Parenting skills classes about attachment, discipline, and parental stress management may also be helpful. Psychoeducation is accompanied by *in vivo* interactions between the therapist, parent, and infant. The therapist observes the parent's interaction with the child and discusses this interaction with the parent. Parents should be taught to attend to the child's cues, especially cues to initiate and terminate parent–child interaction. In many cases, parents must be taught to be less directive and controlling in interactions with the child. Other parents must be taught how to observe the child with sustained, nondirective watching behavior. Interaction components that the child finds appealing may be identified and taught to the parent. Finally, parents often benefit from observing the therapist's interaction with the child.

Related to parent–child therapy, family therapy interventions may also be helpful. These interventions may take several forms, including education of family members, provision of instrumental and emotional support, restructuring of family relationships, and improvement of the marital relationship (Tibbits-Kleber and Howell, 1985; Green, 1989; Fischhoff, 1989). Provision of support may be particularly important for parents who are experiencing significant stresses. These parents may be overwhelmed with their life situation and may regard the child as yet another stressor. Assistance with coping skills such as problem solving (how to care for the child adequately in the context of current stress), cognitive restructuring (seeing the child as a source of happiness as opposed to as a source of stress), and approach-coping (attending to the behavior and needs of the child without feeling overwhelmed) may be a crucial area of needed support. Instrumental support such as financial assistance for food and materials for stimulation may also be necessary. Because providing this support requires a good therapeutic relationship, relationship building is an important component in working with RAD parents.

Marital and family therapy should also attend to issues such as adversarial interactions between family members and disengagement of one or both parents. In some cases, adversarial interactions between spouses occur in front of the child, who withdraws from the environment in order to avoid the negative stimulation. In other cases it is the parent(s) who withdraw from the child, engaging in avoidant or neglectful behavior. The impact of these behaviors on the child should be discussed, and alternative behaviors should be found. Parents should also be encouraged to discuss their feelings about being parents and their feelings toward the child. The effect of the child's behavior on the parents is often an important topic; many parents have never had a chance to process their response to the child. Unrealistic expectations or attributions of the child can be challenged and reframed in order to alter the parents' emotional response to the child.

It is often also necessary to do individual work with one or both parents. In individual psychotherapy, parental psychopathology should be addressed, particularly as this psychopathology affects the parent's relationship with the child. As in family therapy, the parent should be encouraged to discuss expectations, feelings, disappointments, and frustrations related to the child. Many parents will initially deny problems, fearing that their child will be removed from their care. Hence, formation of a trusting therapeutic relationship is generally the first step in this therapy.

Home Monitoring and Protective Removal

Some severe cases of RAD warrant more extreme interventions, such as temporary separation of parent and child, required home visits by a social worker, or even removal of the infant from the parents' care. This decision is usually made based on a combination of four factors: the severity of abuse/neglect, medical status of the child, willingness of the parent to change through psychological intervention, and psychological stability of the parent.

In some cases of hospitalized RAD children who are refusing to eat, a "parental holiday" may be suggested as a way to break the cycle of negative parent–child interactions at mealtimes. This "holiday" serves several purposes: First, it allows the parent to be away from the stress of the child and hospital. A reduction of stress often results in more parental patience and tolerance. Second, it allows greater control of feeding interactions, which are usually conducted by a nurse, psychologist, or feeding specialist in the absence of the parent. Third, the time spent away from the parent may result in a weakening of the child's association of the parent with certain adversarial mealtime behaviors. Ideally, when the parent is returned to the mealtime interaction (typically after 1–3 days), the cycle of adversarial interaction is broken.

Many parents are, understandably, vehemently opposed to separation from their child in the form of a parental holiday. They see that their child is "sick" enough to be in the hospital and want to be there to support and monitor the child. Also, parents are often given the message that their child's NOFT and RAD are their fault; thus, they regard the holiday as a further sign of their failure and possibly as the precursor to permanent separation. Therefore, the parental holiday must be suggested with tact, understanding, and support. Parents should be given a chance to express their concerns. Ideally, a trusted doctor or nurse should be present or should make the suggestion of a holiday. Finally, the rationale for the holiday should be explained, with reassurance that the parents are not being blamed for the problem.

References

Afnan, S., and Carr, A. (1989). Interdisciplinary treatment of a case of elective mutism. *British Journal of Occupational Therapy, 52,* 61–66.

American Psychiatric Association (1987). *Diagnostic and statistical manual of mental disorders* (3d ed., rev.). Washington, DC: Author.

American Psychiatric Association. (1994).*Diagnostic and statistical manual of mental disorders* (4th ed.). Washington, DC: Author.

Atoynatan, T. H. (1986). Elective mutism: Involvement of the mother in the treatment of the child. *Child Psychiatry and Human Development, 17,* 15–27.

Azrin, N. H., and Nunn, R. G. (1973). Habit-reversal: A method of eliminating nervous habits and tics. *Behavior Research and Therapy, 11,* 619–628.

Azrin, N. H., and Peterson, A. L. (1989). Reduction of an eye tic by controlled blinking. *Behavior Therapy, 20,* 467–473.

_____ . (1990). Treatment of Tourette syndrome by habit reversal: A waiting-list control group comparison. *Behavior Therapy, 21,* 305–318.

Bates, J. E., Bentler, P. M., and Thompson, S. K. (1979). Gender deviant boys compared with normal and clinical control boys. *Journal of Abnormal Child Psychology, 7,* 243–259.

Bates, J. E., Bentler, P. M., and Thompson, S. K. (1973). Measurement of deviant gender development in boys. *Child Development, 44,* 591–598.

Beck, A. T., Ward, C. H., Mendelson, M., Mock, J., and Erbaugh, J. (1961). An inventory for measuring depression. *Archives of General Psychiatry, 4,* 561–571.

Benoit, D., Zeanah, C. H., and Barton, M. L. (1989). Maternal attachment disturbances in failure to thrive. *Infant Mental Health Journal, 10,* 185–202.

Blake, P., and Moss, T. (1967). The development of socialization skills in an electively mute child. *Behavior Research and Therapy, 5,* 349–356.

Bleiberg, E., Jackson, L., and Ross, J. L. (1986). Gender Identity Disorder and object loss. *Journal of the American Academy of Child Psychiatry, 25,* 58–67.

Bornstein, R. A. (1990). Neuropsychological performance in children with Tourette's syndrome. *Psychiatry Research, 33,* 73–81.

Bornstein, R. A., and Baker, G. B. (1991). Neuropsychological performance and urinary phenylethylamine in Tourette's syndrome. *Journal of Neuropsychiatry and Clinical Neurosciences, 3,* 417–421.

Bornstein, R. A., Baker, G. B., Bazylewich, T., and Douglass, A. B. (1991). Tourette syndrome and neuropsychological performance. *Acta Psychiatrica Scandinavia, 84,* 212–216.

Bornstein, R. A., and Yang, V. (1991). Neuropsychological performance in medicated and unmedicated patients with Tourette's Disorder. *American Journal of Psychiatry, 148,* 468–471.

Bowlby, J. (1952). *Maternal care and mental health* (2d ed.). New York: Shocken.

Bradley, S. J., Blanchard, R., Coates, S., Green, R., Levine, S. B., Meyer-Bahlburg, H. F. L., Pauly, I. B., and Zucker, K. J. (1991). Interim report of the DSM-IV subcommittee on gender identity disorders. *Archives of Sexual Behavior, 20,* 333–343.

Bradley, S.J., & Zucker, K.J. (1990). Gender Identity Disorder and psychosexual problems in children and adolescents. *Canadian Journal of Psychiatry, 35,* 477–486.

Bronheim, S. (1991). An educator's guide to Tourette syndrome. *Journal of Learning Disabilities, 24,* 17–22.

Brown, B., and Doll, B. (1988). Case illustration of classroom intervention with an elective mute child. *Special Services in the Schools, 5,* 107–125.

Brown, J., and Lloyd, H. (1975). A controlled study of children not speaking at school. *Journal of the Association of Workers with Maladjusted Children, 10,* 49–63.

Brunn, R. D. (1984). Gilles de la Tourette syndrome: An overview of clinical experience. *Journal of the American Academy of Child Psychiatry, 23,* 126–133.

Carr, A., and Afnan, S. (1989). Concurrent individual and family therapy in a case of elective mutism. *Journal of Family Therapy, 11,* 29-44.

Coates, S. (1990). Ontogenesis of boyhood Gender Identity Disorder. *Journal of the American Academy of Psychoanalysis, 18,* 414–438.

Coates, S., and Person, E. (1985). Extreme boyhood femininity: Isolated behavior or pervasive disorder? *Journal of the American Academy of Child and Adolescent Psychiatry, 24,* 702–709.

Dedmon, S. R. (1986). Helping children with Tourette syndrome to cope in the classroom. *Social Work in Education, 8,* 243–257.

Doering, R. W., Zucker, K. J., Bradley, S. J., and MacIntyre, R. B. (1989). Effects of neutral toys on sex-typed play in children with Gender Identity Disorder. *Journal of Abnormal Child Psychology, 17,* 563–574.

Dulcan, M. K., and Popper, C. W. (1991). *Concise guide to child and adolescent psychiatry.* Washington, DC: American Psychiatric Press.

Dunn, L. M., and Dunn, L. M. (1981). *Peabody picture vocabulary test—revised.* Circle Pines, MN: American Guidance Service.

Dykens, E., Leckman, J., Riddle, M., Hardin, M., Schwartz, S., and Cohen, D. (1990). Intellectual, academic, and adaptive functioning of Tourette syndrome children with and without Attention Deficit Disorder. *Journal of Abnormal Child Psychology, 18,* 607–615.

Edell, B. H., and Motta, R. W. (1989). The emotional adjustment of children with Tourette's syndrome. *The Journal of Psychology, 123,* 51–57.

Edell-Fisher, B. H., and Motta, R. W. (1990). Tourette syndrome: Relation to children's and parents' self-concepts. *Psychological Reports, 66,* 539–545.

Fischhoff, J. (1989). Reactive attachment disorder of infancy. *Treatments of psychiatric disorders: A task force report of the American Psychiatric Association* (pp. 734–746). Washington, DC: American Psychiatric Association.

Fisher, W., Conlon, C., Burd, L., and Conlon, R. (1986). Educating children and adults on coping with Tourette syndrome. *Perceptual and Motor Skills, 62,* 530.

Fitts, W. H. (1965). *The Tennessee Self-Concept Scale Manual.* Nashville, TN: Counselor Recordings and Tests.

Furst, A. L. (1989). Elective mutism: Report of a case successfully treated by a family doctor. *Israel Journal of Psychiatry and Related Sciences, 26,* 96–102.

Green, R. (1987). *The "sissy boy" syndrome and the development of homosexuality.* New Haven, NJ: Yale University Press.

Green, W. H. (1989). Reactive Attachment Disorder of infancy or early childhood. In H. I. Kaplan and B. J. Sadock (Eds.), *Comprehensive textbook of psychiatry* (vol. 2, 5th ed., pp. 1894–1903). Baltimore, MD: Williams & Wilkins.

Gunderson, J. G., Kolb, J. E., and Austin, V. (1981). The diagnostic interview for borderline patients. *American Journal of Psychiatry, 138,* 896–905.

Haley, J. (1976). *Problem-solving therapy.* New York: Harper & Row.

Harcherik, D. F., Leckman, J. F., Detlor, J., and Cohen, D. J. (1984). A new instrument for clinical studies of Tourette's syndrome. *Journal of the American Academy of Child Psychiatry, 23,* 153–160.

Hathaway, P. (1989). Failure to thrive: Knowledge for social workers. *Health and Social Work,* 122–126.

Hayden, T. L. (1980). Classification of elective mutism. *Journal of the American Academy of Child Psychiatry, 19,* 18–33.

Hufton, I. W., and Oates, K. (1977). Nonorganic failure to thrive: A long-term follow-up. *Pediatrics, 59,* 73–77.

Kelley, M. L., and Heffer, R. W. (1990). Eating disorders: Food refusal and failure to thrive. In A. M. Gross and R. S. Drabman (Eds.), *Handbook of clinical behavioral pediatrics* (pp. 111–127). New York: Plenum.

Kerbeshian, J., and Burd, L. (1988). A clinical pharmacological approach to treating Tourette syndrome in children and adolescents. *Neuroscience & Behavioral Reviews, 12,* 241–245.

Kohen, D. P., and Botts, P. (1987). Relaxation-imagery (self-hypnosis) in Tourette syndrome: Experience with four children. *American Journal of Clinical Hypnosis, 29,* 227–237.

Kovacs, M. (1992). *Children's Depression Inventory manual.* North Tonawanda, NY: MHS.

Kurlan, R. (1989). Tourette's syndrome: Current concepts. *Neurology, 39,* 1625–1630.

Labbe, E. E., and Williamson, D. A. (1984). Behavioral treatment of elective mutism: A review of the literature. *Clinical Psychology Review, 4,* 273–292.

Laybourne, P. C. (1989). Treatment of elective mutism. In *Treatments of psychiatric disorders: A task force report of the American Psychiatric Association* (vol. 1, pp. 762–771). Washington, DC: American Psychiatric Association.

Leckman, J. F., Dolnansky, E. S., Hardin, M. T., Clubb, M., Walkup, J. T., Stevenson, J., and Pauls, D. L. (1990). Perinatal factors in the expression of Tourette's syndrome: An exploratory study. *Journal of the American Academy of Child and Adolescent Psychiatry, 29,* 220–226.

Leckman, J. F., Hardin, M. T., Riddle, M. A., Stevenson, J., Ort, S. I., and Cohen, D. J. (1991). Clonidine treatment of Gilles de la Tourette's syndrome. *Archives of General Psychiatry, 48,* 324–328.

Leckman, J. F., Riddle, M. A., Hardin, M. T., Ort, S. I., Swartz, K. L., Stevenson, J., and Cohen, D. J. (1989). The Yale Global Tic Severity Scale: Initial testing of a clinician-rated scale of tic severity. *Journal of the American Academy of Child and Adolescent Psychiatry, 28,* 566–573.

Lesser-Katz, M. (1988). The treatment of elective mutism as stranger reaction. *Psychotherapy, 25,* 305–313.

Mace, F. C., and West, B. J. (1986). Analysis of demand conditions associated with reluctant speech. *Journal of Behavior Therapy and Experimental Psychiatry, 17,* 285–294.

Malatesta, V. J. (1990). Behavioral case formulation: An experimental assessment study of Transient Tic Disorder. *Journal of Psychopathology and Behavioral Assessment, 12,* 219–232.

Marantz, S., and Coates, S. (1991). Mothers of boys with Gender Identity Disorder: A comparison of matched controls. *Journal of the American Academy of Child and Adolescent Psychiatry, 30,* 310–315.

Matthews, M., Eustace, C., Grad, G., Pelcovitz, D., and Olson, M. (1985). A family systems perspective on Tourette's syndrome. *International Journal of Family Psychiatry, 6,* 53–66.

Micheli, F., Gatto, M., Lekhuniec, E., Mangone, C., Pardal, M. F., Pikielny, R., and Parera, I. C. (1990). Treatment of Tourette's syndrome with calcium antagonists. *Clinical Neuropharmacology, 13,* 77–83

Minuchin, S. (1974). *Families and family therapy.* Cambridge, MA: Harvard University Press.

Ollendick, T. H. (1981). Self-monitoring and self-administered overcorrection: The modification of tics in children. *Behavior Modification, 5,* 75–84.

Ollendick, T. H., and Ollendick, D. G. (1990). Tics and Tourette syndrome. In A. M. Gross and R. S. Drabman (Eds.), *Handbook of clinical behavioral pediatrics* (pp. 243–252). New York: Plenum.

Olson, D. H. (1986). Circumplex model VII: Validation studies and FACES-III. *Family Process, 25,* 337–351.

Pauls, D. L., and Leckman, J. F. (1986). The inheritance of Gilles de la Tourette's syndrome and associated behaviors: Evidence for autosomal dominant transmission. *New England Journal of Medicine, 315,* 993–997.

Prata, G., and Masson, O. (1985). Short therapy of a child with Gilles de la Tourette's syndrome. *Journal of Family Therapy, 7,* 315–332.

Reed, C. F. (1963). Elective mutism in children. A reappraisal. *Journal of Child Psychology and Psychiatry, 4,* 99–107.

Rekers, G. A., Kilgus, M., and Rosen, A. C. (1991). Long-term effects of treatment for Gender Identity Disorder of Childhood. *Journal of Psychology and Human Sexuality, 3,* 121–153.

Rekers, G. A., and Morey, S. M. (1989). Relationship of maternal report of feminine behaviors and extraversion to clinician's rating of gender disturbance. *Perceptual and Motor Skills, 69,* 387–394.

Rekers, G. A., and Varni, J. W. (1977). Self-regulation of gender-role behaviors: A case study. *Journal of Behavior Therapy and Experimental Psychiatry, 8,* 427–432.

Robertson, M. M., Schnieden, V., and Lees, A. J. (1990). Management of Gilles de la Tourette syndrome using sulpiride. *Clinical Neuropharmacology, 13,* 229–235.

Sarason, I. G., Levine, H. M., Basham, R. B., and Sarason, B. R. (1983). Assessing social support: The Social Support Questionnaire. *Journal of Personality and Social Psychology, 44,* 127–139.

Shapiro, A. K., Shapiro, E., Brunn, R. D., and Sweet, R. D. (1978). *Gilles de la Tourette syndrome.* New York: Raven Press.

Shapiro, E., Shapiro, A. K., Fulop, G., Hubbard, M., Mandeli, J., Nordlie, J., and Phillips, R. A. (1989). Controlled study of haloperidol, pimozide, and placebo for the treatment of Gilles de la Tourette's syndrome. *Archives of General Psychiatry, 46,* 722–730.

Shvartzman, P., Hornshtein, I., Klein, E., Yechezkel, A., Ziv, M., Herman, J. (1990). Elective mutism in family practice. *Journal of Family Practice, 31,* 319–320.

Silver, L. B. (1989). Elective mutism. In H. I. Kaplan and B. T. Sadock (Eds.), *Comprehensive textbook of psychiatry* (vol. 2, 5th ed., pp. 1887–1889). Baltimore, MD: Williams & Wilkins.

Spanier, G. B. (1976). Measuring dyadic adjustment: New scales for assessing the quality of marriage and similar dyads. *Journal of Marriage and the Family, 38,* 15–28.

Spitz, R. A. (1945). Hospitalism: An inquiry into the genesis of psychiatric conditions in early childhood. *Psychoanalytic Study of the Child, 1,* 53–74.

Stoller, R. J. (1968). *Sex and gender.* New York: Science House.

———. (1975). *Sex and gender II. The transsexual experiment.* London: Hogarth Press.

Tibbits-Kleber, A. L., and Howell, R. J. (1985). Reactive Attachment Disorder of Infancy (RAD). *Journal of Clinical Child Psychology, 14,* 304–310.

Tuber, S., and Coates, S. (1989). Indices of psychopathology in the Rorschachs of boys with severe Gender Identity Disorder: A comparison with normal control subjects. *Journal of Personality Assessment, 53,* 100–112.

Turpin, G. (1983). The behavioral management of tic disorders: A critical review. *Advances in Behavior Research and Therapy, 5,* 203-245.

Weininger, O. (1987). Electively mute children: A therapeutic approach. *Journal of the Melanie Klein Society, 5,* 25–42.

Wilkins, R. (1985). A comparison of elective mutism and emotional disorders in children. *British Journal of Psychiatry, 146,* 198–203.

Young, M. H., and Montano, R. J. (1988). A new hypnobehavioral method for the treatment of children with Tourette's Disorder. *American Journal of Clinical Hypnosis, 31,* 97–106.

Zucker, K. J. (1989). Gender identity disorders. In C. G. Last and M. Hersen (Eds.), *Handbook of child psychiatric diagnosis* (pp. 388–406). New York: Wiley.

_____ . (1990a). Gender identity disorders in children: Clinical descriptions and natural history. In R. Blanchard and B. W. Steiner (Eds.), *Clinical management of gender identity disorders in children and adults* (pp. 27–45). Washington, DC: American Psychiatric Association.

_____ . (1990b). Treatment of gender identity disorders in children. In R. Blanchard and B. W. Steiner (Eds.), *Clinical management of gender identity disorders in children and adults* (pp. 3–23). Washington, DC: American Psychiatric Association.

INDEX